Oxford
First Learner's
Spanish
Dictionary

Editor Michael Janes

Consultants Martyn Ellis
Rosa Martin

OXFORD
UNIVERSITY PRESS

Great Clarendon Street, Oxford OX2 6DP

Oxford University Press is a department of the University of Oxford.
It furthers the University's objective of excellence in research,
scholarship, and education by publishing worldwide in

Oxford   New York

Auckland   Cape Town   Dar es Salaam   Hong Kong   Karachi
Kuala Lumpur   Madrid   Melbourne   Mexico City   Nairobi
New Delhi   Shanghai   Taipei   Toronto

With offices in

Argentina   Austria   Brazil   Chile   Czech Republic   France   Greece
Guatemala   Hungary   Italy   Japan   Poland   Portugal   Singapore
South Korea   Switzerland   Thailand   Turkey   Ukraine   Vietnam

Oxford is a registered trade mark of Oxford University Press
in the UK and in certain other countries

© Copyright holder 2007

Database right Oxford University Press (maker)

First published as Oxford Primary Spanish Dictionary 2007
First published as Oxford First Learner's Spanish Dictionary 2010

British Library Cataloguing in Publication Data

Data available

ISBN: 978-0-19-912744-3

10 9 8 7 6 5 4 3 2

Typeset in OUP Argo Infant and OUP Swift Infant

Printed in Malaysia

Contents

Introduction

The *Oxford First Learner's Spanish Dictionary* is a completely new dictionary written for primary school children between the ages of 7 and 11.

This dictionary is much more than a basic resource for looking up translations: it also helps children to see patterns in the way Spanish is used and structured and identify relationships between similar-looking Spanish and English words. It provides an understanding of the basic concepts of grammar and also includes age-appropriate and interesting cultural information.

A selection of the most important Latin American words are included. There are lots of differences between European and Latin American Spanish. For example, the words **tú** and **ustedes** (the familiar word for 'you' in the singular and plural) are not usually used in Latin America - **vos** and **vosotros/vosotras** are used instead.

The layout is modern and clear with Spanish picked out in red and English picked out in blue. Child-friendly example sentences and phrases illustrate common usage and constructions and feature panels present information in a simple graphic way.

The illustrated thematic centre section of the dictionary is a further opportunity to develop key vocabulary skills with its topic based phrases and sentences. The central verb table section provides a simple first step into using and understanding verb tenses.

The *Oxford First Learner's Spanish Dictionary* makes learning another language enjoyable, fun, and easy. It is a vital and effective tool that will enable children to start using Spanish confidently.

The publishers and editor are indebted to all the advisors, consultants, teachers, and readers who were involved in planning and compiling this dictionary. Special thanks go to Martyn Ellis and Rosa Martin.

MJ

Get to know your dictionary

The dictionary is divided into two halves, the *Spanish-English* side and the *English-Spanish* side. These are separated by a picture section and verb tables in the middle.

- **Where do I find the English translation of a Spanish word?**
- Look in the *Spanish-English* half which comes first.

- **Where do I find the Spanish translation of an English word?**
- Look in the *English-Spanish* half towards the back of the book.

b
c
d

- **How do I find a word quickly?**
- Use the alphabet on the edge of each page to find the first letter of the word you need.

carroza ➡ castañuelas

- Then use the guidewords highlighted on the top of the page. They are the first and last words on the page. Think of the order of letters in your word to make sure you are on the right page.

  For example, what does **casi** mean in English?

- Look in the *Spanish-English* half.
- Find where **c** is highlighted in the alphabet on the edge of the page.
- Look at the two words at the top of a page. Find the words beginning with **ca**, then **cas**, until you get to **casi**.

culture panel

guide words

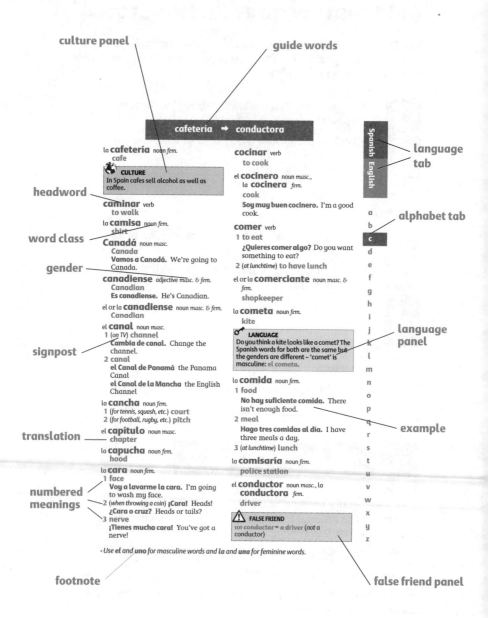

Spanish English

language tab

la **cafetería** noun fem.
cafe

> **CULTURE**
> In Spain cafes sell alcohol as well as coffee.

headword

caminar verb
to walk

la **camisa** noun fem.
shirt

word class

Canadá noun masc.
Canada
Vamos a Canadá. We're going to Canada.

gender

canadiense adjective masc. & fem.
Canadian
Es canadiense. He's Canadian.

el or la **canadiense** noun masc. & fem.
Canadian

el **canal** noun masc.
1 (on TV) channel
Cambia de canal. Change the channel.
2 canal
el Canal de Panamá the Panama Canal
el Canal de la Mancha the English Channel

signpost

la **cancha** noun fem.
1 (for tennis, squash, etc.) court
2 (for football, rugby, etc.) pitch

el **capítulo** noun masc.
chapter

translation

la **capucha** noun fem.
hood

la **cara** noun fem.
1 face
Voy a lavarme la cara. I'm going to wash my face.
2 (when throwing a coin) **¡Cara!** Heads!
¿Cara o cruz? Heads or tails?
3 nerve
¡Tienes mucha cara! You've got a nerve!

numbered meanings

cocinar verb
to cook

el **cocinero** noun masc., la **cocinera** fem.
cook
Soy muy buen cocinero. I'm a good cook.

comer verb
1 to eat
¿Quieres comer algo? Do you want something to eat?
2 (at lunchtime) to have lunch

el or la **comerciante** noun masc. & fem.
shopkeeper

la **cometa** noun fem.
kite

> **LANGUAGE**
> Do you think a kite looks like a comet? The Spanish words for both are the same but the genders are different – 'comet' is masculine: el cometa.

language panel

la **comida** noun fem.
1 food
No hay suficiente comida. There isn't enough food.
2 meal
Hago tres comidas al día. I have three meals a day.
3 (at lunchtime) lunch

example

la **comisaría** noun fem.
police station

el **conductor** noun masc., la **conductora** fem.
driver

> ⚠ **FALSE FRIEND**
> un conductor = a driver (not a conductor)

false friend panel

alphabet tab

a
b
c
d
e
f
g
h
i
j
k
l
m
n
o
p
q
r
s
t
u
v
w
x
y
z

• Use *el* and *uno* for masculine words and *la* and *una* for feminine words.

footnote

headwords
These are the words you look up. The Spanish headwords are in red. The English headwords are in blue.

word classes
Most headwords in the dictionary are nouns, verbs, or adjectives. Sometimes a word can be more than one word class: for example, 'phone' can be a noun (He's on the phone) or a verb (Phone me tomorrow). For nouns, the dictionary gives the Spanish word for 'the', e.g. **el autocar, la barca, los espaguetis, las gafas**.

gender
Spanish nouns and adjectives are either masculine (*masc.*) or feminine (*fem.*). Nouns and adjectives can be singular (just one) or plural (more than one).

translations
These are the headwords translated in English or Spanish.

examples
Examples show you how to use the headword in a typical way.

numbered meanings
If a headword has more than one translation, numbers separate each translation.

signposts
These point you to the right translation, usually when there is more than one meaning of the word you are looking up, e.g. a 'picture' can be a (*drawing*), and the Spanish is **debujo**, or a picture you see (*on TV*) and then the Spanish is **imagen**.

language panels
Vital information about how to use the headwords correctly is shown in the key language panels.

false friend panels
These are important warnings to stop you from using a Spanish word which looks like an English one but which has a completely different meaning!

culture panels
Interesting facts about Spanish culture are shown in these panels.

alphabet tab
To help you navigate your way through the dictionary, the letter you are on is highlighted on the alphabet strip on every page.

language tab
This shows which side of the dictionary you are on.

guide words
These help you to find the word you are looking for easily. They show you the first and last word on the page.

footnotes
These give you useful general language reminders.

Aa

a preposition

🔑 **LANGUAGE**
a + el = al

1 to
a la biblioteca to the library
a España to Spain
Voy al médico. I'm going to the doctor.
He aprendido a leer. I've learnt to read.

2 (*with words of-giving, sending, etc.*) **to**
Doy un regalo a mi amigo. I am giving my friend a present.

3 at
a las siete at seven o'clock
a medianoche at midnight
Llego a casa a las cuatro. I arrive home at four.

4 on
a la derecha on the right
Voy a pie. I go on foot.
Subí al tren. I got on the train.

5 in
a lápiz in pencil
al sol in the sun
Me tiré al agua. I jumped in the water.

6 (*in the distance*) **away**
Está a cinco kilómetros de aquí. It's five kilometres away.

7 (*with dates*)
Estamos a diez de marzo. It's the tenth of March.

8 (*when saying how many times*) **a**
dos veces al día twice a day

9 (*not translated, with a person or a pet*)

🔑 **LANGUAGE**
A is used after verbs in front of nouns for people or pets.

¿Has visto a Rafael? Have you seen Rafael?

Conozco a tu padre. I know your dad.
Lavo a mi perro. I wash my dog.

abajo adverb
1 down
arriba y abajo up and down
No mires abajo. Don't look down.
2 downstairs
Estoy abajo en el salón. I'm downstairs in the living room.
3 de abajo below
el piso de abajo the flat below
4 (*talking about the lowest one*)
de abajo bottom
en el estante de abajo on the bottom shelf

el **abanico** noun *masc.*
fan

el **abecedario** noun *masc.*
alphabet

la **abeja** noun *fem.*
bee

abierto adjective *masc.*,
abierta *fem.*
1 open
La puerta está abierta. The door's open.
2 on
El grifo está abierto. The tap's on.

el **abogado** noun *masc.*,
la **abogada** *fem.*
lawyer
She's a lawyer. Es abogada.

el **abrazo** noun *masc.*
hug
Un abrazo, Antonio. (*in a letter*) With best wishes, Antonio.

el **abrigo** noun *masc.*
coat

• *Languages and nationalities do not take a capital letter in Spanish.*

abril noun *masc.*
April
en abril in April
Mi cumpleaños es en abril.
My birthday's in April.

abrir verb
1 **to open**
Abre la puerta. Open the door.
¿A qué hora abre el supermercado? What time does the supermarket open?
2 **to turn on**
abrir el grifo to turn on the tap

abrochar verb
to do up
Abróchate la chaqueta. Do up your jacket.

el **abuelo** noun *masc.*,
la **abuela** *fem.*
grandfather, grandmother
mis abuelos my grandparents

aburrido adjective *masc.*,
aburrida *fem.*
1 **boring**
Es aburrido. It's boring.
2 **bored**
Estoy aburrido. I'm bored.

aburrirse verb
to get bored
Me aburro. I get bored.

acabar verb
1 **to finish**
He acabado mis deberes. I've finished my homework.
2 **acabar de hacer algo** to have just done something
Acabo de llegar. I've just arrived.

🔑 **LANGUAGE**
Use **acabar de** with the infinitive when you want to say you've done something a short time ago/just now.

acampar verb
to camp

acariciar verb
to stroke
Me gusta acariciar al gato. I like stroking the cat.

el **accidente** noun *masc.*
accident
Mi amigo tuvo un accidente de coche. My friend had a car accident.

la **acción** noun *fem.*
action
una película con mucha acción
a film with lots of action

el **aceite** noun *masc.*
oil
el aceite de oliva olive oil

la **aceituna** noun *fem.*
olive

el **acento** noun *masc.*
accent
'Fútbol' lleva acento en la 'u'.
'Fútbol' has an accent on the 'u'.
María tiene acento español. Maria has a Spanish accent.

aceptar verb
to accept

la **acera** noun *fem.*
pavement

acercarse verb
to get closer
Acércate a la ventana. Get closer to the window.

acertar verb
acertar algo to get something right
¿Acertaste? Did you get it right?

acompañar verb
to go with, to come with
¿Me acompañas? Are you coming with me?

acordarse verb
to remember
No me acuerdo. I don't remember.

• *The months of the year and days of the week do not take a capital letter in Spanish.*

acordarse de algo to remember something
Me acuerdo del número.
I remember the number.
¿Te acuerdas de mí? Do you remember me?

acostarse verb
  to go to bed
  Me acuesto a las ocho. I go to bed at eight.

el or la **acróbata** noun *masc. & fem.*
  acrobat

la **actividad** noun *fem.*
  activity

activo adjective *masc.*, **activa** *fem.*
  active

el **actor** noun *masc.*
  actor

la **actriz** noun *fem.* (plural las **actrices**)
  actress

actuar verb
  (*in a play, film, etc.*) **to act**

el **acuerdo** noun *masc.*
  estar de acuerdo to agree
  Estoy de acuerdo contigo. I agree with you.

acusar verb
  to accuse

el or la **acusica** noun *masc. & fem.*
  telltale

adelantar verb
  1 (*in a car*) **to overtake**
  2 (*in a game*) **to move forward**
  Adelanta una casilla. Move to the next square.

adelante adverb
  forward
  más adelante further on
  ¡Adelante! Come in! (*entering a room*); Go on! (*telling somebody to do something*)

además adverb
  as well, besides

Es inteligente y además trabajador. He's intelligent and hard-working as well.
Es caro y además es feo. It's expensive and it's ugly besides.

adentro adverb
  inside
  Pasa adentro. Come inside.

el **adhesivo** noun *masc.*
  sticker

adiós exclamation
  goodbye

adivinar verb
  to guess

el **adjetivo** noun *masc.*
  adjective

el or la **adolescente** noun *masc. & fem.*
  teenager

adónde adverb
  where
  ¿Adónde vas? Where are you going?

los **adornos** plural noun *masc.*
  decorations
  los adornos de Navidad the Christmas decorations

adrede adverb
  on purpose
  Lo has hecho adrede. You did it on purpose.

el **adulto** noun *masc.*, la **adulta** *fem.*
  adult

el **adverbio** noun *masc.*
  adverb

advertir verb
  to warn
  ¡Te lo advierto! I'm warning you!

el **aeropuerto** noun *masc.*
  airport

• See the centre section for verb tables.

3

a b c d e f g h i j k l m n o p q r s t u v w x y z

a
b
c
d
e
f
g
h
i
j
k
l
m
n
o
p
q
r
s
t
u
v
w
x
y
z

la **afición** noun *fem.*
hobby
¿Qué aficiones tienes? What hobbies do you have?

aficionado adjective *masc.*,
aficionada *fem.*
ser aficionado a algo to be a fan of something
Es aficionado al fútbol. He's a football fan.

África noun *fem.*
Africa

africano adjective *masc.*,
africana *fem.*
African

el **africano** noun *masc.*,
la **africana** *fem.*
African
los africanos Africans

afuera adverb
outside
Vete afuera. Go outside.

agacharse verb
to bend down, to crouch down
¡Agáchate! Bend down!, Crouch down!

agarrar verb
to get hold of
Me agarró del brazo. He got hold of my arm.

agarrarse verb
to hold on
¡Agárrate!, que te caes. Hold on or you'll fall down.

la **agencia de viajes** noun *fem.*
travel agent's

la **agenda** noun *fem.*
diary
la agenda del colegio the school diary

⚠️ **FALSE FRIEND**
una agenda = a diary (*not* an agenda)

agosto noun *masc.*
August
el ocho de agosto the eighth of August
Me voy de vacaciones en agosto. I'm going on holiday in August.

agradable adjective *masc. & fem.*
pleasant

agradecer verb
agradecer algo a alguien to thank somebody for something
Le he agradecido el regalo. I've thanked him for the present.

el **agricultor** noun *masc.*,
la **agricultora** *fem.*
farmer

agrio adjective *masc.*, **agria** *fem.*
sour
La naranja está agria. The orange is sour.

el **agua** noun *fem.*
water
¿Quieres agua? Do you want some water?
el agua mineral mineral water

🔑 **LANGUAGE**
Be careful: you use **el** with **agua** but it is not a masculine noun.

el or la **aguafiestas** noun *masc. & fem.* (plural los or las **aguafiestas**)
spoilsport

aguantar verb
to stand, to tolerate
No aguanto este ruido. I can't stand this noise.

el **águila** noun *fem.*
eagle

🔑 **LANGUAGE**
Be careful: you use **el** with **águila** but it is not a masculine noun.

la **aguja** noun *fem.*
needle

• Use **el** and **uno** for masculine words and **la** and **una** for feminine words.

4

las agujas del reloj the hands of the clock

el **agujero** noun *masc.*
hole

ahí adverb
there
¡Ahí está! There she is!
ahí abajo down there
buscar por ahí to look around there
Ve por ahí. Go that way.
¿Adónde vas? – Me voy por ahí. Where are you going? – I'm going that way.

la **ahijada** noun *fem.*
goddaughter

el **ahijado** noun *masc.*
godson

ahogarse verb
to drown
Se ahogó en el mar. He drowned in the sea.

ahora adverb
now
Ahora estoy en casa. I'm at home now.
ahora mismo right now

ahorrar verb
to save
Tienes que ahorrar dinero. You have to save money.

el **aire** noun *masc.*
air
Tiré el balón al aire. I threw the ball into the air.
el aire condicionado air conditioning

el **ajedrez** noun *masc.*
1 chess
¿Quieres jugar al ajedrez? Do you want to play chess?
2 chess set

el **ajo** noun *masc.*
garlic

ajustado adjective *masc.*,
ajustada *fem.*
tight
unos vaqueros ajustados tight jeans

al preposition

> **LANGUAGE**
> a + el = al

to the
ir al cine to go to the cinema

> **LANGUAGE**
> For more examples of al look at a.

el **ala** noun *fem.*
wing

> **LANGUAGE**
> Be careful: you use el with ala but it is not a masculine noun.

la **alarma** noun *fem.*
alarm
una alarma contra incendios a fire alarm

el **albañil** noun *masc.*
builder

el **albergue juvenil** noun *masc.*
youth hostel

el **álbum** noun *masc.*
album
un álbum de fotos a photo album

el **alcalde** *masc.*,
la **alcaldesa** noun *fem.*
mayor

alcanzar verb
1 to catch up with
Corre si quieres alcanzarlo. Run if you want to catch up with him.
2 to reach
¿Alcanzas al techo? Can you reach the ceiling?

el **alcohol** noun *masc.*
alcohol

a b c d e f g h i j k l m n o p q r s t u v w x y z

• *Languages and nationalities do not take a capital letter in Spanish.*

alegrarse verb
to be happy
Me alegro de verte. I'm pleased to see you.

alegre adjective *masc. & fem.*
happy
Estás muy alegre hoy. You're looking very happy today.

la **alegría** noun *fem.*
joy

el **alemán** noun *masc.*
(*the language*) **German**
¿Hablas alemán? Do you speak German?

alemán adjective *masc.*,
alemana *fem.*
German
Frank es alemán. Frank is German.

el **alemán** noun *masc.*,
la **alemana** *fem.*
German
los alemanes the Germans

Alemania noun *fem.*
Germany

la **alergia** noun *fem.*
allergy
Tengo alergia a la penicilina. I'm allergic to penicillin.

alérgico adjective *masc.*,
alérgica *fem.*
allergic

alfabético adjective *masc.*
en orden alfabético in alphabetical order

el **alfabeto** noun *masc.*
alphabet

la **alfombra** noun *fem.*
rug

algo pronoun
1 something
¿Buscas algo? Are you looking for something?
algo interesante something interesting
2 anything
¿Algo más? Anything else?

el **algodón** noun *masc.*
cotton
unos calcetines de algodón cotton socks

alguien pronoun
1 somebody
Alguien ha llamado. Somebody phoned.
2 anybody
¿Alguien ha visto mi libro? Has anybody seen my book?

alguno adjective & pronoun *masc.*,
alguna *fem.*

LANGUAGE
The masculine singular **alguno** becomes **algún** when it is used before a noun.

1 some
Algunos niños tienen bicicletas. Some children have bicycles.
alguna vez sometimes
en alguna parte somewhere
Sólo me gustan algunos. I only like some.
2 any
¿Tocas algún instrumento? Do you play any instrument?
Tengo muchos caramelos.
¿Quieres alguno? I've got lots of sweets. Do you want any?

la **alimentación** noun *fem.*
diet
una alimentación sana a healthy diet

allá adverb
over there
La farmacia está más allá. The chemist is further away.

• *The months of the year and days of the week do not take a capital letter in Spanish.*

6

allí adverb
there
Siéntate allí. Sit there.

el **almacén** noun *masc.*
warehouse
unos grandes almacenes
a department store

la **almendra** noun *fem.*
almond

la **almohada** noun *fem.*
pillow

almorzar verb
1 to have lunch
2 to have a mid-morning snack

el **almuerzo** noun *masc.*
1 lunch
2 mid-morning snack

alojarse verb
(*in a hotel etc.*) to stay

alquilar verb
1 to rent
Hemos alquilado un apartamento.
We've rented a flat.
2 to hire
Alquilé una bici. I hired a bike.

alrededor adverb
alrededor de around
alrededor de la mesa around the table
Me acuesto alrededor de las nueve. I go to bed around nine.

el **altavoz** noun *masc.* (plural los **altavoces**)
(*for sound and music*) speaker

alto adverb
loud
Habla más alto. Speak louder.

alto adjective *masc.*, **alta** *fem.*
1 tall
Soy alto. I'm tall.
2 high
Aquella montaña es muy alta.
That mountain's very high.
3 loud

La radio está muy alta. The radio's very loud.
4 **en lo alto de** at the top of

la **alubia** noun *fem.*
bean

el **alumno** noun *masc.*, la **alumna** *fem.*
pupil

amable adjective *masc. & fem.*
kind
Es muy amable. She's very kind.

amanecer verb
to get light
Amanece a las seis. It gets light at six.

amargo adjective *masc.*, **amarga** *fem.*
bitter
La naranja está amarga.
The orange is bitter.

amarillo adjective *masc.*, **amarilla** *fem.*
yellow
una blusa amarilla a yellow blouse

el **amarillo** noun *masc.*
yellow
Prefiero el amarillo. I prefer yellow.

ambos adjective & plural pronoun *masc.*, **ambas** *fem.*
both
Me gustan ambos. I like both of them.

la **ambulancia** noun *fem.*
ambulance

amenazar verb
to threaten

América noun *fem.*
America
América Central Central America
América del Sur South America
América Latina Latin America

• *See the centre section for verb tables.*

a b c d e f g h i j k l m n o p q r s t u v w x y z

a
b
c
d
e
f
g
h
i
j
k
l
m
n
o
p
q
r
s
t
u
v
w
x
y
z

americano adjective masc.,
americana fem.
American

el **americano** noun masc.,
la **americana** fem.
American
los americanos the Americans

el **amigo** noun masc.,
la **amiga** fem.
friend
mi mejor amigo my best friend
Somos muy amigas. We're good
friends.

el **amor** noun masc.
love

ancho adjective masc., **ancha** fem.
1 wide
una calle ancha a wide street
2 loose
Me gusta la ropa ancha. I like
loose clothes.

anciano adjective masc.,
anciana fem.
old
Mi abuela es muy anciana.
My grandmother is very old.

LANGUAGE
This is a polite way of saying 'old' in
Spanish.

el **anciano** noun masc.,
la **anciana** fem.
old man, old lady
los ancianos old people

LANGUAGE
This is a polite way of talking about old
people in Spanish.

Andalucía noun fem.
Andalusia

andar verb
to walk
Voy andando a la escuela. I walk
to school.

el **andén** noun masc. (plural los
andenes)
(in a station) platform

los **Andes** plural noun masc.
the Andes

el **ángel** noun masc.
angel

las **anginas** plural noun fem.
tonsils
Tengo anginas. I've got tonsillitis.

el **anillo** noun masc.
ring

animado adjective masc.,
animada fem.
lively
una fiesta animada a lively party

el **animal** noun masc.
animal

animar verb
to cheer on
Hay que animar al equipo.
We must cheer on the team.

ánimo exclamation
1 come on!
¡Ánimo, que vas a ganar! Come on,
you're going to win!
2 cheer up!

el **aniversario** noun masc.
anniversary

anoche adverb
last night

anteayer adverb
the day before yesterday

la **antena** noun fem.
aerial
una antena parabólica a satellite
dish

los **anteojos** plural noun masc.
(Latin America) glasses

• Use **el** and **uno** for masculine words and **la** and **una** for feminine words.

anterior adjective *masc. & fem.*
before
el día anterior the day before

antes adverb
1 before
He terminado antes. I finished before.
2 **antes de** before
Hago los deberes antes de salir. I do my homework before going out.

el **antibiótico** noun *masc.*
antibiotic

anticuado adjective *masc.*,
anticuada *fem.*
old-fashioned
Mi padre es muy anticuado. My dad's very old-fashioned.

antiguo adjective *masc.*,
antigua *fem.*
old
un libro antiguo an old book
mi antiguo colegio my old school

las **Antillas** plural noun *fem.*
West Indies

antipático adjective *masc.*,
antipática *fem.*
very unfriendly

el **anuncio** noun *masc.*
1 advert
Hay muchos anuncios de juguetes. There are lots of adverts for toys.
2 announcement

añadir verb
to add

el **año** noun *masc.*
1 year
el año pasado last year
el año que viene next year
el Año Nuevo the New Year
2 (*when saying how old somebody is*)
¿Cuántos años tienes? How old are you?
Tengo diez años. I'm ten.

apagado adjective *masc.*,
apagada *fem.*
1 off
La tele está apagada. The TV is off.
2 out
El fuego está apagado. The fire is out.

apagar verb
1 to switch off
Apaga la luz. Switch off the light.
2 to put out
Han apagado el incendio. They've put out the fire.

el **aparato** noun *masc.*
(*for teeth*) **brace**

el **aparcamiento** noun *masc.*
car park

aparcar verb
to park
'Prohibido aparcar' 'No parking'

aparecer verb
to appear

el **apartamento** noun *masc.*
apartment

aparte adverb
1 to one side
poner algo aparte to put something to one side
2 separately

el **apellido** noun *masc.*
surname

apenas adverb
hardly
Apenas salen. They hardly go out.

apetecer verb
¿Te apetece un helado? Do you feel like an ice cream?
Me apetece ir al cine. I feel like going to the cinema.

• *Languages and nationalities do not take a capital letter in Spanish.*

9

a
b
c
d
e
f
g
h
i
j
k
l
m
n
o
p
q
r
s
t
u
v
w
x
y
z

el **apetito** noun *masc.*
appetite

aplaudir verb
to clap, to applaud

el **apodo** noun *masc.*
nickname

apoyar verb
to lean
Apoyé la bici en la pared. I leaned my bike against the wall.

aprender verb
to learn
Aprendemos español. We learn Spanish.
Quiero aprender a nadar. I want to learn to swim.

apretar verb
to press
Aprieta el botón. Press the button.
Me aprietan los zapatos. My shoes are tight.

aprobar verb
to pass
Aprobé el examen. I passed the exam.

el **aprobado** noun *masc.*
pass mark
Tengo un aprobado. I got a pass.

aprovechar verb
¡Que aproveche! Enjoy your meal!

apuntar verb
1 to write down
Apúntalo en la agenda. Write it down in your diary.
2 to point

los **apuntes** plural noun *masc.*
notes
Tengo mis apuntes de español. I have my Spanish notes.

apurarse verb
(*Latin American*) to hurry

aquel adjective *masc.*, **aquella** *fem.*
that
aquel coche that car
aquella casa that house

aquél pronoun *masc.*, **aquélla** *fem.*
1 that one
Quiero aquél. I want that one.
¿Quieres aquélla? Do you want that one?
2 that
Aquélla es mi maestra. That's my teacher.

LANGUAGE
The accent goes on aquél and aquélla to show clearly you're using the pronoun.

aquello pronoun
that
¿Qué es aquello? What's that?

aquellos adjective *masc.*, **aquellas** *fem.*
those
aquellos edificios those buildings
aquellas niñas those girls

aquellos, (or **aquéllos**) pronoun *masc.*, **aquellas**, (or **aquéllas**) *fem.*
those
Quiero aquellos. I want those.
¿Quieres aquellas? Do you want those?

LANGUAGE
The accent can go on aquéllos and aquéllas if you want to show clearly you're using the pronoun.

aquí adverb
here
¡Aquí está! Here he is!
¡Ven aquí! Come here!
Aquí tienes el libro. Here's the book.
¿Hay una farmacia por aquí? Is there a chemist around here?
Pasa por aquí. Come this way.

• The months of the year and days of the week do not take a capital letter in Spanish.

árabe adjective *masc. & fem.*
Arab
los países árabes the Arab
countries

el **árabe** noun *masc.*
Arabic
Yasmina habla árabe. Yasmina
speaks Arabic.

el or la **árabe** noun *masc. & fem.*
Arab

Aragón noun *masc.*
Aragon

la **araña** noun *fem.*
spider

arañar verb
(*animals, fingernails, etc.*) **to scratch**
Mi gato me araña. My cat
scratches me.

el **árbitro** noun *masc.*,
la **árbitra** *fem.*
1 (*in football etc.*) referee
2 (*in cricket, tennis, etc.*) umpire

el **árbol** noun *masc.*
tree
un árbol de Navidad a Christmas
tree

el **arbusto** noun *masc.*
bush

el **archivo** noun *masc.*
(*on a computer*) file

el **arco** noun *masc.*
bow
arcos y flechas bows and arrows

el **arco iris** noun *masc.*
rainbow

la **ardilla** noun *fem.*
squirrel

la **arena** noun *fem.*
sand

Argentina noun *fem.*
Argentina

argentino adjective *masc.*,
argentina *fem.*
Argentinian

el **argentino** *masc.*,
la **argentina** noun *fem.*
Argentinian
los argentinos the Argentinians

el **armario** noun *masc.*
1 wardrobe
Mis camisas están en el armario.
My shirts are in the wardrobe.
2 cupboard
un armario de cocina a kitchen
cupboard

arrancar verb
1 to pull out
arrancar las páginas de un libro to
pull the pages out of a book
2 (*talking about a car*) to start
El coche no arranca. The car won't
start.

arreglado adjective *masc.*,
arreglada *fem.*
tidy
una casa muy arreglada a very
tidy house

arreglar verb
1 to fix
Han arreglado la bici. They've
fixed the bike.
2 to tidy
Arregla tu habitación. Tidy your
room.

arreglarse verb
to get ready
¡Arréglate! Get ready!

arriba adverb
1 up
arriba y abajo up and down
aquí arriba up here
¡Mira hacia arriba! Look up!
2 upstairs
Estoy arriba. I'm upstairs.
3 **de arriba** above
el piso de arriba the flat above

a b c d e f g h i j k l m n o p q r s t u v w x y z

• *See the centre section for verb tables.*

4 (*talking about the highest one*)
de arriba top
en el cajón de arriba in the top drawer

la **arroba** noun *fem.*
(*in email addresses*) **the @ symbol**

arrodillarse verb
to kneel down
¡Arrodíllate! Kneel down!

el **arroyo** noun *masc.*
stream

el **arroz** noun *masc.*
rice

el **arte** noun *masc.*
art
el arte español Spanish art

el **artículo** noun *masc.*
article

LANGUAGE
In Spanish grammar the article is a word such as **el**, **la**, **los**, **lss** (the); or **un**, **una** (a/an).

el or la **artista** noun *masc. & fem.*
artist
Es artista. He's an artist.

el **asa** noun *fem.*
handle

LANGUAGE
Be careful: you use **el** with **asa** but it is not a masculine noun.

asaltar verb
to rob
asaltar un banco to rob a bank

el **ascensor** noun *masc.*
lift

los **aseos** plural noun *masc.*
toilets

asesinar verb
to murder

el **asesinato** noun *masc.*
murder

el **asesino** noun *masc.*,
la **asesina** *fem.*
murderer

así adverb
1 like this
Hazlo así. Do it like this.
2 like that
Dijo algo así. He said something like that.

Asia noun *fem.*
Asia

el **asiento** noun *masc.*
seat
el asiento delantero the front seat

la **asignatura** noun *fem.*
subject
mi asignatura favorita
my favourite subject

asistir verb
to attend
asistir a clase to attend a class

el **asma** noun *fem.*
asthma
Tengo asma. I have asthma.

LANGUAGE
Be careful: you use **el** with **asma** but it is not a masculine noun.

asomar verb
asomar la cabeza por la ventana
to lean your head out of the window
No te asomes a la ventana.
Don't lean out of the window.
¡Asómate! Put your head out of the window!

la **aspiradora** noun *fem.*
vacuum cleaner, **Hoover**®
No me gusta pasar la aspiradora.
I don't like hoovering.

asqueroso adjective *masc.*,
asquerosa *fem.*
disgusting

• *Use* **el** *and* **uno** *for masculine words and* **la** *and* **una** *for feminine words.*

el or la **astronauta** noun masc. & fem.
   astronaut

asustar verb
   to scare
   ¡No me asustes! Don't scare me!

atacar verb
   to attack

el **atajo** noun masc.
   short cut

el **ataque** noun masc.
   attack
   un ataque de asma an asthma
   attack

atar verb
   to tie
   Ata el paquete. Tie up the parcel.
   Átate los cordones. Tie your laces.

el **atasco** noun masc.
   traffic jam

la **atención** noun fem.
   attention
   Julia no presta atención. Julia
   doesn't pay attention.
   ¡Pon más atención! Pay more
   attention!

atender verb
   to pay attention
   **Los niños tienen que atender en
   clase.** The children have to pay
   attention in class.

aterrizar verb
   to land
   ¿Ha aterrizado el avión? Has the
   plane landed?

el **Atlántico** noun masc.
   Atlantic

el **atlas** noun masc. (plural los **atlas**)
   atlas

el or la **atleta** noun masc. & fem.
   athlete

el **atletismo** noun masc.
   athletics

la **atmósfera** noun fem.
   atmosphere

atrás adverb
   1 back
   Da un paso atrás. Take one step
   back.
   2 behind
   Me quedé atrás. I stayed behind.
   3 at the back
   Los niños se sientan atrás. The
   children sit at the back.
   4 de atrás back
   la puerta de atrás the back door

atrevido adjective masc.,
   atrevida fem.
   daring

atropellar verb
   to run over

el **atún** noun
   tuna

el **aula** noun fem.
   classroom

⚷ **LANGUAGE**
Be careful: you use **el** with **aula** but it is
not a masculine noun.

aumentar verb
   to increase

aún adverb
   1 still
   ¿Aún vives en Londres? Do you still
   live in London?
   2 yet
   Aún no he comido. I haven't eaten
   yet.

aunque conjunction
   although

los **auriculares** plural noun masc.
   headphones

ausente adjective masc. & fem.
   absent
   Juan está ausente hoy. Juan is
   absent today.

a
b
c
d
e
f
g
h
i
j
k
l
m
n
o
p
q
r
s
t
u
v
w
x
y
z

• Languages and nationalities do not take a capital letter in Spanish.

Australia ➜ azul

Australia noun fem.
Australia

australiano adjective masc.,
australiana fem.
Australian

el **australiano** noun masc.,
la **australiana** fem.
Australian
los australianos the Australians

Austria noun fem.
Austria

el **autobús** noun masc. (plural los
autobuses)
bus
en autobús by bus

el **autocar** noun masc.
coach
en autocar by coach

la **autopista** noun fem.
motorway

el **autor** noun masc., la **autora** fem.
author

avanzar verb
1 to move forward
2 to make progress
Has avanzado en tu español.
You've made progress in your
Spanish.

el **ave** noun fem.
bird

LANGUAGE
Be careful: you use **el** with **ave** but it is not
a masculine noun.

la **avenida** noun fem.
avenue

la **aventura** noun fem.
adventure

LANGUAGE
Spanish = aventura
English = adventure

el **avión** noun masc. (plural los
aviones)
plane
ir en avión to go by plane
mandar algo por avión to send
something by airmail

avisar verb
to warn

el **aviso** noun masc.
warning

la **avispa** noun fem.
wasp

ay exclamation
1 ouch!
¡Ay, me haces daño! Ouch, you're
hurting me!
2 oh!
¡Ay, qué susto! Oh, what a fright
you gave me!

ayer adverb
yesterday
ayer por la mañana yesterday
morning
ayer por la noche yesterday night

la **ayuda** noun fem.
help

ayudar verb
to help
Ayúdame a lavar el coche.
Help me wash the car.

el **ayuntamiento** noun masc.
town hall

el **azúcar** noun masc.
sugar
Echo azúcar en los cereales.
I put sugar on my cereal.

azul adjective masc. & fem.
blue
Tengo los ojos azules. I have blue
eyes.

el **azul** noun masc.
blue
Me encanta el azul. I love blue.

• The months of the year and days of the week do not take a capital letter in Spanish.

Bb

el **bacalao** noun *masc.*
cod

el **bachillerato** noun *masc.*

 CULTURE
El bachillerato is a course taken in the last two years of school for students who want to go to university.

bailar verb
to dance
Me gusta bailar. I like to dance.

el **bailarín** noun *masc.*,
la **bailarina** *fem.*
dancer

🔑 **LANGUAGE**
The plural of bailarín is bailarines.

el **baile** noun *masc.*
1 dance
Voy a clase de baile. I go to dance classes.
2 dancing

bajar verb
1 to go down
Baja al sótano. Go down to the basement.
Bajó en el ascensor. He went down in the lift.
2 to come down
¡Ya bajo! I'm coming down!
Bajé las escaleras. I came down the stairs.
3 to get off
¡Baja de la bici! Get off your bike!
4 to get down
¿Me puedes bajar ese libro? Can you get that book down for me?
5 to put down
Baja la persiana. Put the blind down.

6 to turn down
¿Puedes bajar la tele, por favor? Can you turn down the TV, please?
7 to download
He bajado una canción de Internet. I've downloaded a song from the Internet.

bajarse verb
1 to get off
Me bajé del autobús en el centro. I got off the bus in the centre.
2 to get out
Dave se bajó del coche. Dave got out of the car.
3 to get down
¡Bájate del árbol! Get down from the tree!

bajo adverb
quietly
Habla más bajo. Speak more quietly.

bajo preposition
below
tres grados bajo cero three degrees below zero

bajo adjective *masc.*, **baja** *fem.*
1 short
Soy muy bajo. I'm very short.
2 low
Sus notas son muy bajas. His marks are very low.

el **balancín** noun *masc.* (plural los **balancines**)
seesaw

• *See the centre section for verb tables.*

15

el **balcón** noun masc. (plural los
balcones)
balcony

las **Baleares** plural noun fem.
the Balearic Islands

la **ballena** noun fem.
whale

el **balón** noun masc. (plural los
balones)
ball
un balón de fútbol a football

⚠ **FALSE FRIEND**
un balón = a ball (not a balloon)

el **baloncesto** noun masc.
basketball
jugar al baloncesto to play
basketball

el **banco** noun masc.
1 (for sitting on) **bench**
2 (for money) **bank**
3 **un banco de datos** a database

la **banda** noun fem.
1 (of criminals) **gang**
2 (playing music) **band**

la **bandeja** noun fem.
tray

la **bandera** noun fem.
flag

la **banqueta** noun fem.
stool

el **bañador** noun masc.
1 (for girls) **swimming costume**
2 (for boys) **swimming trunks**

bañarse verb
1 **to have a bath**
2 **to have a swim**
Me bañé en el mar. I had a swim in
the sea.

la **bañera** noun fem.
bath
Hay mucha agua en la bañera.
There's a lot of water in the bath.

el **baño** noun masc.
1 **bath**
Quiero darme un baño. I want to
have a bath.
2 **swim**
Me doy un baño en la piscina.
I go for a swim in the pool.
3 **bathroom**

el **bar** noun masc.
bar

barato adjective masc., **barata** fem.
cheap

la **barba** noun fem.
beard
Mi abuelo tiene barba.
My grandfather has a beard.

la **barbacoa** noun fem.
barbecue
hacer una barbacoa to have a
barbecue

la **barbilla** noun fem.
chin

la **barca** noun fem.
boat

el **barco** noun masc.
1 **boat**
en barco by boat
un barco de vela a sailing boat
2 **ship**

la **barra** noun fem.
1 (for drinks) **bar**
2 (of metal) **bar**
una barra de hierro an iron bar
3 **una barra de pan** a loaf of bread

la **barriga** noun fem.
tummy, stomach
Me duele la barriga. I have a
tummy ache.

borracho masc. adjective,
borracha fem.
drunk
Está borracho. He's drunk.

• Use **el** and **uno** for masculine words and **la** and **una** for feminine words.

16

el **barrio** noun masc.
 area
 Vivo en el barrio. I live in the area.

el **barro** noun masc.
 mud
 lleno de barro covered in mud

basta exclamation
 that's enough!

bastante adverb & pronoun
 1 enough
 Tengo bastante. I have enough.
 2 quite
 Hablo español bastante bien.
 I speak Spanish quite well.
 un libro bastante bueno quite a
 good book
 3 quite a lot
 El maestro me ayuda bastante.
 The teacher helps me quite a lot.

bastante adjective masc. & fem.
 1 enough
 ¿Tienes bastante dinero? Do you
 have enough money?
 2 quite a lot of
 Hay bastantes coches. There are
 quite a lot of cars.

el **bastón** noun masc. (plural los
 bastones)
 walking stick

la **basura** noun fem.
 rubbish
 sacar la basura to put out the
 rubbish
 tirar algo a la basura to throw
 something into the rubbish bin

la **bata** noun fem.
 1 dressing gown
 2 (of a doctor etc.) white coat
 3 (of a schoolboy or girl) overall

la **batalla** noun fem.
 battle

la **batería** noun fem.
 1 (in a car) battery
 2 drums
 tocar la batería to play the drums

el **batido** noun masc.
 milk shake

batir verb
 batir un récord to break a record

el **bebé** noun masc.
 baby

beber verb
 to drink
 Estoy bebiendo agua. I'm drinking
 some water.

la **bebida** noun fem.
 drink
 una bebida caliente a hot drink

el **béisbol** noun masc.
 baseball
 jugar al béisbol to play baseball

belga adjective masc. & fem.
 Belgian

el or la **belga** noun masc. & fem.
 Belgian

Bélgica noun fem.
 Belgium

besar verb
 to kiss

el **beso** noun masc.
 kiss
 Dame un beso. Give me a kiss.

la **Biblia** noun fem.
 Bible

la **biblioteca** noun fem.
 library

el **bicho** noun masc.
 insect

la **bici** noun fem.
 bike

la **bicicleta** noun fem.
 bicycle
 ir en bicicleta to go by bicycle
 Yo sé montar en bicicleta. I can
 ride a bicycle.

a
b
c
d
e
f
g
h
i
j
k
l
m
n
o
p
q
r
s
t
u
v
w
x
y
z

• *Languages and nationalities do not take a capital letter in Spanish.*

bien adverb & adjective
1 well
Hablo español muy bien. I speak Spanish very well.
No me encuentro bien. I don't feel well.
¿Cómo estás? - Bien. How are you? – Fine.
2 all right, okay
¿Estás bien? Are you all right?
Esta película está bien. This film's okay.
3 nice
Huele bien. It smells nice.
4 right
No lo estás haciendo bien. You're not doing it right.

bienvenido adjective *masc.*, **bienvenida** *fem.*
welcome
¡Bienvenido a España! Welcome to Spain!

el **bigote** noun *masc.*
moustache

el **bikini** noun *masc.*
bikini

bilingüe adjective *masc. & fem.*
bilingual

el **billete** noun *masc.*
1 ticket
un billete de autobús a bus ticket
sacar un billete to get a ticket
2 (*money*) **note**
un billete de veinte euros a twenty-euro note

la **biología** noun *fem.*
biology

el **biquini** noun *masc.*
bikini

el **bistec** noun *masc.*
steak

blanco adjective *masc.*, **blanca** *fem.*
white
una camisa blanca a white shirt

el **blanco** noun *masc.*
white
Me gusta el blanco. I like white.

blando adjective *masc.*, **blanda** *fem.*
soft
Esta cama es muy blanda. This bed's very soft.

el **bloc** noun *masc.* (plural los **blocs**)
writing pad

el **bloque** noun *masc.*
un bloque de pisos a block of flats

la **blusa** noun *fem.*
blouse

bobo adjective *masc.*, **boba** *fem.*
silly
Eres boba. You're silly.

la **boca** noun *fem.*
mouth
Abre la boca. Open your mouth.
Duermo boca arriba. I sleep on my back.
Duermo boca abajo. I sleep face down.

> **🔑 LANGUAGE**
> Word for word boca arriba means 'with your mouth up', and boca abajo 'with your mouth down'.

el **bocadillo** noun *masc.*
sandwich
un bocadillo de queso a cheese sandwich

> **🌍 CULTURE**
> A bocadillo is made from French bread.

la **bocina** noun *fem.*
(*on a car*) **horn**

la **boda** noun *fem.*
wedding

la **bodega** noun *fem.*
(*for wines etc.*) **cellar**

• *The months of the year and days of the week do not take a capital letter in Spanish.*

la **bola** noun *fem.*
ball
una bola de nieve a snowball

la **bolera** noun *fem.*
bowling alley

el **boleto** noun *masc.*
(*Latin America*) ticket

el **boli** noun *masc.*
pen

> 🔑 **LANGUAGE**
> **Boli** is short for **bolígrafo**.

el **bolígrafo** noun *masc.*
ballpoint pen

Bolivia noun *fem.*
Bolivia

el **bollo** noun *masc.*
bun
un bollo de chocolate a chocolate bun

los **bolos** plural noun *masc.*
tenpin bowling
jugar a los bolos to go bowling

la **bolsa** noun *fem.*
bag
una bolsa de plástico a plastic bag

el **bolsillo** noun *masc.*
pocket
Tengo el pañuelo en el bolsillo. I've got my handkerchief in my pocket.

el **bolso** noun *masc.*
handbag
La mujer ha perdido el bolso. The woman has lost her bag.

la **bomba** noun *fem.*
1 bomb
Estalló una bomba. A bomb went off.
2 pump
una bomba de bicicleta a bicycle pump
3 **¡Me lo pasé bomba!** I had a great time!

el **bombero** noun *masc.*, la **bombera** *fem.*
fireman, firefighter
Mi padre es bombero. My dad's a fireman.
llamar a los bomberos to call the fire brigade

> 🔑 **LANGUAGE**
> **Bombero** comes from the **bomba** (pump) for pumping water on to fires.

la **bombilla** noun *fem.*
light bulb

el **bombón** noun *masc.* (plural los **bombones**)
chocolate
¿Quieres un bombón? Do you want a chocolate?

bonito adjective *masc.*, **bonita** *fem.*
pretty
un vestido muy bonito a very pretty dress

el **bonobús** noun *masc.* (plural los **bonobuses**)
bus pass

borrar verb
1 to rub out
Borra esta palabra. Rub this word out.
2 to delete
He borrado ese fichero. I've deleted that file.

el **bosque** noun *masc.*
1 (*big*) forest
2 (*small*) wood
Hay un bosque aquí. There's a wood here.
Se perdió en el bosque. He got lost in the woods.

bostezar verb
to yawn

la **bota** noun *fem.*
boot
las botas de fútbol football boots
las botas de goma wellingtons

• *See the centre section for verb tables.*

a
b
c
d
e
f
g
h
i
j
k
l
m
n
o
p
q
r
s
t
u
v
w
x
y
z

a
b
c
d
e
f
g
h
i
j
k
l
m
n
o
p
q
r
s
t
u
v
w
x
y
z

botar verb
   to bounce
   Esta pelota no bota. This ball doesn't bounce.

el **bote** noun masc.
   1 tin
   un bote de pintura a tin of paint
   2 jar
   un bote de mermelada a jar of jam
   3 boat
   un bote de remos a rowing boat
   un bote salvavidas a lifeboat

la **botella** noun fem.
   bottle

el **botiquín** noun masc. (plural los **botiquines**)
   first-aid box

el **botón** noun masc. (plural los **botones**)
   button

el **boxeo** noun masc.
   boxing

las **bragas** plural noun fem.
   knickers

Brasil noun masc.
   Brazil

bravo exclamation
   well done!

el **brazo** noun masc.
   arm

brillante adjective masc. & fem.
   1 (metal, hair, etc.) shiny
   2 (light, sun) bright
   3 (student) brilliant

brillar verb
   to shine
   El sol brilla. The sun is shining.

la **brisa** noun fem.
   breeze

británico adjective masc., **británica** fem.
   British
   Soy británico. I'm British.

el **británico** noun masc., la **británica** fem.
   British man, British woman
   los británicos the British

la **broma** noun fem.
   joke
   ¡Es una broma! It's a joke!

bromear verb
   to joke

el **bronceado** noun masc.
   suntan

broncearse verb
   to get a suntan

la **bruja** noun fem.
   witch

la **brújula** noun fem.
   compass

bruto adjective masc., **bruta** fem.
   rough
   ¡Qué bruto! You're so rough!

bucear verb
   to dive
   Nos vamos a bucear. We're going diving.

budista adjective masc. & fem.
   Buddhist

bueno adjective masc., **buena** fem.

> 🔑 **LANGUAGE**
> The masculine singular **bueno** becomes **buen** when it is used before a noun.

   1 good
   Este libro es muy bueno. This book is very good.
   Es un buen libro. It's a good book.
   2 (when wishing somebody something)
   ¡Buenos días! Good morning!
   ¡Buenas tardes! Good afternoon!
   ¡Buenas noches! Good night!
   ¡Buen viaje! Have a good trip!
   3 (as exclamation) all right!, OK!
   ¿Vienes conmigo? – ¡Bueno! Are you coming with me? – All right!

• Use **el** and **uno** for masculine words and **la** and **una** for feminine words.

el **búho** noun *masc.*
owl

la **burbuja** noun *fem.*
bubble

el **burro** noun *masc.*
donkey

burro adjective *masc.*,
burra *fem.*
stupid
¡Qué burro! You're so stupid!

buscar verb
1 **to look for**
Estoy buscando mi boli.
I'm looking for my pen.
2 **to look**
¿Has buscado en el salón?
Have you looked in the living room?
3 **to look up**

Búscalo en el diccionario. Look it up in the dictionary.
4 **ir a buscar** to get
Voy a buscar tus gafas. I'll get your glasses.
Te voy a buscar al colegio.
I'll come and get you at school.

la **butaca** noun *fem.*
1 **armchair**
2 (*in a cinema or theatre*) **seat in the stalls**

el **buzón** noun *masc.* (plural los **buzones**)
1 (*for posting letters*) **postbox**
2 (*at the house*) **letter box**
3 (*for getting email*) **mailbox**

 CULTURE
In Spain postboxes are usually yellow.

Cc

la **cabalgata** noun *fem.*
parade

 CULTURE
La cabalgata de Reyes (the parade of the Three Wise Men) takes place on 5th January , the day before Spanish children usually receive their Christmas presents.

el **caballero** noun *masc.*
gentleman
'caballeros' (*sign on toilet*) 'gents'

los **caballitos** plural noun *masc.*
merry-go-round

el **caballo** noun *masc.*
horse
montar a caballo to ride a horse

caber verb
caber en algo to fit into something
Esto no cabe en la caja. This doesn't fit into the box.

la **cabeza** noun *fem.*
head
Me di un golpe en la cabeza. I hit my head.

los **cabezudos** plural noun *masc.*

 CULTURE
In many Spanish festivals **cabezudos** are people in fancy dress with big heads (**cabeza** is 'head').

la **cabina** noun *fem.*
1 **una cabina telefónica** a phone box
2 (*in a plane*) **cockpit**

el **cable** noun *masc.*
1 (*of TV, phone, etc.*) **wire**
2 **cable**
la televisión por cable cable television

la **cabra** noun *fem.*
goat

el **cacahuete** noun *masc.*
peanut

• *Languages and nationalities do not take a capital letter in Spanish.*

Spanish English

a
b
c
d
e
f
g
h
i
j
k
l
m
n
o
p
q
r
s
t
u
v
w
x
y
z

el **cacao** noun *masc.*
　cocoa

la **cacerola** noun *fem.*
　saucepan

el **cachorro** noun *masc.*,
　la **cachorra** *fem.*
　puppy

cada adjective *masc. & fem.*
　1 each
　**Cada alumno tiene su propio
　ordenador.** Each pupil has his own
　computer.
　cada uno each one
　cada uno de nosotros each of us
　2 every
　cada vez every time
　cada cinco días every five days

la **cadena** noun *fem.*
　1 chain
　una cadena de plata a silver chain
　2 channel
　una cadena de televisión
　a television channel

la **cadera** noun *fem.*
　hip

caer verb
　(*talking about rain, snow, bombs, etc.*) **to
　fall**
　Ha caído una bomba. A bomb fell.

caerse verb
　to fall
　Me caí de la silla. I fell off the chair.
　Luisa se cayó por la escalera. Luisa
　fell down the stairs.
　Corrí y me caí. I ran and fell over.
　Se ha caído un botón. A button has
　fallen off.

el **café** noun *masc.*
　coffee
　¿Vas a tomar un café? Are you
　going to have a coffee?
　un café con leche a white coffee
　un café solo a black coffee

la **cafetería** noun *fem.*
　cafe

el **caimán** noun *masc.* (plural los
　caimanes)
　alligator

la **caja** noun *fem.*
　1 box
　una caja de cartón a cardboard
　box
　2 (*in a supermarket*) **checkout**
　No me gusta hacer cola en la caja.
　I don't like queueing at the
　checkout.
　3 (*in a shop*) **till**
　4 una caja fuerte a safe

el **cajero** noun *masc.*, la **cajera** *fem.*
　1 cashier
　2 (*in a supermarket*) **checkout assistant**
　3 un cajero automático a cash
　machine

el **cajón** noun *masc.* (plural los
　cajones)
　drawer

el **calabacín** noun *masc.* (plural los
　calabacines)
　courgette

la **calabaza** noun *fem.*
　pumpkin
　**Me han dado calabazas en
　matemáticas.** I've failed maths.

🔑 **LANGUAGE**
Dar calabazas means to fail somebody
in an exam; word for word it means 'to
give pumpkins'.

el **calamar** noun *masc.*
　squid

el **calambre** noun *masc.*
　cramp

calcar verb
　to trace
　calcar un dibujo to trace a picture

el **calcetín** noun *masc.* (plural los
　calcetines)
　sock

• *The months of the year and days of the week do not take a capital letter in Spanish.*

la **calculadora** noun *fem.*
  calculator

calcular verb
  to calculate

la **calefacción** noun *fem.*
  heating
  la calefacción central central
  heating

el **calendario** noun *masc.*
  calendar

la **calidad** noun *fem.*
  quality
  un vestido de buena calidad
  a dress of good quality

caliente adjective *masc. & fem.*
1 **hot**
  Esta sopa está muy caliente.
  This soup is very hot.
2 **warm**
  Este jersey es muy caliente.
  This sweater is very warm.

callar verb
  to be quiet, to shut up
  ¡Todos a callar! Everybody shut
  up!

callarse verb
  to be quiet, to shut up
  ¡Cállate! Be quiet!

la **calle** noun *fem.*
  street
  al otro lado de la calle on the
  other side of the street

LANGUAGE
You can also say 'road' in English,
e.g. cruzar la calle ('to cross the
road').

calmarse verb
  to calm down
  ¡Cálmate! Calm down!

el **calor** noun *masc.*
1 **heat**
  No me gusta este calor. I don't like
  this heat.

2 **tener calor** to be hot
  Tengo calor. I'm hot.

LANGUAGE
Spanish = tener calor   Tengo calor.
English = to be hot   I'm hot.

3 **Hace calor.** It's hot.
  ¡Qué calor hace! It's so hot!

calvo adjective *masc.*, **calva** *fem.*
  bald
  Mi padre es calvo. My dad's bald.

los **calzoncillos** plural noun *masc.*
  underpants

la **cama** noun *fem.*
  bed
  Estoy en la cama. I'm in bed.
  Me voy a la cama. I'm going to
  bed.

la **cámara** noun *fem.*
  camera
  una cámara digital a digital
  camera

el **camarero** noun *masc.*,
  la **camarera** *fem.*
  waiter, waitress

cambiar verb
1 **to change**
  cambiar la fecha to change the
  date
  No has cambiado mucho. You
  haven't changed much.
2 **cambiar de algo** to change
  something
  cambiar de autobús to change
  buses
  ¿Quieres cambiar de sitio? Do you
  want to change places?

LANGUAGE
You use cambiar de when you mean to
change one thing for another.

3 **to swap**
  **Te cambio mi compacto por tu
  libro.** I'll swap my CD for your
  book.

• See the centre section for verb tables.

cambiarse verb
 1 to get changed
   Me voy a cambiar. I'm going to get changed.
 2 cambiarse de algo to change something
   Me voy a cambiar de calcetines. I'm going to change my socks.
   cambiarse de casa to move house

el **cambio** noun *masc.*
   change
   ¿Tienes cambio para la máquina? Do you have change for the machine?
   un cambio de planes a change of plan

el **camello** noun *masc.*
   camel

caminar verb
   to walk

el **camino** noun *masc.*
 1 road
   Tomé el camino más corto. I took the shortest road.
 2 path
   un camino por el bosque a path through the forest
 3 way
   Yo no sé el camino. I don't know the way.

el **camión** noun *masc.* (plural los **camiones**)
   lorry
   un camión de bomberos a fire engine

el **camionero** noun *masc.*, la **camionera** *fem.*
   lorry driver

la **camioneta** noun *fem.*
   van

la **camisa** noun *fem.*
   shirt

la **camiseta** noun *fem.*
 1 T-shirt
 2 (*under a shirt*) **vest**
 3 (*for football, rugby*) **shirt**
   una camiseta de fútbol a football shirt

el **camisón** noun *masc.* (plural los **camisones**)
   nightdress

el **campamento** noun *masc.*
   camp
   un campamento de verano a summer camp

la **campana** noun *fem.*
   bell
   la campana de la iglesia the church bell

el **campeón** noun *masc.*, la **campeona** *fem.*
   champion

LANGUAGE
The plural of **campeón** is **campeones**.

el **campesino** noun *masc.*, la **campesina** *fem.*
   country person
   los campesinos country people

el **camping** noun *masc.* (plural los **campings**)
 1 camping
   ir de camping to go camping
 2 campsite

el **campo** noun *masc.*
 1 country
   una casa en el campo a house in the country
 2 countryside
   El campo está muy bonito. The countryside looks very pretty.
 3 (*for growing food*) **field**
 4 pitch
   un campo de fútbol a football pitch
   un campo de deportes a sports ground

• *Use* **el** *and* **uno** *for masculine words and* **la** *and* **una** *for feminine words.*

Canadá noun *masc.*
Canada
Vamos a Canadá. We're going to Canada.

canadiense adjective *masc. & fem.*
Canadian
Es canadiense. He's Canadian.

el or la **canadiense** noun *masc. & fem.*
Canadian

el **canal** noun *masc.*
1 (*on TV*) channel
Cambia de canal. Change the channel.
2 canal
el Canal de Panamá the Panama Canal
el Canal de la Mancha the English Channel

el **canario** noun *masc.*
canary

cancelar verb
to cancel

el **cáncer** noun *masc.*
cancer
Tiene cáncer. She has cancer.

la **cancha** noun *fem.*
1 (*for tennis, squash, etc.*) court
2 (*for football, rugby, etc.*) pitch

la **canción** noun *fem.* (plural las canciones)
song

el **cangrejo** noun *masc.*
crab

el **canguro** noun *masc.*
kangaroo

el or la **canguro** noun *masc. & fem.*
babysitter

la **canoa** noun *fem.*
canoe

cansado adjective *masc.*,
cansada *fem.*
tired
Estoy cansado. I'm tired.

cansarse verb
to get tired
Me cansé mucho en la excursión.
I got very tired on the trip.

el or la **cantante** noun *masc. & fem.*
singer

cantar verb
to sing

la **cantidad** noun *fem.*
1 amount
una gran cantidad de dinero
a large amount of money
cantidad de lots of
Tengo cantidad de amigos. I've got lots of friends.
2 quantity

la **caña de pescar** noun *fem.*
fishing rod

la **capital** noun *fem.*
capital
Madrid es la capital de España.
Madrid is the capital of Spain.

el **capitán** *masc.*,
la **capitana** noun *fem.*
captain

⚡ **LANGUAGE**
The plural of **capitán** is **capitanes**.

---

el **capítulo** noun *masc.*
chapter

la **capucha** noun *fem.*
hood

la **cara** noun *fem.*
1 face
Voy a lavarme la cara. I'm going to wash my face.
2 (*when throwing a coin*) ¡Cara! Heads!
¿Cara o cruz? Heads or tails?
3 nerve
¡Tienes mucha cara! You've got a nerve!

• *Languages and nationalities do not take a capital letter in Spanish.*

a
b
c
d
e
f
g
h
i
j
k
l
m
n
o
p
q
r
s
t
u
v
w
x
y
z

a
b
c
d
e
f
g
h
i
j
k
l
m
n
o
p
q
r
s
t
u
v
w
x
y
z

el **caracol** noun masc.
snail

el **carácter** noun masc.
character

el **caramelo** noun masc.
sweet
Me encantan los caramelos. I love sweets.

⚠️ **FALSE FRIEND**
un caramelo = a sweet (not a caramel)

la **caravana** noun fem.
1 (traffic jam) **tailback**
2 caravan

el **carbón** noun masc.
coal

la **cárcel** noun fem.
prison
Están en la cárcel. They're in prison.

el **Caribe** noun masc.
el Caribe the Caribbean

caribeño adjective masc.,
caribeña fem.
Caribbean

el **cariño** noun masc.
1 love
Siento cariño por mi gato. I'm very fond of my cat.
2 (when calling somebody)
¡cariño! darling!

cariñoso adjective masc.,
cariñosa fem.
affectionate

el **carnaval** noun masc.
carnival

🌎 **CULTURE**
Spanish people celebrate the festival known as carnaval in the second week of February just before Christian Lent. They put on fancy dress, play music, and dance. Two famous carnavales are those of Tenerife and Cadiz.

la **carne** noun fem.
meat
la carne picada minced meat
la carne de vaca beef

el **carné**, **carnet** noun masc.
card
el carné de identidad identity card
el carné de conducir driving licence

la **carnicería** noun fem.
butcher's shop

el **carnicero** noun masc.,
la **carnicera** fem.
butcher

caro adjective masc., **cara** fem.
expensive
Es demasiado caro. It's too expensive.

la **carpeta** noun fem.
(for papers, and on a computer) **folder**

el **carpintero** noun masc.,
la **carpintera** fem.
carpenter

la **carrera** noun fem.
race
Te echo una carrera. I'll have a race with you.
una carrera universitaria a university course

la **carretera** noun fem.
road
la carretera de Valencia the road to Valencia

el **carril** noun masc.
(part of a road) **lane**
un carril bus a bus lane
un carril bici a cycle path

el **carrito** noun masc.
(for shopping etc.) **trolley**

el **carro** noun masc.
1 cart
2 (Latin America) car

• The months of the year and days of the week do not take a capital letter in Spanish.

la **carroza** noun *fem.*
  (*in a Spanish carnival*) **float**

la **carta** noun *fem.*
  1 **letter**
    Escribo una carta. I am writing a letter.
  2 **card**
    jugar a las cartas to play cards
  3 (*in a restaurant*) **menu**

el **cartel** noun *masc.*
  1 **poster**
  2 **sign**
    un cartel de 'se vende' a 'for sale' sign

la **cartera** noun *fem.*
  1 (*for money*) **wallet**
  2 (*for papers*) **document case**
  3 (*for schoolbooks*) **schoolbag**

el **cartero** noun *masc.*,
  la **cartera** *fem.*
  postman, postwoman

el **cartón** noun *masc.*
  cardboard
  una caja de cartón a cardboard box

la **casa** noun *fem.*
  1 **house**
    una casa pequeña a small house
    Estoy en casa de Aurelio. I'm in Aurelio's house.
  2 **home**
    Estoy en casa. I'm at home.
    Me fui a casa. I went home.

casado adjective *masc.*,
  casada *fem.*
  married
  Está casada con un inglés. She's married to an Englishman.

casarse verb
  to get married
  casarse con alguien to get married to somebody

• *See the centre section for verb tables.*

la **cascada** noun *fem.*
  waterfall

la **cáscara** noun *fem.*
  (*of an egg or nut*) **shell**

el **casco** noun *masc.*
  helmet

los **cascos** plural noun *masc.*
  headphones

la **caseta** noun *fem.*
  1 (*for a dog*) **kennel**
  2 **hut, shed**

el or la **casete** noun *masc. & fem.*
  cassette

casi adverb
  1 **almost**
    Son casi las nueve. It's almost nine o'clock.
  2 (*in negative sentences*) **hardly**
    casi nunca hardly ever
    casi nada hardly anything

la **casilla** noun *fem.*
  1 (*on forms, worksheets, etc.*) **box**
  2 (*in crosswords etc.*) **square**

el **caso** noun *masc.*
  hacer caso a alguien to take notice of somebody
  No me haces caso. You don't take any notice of me.

la **castaña** noun *fem.*
  chestnut

castaño adjective *masc.*,
  castaña *fem.*
  (*hair, eyes*) **brown**
  Tengo el pelo castaño. I have brown hair.

las **castañuelas** plural noun *fem.*
  castanets

 CULTURE
Castanets are held in the hand and make clicking sounds in flamenco dancing.

el **castellano** noun *masc.*
Spanish
Hablo castellano. I speak Spanish.

 CULTURE
Spanish is known as español or castellano. Other languages in Spain are catalán (Catalan), gallego (Galician), and vasco (Basque).

castigar verb
to punish
Mi padre me ha castigado. My dad has punished me.
El maestro lo dejó castigado. The teacher gave him a detention.

el **castigo** noun *masc.*
punishment

Castilla noun *fem.*
Castile

el **castillo** noun *masc.*
castle
un castillo de arena a sand castle

la **casualidad** noun *fem.*
coincidence
¡Qué casualidad! What a coincidence!
por casualidad by chance

el **catalán** noun *masc.*
Catalan
¿Hablas catalán? Do you speak Catalan?

Cataluña noun *fem.*
Catalonia

la **catarata** noun *fem.*
waterfall

el **catarro** noun *masc.*
cold
Tengo un catarro. I have a cold.

la **catedral** noun *fem.*
cathedral

católico adjective *masc.*, **católica** *fem.*
Catholic
Soy católica. I'm a Catholic.

catorce number
1 fourteen
Mi prima tiene catorce años. My cousin is fourteen.
2 (*with dates*) fourteenth
el catorce de agosto the fourteenth of August

cavar verb
to dig

el **cazo** noun *masc.*
saucepan

el **CD** noun *masc.* (plural los **CDs**)
CD
un reproductor CD a CD player

la **cebolla** noun *fem.*
onion

la **cebra** noun *fem.*
zebra

la **ceja** noun *fem.*
eyebrow

celebrar verb
to celebrate
celebrar un cumpleaños to celebrate a birthday
¡Vamos a celebrarlo! Let's celebrate!

el **celo** noun *masc.*
Sellotape®

celoso adjective *masc.*, **celosa** *fem.*
jealous

el **celular** noun *masc.*
(*Latin America*) mobile phone

el **cementerio** noun *masc.*
cemetery

la **cena** noun *fem.*
dinner
¿Qué hay de cena? What's for dinner?

cenar verb
to have dinner

el **centavo** noun *masc.*
cent

• *Use el and uno for masculine words and la and una for feminine words.*

centígrado adjective masc.,
centígrada fem.
centigrade
ocho grados centígrados eight
degrees centigrade

el **centímetro** noun masc.
centimetre

el **céntimo** noun masc.
(part of a euro) cent

central adjective masc. & fem.
central

céntrico adjective masc.,
céntrica fem.
central
Vivo en un barrio céntrico. I live in
a central part of town.

el **centro** noun masc.
centre
el centro de la ciudad the town
centre
ir al centro to go into town
un centro comercial a shopping
centre

cepillar verb
to brush

el **cepillo** noun masc.
brush
un cepillo de dientes a toothbrush

cerca adverb
1 near
Mi escuela está muy cerca. My
school is very near.
2 nearby
La piscina está cerca. The
swimming pool is nearby.
3 (with nouns and pronouns)
cerca de near
cerca de la ventana near the
window
cerca de mí near me

el **cerdo** noun masc.
1 pig
2 pork
No como cerdo. I don't eat pork.

los **cereales** plural noun masc.
cereal
Siempre desayunamos cereales.
We always have cereal for
breakfast.

LANGUAGE
Spanish = los cereales is plural
English = cereal is singular

el **cerebro** noun masc.
brain

la **cereza** noun fem.
cherry

la **cerilla** noun fem.
match
una caja de cerillas a box of
matches

el **cero** noun masc.
1 zero
2 nil
El equipo ha ganado dos a cero.
The team won two nil.

cerrado adjective masc.,
cerrada fem.
1 closed
La puerta está cerrada. The door's
closed.
2 off
El grifo está cerrado. The tap's off.

cerrar verb
1 to close
Cierra la ventana. Close the
window.
El museo cierra a las seis. The
museum closes at six.
2 to turn off
Cierra el grifo. Turn off the tap.

el **certificado** noun masc.
certificate

la **cerveza** noun fem.
beer

la **cesta** noun fem.
basket

• Languages and nationalities do not take a capital letter in Spanish.

el **chalet** noun *masc.*
house

el **champiñón** noun *masc.* (plural los **champiñones**)
mushroom

el **champú** noun *masc.*
shampoo

el **chándal** noun *masc.*
tracksuit

la **chancleta** noun *fem.*
flip-flop

chao exclamation
(*Latin American*) bye, bye-bye

la **chapa** noun *fem.*
badge
una chapa de policía a police badge

el **chaparrón** noun *masc.* (plural los **chaparrones**)
downpour

la **chaqueta** noun *fem.*
1 jacket
2 cardigan

el **charco** noun *masc.*
puddle

charlar verb
to chat

el **chat** noun *masc.*
chatroom

el **cheque** noun *masc.*
cheque

chévere adjective
(*Latin American*) great, fantastic

la **chica** noun *fem.*
girl
una chica de diez años a girl of ten

el **chichón** noun *masc.*
(*on your head*) bump

el **chicle** noun *masc.*
chewing gum

el **chico** noun *masc.*
boy
un chico de dieciséis años a boy of sixteen

Chile noun *masc.*
Chile

chileno adjective *masc.*, **chilena** *fem.*
Chilean

el **chileno** noun *masc.*, la **chilena** *fem.*
Chilean

chillar verb
to scream, to shout

la **chimenea** noun *fem.*
1 chimney
2 fireplace
Hay una chimenea en el salón. There's a fireplace in the lounge.

China noun *fem.*
China

la **chincheta** noun *fem.*
drawing pin

el **chino** noun *masc.*
Chinese
¿Hablas chino? Do you speak Chinese?

chino adjective *masc.*, **china** *fem.*
Chinese
Es china. She's Chinese.

el **chino** noun *masc.*, la **china** *fem.*
Chinese man, Chinese woman
los chinos the Chinese

el **chiste** noun *masc.*
1 joke
contar un chiste to tell a joke
2 (*funny drawing*) cartoon
los chistes del periódico the newspaper cartoons

el **chivato** noun *masc.*, la **chivata** *fem.*
telltale

• The months of the year and days of the week do not take a capital letter in Spanish.

chocar verb
chocar con to crash into
El coche chocó con un árbol.
The car crashed into a tree.

el **chocolate** noun *masc.*
chocolate
un helado de chocolate
a chocolate ice cream

la **chocolatina** noun *fem.*
bar of chocolate

el **choque** noun *masc.*
(*between cars, trains, etc.*) **crash**
los autos or **los coches de choque**
the dodgems

el **chorizo** noun *masc.*
spicy pork sausage

la **chuleta** noun *fem.*
1 chop
una chuleta de cerdo a pork chop
2 (*for cheating at exams*) **crib sheet**

el **chupachups**® noun *masc.*
lollipop

el **chupete** noun *masc.*
dummy

el **churro** noun *masc.*

el **cibercafé** noun *masc.*
Internet cafe

la **cicatriz** noun *fem.* (plural las
cicatrices)
scar

el **ciclismo** noun *masc.*
cycling

• *See the centre section for verb tables.*

el or la **ciclista** noun *masc. & fem.*
cyclist

ciego adjective *masc.*, **ciega** *fem.*
blind
Es ciega. She's blind.

el **ciego** *masc.*, la **ciega** noun *fem.*
blind man, blind woman

el **cielo** noun *masc.*
1 sky
2 heaven
3 angel
Eres un cielo. You're an angel.

el **ciempiés** noun *masc.* (plural los
ciempiés)
centipede

cien number
hundred
cien euros a hundred euros

la **ciencia** noun *fem.*
science
Me encantan las ciencias. I love
science.

el **científico** noun *masc.*,
la **científica** *fem.*
scientist

ciento number
hundred
ciento cincuenta a hundred and
fifty
cientos de personas hundreds of
people

cierto adjective *masc.*, **cierta** *fem.*
true
No es cierto. It's not true.

el **ciervo** noun *masc.*
deer

la **cifra** noun *fem.*
figure
Se escribe en cifras. It is written in
figures.

a
b
c
d
e
f
g
h
i
j
k
l
m
n
o
p
q
r
s
t
u
v
w
x
y
z

la **cima** noun *fem.*
top
la cima de la montaña the top of the mountain

cinco number
1 five
Mi hermano tiene cinco años. My brother is five.
Son las cinco. It's five o'clock.
Son las nueve menos cinco. It's five to nine.
Son las diez y cinco. It's five past ten.
2 (*with dates*) fifth
el cinco de junio the fifth of June

cincuenta number
fifty
Mi abuela tiene cincuenta años. My grandma is fifty.

el **cine** noun *masc.*
cinema
Fui al cine. I went to the cinema.

la **cinta** noun *fem.*
1 ribbon
2 tape
Tengo una cinta para grabar la película. I have a tape to record the film.
la cinta adhesiva sticky tape

la **cintura** noun *fem.*
waist

el **cinturón** noun *masc.* (plural los cinturones)
belt
un cinturón de seguridad a seatbelt

el **circo** noun *masc.*
circus

el **círculo** noun *masc.*
circle
sentarse en círculo to sit in a circle

la **ciruela** noun *fem.*
plum

el **cisne** noun *masc.*
swan

la **cita** noun *fem.*
1 appointment
2 date
Tiene una cita con su novia. He has a date with his girlfriend.

la **ciudad** noun *fem.*
1 city
Madrid es una gran ciudad. Madrid is a big city.
2 town
ir a la ciudad to go into town

el **clarinete** noun *masc.*
clarinet
Yo toco el clarinete. I play the clarinet.

claro adverb
1 clearly
No oigo muy claro. I can't hear very clearly.
2 of course
¡Claro que sí! Yes, of course!
¡Claro que no! Of course not!

claro adjective *masc.*, **clara** *fem.*
1 clear
una explicación clara a clear explanation
Está claro. That's clear.
2 light
los colores claros light colours
blusas azul claro light blue blouses

LANGUAGE
When claro follows the name of a colour (e.g. verde, azul), use claro and the colour word in the masculine singular form only.

la **clase** noun *fem.*
1 class
Hassan está en mi clase. Hassan is in my class.
Hoy tenemos clase de español. We have a Spanish class today.
2 classroom
3 kind
libros de todas clases books of all kinds

• Use **el** and **uno** for masculine words and **la** and **una** for feminine words.

la **clave** noun *fem.*
  code
  un mensaje en clave a message in code

el **clavo** noun *masc.*
  nail

el **clic** noun *masc.*
  click
  hacer clic en algo to click on something

el **cliente** noun *masc.*,
la **clienta** *fem.*
 1 (*in a shop etc.*) **customer**
 2 (*in a hotel*) **guest**

el **clima** noun *masc.*
  climate

> 🔑 **LANGUAGE**
> Be careful: **clima** ends in an -**a** but it is not a feminine noun.

climatizado adjective *masc.*,
  climatizada *fem.*
  air-conditioned

el **clip** noun *masc.* (plural los **clips**)
 1 paperclip
 2 music video

el **club** noun *masc.* (plural los **clubs**)
  club
  un club de fútbol a football club

el or la **cobaya** noun *masc. & fem.*
  guinea pig

la **Coca-Cola**® noun *fem.*
  Coke®

el **coche** noun *masc.*
 1 car
  Me gusta ir en coche. I like to go by car.
  un coche de carreras a racing car
  un coche de bomberos a fire engine
 2 (*of a train*) carriage

el **cochecito** noun *masc.*
  baby buggy

el **cocido** noun *masc.*
  stew (*made of meat, vegetables, and chickpeas*)

la **cocina** noun *fem.*
 1 kitchen
  en la cocina in the kitchen
 2 cooker
  una cocina de gas a gas cooker
 3 cooking
  la cocina española Spanish cooking
  un libro de cocina a cookery book

cocinar verb
  to cook

el **cocinero** noun *masc.*,
  la **cocinera** *fem.*
  cook
  Soy muy buen cocinero. I'm a good cook.

el **coco** noun *masc.*
  coconut

el **cocodrilo** noun *masc.*
  crocodile

> 🔑 **LANGUAGE**
> Spanish = co**c**o**d**ri**l**o
> English = cro**c**o**d**i**l**e

el **cocotero** noun *masc.*
  coconut tree

el **código** noun *masc.*
  code
  el código postal the postcode

el **codo** noun *masc.*
  elbow

coger verb
 1 to take
  Coge un bombón. Take a chocolate.
  coger el autobús to take the bus
 2 to catch
  Cogí un resfriado. I caught a cold.
  Coge la pelota. Catch the ball.

a
b
c
d
e
f
g
h
i
j
k
l
m
n
o
p
q
r
s
t
u
v
w
x
y
z

• *Languages and nationalities do not take a capital letter in Spanish.*

a
b
c
d
e
f
g
h
i
j
k
l
m
n
o
p
q
r
s
t
u
v
w
x
y
z

Han cogido al ladrón. They've caught the thief.

3 to get
coger los billetes to get the tickets

> **CULTURE**
> **Coger** is used especially in Spain; in Latin America use **tomar** instead.

el **cohete** noun *masc.*
rocket

el **cojín** noun *masc.* (plural los **cojines**)
cushion

la **col** noun *fem.*
cabbage

la **cola** noun *fem.*
1 tail
El perro está moviendo la cola. The dog's wagging its tail.
2 queue
Hay cola. There's a queue.
hacer cola to queue up
3 glue
4 una cola de caballo a ponytail

el **colchón** noun *masc.* (plural los **colchones**)
mattress

el **cole** noun *masc.*
school

> **LANGUAGE**
> **Cole** is short for **colegio**.

la **colección** noun *fem.* (plural las **colecciones**)
collection

coleccionar verb
to collect
Colecciono sellos. I collect stamps.

el **colegial** noun *masc.*,
la **colegiala** *fem.*
schoolboy, schoolgirl
los colegiales schoolchildren

el **colegio** noun *masc.*
school
en el colegio at school
ir al colegio to go to school

> **LANGUAGE**
> **Colegio** is related to 'college'.

la **coleta** noun *fem.*
ponytail

colgar verb
to hang
Cuelga el abrigo de la percha. Hang your coat on the hook.

la **coliflor** noun *fem.*
cauliflower

la **colina** noun *fem.*
hill

el **collar** noun *masc.*
1 necklace
2 (*on a dog or cat*) **collar**

colocar verb
to put

Colombia noun *fem.*
Colombia

la **colonia** noun *fem.*
summer camp
pasar el mes de agosto en las colonias to spend August in a summer camp

el **color** noun *masc.*
colour
¿De qué color es? What colour is it?

colorado adjective *masc.*,
colorada *fem.*
red
ponerse colorado to go red, to blush

colorear verb
to colour in
colorear un dibujo to colour in a picture

• *The months of the year and days of the week do not take a capital letter in Spanish.*

la **columna** noun fem.
   column

columpiar verb
   to push (on a swing)

el **columpio** noun masc.
   swing

la **coma** noun fem.
   1 comma
   2 decimal point
      tres coma cinco three point five

la **comba** noun fem.
   skipping rope
   jugar a la comba to skip

el **comedor** noun masc.
   1 (in a house) **dining room**
   2 (in a factory, school, etc.) **canteen**

comenzar verb
   to begin
      La clase comienza a las nueve.
      The class begins at nine.

comer verb
   1 to eat
      ¿Quieres comer algo? Do you want
      something to eat?
   2 (at lunchtime) **to have lunch**

el or la **comerciante** noun masc. &
   fem.
   shopkeeper

la **cometa** noun fem.
   kite

> ⚷ **LANGUAGE**
> Do you think a kite looks like a comet? The
> Spanish words for both are the same but
> the genders are different – 'comet' is
> masculine: **el cometa.**

el **cómic** noun masc.
   comic
      Me gusta leer cómics. I like
      reading comics.

cómico adjective masc.,
   cómica fem.
   funny

la **comida** noun fem.
   1 food
      No hay suficiente comida. There
      isn't enough food.
   2 meal
      Hago tres comidas al día. I have
      three meals a day.
   3 (at lunchtime) **lunch**

la **comisaría** noun fem.
   police station

como preposition & conjunction
   1 like
      Soy como mi padre. I'm like my
      father.
   2 as
      Hazlo como te he dicho. Do it as I
      told you to.
   3 (when comparing)
      tan ... como as ... as
      Soy tan inteligente como tú. I'm as
      clever as you.

cómo adverb
   1 how
      ¿Cómo estás? How are you?
      ¿Cómo se dice 'sky' en español?
      How do you say 'sky' in Spanish?
   2 what
      ¿Cómo es? What's it like?
      ¿Cómo es tu hermana? What's
      your sister like?
      ¿Cómo has dicho? What did you
      say?
      ¡Cómo! What!

la **cómoda** noun fem.
   chest of drawers

cómodo adjective masc.,
   cómoda fem.
   (chair, shoes, etc.) **comfortable**

el **compacto** noun masc.
   CD

el **compañero** masc.,
   la **compañera** noun fem.
   1 (in school) **school friend**
   2 (boyfriend, girlfriend) **partner**

• See the centre section for verb tables.

a
b
c
d
e
f
g
h
i
j
k
l
m
n
o
p
q
r
s
t
u
v
w
x
y
z

a
b
c
d
e
f
g
h
i
j
k
l
m
n
o
p
q
r
s
t
u
v
w
x
y
z

la **compañía** noun *fem.*
company
Mi padre trabaja en una compañía irlandesa. My dad works for an Irish company.

comparar verb
to compare

compartir verb
to share

el **compás** noun *masc.* (plural los **compases**)
pair of compasses

la **competición** noun *fem.*
competition
una competición de natación a swimming competition

completamente adverb
completely

completar verb
to complete

completo adjective *masc.*, **completa** *fem.*
1 (*sentence, list, etc.*) complete
2 (*hotel, plane, etc.*) full

complicado adjective *masc.*, **complicada** *fem.*
complicated

el **comportamiento** noun *masc.*
behaviour

la **compra** noun *fem.*
shopping
hacer la compra to do the shopping
ir de compras to go shopping
una bolsa de la compra a shopping bag
una lista de la compra a shopping list

comprar verb
to buy
Quiero comprar un libro. I want to buy a book.
¿Me compras un helado? Can you buy me an ice cream?

comprender verb
to understand

comprobar verb
to check

el **computador** noun *masc.*, la **computadora** *fem.*
(*Latin America*) computer

común adjective *masc. & fem.*
common
en común in common
Tenemos muchas cosas en común. We have a lot in common.

comunicar verb
(*talking about the phone*) to be engaged
Está comunicando. It's engaged.

con preposition
1 with
beber con una pajita to drink with a straw
con mis amigas with my friends
Son tres euros con cinco. That's three euros and five cents.
2 to
Soy malo con mi hermano. I'm mean to my brother.
hablar con alguien to speak to somebody

concentrarse verb
to concentrate

la **concha** noun *fem.*
shell

el **concierto** noun *masc.*
concert
un concierto de rock a rock concert

el **concurso** noun *masc.*
1 competition
un concurso de fotografía a photo competition
2 quiz
un programa concurso a quiz show

conducir verb
to drive
conducir un coche to drive a car

• *Use **el** and **uno** for masculine words and **la** and **una** for feminine words.*

el **conductor** noun masc.,
la **conductora** fem.
driver

⚠ **FALSE FRIEND**
un conductor = a driver (not a conductor)

conectarse verb
conectarse a Internet to connect to the Internet
Estamos conectados a Internet. We're connected to the Internet.

el **conejo** noun masc.
rabbit

confortable adjective masc. & fem.
comfortable

confundir verb
to confuse
Me confundí en el examen. I got confused in the exam.

congelado adjective masc.,
congelada fem.
frozen

el **congelador** noun masc.
freezer

congelar verb
(in a freezer) **to freeze**

la **conjugación** noun fem. (plural las **conjugaciones**)
conjugation

la **conjunción** noun fem. (plural las **conjunciones**)
conjunction

conmigo pronoun
1 with me
Ven conmigo. Come with me.
2 to me
¿Quieres hablar conmigo? Do you want to speak to me?

conocer verb
1 to know
Conozco a tu primo. I know your cousin.

¿Conoces Madrid? Do you know Madrid?
2 to meet
Conocí a una chica en la playa. I met a girl at the beach.
Nos conocimos en la escuela. We met at school.

los **conocimientos** plural noun masc.
(of Spanish, maths, etc.) **knowledge**

el or la **conserje** noun masc. & fem.
(in a school) **caretaker**

la **consigna** noun fem.
left-luggage office

la **consola** noun fem.
(for games) console

la **consonante** noun fem.
consonant

constipado adjective masc.,
constipada fem.
estar constipado to have a cold

⚠ **FALSE FRIEND**
estar constipado = to have a cold (not to be constipated)

construir verb
to build

el or la **contable** noun masc. & fem.
accountant

🔑 **LANGUAGE**
Contable comes from contar (to count).

contar verb
1 to count
Cuenta hasta veinte. Count up to twenty.
2 to tell
Cuéntame un cuento. Tell me a story.

contento adjective masc.,
contenta fem.
happy
Estoy muy contento. I'm very happy.

• Languages and nationalities do not take a capital letter in Spanish.

contestar verb
to answer
No contesta. He isn't answering.
Contesté a la pregunta. I answered the question.

contigo pronoun
1 **with you**
¿Puedo ir contigo? Can I go with you?
2 **to you**
Quiero hablar contigo. I want to speak to you.

el **continente** noun masc.
continent

continuar verb
to continue
Continúa leyendo. Continue reading.

contra preposition
against
contra la pared against the wall

contrario adjective masc.,
contraria fem.
1 **opposite**
la dirección contraria the opposite direction
¿Qué es lo contrario de 'largo'? What's the opposite of 'long'?
2 **opposing**
el equipo contrario the opposing team

la **contraseña** noun fem.
password

el **control** noun masc.
1 **control**
2 **check**
el control de pasaportes passport check

controlar verb
1 **to control**
¡Contrólate! Control yourself!
2 (passports etc.) **to check**

la **conversación** noun fem. (plural las **conversaciones**)
conversation

convertirse verb
to turn into
¡El príncipe se convirtió en rana! The prince turned into a frog!

la **copa** noun fem.
1 **glass**
una copa de vino a glass of wine
2 **drink**
tomar una copa to have a drink
3 (prize) **cup**
la Copa del Mundo the World Cup

la **copia** noun fem.
copy

copiar verb
to copy

el **Corán** noun masc.
Koran

el **corazón** noun masc. (plural los **corazones**)
heart

la **corbata** noun fem.
tie
Llevo corbata. I'm wearing a tie.

el **cordero** noun masc.
lamb
una chuleta de cordero a lamb chop

el **cordón** noun masc.
(for shoes) **lace**
¿Puedes atarme los cordones? Can you do up my laces?

el **coro** noun masc.
choir
cantar en el coro to sing in the choir

la **corona** noun fem.
crown

el **corral** noun masc.
(for chickens etc.) **farmyard**

• The months of the year and days of the week do not take a capital letter in Spanish.

la **correa** noun *fem.*
(*on a watch, handbag, etc.*) **strap**

correcto adjective *masc.*,
correcta *fem.*
correct
Mis respuestas son correctas.
My answers are correct.

el **corredor** noun *masc.*,
la **corredora** *fem.*
runner

corregir verb
1 (*mistakes etc.*) **to correct**
2 (*exercises, homework, etc.*) **to mark**

el **correo** noun *masc.*
post
mandar algo por correo to send
something by post
por correo aéreo by airmail
correo electrónico email

Correos noun *masc.*
post office
Voy a Correos. I'm going to the
post office.

> **LANGUAGE**
> Be careful: Correos is spelt with a capital
> 'C' and ends with an 's'. Never use el with
> it.

correr verb
1 to run
Rafael corre muy rápido. Rafael
runs very fast.
2 to hurry
¡Corre, cierra la puerta! Hurry,
close the door!

corresponder verb
to match
**Esta palabra corresponde a ese
dibujo.** This word matches that
drawing.

la **corrida** noun *fem.*
bullfight

corriente adjective *masc. & fem.*
common
un problema muy corriente a very
common problem

la **corriente** noun *fem.*
1 draught
Hay corriente. There's a draught.
2 electricity
No hay corriente en la casa.
There's no electricity in the house.

cortar verb
to cut
Corta el pan. Cut the bread.
Me he cortado el dedo. I've cut my
finger.
Me he cortado el pelo. I've had my
hair cut.

el **corte** noun *masc.*
cut
Tengo un corte en el dedo. I have a
cut on my finger.
un corte de pelo a haircut

la **cortina** noun *fem.*
curtain

corto adjective *masc.*, **corta** *fem.*
short
Tengo el pelo corto. I have short
hair.

la **cosa** noun *fem.*
thing
Tengo muchas cosas que hacer.
I have lots of things to do.
Quiero otra cosa. I want
something else.
¿Quieres otra cosa? Do you want
anything else?

coser verb
to sew

las **cosquillas** plural noun *fem.*
Tengo cosquillas. I'm ticklish.

la **costa** noun *fem.*
coast
en la costa on the coast

• See the centre section for verb tables.

a
b
c
d
e
f
g
h
i
j
k
l
m
n
o
p
q
r
s
t
u
v
w
x
y
z

costar verb
1 **to cost**
   ¿Cuánto cuesta? How much does it cost?
   Cuesta mucho. It costs a lot.
2 (*talking about time*) **to take**
   ¿Cuánto cuesta llegar? How long does it take to get there?

la **costilla** noun *fem.*
   rib

la **costumbre** noun *fem.*
1 **habit**
   una mala costumbre a bad habit
2 **custom**
   una costumbre española a Spanish custom

crear verb
   to create

crecer verb
   to grow
   He crecido mucho. I've grown a lot.

creer verb
1 **to think**
   Creo que está en la cocina. I think he's in the kitchen.
   Creo que sí. I think so.
   Creo que no. I don't think so.
2 **to believe**
   Te creo. I believe you.

la **crema** noun *fem.*
   cream

la **cremallera** noun *fem.*
   zip
   subir la cremallera to do up the zip

el **crimen** noun *masc.* (plural los **crímenes**)
1 **murder**
2 **(serious) crime**

el or la **criminal** noun *masc. & fem.*
   criminal

el **cristal** noun *masc.*
1 **glass**
   Es de cristal. It's made of glass.

una botella de cristal a glass bottle
   cristales rotos broken glass
2 **window**
   Has roto el cristal. You've broken the window.

cristiano adjective *masc.*, **cristiana** *fem.*
   Christian

criticar verb
   to criticize

el **cruce** noun *masc.*
1 **crossroads**
   en el cruce at the crossroads
2 **crossing**
   un cruce de peatones a pedestrian crossing

el **crucigrama** noun *masc.*
   crossword

⚷ **LANGUAGE**
Be careful: **crucigrama** ends in an **-a** but it is not a feminine noun.

crudo adjective *masc.*, **cruda** *fem.*
   raw
   una zanahoria cruda a raw carrot

cruel adjective *masc. & fem.*
   cruel
   un hombre cruel a cruel man

la **cruz** noun *fem.* (plural las **cruces**)
1 **cross**
2 (*when throwing a coin*) **¡Cruz!** Tails!
   ¿Cara o cruz? Heads or tails?

cruzar verb
   to cross
   cruzar la calle to cross the road
   cruzar los brazos to cross your arms

el **cuaderno** noun *masc.*
   exercise book
   mi cuaderno de español my Spanish exercise book

la **cuadra** noun *fem.*
   stable

• *Use **el** and **uno** for masculine words and **la** and **una** for feminine words.*

el **cuadrado** noun masc.
  square

cuadrado adjective masc.,
  cuadrada fem.
  square
  una caja cuadrada a square box

el **cuadro** noun masc.
  1 picture
    Hay un cuadro en la pared. There's a picture on the wall.
  2 painting
    un cuadro de Dalí a painting by Dali

cuál pronoun masc. & fem.
  1 what
    ¿Cuál es tu número de teléfono? What's your phone number?
    ¿Cuáles son tus colores favoritos? What are your favourite colours?
  2 which
    Tengo dos libros. ¿Cuál quieres? I have two books. Which do you want?
  3 which one
    ¿Cuál quieres? Which one do you want?
    ¿Cuáles quieres? Which ones do you want?

la **cualidad** noun fem.
  quality
  El niño tiene muchas cualidades. The boy has many qualities.

cuando conjunction
  when
  Voy a ir a casa cuando termine. I'm going home when I finish.

cuándo adverb
  (in questions) when
  ¿Cuándo vas a venir? When are you coming?

> **LANGUAGE**
> Remember to put the accent on cuándo in questions.

cuánto adjective & pronoun masc.,
  cuánta fem.
  1 how much
    ¿Cuánto dinero tienes? How much money do you have?
    ¿Cuánta agua? How much water?
    ¿Cuánto cuesta? How much does it cost?
    ¿Cuánto tiempo llevas aquí? How long have you been here?
  2 how many
    ¿Cuántos bombones quieres? How many chocolates do you want?
    ¿Cuántas niñas hay en tu clase? How many girls are there in your class?
    ¿Cuántos años tienes? How old are you?

cuarenta number
  forty
  Mi padre tiene cuarenta años. My dad is forty.

el **cuarto** noun masc.
  1 room
    el cuarto de baño the bathroom
  2 quarter
    un cuarto de hora a quarter of an hour
    Son las tres y cuarto. It's a quarter past three.
    a las ocho menos cuarto at a quarter to eight

cuarto adjective masc.,
  cuarta fem.
  fourth
  en el cuarto piso on the fourth floor

cuatro number
  1 four
    Mi primo tiene cuatro años. My cousin is four.
    Son las cuatro. It's four o'clock.
  2 (with dates) fourth
    el cuatro de septiembre the fourth of September

a b c d e f g h i j k l m n o p q r s t u v w x y z

• Languages and nationalities do not take a capital letter in Spanish.

cuatrocientos number *masc.*,
cuatrocientas *fem.*
four hundred

Cuba noun *fem.*
Cuba

cubano adjective *masc.*,
cubana *fem.*
Cuban

los **cubiertos** plural noun *masc.*
cutlery

el **cubito de hielo** noun *masc.*
ice cube

el **cubo** noun *masc.*
1 bucket
un cubo de agua a bucket of water
2 cube
3 **un cubo de basura** a dustbin

cubrir verb
to cover

la **cucaracha** noun *fem.*
cockroach

la **cuchara** noun *fem.*
spoon

la **cucharilla** noun *fem.*
teaspoon

> **LANGUAGE**
> You can also say **la cucharita** in Spanish.

el **cuchillo** noun *masc.*
knife

el **cuello** noun
1 neck
2 collar
el cuello de mi camisa my shirt collar

la **cuenta** noun *fem.*
1 bill
¡La cuenta, por favor! The bill, please!
2 **darse cuenta de algo** to realize something
No me di cuenta. I didn't realize.

el **cuento** noun *masc.*
1 story
Cuéntame un cuento. Tell me a story.
2 tale
un cuento de hadas a fairy tale

la **cuerda** noun *fem.*
1 rope
2 string
Ata el paquete con una cuerda. Tie the parcel with string.
3 **saltar a la cuerda** to skip

el **cuero** noun *masc.*
leather
una chaqueta de cuero a leather jacket

el **cuerpo** noun *masc.*
body

la **cuesta** noun *fem.*
1 hill
Tienes que subir la cuesta. You have to go up the hill.
2 slope

la **cueva** noun *fem.*
cave

el **cuidado** noun *masc.*
care
con cuidado carefully
tener cuidado to be careful
¡Cuidado con el escalón! Be careful of the step!

cuidar verb
to look after
cuidar a alguien to look after somebody
Yo cuido a los niños. I look after the children.

la **culpa** noun *fem.*
fault
No es mi culpa. It's not my fault.
Tú tienes la culpa. It's your fault.

• *The months of the year and days of the week do not take a capital letter in Spanish.*

culpable adjective *masc. & fem.*
guilty

el **cumpleaños** noun *masc.*
.birthday
Ayer fue mi cumpleaños.
My birthday was yesterday.
¡Feliz cumpleaños! Happy
birthday!
una fiesta de cumpleaños
a birthday party

cumplir verb
Mañana cumplo ocho años.
Tomorrow I'll be eight.

la **cuna** noun *fem.*
cot

el **cura** noun *masc.*
priest

curioso adjective *masc.*,
curiosa *fem.*
curious

el **curso** noun *masc.*
1 year
¿En qué curso estás? What year
are you in?
2 course
un curso de español a Spanish
course

el **cursor** noun *masc.*
cursor

la **curva** noun
1 (*in the road*) bend
2 curve
dibujar una curva to draw a curve

curvo adjective *masc.*, **curva** *fem.*
curved
una línea curva a curved line

Dd

el **dado** noun *masc.*
dice
Tira los dados. Throw the dice.

la **dama** noun *fem.*
1 lady
2 **las damas** draughts
jugar a la damas to play draughts

el **daño** noun *masc.*
hacer daño a alguien to hurt
somebody
Me he hecho daño. I've hurt
myself.

los **daños** plural noun *masc.*
damage

> **LANGUAGE**
> Spanish = **los daños** is plural
> English = **damage** is singular

dar verb
1 to give
Dame el libro. Give me the book.
Ricardo le dio el dinero a su padre.
Ricardo gave the money to his
dad.
2 to go for
dar un paseo to go for a walk
dar una vuelta en coche to go for a
drive
3 to make
Me da sed. It makes me thirsty.
Me da sueño. It makes me sleepy.
Me dio miedo. It scared me.
4 to put on
¿Qué dan en la tele? What's
on TV?
Dan una película. They're putting
on a film.

• *See the centre section for verb tables.*

darse verb
  to have
    darse un baño to have a bath
    Me he dado una ducha. I've had a shower.
    Me di un golpe en la cabeza. I bumped my head.

de preposition

> 🔑 **LANGUAGE**
> de + el = del

1 **of**
    un vaso de agua a glass of water
    una niña de ocho años a girl of eight
    dos páginas del libro two pages of the book
2 (*talking about belonging to somebody, being made of something, etc.*)
    los calcetines de Alberto Alberto's socks
    la casa de mis padres my parents' house
    la puerta de la cocina the kitchen door
    una bolsa de plástico a plastic bag

> 🔑 **LANGUAGE**
> In English you usually use -'s or -s', and you can leave out 'of' completely.

3 **from**
    Soy de Bilbao. I come from Bilbao.
4 **by**
    un cuadro de Picasso a painting by Picasso
5 **about**
    hablar de algo to talk about something
6 **in**
    el mejor alumno de la clase the best student in the class
    a las seis de la mañana at six in the morning

debajo adverb
1 **underneath**
    Está debajo. It's underneath.
2 **debajo de** under
    debajo de la silla under the chair

deber verb
1 **must**
    Debo ir al colegio. I must go to school.
2 **should**
    Deberías hacerlo. You should do it.
3 **to owe**
    Te debo cinco euros. I owe you five euros.

los **deberes** plural noun *masc.*
  homework
    mis deberes de español my Spanish homework

> 🔑 **LANGUAGE**
> Spanish = los deberes is plural
> English = homework is singular

débil adjective *masc. & fem.*
  weak

decidir verb
  to decide
    He decidido venir contigo. I've decided to come with you.
    ¡Decídete! Make up your mind!

décimo adjective *masc.*,
décima *fem.*
  tenth
    en el décimo piso on the tenth floor

decir verb
1 **to say**
    No he dicho nada. I haven't said anything.
    Dice que no quiere venir. He says he doesn't want to come.
    ¿Cómo se dice 'coche' en inglés? How do you say 'coche' in English?
2 **to tell**
    decir algo a alguien to tell somebody something
    Te he dicho la verdad. I've told you the truth.
3 (*when answering the phone*)
    ¡Diga! Hello?

• Use **el** and **uno** for masculine words and **la** and **una** for feminine words.

la **decisión** noun *fem.* (plural las **decisiones**)
decision
tomar una decisión to make a decision

decorar verb
to decorate

el **dedo** noun *masc.*
1 finger
2 **el dedo del pie** the toe
el dedo gordo del pie the big toe

defender verb
to defend

dejar verb
1 to leave
Déjalo aquí. Leave it here.
¡Déjame en paz! Leave me alone!
2 to let
No me dejan salir. They don't let me go out.
3 to lend
¿Me dejas tu bici? Can you lend me your bike?
4 **dejar de hacer algo** to stop doing something
¡Deja de molestarme! Stop annoying me!

del preposition

LANGUAGE
de + el = del

1 of the
una página del libro a page of the book
la hermana del panadero the baker's sister
2 from the
Vengo del hotel. I've come from the hotel.

el **delantal** noun *masc.*
apron

delante adverb
1 in front
Ve delante. Go in front.
2 **delante de** in front of

delante de la biblioteca in front of the library
3 **pasar por delante de** to go past
El autobús pasa por delante de la escuela. The bus goes past the school.

delantero adjective *masc.*, **delantera** *fem.*
front
el asiento delantero the front seat

deletrear verb
to spell
¿Me lo deletreas? Can you spell it?

el **delfín** noun *masc.* (plural los **delfines**)
dolphin

delgado adjective *masc.*, **delgada** *fem.*
thin
Soy delgada. I'm thin.

delicioso adjective *masc.*, **deliciosa** *fem.*
delicious
Está delicioso. It's delicious.

el or la **delincuente** noun *masc. & fem.*
criminal

demás adjective & pronoun
1 other
los demás niños the other children
2 **lo demás** the rest
los demás the others
¿Dónde están los demás? Where are the others?

demasiado adverb
1 too
Es demasiado pequeño. It's too small.
2 too much
Comes demasiado. You eat too much.

• *Languages and nationalities do not take a capital letter in Spanish.*

Spanish English

a
b
c
d
e
f
g
h
i
j
k
l
m
n
o
p
q
r
s
t
u
v
w
x
y
z

demasiado adjective & pronoun *masc.*,
demasiada *fem.*
1 **too much**
demasiado dinero too much
money
Tengo demasiados deberes.
I've got too much homework.
2 **too many**
demasiadas veces too many times
¿Hay demasiados? Are there too
many?

el or la **dentista** noun *masc. & fem.*
dentist
ir al dentista to go to the dentist

dentro adverb
1 **inside**
Está dentro. It's inside.
aquí dentro in here
dentro de algo inside something
dentro del edificio inside the
building
2 **dentro de una semana** within a
week

el **departamento** noun *masc.*
1 **department**
2 (*Latin America*) **apartment, flat**

depender verb
to depend
depender de algo to depend on
something
Depende. It all depends.

el **dependiente** noun *masc.*,
la **dependienta** *fem.*
shop assistant

el **deporte** noun *masc.*
sport
mi deporte favorito my favourite
sport
hacer deporte to play sports

deportista adjective *masc. & fem.*
sporty

el or la **deportista** noun *masc. & fem.*
sportsman, sportswoman

deportivo adjective *masc.*,
deportiva *fem.*
sports
un coche deportivo a sports car
ropa deportiva sports clothes

deprisa adverb
quickly
Lo he hecho deprisa. I did it
quickly.

la **derecha** noun *fem.*
right
Está a la derecha. It's on the right.
Gira a la derecha. Turn right.
conducir por la derecha to drive on
the right

derecho adverb
straight
Siga derecho. Go straight on.

derecho adjective *masc.*,
derecha *fem.*
1 **right**
Escribo con la mano derecha.
I write with my right hand.
2 (*talking about pictures, hats, etc.*) **straight**
No está derecho. It isn't straight.
Siéntate derecho. Sit up straight.

derramar verb
to spill

desabrochar verb
to undo
Desabróchate la chaqueta.
Undo your jacket.

desagradable adjective *masc. & fem.*
unpleasant

desaparecer verb
1 **to disappear**
2 (*talking about people*) **to go missing**

el **desastre** noun *masc.*
disaster

desatar verb
to untie

• *The months of the year and days of the week do not take a capital letter in Spanish.*

desayunar verb
to have breakfast

el **desayuno** noun *masc.*
breakfast

descalzo adjective *masc.*,
descalza *fem.*
in bare feet
correr descalzo to run in bare feet

descansar verb
to rest
Tengo que descansar. I have to
have a rest.

el **descanso** noun *masc.*
rest
Necesito un descanso. I need a rest.

descarado adjective *masc.*,
descarada *fem.*
cheeky

descargar verb
1 to download
**He descargado un programa de
Internet.** I've downloaded a
program from the Internet.
2 to unload

desconectar verb
1 (*a computer, lamp, etc.*) to unplug
2 to disconnect

el **desconocido** noun *masc.*,
la **desconocida** *fem.*
stranger

describir verb
to describe

la **descripción** noun *fem.* (plural las
descripciones)
description

el **descubrimiento** noun *masc.*
discovery

descubrir verb
to discover

descuidado adjective *masc.*,
descuidada *fem.*
careless

desde preposition
1 from
desde Londres from London
desde ahora from now on
2 since
No le he visto desde ayer. I haven't
seen him since yesterday.
Vivo aquí desde el año pasado.
I've been living here since last
year.
3 **desde hace** for
Vivo aquí desde hace dos años.
I've been living here for two years.

desear verb
1 to wish
Te deseo buena suerte. I wish you
good luck.
2 (*used for saying 'would like'*)
¿Qué desea, señor? What would
you like, sir?

desenchufar verb
to unplug

el **deseo** noun *masc.*
wish
pedir un deseo to make a wish

el **desfile** noun *masc.*
parade

deshacer verb
1 to unpack
deshacer las maletas to unpack
the cases
2 to undo
deshacer un nudo to undo a knot

el **desierto** noun *masc.*
desert

deslizarse verb
to slide

desmayarse verb
to faint

desnudarse verb
to get undressed

• *See the centre section for verb tables.*

a
b
c
d
e
f
g
h
i
j
k
l
m
n
o
p
q
r
s
t
u
v
w
x
y
z

desnudo adjective *masc.*,
desnuda *fem.*
1 naked
2 bare
con los brazos desnudos with bare arms

desobedecer verb
to disobey

desobediente adjective *masc. & fem.*
disobedient

el **desorden** noun *masc.*
mess
¡Qué desorden! What a mess!

desordenado adjective *masc.*,
desordenada *fem.*
untidy

desordenar verb
to mess up

el **despacho** noun *masc.*
office

despacio adverb
slowly

despegar verb
to take off
El avión ha despegado. The plane has taken off.

el **despegue** noun *masc.*
(of a plane) take-off

el **despertador** noun *masc.*
alarm clock
¿Has puesto el despertador? Have you set the alarm?

despertar verb
to wake up
¿Me puedes despertar a las ocho? Can you wake me up at eight?

despertarse verb
to wake up
Me despierto a las seis. I wake up at six.

despierto adjective *masc.*,
despierta *fem.*
awake
Está despierta. She's awake.

después adverb
1 afterwards
poco después soon afterwards
2 later
dos años después two years later
3 (with nouns)
después de after
después de las vacaciones after the holidays
Llegó después que yo. He arrived after me.

el **destino** noun *masc.*
destination

destruir verb
to destroy

el **detalle** noun *masc.*
detail
con todo detalle in detail

el or la **detective** noun *masc. & fem.*
detective

detener verb
1 to stop
detener el coche to stop the car
2 to arrest
Han detenido al ladrón They've arrested the thief

detrás adverb
1 behind
Ponte detrás. Stand behind.
2 (with nouns and pronouns)
detrás de behind
detrás del árbol behind the tree
detrás de mí behind me

devolver verb
1 to take back
devolver un libro a la biblioteca to take a book back to the library
2 to give back

• Use **el** and **uno** for masculine words and **la** and **una** for feminine words.

¿Puedes devolverme la bici mañana? Can you give me back my bike tomorrow?

3 to throw up

Voy a devolver. I'm going to throw up.

el **día** noun *masc.*
  day
  ¿Qué día es hoy? What day is it today?
  todos los días every day
  todo el día all day
  Es de día. It's light outside.
  un día de fiesta a holiday
  el día de la Madre Mother's Day
  el día del Padre Father's Day

🔑 LANGUAGE
Be careful: **día** ends in an **-a** but it is not a feminine noun.

---

el **diablo** noun *masc.*
  devil

el **diagrama** noun *masc.*
  diagram

🔑 LANGUAGE
Be careful: **diagrama** ends in an **-a** but it is not a feminine noun.

---

el **diamante** noun *masc.*
  diamond
  un anillo de diamantes a diamond ring

el **diario** noun *masc.*
  1 diary
  Escribo en mi diario. I write in my diary.
  2 newspaper

diario adjective *masc.*, **diaria** *fem.*
  daily

dibujar verb
  to draw
  Dibujé un caballo. I drew a horse.

el **dibujo** noun *masc.*
  1 drawing
  hacer un dibujo to do a drawing, to draw a picture
  2 los dibujos animados cartoons

el **diccionario** noun *masc.*
  dictionary
  buscar una palabra en el diccionario to look up a word in the dictionary

diciembre noun *masc.*
  December
  Mi cumpleaños fue en diciembre. My birthday was in December.
  Se van el diez de diciembre. They leave on the tenth of December.

diecinueve number
  1 nineteen
  Mi hermana tiene diecinueve años. My sister is nineteen.
  2 (*with dates*) **nineteenth**
  el diecinueve de mayo the nineteenth of May

dieciséis number
  1 sixteen
  Mi hermano tiene dieciséis años. My brother is sixteen.
  2 (*with dates*) **sixteenth**
  el dieciséis de abril the sixteenth of April

diecisiete number
  1 seventeen
  Mi primo tiene diecisiete años. My cousin is seventeen.
  2 (*with dates*) **seventeenth**
  el diecisiete de octubre the seventeenth of October

dieciocho number
  1 eighteen
  Mi prima tiene dieciocho años. My cousin is eighteen.
  2 (*with dates*) **eighteenth**
  el dieciocho de julio the eighteenth of July

a
b
c
d
e
f
g
h
i
j
k
l
m
n
o
p
q
r
s
t
u
v
w
x
y
z

• *Languages and nationalities do not take a capital letter in Spanish.*

el **diente** noun *masc.*
tooth
Me estoy lavando los dientes.
I'm brushing my teeth.

🔑 **LANGUAGE**
Diente is related to 'dentist'.

la **dieta** noun *fem.*
diet

diez number
1 **ten**
Tengo diez años. I'm ten.
Son las diez. It's ten o'clock.
Son las tres menos diez. It's ten to three.
Son las siete y diez. It's ten past seven.
2 (*with dates*) **tenth**
el diez de febrero the tenth of February

la **diferencia** noun *fem.*
difference

diferente adjective *masc. & fem.*
different
Son muy diferentes. They're very different.

difícil adjective *masc. & fem.*
difficult
un problema difícil a difficult problem

la **dificultad** noun *fem.*
difficulty

digital adjective *masc. & fem.*
digital
una cámara digital a digital camera

el **dinero** noun *masc.*
money
No tengo dinero. I haven't got any money.

el **dinosaurio** noun *masc.*
dinosaur

Dios noun *masc.*
God

la **dirección** noun *fem.* (plural las **direcciones**)
1 **address**
¿Cuál es tu dirección? What's your address?
2 **direction**
¿En qué dirección se fue? What direction did she go in?

directamente adverb
straight, **directly**
Fuimos directamente a Madrid. We went straight to Madrid.

directo adjective *masc.*,
directa *fem.*
1 **direct**
un vuelo directo a direct flight
2 **straight**
Fui directo a casa. I went straight home.

el **director** noun *masc.*,
la **directora** *fem.*
1 **headmaster**, **headmistress**
2 (*of a company*) **manager**
3 (*of an orchestra*) **conductor**

el **disco** noun *masc.*
1 **disk**
Graba los archivos en un disco. Copy the files onto a disk.
un disco compacto a CD, a compact disc
2 **record**
un disco viejo an old record

la **discoteca** noun *fem.*
disco

la **disculpa** noun *fem.*
apology
Tienes que pedir disculpas. You have to apologize.

disculparse verb
to apologize

el **discurso** noun *masc.*
speech

• *The months of the year and days of the week do not take a capital letter in Spanish.*

la **discusión** noun fem.
1 **argument**
  tener una discusión to have an argument
2 **discussion**

discutir verb
1 **to argue**
  discutir con alguien to argue with somebody
2 **to discuss**

diseñar verb
  to design

el **diseño** noun masc.
  design

el **disfraz** noun masc. (plural los **disfraces**)
  costume, fancy dress
  un disfraz de pirata a pirate costume
  una fiesta de disfraces a fancy dress party

disfrazarse verb
  to dress up
  Me disfracé de pirata. I dressed up as a pirate.

disléxico adjective masc., **disléxica** fem.
  dyslexic
  Soy disléxica. I'm dyslexic.

la **distancia** noun fem.
  distance
  una distancia de cien metros a distance of a hundred metres
  ¿A qué distancia está la biblioteca? How far is the library?

distinto adjective masc., **distinta** fem.
  different
  Soy muy distinto a mi hermano. I'm very different from my brother.

divertido adjective masc., **divertida** fem.
1 **funny**
  Mis amigos son muy divertidos. My friends are very funny.

2 **enjoyable**
  La fiesta fue divertida. The party was enjoyable.
  ¡Qué divertido! What fun!

divertirse verb
  to have fun
  Me divertí mucho. I had a lot of fun.

dividir verb
  to divide
  Doce dividido por dos son seis. Twelve divided by two is six.

divorciado adjective masc., **divorciada** fem.
  divorced
  Mis padres están divorciados. My parents are divorced.

doblar verb
1 **to fold**
  doblar algo por la mitad to fold something in half
2 **to bend**
  doblar el brazo to bend your arm
3 **to turn**
  Dobla a la derecha. Turn right.
4 **to double**

doble adjective masc. & fem.
  double
  una habitación doble a double room

el **doble** noun masc.
  twice as much
  Este vestido cuesta el doble. This dress costs twice as much.

doce number
1 **twelve**
  Mi hermana tiene doce años. My sister is twelve (years old).
  Son las doce. It's twelve o'clock.
2 (with dates) **twelfth**
  el doce de marzo the twelfth of March

• See the centre section for verb tables.

a
b
c
d
e
f
g
h
i
j
k
l
m
n
o
p
q
r
s
t
u
v
w
x
y
z

la **docena** noun fem.
dozen
una docena de huevos a dozen eggs
dos docenas two dozen

el **doctor** noun masc.,
la **doctora** fem.
doctor

el **dólar** noun masc.
dollar

doler verb
to hurt
Me duele la pierna. My leg hurts.
Me duele mucho. It hurts a lot.
Me duele la cabeza. I have a headache.

el **dolor** noun masc.
1 pain
Siento mucho dolor. I'm in a lot of pain.
2 ache
Tengo dolor de cabeza. I have a headache.
Tengo dolor de muelas. I have a toothache.

el **domingo** noun masc.
Sunday
Hoy es domingo. It's Sunday today.
el domingo on Sunday
Te veo el domingo. I'll see you on Sunday.
los domingos on Sundays
Voy a la piscina los domingos. I go swimming on Sundays.

LANGUAGE
Remember the difference between el domingo (one Sunday only) and los domingos (every Sunday).

el **dominó** noun masc.
dominoes
jugar al dominó to play dominoes

donde adverb
where
Es la ciudad donde nací. It's the town where I was born.

dónde adverb
(in questions) where
¿Dónde estás? Where are you?
¿Dónde vas? Where are you going?
¿De dónde eres? Where are you from?
¿por dónde? which way?

LANGUAGE
Remember to put the accent on dónde in questions.

dorado adjective masc.,
dorada fem.
golden

dormir verb
to sleep
Están durmiendo. They're sleeping.
estar medio dormido to be half asleep

dormirse verb
to fall asleep
Me dormí. I fell asleep.

el **dormitorio** noun masc.
1 bedroom
2 (in a school etc.) dormitory

LANGUAGE
Both dormitorio and 'dormitory' are related to dormir (to sleep) because you sleep there.

dos number
1 two
Mi hermano tiene dos años. My brother is two.
Son las dos. It's two o'clock.
2 (with dates) second
el dos de agosto the second of August
3 both
Están cansados los dos. They're both tired.

• Use el and uno for masculine words and la and una for feminine words.

doscientos number *masc.*,
doscientas *fem.*
two hundred

el **dragón** noun *masc.* (plural los
dragones)
dragon

la **ducha** noun *fem.*
shower
La ducha no funciona. The shower
doesn't work.
darse una ducha to have a
shower

ducharse verb
to have a shower
Me estoy duchando. I'm having a
shower.

la **duda** noun *fem.*
doubt

dudar verb
to doubt
Lo dudo. I doubt it.

dulce adjective *masc. & fem.*
sweet
una manzana muy dulce a very
sweet apple

el **dulce** noun *masc.*
sweet
Me gustan los dulces. I like sweets.

durante preposition
1 during
durante la noche during the night
2 for
**Me quedé en casa durante una
semana.** I stayed at home for a
week.

durar verb
to last
Las vacaciones duran un mes.
The holidays last for a month.
¿Cuánto tiempo dura la película?
How long is the film?
La película dura dos horas.
The film is two hours long.

duro adjective *masc.*, **dura** *fem.*
1 hard
Las patatas están duras.
The potatoes are hard.
2 strict
La maestra es muy dura.
The teacher is very strict.

el **DVD** noun *masc.* (plural los **DVDs**)
DVD
un reproductor DVD a DVD player

Ee

e conjunction
and
español e inglés Spanish and
English
padre e hijo father and son

🔑 **LANGUAGE**
In Spanish you use **e** instead of the normal
y before words beginning with **i** or **hi**, but
not before **hie**.

echar verb
1 to throw

echar algo a la basura to throw
something into the bin
Me eché al agua. I jumped into the
water.
2 to put
echar gasolina al coche to put
petrol in the car
3 to put on
Echan una buena película. They're
putting on a good film.
4 **echar de menos** to miss
Te echo de menos. I miss you.
Echo de menos a mis padres. I miss
my parents.

a b c d e f g h i j k l m n o p q r s t u v w x y z

• *Languages and nationalities do not take a capital letter in Spanish.*

a
b
c
d
e
f
g
h
i
j
k
l
m
n
o
p
q
r
s
t
u
v
w
x
y
z

echarse verb
(*on a bed, sofa, etc.*) **to lie down**
Échate en la cama. Lie down on the bed.

Ecuador noun *masc.*
Ecuador

la **edad** noun *fem.*
age
a la edad de ocho años at the age of eight
¿Qué edad tienes? How old are you?

el **edificio** noun *masc.*
building

Edimburgo noun *masc.*
Edinburgh

la **educación** noun *fem.*
1 education
2 manners
Eso es de mala educación. That's bad manners.

educado adjective *masc.*,
educada *fem.*
polite
una niña bien educada a polite girl
un niño mal educado a rude boy

egoísta adjective *masc. & fem.*
selfish

el **ejemplo** noun *masc.*
example
por ejemplo for example

el **ejercicio** noun *masc.*
exercise
un ejercicio de español a Spanish exercise
Hago mucho ejercicio. I do a lot of exercise.

el **ejército** noun *masc.*
army

el determiner *masc.*
1 (*before masculine singular nouns*) **the**
el niño the boy
el tren the train

2 (*before feminine singular nouns beginning with a stressed 'a' sound*) **the**
el agua the water
el hada the fairy
3 (*no translation*)
Me gusta el chocolate. I like chocolate.
Tengo el pelo largo. I have long hair.
4 (*with adjectives used as nouns*) **the**
el rojo the red one
el pequeño the small one
5 (*with parts of the body, clothes, etc.*)
my, your, his (*etc.*)
Me he cortado el dedo. I've cut my finger.
Ponte el sombrero. Put your hat on.
Le han robado el móvil. Someone has stolen his mobile.

él pronoun *masc.*
1 he
Él lee libros pero su hermano prefiere ver la tele. He reads books but his brother prefers to watch TV.

LANGUAGE
Él is used for giving special importance to the word 'he'.

2 (*after a preposition etc.*) **him**
con él with him
Soy más alta que él. I'm taller than him.
Es él. It's him.
él mismo himself

la **elección** noun *fem.*
choice
una buena elección a good choice

la **electricidad** noun *fem.*
electricity

el or la **electricista** noun *masc. & fem.*
electrician
Mi tío es electricista. My uncle is an electrician.

eléctrico adjective *masc.*,
eléctrica *fem.*
electric

• *The months of the year and days of the week do not take a capital letter in Spanish.*

electrónico adjective *masc.*,
electrónica *fem.*
electronic
un correo electrónico an email
por correo electrónico by email

el **elefante** noun *masc.*
elephant

elegante adjective *masc. & fem.*
smart
Estás muy elegante. You look very
smart.

elegir verb
to choose

ella pronoun *fem.*
1 she
Ella ha venido pero los otros no.
She has come but the others
haven't.

🔑 **LANGUAGE**
Élla is used for giving special importance
to the word 'she'.

2 *(after a preposition etc.)* **her**
con ella with her
Juego mejor que ella. I play better
than her.
Es ella. It's her.
ella misma herself

ellas pronoun *fem.*
1 they
Ellas van al parque pero yo no.
They're going to the park but I'm
not.

🔑 **LANGUAGE**
Éllas is used for giving special importance
to the word 'they'.

2 *(after a preposition etc.)* **them**
con ellas with them
Somos más inteligentes que ellas.
We're cleverer than them.
Son ellas. It's them.
ellas mismas themselves

• *See the centre section for verb tables.*

ellos pronoun *masc.*
1 they
**Ellos vienen a la fiesta pero
nosotros no.** They're coming to the
party but we are not.

🔑 **LANGUAGE**
Éllos is used for giving special importance
to the word 'they'.

2 *(after a preposition etc.)* **them**
con ellos with them
Soy más alto que ellos. I'm taller
than them.
Son ellos. It's them.
ellos mismos themselves

embarazada adjective *fem.*
pregnant
Está embarazada de seis meses.
She's six months pregnant.

la **emergencia** noun *fem.*
emergency
una salida de emergencia an
emergency exit

emocionante adjective *masc. & fem.*
exciting
una película emocionante
an exciting film

la **empanadilla** noun *fem.*
pastie

empatar verb
(talking about teams) **to draw**

el **empate** noun *masc.*
(in a match) **draw**

empezar verb
to start
La película empieza a las dos.
The film starts at two.
**Hemos empezado a aprender
español.** We've started to learn
Spanish.

a
b
c
d
e
f
g
h
i
j
k
l
m
n
o
p
q
r
s
t
u
v
w
x
y
z

el **empleado** noun masc.,
la **empleada** fem.
1 office worker
2 (in a bank) bank worker

el **empleo** noun masc.
job
buscar empleo to look for a job

la **empresa** noun fem.
company

empujar verb
to push
¡No me empujes! Don't push me!

en preposition
1 in
en la caja in the box
en Escocia in Scotland
en inglés in English
2 into
Entré en la cocina. I went into the kitchen.
3 on
en la mesa on the table
en la tele on TV
4 by
en autobús by bus
5 at
en la estación at the station
en casa at home

enamorado adjective masc.,
enamorada fem.
in love
estar enamorado de alguien to be in love with somebody

enamorarse verb
to fall in love

el **enano** noun masc., la **enana** fem.
dwarf

encantado adjective masc.,
encantada fem.
pleased
Encantado de conocerte. Pleased to meet you.
Estoy encantada con los regalos. I'm very pleased with the presents.

encantador adjective masc.,
encantadora fem.
lovely

encantar verb
to love
Me encanta el fútbol. I love football.
Me encantan las películas. I love films.
A Zafir le encanta leer. Zafir loves to read.

🔑 **LANGUAGE**
Encantar means 'to please very much' so the order of the words in the Spanish sentence is different, e.g. *Me encanta el fútbol* is, word for word, 'Football pleases me very much'.

el **encargado** noun masc.,
la **encargada** fem.
manager, person in charge

encender verb
1 to light
encender una vela to light a candle
2 to switch on
encender la luz to switch on the light

encendido adjective masc.,
encendida fem.
1 (light, computer, etc.) on
La tele está encendida. The TV is on.
2 burning
El fuego está encendido. The fire is burning.

enchufar verb
to plug in

la **enciclopedia** noun fem.
encyclopedia

• Use **el** and **uno** for masculine words and **la** and **una** for feminine words.

56

encima adverb
1 **on top**
Pon el libro aquí encima. Put the book here on top.
2 **encima de** on top of
encima del armario on top of the wardrobe
3 **por encima de** over
El balón pasó por encima de la portería. The ball went over the goal.

⚷ **LANGUAGE**
Use por encima de with verbs of movement like pasar (go) or saltar (jump).

encontrar verb
to find
No encuentro mi reloj. I can't find my watch.

encontrarse verb
1 **to meet**
Nos encontramos en la calle. We met in the street.
encontrarse con alguien to meet somebody
2 **to feel**
No me encuentro bien. I don't feel well.

el **enemigo** noun masc.,
la **enemiga** fem.
enemy

la **energía** noun fem.
energy

enero noun masc.
January
Ven a mi fiesta en enero. Come to my party in January.
el seis de enero on the sixth of January

enfadado adjective masc.,
enfadada fem.
angry
¿Estás enfadada conmigo?
Are you angry with me?

enfadarse verb
to get angry

la **enfermedad** noun fem.
illness

el **enfermero** noun masc.,
la **enfermera** fem.
nurse
Mi madre es enfermera.
My mother's a nurse.

enfermo adjective masc.,
enferma fem.
ill
Estoy enferma. I'm ill.
ponerse enfermo to get ill

el **enfermo** noun masc.,
la **enferma** fem.
1 **sick person**
los enfermos sick people
2 (in a hospital etc.) **patient**

enfrente adverb
1 **opposite**
Siéntate enfrente. Sit down opposite.
2 (with nouns and pronouns)
enfrente de opposite
enfrente de la estación opposite the station
Gabriel está sentado enfrente de mí. Gabriel is sitting opposite me.
3 de enfrente opposite
la casa de enfrente the opposite house

enhorabuena exclamation
congratulations!

el **enlace** noun masc.
(on a web page) **link**
Sigue el enlace. Follow the link.

enorme adjective masc. & fem.
huge, enormous

la **ensalada** noun fem.
salad
una ensalada de frutas a fruit salad

• Languages and nationalities do not take a capital letter in Spanish.

a
b
c
d
e
f
g
h
i
j
k
l
m
n
o
p
q
r
s
t
u
v
w
x
y
z

a
b
c
d
e
f
g
h
i
j
k
l
m
n
o
p
q
r
s
t
u
v
w
x
y
z

la **ensaladilla** noun *fem.*
 Russian salad

 CULTURE
A Russian salad is made with boiled potatoes, carrots, hard-boiled eggs, peas, etc. mixed with mayonnaise.

el **ensayo** noun *masc.*
 rehearsal
 Tenemos ensayo. We have a rehearsal.

enseguida adverb
 straight away
 Enseguida vuelvo. I'm coming straight back.

la **enseñanza** noun *fem.*
 education
 la enseñanza primaria primary education

enseñar verb
 1 to teach
 La señora Campbell enseña inglés. Mrs Campbell teaches English.
 Mi madre me enseñó a leer. My mum taught me to read.
 2 to show
 Enséñame el cuaderno. Show me the exercise book.

entender verb
 to understand
 Entiendo el español. I understand Spanish.
 ¿Entiendes? Do you understand?

entenderse verb
 to get on
 Nos entendemos bien. We get on well.

entero adjective *masc.*, **entera** *fem.*
 whole
 una semana entera a whole week

entonces adverb
 1 then
 Entonces no había coches. There were no cars then.
 desde entonces since then
 2 so, then
 Entonces, ¿qué vas a hacer? So, what are you going to do?, What are you going to do, then?

la **entrada** noun *fem.*
 1 entrance
 ¿Dónde está la entrada? Where's the entrance?
 2 (*for the cinema, museum, etc.*) ticket

entrar verb
 1 to go in
 Entra tú, yo te espero. You go in, and I'll wait for you.
 Entré en la tienda. I went into the shop.
 2 to come in
 ¿Puedo entrar? Can I come in?
 3 (*used for saying you're starting to get hungry, cold, etc.*)
 Me está entrando hambre. I'm getting hungry.

entre preposition
 1 between
 entre la escuela y la estación. between the school and the station.
 2 **entre todos** together
 Decoramos la clase entre todos. We decorated the classroom all together.

entregar verb
 1 to deliver
 entregar un paquete to deliver a parcel
 2 to hand in
 entregar los deberes to hand in the homework

el **entrenamiento** noun *masc.*
 training

entrenar verb
 (*for football etc.*) to train

la **entrevista** noun *fem.*
 interview

entusiasmado adjective *masc.*, **entusiasmada** *fem.*
 excited

• *The months of the year and days of the week do not take a capital letter in Spanish.*

enviar verb
to send

envidioso adjective *masc.*,
envidiosa *fem.*
jealous, envious

envolver verb
to wrap up
envolver un regalo to wrap up a
present

el **episodio** noun *masc.*
episode

la **época** noun *fem.*
time
esta época del año this time of the
year

el **equilibrio** noun *masc.*
balance
Perdí el equilibrio. I lost my
balance.

el **equipaje** noun *masc.*
luggage

el **equipo** noun *masc.*
1 team
un equipo de fútbol a football
team
2 equipment
el equipo de camping the camping
equipment
un equipo de música a stereo

la **equitación** noun *fem.*
horse riding
hacer equitación to go riding

equivocado adjective *masc.*,
equivocada *fem.*
wrong
Estás equivocado. You're
wrong.
la respuesta equivocada the
wrong answer

equivocarse verb
1 to be wrong
Te equivocas. You're wrong.
Me he equivocado de autobús.
I got on the wrong bus.

2 to make a mistake
Lo siento, me he equivocado.
Sorry, I made a mistake.

era verb SEE **ser**
was
Era cierto. It was true.

eran verb SEE **ser**
were
Mis amigos eran españoles.
My friends were Spanish.

eres verb SEE **ser**
are
Eres mi mejor amiga. You're my
best friend.

el **error** noun *masc.*
mistake
cometer un error to make a
mistake

es verb SEE **ser**
is
Es inglesa. She's English.
No es difícil. It isn't hard.

esa, **ésa** adjective & pronoun *fem.*
SEE **ese, ése** adjective & pronoun
that, that one

esas, **ésas** adjective & pronoun *fem.*
SEE **esos, ésos** adjective & pronoun
those

la **escalera** noun *fem.*
1 staircase
2 stairs
bajar la escalera to go down the
stairs

> 🔑 **LANGUAGE**
> You can also say **las escaleras** in the
> plural in Spanish.

3 ladder
subirse a una escalera to climb a
ladder
una escalera de mano a ladder
4 **una escalera mecánica** an
escalator

• *See the centre section for verb tables.*

el **escalón** noun masc. (plural los **escalones**)
step
¡Cuidado con el escalón! Mind the step!

el **escáner** noun masc.
scanner

el **escaparate** noun masc.
shop window

escaparse verb
1 to escape
2 to run away
Se escapó de la escuela. He ran away from school.

el **escarabajo** noun masc.
beetle

la **escayola** noun fem.
plaster (for broken bones)

escayolado adjective masc., **escayolada** fem.
in plaster
Tengo la pierna escayolada. I've got my leg in plaster.

la **escoba** noun fem.
broom

escocés adjective masc., **escocesa** fem.
Scottish

LANGUAGE
The plural of escocés is escoceses.

el **escocés** masc., la **escocesa** noun fem.
Scot

LANGUAGE
The plural of escocés is escoceses.

Escocia noun fem.
Scotland

escoger verb
to choose
He escogido el verde. I've chosen the green one.

escolar adjective masc. & fem.
school
un autobús escolar a school bus
las vacaciones escolares the school holidays

el or la **escolar** noun masc. & fem.
schoolboy, schoolgirl
los escolares schoolchildren

esconder verb
to hide
Esconde los regalos. Hide the presents.

esconderse verb
to hide
Me escondí detrás de la puerta. I hid behind the door.

escondido adjective masc., **escondida** fem.
hidden
Está escondido allí. It's hidden there.

el **escondite** noun masc.
hiding place
jugar al escondite to play hide-and-seek

escribir verb
1 to write
Escribe las palabras en tu cuaderno. Write the words in your exercise book.
Nos escribimos. We write to each other.
2 to spell
Lo has escrito mal. You've spelled it wrong.
¿Cómo se escribe tu nombre? How do you spell your name?

el **escritor** noun masc., la **escritora** fem.
writer

el **escritorio** noun masc.
desk

• Use el and uno for masculine words and la and una for feminine words.

60

escuchar verb
to listen, to listen to
¡Escucha! Listen!
Me gusta escuchar música. I like to listen to music.

🔑 **LANGUAGE**
Spanish = escuchar algo/a alguien
English = to listen to something/
          somebody

el **escudo** noun *masc.*
shield

la **escuela** noun *fem.*
school
en la escuela at school
ir a la escuela to go to school

escupir verb
to spit

ese adjective *masc.*, **esa** *fem.*
that
ese niño that boy
esa bicicleta that bicycle

ése pronoun *masc.*, **ésa** *fem.*
1 **that one**
Me gusta ése. I like that one.
Toma ésa. Take that one.
2 **that**
¿Quién es ésa? Who's that?

🔑 **LANGUAGE**
The accent goes on ése and ésa to show clearly you're using the pronoun.

el **esfuerzo** noun *masc.*
effort
hacer un esfuerzo to make an effort

el **esguince** noun *masc.*
sprain
Tengo un esguince en el tobillo. I've sprained my ankle.

el **esmalte** noun *masc.*
el esmalte de uñas nail varnish

eso pronoun
that
¿Qué es eso? What's that?
¡Eso es! That's it!

esos adjective *masc.*, **esas** *fem.*
those
esos libros those books
esas sillas those chairs

ésos pronoun *masc.*, **ésas** *fem.*
those
Quiero ésos. I want those.
Ésas son mejores. Those are better.

🔑 **LANGUAGE**
The accent goes on ésos and ésas to show clearly you're using the pronoun.

espacial adjective *masc. & fem.*
space
una estación espacial a space station
una nave espacial a spaceship

el **espacio** noun *masc.*
1 **room, space**
No hay suficiente espacio. There isn't enough room.
2 **space**
Deja un espacio. Leave a space.
un viaje en el espacio a journey into space

la **espada** noun *fem.*
sword

los **espaguetis** plural noun *masc.*
spaghetti

🔑 **LANGUAGE**
Spanish = los espaguetis is plural
English = spaghetti is singular

la **espalda** noun *fem.*
back
Me duele la espalda. My back hurts.

España noun *fem.*
Spain
Estamos en España. We're in Spain.
Quiero ir a España. I want to go to Spain.

a b c d e f g h i j k l m n o p q r s t u v w x y z

• *Languages and nationalities do not take a capital letter in Spanish.*

el **español** noun *masc.*
Spanish
Hablo español. I speak Spanish.

español adjective *masc.*,
española *fem.*
Spanish
Soy español. I'm Spanish.

el **español** noun *masc.*,
la **española** *fem.*
Spaniard
los españoles the Spanish

especial adjective *masc. & fem.*
special

especialmente adverb
especially

espectacular adjective *masc. & fem.*
spectacular

el **espectáculo** noun *masc.*
(*with actors, musicians, etc.*) **show**

el **espejo** noun *masc.*
mirror
en el espejo in the mirror

la **espera** noun *fem.*
wait
una larga espera a long wait
una sala de espera a waiting room

esperar verb
1 **to wait**, **to wait for**
Espera aquí. Wait here.
Espérame. Wait for me.

LANGUAGE
Spanish = **esperar** a alguien
English = **to wait for** somebody

2 **to hope**
Espero tener buen tiempo. I hope I
have good weather.
Espero que sí. I hope so.
3 **to expect**
Te espero a las cinco. I'll expect
you at five.
Está esperando un niño. She's
expecting a baby.

espeso adjective *masc.*, **espesa** *fem.*
thick

las **espinacas** plural noun *fem.*
spinach

LANGUAGE
Spanish = **las espinacas** is plural
English = **spinach** is singular

la **esponja** noun *fem.*
sponge

la **esposa** noun *fem.*
wife

el **esposo** noun *masc.*
husband

el **esqueleto** noun *masc.*
skeleton

el **esquí** noun *masc.*
1 **ski**
un par de esquís a pair of skis
una pista de esquí a ski slope
2 **skiing**
Me encanta el esquí. I love skiing.

esquiar verb
to ski

la **esquina** noun *fem.*
corner
doblar la esquina to turn the
corner

esta, **ésta** adjective & pronoun *fem.*
SEE **este, éste** adjective & pronoun
this, **this one**

está verb SEE **estar**
is
La puerta está abierta. The door's
open.
Papá está en el jardín. Dad's in the
garden.

estaba verb SEE **estar**
was
Estaba en Toledo. He was in
Toledo.

• *The months of the year and days of the week do not take a capital letter in Spanish.*

estaban verb SEE **estar**
were
Estaban en la escuela. They were in school.

la **estación** noun *fem.* (plural las **estaciones**)
1 station
en la estación at the station
una estación de autobuses a bus station
2 season
la estación de las lluvias the rainy season

estacionar verb
to park
'Prohibido estacionar' 'No parking'

el **estadio** noun *masc.*
stadium

el **estado** noun *masc.*
condition
en buen estado in good condition

Estados Unidos noun *masc.*
United States
Voy a Estados Unidos. I'm going to the United States.

estadounidense adjective *masc. & fem.*
American

estáis verb SEE **estar**
are
Tomás y Rafael, ¿dónde estáis? Tomás and Rafael, where are you?

estallar verb
to explode
Una bomba estalló. A bomb exploded.

estamos verb SEE **estar**
are

• *See the centre section for verb tables.*

Estamos en la cocina. We're in the kitchen.

están verb SEE **estar**
are
Están cansados. They're tired.
Están en la playa. They're on the beach.

la **estancia** noun *fem.*
stay
mi estancia en Barcelona my stay in Barcelona

el **estanco** noun *masc.*
tobacconist's shop

el **estanque** noun *masc.*
pond

el **estante** noun *masc.*
shelf

la **estantería** noun *fem.*
bookcase

estar verb
1 to be
Estoy en mi habitación. I'm in my room.
¿Dónde está mi libro? Where's my book?
Tu hermano no está. Your brother isn't here.
¿Cómo estás? How are you?
¿Estáis cansadas? Are you tired?
Estamos jugando. We're playing.
¿Qué están haciendo? What are they doing?
Han estado de vacaciones. They've been on holiday.
2 (*with dates*)
¿A cuántos estamos? What's the date?

Estamos a cinco de junio. It's the fifth of June.

estas, **éstas** adjective & pronoun *fem.*
SEE **estos, éstos** adjective & pronoun
these

estás verb SEE **estar**
are
¿Dónde estás, Maite? Where are you, Maite?

la **estatua** noun *fem.*
statue

la **estatura** noun *fem.*
height

este noun *masc.* & adjective
east
en el este in the east
la costa este the east coast

este adjective *masc.*, **esta** *fem.*
this
este coche this car
esta niña this girl

éste pronoun *masc.*, **ésta** *fem.*
1 **this one**
Me gusta éste. I like this one.
Mira ésta. Look at this one.
2 **this**
¿Quién es ésta? Who's this?

estirar verb
to stretch
Estira las piernas. Stretch your legs.

estirarse verb
(*after waking up etc.*) **to stretch**

esto pronoun
this
¿Qué es esto? What's this?

el **estofado** noun *masc.*
stew

el **estómago** noun *masc.*
stomach
Me duele el estómago. I have a stomach ache.

estornudar verb
to sneeze

estos adjective *masc.*, **estas** *fem.*
these
estos compactos these CDs
estas cajas these boxes

éstos *masc.*, **éstas** *fem.* pronoun
these
Quiero éstos. I want these.
Éstas son más grandes. These are bigger.

estoy verb SEE **estar**
am
Estoy triste. I'm sad.
Estoy en mi habitación. I'm in my room.

estrecho adjective *masc.*, **estrecha** *fem.*
1 **narrow**
una calle estrecha a narrow street
2 **tight**

• Use **el** and **uno** for masculine words and **la** and **una** for feminine words.

La falda está estrecha. The skirt is too tight.

la **estrella** noun fem.
  star
  una estrella de cine a film star

estresado adjective masc.,
  estresada fem.
  stressed out

estricto adjective masc.,
  estricta fem.
  strict

estropear verb
  1 (a toy, the TV, etc.) **to break**
  2 (clothes, holidays, etc.) **to ruin**

estropearse verb
  to break down
  Se ha estropeado el coche. The car has broken down.

el **estuche** noun masc.
  case
  un estuche para lápices a pencil case

el or la **estudiante** noun masc. & fem.
  student
  Mi hermano es estudiante. My brother is a student.

estudiar verb
  to study

el **estudio** noun masc.
  1 studio
  un estudio de televisión a TV studio
  2 studio flat

los **estudios** plural noun masc.
  (in school) **studies**

estupendo adjective masc.,
  estupenda fem.
  great
  ¡Estupendo! Great!

estúpido adjective masc.,
  estúpida fem.
  stupid

la **etiqueta** noun fem.
  label

el **euro** noun masc.
  euro

Europa noun fem.
  Europe

europeo adjective masc.,
  europea fem.
  European
  la Unión Europea the European Union

el **europeo** noun masc.,
  la **europea** fem.
  European

Euskadi noun
  the Basque Country

el **euskera** noun masc.
  Basque (the language)

evitar verb
  to avoid

exacto adjective masc.,
  exacta fem.
  exact

exagerar verb
  to exaggerate

el **examen** noun masc. (plural los **exámenes**)
  exam
  un examen de español a Spanish exam

excelente adjective masc. & fem.
  excellent

excepto preposition
  except
  todos excepto yo everybody except me

• Languages and nationalities do not take a capital letter in Spanish.

la **excursión** noun *fem.* (plural las **excursiones**)
trip
Voy de excursión al campo.
I'm going on a trip to the country.

la **excusa** noun *fem.*
excuse

existir verb
to exist

el **éxito** noun *masc.*
success

⚠ **FALSE FRIEND**
el éxito = success (*not* exit)

la **experiencia** noun *fem.*
experience

el **experimento** noun *masc.*
experiment

el **experto** noun *masc.*,
la **experta** *fem.*
expert

la **explicación** noun *fem.* (plural las **explicaciones**)
explanation

explicar verb
to explain
¿Puede explicarme esto? Can you explain this to me?

explorar verb
to explore

la **explosión** noun *fem.* (plural las **explosiones**)
explosion

la **exposición** noun *fem.* (plural las **exposiciones**)
exhibition

la **expresión** noun *fem.* (plural las **expresiones**)
expression

extender verb
1 (*butter, glue, etc.*) **to spread**
Extiende el pegamento. Spread the glue.

2 **to stretch**
extender la mano to stretch out your hand

el **exterior** noun *masc.*
outside
el exterior de la casa the outside of the house

el **extranjero** noun *masc.*
1 **en el extranjero** abroad
vivir en el extranjero to live abroad
2 (*with verbs showing movement*)
al extranjero abroad
ir al extranjero to go abroad

extranjero adjective *masc.*,
extranjera *fem.*
foreign

el **extranjero** noun *masc.*,
la **extranjera** *fem.*
foreigner
Soy extranjera. I'm a foreigner.

extraño adjective *masc.*,
extraña *fem.*
strange

extraordinario adjective *masc.*,
extraordinaria *fem.*
1 **unusual**
2 (*success, beauty, etc.*) **outstanding**

el or la **extraterrestre** noun *masc. & fem.*
extraterrestrial

el **extremo** noun *masc.*
end
Ponte al otro extremo de la fila.
Go to the other end of the line.
al otro extremo de la ciudad at the other end of town

• *The months of the year and days of the week do not take a capital letter in Spanish.*

Ff

la **fábrica** noun *fem.*
factory

fabricar verb
to make
'**Fabricado en España.**' 'Made in
Spain.'

fácil adjective *masc. & fem.*
easy
Es fácil de entender. It's easy to
understand.

fácilmente adverb
easily

la **factura** noun *fem.*
(*for gas, phone, etc.*) **bill**

la **falda** noun *fem.*
skirt

las **Fallas** plural noun *fem.*
the festival of San José (Saint
Joseph) in Valencia

CULTURE
Every March the people of Valencia make
fallas: cardboard figures of famous
people that they display in the streets.
The most important part of the festival is
the burning of the **fallas** on 19th March.

falso adjective *masc.*, **falsa** *fem.*
false
¿Verdadero o falso? True or false?

la **falta** noun *fem.*
1 mistake
hacer una falta de ortografía to
make a spelling mistake
2 (*in sport*) **foul**

faltar verb
to be missing
Falta una página. There's a page
missing.
¿Quién falta? Who's missing?

• *See the centre section for verb tables.*

la **familia** noun *fem.*
family
en familia with the family
una familia numerosa a big family

famoso adjective *masc.*,
famosa *fem.*
famous

el **fantasma** noun *masc.*
ghost

LANGUAGE
Be careful: **fantasma** ends in an -**a** but it is
not a feminine noun.

fantástico adjective *masc.*,
fantástica *fem.*
fantastic

el **farmacéutico** *masc.*,
la **farmacéutica** noun *fem.*
chemist

la **farmacia** noun *fem.*
chemist's, pharmacy

el **faro** noun *masc.*
1 (*on the coast*) **lighthouse**
2 (*of a car*) **headlamp**

la **farola** noun *fem.*
1 lamp-post
chocar contra una farola to crash
into a lamp-post
2 streetlight

fatal adjective *masc. & fem.*
1 fatal
un accidente fatal a fatal accident
2 really awful
Me siento fatal. I feel really awful.

fatal adverb
really badly
Lo has hecho fatal. You've done it
really badly.

a
b
c
d
e
f
g
h
i
j
k
l
m
n
o
p
q
r
s
t
u
v
w
x
y
z

el **favor** noun masc.
favour
¿Me haces un favor? Can you do me a favour?
por favor please
Apaga la luz, por favor. Turn the light off, please.

favorito adjective masc.,
favorita fem.
favourite

febrero noun masc.
February
Mi cumpleaños es en febrero. My birthday is in February.
el tres de febrero on the third of February

la **fecha** noun fem.
date
mi fecha de nacimiento my date of birth
¿A qué fecha estamos hoy? What's the date today?

la **felicidad** noun fem.
1 happiness
2 ¡Felicidades! Congratulations!
¿Es tu cumpleaños? – ¡Felicidades! Is it your birthday? – Happy birthday!

feliz adjective masc. & fem. (plural **felices**)
happy
Soy muy feliz aquí. I'm very happy here.
¡Feliz cumpleaños! Happy birthday!
¡Feliz Año Nuevo! Happy New Year!
¡Feliz Navidad! Happy Christmas!

femenino adjective masc.,
femenina fem.
1 (in grammar) feminine
el género femenino the feminine gender

2 women's
el equipo femenino the women's team

LANGUAGE
Spanish = femenino
English = feminine

fenomenal adjective masc. & fem.
fantastic

feo adjective masc., **fea** fem.
ugly

la **feria** noun fem.
fair

feroz adjective masc. & fem. (plural **feroces**)
fierce

el **ferrocarril** noun masc.
railway
una línea de ferrocarril a railway line

festivo adjective masc.
un día festivo a holiday

la **ficha** noun fem.
1 (in a game) counter
2 card

el **fichero** noun masc.
(on a computer) file

los **fideos** plural noun masc.
noodles

la **fiebre** noun fem.
1 temperature
tener fiebre to have a temperature
2 fever
Tengo fiebre del heno. I have hay fever.

la **fiesta** noun fem.
1 party
Van a dar una fiesta. They're going to have a party.
una fiesta de cumpleaños a birthday party
2 holiday
El martes es fiesta. Tuesday is a holiday.

• Use **el** and **uno** for masculine words and **la** and **una** for feminine words.

un día de fiesta a holiday

la **fila** noun *fem.*
1 **line**
   ponerse en fila to get into line
   en fila india in single file
2 (*in the cinema etc.*) **row**
   en la primera fila in the front row

el **fin** noun *masc.*
1 **end**
   el fin del año escolar the end of the school year
   la fiesta de fin de curso the end-of-year party
   el fin de semana the weekend
2 **¡por fin!** at last!

el **final** noun *masc.*
1 **end**
   al final de ha calle at the end of the street
   al final in the end
   a finales de agosto at the end of August
2 (*of a book, film, or play*) **ending**
   un final feliz a happy ending

la **final** noun *fem.*
   final
   Nuestro equipo la ganado la final. Our team has won the final.

fino adjective *masc.*, **fina** *fem.*
   thin
   una rebanada fina a thin slice

la **firma** noun *fem.*
   signature

firmar verb
   to sign

físico adjective *masc.*, **física** *fem.*
   physical

flaco adjective *masc.*, **flaca** *fem.*
   skinny

el **flamenco** noun *masc.*
   flamenco

CULTURE
Flamenco is a type of popular music with dancing, singing, and guitar playing that started in Andalusia in the south of Spain.

la **flauta** noun *fem.*
   flute
   Joaquín toca la flauta. Joaquín plays the flute.
   la flauta dulce the recorder

LANGUAGE
Word for word flauta dulce means 'sweet flute'.

la **flecha** noun *fem.*
   arrow

el **flequillo** noun *masc.*
   fringe
   Llevo flequillo. I have a fringe.

flojo adjective *masc.*, **floja** *fem.*
1 (*knot, wire, etc.*) **loose**
2 **weak**
   Está flojo. He's weak.

la **flor** noun *fem.*
   flower
   un ramo de flores a bunch of flowers

el **florero** noun *masc.*
   vase

el or la **florista** noun *masc. & fem.*
   florist

la **floristería** noun *fem.*
   florist's

flotar verb
   to float

la **foca** noun *fem.*
   seal

el **fondo** noun *masc.*
1 **bottom**
   en el fondo del mar at the bottom of the sea

• *Languages and nationalities do not take a capital letter in Spanish.*

2 end
al fondo del pasillo at the end of the corridor
3 back
al fondo de la clase at the back of the class

el **fontanero** noun *masc.*,
la **fontanera** *fem.*
plumber
Mi padre es fontanero. My dad's a plumber.

el **footing** noun *masc.*
jogging
hacer footing to go jogging

la **forma** noun *fem.*
1 shape
en forma de cruz in the shape of a cross
2 en forma fit
Carlos está en forma. Carlos is fit.

formar verb
1 to form
formar un círculo to form a circle
Han formado un grupo. They've formed a band.
¡Formad parejas! Get into pairs!
2 to make up
El equipo está formado por niños y niñas. The team is made up of boys and girls.

el **formulario** noun *masc.*
form
rellenar un formulario to fill in a form

la **foto** noun *fem.*
photo
He hecho una foto de mi casa. I've taken a photo of my house.
¿Puede hacernos una foto? Could you take a photo of us?

la **fotocopia** noun *fem.*
photocopy

la **fotocopiadora** noun *fem.*
photocopier

fotocopiar verb
to photocopy

la **fotografía** noun *fem.*
photograph
hacer una fotografía to take a photograph

el **fotógrafo** noun *masc.*,
la **fotógrafa** *fem.*
photographer

la **frambuesa** noun *fem.*
raspberry
la mermelada de frambuesa raspberry jam

el **francés** noun *masc.*
French
¿Hablas francés? Do you speak French?

francés adjective *masc.*,
francesa *fem.*
French
Alain es francés. Alain is French.

LANGUAGE
The plural of **francés** is **franceses**.

el **francés** noun *masc.*,
la **francesa** *fem.*
Frenchman, Frenchwoman
los franceses the French

Francia noun *fem.*
France

la **frase** noun *fem.*
1 sentence
Esta frase tiene dos verbos. This sentence has two verbs.
2 phrase
una frase hecha a set phrase

frecuente adjective *masc. & fem.*
1 common
un error frecuente a common mistake
2 frequent

frecuentemente adverb
frequently

• *The months of the year and days of the week do not take a capital letter in Spanish.*

el **fregadero** noun masc.
(in the kitchen) **sink**

fregar verb
to wash
fregar los platos to wash the dishes

frenar verb
to put on the brakes

el **freno** noun masc.
brake

la **frente** noun fem.
forehead

frente a preposition
opposite
frente al colegio opposite the school

la **fresa** noun fem.
strawberry
la mermelada de fresa strawberry jam

fresco adjective masc., **fresca** fem.
1 **cool**
una bebida fresca a cool drink
Hace fresco. The weather's cool.
2 **fresh**
huevos frescos fresh eggs

el **frigorífico** noun masc.
fridge

el **frío** noun masc.
1 **cold**
No me gusta el frío. I don't like the cold.
2 **tener frío** to be cold
Tengo frío. I'm cold.

🔑 **LANGUAGE**
Spanish = **tener** frío   **Tengo frío.**
English = **to be** cold   **I'm cold.**

---

3 **Hace frío.** It's cold.
¡Qué frío hace! It's so cold!

frío adjective masc., **fría** fem.
cold
La sopa está fría. The soup's cold.

• See the centre section for verb tables.

frito adjective masc., **frita** fem.
fried
un huevo frito a fried egg

la **frontera** noun fem.
border

la **fruta** noun fem.
fruit
Me gusta la fruta. I like fruit.
un zumo de fruta a fruit juice

la **frutería** noun fem.
fruit shop

fue verb
1 **went** SEE **ir**
Fue a casa. He went home.
2 **was** SEE **ser**
Ayer fue mi cumpleaños.
Yesterday was my birthday.

el **fuego** noun masc.
fire
encender el fuego to light the fire
los fuegos artificiales fireworks

la **fuente** noun fem.
1 **fountain**
2 **serving dish**

fuera adverb
1 **out**
Estoy aquí fuera. I'm out here.
Mi madre está fuera del país.
My mum's out of the country.
2 **outside**
Están jugando fuera. They're playing outside.
fuera de nuestra casa outside our house
3 **away**
Javier está fuera hasta el domingo.
Javier is away until Sunday.

fueron verb
1 **went** SEE **ir**
Fueron al supermercado. They went to the supermarket.
2 **were** SEE **ser**
Las vacaciones fueron muy buenas. The holidays were very good.

fuerte adjective *masc. & fem.*
1 **strong**
Soy fuerte. I'm strong.
2 **loud**
La música está muy fuerte. The music's very loud.
hablar más fuerte to speak louder
3 **bad**
un dolor fuerte a bad pain
un resfriado muy fuerte a very bad cold

la **fuerza** noun *fem.*
strength

🔑 **LANGUAGE**
Fuerza is related to 'force', another word for 'strength'.

fui verb
1 **went** SEE **ir**
Fui al colegio. I went to school.
2 **was** SEE **ser**
Fui la primera en llegar. I was the first to arrive.

funcionar verb
to work
El ordenador no funciona. The computer isn't working.

la **funda** noun *fem.*
1 (*for glasses, guitar, etc.*) **case**
2 (*for cushion, sofa, etc.*) **cover**

el **funeral** noun *masc.*
funeral

la **furgoneta** noun *fem.*
van

furioso adjective *masc.*,
furiosa *fem.*
furious
Estoy furioso contigo. I'm furious with you.

el **fútbol** noun *masc.*
football
Me gusta jugar al fútbol. I like to play football.
un balón de fútbol a football

el or la **futbolista** noun *masc. & fem.*
footballer
Quiero ser futbolista. I want to be a footballer.

el **futuro** noun *masc.*
future
en el futuro in the future

Gg

las **gafas** plural noun *fem.*
Llevo gafas. I wear glasses.
las gafas de sol sunglasses

la **galería** noun *fem.*
una galería comercial a shopping mall

Gales noun *masc.*
Wales
el País de Gales Wales

el **galés** noun *masc.*
Welsh
David habla galés. David speaks Welsh.

galés adjective *masc.*,
galesa *fem.*
Welsh

🔑 **LANGUAGE**
The plural of **galés** is **galeses**.

el **galés** noun *masc.*,
la **galesa** *fem.*
Welshman, Welshwoman
los galeses the Welsh

Galicia noun *fem.*
Galicia

• Use **el** and **uno** for masculine words and **la** and **una** for feminine words.

el **gallego** noun *masc.*
  Galician
  ¿Hablas gallego? Do you speak Galician?

la **galleta** noun *fem.*
  biscuit

la **gallina** noun *fem.*
 1 hen
 2 chicken
   darles de comer a las gallinas to feed the chickens

el **gallo** noun *masc.*
  cockerel, rooster

la **gamba** noun *fem.*
  prawn

la **gana** noun *fem.*
  tener ganas de hacer algo to feel like doing something
  No me da la gana. I don't feel like it.

el **ganador** noun *masc.*,
la **ganadora** *fem.*
  winner

ganar verb
 1 to win
   ganar una carrera to win a race
 2 to beat
   Les ganamos tres a cero. We beat them three nil.
 3 to earn
   ganar mucho dinero to earn lots of money

el **gancho** noun *masc.*
  hook

el **ganso** noun *masc.*, la **gansa** *fem.*
  goose

el **garaje** noun *masc.*
  garage

> 🔑 **LANGUAGE**
> Spanish = garaje
> English = garage

la **garganta** noun *fem.*
  throat

Me duele la garganta. I have a sore throat.

el **gas** noun *masc.*
  gas
  una cocina de gas a gas cooker
  agua con gas fizzy water

la **gaseosa** noun *fem.*
  lemonade

la **gasolina** noun *fem.*
  petrol
  echar gasolina to fill up with petrol

la **gasolinera** noun *fem.*
  petrol station

gastar verb
 1 to spend
   He gastado mucho dinero. I've spent a lot of money.
 2 to use
   ¿Has gastado toda el agua? Have you used all the water?

el **gato** noun *masc.*, la **gata** *fem.*
  cat

el **gazpacho** noun *masc.*
  gazpacho

> 🌎 **CULTURE**
> Gazpacho is a cold soup made from tomatoes and other vegetables. It's especially common in Andalusia in the south of Spain.

la **gelatina** noun *fem.*
  jelly

el **gemelo** noun *masc.*,
la **gemela** *fem.*
  identical twin

los **gemelos** plural noun *masc.*
  binoculars

general adjective *masc. & fem.*
  general
  en general generally

generalmente adverb
  generally

• *Languages and nationalities do not take a capital letter in Spanish.*

a
b
c
d
e
f
g
h
i
j
k
l
m
n
o
p
q
r
s
t
u
v
w
x
y
z

el **género** noun *masc.*
 gender
 'Cristal' es del género masculino.
 'Cristal' is masculine.

generoso adjective *masc.*,
 generosa *fem.*
 generous

genial adjective *masc. & fem.*
 brilliant
 ¡Es genial! It's brilliant!

el **genio** noun *masc.*
 1 genius
 Rosa es un genio. Rosa is a
 genius.
 2 temper
 José tiene mal genio. José has a
 bad temper.
 3 genie

la **gente** noun *fem.*
 people
 Hay mucha gente aquí. There are a
 lot of people here.
 No hay gente en la playa.
 There isn't anybody on the
 beach.

> **LANGUAGE**
> Gente is a singular noun.

la **geografía** noun *fem.*
 geography

gigante adjective *masc. & fem.*
 giant
 una pantalla gigante a giant
 screen

el **gigante** noun *masc.*,
 la **giganta** *fem.*
 giant

> **CULTURE**
> Los gigantes y cabezudos are giant
> carnival figures with big heads that you
> see in many Spanish festivals.

la **gimnasia** noun *fem.*
 1 exercise
 hacer gimnasia to do exercise

2 (*in school*) PE
 Hoy tenemos gimnasia. Today we
 have PE.
 3 gymnastics

el **gimnasio** noun *masc.*
 gym

girar verb
 1 to turn
 Gira a la izquierda. Turn left.
 girar el volante to turn the
 steering wheel
 2 to go round
 La tierra gira alrededor del sol.
 The earth goes round the sun.

el **girasol** noun *masc.*
 sunflower

> **LANGUAGE**
> The Spanish means 'turns towards the
> sun'.

el **gitano** noun *masc.*, la **gitana** *fem.*
 gypsy

el **globo** noun *masc.*
 1 balloon
 inflar un globo to blow up a
 balloon
 2 globe

glotón adjective *masc.*,
 glotona *fem.*
 greedy

> **LANGUAGE**
> The plural of glotón is glotones.

el **gol** noun *masc.*
 goal
 marcar un gol to score a goal

el **golf** noun *masc.*
 golf
 Mi hermano juega al golf.
 My brother plays golf.

la **golosina** noun *fem.*
 sweet
 una tienda de golosinas a sweet
 shop

• *The months of the year and days of the week do not take a capital letter in Spanish.*

el **golpe** noun masc.
knock
Recibió un golpe en la cabeza.
He got a hit on the head.
Me he dado un golpe en la rodilla.
I've knocked my knee.
Beatriz me ha dado un golpe.
Beatriz has hit me.

golpear verb
1 **to hit**
La pelota me golpeó en la cara.
The ball hit me in the face.
2 **to bang**
Están golpeando la mesa. They're
banging the table.

la **goma** noun fem.
1 **rubber**
¿Me prestas la goma? Can you
lend me your rubber?
2 **elastic band**

el **gordo** noun masc.
first prize in the Spanish lottery

gordo adjective masc., **gorda** fem.
fat
Estoy gordo. I'm fat.

el **gorila** noun masc.
gorilla

> **LANGUAGE**
> Be careful: **gorila** ends in an **-a** but it is not
> a feminine noun.

la **gorra** noun fem.
cap

el **gorro** noun masc.
hat
un gorro de lana a woolly hat

la **gota** noun fem.
drop
una gota de agua a drop of water

grabar verb
1 **to record**
¿Has grabado la película? Have
you recorded the film?
2 **to save**
Graba el archivo. Save the file.

gracias exclamation
thank you!
¡Muchas gracias! Thank you very
much!

las **gracias** plural noun fem.
dar las gracias a alguien to thank
somebody

gracioso adjective masc.,
graciosa fem.
funny

el **grado** noun masc.
(of temperature) **degree**
Estamos a veinte grados.
It's twenty degrees.

la **gramática** noun fem.
grammar

el **gramo** noun masc.
gram

Gran Bretaña noun fem.
Great Britain
Vivimos en Gran Bretaña. We live
in Great Britain.

grande adjective masc. & fem.

> **LANGUAGE**
> **Grande** becomes **gran** when it is used
> before a singular noun.

big
una casa grande a big house
un gran incendio a big fire

los **grandes almacenes** plural
noun masc.
department store

granizar verb
to hail
Está granizando. It's hailing.

el **granizo** noun masc.
hail

la **granja** noun fem.
farm

el **granjero** noun masc.,
la **granjera** fem.
farmer

a b c d e f **g** h i j k l m n o p q r s t u v w x y z

• The months of the year and days of the week do not take a capital letter in Spanish.

a
b
c
d
e
f
g
h
i
j
k
l
m
n
o
p
q
r
s
t
u
v
w
x
y
z

el **grano** noun masc.
1 **spot**
Tengo muchos granos. I've got lots of spots.
2 (of salt, sand, etc.) **grain**

la **grapa** noun fem.
staple

la **grapadora** noun fem.
stapler

gratis adjective & adverb
free
Es gratis. It's free.
dos entradas gratis two free tickets
Entré gratis. I got in free.

grave adjective masc. & fem.
serious
un problema grave a serious problem
El abuelo está grave. Grandfather is seriously ill.

gravemente adverb
seriously
gravemente herido seriously injured

Grecia noun fem.
Greece

griego adjective masc., **griega** fem.
Greek

el **griego** noun masc., la **griega** fem.
Greek
los griegos the Greeks

el **grifo** noun masc.
tap
abrir el grifo to turn on the tap

la **gripe** noun fem.
flu
Tengo gripe. I have the flu.

gris adjective masc. & fem.
grey
una camisa gris a grey shirt

el **gris** noun masc.
grey
No me gusta el gris. I don't like grey.

gritar verb
1 **to shout**
No me grites. Don't shout at me.
2 (with pain etc.) **to scream**

el **grito** noun masc.
1 **shout**
2 **scream**

grueso adjective masc., **gruesa** fem.
1 (wall, slice, etc.) **thick**
2 (person) **fat**

gruñón adjective masc., **gruñona** fem.
grumpy

LANGUAGE
The masculine plural of **gruñón** is **gruñones.**

---

el **grupo** noun masc.
group

el **guante** noun masc.
glove

guapo adjective masc., **guapa** fem.
1 **pretty**
una niña muy guapa a very pretty girl
2 **good-looking**
Carlos es muy guapo. Carlos is very good-looking.

guardar verb
1 **to keep**
Guarda el billete. Keep the ticket.
2 **to put away**
Guarda los juguetes. Put the toys away.
3 **to save**
¿Me guardas el sitio? Can you save my place?
He guardado el archivo. I've saved the file.

• See the centre section for verb tables.

el **guardarropa** noun *masc.*
  cloakroom

⚷ **LANGUAGE**
Be careful: **guardarropa** ends in an -**a** but it is not a feminine noun.

la **guardería** noun *fem.*
  nursery

el or la **guardia** noun *masc. & fem.*
  policeman, policewoman

guay adjective *masc. & fem.*
  cool
  ¡Qué película más guay! What a cool film!

la **guayaba** noun *fem.*
  guava

la **guerra** noun *fem.*
  war

la **guía** noun *fem.*
  (*book*) guide
  una guía de Madrid a guide to Madrid
  la guía telefónica the phone book

el or la **guía** noun *masc. & fem.*
  (*person*) guide

guiar verb
  to guide

el **guión** noun *masc.* (plural los **guiones**)
  hyphen

Se escribe con un guión. It's spelled with a hyphen.

el **guisante** noun *masc.*
  pea

la **guitarra** noun *fem.*
  guitar
  Toco la guitarra. I play the guitar.

el **gusano** noun *masc.*
  worm

gustar verb
  to like
  Me gusta el chocolate. I like chocolate.
  Me gusta. I like it.
  Me gustan los perros. I like dogs.
  A Raúl le gusta leer. Raúl likes to read.
  ¿Te gusta la música? Do you like music?

⚷ **LANGUAGE**
Gustar means 'to please' so the order of the words in the Spanish is different, e.g. **Me gusta el chocolate** is 'Chocolate pleases me'.

el **gusto** noun *masc.*
  (*when being introduced to somebody*)
  ¡Mucho gusto! Pleased to meet you!

Hh

ha verb
1 has
  ¿Ha llegado Javier? Has Javier arrived?
2 have SEE **haber**
  Usted no ha dicho nada. You haven't said anything.

habéis verb SEE **haber**
  have

Niños, ¿habéis leído el libro? Have you read the book, children?

haber verb
  (*used for making past tenses*) **to have**
  He visto la película. I've seen the film.
  Ha hecho sus deberes. He has done his homework.
  Han cerrado la puerta. They've closed the door.

• *Use* **el** *and* **uno** *for masculine words and* **la** *and* **una** *for feminine words.*

a
b
c
d
e
f
g
h
i
j
k
l
m
n
o
p
q
r
s
t
u
v
w
x
y
z

había verb
1 **there was**
Había un libro en la mesa. There was a book on the table.
2 **there were** SEE **hay**
Había dos libros en la mesa. There were two books on the table.

la **habitación** noun *fem.* (plural las **habitaciones**)
room
La casa tiene cinco habitaciones. The house has five rooms.

el or la **habitante** noun *masc. & fem.*
inhabitant

habitual adjective *masc. & fem.*
usual

hablador adjective *masc.*,
habladora *fem.*
talkative

hablar verb
1 **to speak**
¿Hablas español? Do you speak Spanish?
'Se habla inglés.' 'English spoken.'
2 **to talk**
Gabriel habla demasiado. Gabriel talks too much.
Estoy hablando con mis amigas. I'm talking to my friends.

hacer verb
1 **to do**
¿Qué estás haciendo? What are you doing?
No hago nada. I'm not doing anything.
Hace mucho deporte. He does a lot of sport.
2 **to make**
Hacen mucho ruido. They're making a lot of noise.
Me hace reír. He makes me laugh.
He hecho un pastel. I've made a cake.
3 **to be**
Hace frío. It's cold.

Hace buen tiempo. It's a lovely day.

🔑 **LANGUAGE**
With the weather **hace** = **it is**

4 **ago**
Se fue hace una semana. She left a week ago.

🔑 **LANGUAGE**
Hace goes before the amount of time but **ago** goes after.

5 **for**
Hace un mes que estudio español. I've been studying Spanish for a month.

hacerse verb
to become
hacerse famoso to become famous
Nos hicimos amigos. We became friends.

hacia preposition
1 **towards**
hacia la puerta towards the door
2 **around**
hacia las nueve de la mañana around nine in the morning
3 **hacia arriba** up
hacia abajo down
hacia atrás backwards

el **hada** noun *fem.*
fairy
un cuento de hadas a fairy tale

🔑 **LANGUAGE**
Be careful: you use **el** with **hada** but it is not a masculine noun.

hago verb SEE **hacer**
1 **do**
Hago mis deberes. I do my homework.
2 **make**
Hago mucho ruido. I make a lot of noise.

la **hamaca** noun *fem.*
(*on the beach*) **deckchair**

• *Languages and nationalities do not take a capital letter in Spanish.*

el **hambre** noun *fem.*
hunger
tener hambre to be hungry
Tengo mucha hambre. I'm very hungry.

> **LANGUAGE**
> Spanish = **tener** hambre **Tengo hambre.**
> English = **to be** hungry **I'm hungry.**

> **LANGUAGE**
> Be careful: you use **el** with **hambre** but it is not a masculine noun.

la **hamburguesa** noun *fem.*
hamburger

el **hámster** noun *masc.*
hamster

han verb SEE **haber**
have
Los chicos han llegado. The boys have arrived.

la **harina** noun *fem.*
flour

harto adjective *masc.*, **harta** *fem.*
fed up
Estoy harto de ti. I'm fed up with you.

has verb SEE **haber**
have
¿Has terminado los deberes? Have you finished your homework?

hasta preposition
1 until
Está abierto hasta las seis. It's open until six.
2 up to
Cuenta hasta diez. Count up to ten.
hasta ahora up to now
3 (*in greetings*)
¡Hasta mañana! See you tomorrow!
¡Hasta las nueve! See you at nine!
¡Hasta luego! See you!

hay verb
1 there is

Hay una biblioteca muy cerca. There's a library nearby.
No hay pan. There isn't any bread.
2 there are
Hay juguetes en el suelo. There are toys on the floor.
3 (*for saying 'must'*)
Hay que esperar. We must wait.

> **LANGUAGE**
> **Hay** is a special form of the verb **haber** (to have).

he verb SEE **haber**
have
He comprado una bici. I've bought a bike.

el **hechizo** noun *masc.*
magic spell

el **hecho** noun *masc.*
fact

hecho adjective *masc.*, **hecha** *fem.*
1 made
Está bien hecho. It's well made.
hecho a mano made by hand
2 done
¡Bien hecho! Well done!

la **helada** noun *fem.*
frost

el **helado** noun *masc.*
ice cream
un helado de chocolate a chocolate ice cream

helado adjective *masc.*, **helada** *fem.*
1 frozen
El río está helado. The river is frozen.
2 freezing
La habitación está helada. The room is freezing.
¡Estoy helado! I'm freezing!

helar verb
to be frosty
Esta noche ha helado. It was frosty last night.

• *The months of the year and days of the week do not take a capital letter in Spanish.*

a
b
c
d
e
f
g
h
i
j
k
l
m
n
o
p
q
r
s
t
u
v
w
x
y
z

helarse verb
to freeze
El agua se ha helado. The water has frozen.

el **helicóptero** noun *masc.*
helicopter

la **hembra** noun *fem.*
female
un elefante hembra a female elephant

hemos verb SEE **haber**
have
Hemos terminado el ejercicio.
We've finished the exercise.

la **herida** noun *fem.*
injury

herido adjective *masc.*, **herida** *fem.*
injured
Está herida. She's injured.

la **hermana** noun *fem.*
sister

la **hermanastra** noun *fem.*
stepsister

el **hermanastro** noun *masc.*
stepbrother

el **hermano** noun *masc.*
brother
mi hermano mayor my big brother
¿Tienes hermanos? Do you have any brothers or sisters?

hermoso adjective *masc.*,
hermosa *fem.*
beautiful

el **héroe** noun *masc.*
hero

la **heroína** noun *fem.*
heroine

las **herramientas** plural noun *fem.*
tools

hervir verb
to boil
hervir la leche to boil the milk
estar hirviendo to be boiling

el **hielo** noun *masc.*
ice
un cubito de hielo an ice cube

la **hierba** noun *fem.*
1 grass
2 herb

el **hierro** noun *masc.*
iron

la **hija** noun *fem.*
daughter

la **hijastra** noun *fem.*
stepdaughter

el **hijastro** noun *masc.*
stepson

el **hijo** noun *masc.*
1 son
Tienen un hijo. They have a son.
2 hijos children
¿Cuántos hijos tienen? How many children do they have?

LANGUAGE
Hijos is the Spanish for 'sons' but can also mean children – either boys or girls.

el **himno** noun *masc.*
hymn
el himno nacional the national anthem

el or la **hincha** noun *masc. & fem.*
fan
un hincha del fútbol a football fan

hinchado adjective *masc.*,
hinchada *fem.*
swollen

hindú adjective *masc. & fem.* (plural
hindúes)
Hindu

el **hipermercado** noun *masc.*
superstore

el **hipo** noun *masc.*
tener hipo to have hiccups

• *See the centre section for verb tables.*

la **historia** noun *fem.*
 1 **story**
  El libro cuenta la historia de ... The book tells the story of ...
 2 **history**
  la historia de Inglaterra English history

el **hogar** noun *masc.*
 home

la **hoguera** noun *fem.*
 bonfire

la **hoja** noun *fem.*
 1 **leaf**
  las hojas del árbol the leaves of the tree
 2 **sheet**
  una hoja de papel a sheet of paper
 3 **page**
  las hojas del libro the pages of the book

hola exclamation
 hello!

Holanda noun *fem.*
 Holland

el **holandés** noun *masc.*
 Dutch
 hablar holandés to speak Dutch

holandés adjective *masc.*,
 holandesa *fem.*
 Dutch

🔑 **LANGUAGE**
The plural of holandés is holandeses.

el **holandés** noun *masc.*,
 la **holandesa** *fem.*
 Dutchman, Dutchwoman
 los holandeses the Dutch

el **hombre** noun *masc.*
 man
 un hombre y una mujer a man and a woman

el **hombro** noun *masc.*
 shoulder

hondo adjective *masc.*, **honda** *fem.*
 deep

la **hora** noun *fem.*
 1 **hour**
  media hora half an hour
  un cuarto de hora a quarter of an hour
  una hora y cuarto an hour and a quarter
  la hora punta the rush hour
 2 **time**
  ¿Qué hora es? What time is it?
  ¿Tienes hora? Do you have the time?
  ¿a qué hora ...? what time ...?
  Es hora de ir a la escuela. It's time to go to school.
  mis horas libres my free time
  llegar a la hora to arrive on time
 3 *(with a doctor etc.)* **appointment**
  pedir hora to make an appointment

el **horario** noun *masc.*
 timetable
 el horario de clases the school timetable

la **hormiga** noun *fem.*
 ant

el **horno** noun *masc.*
 oven
 un horno microondas a microwave oven

horrible adjective *masc. & fem.*
 horrible

el **horror** noun *masc.*
 horror
 ¡Qué horror! That's horrible!

el **hospital** noun *masc.*
 hospital
 estar en el hospital to be in hospital

• Use **el** and **uno** for masculine words and **la** and **una** for feminine words.

a
b
c
d
e
f
g
h
i
j
k
l
m
n
o
p
q
r
s
t
u
v
w
x
y
z

el **hotel** noun *masc.*
hotel

hoy adverb
today
Hoy es mi cumpleaños. Today is my birthday.
¿A qué fecha estamos hoy? What's the date today?

hubo verb
1 there was
Hubo un accidente. There was an accident.
2 there were
Hubo dos accidentes. There were two accidents.

⚷ **LANGUAGE**
Hubo is the past tense of hay.

la **hucha** noun *fem.*
money box

el **hueco** noun *masc.*
1 space
Aquí hay un hueco. There's a space here.
2 (*in a timetable, fence, etc.*) gap

la **huella** noun *fem.*
footprint
una huella dactilar a fingerprint

el **huérfano** noun *masc.*,
la **huérfana** *fem.*
orphan

el **hueso** noun *masc.*
bone

el or la **huésped** noun *masc. & fem.*
guest

el **huevo** noun *masc.*
egg
un huevo duro a hard-boiled egg
un huevo pasado por agua a soft-boiled egg
huevos revueltos scrambled eggs

huir verb
1 to run away
2 to escape
El ladrón huyó en una moto. The thief escaped on a motorbike.

humano adjective *masc.*,
humana *fem.*
human
un ser humano a human being

húmedo adjective *masc.*,
húmeda *fem.*
damp

el **humo** noun *masc.*
smoke

el **humor** noun *masc.*
mood
estar de buen humor to be in a good mood
tener sentido del humor to have a sense of humour

hundirse verb
to sink
El barco se hundió. The boat sank.

el **huracán** noun *masc.* (plural los **huracanes**)
hurricane

Ii

el **icono** noun *masc.*
icon
Haz clic en el icono. Click on the icon.

la **ida** noun *fem.*
un billete de ida a single ticket
un billete de ida y vuelta a return ticket

• *Languages and nationalities do not take a capital letter in Spanish.*

82

la **idea** noun fem.
idea
Tengo una idea. I have an idea.
cambiar de idea to change your mind

idéntico adjective masc.,
idéntica fem.
identical

la **identidad** noun fem.
identity
el carné de identidad identity card

el **idioma** noun masc.
language
Hablo dos idiomas. I speak two languages.

LANGUAGE
Be careful: **idioma** ends in an **-a** but it is not a feminine noun.

idiota adjective masc. & fem.
stupid

el or la **idiota** noun masc. & fem.
idiot

la **iglesia** noun fem.
church
ir a la iglesia to go to church

igual adjective masc. & fem.& adverb
1 **equal**
dos grupos iguales two equal groups
2 **the same**
Estos colores son iguales. These colours are the same.
Se escriben igual. They're spelled the same.
Eres igual a tu hermana. You're the same as your sister.
Me da igual. I don't mind.

la **imagen** noun fem.
(on TV screen) **picture**

la **imaginación** noun fem. (plural las **imaginaciones**)
imagination

imaginar verb
to imagine

imaginarse verb
to imagine
¡Imagínate! Imagine that!

imaginario adjective masc.,
imaginaria fem.
imaginary
un amigo imaginario an imaginary friend

el **imán** noun masc. (plural los **imanes**)
magnet

imbécil adjective masc. & fem.
stupid
¡Qué imbécil eres! You're so stupid!

el or la **imbécil** noun masc. & fem.
idiot

imitar verb
to imitate

impaciente adjective masc. & fem.
impatient

impar adjective masc.
un número impar an odd number

el **impermeable** noun masc.
raincoat

la **importancia** noun fem.
importance
Tiene mucha importancia. It's very important.

importante adjective masc. & fem.
important
una persona importante an important person

importar verb
1 **to matter**
No importa. It doesn't matter.
2 **to mind**
¿le importa ...? do you mind ...?
¿Le importa si me siento aquí? Do you mind if I sit here?
No me importa. I don't mind.

imposible adjective masc. & fem.
impossible

• The months of the year and days of the week do not take a capital letter in Spanish.

impresionante adjective *masc. & fem.*
amazing, impressive

la **impresora** noun *fem.*
printer

imprimir verb
(*on a computer etc.*) to print

incapaz adjective *masc. & fem.* (plural **incapaces**)
ser incapaz de hacer algo to be unable to do something

el **incendio** noun *masc.*
fire
apagar el incendio to put out the fire

inclinarse verb
1 to bend down
inclinarse para recoger algo to bend down to pick something up
2 to lean over
Inclínate hacia delante. Lean forward.

incluido adjective *masc.*, **incluida** *fem.*
included
El servicio está incluido. The service is included.

incluir verb
to include
todos, incluyendo a mi hermana everybody, including my sister

incluso adverb
even
Incluso yo puedo hacerlo. Even I can do it.

incómodo adjective *masc.*, **incómoda** *fem.*
uncomfortable

incorrecto adjective *masc.*, **incorrecta** *fem.*
incorrect

increíble adjective *masc. & fem.*
incredible

independiente adjective *masc. & fem.*
independent

la **India** noun *fem.*
India

las **indicaciones** plural noun *fem.*
instructions
seguir las indicaciones to follow the instructions

indicar verb
to show
indicar el camino to show the way

indio adjective *masc.*, **india** *fem.*
Indian
una lengua india an Indian language

🌎 **CULTURE**
In Latin America indio means American Indian, not from India.

el **indio** noun *masc.*, la **india** *fem.*
Indian

individual adjective *masc. & fem.*
1 (*bed, portion, etc.*) single
una habitación individual a single room
2 individual

inesperado adjective *masc.*, **inesperada** *fem.*
unexpected

infantil adjective *masc. & fem.*
1 children's
un cuento infantil a children's story
2 childish
Eres muy infantil. You're very childish.

• *See the centre section for verb tables.*

la **infección** noun fem. (plural las **infecciones**)
infection

el **infinitivo** noun masc.
infinitive

inflar verb
to blow up
inflar un globo to blow up a balloon

la **información** noun fem.
1 information
buscar información to look for information
2 (on TV or in the newspaper) news

la **informática** noun fem.
IT, computing

informático adjective masc., **informática** fem.
computer
un programa informático a computer program

el **ingeniero** noun masc., la **ingeniera** fem.
engineer

Inglaterra noun fem.
England
Vivo en Inglaterra. I live in England.
¿Quieres venir a Inglaterra? Do you want to come to England?

el **inglés** noun masc.
English
¿Hablas inglés? Do you speak English?

inglés adjective masc., **inglesa** fem.
English
Soy inglesa. I'm English.

> **LANGUAGE**
> The plural of inglés is ingleses.

el **inglés** noun masc., la **inglesa** fem.
Englishman, Englishwoman
los ingleses the English

el **ingrediente** noun masc.
ingredient

las **iniciales** plural noun fem.
initials

el **inicio** noun masc.
(on a web page) home
la página de inicio the home page

injusto adjective masc., **injusta** fem.
unfair

inmediatamente adverb
immediately

> **LANGUAGE**
> Spanish = inmediatamente
> English = immediately

inmenso adjective masc., **inmensa** fem.
huge, immense

> **LANGUAGE**
> Spanish = inmenso
> English = immense

inocente adjective masc. & fem.
innocent

inquieto adjective masc., **inquieta** fem.
worried

el **insecto** noun masc.
insect

insolente adjective masc. & fem.
cheeky

instalar verb
to install
instalar un programa to install a program

el **instante** noun masc.
moment
hace un instante a moment ago

• Use **el** and **uno** for masculine words and **la** and **una** for feminine words.

el **instituto** noun masc.
(secondary) school

las **instrucciones** plural noun fem.
instructions

el **instrumento** noun masc.
instrument
tocar un instrumento to play an instrument

inteligente adjective masc. & fem.
intelligent

intentar verb
to try
intentar hacer algo to try to do something
Inténtalo otra vez. Try again.

interesante adjective masc. & fem.
interesting

interesar verb
to interest
Me interesan los idiomas. I'm interested in languages.
No me interesa. I'm not interested.

el **interior** noun masc.
inside
el interior de la caja the inside of the box

el **intermedio** noun masc.
interval

internacional adjective masc. & fem.
international

el **internado** noun masc.
boarding school

el or la **internauta** noun masc. & fem.
Internet user

Internet noun masc. & fem.
Internet
en Internet on the Internet

> **LANGUAGE**
> **El** or **la** are not used with **Internet**.

interrumpir verb
to interrupt
¡No me interrumpas! Don't interrupt!

el **interruptor** noun masc.
switch

la **inundación** noun fem. (plural las **inundaciones**)
flood

inútil adjective masc. & fem.
useless

inventar verb
to invent

el **invento** noun masc.
invention

el **invierno** noun masc.
winter
en invierno in the winter

invisible adjective masc. & fem.
invisible

la **invitación** noun fem. (plural las **invitaciones**)
invitation

el **invitado** noun masc.,
la **invitada** fem.
guest

invitar verb
to invite
Isabel me ha invitado a una fiesta. Isabel has invited me to a party.

la **inyección** noun fem. (plural las **inyecciones**)
injection
La enfermera me ha puesto una inyección. The nurse has given me an injection.

ir verb
1 to go
Voy al colegio en autobús. I go to school by bus.
¿Adónde vas? Where are you going?

• Languages and nationalities do not take a capital letter in Spanish.

Ha ido al parque. He's gone to the park.

Fueron de compras. They went shopping.

2 (*used with another verb when talking about the future*)

ir a ... to be going to ...

¿Qué vas a hacer? What are you going to do?

Voy a ver la tele. I'm going to watch TV.

3 (*used for making suggestions*)

Vamos a ... Let's ...

Vamos a jugar. Let's play.

¡Vamos a ver! Let's see!

Vamos. Let's go.

4 **to come**

¡Ya voy! I'm coming!

¡Vamos! ¡Ayúdame! Come on! Help me!

5 **to suit**

El verde te va bien. Green suits you.

irse verb

1 **to leave**

Tengo que irme. I have to leave.

Me voy el lunes. I'm leaving on Monday.

Se ha ido del hotel. She has left the hotel.

2 **to go away**

¡Vete! Go away!

¡Vámonos! Let's go!

Irlanda noun *fem.*

Ireland

el **irlandés** noun *masc.*

Irish

Hablan irlandés. They speak Irish.

irlandés adjective *masc.*,
irlandesa *fem.*

Irish

🔑 LANGUAGE
The plural of irlandés is irlandeses.

---

el **irlandés** *masc.*,
la **irlandesa** noun *fem.*

Irishman, Irishwoman

los irlandeses the Irish

la **isla** noun *fem.*

island

las Islas Baleares the Balearic Islands

las Islas Británicas the British Isles

islámico adjective *masc.*,
islámica *fem.*

Islamic

Italia noun *fem.*

Italy

el **italiano** noun *masc.*

Italian

¿Hablas italiano? Do you speak Italian?

italiano adjective *masc.*,
italiana *fem.*

Italian

Son italianos. They're Italian.

el **italiano** noun *masc.*,
la **italiana** *fem.*

Italian

la **izquierda** noun *fem.*

left

Está a la izquierda. It's on the left.

girar a la izquierda to turn left

conducir por la izquierda to drive on the left

izquierdo adjective *masc.*,
izquierda *fem.*

left

Escribo con la mano izquierda. I write with my left hand.

• *The months of the year and days of the week do not take a capital letter in Spanish.*

Jj

el **jabón** noun *masc.*
soap
una pastilla de jabón a bar of soap

jamás adverb
never
¡Jamás he visto eso! I've never seen that!
nunca jamás never ever

el **jamón** noun *masc.*
ham
un bocadillo de jamón a ham sandwich

LANGUAGE
The plural of **jamón** is **jamones**.

Japón noun *masc.*
Japan

el **japonés** noun *masc.*
Japanese
hablar japonés to speak Japanese

japonés adjective *masc.*,
japonesa *fem.*
Japanese
Es japonés. He's Japanese.

el **japonés** noun *masc.*,
la **japonesa** *fem.*
Japanese man, Japanese woman
los japoneses the Japanese

el **jardín** noun *masc.*
garden
Nuestra casa tiene jardín.
Our house has a garden.
el jardín de infancia nursery school

LANGUAGE
The plural of **jardín** is **jardines**.

el **jardinero** noun *masc.*,
la **jardinera** *fem.*
gardener

la **jarra** noun *fem.*
jug

el **jarrón** noun *masc.* (plural los **jarrons**)
vase

la **jaula** noun *fem.*
cage

el **jefe** noun *masc.*, la **jefa** *fem.*
1 boss
2 (*of a group or gang*) leader
3 (*of a department*) head

el **jersey** noun *masc.* (plural los **jerseys** or los **jerséis**)
sweater

Jesús exclamation
(*when somebody sneezes*) Bless you!

la **jirafa** noun *fem.*
giraffe

joven adjective *masc. & fem.*
young
Eres más joven que yo. You're younger than me.

el or la **joven** noun *masc. & fem.*
young man, young woman
los jóvenes young people

la **joya** noun *fem.*
jewel

la **joyería** noun *fem.*
jewellery shop

jubilado adjective *masc.*,
jubilada *fem.*
retired

la **judía** noun *fem.*
bean
las judías verdes green beans

judío adjective *masc.*, la **judía** *fem.*
Jewish

• *See the centre section for verb tables.*

el **judo** noun *masc.*
judo
hacer judo to do judo

el **juego** noun *masc.*
game
un juego de mesa a board game
los Juegos Olímpicos the Olympic
Games

el **jueves** noun *masc.*
Thursday
Hoy es jueves. It's Thursday today.
el jueves on Thursday
¡Hasta el jueves! See you on
Thursday!
los jueves on Thursdays
Voy a la biblioteca los jueves. I go
to the library on Thursdays.

> **LANGUAGE**
> Remember the difference between
> el jueves (one Thursday only) and
> los jueves (every Thursday)

el or la **juez** noun *masc. & fem.*
judge

el **jugador** noun *masc.*,
la **jugadora** *fem.*
player
una jugadora de tenis a tennis
player

jugar verb
to play
Estamos jugando en el jardín.
We're playing in the garden.
jugar al fútbol to play football
jugar a la pelota to play ball

> **LANGUAGE**
> Use jugar + a with games and sports.

el **jugo** noun *masc.*
juice

el **juguete** noun *masc.*
toy

> **LANGUAGE**
> Juguete comes from jugar (to play).

la **juguetería** noun *fem.*
toy shop

julio noun *masc.*
July
en julio in July
Vamos a Barcelona en julio. We're
going to Barcelona in July.
Nací el tres de julio. I was born on
the third of July.

la **jungla** noun *fem.*
jungle

junio noun *masc.*
June
Mi cumpleaños es en junio.
My birthday is in June.
**Dan una fiesta el lunes nueve de
junio.** They're having a party on
Monday, the ninth of June.

junto a preposition
next to
La silla está junto a la ventana.
The chair is next to the window.

juntos adjective *masc. plural,*
juntas *fem. plural*
together
Han llegado juntos. They've
arrived together.
Las mesas están demasiado juntas.
The tables are too close together.

justo adverb
just
Viven justo al lado. They live just
next door.
justo a tiempo just in time

justo adjective *masc.*, **justa** *fem.*
1 fair
¡No es justo! It's not fair!
2 tight
Estos vaqueros me quedan justos.
These jeans are too tight.

juzgar verb
to judge

• Use **el** and **uno** for masculine words and **la** and **una** for feminine words.

Kk

el **kárate** noun *masc.*
karate
hacer kárate to do karate

el **kilo** noun *masc.*
kilo
tres euros el kilo three euros a kilo

el **kilómetro** noun *masc.*
kilometre
Está a diez kilómetros de aquí.
It's ten kilometres away.

el **kiosco** noun *masc.*
1 (*for newspapers*) **news-stand**
2 (*for flowers, ice creams, etc.*) **kiosk**

Ll

la determiner *fem.*
1 (*before feminine singular nouns*) **the**
la silla the chair
la mujer the woman
2 (*no translation*)
No me gusta la leche. I don't like milk.
Me voy a la cama. I'm going to bed.
la hermana de Julio Julio's sister
3 (*with adjectives used as nouns*) **the**
la verde the green one
la grande the big one
4 (*with parts of the body, clothes, etc.*)
my, **your**, **his** (*etc.*)
Me he roto la pierna. I've broken my leg.
Ponte la camisa. Put your shirt on.
Levantó la mano. He put up his hand.

la pronoun *fem.*
1 **her**
La conozco. I know her.
Quiero ayudarla. I want to help her.
2 **it**
¿Dónde está mi chaqueta? – No la veo. Where's my jacket? – I can't see it.
3 **you**
La acompaño, señora López. I'll go with you, Mrs López.

el **laberinto** noun *masc.*
maze

el **labio** noun *masc.*
lip

el **lado** noun *masc.*
1 side
al otro lado de la calle on the other side of the road
2 **al lado de** next to
Siéntate al lado de Carlos. Sit next to Carlos.
a mi lado next to me
al lado next door
Viven al lado. They live next door.
3 **por todos lados** everywhere
por ningún lado nowhere

ladrar verb
to bark

el **ladrillo** noun *masc.*
brick

el **ladrón** noun *masc.*,
la **ladrona** *fem.*
1 thief
2 burglar

🔑 LANGUAGE
The plural of **ladrón** is **ladrones**.

el **lagarto** noun *masc.*
lizard

• *Languages and nationalities do not take a capital letter in Spanish.*

el **lago** noun *masc.*
lake

la **lágrima** noun *fem.*
tear

la **lámpara** noun *fem.*
lamp

la **lana** noun *fem.*
wool
una bufanda de lana a woolly scarf

la **langosta** noun *fem.*
lobster

lanzar verb
to throw
Lánzame la pelota. Throw the ball to me.
Me han lanzado una piedra. They've thrown a stone at me.

el **lápiz** noun *masc.* (plural los **lápices**)
pencil
a lápiz in pencil

largo adjective *masc.*, **larga** *fem.*
long
Tengo el pelo largo. I have long hair.

⚠ **FALSE FRIEND**
largo = long (*not* large)

las determiner *fem. plural*
1 (*before feminine plural nouns*) **the**
las casas the houses
las hermanas the sisters
2 (*no translation*)
Odio las naranjas. I hate oranges.
las amigas de María María's friends
3 (*with adjectives used as nouns*) **the**
las azules the blue ones
las largas the long ones
4 (*with parts of the body, clothes, etc.*)
my, your, his (*etc.*)
Me he lavado las manos. I've washed my hands.

Ponte las gafas. Put your glasses on.
Se quitó las botas. He took his boots off.

las pronoun *fem. plural*
1 **them**
Las conozco. I know them.
Dámelas. Give them to me.
2 **you**
Las esperan, señoras. They're waiting for you, ladies.

la **lástima** noun *fem.*
pity
¡Qué lástima! What a pity!

la **lata** noun *fem.*
1 tin
una lata de tomates a tin of tomatoes
2 can
una lata de cerveza a can of beer

Latinoamérica noun *fem.*
Latin America

latinoamericano adjective *masc.*, **latinoamericana** *fem.*
Latin American
Soy latinoamericano. I'm a Latin American.

el **latinoamericano** *masc.*, la **latinoamericana** noun *fem.*
Latin American

el **lavabo** noun *masc.*
1 sink
Lávate las manos en el lavabo. Wash your hands in the sink.
2 toilet
Voy al lavabo. I'm going to the toilet.

la **lavadora** noun *fem.*
washing machine

el **lavaplatos** noun *masc.* (plural los **lavaplatos**)
dishwasher

• *The months of the year and days of the week do not take a capital letter in Spanish.*

Spanish English

lavar verb
to wash
lavar la ropa to wash the clothes

lavarse verb
to wash
Me estoy lavando. I'm washing.
Me he lavado las manos. I've washed my hands.
Se está lavando los dientes. She's cleaning her teeth.

el **lavavajillas** noun *masc.* (plural los **lavavajillas**)
dishwasher

Le pronoun *masc. & fem.*
1 **him, to him**
Le he mandado una carta. I've sent him a letter., I've sent a letter to him.
Dale el disco compacto. Give him the CD.
2 **her, to her**
Le he dado el dinero. I've given her the money., I've given the money to her.
Quiero decirle algo. I want to tell her something.
3 **you, to you**
Voy a decirle la verdad, señor. I'm going to tell you the truth, sir.
Le doy esto a usted. I'm giving this to you.

la **lección** noun *fem.* (plural las **lecciones**)
lesson

la **leche** noun *fem.*
milk

la **lechuga** noun *fem.*
lettuce

leer verb
to read
Yo sé leer. I know how to read.
Me gusta leer. I like reading.

• *See the centre section for verb tables.*

las **legumbres** plural noun *fem.*
pulses

⚷ **LANGUAGE**
Pulses are vegetables like beans and peas.

lejos adverb
far
¿Está lejos? Is it far?
No está muy lejos. It's not very far.
Montevideo está lejos. Montevideo is a long way away.
Está un poco más lejos. It's a bit further.

la **lengua** noun *fem.*
1 **tongue**
2 **language**
Hablo dos lenguas. I speak two languages.

lento adverb
slowly

lento adjective *masc.*, **lenta** *fem.*
slow
Soy muy lento. I'm very slow.

el **león** noun *masc.* (plural los **leones**)
lion

el **leopardo** noun *masc.*
leopard

les pronoun *masc. & fem.*
1 **them, to them**
Les he mandado un regalo. I've sent them a present., I've sent a present to them.
Dales los libros. Give them the books.
2 **you, to you**
Les doy esto a ustedes. I'm giving this to you.

la **lesión** noun *fem.* (plural las **lesiones**)
(*in sports etc.*) injury

la **letra** noun *fem.*
1 (*of the alphabet*) letter
la letra Q the letter Q

2 handwriting
Tengo muy buena letra. I've got very good handwriting.
3 la letra de una canción the words of a song

el **letrero** noun *masc.*
sign

levantar verb
1 to lift
Levanta esta maleta. Lift up this case.
2 to put up
Levantad la mano. Put your hands up.

levantarse verb
1 to get up
Me levanto a las siete. I get up at seven.
2 to stand up, to get up
Levántate. Stand up., Get up.

la **libertad** noun *fem.*
freedom

la **libra** noun *fem.*
(*money and weight*) **pound**

libre adjective *masc. & fem.*
free
Este asiento está libre. This seat is free.
un día libre a day off

la **librería** noun *fem.*
1 bookshop
La librería está cerrada. The bookshop's closed.
2 bookcase

⚠ **FALSE FRIEND**
una librería = a bookshop (*not* a library)

el **libro** noun *masc.*
book
He leído este libro. I've read this book.
un libro de bolsillo a paperback

el or la **líder** noun *masc. & fem.*
leader

ligero adjective *masc.*, **ligera** *fem.*
1 light
un paquete ligero a light parcel
2 slight
un ligero acento francés a slight French accent

el **limón** noun *masc.* (plural los **limones**)
lemon

la **limonada** noun *fem.*
lemon drink (*with fresh lemons and lemonade*)

limpiar verb
to clean
limpiar la casa to clean the house

la **limpieza** noun *fem.*
cleaning
hacer la limpieza to do the cleaning

limpio adjective *masc.*, **limpia** *fem.*
clean
una casa limpia a clean house

la **línea** noun *fem.*
line
una línea recta a straight line
en línea online

la **linterna** noun *fem.*
torch

el **líquido** noun *masc.*
liquid

liso adjective *masc.*, **lisa** *fem.*
smooth
tener la piel lisa to have smooth skin
tener el pelo liso to have straight hair

la **lista** noun *fem.*
1 list
una lista de la compra a shopping list
2 register
pasar lista to take the register

a b c d e f g h i j k l m n o p q r s t u v w x y z

• *Use* **el** *and* **uno** *for masculine words and* **la** *and* **una** *for feminine words.*

listo adjective *masc.*, **lista** *fem.*
1 smart
un chico muy listo a very smart boy
2 ready
Estamos listas. We're ready.

la **litera** noun *fem.*
bunk bed
Dormimos en una litera. We sleep in bunk beds.

la **literatura** noun *fem.*
literature

el **litro** noun *masc.*
litre

la **llama** noun *fem.*
flame

la **llamada** noun *fem.*
call
hacer una llamada to make a phone call

llamar verb
1 to call
Tu padre te llama. Your father is calling you.
llamar al médico to call the doctor
2 to phone
Te llamo mañana. I'll phone you tomorrow.
3 **Están llamando a la puerta.** There's somebody at the door.

llamarse verb
to be called
¿Cómo se llama el libro? What's the book called?
¿Cómo te llamas? What's your name?
Me llamo Miguel. My name's Miguel.
Se llama Yasmina. Her name is Yasmina.

llano adjective *masc.*, **llana** *fem.*
flat
un país llano a flat country

la **llave** noun *fem.*
1 key
2 (*Latin America*) tap

la **llegada** noun *fem.*
1 arrival
2 (*in a race*) finish

llegar verb
1 to arrive
Llegan a las ocho. They arrive at eight.
2 **llegar tarde** to be late
Siempre llegas tarde. You're always late.
3 to reach
No llego a la lámpara. I can't reach the lamp.
4 **llegar a ser** to become
Más tarde llegó a ser famosa. She later became famous.

llenar verb
to fill
llenar una bañera de agua to fill a bath with water

lleno adjective *masc.*, **llena** *fem.*
full
El cubo está lleno de agua. The bucket's full of water.

llevar verb
1 to take
Mi madre me lleva al colegio. My mum takes me to school.
Lleva el cuaderno a la maestra. Take the exercise book to the teacher.
2 to wear
Llevo vaqueros. I'm wearing jeans.
3 to carry
Lleva una maleta. He's carrying a suitcase.
4 (*talking about time*) to be
¿Cuánto tiempo llevas aquí? How long have you been here?
Llevo una hora esperando. I've been waiting for an hour.

llevarse verb
1 to take

• *Languages and nationalities do not take a capital letter in Spanish.*

Spanish English

a b c d e f g h i j k l m n o p q r s t u v w x y z

¿Quién se ha llevado mi boli?
Who's taken my pen?
2 **llevarse bien con alguien** to get on
with somebody
Me llevo bien con mi hermana.
I get on well with my sister.

llorar verb
to cry
¿Por qué lloras? Why are you
crying?

llover verb
to rain
Está lloviendo. It's raining.

la **lluvia** noun *fem.*
rain
Me gusta la lluvia. I like rain.

lo determiner *masc.*
1 (*used with adjectives*) **the ... thing**
lo bueno the good thing
lo mejor the best thing
2 **lo que** what
Dime lo que quieres. Tell me what
you want.

lo pronoun *masc.*
1 **him**
Lo conozco. I know him.
No quiero verlo. I don't want to see
him.
2 **it**
Lo he leído. I've read it.
3 **you**
Lo acompaño, señor Gallego.
I'll go with you, Mr Gallego.

el **lobo** noun *masc.*
wolf
el lobo feroz the big bad wolf

loco adjective *masc.*, **loca** *fem.*
mad
¡Estás loca! You're mad!

la **locomotora** noun *fem.*
(*of a train*) **engine**

el **lomo** noun *masc.*
back
el lomo de un caballo the back of
a horse

la **loncha** noun *fem.*
slice

Londres noun *masc.*
London

la **longitud** noun *fem.*
length

el **loro** noun *masc.*
parrot

los determiner *masc. plural*
1 (*before masculine plural nouns*) **the**
los jardines the gardens
los niños the children
2 (*no translation*)
Me gustan los tomates. I love
tomatoes.
los libros de mi hermana my
sister's books
3 (*with adjectives used as nouns*) **the**
los rojos the red ones
los pequeños the small ones
4 (*with parts of the body, clothes, etc.*)
my, **your**, **his**, etc.
Me pongo los calcetines. I put my
socks on.
¿Te duelen los pies? Do your feet
hurt?
Se quitaron los zapatos. They took
off their shoes.

los pronoun *masc. plural*
1 **them**
Los veo. I can see them.
¿Puedo comerlos? Can I eat them?
2 **you**
Los han llamado a ustedes.
They've called you.

la **lotería** noun *fem.*
lottery
jugar a la lotería to play the
lottery
Me ha tocado la lotería. I've won
the lottery.

a
b
c
d
e
f
g
h
i
j
k
l
m
n
o
p
q
r
s
t
u
v
w
x
y
z

• The months of the year and days of the week do not take a capital letter in Spanish.

Spanish English

luego adverb
1 then
Primero está Juan y luego yo. Juan is first and then it's me.
2 later
Mi padre viene luego. My dad's coming later.
¡Hasta luego! See you later!

el **lujo** noun masc.
luxury
un hotel de lujo a luxury hotel

la **luna** noun fem.
moon

el **lunes** noun masc.
Monday
Hoy es lunes. Today is Monday.
el lunes on Monday

Voy a la piscina el lunes. I'm going swimming on Monday.
los lunes on Mondays
Los lunes tenemos clase de gimnasia. On Mondays we have PE.

LANGUAGE
Remember the difference between el lunes (one Monday only) and los lunes (every Monday).

la **lupa** noun fem.
magnifying glass

la **luz** noun fem.
1 light
encender la luz to turn on the light
apagar la luz to turn off the light
2 electricity
No hay luz en la casa. There's no electricity in the house.

Mm

los **macarrones** plural noun masc.
macaroni

LANGUAGE
Spanish = los macarrones is plural
English = macaroni is singular

la **maceta** noun fem.
flowerpot

el **macho** masc.
male
un cachorro macho a male puppy

la **madera** noun fem.
wood
Es de madera. It's made of wood.
un juguete de madera a wooden toy

la **madrastra** noun fem.
stepmother

la **madre** noun fem.
mother, mum

Mi madre es maestra. My mother's a teacher.

Madrid noun masc.
Madrid
Estoy en Madrid. I'm in Madrid.
Voy a Madrid. I'm going to Madrid.

madrileño adjective masc.,
madrileña fem.
from Madrid
Soy madrileño. I'm from Madrid.

la **madrina** noun fem.
godmother

la **madrugada** noun fem.
1 dawn
de madrugada at dawn
2 (between midnight and dawn) **morning**
las tres de la madrugada three o'clock in the morning
de madrugada early in the morning

• See the centre section for verb tables.

a b c d e f g h i j k l m n o p q r s t u v w x y z

maduro adjective *masc.*, **madura** *fem.*
ripe
un tomate maduro a ripe tomato

el **maestro** *masc.*, la **maestra** noun *fem.*
teacher
Mi maestra se llama Antonia. My teacher's name is Antonia.

la **magia** noun *fem.*
magic
un truco de magia a magic trick

mágico adjective *masc.*, **mágica** *fem.*
magic
una varita mágica a magic wand

el **magnetófono** noun *masc.*
tape recorder

magnífico adjective *masc.*, **magnífica** *fem.*
superb

el **mago** noun *masc.*, la **maga** *fem.*
1 magician
2 (*in stories*) **wizard**

el **maíz** noun *masc.*
sweetcorn

mal adjective *masc. & fem.*
1 bad
un mal ejemplo a bad example
No está mal. It isn't bad.
2 wrong
La fecha está mal. The date's wrong.
3 ill
Me siento mal. I feel ill.

LANGUAGE
Mal is used instead of malo before a masculine singular noun, e.g. mal ejemplo instead of ejemplo malo.

mal adverb
1 badly
Canto muy mal. I sing very badly.
2 wrong
Lo has escrito mal. You've spelled it wrong.
3 bad
Huele mal. It smells bad.

la **malanga** noun *fem.*
eddo (*a vegetable*)

maleducado adjective *masc.*, **maleducada** *fem.*
rude

la **maleta** noun *fem.*
suitcase
He hecho la maleta. I've packed my case.

Mallorca noun *fem.*
Majorca

malo adjective *masc.*, **mala** *fem.*

LANGUAGE
The masculine singular malo becomes mal when it is used before a noun.

1 bad
un hotel malo a bad hotel
La película es muy mala. The film's very bad.
un mal ejemplo a bad example
Hace mal tiempo. The weather's bad.
2 naughty
un niño malo a naughty boy
3 ill
Papá está malo. Dad's ill.

la **mamá** noun *fem.*
mum
Sí, mamá. Yes, mum.

la **mancha** noun *fem.*
stain
una mancha de chocolate a chocolate stain

mandar verb
1 to send
mandar una carta a alguien to send somebody a letter
2 to be in charge
¡Aquí mando yo! I'm in charge here!

• *Use* **el** *and* **uno** *for masculine words and* **la** *and* **una** *for feminine words.*

la **mandarina** noun *fem.*
mandarin orange

el **mando a distancia** noun *masc.*
remote control

la **manecilla** noun *fem.*
hand
las manecillas del reloj the hands
of the clock

la **manera** noun *fem.*
way
Hazlo de esta manera. Do it this
way.
Lo hago a mi manera. I'll do it my
way.

la **manga** noun *fem.*
sleeve
una camisa de manga corta a shirt
with short sleeves

el **mango** noun *masc.*
handle
el mango de la sartén the handle
of the frying pan

el **manillar** noun *masc.*
handlebars

LANGUAGE
Spanish = **el manillar** is singular
English = **handlebars** is plural

la **mano** noun *fem.*
hand
¿Tienes algo en la mano? Have
you got anything in your hand?
levantar la mano to put your hand
up
dar la mano a alguien to shake
hands with somebody
Se dan la mano. They shake hands.

la **manta** noun *fem.*
blanket

el **mantel** noun *masc.*
tablecloth

mantener verb
to keep
mantenerse en forma to keep fit

la **mantequilla** noun *fem.*
butter

la **manzana** noun *fem.*
apple
zumo de manzana apple juice

el **manzano** noun *masc.*
apple tree

mañana adverb
tomorrow
pasado mañana the day after
tomorrow
mañana por la mañana tomorrow
morning
mañana por la noche tomorrow
night

la **mañana** noun *fem.*
morning
por la mañana in the morning
ayer por la mañana yesterday
morning
a las siete de la mañana at seven
in the morning

el **mapa** noun *masc.*
map

LANGUAGE
Be careful: **mapa** ends in an -**a** but it is not
a feminine noun.

el **maquillaje** noun *masc.*
make-up

maquillarse verb
to put your make-up on

la **máquina** noun *fem.*
machine
una máquina de afeitar a razor,
a shaver

el **mar** noun *masc.*
sea

el or la **maratón** noun *masc. & fem.*
(plural los **maratones**)
marathon

maravilloso adjective *masc.*,
maravillosa *fem.*
wonderful, marvellous

• *Languages and nationalities do not take a capital letter in Spanish.*

la **marca** noun *fem.*
 1 mark
  dejar una marca to leave a mark
 2 make
  ¿De qué marca es tu ordenador?
  What make is your computer?

marcar verb
 1 to mark
 2 to dial
  marcar un número to dial a
  number
 3 to score
  marcar un gol to score a goal

la **marcha** noun *fem.*
  (*in a car*)
  dar marcha atrás to reverse

el **marciano** noun *masc.*,
la **marciana** *fem.*
  Martian

la **marea** noun *fem.*
  tide
  La marea está alta. The tide's in.
  La marea está baja. The tide's out.

mareado adjective *masc.*,
 mareada *fem.*
 1 sick
  Estoy mareado. I feel sick.
 2 (*in a boat*) seasick
 3 (*losing your balance etc.*) dizzy

marearse verb
 1 to get sick
 2 to get seasick
  Me mareo en los barcos. I get sick
  on boats.
 3 to get dizzy

la **margarina** noun *fem.*
  margarine

el **margen** noun *masc.*
  margin
  No escribas en el margen.
  Don't write in the margin.

el **marido** noun *masc.*
  husband

el **marinero** noun *masc.*
  sailor

la **mariposa** noun *fem.*
  butterfly

la **masiquita** noun *fem.*
  ladybird

el **marisco** noun *masc.*
  seafood

marrón adjective *masc. & fem.*
  brown
  una falda marrón a brown skirt

LANGUAGE
The singular form marrón is the same in the masculine and feminine, and the plural is marrones.

el **marrón** noun *masc.*
  brown
  Me gusta el marrón. I like brown.

el **martes** noun *masc.*
  Tuesday
  Hoy es martes. Today is Tuesday.
  el martes on Tuesday
  Es mi cumpleaños el martes.
  It's my birthday on Tuesday.
  los martes on Tuesdays
  Los martes jugamos al fútbol.
  On Tuesdays we play football.

LANGUAGE
Remember the difference between el martes (one Tuesday only) and los martes (every Tuesday).

el **martillo** noun *masc.*
  hammer

marzo noun *masc.*
  March
  Nací en marzo. I was born in
  March.
  El avión sale de Londres el tres de marzo. The plane leaves London on the third of March.

• *The months of the year and days of the week do not take a capital letter in Spanish.*

a
b
c
d
e
f
g
h
i
j
k
l
m
n
o
p
q
r
s
t
u
v
w
x
y
z

más adverb, adjective & pronoun
1 more
Comes más que yo. You eat more than me.
Eres más alta que él. You're taller than him.
¿Quieres más azúcar? Do you want any more sugar?
Quiero más. I want some more.
2 (*talking about numbers*)
más de more than
más de cinco manzanas more than five apples
3 else
nadie más nobody else
nada más nothing else
4 most
Es el que más me gusta. It's the one I like most.
la niña más inteligente the most intelligent girl
el edificio más alto the tallest building
el más pequeño de todos the smallest of them all
5 plus
Cinco más dos son siete. Five plus two is seven.

la **máscara** noun *fem.*
mask

masculino adjective *masc.*,
masculina *fem.*
1 (*in grammar*) **masculine**
el género masculino the masculine gender
2 men's
el equipo masculino the men's team

masticar verb
to chew

matar verb
to kill

las **matemáticas** plural noun *fem.*
maths

el **matrimonio** noun *masc.*
marriage

maullar verb
to miaow

el **máximo** noun *masc.*
maximum

máximo adjective *masc.*,
máxima *fem.*
maximum

mayo noun *masc.*
May
Llovió mucho en mayo. It rained a lot in May.
Es mi cumpleaños el domingo ocho de mayo. It's my birthday on Sunday, the eighth of May

la **mayonesa** noun *fem.*
mayonnaise

mayor adjective *masc. & fem.*
1 older
Eres mayor que yo. You're older than me.
mi hermano mayor my older brother
2 eldest
la hija mayor the eldest daughter
3 bigger
un tamaño mayor a bigger size
4 biggest
el mayor edificio del pueblo the biggest building in the village
la mayor parte de ... most of ...
5 grown-up
Ya eres mayor. You're grown-up now.

el or la **mayor** noun *masc. & fem.*
1 oldest
la mayor de las hermanas the oldest of the sisters
2 grown-up
una película para mayores a film for grown-ups

• *See the centre section for verb tables.*

la **mayoría** noun *fem.*
　la mayoría de ... most of ...
　la mayoría de los niños most of the
　children

la **mayúscula** noun *fem.*
　capital letter
　en mayúsculas in capital letters
　Se escribe con S mayúscula.
　It's written with a capital S.

me pronoun
1 me
　¿Me conoces? Do you know me?
　Llámame mañana. Call me
　tomorrow.
　Me ha dado el compacto.
　She's given me the CD.
2 to me
　Me lo ha mandado. He has sent it
　to me.
　Dámela. Give it to me.
3 myself
　Me estoy lavando. I'm washing
　myself.
4 *(with parts of the body, clothes, etc.)* **my**
　Me he roto el brazo. I've broken
　my arm.
　Me pongo la camisa. I'm putting
　my shirt on.

el **mecánico** noun *masc.*,
　la **mecánica** *fem.*
　mechanic

la **medalla** noun *fem.*
　medal
　una medalla de plata a silver
　medal

la **media** noun *fem.*
1 *(talking about time)* **half**
　a las ocho y media at half past
　eight
　dos horas y media two and a half
　hours
2 *(Latin America)* **sock**

mediano adjective *masc.*,
　mediana *fem.*
　medium

de tamaño mediano of medium
size

la **medianoche** noun *fem.*
　midnight
　a medianoche at midnight

las **medias** plural noun *fem.*
　tights

el **medicamento** noun *masc.*
　medicine

la **medicina** noun *fem.*
　medicine

el **médico** noun *masc.*,
　la **médica** *fem.*
　doctor
　Mi padre es médico. My dad's a
　doctor.
　ir al médico to go to the doctor

medio adverb
　half
　Está medio dormido. He's half
　asleep.

el **medio** noun *masc.*
　middle
　Ponlo en el medio. Put it in the
　middle.
　en medio de in the middle of

el **medio ambiente** noun *masc.*
　environment

medio adjective *masc.*, **media** *fem.*
　half
　medio litro half a litre
　media hora half an hour
　siete y medio seven and a half
　una hora y media an hour and a
　half
　Son las cuatro y media. It's half
　past four.

el **mediodía** noun *masc.*
　midday
　a mediodía at midday

medir verb
　to measure
　medir una habitación to measure a
　room

• Use el and uno for masculine words and la and una for feminine words.

¿Cuánto mides? How tall are you?
Mido un metro cincuenta. I'm one metre fifty.

el **Mediterráneo** noun masc.
   Mediterranean

la **mejilla** noun fem.
   cheek

mejor adjective masc. & fem.
 1 better
   Mi casa es mejor que la tuya.
   My house is better than yours.
   Me encuentro mejor. I'm feeling better.
 2 best
   mi mejor amigo my best friend
   uno de los mejores alumnos de la clase one of the best pupils in the class

mejor adverb
 1 better
   Juegas al fútbol mejor que yo.
   You play football better than me.
 2 best
   ¿Quién lo ha hecho mejor?
   Who's done it best?
 3 **a lo mejor** maybe

el or la **mejor** noun masc. & fem.
   best
   Esta bici es la mejor. This bike is the best.
   Elige los mejores. Pick the best ones.

mejorar verb
 1 to get better
   El tiempo está mejorando.
   The weather's getting better.
   ¡Que te mejores! Get well soon!
 2 to improve
   Quiero mejorar mi español. I want to improve my Spanish.

el **mellizo** noun masc.,
   la **melliza** fem.
   twin
   Son mellizos. They're twins.

el **melocotón** noun masc. (plural los **melocotones**)
   peach

la **melodía** noun fem.
   tune

el **melón** noun masc. (plural los **melones**)
   melon

la **memoria** noun fem.
   memory
   Tengo buena memoria. I've got a good memory.
   aprender algo de memoria
   to learn something by heart

menor adjective masc. & fem.
 1 younger
   Soy menor que tú. I'm younger than you.
   mi hermana menor my younger sister
 2 youngest
   el hijo menor the youngest son

el or la **menor** noun masc. & fem.
   youngest
   el menor de los hermanos
   the youngest of the brothers

menos adverb, adjective, pronoun & preposition
 1 less
   Hablo menos que tú. I talk less than you.
   Esta película es menos interesante. This film is less interesting.
   Tengo menos dinero que ella.
   I have less money than her.
 2 not as
   Eres menos alto que yo. You're not as tall as me.
 3 not as many, fewer
   Tengo menos amigos que mi hermano. I don't have as many friends as my brother., I have fewer friends than my brother.
 4 (talking about numbers)
   menos de less than

• Languages and nationalities do not take a capital letter in Spanish.

menos de cinco euros less than five euros

5 **least**
Es la que menos me gusta. It's the one I like least.
el libro menos interesante the least interesting book
los menos caros the least expensive ones
por lo menos at least

6 **minus**
Nueve menos tres son seis. Nine minus three is six.

7 **except**
todos menos Javier everybody except Javier

8 (*when telling the time*) **to**
Son las seis menos cinco. It's five to six.

el **mensaje** noun *masc.*
message
un mensaje de texto a text message

la **menta** noun *fem.*
mint
un caramelo de menta a mint

mentir verb
to lie
No miento. I'm not lying.

la **mentira** noun *fem.*
lie
decir mentiras to tell lies
¿Verdad o mentira? True or false?

el **mentiroso** noun *masc.*,
la **mentirosa** *fem.*
liar

el **menú** noun *masc.* (plural los **menús**)
menu

a menudo adverb
often
La veo a menudo. I see her often.

el **mercado** noun *masc.*
market

merecer verb
to deserve

merendar verb
to have an afternoon snack

la **merienda** noun *fem.*
(late) afternoon snack

la **mermelada** noun *fem.*
1 jam
la mermelada de fresa strawberry jam
2 marmalade

el **mes** noun *masc.*
month
el mes pasado last month
el mes que viene next month

la **mesa** noun *fem.*
table
en la mesa on the table
poner la mesa to lay the table
quitar la mesa to clear the table

el **metal** noun *masc.*
metal
una caja de metal a metal box

el **mesero** noun *masc.*,
la **mesera** *fem.*
(*Latin America*) **waiter, waitress**

meter verb
to put
Mete la carta en el sobre. Put the letter in the envelope.

meterse verb
meterse en to get into
Me metí en el agua. I got into the water.

el **metro** noun *masc.*
1 metre
2 underground
en metro by underground
coger el metro to take the underground

México noun *masc.*
Mexico

a
b
c
d
e
f
g
h
i
j
k
l
m
n
o
p
q
r
s
t
u
v
w
x
y
z

• *The months of the year and days of the week do not take a capital letter in Spanish.*

mexicano adjective *masc.*,
mexicana *fem.*
Mexican

el **mexicano** noun *masc.*,
la **mexicana** *fem.*
Mexican

la **mezcla** noun *fem.*
mixture

mezclar verb
to mix

la **mezquita** noun *fem.*
mosque

mi adjective *masc. & fem.*
my
mi casa my house
mis libros my books

> 🔑 **LANGUAGE**
> **Mis** is used before a plural noun.

mí pronoun
me
para mí for me
detrás de mí behind me
A mí me gusta. I like it.

los **microbios** plural noun *masc.*
germs

el **micrófono** noun *masc.*
microphone

el **microondas** noun *masc.* (plural
los **microondas**)
microwave

el **microscopio** noun *masc.*
microscope

el **miedo** noun *masc.*
fear
tener miedo to be afraid
Tengo miedo a la oscuridad.
I'm afraid of the dark.
Tengo miedo de caerme. I'm afraid
of falling.

> 🔑 **LANGUAGE**
> Spanish = **Tengo** miedo (= I have fear)
> English = **I am** afraid

el **miembro** noun *masc.*
member

mientras conjunction
while
Espera aquí mientras me visto.
Wait here while I get dressed.

el **miércoles** noun *masc.*
Wednesday
Hoy es miércoles. Today is
Wednesday.
el miércoles on Wednesday
Voy al cine el miércoles. I'm going
to the cinema on Wednesday.
los miércoles on Wednesdays
Hago deportes los miércoles.
I do sports on Wednesdays.

> 🔑 **LANGUAGE**
> Remember the difference between **el**
> **miércoles** (one Wednesday only) and **los**
> **miércoles** (every Wednesday).

las **migas** plural noun *fem.*
crumbs

> 🌍 **CULTURE**
> In Spain **migas** is also a dish of
> breadcrumbs, olive oil, and grapes.

mil number
thousand
mil personas a thousand people
dos mil personas two thousand
people
miles de euros thousands of euros

el **milagro** noun *masc.*
miracle

el **millón** noun *masc.*
million
un millón de personas a million
people
dos millones two million

> 🔑 **LANGUAGE**
> Spanish = **un millón de** + noun
> English = **a million** + noun

• *See the centre section for verb tables.*

el **millonario** noun *masc.*,
la **millonaria** *fem.*
millionaire

mineral adjective *masc. & fem.*
mineral
el agua mineral mineral water

la **minifalda** noun *fem.*
miniskirt

el **mínimo** noun *masc.*
minimum

mínimo adjective *masc.*,
mínima *fem.*
minimum

la **minúscula** noun *fem.*
small letter
Se escribe con minúscula.
It's written with a small letter.

minusválido adjective *masc.*,
minusválida *fem.*
disabled

el **minusválido** noun *masc.*,
la **minusválida** *fem.*
disabled man, disabled woman

el **minuto** noun *masc.*
minute
Espera un minuto. Wait a minute.

mío adjective *masc.*, **mía** *fem.*
mine
Este libro es mío. This book is mine.
Estas bicis son mías. These bikes are mine.
un amigo mío a friend of mine

el **mío** pronoun *masc.*, la **mía** *fem.*
mine
tu hermano y el mío your brother and mine
Tu casa es más grande que la mía.
Your house is bigger than mine.

mirar verb
to look, to look at
mirar por la ventana to look out of the window

¡Mira! Look!
Estoy mirando las fotos.
I'm looking at the photos.

🔑 **LANGUAGE**
Spanish = **mirar** algo/a alguien
English = **to look at** something/somebody

la **misa** noun *fem.*
mass
ir a misa to go to mass

mismo adverb
right
ahora mismo right now
aquí mismo right here

mismo adjective *masc.*, **misma** *fem.*
1 same
Tienes la misma blusa que yo.
You have the same blouse as me.
al mismo tiempo at the same time
2 ...self (plural **...selves**)
yo mismo myself
ella misma herself
nosotros mismos ourselves

el **mismo** pronoun *masc.*,
la **misma** *fem.*
1 same one
Tengo el mismo. I've got the same one.
2 **lo mismo** the same thing
Siempre dice lo mismo. She always says the same thing.

el **misterio** noun *masc.*
mystery

misterioso adjective *masc.*,
misteriosa *fem.*
mysterious

la **mitad** noun *fem.*
half
la mitad de los alumnos half the pupils
Corta el pastel por la mitad.
Cut the cake in half.
a mitad de camino halfway

a
b
c
d
e
f
g
h
i
j
k
l
m
n
o
p
q
r
s
t
u
v
w
x
y
z

• Use **el** and **uno** for masculine words and **la** and **una** for feminine words.

a
b
c
d
e
f
g
h
i
j
k
l
m
n
o
p
q
r
s
t
u
v
w
x
y
z

la **mochila** noun *fem.*
1 backpack
2 schoolbag

🔑 **LANGUAGE**
Schoolchildren carry a mochila on their backs.

los **mocos** plural noun *masc.*
tener mocos to have a runny nose

la **moda** noun *fem.*
fashion
una revista de modas a fashion magazine
estar de moda to be fashionable

los **modales** plural noun *masc.*
manners
buenos modales good manners

el **modelo** noun *masc.*
model
el último modelo the latest model

el or la **modelo** noun *masc. & fem.*
model
Es una modelo española. She's a Spanish model.

moderno adjective *masc.*,
moderna *fem.*
modern

mojado adjective *masc.*,
mojada *fem.*
wet
una toalla mojada a wet towel

mojarse verb
to get wet
Me he mojado con la lluvia. I got wet in the rain.

molestar verb
1 to bother
Siento molestarle. I'm sorry to bother you.
¿Le molesta si abro la ventana? Will it bother you if I open the window?
2 to annoy
Mi hermano me molesta. My brother annoys me.

el **momento** noun *masc.*
moment
¡Un momento! Just a moment!
en este momento at the moment

la **moneda** noun *fem.*
coin
una moneda de dos euros a two euro coin

el **monedero** noun *masc.*
purse

el **monitor** noun *masc.*
(computer screen) monitor

el **monitor** noun *masc.*,
la **monitora** *fem.*
instructor
un monitor de esquí a ski instructor

la **monja** noun *fem.*
nun

mono adjective *masc.*, **mona** *fem.*
lovely
un niño mono a lovely baby

el **mono** noun *masc.*, la **mona** *fem.*
monkey

el **monopatín** noun *masc.* (plural los **monopatines**)
skateboard

el **monstruo** noun *masc.*
monster

la **montaña** noun *fem.*
mountain
en la montaña in the mountains
la montaña rusa the roller coaster
una bicicleta de montaña a mountain bike

montar verb
1 to ride
montar en bici to ride a bike
montar a caballo to ride a horse
2 montar una tienda to put up a tent

• Languages and nationalities do not take a capital letter in Spanish.

el **montón** noun *masc.* (plural los **montones**)
1 **pile**
un montón de libros a pile of books
2 **un montón de** loads of
Hay un montón de niños. There are loads of children.

el **monumento** noun *masc.*
historic building

la **moqueta** noun *fem.*
(fitted) carpet

la **mora** noun *fem.*
blackberry

morado adjective *masc.*,
morada *fem.*
purple
una camisa morada a purple shirt

el **morado** noun *masc.*
purple
Prefiero el morado. I prefer purple.

morder verb
to bite
Me muerdo las uñas. I bite my nails.

moreno adjective *masc.*,
morena *fem.*
1 **dark**
Tengo el pelo moreno. I've got dark hair.
2 **brown, tanned**
Estoy muy moreno. I'm very brown., I'm very tanned.

morir verb
to die
Mi gato murió ayer. My cat died yesterday.
¡Me muero de hambre! I'm starving!

la **mosca** noun *fem.*
fly

el **mosquito** noun *masc.*
mosquito

la **mostaza** noun *fem.*
mustard

el **mostrador** noun *masc.*
1 (*in a shop*) **counter**
2 (*at an airport*) **check-in desk**

mostrar verb
to show

el **motivo** noun *masc.*
reason
el motivo de algo the reason for something

la **moto** noun *fem.*
motorbike

la **motocicleta** noun *fem.*
motorcycle

el **motor** noun *masc.*
(*of a car*) **engine**

el or la **motorista** noun *masc. & fem.*
motorcyclist

⚠ **FALSE FRIEND**
motorista = motorcyclist (*not* motorist)

mover verb
to move
He movido la silla. I've moved the chair.

moverse verb
to move
No puedo moverme. I can't move.
No te muevas. Don't move.

el **móvil** noun *masc.*
mobile phone
Llámame al móvil. Call me on my mobile.

el **movimiento** noun *masc.*
movement

la **muchacha** noun *fem.*
girl

el **muchacho** noun *masc.*
boy

a
b
c
d
e
f
g
h
i
j
k
l
m
n
o
p
q
r
s
t
u
v
w
x
y
z

• *The months of the year and days of the week do not take a capital letter in Spanish.*

mucho adverb
1 a lot
Leo mucho. I read a lot.
mucho más grande a lot bigger
2 much
No leo mucho. I don't read much.
No me gusta mucho. I don't like it
very much.
mucho más grande much bigger

mucho adjective & pronoun *masc.*,
mucha *fem.*
1 a lot of
mucho dinero a lot of money
muchos coches a lot of cars
Me has dado mucho. You've given
me a lot.
hace mucho tiempo a long time
ago
2 much
No tengo mucho dinero. I don't
have much money.
No tengo mucho. I don't have
much.
3 many
No hay muchas casas. There aren't
many houses.
¿Tienes muchos? Do you have
many?
Muchas gracias. Many thanks.
4 very
Hace mucho calor. It's very hot.
Tengo mucha hambre. I'm very
hungry.

mudarse verb
to move house
Se mudan mañana. They're
moving tomorrow.

el **mueble** noun *masc.*
los muebles furniture
un mueble a piece of furniture

la **muela** noun *fem.*
back tooth
Tengo dolor de muelas. I have a
toothache.

la **muerte** noun *fem.*
death

muerto adjective *masc.*,
muerta *fem.*
dead
Está muerta. She's dead.
Hay muchos muertos. Lots of
people have been killed.

la **mujer** noun *fem.*
1 woman
un hombre y una mujer a man and
a woman
2 wife
la mujer de mi primo my cousin's
wife

la **muleta** noun *fem.*
crutch
Anda con muletas. He's on
crutches.

multiplicar verb
to multiply
Multiplica ocho por cinco.
Multiply eight by five.
las tablas de multiplicar the times
tables

el **Mundial** noun *masc.*
(*in football*) **the World Cup**

el **mundo** noun *masc.*
1 world
el mejor del mundo the best in the
world
2 todo el mundo everybody
Todo el mundo ha leído este libro.
Everybody has read this book.

la **muñeca** noun *fem.*
1 doll
una casa de muñecas a doll's
house
2 wrist

el **muñeco de nieve** noun *masc.*
snowman

el **murciélago** noun *masc.*
bat

el **muro** noun *masc.*
wall

• *See the centre section for verb tables.*

el **músculo** noun *masc.*
muscle

el **museo** noun *masc.*
1 museum
2 (*for paintings*) **art gallery**

la **música** noun *fem.*
music

el **músico** noun *masc.*,
la **música** *fem.*
musician

el **muslo** noun *masc.*
un muslo de pollo a chicken leg

musulmán adjective *masc.*,
musulmana *fem.*
Muslim

🔑 **LANGUAGE**
The plural of **musulmán** is **musulmanes**.

muy adverb
very
muy bueno very good
muy bien very well

Nn

nacer verb
to be born
Nací en Madrid. I was born in Madrid.

el **nacimiento** noun *masc.*
birth
mi fecha de nacimiento my date of birth

nacional adjective *masc. & fem.*
national

la **nacionalidad** noun *fem.*
nationality

nada pronoun & adverb
1 nothing
¿Qué haces? – Nada. What are you doing? – Nothing.
nada más nothing else
2 anything
No he dicho nada. I haven't said anything.
No quiero nada más. I don't want anything else.

🔑 **LANGUAGE**
No + *verb* + nada, for example: No quiero nada.

3 at all
No me gusta nada. I don't like it at all.

4 **de nada** you're welcome
¡Gracias! – De nada. Thank you! – You're welcome.

nadar verb
to swim

nadie pronoun
1 nobody
No hay nadie en la cocina. There's nobody in the kitchen.
2 anybody
No conozco a nadie. I don't know anybody.

🔑 **LANGUAGE**
No + *verb* + nadie, for example: No hay nadie.

naranja adjective *masc. & fem.*
orange
calcetines naranja orange socks

🔑 **LANGUAGE**
Naranja is the same in the masculine, feminine, and plural.

el **naranja** noun *masc.*
(*colour*) orange
El naranja te queda bien. Orange looks good on you.

• Use **el** and **uno** for masculine words and **la** and **una** for feminine words.

a
b
c
d
e
f
g
h
i
j
k
l
m
n
o
p
q
r
s
t
u
v
w
x
y
z

a
b
c
d
e
f
g
h
i
j
k
l
m
n
o
p
q
r
s
t
u
v
w
x
y
z

la **naranja** noun *fem.*
orange
un zumo de naranja an orange juice

la **nariz** noun *fem.* (plural las **narices**)
nose

la **nata** noun *fem.*
cream
fresas con nata strawberries and cream

la **natación** noun *fem.*
swimming

natural adjective *masc. & fem.*
natural

la **naturaleza** noun *fem.*
nature

la **navaja** noun *fem.*
penknife

la **nave** noun *fem.*
ship
una nave espacial a spaceship

navegar verb
1 **navegar en Internet** to surf the Internet
2 to sail

la **Navidad** noun *fem.*
Christmas
en Navidad at Christmas
¡Feliz Navidad! Happy Christmas!
el día de Navidad Christmas Day

necesario adjective *masc.*, **necesaria** *fem.*
necessary

necesitar verb
to need
Necesito un libro nuevo. I need a new book.

la **nectarina** noun *fem.*
nectarine

el **negativo** noun *masc.*
(*in grammar*) negative

los **negocios** plural noun *masc.*
business
estar en un viaje de negocios to be on a business trip

negro adjective *masc.*, **negra** *fem.*
black
un traje negro a black suit

el **negro** noun *masc.*
black
Yo prefiero el negro. I prefer black.

el **nervio** noun *masc.*
nerve
un ataque de nervios an attack of nerves

nervioso adjective *masc.*, **nerviosa** *fem.*
nervous
Estoy nerviosa. I'm nervous.

el **neumático** noun *masc.*
tyre

la **nevada** noun *fem.*
snowfall

nevar verb
to snow
Está nevando. It's snowing.

la **nevera** noun *fem.*
fridge

ni conjunction
1 or
No sabes leer ni escribir. You can't read or write.
2 nor
Isabel no viene. – Ni yo tampoco. Isabel isn't coming. – Nor am I.
3 **ni ... ni** not either ... or
No quiero ni pescado ni carne. I don't want either fish or meat.
4 **ni ... ni** neither ... nor
ni María ni su hermano neither María nor her brother

el **nido** noun *masc.*
nest

•*Languages and nationalities do not take a capital letter in Spanish.*

la **niebla** noun *fem.*
fog
Hay niebla. It's foggy.

la **nieta** noun *fem.*
granddaughter

el **nieto** noun *masc.*
grandson
los nietos grandchildren

la **nieve** noun *fem.*
snow

ninguno adjective & pronoun *masc.*,
ninguna *fem.*

LANGUAGE
The masculine singular **ninguno**
becomes **ningún** when it is used before a
noun.

1 not any
No toco ningún instrumento.
I don't play any instrument.
No he comprado ninguno.
I haven't bought any.
2 neither, not either
**¿Quieres la bici negra o la roja? –
Ninguna.** Do you want the black
bike or the red one? – Neither.
No me gusta ninguno de los dos.
I don't like either of them.
3 none
¿Cuántos libros tienes? – Ninguno.
How many books do you have? –
None.
ninguno de los niños none of the
children

la **niña** noun *fem.*
1 girl
**Mi hermana tiene una niña de dos
años.** My sister has a little girl of
two.
2 child
Es una niña tímida. She's a shy
child.
3 baby
Mi prima espera una niña.
My cousin is expecting a baby girl.

la **niñera** noun *fem.*
nanny

el **niño** noun *masc.*
1 boy
**Mi prima tiene un niño de cuatro
años.** My cousin has a little boy of
four.
2 child
Es un niño tímido. He's a shy child.
3 **los niños** children, boys and girls
Hay veinte niños en la clase. There
are twenty children in the class.
4 baby
Ha tenido un niño. She's had a
baby boy.

el **nivel** noun *masc.*
level

no adverb
1 no
¿Has visto esta película? - No.
Have you seen this film? - No.
No, gracias. No thanks.
2 not
No soy alta. I'm not tall.
No me gusta. I don't like it.
todavía no not yet
no mucho not much
3 (*with negatives such as* **nunca, nada**)
No hace nunca los deberes. He
never does his homework.
No tengo nada. I don't have
anything.
4 (*in questions*)
Vas a la biblioteca, ¿no? You're
going to the library, aren't you?
Es inglés, ¿no? He's English, isn't
he?

LANGUAGE
English uses questions such as 'aren't
you?', 'isn't he?' but Spanish simply puts
¿no? at the end.

la **noche** noun *fem.*
1 night
por la noche at night
ayer por la noche yesterday night

a b c d e f g h i j k l m n o p q r s t u v w x y z

• *The months of the year and days of the week do not take a capital letter in Spanish.*

a b c d e f g h i j k l m **n** o p q r s t u v w x y z

a las diez de la noche at ten o'clock at night
esta noche tonight
¡Buenas noches! Good night!
Es de noche. It's dark.
2 evening
por la noche in the evening
a las ocho de la noche at eight o'clock in the evening
¡Buenas noches! Good evening!

la **Nochebuena** noun *fem.*
Christmas Eve

CULTURE
In Spain the main Christmas meal is on Nochebuena, and it is eaten before Midnight Mass.

la **Nochevieja** noun *fem.*
New Year's Eve

nocturno adjective *masc.*,
nocturna *fem.*
1 night
el tren nocturno the night train
2 evening
una clase nocturna an evening class

el **nombre** noun *masc.*
1 name
No sé su nombre. I don't know her name.
2 noun
'Mesa' y 'silla' son nombres. 'Table' and 'chair' are nouns.

normal adjective *masc. & fem.*
normal

normalmente adverb
normally

norte noun masculine & adjective
north
en el norte in the north
la costa norte the north coast
el Mar del Norte the North Sea

Norteamérica noun *fem.*
North America

norteamericano adjective *masc.*,
norteamericana *fem.*
American
Es norteamericana. She's American.

el **norteamericano** noun *masc.*,
la **norteamericana** *fem.*
American

nos pronoun
1 us
Nos han visto. They've seen us.
Quiere vernos. He wants to see us.
2 to us
Nos ha dicho algo. He said something to us.
3 ourselves
Nos estamos lavando. We're washing ourselves.
4 (*with parts of the body, clothes, etc.*) **our**
Nos quitamos los zapatos. We took our shoes off.
5 each other
Nos escribimos. We write to each other.

nosotros pronoun *masc.*,
nosotras *fem.*
1 we
Nosotros hemos venido pero nuestros padres no. We've come but our parents haven't.

LANGUAGE
Nosotros/nosotras is used for giving special importance to the word 'we'.

2 (*after a preposition etc.*) **us**
con nosotros with us
Somos nosotras. It's us.
nosotros mismos ourselves

la **nota** noun *fem.*
1 mark
He sacado buenas notas. I've got good marks.
2 note
Escribe una nota. Write a note.

• *See the centre section for verb tables.*

notar verb
to notice

la **noticia** noun *fem.*
1 news
Tengo una buena noticia. I have some good news.
No tenemos noticias de Raúl. We don't have any news of Raúl.

⚷ **LANGUAGE**
las noticias = more than one piece of news

2 **las noticias** the news (*on TV or the radio*)
las noticias de las nueve the nine o'clock news

la **novela** noun *fem.*
novel

noveno adjective *masc.*,
novena *fem.*
ninth
en el noveno piso on the ninth floor

noventa number
ninety

la **novia** noun *fem.*
1 girlfriend
Mi hermano tiene novia. My brother has a girlfriend.
2 bride

noviembre noun *masc.*
November
Es mi cumpleaños en noviembre. It's my birthday in November.
Voy a Madrid el cinco de noviembre. I'm going to Madrid on the fifth of November.

el **novio** noun *masc.*
1 boyfriend
Mi hermana tiene novio. My sister has a boyfriend.
2 bridegroom
los novios the bride and groom

la **nube** noun *fem.*
cloud

nublado adjective *masc.*,
nublada *fem.*
cloudy
Está nublado. It's cloudy.

el **nudo** noun *masc.*
knot
hacer un nudo to tie a knot

nuestro adjective *masc.*,
nuestra *fem.*
1 our
nuestra escuela our school
nuestros padres our parents
2 ours
Este ordenador es nuestro. This computer is ours.
Estos libros son nuestros. These books are ours.
un amigo nuestro a friend of ours

⚷ **LANGUAGE**
Nuestros/nuestras is used with a plural noun.

el **nuestro** pronoun *masc.*,
la **nuestra** *fem.*
ours
Su piscina es mejor que la nuestra. His pool is better than ours.
tus libros y los nuestros your books and ours

Nueva Zelanda noun *fem.*
New Zealand

nueve number
1 nine
Tengo nueve años. I'm nine.
Son las nueve. It's nine o'clock.
2 (*with dates*) ninth
el nueve de diciembre the ninth of December

• Use el and uno for masculine words and la and una for feminine words.

a
b
c
d
e
f
g
h
i
j
k
l
m
n
o
p
q
r
s
t
u
v
w
x
y
z

nuevo adjective *masc.*, **nueva** *fem.*
new
una bicicleta nueva a new bicycle
mis nuevos amigos my new friends
el Año Nuevo the New Year

la **nuez** noun *fem.* (plural las **nueces**)
walnut

el **número** noun *masc.*
number
¿Cuál es tu número de teléfono?
What's your phone number?
un gran número de a large number
of

nunca adverb
1 never
No llego tarde nunca. I never
arrive late.
Nunca salgo sola. I never go out by
myself.
2 ever
No salgo casi nunca. I hardly ever
go out.
más que nunca more than ever

🔑 **LANGUAGE**
no + *verb* + nunca, for example: No salgo
nunca.

Oo

o conjunction
or
hoy o mañana today or tomorrow
¿Vienes o no? Are you coming or
not?

obedecer verb
to obey
Ese niño no obedece al maestro.
That child doesn't obey the
teacher.

el **objeto** noun *masc.*
object

obligar verb
to make, to force
Lo han obligado a salir. They've
made him leave.

la **obra** noun *fem.*
play
hacer una obra to put on a play

las **obras** plural noun *fem.*
roadworks

el **obrero** noun *masc.*,
la **obrera** *fem.*
worker

obtener verb
to get
He obtenido el primer premio.
I got the first prize.

la **ocasión** noun *fem.*
1 opportunity
una buena ocasión a good
opportunity
2 occasion
en varias ocasiones on several
occasions

el **océano** noun *masc.*
ocean

ochenta number
eighty

ocho number
1 eight
Tengo ocho años. I'm eight.
Son las ocho. It's eight o'clock.
2 (*with dates*) **eighth**
el ocho de mayo the eighth of
May

el **ócorro** noun *masc.*
okra

octavo *masc.*, **octava** adjective *fem.*
eighth

• Languages and nationalities do not take a capital letter in Spanish.

octubre noun *masc.*
October
Mis abuelos llegan en octubre.
My grandparents are coming in October.
¿Qué haces el dos de octubre?
What are you doing on the second of October?

 CULTURE
On 12th October people in Spain and Latin America celebrate the finding of America by Christopher Columbus. In Spain this is called **el día de la Hispanidad**.

ocupado *masc.*,
ocupada adjective *fem.*
1 busy
Estoy ocupada. I'm busy.
2 (*talking about a toilet etc.*) **engaged**
3 taken
Este asiento está ocupado.
This seat is taken.

ocurrir verb
to happen

LANGUAGE
Ocurrir is similar to the English 'occur'.

odiar verb
to hate
Odio el pescado. I hate fish.

oeste noun *masc.* & adjective
west
en el oeste in the west
la costa oeste the west coast

la **oficina** noun *fem.*
office
la oficina de correos the post office
la oficina de turismo the tourist office

ofrecer verb
to offer
ofrecer algo a alguien to offer somebody something

el **oído** noun *masc.*
ear

oír verb
to hear
No te oigo. I can't hear you.
¡Oiga, por favor! Excuse me!

el **ojo** noun *masc.*
eye
Tengo los ojos verdes. I have green eyes.

la **ola** noun *fem.*
wave

oler verb
to smell
oler las flores to smell the flowers
oler a algo to smell of something
Huele a pescado. It smells of fish.
Huele bien. It smells nice.

olímpico adjective *masc.*,
olímpica *fem.*
Olympic
los Juegos Olímpicos the Olympic Games

el **olor** noun *masc.*
smell
Hay olor a gas. There's a smell of gas.

olvidar verb
to forget

olvidarse verb
to forget
Me olvido de todo. I forget everything.
Se me ha olvidado tu dirección. I've forgotten your address.
¡Se me olvidó! I forgot!

once number
1 eleven
Tengo once años. I'm eleven.
Son las once. It's eleven o'clock.
2 (*with dates*) **eleventh**
el once de enero the eleventh of January

a b c d e f g h i j k l m n **o** p q r s t u v w x y z

• *The months of the year and days of the week do not take a capital letter in Spanish.*

a
b
c
d
e
f
g
h
i
j
k
l
m
n
o
p
q
r
s
t
u
v
w
x
y
z

ondulado adjective masc.,
  ondulada fem.
  wavy
  Tengo el pelo ondulado. I've got
  wavy hair.

operar verb
  to operate on
  Van a operarme. I'm going to have
  an operation.
  Me han operado del hombro.
  I've had an operation on my
  shoulder.

operarse verb
  to have an operation
  Tiene que operarse del brazo.
  He has to have an operation on his
  arm.

la **opinión** noun fem. (plural las
  opiniones)
  opinion
  en mi opinión in my opinion
  He cambiado de opinión.
  I've changed my mind.

la **oportunidad** noun fem.
  chance, opportunity
  una segunda oportunidad
  a second chance

la **óptica** noun fem.
  optician's
  ir a la óptica to go to the
  optician's

optimista adjective masc. & fem.
  optimistic

opuesto adjective masc.,
  opuesta fem.
  opposite
  en direcciones opuestas
  in opposite directions

la **oración** noun fem. (plural las
  oraciones)
  1 (in grammar) **sentence**
  2 **prayer**

el **orden** noun masc.
  order
  en orden alfabético in
  alphabetical order
  La habitación está en orden.
  The room's tidy.

ordenado adjective masc.,
  ordenada fem.
  tidy

el **ordenador** noun masc.
  computer
  un ordenador portátil a laptop

ordenar verb
  to tidy

la **oreja** noun fem.
  ear

organizar verb
  to organize

orgulloso adjective masc.,
  orgullosa fem.
  proud
  Estoy muy orgullosa de ti.
  I'm very proud of you.

original adjective masc. & fem.
  original

la **orilla** noun fem.
  bank
  sentarse a la orilla del río to sit
  down on the river bank
  la orilla del mar the seashore

el **oro** noun masc.
  gold
  una medalla de oro a gold medal

la **orquesta** noun fem.
  1 (playing dance music etc.) **band**
  2 **orchestra**

la **ortografía** noun fem.
  spelling
  una falta de ortografía a spelling
  mistake

• See the centre section for verb tables.

la **oruga** noun *fem.*
caterpillar

os pronoun
1 **you**
Os conozco. I know you.
Queremos ayudaros. We want to help you.
2 **to you**
Os ha escrito. He has written to you.
3 **yourselves**
¿Os habéis cortado? Have you cut yourselves?
4 *(with parts of the body, clothes, etc.)* **your**
Os podéis lavar las manos. You can wash your hands.
¡Lavaos las manos! Wash your hands!
5 **each other**
¿Os conocéis? Do you know each other?

🔑 **LANGUAGE**
Use **os** when you are talking to two or more friends, people in your family, or people your own age.

la **oscuridad** noun *fem.*
dark
Está sentado en la oscuridad. He's sitting in the dark.

oscuro adjective *masc.*, **oscura** *fem.*
dark
Aquí está oscuro. It's dark here.
faldas verde oscuro dark green skirts

🔑 **LANGUAGE**
When **oscuro** follows the name of a colour (e.g. verde, azul), use the colour word in the masculine singular form only.

el **osito de peluche** noun *masc.*
teddy bear

el **oso** noun *masc.*
bear

el **otoño** noun *masc.*
autumn
en otoño in the autumn

otro adjective & pronoun *masc.*, **otra** *fem.*
1 **another**
Quiero otro libro. I want another book.
Tengo otro. I have another one.
2 **other**
el otro día the other day
las otras niñas the other girls
Tengo otros. I have others.
3 **otra cosa** something else
Dame otra cosa. Give me something else.
4 **otra vez** again
¿Puedo leerlo otra vez? Can I read it again?

el **otro** pronoun *masc.*, la **otra** *fem.*
the other one
¿Dónde está el otro? Where is the other one?
Las otras están en la mesa. The others are on the table.

la **oveja** noun *fem.*
sheep

el **OVNI** noun *masc.*
UFO

🔑 **LANGUAGE**
The Spanish stands for objeto volador no identificado, matching the English 'unidentified flying object'.

oxidado *masc.*, **oxidada** adjective *fem.*
rusty

el **oxígeno** noun *masc.*
oxygen

a
b
c
d
e
f
g
h
i
j
k
l
m
n
o
p
q
r
s
t
u
v
w
x
y
z

• Use **el** and **uno** for masculine words and **la** and **una** for feminine words.

Pp

la **paciencia** noun *fem.*
  patience
  tener paciencia to be patient

el or la **paciente** noun *masc. & fem.*
  (*of a doctor*) **patient**

el **Pacífico** noun *masc.*
  Pacific

el **padrastro** noun *masc.*
  stepfather

el **padre** noun *masc.*
  father, dad
  Mi padre es fontanero. My father's
  a plumber., My dad's a plumber.
  mis padres my parents

⚠ **FALSE FRIEND**
mis padres = my parents (*not* my
fathers)

el **padrino** noun *masc.*
  godfather
  mis padrinos my godparents

la **paella** noun *fem.*
  paella

🌏 **CULTURE**
Paella is made from rice, cooked with
chicken, vegetables, and shellfish.

la **paga** noun *fem.*
 1 **pay**
 2 (*for children*) **pocket money**

pagar verb
 1 **to pay**
  Pagué diez euros. I paid ten euros.
 2 **to pay for**
  ¿Has pagado la entrada? Have you
  paid for the ticket?

la **página** noun *fem.*
  page
  en la página siete on page seven

el **país** noun *masc.*
 1 **country**
  un país extranjero a foreign
  country
 2 **el País de Gales** Wales
  los Países Bajos the Netherlands
  el País Vasco the Basque Country

el **paisaje** noun *masc.*
  scenery, landscape
  Mira el paisaje. Look at the
  scenery.

la **paja** noun *fem.*
  straw
  un sombrero de paja a straw hat

el **pájaro** noun *masc.*
  bird

la **pajita** noun *fem.*
  (*for drinking*) **straw**
  beber con una pajita to drink with
  a straw

la **pala** noun *fem.*
 1 **shovel**
 2 **spade**
  un cubo y una pala a bucket and
  spade
 3 (*for table tennis*) **bat**

el **palacio** noun *masc.*
  palace

pálido adjective *masc.*,
pálida *fem.*
  pale
  Estás muy pálido. You look very
  pale.

• *Languages and nationalities do not take a capital letter in Spanish.*

los **palillos** plural noun *masc.*
chopsticks

la **palmera** noun *fem.*
palm tree

el **palo** noun *masc.*
stick
Me ha pegado con un palo. He hit me with a stick.

la **paloma** noun *fem.*
pigeon

las **palomitas** plural noun *fem.*
popcorn

⚷ **LANGUAGE**
Spanish = **las palomitas** is plural
English = **popcorn** is singular

el **pan** noun *masc.*
1 bread
¿Quieres pan con mantequilla? Do you want some bread and butter?
el pan tostado toast
una barra de pan a loaf of bread
2 loaf
un pan a loaf of bread

la **panadería** noun *fem.*
baker's shop

Panamá noun *masc.*
Panama

el **panda** noun *masc.*
panda
un oso panda a panda

⚷ **LANGUAGE**
Be careful: **panda** ends in an -a but it is not a feminine noun.

la **pandilla** noun *fem.*
gang

el **panecillo** noun *masc.*
bread roll

la **pantalla** noun *fem.*
screen
la pantalla del ordenador the computer screen

los **pantalones** plural noun *masc.*
trousers
unos pantalones a pair of trousers

el **pañal** noun *masc.*
nappy

el **paño** noun *masc.*
cloth

el **pañuelo** noun *masc.*
1 handkerchief
2 scarf
un pañuelo de seda a silk scarf

la **papa** noun *fem.*
(*Latin America*) potato

el **Papa** noun *masc.*
Pope

⚷ **LANGUAGE**
Be careful: **Papa** ends in an -a but it is not a feminine noun.

el **papá** noun *masc.*
dad
Gracias, papá Thanks, dad
mis papás my mum and dad
Papá Noel Father Christmas

la **papaya** noun *fem.*
pawpaw

el **papel** noun *masc.*
1 paper
una bolsa de papel a paper bag
el papel higiénico toilet paper
el papel pintado wallpaper
el papel de aluminio tinfoil
2 piece of paper
Escribe tu nombre en un papel. Write your name on a piece of paper.
3 (*in a play or film*) part
Hace el papel del mago. He plays the part of the wizard.

la **papelera** noun *fem.*
1 wastepaper basket
2 (*in the street*) litter bin

a b c d e f g h i j k l m n o **p** q r s t u v w x y z

• *The months of the year and days of the week do not take a capital letter in Spanish.*

la **papelería** noun fem.
stationery shop

las **paperas** plural noun fem.
mumps

el **paquete** noun masc.
1 packet
un paquete de galletas a packet of biscuits
2 parcel

Paquistán noun masc.
Pakistan

par adjective masc. & fem.
un número par an even number

el **par** noun masc.
1 pair
un par de zapatos a pair of shoes
2 un par de a couple of
un par de veces a couple of times

para preposition
1 for
Es para mí. It's for me.
¿Para qué? What for?
para siempre for ever
2 to
el próximo vuelo para Barcelona the next flight to Barcelona
Dame dinero para comprar un helado. Give me some money to buy an ice cream.

la **parada** noun fem.
stop
bajar en la próxima parada to get off at the next stop
una parada de autobús a bus stop

el **paracaídas** noun masc. (plural los **paracaídas**)
parachute

parado adjective masc., **parada** fem.
unemployed

el **paraguas** noun masc. (plural los **paraguas**)
umbrella

Paraguay noun masc.
Paraguay

parar verb
1 to stop
¿Puedes parar el coche? Can you stop the car?
El autobús para delante del colegio. The bus stops in front of the school.
2 (Latin America) to stand up

pararse verb
to stop
Mi reloj se ha parado. My watch has stopped.

parecer verb
1 to look
Parecen iguales. They look the same.
Parece que va a llover. It looks like rain.
2 to think
¿Qué te parece el libro? What do you think of the book?
Me parece difícil. I think it's difficult.
Me parece que sí. I think so.

parecerse verb
to look like
Te pareces a tu prima. You look like your cousin.
Las dos hermanas se parecen. The two sisters look alike.

parecido adjective masc., **parecida** fem.
similar
Tus pantalones son parecidos a los míos. Your trousers are similar to mine.

la **pared** noun fem.
wall
en la pared on the wall

• See the centre section for verb tables.

la **pareja** noun *fem.*
  1 **pair**
    trabajar en parejas to work in pairs
  2 **couple**
    una pareja de casados a married couple
  3 (*in a game, school play, etc.*) **partner**

el or la **pariente** noun *masc. & fem.*
  relative

 FALSE FRIEND
los parientes = **relatives** (*not* parents)

el **párpado** noun *masc.*
  eyelid

el **parque** noun *masc.*
  park
  un parque de atracciones an amusement park

el **párrafo** noun *masc.*
  paragraph

la **parte** noun *fem.*
  1 **part**
    la primera parte de la película the first part of the film
    en parte partly
  2 **la mayor parte de** most of
    la mayor parte del día most of the day
  3 (*for saying 'somewhere' etc.*)
    estar en alguna parte to be somewhere
    ir a alguna parte to go somewhere
    No vamos a ninguna parte. We're going nowhere.
    por todas partes everywhere

participar verb
  to take part
  participar en algo to take part in something

particular adjective *masc. & fem.*
  private
  clases particulares private lessons

la **partida** noun *fem.*
  game

una partida de ajedrez a game of chess

el **partido** noun *masc.*
  match
  un partido de fútbol a football match

la **pasa** noun *fem.*
  raisin

el **pasado** noun *masc.*
  1 **past**
    en el pasado in the past
  2 (*in grammar*) **past tense**

pasado adjective *masc.*,
  pasada *fem.*
  last
  la semana pasada last week
  el jueves pasado last Thursday

el **pasajero** noun *masc.*,
  la **pasajera** *fem.*
  passenger

el **pasaporte** noun *masc.*
  passport

pasar verb
  1 **to pass**
    ¿Me pasas el azúcar, por favor? Can you pass me the sugar, please?
  2 **to go past**
    El autobús pasa por el colegio. The bus goes past the school.
  3 **to go through**
    pasar por un túnel to go through a tunnel
    ¡Déjame pasar! Let me go through!
  4 **to come**
    Pasaré mañana. I'll come tomorrow.
    ¿Puedo pasar? Can I come in?
  5 **to happen**
    ¿Qué pasa? What's happening?
    No pasó nada. Nothing happened.
  6 **to be the matter**
    ¿Qué pasa? What's the matter?
    ¿Qué te pasa? What's the matter with you?

• *Use* **el** *and* **uno** *for masculine words and* **la** *and* **una** *for feminine words.*

7 **to spend**
He pasado una semana en Bilbao.
I've spent a week in Bilbao.
pasar las vacaciones en ...
to spend the holidays in ...
8 **pasarlo bien** to have a good time
Lo pasé muy bien. I had a very
good time.

el **pasatiempo** noun *masc.*
hobby

la **Pascua** noun *fem.*
Easter
un huevo de Pascua an Easter egg

pasear verb
1 **to walk**
Me gusta pasear por el parque.
I like walking in the park.
ir a pasear to go for a walk
2 (*by bike, car, etc.*) **to ride**
Fui a pasear en bici. I went for a
ride on my bike.

el **paseo** noun *masc.*
1 **walk**
ir a dar un paseo to go for a walk
2 (*by car, bike, etc.*) **ride**
ir a dar un paseo en coche to go for
a ride in the car

el **pasillo** noun *masc.*
corridor
al final del pasillo at the end of the
corridor

el **paso** noun *masc.*
1 **step**
Da un paso hacia adelante.
Take one step forward.
oír pasos to hear footsteps
2 **way**
cerrar el paso to block the way
un paso subterráneo a subway
un paso de peatones a pedestrian
crossing

la **pasta** noun *fem.*
pasta
Me gusta la pasta. I like pasta.
la pasta de dientes toothpaste

el **pastel** noun *masc.*
1 **cake**
Me gustan los pasteles. I like
cakes.
2 **pie**
un pastel de manzana an apple
pie

la **pastelería** noun *fem.*
cake shop

la **pastilla** noun *fem.*
tablet
tomar una pastilla to take a tablet
una pastilla de jabón a bar of soap

el **pasto** noun *masc.*
(*Latin America*) **grass**

la **pata** noun *fem.*
leg
la pata del perro the dog's leg

la **patada** noun *fem.*
kick
dar una patada a algo to kick
something
Me dio una patada. He kicked me.

la **patata** noun *fem.*
potato
patatas asadas baked potatoes
patatas fritas chips
una bolsa de patatas fritas
a bag of crisps

🔑 **LANGUAGE**
Word for word **patatas fritas** means
'fried potatoes'. This is the Spanish for
'chips' as well as 'crisps'.

el **patinaje** noun *masc.*
skating
el patinaje sobre hielo ice skating
el patinaje sobre ruedas
rollerskating

patinar verb
to skate

los **patines** plural noun *masc.*
skates
los patines de ruedas roller skates
los patines en línea rollerblades

•*Languages and nationalities do not take a capital letter in Spanish.*

el **patinete** noun *masc.*
scooter

el **patio** noun *masc.*
1 playground
   el patio de la escuela the school playground
2 (*between houses*) courtyard

el **pato** noun *masc.*
duck

el **pavo** noun *masc.*
turkey
un pavo real a peacock

el **payaso** noun *masc.*,
la **payasa** *fem.*
clown

la **paz** noun *fem.*
peace
vivir en paz to live in peace
¡Déjame en paz! Leave me alone!

el **peatón** noun *masc.* (plural los **peatones**)
pedestrian

las **pecas** plural noun *fem.*
freckles

la **pecera** noun *fem.*
fish tank

el **pecho** noun *masc.*
chest

el **pedal** noun *masc.*
pedal

el **pedazo** noun *masc.*
piece
un pedazo de pan a piece of bread

pedir verb
1 to ask for
   He pedido otro plato. I asked for another plate.
2 to ask
   pedir un favor to ask a favour
3 (*in a restaurant*) to order
   Hemos pedido pollo. We've ordered chicken.
4 **pedir perdón** to apologize

5 **pedir prestado** to ask to borrow
   Pedí prestado un boli. I asked to borrow a pen.
   Le pedí un libro. I asked to borrow a book from him., I borrowed a book from him.

pegajoso adjective *masc.*,
pegajosa *fem.*
sticky

el **pegamento** noun *masc.*
glue

pegar verb
1 to stick
   He pegado la foto con celo. I stuck the photo with Sellotape.
2 to hit
   Me han pegado. They hit me.
3 to give
   Me pegó una patada. She gave me a kick.

la **pegatina** noun *fem.*
sticker

el **peinado** noun *masc.*
hairstyle

peinarse verb
1 to comb your hair
2 to brush your hair

el **peine** noun *masc.*
comb

p. ej. abbreviation
e.g.

🔑 **LANGUAGE**
p. ej. is short for **por ejemplo** ('for example').

pelar verb
to peel
pelar una manzana to peel an apple

la **pelea** noun *fem.*
1 fight
2 argument
   tener una pelea con alguien to have an argument with somebody

a
b
c
d
e
f
g
h
i
j
k
l
m
n
o
p
q
r
s
t
u
v
w
x
y
z

• *The months of the year and days of the week do not take a capital letter in Spanish.*

a
b
c
d
e
f
g
h
i
j
k
l
m
n
o
P
q
r
s
t
u
v
w
x
y
z

pelearse verb
1 **to fight**
José y Gabriel se están peleando.
José and Gabriel are fighting.
2 **to argue**
Sus padres siempre se pelean.
His parents are always arguing.

la **película** noun *fem.*
film
¿A qué hora es la película? What
time is the film on?

el **peligro** noun *masc.*
danger

peligroso *masc.*,
peligrosa adjective *fem.*
dangerous

pelirrojo adjective *masc.*,
pelirroja *fem.*
ser pelirrojo to have red hair
Soy pelirroja. I have red hair.

el **pelo** noun *masc.*
1 **hair**
Tengo el pelo rubio. I have fair
hair.
2 (*of an animal*) **fur**
el pelo del gato the cat's fur
pelos de gato cat hairs

la **pelota** noun *fem.*
ball
jugar a la pelota to play ball

peludo adjective *masc.*,
peluda *fem.*
hairy

la **peluquería** noun *fem.*
hairdresser's
ir a la peluquería to go to the
hairdresser's

el **peluquero** noun *masc.*,
la **peluquera** *fem.*
hairdresser

la **pena** noun *fem.*
1 **shame**
¡Qué pena! What a shame!

2 Vale la pena. It's worth it.
No vale la pena hacerlo. It's not
worth doing it.

el **pendiente** noun *masc.*
earring

pensar verb
1 **to think**
¿Qué piensas? What do you think?
Estoy pensando en ti. I'm thinking
about you.
2 **pensar hacer algo** to intend to do
something

peor adjective *masc. & fem.*
1 **worse**
Este libro es peor que el otro. This
book is worse than the other one.
Me siento peor. I feel worse.
2 **worst**
el peor alumno de la clase the
worst pupil in the class

peor adverb
1 **worse**
Yo juego peor que tú. I play worse
than you.
2 **worst**
¿Quién escribe peor? Who writes
the worst?

el or la **peor** noun *masc. & fem.*
worst, worst one
Eres el peor del equipo. You're the
worst in the team., You're the
worst one in the team.

el **pepino** noun *masc.*
cucumber

pequeño adjective *masc.*,
pequeña *fem.*
1 **small**
una casa pequeña a small house
Soy más pequeño que tú. I'm
smaller than you.
2 **little**
mi hermano pequeño my little
brother

• *See the centre section for verb tables.*

el **pequeño** noun masc.,
la **pequeña** fem.
1 little boy, little girl
los pequeños little children
2 youngest
Es la pequeña de la familia. She's the youngest in the family.

la **pera** noun fem.
pear

la **percha** noun fem.
1 coat hanger
2 coat peg

perder verb
1 to lose
He perdido el cuaderno. I've lost my exercise book.
2 to miss
He perdido el autobús. I've missed the bus.
3 to waste
perder el tiempo to waste time

perderse verb
1 to get lost
Nos perdimos. We got lost.
2 to miss
Te has perdido la fiesta. You've missed the party.

la **pérdida** noun fem.
Es una pérdida de tiempo. It's a waste of time.

perdido adjective masc.,
perdida fem.
lost
Estoy perdido. I'm lost.
los objetos perdidos lost property

perdón exclamation
1 sorry
Perdón, no te vi. Sorry, I didn't see you.
2 excuse me
Perdón, ¿dónde está la estación? Excuse me, where is the station?

el **perdón** noun masc.
pedir perdón to apologize

perdonar verb
to forgive
Te perdono. I forgive you.
¡Perdona! Sorry!
¡Perdona! ¿Tienes hora? Excuse me, do you have the time?

perezoso adjective masc.,
perezosa fem.
lazy
Es perezosa. She's lazy.

perfeccionar verb
to improve
Necesito perfeccionar mi español. I need to improve my Spanish.

perfectamente adverb
perfectly

perfecto adjective masc.,
perfecta fem.
perfect

el **perfume** noun masc.
perfume

el **periódico** noun masc.
newspaper

el **periodo** noun masc.
period

el **periquito** noun masc.
budgie

permanecer verb
to stay

el **permiso** noun masc.
permission
tener permiso para hacer algo to have permission to do something
un permiso de conducir a driving licence

permitir verb
to allow

pero conjunction
but
Quiero salir, pero está lloviendo. I want to go out but it's raining.

a
b
c
d
e
f
g
h
i
j
k
l
m
n
o
p
q
r
s
t
u
v
w
x
y
z

• Use **el** and **uno** for masculine words and **la** and **una** for feminine words.

a
b
c
d
e
f
g
h
i
j
k
l
m
n
o
p
q
r
s
t
u
v
w
x
y
z

el **perrito** noun *masc.*
1 **puppy**
2 **un perrito caliente** a hot dog

el **perro** noun *masc.*, la **perra** *fem.*
dog

perseguir verb
to chase

la **persiana** noun *fem.*
blind
bajar las persianas to pull down the blinds

la **persona** noun *fem.*
person
una persona inteligente an intelligent person
las personas people
veinte personas twenty people

el **personaje** noun *masc.*
character
los personajes del libro the characters in the book

la **personalidad** noun *fem.*
personality

pertenecer verb
to belong
Esta casa pertenece a mi tío. This house belongs to my uncle.

Perú noun *masc.*
Peru

peruano adjective *masc.*, **peruana** *fem.*
Peruvian

el **peruano** noun *masc.*, la **peruana** *fem.*
Peruvian (*the person*)

la **pesadilla** noun *fem.*
nightmare

pesado adjective *masc.*, **pesada** *fem.*
1 heavy
Es muy pesado. It's very heavy.
2 **¡Qué pesado eres!** You're a real pest!

pesar verb
1 to weigh
Peso treinta kilos. I weigh thirty kilos.
2 to be heavy
Esta mochila pesa mucho. This schoolbag is heavy.

la **pescadería** noun *fem.*
fishmonger's

el **pescado** noun *masc.*
fish
Me gusta el pescado. I like fish.

el **pescador** noun *masc.*
fisherman

pescar verb
to fish
ir a pescar to go fishing

pesimista adjective *masc. & fem.*
pessimistic

el **peso** noun *masc.*
1 weight
perder peso to lose weight
2 peso

CULTURE
The peso is the money used in many Latin American countries.

el **pez** noun *masc.* (plural los **peces**)
fish
Hay muchos peces en el río. There are lots of fish in the river.
un pez de colores a goldfish

el or la **pianista** noun *masc. & fem.*
pianist

el **piano** noun *masc.*
piano
tocar el piano to play the piano

la **picadura** noun *fem.*
1 sting
una picadura de abeja a bee sting
2 bite
una picadura de mosquito a mosquito bite

• *Languages and nationalities do not take a capital letter in Spanish.*

picar verb
1 **to sting**
Me ha picado una avispa. I've been stung by a wasp.
2 **to bite**
Me ha picado un mosquito. I've been bitten by a mosquito.
3 **to itch**
Me pica la pierna. My leg itches.

el **pico** noun *masc.*
beak
Tiene un pico muy largo. It has a very long beak.

el **pie** noun *masc.*
foot
a pie on foot
estar de pie to be standing
ponerse de pie to stand up

la **piedra** noun *fem.*
stone
Me están tirando piedras. They're throwing stones at me.

la **piel** noun *fem.*
1 **skin**
la piel suave soft skin
2 **leather**
un bolso de piel a leather bag
3 (*of an apple etc.*) **peel**

la **pierna** noun *fem.*
leg

la **pieza** noun *fem.*
piece
las piezas del rompecabezas the pieces of the jigsaw puzzle

el **pijama** noun *masc.*
pyjamas
Estoy en pijama. I'm in pyjamas.
un pijama a pair of pyjamas

🔑 **LANGUAGE**
Spanish = **el pijama** is singular
English = **pyjamas** is plural

🔑 **LANGUAGE**
Be careful: **pijama** ends in an **-a** but it is not a feminine noun.

la **pila** noun *fem.*
1 **battery**
Funciona con pilas. It works on batteries.
2 **pile**
una pila de libros a pile of books

la **píldora** noun *fem.*
pill

pillar verb
to catch
¡A que no me pillas! I bet you can't catch me!

el or la **piloto** noun *masc. & fem.*
pilot

la **pimienta** noun *fem.*
pepper
¿Quieres sal o pimienta? Would you like salt or pepper?

el **pimiento** noun *masc.*
pepper
un pimiento rojo a red pepper

el **pincel** noun *masc.*
paintbrush

el **ping-pong** noun *masc.*
ping-pong
jugar al ping-pong to play ping-pong

el **pingüino** noun *masc.*
penguin

el **pino** noun *masc.*
pine tree

el **pintalabios** noun *masc.* (plural los **pintalabios**)
lipstick

pintar verb
to paint
Pinta esto en verde. Paint this green.

pintarse verb
to put on make-up
Mi hermana se pinta los labios. My sister wears lipstick.

a
b
c
d
e
f
g
h
i
j
k
l
m
n
o
p
q
r
s
t
u
v
w
x
y
z

• *The months of the year and days of the week do not take a capital letter in Spanish.*

a
b
c
d
e
f
g
h
i
j
k
l
m
n
o
P
q
r
s
t
u
v
w
x
y
z

el **pintor** noun *masc.*,
la **pintora** *fem.*
painter

la **pintura** noun *fem.*
1 paint
un bote de pintura a tin of paint
2 painting
una pintura de ... a painting by ...

la **piña** noun *fem.*
pineapple

la **pirámide** noun *fem.*
pyramid

el or la **pirata** noun *masc. & fem.*
pirate

los **Pirineos** plural noun *masc.*
Pyrenees

pisar verb
to tread on
pisar las flores to tread on the
flowers
pisar a alguien to tread on
somebody's foot

la **piscina** noun *fem.*
swimming pool

el **piso** noun *masc.*
1 floor
en el segundo piso on the second
floor
2 flat
Tenemos un piso en Toledo.
We have a flat in Toledo.

la **pista** noun *fem.*
1 (*for races*) track
una pista de esquí a ski slope
una pista de hielo an ice rink
una pista de tenis a tennis court
2 clue
Dame una pista. Give me a clue.

la **pistola** noun *fem.*
gun

el **pito** noun *masc.*
whistle

la **pizarra** noun *fem.*
blackboard
escribir algo en la pizarra
to write something on the
board

la **pizza** noun *fem.*
pizza

el **plan** noun *masc.*
plan
No tengo planes para mañana.
I don't have any plans for
tomorrow.

la **plancha** noun *fem.*
iron
No necesita plancha. It doesn't
need ironing.

planchar verb
to iron
planchar una falda to iron a
skirt

planear verb
to plan

el **planeta** noun *masc.*
planet

⚷ **LANGUAGE**
Be careful: **planeta** ends in an **-a** but it is
not a feminine noun.

el **plano** noun *masc.*
1 map
un plano de Londres a map of
London
un plano del metro an
underground map
2 plan
el plano de la casa the plan of the
house

• *See the centre section for verb tables.*

plano adjective masc.,
  plana fem.
  flat
  zapatos planos flat shoes

la **planta** noun fem.
 1 **plant**
  regar las plantas to water the plants
 2 **floor**
  la planta baja the ground floor

plantar verb
  to plant

el **plástico** noun masc.
  plastic
  una bolsa de plástico a plastic bag

la **plastilina**® noun fem.
  Plasticine®

la **plata** noun fem.
 1 **silver**
  una medalla de plata a silver medal
 2 (Latin America) **money**

el **plátano** noun masc.
  banana

platicar verb
  (Latin America) **to talk**

el **platillo** noun masc.
  saucer
  un platillo volante a flying saucer

el **plato** noun masc.
 1 **plate**
  Pásame tu plato. Pass me your plate.
 2 **dish**
  lavar los platos to wash the dishes
  el plato del día today's special
 3 (part of a meal) **course**
  el primer plato the first course

la **playa** noun fem.
  beach

la **plaza** noun fem.
 1 (in a town or village) **square**
  la plaza mayor the main square
 2 (on a bus, in a car, etc.) **place**

la **pluma** noun fem.
 1 **feather**
 2 **pen, fountain pen**

el **plural** noun masc.
  plural
  en plural in the plural

pobre adjective masc. & fem.
  poor
  una familia pobre a poor family
  ¡Pobre Isabel! Poor Isabel!
  los pobres the poor

LANGUAGE
Use **pobre** after the noun when it means the opposite of 'rich', and before the noun when you feel sad about somebody.

poco adverb
 1 **not much**
  Hablo muy poco. I don't talk very much.
  poco después soon after
 2 **not very**
  muy poco conocido not very well known
 3 **un poco** a bit
  Estoy un poco cansada. I'm a bit tired.
  un poco de pastel a bit of cake
  ¿Quieres un poco de agua? Do you want some water?

poco adjective & pronoun masc.,
  poca fem.
 1 **not much**
  Tenemos poco dinero. We don't have much money.
  Comió poco. He didn't eat much.
 2 **not many**
  Tiene pocas amigas. She doesn't have many friends.
 3 **few**
  Cuesta unos pocos euros. It costs a few euros.

a
b
c
d
e
f
g
h
i
j
k
l
m
n
o
p
q
r
s
t
u
v
w
x
y
z

• Use **el** and **uno** for masculine words and **la** and **una** for feminine words.

poder verb
can
Puedo hacerlo ahora. I can do it now.
¿Puedo ir al cine? Can I go to the cinema?
Puedes esperar aquí. You can wait here.
¿Puedes ayudarme? – Sí, puedo. Can you help me? – Yes, I can.
¡No puede ser! It can't be true!
Puede ser. Maybe.

podrido adjective masc.,
podrida fem.
rotten

el **poema** noun masc.
poem

LANGUAGE
Be careful: **poema** ends in an **-a** but it is not a feminine noun.

el or la **poeta** noun masc. & fem.
poet

polar adjective masc. & fem.
polar
un oso polar a polar bear

el **policía** noun masc.
policeman

la **policía** noun fem.
1 **police**
llamar a la policía to call the police
2 **policewoman**

el **polideportivo** noun masc.
sports centre

el **pollito** noun masc.
chick

el **pollo** noun masc.
chicken

el **polo** noun masc.
ice lolly

el **Polo** noun masc.
el Polo Norte the North Pole
el Polo Sur the South Pole

Polonia noun fem.
Poland

el **polvo** noun masc.
dust
lleno de polvo full of dust
quitar el polvo to do the dusting

el **pomelo** noun masc.
grapefruit

el **pomo** noun masc.
handle

poner verb
1 **to put**
¿Dónde pongo mi mochila? Where shall I put my schoolbag?
Ponla aquí. Put it here.
2 (music, the radio, etc.) **to put on**
¿Puedo poner la tele? Can I put the TV on?
Ponen una película esta noche. They're putting on a film tonight.
3 **to get**
poner gasolina to get petrol
4 **to set**
poner la mesa to set the table
Hay que poner el despertador. We have to set the alarm clock.
5 **to make**
Eso me pone nervioso. This makes me nervous.

ponerse verb
1 **to put on**
Me pongo los zapatos. I'm putting my shoes on.
2 **to wear**
¿Qué te vas a poner? What are you going to wear?
3 **to stand**
Ponte ahí. Stand over there.
Poneos en fila. Stand in line.
Todo el mundo se puso de pie. Everybody stood up.
4 (with adjectives) **to get**
ponerse nervioso to get nervous
5 **to set**
El sol se pone a las ocho. The sun sets at eight.

• Languages and nationalities do not take a capital letter in Spanish.

el **poni** noun *masc.*
pony

popular adjective *masc. & fem.*
popular

por preposition
1 **through**
pasar por un túnel to go through a tunnel
por la ventana through the window
2 **for**
Vendo este libro por diez euros. I'm selling this book for ten euros.
por ejemplo for example
3 **by**
por correo by post
un libro escrito por ... a book written by ...
4 **because of**
por el mal tiempo because of the bad weather
5 (*saying where*)
viajar por España to travel around Spain
andar por la calle to walk along the street
6 (*saying when*)
por la mañana in the morning
por la noche at night
7 (*with numbers*)
Tres por tres son nueve. Three times three is nine.
cinco por ciento five per cent
8 **¿por qué?** why?
No sé por qué. I don't know why.

porque conjunction
because
Lo hago porque me gusta. I do it because I like it.

portarse verb
to behave
Los niños se portan muy bien. The children behave very well.

portátil adjective *masc. & fem.*
portable

el **portátil** noun *masc.*
laptop

el **portazo** noun *masc.*
dar un portazo to slam the door

la **portería** noun *fem.*
goal

el **portero** noun *masc.*,
la **portera** *fem.*
1 goalkeeper
2 (*in a building*) caretaker

Portugal noun *masc.*
Portugal

el **portugués** noun *masc.*
Portuguese
¿Hablas portugués? Do you speak Portuguese?

portugués adjective *masc.*,
portuguesa *fem.*
Portuguese
Fernando es portugués. Fernando is Portuguese.

🔑 **LANGUAGE**
The plural of **portugués** is **portugueses**.

el **portugués** noun *masc.*,
la **portuguesa** *fem.*
Portuguese man,
Portuguese woman
los portugueses the Portuguese

la **posibilidad** noun *fem.*
1 chance
tener posibilidades de hacer algo to have a good chance of doing something
2 possibility

posible adjective *masc. & fem.*
possible
Es posible. It's possible.

la **posición** noun *fem.* (plural las **posiciones**)
position

a
b
c
d
e
f
g
h
i
j
k
l
m
n
o
p
q
r
s
t
u
v
w
x
y
z

• *The months of the year and days of the week do not take a capital letter in Spanish.*

a
b
c
d
e
f
g
h
i
j
k
l
m
n
o
p
q
r
s
t
u
v
w
x
y
z

la **postal** noun *fem.*
  postcard

el **póster** noun *masc.* (plural los **pósters**)
  poster

el **postre** noun *masc.*
  dessert
  ¿Qué hay de postre? What's for dessert?

el **pozo** noun *masc.*
  well
  El agua del pozo es buena. The water from the well is good.

practicar verb
  to practise
  Tienes que practicar tu inglés. You have to practise your English.

práctico adjective *masc.*, **práctica** *fem.*
  1 handy
  El móvil es muy práctico. The mobile is very handy.
  2 practical
  una falda muy práctica a very practical skirt

el **precio** noun *masc.*
  price

precioso adjective *masc.*, **preciosa** *fem.*
  beautiful

el **precipicio** noun *masc.*
  cliff

preferir verb
  to prefer
  Prefiero el pescado a la carne. I prefer fish to meat.
  Prefiero ver la tele. I prefer to watch TV.

la **pregunta** noun *fem.*
  question
  hacer una pregunta to ask a question

preguntar verb
  to ask
  Pregúntale a tu padre. Ask your dad.
  Le pregunté la hora. I asked him the time.

preguntarse verb
  to wonder
  Me pregunto por qué has hecho eso. I wonder why you did that.

prehistórico adjective *masc.*, **prehistórica** *fem.*
  prehistoric

el **premio** noun *masc.*
  prize
  ganar un premio to win a prize

prender verb
  1 **prender fuego a algo** to set fire to something
  2 (*Latin America*) **to turn on** (*the radio, the lights, etc.*)

preocupado adjective *masc.*, **preocupada** *fem.*
  worried
  Estoy preocupada por mi hermana. I'm worried about my sister.

preocupar verb
  to worry
  ¿Qué te preocupa? What are you worried about?
  preocuparse por algo to worry about something
  ¡No te preocupes! Don't worry!

preparado adjective *masc.*, **preparada** *fem.*
  ready
  Estoy preparado. I'm ready.

preparar verb
  1 to get ready
  Me estoy preparando para salir. I'm getting ready to go out.

• See the centre section for verb tables.

2 to make
Papá está preparando la comida.
Dad's making lunch.
3 to prepare
preparar la clase to prepare the
lesson

la **preposición** noun *fem.* (plural las
preposiciones)
preposition

presentar verb
1 to introduce
Te presento a mi hermano. Can I
introduce you to my brother?
2 to present
presentar un programa to present
a programme
presentarse a un concurso to enter
a competition

presente adjective *masc. & fem.*
present
¿Está presente Javier? Is Javier
present?
¡Presente! Here!

el **presente** noun *masc.*
1 present
el presente y el pasado the present
and the past
2 (*in grammar*) **present tense**

el **presidente** noun *masc.*,
la **presidenta** *fem.*
president

el **preso** noun *masc.*, la **presa** *fem.*
prisoner

prestado adjective *masc.*,
prestada *fem.*
Me ha dejado la bici prestada.
He's lent me his bike.
Pedí dinero prestado. I borrowed
some money.

prestar verb
to lend
¿Me prestas el libro? Can you lend
me the book?

primaria adjective *fem.*
la escuela primaria primary
school

CULTURE
La escuela primaria is for children from 6
to 12.

la **primavera** noun *fem.*
spring
en primavera in the spring

primero adverb
first
Primero cojo el autobús. First I
take the bus.

primero adjective *masc.*,
primera *fem.*

LANGUAGE
The masculine singular primero becomes
primer when it is used before a noun.

1 first
la primera página the first page
el primer día the first day
Quedé primero en la carrera.
I came first in the race.
los primeros auxilios first aid
2 el primer ministro the Prime
Minister

el **primero** pronoun *masc.*,
la **primera** *fem.*
first, first one
Soy el primero. I'm the first.,
I'm the first one.

el **primo** noun *masc.*, la **prima** *fem.*
cousin

la **princesa** noun *fem.*
princess

principal adjective *masc. & fem.*
main
la calle principal the main street

el **príncipe** noun *masc.*
prince

• Use **el** and **uno** for masculine words and **la** and **una** for feminine words.

Spanish English

a b c d e f g h i j k l m n o **p** q r s t u v w x y z

el or **la principiante** noun masc. & fem.
  beginner

el principio noun masc.
  beginning
  el principio del libro the beginning of the book
  a principios de junio at the beginning of June
  al principio at first

la prisa noun fem.
  tener prisa to be in a hurry
  Tengo prisa. I'm in a hurry.
  ¡Date prisa! Hurry up!

los prismáticos plural noun masc.
  binoculars

privado adjective masc., **privada** fem.
  private
  una escuela privada a private school

probable adjective masc. & fem.
  likely

probablemente adverb
  probably

el probador noun masc.
  changing room

probar verb
  (food, machine, etc.) **to try**
  Prueba este pastel. – ¿Te gusta? Try this cake. – Do you like it?

probarse verb
  to try on
  Quiero probarme estos vaqueros. I want to try on these jeans.

el problema noun masc.
  problem

> **LANGUAGE**
> Be careful: problema ends in an -a but it is not a feminine noun.

producir verb
  to produce

el or **la profe** noun masc. & fem.
  teacher

> **LANGUAGE**
> Profe is short for profesor.

la profesión noun fem. (plural las profesiones)
  profession

el profesor noun masc., **la profesora** fem.
  teacher
  Es profesor de español. He's a Spanish teacher.

> ⚠ **FALSE FRIEND**
> un profesor = a teacher (not a professor)

profundo adjective masc., **profunda** fem.
  deep

el programa noun masc.
  1 programme
  un programa de televisión a TV programme
  2 program
  He bajado un programa de Internet. I've downloaded a program from the Internet.

> **LANGUAGE**
> Be careful: programa ends in an -a but it is not a feminine noun.

prohibir verb
  to forbid
  Está prohibido fumar. Smoking is forbidden.
  'Prohibido fumar.' 'No smoking.'

la promesa noun fem.
  promise
  cumplir una promesa to keep a promise

prometer verb
  to promise
  Te lo prometo. I promise.
  Ha prometido trabajar más. He has promised to work harder.

• Languages and nationalities do not take a capital letter in Spanish.

el **pronombre** noun *masc.*
  pronoun

el **pronóstico** noun *masc.*
  forecast
  el pronóstico del tiempo
  the weather forecast

pronto adverb
1 soon
  lo más pronto posible as soon as possible
  ¡Hasta pronto! See you soon!
2 early
  Has llegado pronto. You've arrived early.

la **pronunciación** noun *fem.*
  pronunciation

pronunciar verb
  to pronounce
  ¿Cómo se pronuncia este nombre?
  How do you pronounce this name?

propio adjective *masc.*, **propia** *fem.*
  own
  mi propia habitación my own room

a propósito adverb
  on purpose
  hacer algo a propósito to do something on purpose

el **protagonista** noun *masc.*
  main character
  el protagonista de la película
  the main character in the film

proteger verb
  to protect

protestante adjective *masc. & fem.*
  Protestant

protestar verb
  to complain
  ¡No protestes! Don't complain!

el **proverbio** noun *masc.*
  proverb

próximo adjective *masc.*, **próxima** *fem.*
  next
  la próxima vez next time
  la próxima semana next week

la **prueba** noun *fem.*
  test
  una prueba de ortografía
  a spelling test

el **público** noun *masc.*
1 public
  Está abierto al público. It's open to the public.
2 audience

público adjective *masc.*, **pública** *fem.*
  public
  una biblioteca pública a public library

el **pueblo** noun *masc.*
1 village
2 small town

el **puente** noun *masc.*
  bridge

la **puerta** noun *fem.*
1 door
  Llaman a la puerta. There's somebody at the door.
2 gate
  la puerta del jardín the garden gate

el **puerto** noun *masc.*
  port

pues adverb
1 well
  ¡Pues mira! Well, look!
  ¡Pues claro! Well, of course!
2 then
  Estoy cansado. – Pues vete a la cama. I'm tired. – Then go to bed.

el **pulgar** noun *masc.*
  thumb

a
b
c
d
e
f
g
h
i
j
k
l
m
n
o
p
q
r
s
t
u
v
w
x
y
z

• *The months of the year and days of the week do not take a capital letter in Spanish.*

el **pulmón** noun masc. (plural
los **pulmones**)
lung

el **pulpo** noun masc.
octopus

pulsar verb
to press
Pulsa el botón. Press the button.

la **pulsera** noun fem.
bracelet

la **punta** noun fem.
1 (of a pencil, knife, etc.) **point**
sacar punta a un lápiz to sharpen a
pencil
2 **tip**
la punta de la nariz the tip of my
nose

de puntillas adverb
on tiptoe

el **punto** noun masc.
1 **point**
sacar un punto to score a point
2 (in a sentence) **full stop**
punto y aparte full stop, new
paragraph
3 **dot**
el punto sobre la 'i' the dot on
the 'i'
4 **stitch**
El médico me puso tres puntos.
The doctor gave me three stitches.

5 **knitting**
hacer punto to knit
una chaqueta de punto a knitted
cardigan
6 **estar a punto de hacer algo** to be
about to do something

la **puntuación** noun fem.
punctuation

LANGUAGE
Spanish = **puntuación**
English = **punctuation**

puntual adjective masc. & fem.
punctual
Es muy puntual. He's very
punctual.

LANGUAGE
Spanish = **puntual**
English = **punctual**

el **puñetazo** noun masc.
punch
dar un puñetazo a alguien
to punch somebody
Me ha dado un puñetazo.
He punched me.

el **puño** noun masc.
fist

puro adjective masc., **pura** fem.
pure

Qq

que pronoun
1 **who**
mi amigo que tiene el pelo largo
my friend who has long hair
2 **that**, **which**
los libros que están en la mesa
the books that are on the table,
the books which are on the table

los animales que tengo
the animals (that) I have

que conjunction
1 **that**
Creo que está lloviendo. I think
(that) it's raining.
2 (when comparing) **than**
Soy más alta que tú. I'm taller
than you.

• See the centre section for verb tables.

qué pronoun & adjective

1 (*in questions*) **what**

¿Qué estás haciendo? What are you doing?

¿Qué es? What is it?

¿Qué? What?

¿Qué hora es? What time is it?

¿Qué tal? How are you doing?

2 **which**, **what**

¿Qué libro quieres leer? Which book do you want to read?, What book do you want to read?

¿Qué coche es? Which car is it?

3 (*in exclamations*) **what**

¡Qué lástima! What a pity!

¡Qué vestidos tan bonitos! What pretty dresses!

qué adverb

¡Qué bonito! It's really pretty!

¡Qué difícil! It's really difficult!

quedar verb

1 **to be left**

Quedan tres manzanas. There are three apples left.

Me quedan diez euros. I have ten euros left.

2 **to suit**

El azul te queda bien. Blue suits you.

3 **to meet**, **to plan to meet**

He quedado con una amiga. I'm meeting a friend., I've planned to meet a friend.

¿Dónde quedamos? Where shall we meet?

quedarse verb

1 **to stay**

Me quedé en casa. I stayed at home.

Me quedé dormido. I fell asleep.

2 **quedarse con algo** to keep something

Quédate con el libro. You can keep the book.

quejarse verb

to complain

Se queja de todo. He complains about everything.

quemar verb

to burn

Quemó la basura. He burned the rubbish.

quemarse verb

1 **to burn**

Se está quemando algo. Something's burning.

Se ha quemado la casa. The house has burnt down.

2 **to burn yourself**

Se quemó. He burned himself.

Me he quemado el dedo. I've burnt my finger.

querer verb

1 **to want**

¿Qué quieres? What do you want?

Quiero ir al cine. I want to go to the cinema.

2 **to love**

María quiere a Juan. María loves Juan.

3 (*in polite questions*)

¿Quieres ...? Would you like ...?

¿Quieres beber algo? Would you like something to drink?

4 (*when asking for something*) **Quisiera ...** I would like ...

Quisiera hablar con la maestra. I would like to speak to the teacher.

5 **querer decir** to mean

¿Qué quiere decir esta palabra? What does this word mean?

querido adjective *masc.*, **querida** *fem.*

dear

Querido Pedro ... Dear Pedro ...

el **queso** noun *masc.*

cheese

• Use **el** and **uno** for masculine words and **la** and **una** for feminine words.

quién pronoun
1 (in questions) **who**
¿Quién es? Who is it?
¿Quiénes son? Who are they?
2 ¿de quién? **whose?**
¿De quién es? Whose is it?
¿De quién son estos calcetines?
Whose socks are these?

quieto adjective masc., **quieta** fem.
still
Estate quieta. Keep still.

quince number
1 **fifteen**
Mi primo tiene quince años.
My cousin is fifteen.
2 (with dates) **fifteenth**
el quince de mayo the fifteenth of
May

quinientos number masc.,
quinientas fem.
five hundred

quinto adjective masc., **quinta** fem.
fifth
en el quinto piso on the fifth floor

el **quiosco** noun masc.
1 (for newspapers) **news-stand**
2 (for flowers, ice creams, etc.) **kiosk**

quisiera verb SEE **querer**
would like
Quisiera una taza de té. I would
like a cup of tea.

quitar verb
1 **to take away**
Quita tus libros de aquí. Take your
books away from here.
2 **to take off**
¿Puedes quitarte los zapatos?
Can you take your shoes off?
3 **to take**
¿Quién me ha quitado la mochila?
Who's taken my bag?

quizá, **quizás** adverb
maybe, **perhaps**

Rr

el **rabo** noun masc.
tail

la **ración** noun fem. (plural las
raciones)
portion
una ración de patatas fritas
a portion of chips

el **radiador** noun masc.
radiator

> **⚬ LANGUAGE**
> Spanish = radia**d**or
> English = radia**t**or

la **radio** noun fem.
radio
Lo oí por la radio. I heard it on the
radio.

la **radiografía** noun fem.
X-ray
Me han hecho una radiografía.
I've had an X-ray.

la **raíz** noun fem. (plural las **raíces**)
root

la **rama** noun fem.
branch

el **ramo** noun masc.
bunch
un ramo de flores a bunch of
flowers

la **rana** noun fem.
frog

rápidamente adverb
quickly

• Languages and nationalities do not take a capital letter in Spanish.

rápido adverb
fast
Hablas muy rápido. You speak too fast.
¡Rápido! Quick!

rápido adjective *masc.*, **rápida** *fem.*
1 quick
una respuesta rápida a quick reply
2 fast
un coche rápido a fast car

la **raqueta** noun *fem.*
racket
una raqueta de tenis a tennis racket

raro adjective *masc.*, **rara** *fem.*
strange
Aurelia es un poco rara. Aurelia is a bit strange.

el **rascacielos** noun *masc.* (plural los **rascacielos**)
skyscraper

rascarse verb
to scratch
Me rasco la nariz. I scratch my nose.

la **rata** noun *fem.*
rat

el **rato** noun *masc.*
while
quedarse un rato to stay a while

el **ratón** noun *masc.* (plural los **ratones**)
mouse
una alfombrilla de ratón a mouse mat

 LANGUAGE
As in English, a **ratón** is an animal *and* a part of your computer.

⚠ **FALSE FRIEND**
un ratón = a mouse (*not* a rat)

el **ratoncito** noun *masc.*
little mouse
el ratoncito Pérez the tooth fairy

🌍 **CULTURE**
Spanish children leave their tooth under the pillow at bedtime and in the morning find some money or a present there instead. It's not a fairy but a little mouse (**ratoncito**) that comes to take the tooth away.

la **raya** noun *fem.*
1 stripe
una camisa con rayas azules a shirt with blue stripes
2 (*in your hair*) **parting**

el **rayo** noun *masc.*
lightning
los rayos lightning

la **raza** noun *fem.*
1 (*of dog, cat, etc.*) **breed**
2 race
la raza humana the human race

la **razón** noun *fem.*
1 reason
¿Por qué razón? For what reason?
2 **tener razón** to be right
Tengo razón. I'm right.
No tienes razón. You're wrong.

🔑 **LANGUAGE**
Spanish = **tener** razón   **Tengo razón.**
English = **to be** right   **I'm right.**

real adjective *masc. & fem.*
1 real
la vida real real life
2 royal
la familia real the royal family

la **realidad** noun *fem.*
reality
en realidad actually

• *The months of the year and days of the week do not take a capital letter in Spanish.*

a
b
c
d
e
f
g
h
i
j
k
l
m
n
o
p
q
r
s
t
u
v
w
x
y
z

a
b
c
d
e
f
g
h
i
j
k
l
m
n
o
p
q
r
s
t
u
v
w
x
y
z

las **rebajas** plural noun *fem.*
  sales
  ¿Cuándo empiezan las rebajas?
  When do the sales start?

la **rebanada** noun *fem.*
  slice
  una rebanada de pan a slice of
  bread

rebobinar verb
  to rewind
  rebobinar un vídeo to rewind a
  video

la **recepción** noun *fem.*
  (*desk in a hotel*) reception

el or la **recepcionista** noun *masc. &
  fem.*
  receptionist

la **receta** noun *fem.*
  recipe
  la receta de un pastel the recipe
  for a cake

recibir verb
  to get, to receive
  ¿Has recibido mi carta? Have you
  got my letter?

el **recibo** noun *masc.*
  1 bill
    el recibo del teléfono the phone
    bill
  2 receipt

recién adverb
  just
  Está recién pintado. It's just been
  painted.

reciente adjective *masc. & fem.*
  recent

recientemente adverb
  recently

recoger verb
  1 to pick up
    Recoge estos libros del suelo.
    Pick up these books from the floor.
    ¿Me puedes recoger a las dos?
    Can you pick me up at two?

  2 to tidy up
    recoger la habitación to tidy up
    the room
  3 to pick
    recoger flores to pick flowers

recomendar verb
  to recommend

la **recompensa** noun *fem.*
  reward

reconocer verb
  to recognize

el **récord** noun *masc.* (plural los
  récords)
  record
  batir el récord mundial to beat the
  world record

recordar verb
  1 to remember
    No recuerdo su nombre. I don't
    remember his name.
  2 to remind
    Recuérdame cómo se llama.
    Remind me what his name is.
    Me recuerdas a mi hermana.
    You remind me of my sister.

recortar verb
  to cut out
  recortar una foto to cut out a
  picture

el **recreo** noun *masc.*
  playtime
  Salimos al recreo a las dos.
  We have playtime at two.

el **rectángulo** noun *masc.*
  rectangle

recto adverb
  seguir todo recto to go straight
  ahead

recto adjective *masc.*, **recta** *fem.*
  straight
  una línea recta a straight line

• *See the centre section for verb tables.*

el recuerdo noun masc.
1 memory
tener buenos recuerdos de algo
to have good memories of
something
2 souvenir
**Tráeme un recuerdo de tu
viaje.** Bring me a souvenir of your
trip.
una tienda de recuerdos a souvenir
shop
3 recuerdos best wishes
Recuerdos a tu mamá. Best wishes
to your mum.

la red noun fem.
1 net
La pelota ha tocado la red.
The ball has touched the net.
2 la Red the Net
navegar por la Red to surf the Net

redondo adjective masc.,
redonda fem.
round
una mesa redonda a round table

reducir verb
to reduce

reflexivo masc. adjective
(in grammar)
un verbo reflexivo
a reflexive verb

🔑 **LANGUAGE**
A **verbo reflexivo** is a verb that is used
with a pronoun, e.g. **despertarse** (to
wake up): **me despierto** is 'I wake up',
te despiertas is 'you wake up', etc.
---

el refrán noun masc. (plural los
refranes)
saying

el refresco noun masc.
soft drink

regalar verb
to give (as a present)
**Me han regalado una bici para mi
cumpleaños.** They've given me a
bike for my birthday.

el regalo noun masc.
present
hacer un regalo a alguien to give
somebody a present
un regalo de cumpleaños
a birthday present

regañar verb
to tell off

regar verb
to water

la región noun fem. (plural las
regiones)
region

la regla noun fem.
1 ruler
2 rule
las reglas del juego the rules of the
game

el reglamento noun masc.
rules
el reglamento del colegio the
school rules

regular adjective masc. & fem.
1 regular
un verbo regular a regular verb
2 not very good
Es una película regular. It's not a
very good film.
3 not too bad
¿Cómo estás? – Regular. How are
you? – Not too bad.

la reina noun fem.
queen

el reino noun masc.
kingdom
el Reino Unido the United Kingdom

reír verb
to laugh
Me ha hecho reír. He made me
laugh.

reírse verb
to laugh
Me río con mis amigos. I laugh a
lot with my friends.

a b c d e f g h i j k l m n o p q **r** s t u v w x y z

• Use **el** and **uno** for masculine words and **la** and **una** for feminine words.

a
b
c
d
e
f
g
h
i
j
k
l
m
n
o
p
q
r
s
t
u
v
w
x
y
z

relajar verb
to relax
Me relaja. It relaxes me.
Voy a relajarme. I'm going to relax.

el **relámpago** noun *masc.*
flash of lightning
los relámpagos lightning

la **religión** noun *fem.* (plural las **religiones**)
religion

religioso adjective *masc.*,
religiosa *fem.*
religious

rellenar verb
to fill in
rellenar un formulario to fill in a form

el **reloj** noun *masc.*
1 clock
un reloj de pared a wall clock
2 watch
mi reloj digital my digital watch

remar verb
to row

el **remedio** noun *masc.*
No hay más remedio. There's no other choice.

el **renacuajo** noun *masc.*
tadpole

el **reno** noun *masc.*
reindeer

reñir verb
1 to tell off
Me ha reñido. She told me off.
2 to have a fight
He reñido con mi hermano. I had a fight with my brother.

reparar verb
to repair

repartir verb
1 to hand out
Reparte los libros. Hand out the books.
2 to deliver
repartir el correo to deliver the mail
3 to share

repasar verb
to revise
Tengo que repasar. I have to revise.

el **repaso** noun *masc.*
revision
un ejercicio de repaso a revision exercise

de **repente** adverb
suddenly

repetir verb
1 to repeat
¿Puedes repetir la pregunta? Can you repeat the question?
2 to say again
Repite, por favor. Can you say that again, please?

representar verb
1 to put on
representar una obra to put on a play
2 to show
¿Qué representa este dibujo? What does this picture show?

el **reproductor** noun *masc.*
player
un reproductor CD a CD player
un reproductor MP3 an MP3 player

el **reptil** noun *masc.*
reptile

resbalarse verb
to slip
resbalarse en el suelo to slip on the floor

• *Languages and nationalities do not take a capital letter in Spanish.*

reservar verb
to reserve
Esta mesa está reservada.
This table is reserved.

el resfriado noun *masc.*
cold
Tengo un resfriado. I have a cold.

resfriado adjective *masc.*,
resfriada *fem.*
estar resfriado to have a cold

resolver verb
to solve

respetar verb
to obey
respetar las reglas to obey the
rules

respirar verb
to breathe

responder verb
to answer
No responde. He's not answering.
responder a una pregunta
to answer a question

responsable adjective *masc. & fem.*
responsible
Es un niño muy responsable.
He's a very responsible boy.

LANGUAGE
Spanish = responsable
English = responsible

el or la responsable noun *masc. &*
fem.
1 person responsible
2 person in charge
¿Quién es el responsable?
Who's the person in charge?

la respuesta noun *fem.*
answer
la respuesta correcta the right
answer

el restaurante noun *masc.*
restaurant

el **resto** noun *masc.*
rest
el resto del libro the rest of the
book

el resultado noun *masc.*
1 result
los resultados de los exámenes
the exam results
2 score
El resultado fue tres a dos.
The score was three two.

el retraso noun *masc.*
delay
llegar con retraso to arrive late
El tren lleva retraso. The train is
late.

el retrato noun *masc.*
portrait

la reunión noun *fem.* (plural **las
reuniones**)
meeting

reunirse verb
1 to gather
**Los alumnos se reúnen delante del
colegio.** The pupils gather in front
of the school.
2 to get together
La familia se reúne los domingos.
The family gets together on
Sundays.

revelar verb
to develop
revelar las fotos to develop the
photos

reventar verb
to burst
Reventó el globo. She burst the
balloon.

el revés adverb
1 inside out
Tus calcetines están al revés.
Your socks are inside out.
2 upside down
El cuadro está al revés. The picture
is upside down.

• *The months of the year and days of the week do not take a capital letter in Spanish.*

a
b
c
d
e
f
g
h
i
j
k
l
m
n
o
p
q
r
s
t
u
v
w
x
y
z

3 back to front
Llevas el jersey al revés. You're wearing your sweater back to front.

la **revista** noun *fem.*
magazine

el **rey** noun *masc.*
king
los reyes de España the King and Queen of Spain
los Reyes Magos the Three Wise Men

CULTURE
In Spain the 6th January is known as **el día de Reyes** (the day of the Three Wise Men) and is the day Spanish children usually receive their Christmas presents. They put out their shoes for the Wise Men to leave the presents in.

rezar verb
to pray

rico adjective *masc.*, **rica** *fem.*
1 rich
Es rica. She's rich.
2 delicious
La paella está muy rica. The paella is really delicious.

el **rico** noun *masc.*, la **rica** *fem.*
rich man, rich woman

ridículo adjective *masc.*, **ridícula** *fem.*
ridiculous

la **rima** noun *fem.*
rhyme

el **rincón** noun *masc.* (plural los **rincones**)
corner

el **rinoceronte** noun *masc.*
rhinoceros

el **río** noun *masc.*
river

la **risa** noun *fem.*
laugh

el **ritmo** noun *masc.*
rhythm

rizado adjective *masc.*, **rizada** *fem.*
curly
tener el pelo rizado to have curly hair

robar verb
1 to steal
robar dinero a alguien to steal money from somebody
Me han robado la mochila. Somebody has stolen my schoolbag.
2 to rob
Nos han robado. We've been robbed.

el **robo** noun *masc.*
1 robbery
2 (*of money, things*) **theft**

el **robot** noun *masc.* (plural los **robots**)
robot

la **roca** noun *fem.*
rock

rodar verb
to roll
La pelota está rodando. The ball is rolling.

rodear verb
to surround
rodeado de amigos surrounded by friends

la **rodilla** noun *fem.*
knee
ponerse de rodillas to kneel down
Está de rodillas. He's kneeling down.

rojo adjective *masc.*, **roja** *fem.*
red
una camisa roja a red shirt

el **rojo** noun *masc.*
red
El rojo te queda bien. Red looks good on you.

• *See the centre section for verb tables.*

144

el **rollo** noun masc.
 1 roll
  un rollo de papel a roll of paper
 2 **¡Qué rollo!** How boring!

el **rompecabezas** noun masc.
  (plural los **rompecabezas**)
  jigsaw puzzle

> 🔑 **LANGUAGE**
> The Spanish comes from **rompe** (it breaks) and **cabezas** (heads)!

romper verb
 1 **to break**
  He roto una taza. I've broken a cup.
 2 **to tear**
  Rompí la página. I tore the page.

romperse verb
 1 **to break**
  La lámpara se ha roto. The lamp has broken.
  Se rompió la pierna. He broke his leg.
 2 **to get torn**
  La camisa se ha roto. The shirt has got torn.

la **ropa** noun fem.
  clothes
  La ropa está en el armario.
  The clothes are in the wardrobe.
  la ropa interior underwear

> 🔑 **LANGUAGE**
> Spanish = **la ropa** is singular
> English = **clothes** is plural

rosa adjective masc. & fem.
  pink
  calcetines rosa pink socks

> 🔑 **LANGUAGE**
> The adjective **rosa** is the same in the masculine, feminine, and plural.

el **rosa** noun masc.
  pink
  No me gusta el rosa. I don't like pink.

la **rosa** noun fem.
  rose

roto adjective masc., **rota** fem.
 1 **broken**
  una taza rota a broken cup
 2 **torn**
  una camisa rota a torn shirt

la **rotonda** noun fem.
  (for traffic) **roundabout**

rubio adjective masc., **rubia** fem.
  blond
  tener el pelo rubio to have blond hair
  una niña rubia a blonde girl

la **rueda** noun fem.
 1 **wheel**
  la rueda delantera the front wheel
 2 **tyre**

el **rugby** noun masc.
  rugby
  jugar al rugby to play rugby

rugir verb
  to roar
  El león ruge. The lion roars.

el **ruido** noun masc.
  noise
  hacer ruido to make a noise

las **ruinas** plural noun fem.
  (of a castle etc.) **ruins**
  las ruinas del castillo the ruins of the castle

Rusia noun fem.
  Russia

el **ruso** noun masc.
  Russian
  hablar ruso to speak Russian

ruso adjective masc., **rusa** fem.
  Russian
  Es ruso. He's Russian.

el **ruso** noun masc., la **rusa** fem.
  Russian

• Use **el** and **uno** for masculine words and **la** and **una** for feminine words.

Ss

el **sábado** noun *masc.*
Saturday
Hoy es sábado. Today is Saturday.
el sábado on Saturday
Mis abuelos llegan el sábado.
My grandparents arrive on
Saturday.
los sábados on Saturdays
Los sábados vamos a la biblioteca.
On Saturdays we go to the library.

🔑 **LANGUAGE**
Remember the difference between el
sábado (one Saturday only) and los
sábados (every Saturday).

la **sábana** noun *fem.*
sheet

saber verb
1 to know
¿Sabes dónde están? Do you know
where they are?
Ya lo sé. I know.
No lo sé. I don't know.
2 can, know how to
¿Sabes montar en bicicleta?
Can you ride a bike?
Pedro y Juan saben leer. Pedro and
Juan can read.
3 to taste
Sabe a fresa. It tastes of
strawberry.

sabio adjective *masc.*, **sabia** *fem.*
wise

el **sabor** noun *masc.*
1 taste
Tiene un sabor amargo. It has a
bitter taste.
2 flavour
cuatro sabores diferentes
four different flavours

el **sacapuntas** noun *masc.* (plural
los **sacapuntas**)
pencil sharpener

sacar verb
1 to take out
sacar algo del bolsillo to take
something out of your pocket
sacar la lengua to stick out your
tongue
2 to get
¿Has sacado los billetes? Have you
got the tickets?
Siempre saco buenas notas.
I always get good marks.
3 to take
sacar fotos to take photos
He sacado una foto de mi clase.
I've taken a photo of my class.
4 sacar punta a un lápiz to sharpen a
pencil

el **sacerdote** noun *masc.*
priest

el **saco** noun *masc.*
1 sack
un saco de patatas a sack of
potatoes
un saco de dormir a sleeping bag
2 (*Latin America*) **sweater**

sacudir verb
to shake

sagrado adjective *masc.*,
sagrada *fem.*
holy
una ciudad sagrada a holy city

la **sal** noun *fem.*
salt

la **sala** noun *fem.*
1 room
una sala de espera a waiting room
la sala de estar the living room
la sala de profesores the staff
room
2 hall
una sala de conciertos a concert
hall

• *Languages and nationalities do not take a capital letter in Spanish.*

salado adjective *masc.*, **salada** *fem.*
salty
Está muy salado. It's very salty.

la **salchicha** noun *fem.*
sausage

la **salida** noun *fem.*
1 exit
una salida de emergencia an emergency exit
2 departure
la hora de salida the departure time
3 start
la salida de la carrera the start of the race

salir verb
1 to go out
Ha salido al jardín. He's gone out into the garden.
María sale con mi hermano. María's going out with my brother.
2 to come out
¿A qué hora sales del colegio? What time do you come out of school?
3 to leave
El avión sale a las ocho. The plane leaves at eight.
Salgo de casa a las seis. I leave the house at six.
4 (*from a computer program*) to log off

el **salón** noun *masc.* (plural los **salones**)
living room

la **salsa** noun *fem.*
sauce

saltar verb
to jump
¡Salta! Jump!
saltar el arroyo to jump over the stream
saltar a la cuerda to skip

el **salto** noun *masc.*
jump
dar un salto to jump

la **salud** noun *fem.*
health

saludar verb
1 to say hello
Saluda a la profesora. Say hello to the teacher.
2 to wave
Me saludó con la mano. He waved to me.

el **saludo** noun *masc.*
greeting
Te manda un saludo. He sends you his best wishes.
Saludos de Álex. (*in a letter*) With best wishes, Álex.

salvaje adjective *masc. & fem.*
wild
animales salvajes wild animals

el **salvavidas** noun *masc.* (plural los **salvavidas**)
lifebelt

San adjective *masc.*
Saint
San Pablo Saint Paul

> 🔑 **LANGUAGE**
> **San** is short for **Santo**.

la **sandalia** noun *fem.*
sandal

la **sandía** noun *fem.*
watermelon

el **sándwich** noun *masc.* (plural los **sándwiches**)
sandwich
un sándwich de queso a cheese sandwich

los **Sanfermines** plural noun *masc.*

> **CULTURE**
> This is a festival in honour of St. Fermin that people celebrate in Pamplona every July when they let bulls run through the streets of the town.

• *The months of the year and days of the week do not take a capital letter in Spanish.*

sangrar verb
to bleed

la **sangre** noun *fem.*
blood

sano adjective *masc.*, **sana** *fem.*
healthy
una vida sana a healthy life
sano y salvo safe and sound

santo adjective *masc.*, **santa** *fem.*
holy

el **santo** noun *masc.*, la **santa** *fem.*
1 saint
Es un santo. He's a saint.
el día de Todos los Santos
All Saints' Day
2 name day
Hoy es mi santo. Today it's my
name day.

CULTURE
In Spain every day of the year has its own
saint. If somebody has the same name as
the saint whose day it is, they often
celebrate their special 'name day'.

el **sapo** noun *masc.*
toad

el **sarampión** noun *masc.*
measles

la **sardina** noun *fem.*
sardine

el **sarpullido** noun *masc.*
rash

la **sartén** noun *fem.* (plural las
sartenes)
frying pan

el **satélite** noun *masc.*
satellite
la televisión vía satélite satellite
television

el **saxofón** noun *masc.* (plural los
saxofones)
saxophone
tocar el saxofón to play the
saxophone

• *See the centre section for verb tables.*

se pronoun
1 (*talking about a boy or man*) himself
Se está lavando. He's washing
himself.
2 (*talking about a girl or woman*) herself
Se ha hecho daño. She has hurt
herself.
3 (*talking about a thing or animal*)
itself
El perro se ha cortado. The dog
has cut itself.
4 themselves
Se miran al espejo. They look at
themselves in the mirror.
5 (*polite form*) yourself (plural
yourselves)
¿Se ha hecho daño, señor? Have
you hurt yourself, sir?
6 each other
Se conocen. They know each
other.
7 (*no translation*)
Se sentó. He sat down.
No se acuerdan. They don't
remember.
8 (*with parts of the body, clothes, etc.*)
his, her, its, their, your
Se ha roto la pierna. He's broken
his leg.
Se pone la chaqueta. He puts on
his jacket.
Se lavan las manos. They wash
their hands.

LANGUAGE
Se is used instead of le and les when
there is another pronoun, e.g. se lo
instead of le lo.

9 to him, him
Di a Javier que se lo he mandado.
Tell Javier that I've sent it to
him.
No se lo digas. Don't tell him.
10 to her, her
Isabel lo quiere y su hermana se lo
ha dado. Isabel wants it and her
sister gave it to her.
Dáselo. Give it to her.

11 to them, **them**
Les gusta mi libro. ¿Puedo dárselo? They like my book. Can I give it to them?
Se lo he preguntado. I've asked them.

12 (*polite form*) **to you**, **you**
Se la han mandado, señorita. They've sent it to you, miss.
Se lo dije a usted. I told you.

13 (*in third person phrases*)
Se puede comprar esto en el supermercado. You can buy this in the supermarket.
'Se habla inglés'. 'English is spoken'.

el **secador de pelo** noun *masc.*
hairdryer

secar verb
to dry
secar los platos to dry the dishes
Me estoy secando el pelo. I'm drying my hair.

la **sección** noun *fem.* (plural las **secciones**)
section, department
¿Dónde está la sección de juguetes? Where is the toy section?, Where is the toy department?

seco adjective *masc.*, **seca** *fem.*
dry
La pintura está seca. The paint is dry.

el **secretario** noun *masc.*, la **secretaria** *fem.*
secretary
Mi hermana es secretaria. My sister's a secretary.

el **secreto** noun *masc.*
secret
guardar un secreto to keep a secret

secreto adjective *masc.*, **secreta** *fem.*
secret

la **sed** noun *fem.*
thirst
tener sed to be thirsty
Tengo mucha sed. I'm very thirsty.

> **⚷ LANGUAGE**
> Spanish = **tener** sed **Tengo** sed.
> English = **to be** thirsty **I'm** thirsty.

la **seda** noun *fem.*
silk

en seguida adverb
straight away
Voy en seguida. I'm coming straight away.

seguir verb
1 to follow
Sígueme. Follow me.
2 to carry on
seguir haciendo algo to carry on doing something
Quiero seguir leyendo. I want to carry on reading.
3 (*used for saying something is still going on*) **Sigue lloviendo.** It's still raining.
¿Siguen en clase? Are they still in class?

según preposition
according to

el **segundo** noun *masc.*
second
un minuto y veinte segundos one minute and twenty seconds

segundo adjective *masc.*, **segunda** *fem.*
second
por segunda vez for the second time
Quedé segunda en la carrera. I came second in the race.

la **seguridad** noun *fem.*
safety

a
b
c
d
e
f
g
h
i
j
k
l
m
n
o
p
q
r
s
t
u
v
w
x
y
z

• *Use **el** and **uno** for masculine words and **la** and **una** for feminine words.*

seguro adjective masc.,
segura fem.
1 **safe**
Aquí estoy seguro. I'm safe here.
2 **sure**
No estoy segura. I'm not sure.
3 **certain**
Puedo venir pero no es seguro.
I can come but it's not certain.

seis number
1 **six**
Tengo seis años. I'm six.
Son las seis. It's six o'clock.
2 (with dates) **sixth**
el seis de abril the sixth of April

seleccionar verb
to select

el **sello** noun masc.
stamp
¿Coleccionas sellos? Do you
collect stamps?

la **selva** noun fem.
1 **forest**
una selva tropical a tropical rain
forest
2 **jungle**

el **semáforo** noun masc.
traffic lights
El semáforo está en rojo.
The traffic lights are red.

la **semana** noun fem.
1 **week**
la semana pasada last week
la semana que viene next week
entre semana during the week
2 **la Semana Santa** Holy Week
en Semana Santa at Easter

CULTURE
Semana Santa means the whole Easter
period and can often be translated by
'Easter'. Spanish people take part in
religious processions, such as the famous
one in Seville.

el **semicírculo** noun masc.
semicircle

la **semifinal** noun fem.
semifinal

la **semilla** noun fem.
seed

sencillo adjective masc.,
sencilla fem.
simple
Es muy sencillo. It's very simple.

sensato adjective masc.,
sensata fem.
sensible
un niño sensato a sensible boy

sensible adjective masc. & fem.
sensitive
Raúl es muy sensible. Raúl is very
sensitive.

⚠ **FALSE FRIEND**
sensible = **sensitive** (not sensible)

sentado adjective masc.,
sentada fem.
sitting
Estoy sentado en la silla.
I'm sitting on the chair.

sentarse verb
1 **to sit down**
Me senté en el sillón. I sat down on
the armchair.
¡Siéntate, Rosa! Sit down, Rosa!
¡Niños, sentaos! Sit down,
children!
2 **to sit**
¿Dónde puedo sentarme? Where
can I sit?

el **sentido** noun masc.
sense
No tiene sentido. It doesn't make
sense.
tener sentido del humor to have a
sense of humour

sentir verb
1 **to feel**
sentir un dolor en el brazo to feel a
pain in your arm

• Languages and nationalities do not take a capital letter in Spanish.

2 to be sorry
Lo siento. I'm sorry.
Siento mucho llegar tarde. I'm very sorry I'm late.

sentirse verb
to feel
No me siento bien. I don't feel well.
¿Te sientes mal? Do you feel ill?

la **seña** noun *fem.*
sign
hacer una seña to make a sign

la **señal** noun *fem.*
sign
una buena señal a good sign
una señal de tráfico a road sign

señalar verb
1 (*with your finger*) **to point**
Señala tu colegio con el dedo. Point to your school.
2 to mark
Señala con una cruz. Mark with a cross.

las **señas** plural noun *fem.*
address
Dame tus señas. Give me your address.

el **señor** noun *masc.*
1 man
¿Qué quiere ese señor? What does that man want?
2 ¡Buenos días, señor! Good morning!

LANGUAGE
Used when talking to a man in a polite way and not usually translated, though 'sir' is sometimes used in English, especially at school, e.g. **Sí, señor** (Yes, sir).

3 Mr
el señor Lorca Mr Lorca

LANGUAGE
Señor is usually written on an envelope as Sr., e.g. Sr. Lorca.

la **señora** noun *fem.*
1 lady
Esa señora es mi tía. That lady is my aunt.
2 ¡Adiós, señora! Goodbye!

LANGUAGE
Used when talking to a woman in a polite way and not usually translated, though 'madam' is sometimes used in English.

3 Mrs
la señora González Mrs González

LANGUAGE
Señora is usually written on an envelope as Sra., e.g. Sra. González.

la **señorita** noun *fem.*
1 young lady
Te busca una señorita. A young lady is looking for you.
2 ¡Buenas tardes, señorita! Good afternoon!

LANGUAGE
Used when talking to a young woman in a polite way and not usually translated, though 'miss' is sometimes used in English, especially at school, e.g. Sí, señorita (Yes, miss).

3 Miss
la señorita Almenar Miss Almenar

LANGUAGE
Señorita is usually written on an envelope as Srta., e.g. Srta. Almenar.

separado adjective *masc.*, **separada** *fem.*
separated
Mis padres están separados. My parents are separated.

separar verb
to separate

a b c d e f g h i j k l m n o p q r s t u v w x y z

• *The months of the year and days of the week do not take a capital letter in Spanish.*

a
b
c
d
e
f
g
h
i
j
k
l
m
n
o
p
q
r
s
t
u
v
w
x
y
z

septiembre noun *masc.*
  September
  Nací en septiembre. I was born in September.
  Es mi cumpleaños el martes cinco de septiembre. It's my birthday on Tuesday, the fifth of September.

séptimo adjective *masc.*,
séptima *fem.*
  seventh

ser verb
  to be
  Soy inglés. I'm English.
  Eres mi amiga. You're my friend.
  Mi hermana es enfermera. My sister's a nurse.
  ¿Quién es? Who is it?
  Es de Javier. It's Javier's.
  Somos veinte en la clase. There are twenty of us in the class.
  ¿Sois de Londres? Are you from London?
  Son muy pequeños. They're very small.
  Son las tres. It's three o'clock.
  Ayer fue mi cumpleaños. Yesterday was my birthday.

🔑 **LANGUAGE**
There are two main verbs for saying 'to be': ser and estar. Use ser for saying how something or somebody always is, what job people do, or where they are from. Use it also to talk about times and dates.

el **ser** noun *masc.*
  being
  un ser humano a human being

la **serie** noun *fem.*
  series
  une serie de televisión a TV series

serio adjective *masc.*, **seria** *fem.*
  serious
  Hoy estás muy serio. You look very serious today.

la **serpiente** noun *fem.*
  snake

el **servicio** noun *masc.*
  1 service
    un buen servicio a good service
  2 toilet
    ¿Dónde están los servicios? Where are the toilets?

la **servilleta** noun *fem.*
  napkin

servir verb
  1 to serve
    ¿Te sirvo más sopa? Can I serve you more soup?
  2 to be useful
    Este ordenador no sirve para nada. This computer is useless.
    ¿Para qué sirve esto? What's this for?

servirse verb
  servirse algo to help yourself to something
  ¡Sírvete! Help yourself!

sesenta number
  sixty
  Mi abuela tiene sesenta años. My grandmother is sixty (years old).

la **seta** noun *fem.*
  mushroom

setenta number
  seventy
  Mi abuelo tiene setenta años. My grandfather is seventy.

sexto adjective *masc.*, **sexta** *fem.*
  sixth
  en el sexto piso on the sixth floor

si conjunction
  if
  Dime si puedes hacerlo. Tell me if you can do it.
  si no if not

sí adverb
  yes
  ¿Sabes leer? – Sí Can you read? – Yes

• See the centre section for verb tables.

siempre adverb
  always
  Siempre dices lo mismo. You always say the same thing.
  como siempre as usual
  para siempre forever

la **siesta** noun *fem.*
  nap
  echarse una siesta to have a nap

siete number
 1 seven
  Tengo siete años. I'm seven.
  Son las siete. It's seven o'clock.
 2 (*with dates*) seventh
  el siete de julio the seventh of July

el **siglo** noun *masc.*
  century
  en el siglo veintiuno in the twenty-first century

el **significado** noun *masc.*
  meaning

significar verb
  to mean
  ¿Qué significa? What does it mean?

el **signo** noun *masc.*
 1 sign
  el lenguaje de signos sign language
 2 mark
  un signo de admiración an exclamation mark
  un signo de interrogación a question mark

siguiente adjective *masc. & fem.*
  next
  en la página siguiente on the next page

sij adjective *masc. & fem.*
  Sikh

la **sílaba** noun *fem.*
  syllable

silbar verb
  to whistle

el **silbato** noun *masc.*
  whistle

el **silencio** noun *masc.*
  silence
  ¡Silencio, por favor! Quiet, please!

silencioso adjective *masc.*, **silenciosa** *fem.*
 1 quiet
  un coche silencioso a quiet car
 2 silent

la **silla** noun *fem.*
  chair
  sentarse en una silla to sit down on a chair
  una silla de montar a saddle
  una silla de ruedas a wheelchair

el **sillín** noun *masc.* (plural los **sillines**)
  (*on a bicycle*) saddle

la **sillita** noun *fem.*
  buggy

el **sillón** noun *masc.* (plural los **sillones**)
  armchair

el **símbolo** noun *masc.*
  symbol

simpático adjective *masc.*, **simpática** *fem.*
  nice
  Tu hermana es muy simpática. Your sister is very nice.

sin preposition
  without
  sin paraguas without an umbrella
  sin decir nada without saying anything

la **sinagoga** noun *fem.*
  synagogue

el **singular** noun *masc.*
  singular
  en singular in the singular

a b c d e f g h i j k l m n o p q r s t u v w x y z

• *Use* **el** *and* **uno** *for masculine words and* **la** *and* **una** *for feminine words.*

sino conjunction
but
No es jueves, sino viernes. It's not Thursday, but Friday.

la **sirena** noun *fem.*
mermaid

el **sistema** noun *masc.*
system

> **LANGUAGE**
> Be careful: **sistema** ends in an -a but it is not a feminine noun.

el **sitio** noun *masc.*
1 place
un sitio seguro a safe place
¿Me guardas el sitio? Can you keep my place?
2 room
No hay sitio. There isn't any room.
Hazme sitio. Make room for me.
3 (*for saying 'somewhere' etc.*)
estar en algún sitio to be somewhere
en ningún sitio nowhere

el **sitio web** noun *masc.*
website

la **situación** noun *fem.* (plural las **situaciones**)
situation

el **SMS** noun *masc.*
text message
Te he enviado un SMS. I've sent you a text.

sobre preposition
1 on
sobre la cama on the bed
2 over
un puente sobre el río a bridge over the river
3 about
una película sobre los animales a film about animals
4 **sobre todo** especially

el **sobre** noun *masc.*
envelope

la **sobrina** noun *fem.*
niece

el **sobrino** noun *masc.*
nephew
Mis padres tienen muchos sobrinos. My parents have lots of nieces and nephews.

el **socio** noun *masc.*, la **socia** *fem.*
member
Soy socia del club de tenis. I'm a member of the tennis club.

el **socorro** noun *masc.*
help
¡Socorro! Help!

el **sofá** noun *masc.*
sofa

sois verb SEE **ser**
are
Isabel y Carlos, sois muy inteligentes. Isabel and Carlos, you're very clever.

el **sol** noun *masc.*
sun
al sol in the sun
Hace sol. It's sunny.
tomar el sol to sunbathe

solamente adverb
only

el or la **soldado** noun *masc. & fem.*
soldier

solo adjective *masc.*, **sola** *fem.*
1 alone
Estoy solo. I'm alone.
2 lonely
Me siento sola. I feel lonely.
3 by yourself
Lo he hecho solo. I've done it by myself.

• Languages and nationalities do not take a capital letter in Spanish.

sólo adverb
only
Sólo tengo diez euros. I only have ten euros.

🔑 **LANGUAGE**
Remember to put the accent on sólo when it means 'only'.

soltar verb
to let go of
¡Suéltame! Let go of me!

la **sombra** noun *fem.*
1 shade
Aquí hay mucha sombra. There's a lot of shade here.
2 shadow
Vi una sombra en la pared. I saw a shadow on the wall.

el **sombrero** noun *masc.*
hat

la **sombrilla** noun *fem.*
sunshade

somos verb SEE **ser**
are
Somos amigos. We're friends.

son verb SEE **ser**
are
Mis abuelos son de Bilbao. My grandparents are from Bilbao.

sonar verb
1 to ring
El teléfono está sonando. The phone's ringing.
2 to sound
Tu nombre suena francés. Your name sounds French.

sonarse verb
sonarse la nariz to blow your nose
Suénate. Blow your nose.

el **sonido** noun *masc.*
sound

sonreír verb
to smile
¡Sonríe! Smile!

la **sonrisa** noun *fem.*
smile

soñar verb
to dream
soñar con alguien to dream about somebody

la **sopa** noun *fem.*
soup

soplar verb
1 to blow
Hoy sopla el viento. The wind is blowing today.
2 to blow out
soplar las velas to blow out the candles

soportar verb
to stand
No soporto a Maite. I can't stand Maite.

sordo adjective *masc.*, **sorda** *fem.*
deaf
Es sorda. She's deaf.

sorprender verb
to surprise
Me sorprende. It surprises me.

la **sorpresa** noun *fem.*
surprise
¡Qué sorpresa! What a surprise!

soso adjective *masc.*, **sosa** *fem.*
1 tasteless
La sopa está sosa. The soup is tasteless.
2 dull
Juan es muy soso. Juan is very dull.

sostener verb
to hold
¿Me sostienes la escalera? Can you hold the ladder?

el **sótano** noun *masc.*
basement
en el sótano in the basement

soy verb SEE **ser**
am
Soy delgado. I'm thin.

a
b
c
d
e
f
g
h
i
j
k
l
m
n
o
p
q
r
s
t
u
v
w
x
y
z

• *The months of the year and days of the week do not take a capital letter in Spanish.*

Sr. abbreviation
  Mr

> 🔑 **LANGUAGE**
> Sr. is short for Señor.

Sra. abbreviation
  Mrs

> 🔑 **LANGUAGE**
> Sra. is short for Señora.

Sres. abbreviation
  Mr & Mrs

> 🔑 **LANGUAGE**
> Sres. is short for Señores.

Srta. abbreviation
  Miss

> 🔑 **LANGUAGE**
> Srta. is short for Señorita.

su adjective
1 (talking about a boy or man) his
  su hermana his sister
  sus juguetes his toys
2 (talking about a girl or woman) her
  su hermana her sister
  sus juguetes her toys
3 (talking about a thing or animal) its
  El perro está en su caseta.
  The dog's in its kennel.
  la ciudad y sus habitantes
  the town and its inhabitants
4 their
  Van al cine con su hermano.
  They're going to the cinema with
  their brother.
  Han traído sus libros. They've
  brought their books.
5 (polite form) your
  Aquí tiene su paraguas, señorita.
  Here's your umbrella, miss.
  ¿Me dicen sus nombres? Would
  you tell me your names?

> 🔑 **LANGUAGE**
> Sus is used before a plural noun.

• See the centre section for verb tables.

suave adjective masc. & fem.
1 soft
  la piel suave soft skin
2 smooth
  una superficie suave a smooth
  surface

subir verb
1 to go up
  Sube al primer piso. Go up to the
  first floor.
  Subió la escalera. He went up the
  stairs.
2 to come up
  ¡Ya subo! I'm coming up!
  ¡Sube! Come up!
3 to get on
  ¿Quieres subir al columpio?
  Do you want to get on the
  swing?
4 to get in
  Sube al coche. Get in the car.
5 to take up
  Ayúdame a subir la maleta.
  Help me take up the suitcase.
6 to bring up
  Súbeme una taza de té. Bring me
  up a cup of tea.
7 to pull up
  Sube la ventanilla. Pull the
  window up.
8 to turn up
  Sube la tele, por favor. Turn up the
  TV, please.

subirse verb
1 to get on
  subirse al tren to get on the
  train
2 to get in
  subirse al coche to get in the car
3 to climb
  subirse a un muro to climb a wall

el **submarino** noun masc.
  submarine

subrayar verb
  to underline

subterráneo adjective masc.,
subterránea fem.
underground
un paso subterráneo a subway

los **subtítulos** plural noun masc.
subtitles

sucio adjective masc., **sucia** fem.
dirty
Mis calcetines están sucios.
My socks are dirty.

Sudáfrica noun fem.
South Africa

Sudamérica noun fem.
South America

sudamericano adjective masc.,
sudamericana fem.
South American
Es sudamericano. He's South
American.

el **sudamericano** noun masc.,
la **sudamericana** fem.
South American

sudar verb
to sweat

el **suelo** noun masc.
1 floor
en el suelo on the floor
2 ground
**Encontré un billete de diez euros
en el suelo.** I found a ten-euro note
on the ground.
caerse al suelo to fall down

el **sueño** noun masc.
1 dream
tener un sueño to have a dream
2 sleep
nueve horas de sueño nine hours'
sleep
tener sueño to be sleepy

🔑 **LANGUAGE**
Spanish = tener sueño   Tengo sueño.
English = to be sleepy   I'm sleepy.

la **suerte** noun fem.
luck
Me trae suerte. It brings me luck.
¡Buena suerte! Good luck!
tener suerte to be lucky

🔑 **LANGUAGE**
Spanish = tener suerte   Tengo suerte.
English = to be lucky   I'm lucky.

el **suéter** noun masc.
sweater

suficiente adjective & pronoun masc. &
fem.
enough
No hay suficiente espacio. There
isn't enough room.
¿Tienes suficientes pasteles? Do
you have enough cakes?
No hay suficientes. There aren't
enough.

sufrir verb
to suffer

Suiza noun fem.
Switzerland

suizo adjective masc., **suiza** fem.
Swiss

el **suizo** noun masc., la **suiza** fem.
Swiss man, Swiss woman
los suizos the Swiss

el **sujetador** noun masc.
bra

la **suma** noun fem.
sum
hacer sumas to do sums

súper, **super** adjective masc. & fem. &
adverb
super

la **superficie** noun fem.
surface

el **supermercado** noun masc.
supermarket

a
b
c
d
e
f
g
h
i
j
k
l
m
n
o
p
q
r
s
t
u
v
w
x
y
z

• Use **el** and **uno** for masculine words and **la** and **una** for feminine words.

a
b
c
d
e
f
g
h
i
j
k
l
m
n
o
p
q
r
s
t
u
v
w
x
y
z

el **suplemento** noun *masc.*
extra charge
pagar un suplemento to pay an extra charge

suponer verb
to suppose
Supongo que sí. I suppose so.

por supuesto adverb
of course
¡Por supuesto que no! Of course not!

sur noun masculine & adjective
south
en el sur in the south
la costa sur the south coast

suspender verb
1 to fail
Ha suspendido el examen. He's failed the exam.
2 to call off
Han suspendido el partido. They've called off the match.

el **sustantivo** noun *masc.*
noun

sustituir verb
to replace

el **susto** noun *masc.*
fright
¡Qué susto! What a fright!

suyo adjective *masc.*, **suya** *fem.*
1 (*talking about a boy or man*) **his**

Este ordenador es suyo. This computer is his.
Estas fotos son suyas. These photos are his.
2 (*talking about a girl or woman*) **hers**
Este libro es suyo. This book is hers.
unas amigas suyas friends of hers
3 **theirs**
Esta casa es suya. This house is theirs.
4 (*polite form*) **yours**
Este abrigo es suyo, señorita. This coat is yours, miss.

el **suyo** pronoun *masc.*, la **suya** *fem.*
1 **his**
mi hermana y la suya my sister and his
Nuestro ordenador es más viejo que el suyo. Our computer is older than his.
2 **hers**
mi hermana y la suya my sister and hers
Vuestra casa es más pequeña que la suya. Your house is smaller than hers.
3 **theirs**
mis padres y los suyos my parents and theirs
4 (*polite form*) **yours**
Este paraguas es el suyo, señor. This umbrella is yours.

Tt

la **tabla** noun *fem.*
1 board
una tabla de planchar an ironing board
2 table
las tablas de multiplicar the times tables
la tabla del diez the ten-times table

el **tablero** noun *masc.*
(*for chess, notices, etc.*)
board

la **tableta** noun *fem.*
bar
una tableta de chocolate a bar of chocolate

• Languages and nationalities do not take a capital letter in Spanish.

el **tablón** noun masc. (plural los **tablones**)
board
un tablón de anuncios a notice board

el **taburete** noun masc.
stool

tacaño adjective masc., **tacaña** fem.
mean
Es muy tacaña. She's very mean.

tachar verb
to cross out

el **tacón** noun masc. (plural los **tacones**)
(of a shoe) heel

tal adverb
1 **¿Qué tal?** How are things?
¿Qué tal está tu hermana? How's your sister?
¿Qué tal es tu maestra? What's your teacher like?
¿Qué tal las vacaciones? What were your holidays like?
2 **tal vez** maybe

la **talla** noun fem.
size
¿Qué talla usas? What size do you take?

el **taller** noun masc.
1 workshop
2 (for car repairs) garage

el **talón** noun masc. (plural los **talones**)
heel

el **tamaño** noun masc.
size
¿De qué tamaño es? What size is it?

también adverb
too
Voy al cine hoy y mañana también. I'm going to the cinema today and tomorrow too.
Estoy cansada. – Yo también. I'm tired. – Me too.

el **tambor** noun masc.
drum
tocar un tambor to play a drum

el **Támesis** noun masc.
Thames

tampoco adverb
1 not ... either
Yo tampoco quiero ir. I don't want to go either.
No sabe nadar tampoco. He can't swim either.
2 neither
No tengo dinero. – Yo tampoco. I don't have any money. – Neither do I.

tan adverb
1 so
No es tan alto. He isn't so tall.
2 such
Es un chico tan inteligente. He's such a clever boy.
chicos tan inteligentes such clever boys
3 (when comparing)
tan ... como as ... as
Mi casa no es tan grande como la tuya. My house isn't as big as yours.

tanto adverb
so much
Tengo que estudiar tanto. I have to study so much.

a b c d e f g h i j k l m n o p q r s t u v w x y z

• The months of the year and days of the week do not take a capital letter in Spanish.

159

tanto adjective & pronoun *masc.*,
tanta *fem.*

1 so much
tanto dinero so much money
No quiero tanto. I don't want so
much.

2 so many
tantas cosas so many things
No queremos tantos. We don't
want so many.

3 as much
No tengo tanto trabajo como tú.
I don't have as much work as you.
Hoy no hace tanto calor. Today it's
not as hot.

4 as many
No hay tantos coches como ayer.
There aren't as many cars as
yesterday.

la **tapa** noun *fem.*
1 lid
la tapa de la caja the lid of the box
2 cover
la tapa del libro the cover of the
book
3 bar snack

CULTURE
Tapas are small amounts of food served
with drinks in a bar or cafe.

la **taquilla** noun *fem.*
ticket office

tardar verb
1 to take a long time
Tardas mucho. You're taking a
long time.
No tardo mucho. I won't be long.
2 to take
Tardé dos días en terminar. I took
two days to finish.

tarde adverb
late
llegar tarde to be late, to arrive
late
Es tarde. It's late.
más tarde later

la **tarde** noun *fem.*
1 afternoon
por la tarde in the afternoon
ayer por la tarde yesterday
afternoon
¡Buenas tardes! Good afternoon!
2 evening
por la tarde in the evening
a las siete de la tarde at seven in
the evening
¡Buenas tardes! Good evening!

la **tarjeta** noun *fem.*
card
una tarjeta de cumpleaños
a birthday card
una tarjeta de Navidad
a Christmas card
una tarjeta postal a postcard

el **tarro** noun *masc.*
jar
un tarro de mermelada a jar of
jam

la **tarta** noun *fem.*
1 cake
una tarta de cumpleaños
a birthday cake
2 tart
una tarta de fresa a strawberry
tart

el **tatuaje** noun *masc.*
tattoo

el **taxi** noun *masc.*
taxi
en taxi by taxi

el or la **taxista** noun *masc. & fem.*
taxi driver

la **taza** noun *fem.*
cup
una taza de café a cup of coffee

el **tazón** noun *masc.* (plural los
tazones)
bowl, **big cup**

• *See the centre section for verb tables.*

te pronoun
1 **you**
   Te he llamado. I called you.
   Quiero verte. I want to see you.
2 **to you**
   Te he mandado una carta. I've sent a letter to you.
3 **yourself**
   ¿Te has cortado? Have you cut yourself?
4 (with parts of the body, clothes, etc.) **your**
   ¿Te has cortado el dedo? Have you cut your finger?
   Ponte los zapatos. Put your shoes on.
5 (no translation)
   Siéntate. Sit down.
   ¿Te acuerdas? Do you remember?

LANGUAGE
Use **te** when you are talking to a friend, somebody in your family, or someone your own age.

el **té** noun masc.
   tea
   ¿Quieres té? Do you want some tea?

el **teatro** noun masc.
   theatre

el **tebeo** noun masc.
   comic

el **techo** noun masc.
   ceiling

la **tecla** noun fem.
   (on a computer or piano) **key**

el **teclado** noun masc.
   keyboard

teclear verb
   (on a computer) **to type**

el **técnico** noun masc.,
la **técnica** fem.
   engineer
   El técnico ha arreglado el ordenador. The engineer has fixed the computer.

el **tejado** noun masc.
   roof

la **tela** noun fem.
   cloth

la **telaraña** noun fem.
1 **spider's web**
2 **cobweb**
   lleno de telarañas full of cobwebs

la **tele** noun fem.
   TV
   en la tele on TV

telefónico adjective masc.,
telefónica fem.
   phone
   la guía telefónica the phone book
   una llamada telefónica a phone call

el **teléfono** noun masc.
   phone
   contestar el teléfono to answer the phone
   Estoy hablando por teléfono. I'm on the phone.
   Me llamó por teléfono. He phoned me.
   un teléfono móvil a mobile phone

la **telenovela** noun fem.
   soap opera

el **telescopio** noun masc.
   telescope

la **televisión** noun fem. (plural las **televisiones**)
   television
   Veo la televisión. I watch television.
   en televisión on television

el **tema** noun masc.
   subject
   el tema de la película the subject of the film

LANGUAGE
Be careful: **tema** ends in an **-a** but it is not a feminine noun.

• Use **el** and **uno** for masculine words and **la** and **una** for feminine words.

temblar verb
1 to shake
Te tiemblan las manos. Your hands are shaking.
2 to shiver
Tiemblo de frío. I'm shivering.

la **temperatura** noun *fem.*
temperature

la **tempestad** noun *fem.*
storm

el **templo** noun *masc.*
temple
un templo sij a Sikh temple

la **temporada** noun *fem.*
season
la temporada de esquí the ski season

temprano adverb
early
He llegado temprano. I've arrived early.

tender verb
to hang out
Tiende la ropa. Hang out the cothes to dry.

el **tendedero** noun *masc.*
clothes line

el **tenedor** noun *masc.*
fork

tener verb
1 to have, to have got
Tengo un regalo para ti. I have a gift for you.
¿Qué tienes en la mano? What have you got in your hand?
Álex tiene los ojos azules. Álex has blue eyes.
No tenemos dinero. We haven't got any money.
2 to be
Tengo calor. I'm hot.
Rosa tiene diez años. Rosa is ten.

Tenemos suerte. We're lucky.

> **LANGUAGE**
> Spanish = **Tengo** calor/frío/hambre/sed/miedo/10 años.
> English = **I am** hot/cold/hungry/thirsty/scared/10 years old.

3 **tener que hacer algo** to have to do something
Tengo que ir al médico. I have to go to the doctor.
Tienes que trabajar más. You've got to work harder.

el **tenis** noun *masc.*
tennis
Juego al tenis. I play tennis.
el tenis de mesa table tennis

tercero *masc.*,
tercera adjective *fem.*

> **LANGUAGE**
> The masculine singular **tercero** becomes **tercer** when it is used before a noun.

third
en el tercer piso on the third floor
Quedé tercero en la carrera. I came third in the race.
una tercera parte a third

terco adjective *masc.*, **terca** *fem.*
stubborn

terminar verb
to finish
No he terminado. I haven't finished.

el **termo** noun *masc.*
flask

el **termómetro** noun *masc.*
thermometer

el **ternero** noun *masc.*,
la **ternera** *fem.*
calf

la **terraza** noun *fem.*
1 balcony
2 (*outside a cafe etc.*) **terrace**

• *Languages and nationalities do not take a capital letter in Spanish.*

el **terremoto** noun masc.
  earthquake

el **terreno** noun masc.
  1 land
  2 (for sports) field

terrible adjective masc. & fem.
  terrible

el **tesoro** noun masc.
  treasure

> 🔑 **LANGUAGE**
> Spanish = tesero
> English = treasure

la **tetera** noun fem.
  1 teapot
  2 kettle

el **texto** noun masc.
  text
  un libro de texto a textbook

ti pronoun
  you
  para ti for you
  delante de ti in front of you
  ¿A ti te gusta? Do you like it?

> 🔑 **LANGUAGE**
> Be careful: ti is not written with an accent like mí.

> 🔑 **LANGUAGE**
> You use ti when you are talking to a friend, somebody in your family, or someone your own age.

la **tía** noun fem.
  aunt

el **tiburón** noun masc. (plural los **tiburones**)
  shark

el **tiempo** noun masc.
  1 time
  No tengo tiempo. I don't have time.
  al mismo tiempo at the same time
  mucho tiempo a long time

Hace mucho tiempo que no lo veo. I haven't seen him for a long time.
  2 **¿cuánto tiempo?** how long?
  ¿Cuánto tiempo dura? How long does it last?
  3 weather
  ¿Qué tiempo hace? What's the weather like?
  Hace buen tiempo. The weather's nice.

la **tienda** noun fem.
  1 shop
  una tienda de ropa a clothes shop
  una tienda de comestibles a grocer's
  2 tent
  una tienda de campaña a tent

la **tierra** noun fem.
  1 land
  La tierra es seca. The land is dry.
  2 earth
  Está cubierto de tierra. It's covered with earth.

el **tigre** noun masc.
  tiger

las **tijeras** plural noun fem.
  scissors
  unas tijeras a pair of scissors

el **timbre** noun masc.
  bell
  Sonó el timbre. The bell rang.

tímido adjective masc., **tímida** fem.
  shy

la **tina** noun fem.
  (Latin America) bathtub

la **tinta** noun fem.
  ink
  escribir con tinta to write in ink

tinto adjective masc.
  un vino tinto a red wine

• The months of the year and days of the week do not take a capital letter in Spanish.

a
b
c
d
e
f
g
h
i
j
k
l
m
n
o
p
q
r
s
t
u
v
w
x
y
z

el **tío** noun masc.
1 uncle
Es mi tío. He's my uncle.
mis tíos my uncle and aunt
2 guy
¡Vamos, tíos! Let's go, guys!

el **tiovivo** noun masc.
merry-go-round

el **tipo** noun masc.
1 type
¿Qué tipo de música es? What type of music is it?
2 guy
un tipo simpático a nice guy

el **tirante** noun masc.
1 strap
los tirantes del vestido the straps on the dress
2 los tirantes braces (on trousers)

tirar verb
1 to throw
Tírame la pelota. Throw me the ball.
Me tiró una piedra. He threw a stone at me.
Me tiré al agua. I jumped into the water.
2 to throw away
Tira estos papeles. Throw these papers away.
3 to knock over
No tires el vaso. Don't knock the glass over.
4 to pull
No me tires del pelo. Don't pull my hair.

la **tirita** noun fem.
(for a cut, burn, etc.) **plaster**

el **títere** noun masc.
puppet

el **título** noun masc.
1 title
el título del libro the title of the book
2 certificate

la **tiza** noun fem.
chalk
una tiza a piece of chalk

la **toalla** noun fem.
towel

el **tobillo** noun masc.
ankle

el **tobogán** noun masc. (plural los **toboganes**)
(in a playground) **slide**

tocar verb
1 to touch
No toques la pantalla. Don't touch the screen.
2 (a musical instrument) **to play**
¿Sabes tocar el piano? Can you play the piano?
3 to ring
tocar el timbre to ring the bell
4 ¿A quién le toca? Whose turn is it?
Me toca a mí. It's my turn.

el **tocino** noun masc.
bacon

todavía adverb
1 still
Todavía está durmiendo. He's still asleep.
2 yet
todavía no not yet
Todavía no ha llegado. She hasn't arrived yet.
3 even
todavía más difícil even more difficult

todo adjective masc., **toda** fem.
1 all
todos los libros all the books
todas mis amigas all my friends
2 whole, all
todo el pastel the whole cake, all the cake
toda la mañana the whole morning, all morning
3 every
todos los días every day
todo el mundo everybody

• See the centre section for verb tables.

todo pronoun *masc.*, **toda** *fem.*
1 everything
Todo está listo. Everything's ready.
2 all
Eso es todo. That's all.
Me lo he comido todo. I've eaten it all.
Las he comprado todas. I've bought them all.
3 everybody
Todos han venido. Everybody has come.

tomar verb
1 to take
Toma el autobús. Take the bus.
¿Has tomado la pastilla? Have you taken the tablet?
Toma, cómete esto. Here, eat this.
2 to have
Vamos a tomar el desayuno. We're going to have breakfast.
¿Qué quieres tomar? What do you want to have?
3 tomar el sol to sunbathe
tomar el aire to get some fresh air

el **tomate** noun *masc.*
tomato
una salsa de tomate a tomato sauce

la **tontería** noun *fem.*
1 stupid thing
hacer una tontería to do a stupid thing
2 nonsense
¡Qué tontería! What nonsense!
decir tonterías to talk nonsense

tonto adjective *masc.*, **tonta** *fem.*
stupid, silly

torcer verb
1 to twist
Me he torcido el tobillo. I've twisted my ankle.
2 to turn
Tuerce a la izquierda. Turn left.

torcido adjective *masc.*, **torcida** *fem.*
1 crooked
El cuadro está torcido. The picture's crooked.
2 twisted

el **torero** noun *masc.*, la **torera** *fem.*
bullfighter

la **tormenta** noun *fem.*
storm

el **toro** noun *masc.*
bull

la **torre** noun *fem.*
tower

la **torta** noun *fem.*
flat, round cake

la **tortilla** noun *fem.*
1 omelette
2 (*Mexico*) **tortilla** (*made of corn flour*)

la **tortuga** noun *fem.*
1 tortoise
2 turtle
una tortuga de mar a turtle

la **tos** noun *fem.*
cough
Tengo mucha tos. I have a bad cough.

toser verb
to cough

la **tostada** noun *fem.*
una tostada a piece of toast
¿Quieres tostadas? Do you want some toast?

tostado adjective *masc.*
el pan tostado toasted bread

el **total** noun *masc.*
total

trabajador adjective *masc.*, **trabajadora** *fem.*
hard-working

a
b
c
d
e
f
g
h
i
j
k
l
m
n
o
p
q
r
s
t
u
v
w
x
y
z

• *Use* **el** *and* **uno** *for masculine words and* **la** *and* **una** *for feminine words.*

165

el **trabajador** noun *masc.*,
la **trabajadora** *fem.*
worker

trabajar verb
to work
Mi padre trabaja en una oficina.
My dad works in an office.

el **trabajo** noun *masc.*
1 work
Tengo mucho trabajo. I've got lots
of work.
ir al trabajo to go to work
2 job
encontrar trabajo to find a job

el **tractor** noun *masc.*
tractor

la **traducción** noun *fem.* (plural las
traducciones)
translation

traducir verb
to translate
Tradúcelo del español al inglés.
Translate it from Spanish into
English.

traer verb
to bring
Traigo un regalo para ti. I've
brought a present for you.

el **tráfico** noun *masc.*
traffic
Hay mucho tráfico. There's a lot of
traffic.

tragar verb
to swallow

el **traje** noun *masc.*
1 suit
Javier lleva un traje negro. Javier
is wearing a black suit.
un traje de chaqueta (*for a woman*) a
suit
un traje de baño (*for a man*)
swimming trunks; (*for a
woman*) swimsuit
2 costume
el traje regional regional costume

la **trampa** noun *fem.*
1 trap
2 **hacer trampa** to cheat

tramposo noun *masc.*,
tramposa *fem.*
cheat

tranquilo adjective *masc.*,
tranquila *fem.*
1 quiet
un sitio tranquilo a quiet place
2 calm
Tienes que estar tranquila. You
have to be calm.

el **transbordador** noun *masc.*
el transbordador espacial the
space shuttle

el **transporte** noun *masc.*
el transporte público public
transport

el **tranvía** noun *masc.*
tram

> 🔑 **LANGUAGE**
> Be careful: **tranvía** ends in an **-a** but it is
> not a feminine noun.

el **trapo** noun *masc.*
cloth
un trapo de cocina a tea towel

trasero adjective *masc.*,
trasera *fem.*
back
el asiento trasero the back seat

tratar verb
1 to treat
Trato muy bien a mi perro. I treat
my dog very well.
2 **tratar de hacer algo** to try to do
something
3 **tratar de algo** to be about
something
¿De qué trata el libro? What's the
book about?

• *Languages and nationalities do not take a capital letter in Spanish.*

a través de preposition
through
a través del cristal through the window

trece number
1 thirteen
Mi hermano tiene trece años. My brother is thirteen (years old).
2 (with dates) thirteenth
el trece de octubre the thirteenth of October

treinta number
1 thirty
Mi madre tiene treinta años. My mum is thirty (years old).
2 (with dates) thirtieth
el treinta de marzo the thirtieth of March

el **tren** noun masc.
train
en tren by train
cambiar de tren to change trains

las **trenzas** plural noun fem.
plaits

trepar verb
to climb
trepar a un árbol to climb a tree

tres number
1 three
Mi hermana tiene tres años. My sister is three (years old).
Son las tres. It's three o'clock.
2 (with dates) third
el tres de junio the third of June

trescientos number masc.,
trescientas fem.
three hundred

el **triángulo** noun masc.
triangle

el **trigo** noun masc.
wheat

el **trimestre** noun masc.
term
el primer trimestre del año the first term of the year

el **trineo** noun masc.
sledge

el **triple** noun masc.
three times
Cuesta el triple. It costs three times as much.

la **tripulación** noun fem.
crew

triste adjective masc. & fem.
1 sad
¿Estás triste? Are you sad?
2 gloomy
un día triste a gloomy day

la **tristeza** noun fem.
sadness

el **triunfo** noun masc.
victory

la **trompa** noun fem.
trunk
la trompa del elefante the elephant's trunk

la **trompeta** noun fem.
trumpet
Raúl toca la trompeta. Raúl plays the trumpet.

el **tronco** noun masc.
trunk
el tronco del árbol the trunk of the tree

el **trono** noun masc.
throne

tropezar verb
to trip

el **trozo** noun masc.
piece
¿Quieres un trozo de tarta? Do you want a piece of cake?

el **truco** noun masc.
trick
un truco de magia a magic trick

el **trueno** noun masc.
thunder
Hubo truenos. There was thunder.

a b c d e f g h i j k l m n o p q r s t u v w x y z

• The months of the year and days of the week do not take a capital letter in Spanish.

tu adjective *masc. & fem.*
your
tu hermana your sister
tus dibujos your drawings

> **LANGUAGE**
> Tus is used before a plural noun.

> **LANGUAGE**
> Use tu when you are talking to a friend, somebody in your family, or someone your own age.

tú pronoun
1 (*for giving special importance to the word in the sentence*) you
Tú lo sabes pero las otras no. You know but the others don't.
¿Quieres venir tú? Do you want to come?
2 (*with 'que', 'ser', etc.*) you
Soy más alto que tú. I'm taller than you.
¿Eres tú? Is that you?
tú mismo yourself

> **LANGUAGE**
> Use tú when you are talking to a friend, somebody in your family, or someone your own age.

el **tubo** noun *masc.*
tube

tumbarse verb
to lie down

la **tumbona** noun *fem.*
deckchair

el **túnel** noun *masc.*
tunnel
Pasamos por el túnel. We went through the tunnel.

el **turismo** noun *masc.*
hacer turismo to go sightseeing
una oficina de turismo a tourist office

el or la **turista** noun *masc. & fem.*
tourist

• *See the centre section for verb tables.*

el **turno** noun *masc.*
turn
Es tu turno. It's your turn.

el **turrón** noun *masc.*
nougat

> **CULTURE**
> Turrón is a kind of nougat that Spanish people eat at Christmas.

tuve verb SEE **tener**
had
Tuve un problema. I had a problem.

tuvieron verb SEE **tener**
had
Tuvieron una discusión. They had an argument.

tuvo verb SEE **tener**
had
Tuvo un buen viaje. She had a good trip.

tuyo adjective *masc.*, **tuya** *fem.*
yours
Este paraguas es tuyo. This umbrella is yours.
Estas cajas son tuyas. These boxes are yours.
una amiga tuya a friend of yours

> **LANGUAGE**
> You use tuyo/tuya when you are talking to a friend, somebody in your family, or someone your own age.

el **tuyo** pronoun *masc.*, la **tuya** *fem.*
yours
mi hermano y el tuyo my brother and yours
Mi casa es más pequeña que la tuya. My house is smaller than yours.

> **LANGUAGE**
> Use el tuyo/la tuya when you are talking to a friend, somebody in your family, or someone your own age.

Uu

u conjunction
or
siete u ocho seven or eight

🔑 **LANGUAGE**
The usual word for 'or' is **o** but **u** is used in front of a word starting with **o** or **ho**.

Ud. abbreviation
you

🔑 **LANGUAGE**
Ud. is short for **usted** in the singular.

Uds. abbreviation
you

🔑 **LANGUAGE**
Uds. is short for **ustedes** in the plural.

la **UE** noun *fem.*
EU *(European Union)*

últimamente adverb
lately

último adjective *masc.*,
última *fem.*
1 **last**
la última vez the last time
Quedé último en la carrera. I came last in the race.
2 **latest**
las últimas noticias the latest news
3 **top**
en el último piso on the top floor
4 **back**
en la última fila in the back row

el **último** pronoun *masc.*,
la **última** *fem.*
last one, last
¿Eres la última? Are you the last one?
Es el último de la clase. He's bottom of the class.

un determiner *masc.*, **una** *fem.*
1 **a**
un coche a car
una mesa a table
un ala a wing
un hada a fairy

🔑 **LANGUAGE**
Un is used instead of **una** before feminine nouns (like **ala** or **hada**) beginning with a stressed 'a' sound.

2 **an**
un elefante an elephant
una manzana an apple

un number *masc.*, **una** *fem.*
one
¿Cuesta un euro o dos? Does it cost one euro or two?
Es la una. It's one o'clock.
Mi hermano tiene un año. My brother is one.

único adjective *masc.*,
única *fem.*
only
Es el único vestido que me gusta. It's the only dress I like.
Isabel es hija única. Isabel is an only child.

el **único** noun *masc.*,
la **única** *fem.*
only one
Es el único que tengo. It's the only one I have.

el **uniforme** noun *masc.*
uniform

 CULTURE
In Spain schoolchildren don't usually wear uniforms.

• *Use **el** and **uno** for masculine words and **la** and **una** for feminine words.*

la **Unión Europea** noun *fem.*
European Union

unir verb
to match
Une las dos palabras. Match the two words.

la **universidad** noun *fem.*
university
ir a la universidad to go to university

el **universo** noun *masc.*
universe

uno number & pronoun *masc.*,
una *fem.*
1 one
el número uno number one
Quiero sólo uno. I only want one.
uno de ellos, una de ellas one of them
Es la una. It's one o'clock.
2 (*in dates*) **first**
el uno de marzo the first of March

unos adjective & pronoun *masc. plural*,
unas *fem. plural*
1 some
He comprado unos vaqueros. I've bought some jeans.
Unos quieren venir, otros no. Some want to come, others don't.
2 a few
Voy a invitar a unos amigos. I'm going to invite a few friends.
3 about
unos veinte niños about twenty children

la **uña** noun *fem.*
nail
una uña del dedo del pie a toe nail

la **urgencia** noun *fem.*
emergency
en caso de urgencia in an emergency

urgente adjective *masc. & fem.*
urgent

Uruguay noun *masc.*
Uruguay

usar verb
1 to use
Usa una calculadora. Use a calculator.
2 to take
¿Qué talla usas? What size do you take?

usted pronoun
you
¿Cómo está usted? How are you?
Esto es para usted. This is for you.

LANGUAGE
You use **usted** when talking in a polite way to a grown-up or a stranger.

ustedes plural pronoun
you
¿Cómo están ustedes? How are you?
Esto es para ustedes. This is for you.

LANGUAGE
You use **ustedes** when talking in a polite way to two or more grown-ups or strangers.

útil adjective *masc. & fem.*
useful

utilizar verb
to use

la **uva** noun *fem.*
grape

• *Languages and nationalities do not take a capital letter in Spanish.*

Vv

va verb SEE **ir**
Va al cine. He goes to the cinema.
¿Qué va a hacer? What's she going to do?

la **vaca** noun *fem.*
cow

las **vacaciones** plural noun *fem.*
holiday, holidays
Estamos de vacaciones. We're on holiday.
Me voy de vacaciones en julio. I'm going on holiday in July.
las vacaciones de Navidad the Christmas holidays
las vacaciones de verano the summer holidays

vaciar verb
to empty

vacío adjective *masc.*, **vacía** *fem.*
empty
El vaso está vacío. The glass is empty.

vago adjective *masc.*, **vaga** *fem.*
lazy

el **vagón** noun *masc.* (plural los **vagones**)
(*on a train*) carriage

la **vainilla** noun *fem.*
vanilla
un helado de vainilla a vanilla ice cream

🔑 **LANGUAGE**
Spanish = vainilla
English = vanilla

la **vajilla** noun *fem.*
dishes
lavar la vajilla to wash the dishes

vale exclamation
okay
¿Quieres ir a la piscina? – ¡Vale! Do you want to go to the pool? – Okay!

el **vale** noun *masc.*
voucher
un vale de regalo a gift voucher

valer verb
1 to cost
¿Cuánto vale? How much does it cost?
2 to be worth
La bici vale mucho dinero. The bike is worth a lot of money.
3 **valer la pena** to be worth it
No vale la pena. It's not worth it.

valiente adjective *masc. & fem.*
brave

la **valla** noun *fem.*
fence

el **valle** noun *masc.*
valley

el **valor** noun *masc.*
value
un anillo de gran valor a very valuable ring

vamos verb SEE **ir**
Vamos al cole. We go to school.
¿Qué vamos a hacer? What are we going to do?
Vamos a ver la tele. Let's watch TV.

van verb SEE **ir**
Van en bici. They go by bike.
Van a comprar vaqueros. They're going to buy jeans.

el **vapor** noun *masc.*
steam

• *The months of the year and days of the week do not take a capital letter in Spanish.*

a
b
c
d
e
f
g
h
i
j
k
l
m
n
o
p
q
r
s
t
u
v
w
x
y
z

vaquero adjective *masc.*,
vaquera *fem.*
denim
una camisa vaquera a denim shirt

el **vaquero** noun *masc.*
cowboy
una película de vaqueros
a western

los **vaqueros** plural noun *masc.*
jeans
unos vaqueros a pair of jeans

la **varicela** noun *fem.*
chickenpox
Tengo la varicela. I have
chickenpox.

varios adjective *masc. plural*,
varias *fem. plural*
several
varios días several days

la **varita** noun *fem.*
wand
una varita mágica a magic wand

vas verb SEE **ir**
¿Adónde vas? Where are you
going?
¿Vas a ayudarme? Are you going
to help me?

el **vasco** noun *masc.*
(*the language*) Basque

vasco adjective *masc.*, **vasca** *fem.*
Basque
el País Vasco the Basque Country

el **vasco** noun *masc.*,
la **vasca** *fem.*
Basque
los vascos the Basques

el **vaso** noun *masc.*
glass
un vaso de agua a glass of water
un vaso de plástico a plastic cup

• *See the centre section for verb tables.*

172

Vd. abbreviation
you

🔑 **LANGUAGE**
Vd. is short for **usted** in the singular.

Vds. abbreviation
you

🔑 **LANGUAGE**
Vds. is short for **ustedes** in the plural.

el **vecino** noun *masc.*, la **vecina** *fem.*
1 neighbour
Es mi vecina. She's my neighbour.
2 resident
los vecinos del pueblo the
residents of the village

vegetariano adjective *masc.*,
vegetariana *fem.*
vegetarian
Soy vegetariano. I'm vegetarian.

el **véhiculo** noun *masc.*
vehicle

veinte number
1 twenty
Mi primo tiene veinte años.
My cousin is twenty.
2 (*with dates*) twentieth
el veinte de septiembre the
twentieth of September

la **vela** noun *fem.*
1 candle
encender una vela to light a
candle
2 sailing
hacer vela to go sailing

la **velocidad** noun *fem.*
speed

vencer verb
1 to beat
vencer a un equipo to beat a team
2 to win

la **venda** noun *fem.*
bandage

el **vendedor** noun masc.,
la **vendedora** fem.
sales person

vender verb
to sell
He vendido mi bici a mi amigo.
I've sold my bike to my friend.
'Se vende'. 'For sale'.

el **veneno** noun masc.
poison

venenoso adjective masc.,
venenosa fem.
poisonous

Venezuela noun fem.
Venezuela

venir verb
1 to come
¿Quieres venir conmigo? Do you
want to come with me?
Vengo a verte. I'm coming to see
you.
Ya viene el autobús. Here comes
the bus.
Ven aquí. Come here.
¡Venga! Come on!
Vine en coche. I came by car.
2 **que viene** next
la semana que viene next week

la **ventana** noun fem.
window
Abre la ventana. Open the
window.

la **ventanilla** noun fem.
(of a car) window
Baja la ventanilla. Open the
window.

el **ventilador** noun masc.
fan

el **veo veo** noun masc.
I spy
jugar al veo veo to play I spy

ver verb
1 to see
¿Has visto a mi hermana?
Have you seen my sister?
No la veo. I can't see her.
Te vi en el supermercado.
I saw you in the supermarket.
A ver … Let's see …
2 to watch
ver la tele to watch TV

el **verano** noun masc.
summer
en verano in the summer

el **verbo** noun masc.
verb

la **verdad** noun fem.
1 truth
¿Me dices la verdad? Are you
telling me the truth?
Eso es verdad. That's true.
2 (in questions)
Hace calor, ¿verdad? It's hot, isn't
it?
Te gusta, ¿verdad? You like it,
don't you?

> **LANGUAGE**
> **¿Verdad?** is often used to say 'isn't it?',
> 'don't you?', 'hasn't she?', etc.

verdadero adjective masc.,
verdadera fem.
1 real
su verdadero nombre her real
name
2 true
una historia verdadera
a true story

verde adjective masc. & fem.
green
Tengo los ojos verdes. I have green
eyes.

el **verde** noun masc.
green
El verde es mi color favorito.
Green is my favourite colour.

a
b
c
d
e
f
g
h
i
j
k
l
m
n
o
p
q
r
s
t
u
v
w
x
y
z

• Use **el** and **uno** for masculine words and **la** and **una** for feminine words.

la **verdulería** noun *fem.*
  greengrocer's

la **verdura** noun *fem.*
  vegetable
  sopa de verduras vegetable soup

la **vergüenza** noun *fem.*
  1 shame
    Me da vergüenza. I'm ashamed.
  2 shyness
    Tiene vergüenza. He's shy.

el **vestíbulo** noun *masc.*
  1 (*in a house*) **hall**
  2 (*in a hotel etc.*) **lobby**

el **vestido** noun *masc.*
  dress
  un vestido rojo a red dress

vestido adjective *masc.*,
  vestida *fem.*
  dressed
  No estoy vestido. I'm not dressed.
  Está vestida de azul. She's dressed in blue.

vestir verb
  to dress
  Viste muy bien. He dresses very well.

vestirse verb
  1 to get dressed
    Vístete. Get dressed.
  2 to dress
    Se viste de verde. She dresses in green.
    Se vistió de pirata. He dressed up as a pirate.

el **vestuario** noun *masc.*
  (*for sports*) **changing room**, **cubicle**

el **veterinario** noun *masc.*,
  la **veterinaria** *fem.*
  vet
  Mi madre es veterinaria.
  My mum's a vet.

la **vez** noun *fem.*
  time
  por primera vez for the first time
  una vez once
  dos veces al mes twice a month
  a veces sometimes
  otra vez again
  tal vez maybe
  en vez de instead of
  'Érase una vez ...' (*in stories*) 'Once upon a time there was ...'

la **vía** noun *fem.*
  1 way, road
    vías romanas Roman roads
  2 (*for trains*) platform
  3 **la vía del tren** the railway line
    Se cayó a la vía. He fell onto the line.

viajar verb
  to travel
  ¿Te gusta viajar? Do you like travelling?

el **viaje** noun *masc.*
  1 trip
    hacer un viaje to go on a trip
    ¡Buen viaje! Have a good trip!
  2 journey
    un viaje muy largo a very long journey

el **viajero** noun *masc.*,
  la **viajera** *fem.*
  passenger

la **victoria** noun *fem.*
  victory

la **vida** noun *fem.*
  life
  toda mi vida all my life

el **vídeo** noun *masc.*
  video
  Estamos viendo un vídeo.
  We're watching a video.
  en vídeo on video

• *Languages and nationalities do not take a capital letter in Spanish.*

la **videoconsola** noun fem.
  games console

el **videojuego** noun masc.
  video game

el **vidrio** noun masc.
  glass

viejo adjective masc., **vieja** fem.
  old
  Mi abuelo es muy viejo.
  My grandfather's very old.

el **viejo** noun masc., la **vieja** fem.
  old man, old woman

el **viento** noun masc.
  wind
  Hace viento. It's windy.

la **viernes** noun masc.
  Friday
  Hoy es viernes. Today is Friday.
  el viernes on Friday
  Mis primos se van el viernes.
  My cousins are leaving on
  Friday.
  los viernes on Fridays
  Voy al parque los viernes. I go to
  the park on Fridays.

LANGUAGE
Remember the difference between el
viernes (one Friday only) and los viernes
(every Friday).

el **Viernes Santo** noun masc.
  Good Friday

el **villancico** noun masc.
  Christmas carol

el **vinagre** noun masc.
  vinegar

el **vino** noun masc.
  wine
  el vino tinto red wine

violeta adjective masc. & fem.
  violet
  faldas violeta violet skirts

LANGUAGE
The form violeta is the same in the
masculine, feminine, and plural.

el **violín** noun masc. (plural los
  violines)
  violin
  Toco el violín. I play the violin.

el **violonchelo** noun masc.
  cello
  Hakim toca el violonchelo. Hakim
  plays the cello.

la **Virgen** noun fem.
  Virgin
  la Virgen María the Virgin
  Mary

el **virus** noun masc. (plural los **virus**)
  virus

la **visita** noun fem.
  1 visit
    la visita de mis primos my cousins'
    visit
  2 visitor
    Tenemos visitas. We have
    visitors.

el or la **visitante** noun masc. & fem.
  visitor

visitar verb
  to visit

la **vista** noun fem.
  1 view
    una vista maravillosa a wonderful
    view
    ¡Hasta la vista! See you!
  2 eyesight

viva exclamation
  hip hip hurrah!

• The months of the year and days of the week do not take a capital letter in Spanish.

a
b
c
d
e
f
g
h
i
j
k
l
m
n
o
p
q
r
s
t
u
v
w
x
y
z

a
b
c
d
e
f
g
h
i
j
k
l
m
n
o
p
q
r
s
t
u
v
w
x
y
z

vivir verb
to live
¿Dónde vives? Where do you live?
Vivo en Toledo. I live in Toledo.

vivo adjective *masc.*,
viva *fem.*
alive
¿Está vivo? Is it alive?

el **vocabulario** noun *masc.*
vocabulary

la **vocal** noun *fem.*
vowel

el **volante** noun *masc.*
steering wheel

volar verb
1 to fly
Me gusta volar. I like to fly.
2 to blow up
Han volado un edificio. They've blown up a building.

el **volcán** noun *masc.* (plural los **volcanes**)
volcano

el **voleibol** noun *masc.*
volleyball
jugar al voleibol to play volleyball

el **volumen** noun *masc.*
volume
Sube el volumen. Turn up the volume.

el **voluntario** noun *masc.*,
la **voluntaria** *fem.*
volunteer

volver verb
1 to go back
Tengo que volver al colegio. I have to go back to school.
2 to come back
¿Cuándo vuelves de Madrid? When do you come back from Madrid?

3 to turn
Volví la cabeza. I turned my head.
4 (*for saying 'again'*)
volver a hacer algo to do something again
Volveré a verlos mañana. I'll see them again tomorrow.

volverse verb
1 to turn round
Me volví a mirar. I turned round to look.
2 **volver loco a alguien** to drive somebody mad
La música me vuelve loco. The music is driving me mad.

vosotros pronoun *masc.*,
vosotras *fem.*
1 you
Vosotros podéis hacerlo. You can do it.

LANGUAGE
Vosotros/vosotras is used for giving special importance to the word 'you'.

2 (*after a preposition etc.*) **you**
con vosotros with you
Somos más altas que vosotras. We're taller than you.
vosotros mismos yourselves

LANGUAGE
Use **vosotros/vosotras** when you are talking to two or more friends, people in your family, or people your own age.

votar verb
to vote

voy verb SEE **ir**
Voy en coche. I go by car.
Voy a sentarme aquí. I'm going to sit here.

la **voz** noun *fem.* (plural las **voces**)
voice
Tiene una voz muy bonita. She has a lovely voice.

• *The months of the year and days of the week do not take a capital letter in Spanish.*

Lee esto en voz alta. Read this aloud.
Maite habla en voz baja. Maite speaks quietly.

el **vuelo** noun *masc.*
flight
El vuelo dura dos horas. The flight lasts two hours.

la **vuelta** noun *fem.*
1 **return**
la vuelta al colegio the return to school
2 **change**
Aquí tienes la vuelta. Here's your change.
3 **walk**
¿Quieres dar una vuelta? Do you want to go for a walk?
4 *(in a car, on a horse, etc.)* **ride**
Quiero dar una vuelta en bici. I want to go for a ride on my bike.
5 **dar la vuelta a una página** to turn a page
darse la vuelta to turn round
Me di la vuelta. I turned round.

vuestro adjective *masc.*,
vuestra *fem.*
1 **your**
vuestro colegio your school
vuestros juguetes your toys
2 **yours**
Este boli es vuestro. This pen is yours.
¿Son vuestros? Are they yours?
unas amigas vuestras some friends of yours

> **⚷ LANGUAGE**
> Use vuestro/vuestra when you are talking to two or more friends, people in your family, or people your own age.

el **vuestro** pronoun *masc.*,
la **vuestra** *fem.*
yours
Nuestro perro es más grande que el vuestro. Our dog is bigger than yours.
mis libros y los vuestros my books and yours

> **⚷ LANGUAGE**
> Use el vuestro/la vuestra when you are talking to two or more friends, people in your family, or people your own age.

Ww

la **web** noun *fem.*
web
una página web a web page
un sitio web a website

Xx

el **xilófono** noun *masc.*
xylophone
tocar el xilófono to play the xylophone

• *See the centre section for verb tables.*

a
b
c
d
e
f
g
h
i
j
k
l
m
n
o
p
q
r
s
t
u
v
w
x
y
z

Yy

y conjunction
and
rojo y verde red and green

ya adverb
1 already
Ya he comido. I've already eaten.
2 yet
¿Ya has terminado? Have you
finished yet?
3 now
Ya es hora de irnos. It's time to go
now.
4 ya no ... not ... any more
Ya no vivo en Londres. I don't live
in London any more.
5 (*no translation*)
Ya lo sé. I know.
¡Ya voy! I'm coming!

el **yate** noun *masc.*
yacht

la **yema** noun *fem.*
yolk

yo pronoun
1 (*for giving special importance to the word in
the sentence*) **I**
**Yo soy inglesa pero las otras son
españolas.** I'm English but the
others are Spanish.
Pedro y yo fuimos a casa. Pedro
and I went home.
2 (*with* **que**, **ser**, *etc.*) **me**
Eres más rápido que yo. You're
faster than me.
Soy yo. It's me.
yo mismo myself

el **yogur** noun *masc.*
yoghurt

el **yoyó** noun *masc.*
yo-yo

Zz

la **zanahoria** noun *fem.*
carrot

la **zapatería** noun *fem.*
shoe shop

el **zapatero** noun *masc.*,
la **zapatera** *fem.*
1 shoemaker
2 shoe repairer's

la **zapatilla** noun *fem.*
slipper
Llevo zapatillas en casa. I wear
slippers at home.
zapatillas de deporte trainers

el **zapato** noun *masc.*
shoe
un par de zapatos a pair of shoes

la **zarzamora** noun *fem.*
blackberry

la **zona** noun *fem.*
area
Vivo en una zona tranquila. I live
in a quiet area.

el **zoo** noun *masc.*
zoo

el **zoológico** noun *masc.*
zoo

el **zorro** noun *masc.*
fox

el **zumo** noun *masc.*
juice
zumo de naranja orange juice

zurdo adjective *masc.*, **zurda** *fem.*
left-handed

• *Use* **el** *and* **uno** *for masculine words and* **la** *and* **una** *for feminine words.*

Animals
Clothes and colours
Calendar

Time
Body
Numbers

In the classroom
Friends
The weather

Shopping
Countries and places
Family

Healthy eating
Jobs
Where are you?

Feelings
A letter, a text, an email
Where I live

Sports
Hobbies
Story time

179

Los animales / Animals
¿Tienes un animal? / Do you have a pet?

No, no tengo animales.
No, I don't have any pets.

Sí, tengo …
Yes, I have …

un animal / animales	an animal / animals
un gato / gatos	a cat / cats
un perro / perros	a dog / dogs
un pájaro / pájaros	a bird / birds
un caballa / caballas	a horse / horses
un pez / peces	a fish / fish
un ratón / ratones	a mouse / mice
un hámster / hámsters	a hamster / hamsters
un cobaya / cobayas	a guinea pig / guinea pigs
un conejo / conejos	a rabbit / rabbits
una serpiente / serpientes	a snake / snakes
un camaleón / camaleones	a chameleon / chameleons

pío pío
tweet, tweet

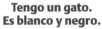

guau guau
woof, woof

Tengo un gato.
Es blanco y negro.
I have a cat.
He is black and white.

No tengo caballo.
I don't have a horse.

No tengo perro.
I don't have a dog.

miau
miaow

La ropa y los colores / Clothes and colours

Mi color favorito es el azul.
My favourite colour is blue.

Odio el azul.
I hate blue.

Me encanta el rojo.
I love red.

la camisa
shirt

los zapatos
shoes

la camiseta
T-shirt

la sudadera
sweatshirt

los pantalones
trousers

los vaqueros
jeans

el suéter
sweater

la falda
skirt

el sombrero
hat

los calcetines
socks

¿De qué color es? / What colour is it?

blanco / blanca
white

azul
blue

rojo / roja
red

marrón
brown

negro / negra
black

rosa
pink

amarillo / amarilla
yellow

verde
green

gris
grey

naranja
orange

morado / morada
purple

El calendario / Calendar

Los días de la semana / Days of the week

lunes	Monday
martes	Tuesday
miércoles	Wednesday
jueves	Thursday
viernes	Friday
sábado	Saturday
domingo	Sunday

Hoy es lunes.
It is Monday.

¿Qué día es hoy?
What day is it?

Los meses / Months

enero	January
febrero	February
marzo	March
abril	April
mayo	May
junio	June
julio	July
agosto	August
septiembre	September
octubre	October
noviembre	November
diciembre	December
el día de Reyes	Twelfth Night (6th January)

¿Qué fecha es hoy?
What is today's date?

El 24 de enero.
24th January.

Days and months don't start with a capital letter in Spanish.

¡Feliz Navidad!
Happy Christmas!

los lunes
on Mondays

Las estaciones / Seasons

la primavera	spring
el verano	summer
el otoño	autumn
el invierno	winter

¡Feliz cumpleaños!
Happy birthday!

¡Feliz Año Nuevo!
Happy New Year!

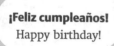

La hora / Time

¿Qué hora es?
What time is it?

Es la una.
It is one o'clock.

Son las tres.
It is three o'clock.

Son las cinco.
It is five o'clock.

Son las siete.
It is seven o'clock.

Son las dos.
It is two o'clock.

Son las cuatro.
It is four o'clock.

Son las seis.
It is six o'clock.

Son las ocho.
It is eight o'clock.

Son las diez.
It is ten o'clock.

Es mediodía.
It is noon / midday.

Son las nueve.
It is nine o'clock.

Son las once.
It is eleven o'clock.

Es medianoche.
It is midnight.

Es mediodía.	It is midday.	**Son las doce y media de la noche.**	It is half past midnight.
Es la una.	It is one o'clock.	**Es la una y media.**	It is half past one.
Es la una y cuarto.	It is quarter past one.	**Es la una menos cuarto.**	It is quarter to one.

por la mañana
morning

por la tarde
in the afternoon / evening

por la noche
at night / in the evening

¿A qué hora es?
At what time is it?

El colegio empieza a las nueve menos cuarto.
School starts at 8.45.

Me acuesto a las ocho.
I go to bed at 8 o'clock.

Es a la una y veinticinco.
It is at 1.25.

Cenamos a las seis y media.
We eat at 6.30.

Salimos al recreo a las once.
Playtime is at 11.

Me levanto a las siete.
I get up at 7.

Salimos de clase a las cuatro y media.
School finishes at 4.30.

183

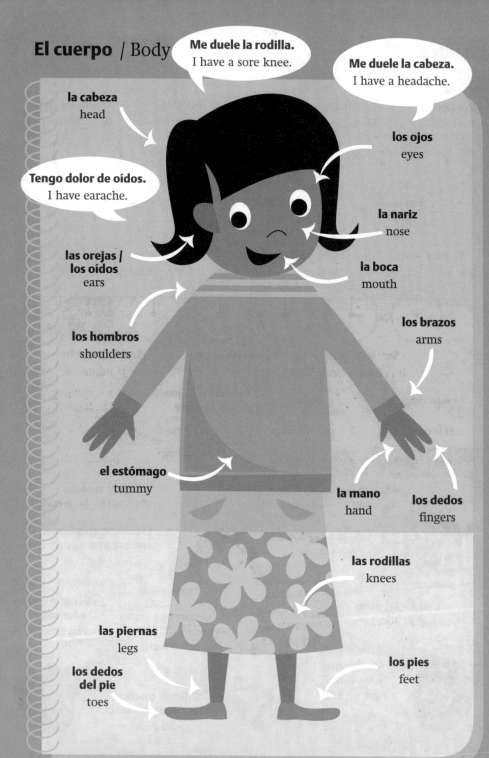

Los números / Numbers

cero	zero					
uno, un/una	one	**once**	eleven	**veintiuno,**	twenty-one	
dos	two	**doce**	twelve	**veintiún /**		
tres	three	**trece**	thirteen	**veintiuna**		
cuatro	four	**catorce**	fourteen	**treinta**	thirty	
cinco	five	**quince**	fifteen	**cuarenta**	forty	
seis	six	**dieciséis**	sixteen	**cincuenta**	fifty	
siete	seven	**diecisiete**	seventeen	**sesenta**	sixty	
ocho	eight	**dieciocho**	eighteen			
nueve	nine	**diecinueve**	nineteen			
diez	ten	**veinte**	twenty			

1° / 1st

**primero,
primer / primera**

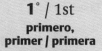

2°/ 2nd
segundo /segunda

3° / 3rd
tercero, tercer /tercera

más + add

Cinco más dos son siete.
Five plus two is seven.
5 + 2 = 7

menos - subtract

Seis menos dos son cuatro.
Six minus two is four.
6 - 2 = 4

por x multiplied by

Dos por cinco son diez.
Two times five is ten.
2 x 5 = 10

dividido entre ÷ divided by

**Doce dividido entre
dos son seis.**
Twelve divided by two is six.
12 ÷ 2 = 6

En la clase / In the classroom

¡Excelente!
¡Bien hecho!
Excellent!
Well done!

¿Qué es?
What is it?

¿Puedo ir al baño?
May I go to the toilet?

Tomad un lápiz.
Take a pencil.

un libro
a book

una goma
a rubber

un estuche
a pencil case

una mesa
a table

un maestro /
una maestra
a teacher

¡Silencio!
Silence!

¡Escribid!
Write!

¡Levantaos!
Stand up!

¡Dámelo!
Give it to me!

¡Sentaos!
Sit down!

¡Mirad!
Look!

¡Miradme!
Watch me!

¡Escuchad!
Listen!

He perdido mi lápiz.
I've lost my pencil.

un alumno / una alumna
a pupil

Presente.
Here.

Ausente.
Absent.

una silla
a chair

He terminado.
I've finished.

una cartera
a schoolbag

un lápiz
a pencil

un bolígrafo
a pen

un cuaderno
an exercise book

un sacapuntas
a pencil sharpener

un rotulador
a felt-tip pen

una regla
a ruler

Los amigos / Friends

¡Hola! Hello!	**¡Hola!** Hi!
¿Cómo te llamas? What is your name?	**Me llamo Felipe.** My name is Philip.
¿Cuántos años tienes? How old are you?	**Tengo ocho años.** I am eight.
¿Dónde vives? Where do you live?	**Vivo en York.** I live in York.
¡Adiós! Goodbye!	**¡Hasta pronto!** See you soon!

¿Cómo estás? How are you?	**Bien, gracias.** Fine, thanks.
	No muy bien. Not very well.
¿Hablas español? Do you speak Spanish?	**Sí, un poco.** Yes, a little.
	No muy bien. Not very well.

¿Cuándo es tu cumpleaños?
When is your birthday?

Es el diez de diciembre. ¿Y tú?
It's the tenth of December. And you?

Mi cumpleaños es el primero de abril.
My birthday is the first of April.

¡Feliz cumpleaños!
Happy birthday!

Voy al cine el sábado. ¿Quieres ir al cine el sábado?
I am going to the cinema on Saturday. Would you like to go to the cinema on Saturday?

Sí, gracias.
Yes, thanks.

¿Cuál es tu dirección de email?
What is your email address?

Es …
It is …

El tiempo / The weather

Hace mucho frío.
It's very cold.

Está nevando.
It's snowing.

Hace frío.
It's cold.

Hace un tiempo estupendo.
It's beautiful.

Hace sol.
It's sunny.

¿Qué tiempo hace?
What is the weather like?

¿Qué tiempo hace en Madrid?
What is the weather like in Madrid?

Hace viento.
It's windy.

Está nublado.
It's cloudy.

Está lloviendo.
It's raining.

Hay tormenta.
It's stormy.

Hace calor.
It's hot.

Hay niebla.
It's foggy.

191

Las compras / Shopping

¡Hola!
Hello!

¿Qué desea?
What would you like?

¿De qué sabor?
What flavour?

Cinco euros.
Five euros.

una Coca-Cola
a Coke

un zumo de naranja
an orange juice

¡Hola!
Hello!

Quiero un helado, por favor.
I would like an ice cream, please.

Aquí tiene. Gracias.
Here you are.
Thank you.

una taza de té
a cup of tea

un helado
an ice cream

un café
a coffee

Quiero ...
I would like ...

una limonada
a lemonade

un bocadillo de queso
a cheese sandwich

El chocolate. ¿Cuánto es?
Chocolate. How much is that?

... por favor
... please

una postal
a postcard

un sello
a stamp

un pan
some bread

una revista
a magazine

un pastel
a cake

la farmacia
chemist

la panadería
baker

la pastelería
cake shop

la tienda de periódicos
newsagent

193

Los países y los lugares / Countries and places

¿Qué país es?
What country is this?

Es ...
This is ...

Gales
Wales

Irlanda
Ireland

Francia
France

Reino Unido
United Kingdom

Escocia
Scotland

España
Spain

¿Dónde está ...?
Where is ...?

Está ...	en el norte.	en el sur.	en el este.	en el oeste.
It is ...	in the north.	in the south.	in the east.	in the west.
	el noreste	**el suroeste**	**el sureste**	**el noroeste**
	north-east	south-west	south-east	north-west

¿De qué nacionalidad eres?
What nationality are you?

Soy inglés / inglesa.	I am English.
Soy británico / británica.	I am British.
Soy galés / galesa.	I am Welsh.
Soy escocés / escocesa.	I am Scottish.
Soy irlandés / irlandesa.	I am Irish.

¿Qué idioma hablas?
What language do you speak?

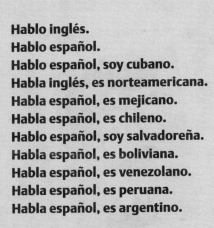

Hablo inglés.	I speak English.
Hablo español.	I speak Spanish.
Hablo español, soy cubano.	I speak Spanish, I am Cuban.
Habla inglés, es norteamericana.	She speaks English, she is American.
Habla español, es mejicano.	He speaks Spanish, he is Mexican.
Habla español, es chileno.	He speaks Spanish, he is Chilean.
Hablo español, soy salvadoreña.	I speak Spanish, I am from El Salvador.
Habla español, es boliviana.	She speaks Spanish, she is Bolivian.
Habla español, es venezolano.	He speaks Spanish, he is Venezuelan.
Habla español, es peruana.	She speaks Spanish, she is Peruvian.
Habla español, es argentino.	He speaks Spanish, he is Argentinian.

La familia / Family

¿Tienes hermanos?
Do you have any brothers and sisters?

Soy hijo único / hija única.
I am an only child.

Tengo un hermano mayor / pequeño.
I have a big / little brother.

Tengo una hermana mayor / pequeña que se llama ...
I have a big / little sister who is called ...

No tengo hermano / hermana.
I don't have a brother / sister.

¿Quién es éste/ésta?
Who is this?

Te presento a ...
This is ...

mi madre | mi madrastra
my mother / stepmother

Soy yo.
This is me.

mi hermana | mi hermanastra
my sister / stepsister

mi padre | mi padrastro
my father / stepfather

mi abuelo
my grandfather

mi abuela
my grandmother

mi hermano | mi hermanastro
my brother / stepbrother

alto | alta
tall

pequeño | pequeña
small

grande
big

delgado | delgada
slim

moreno | morena
brown

rubio | rubia
blond / blonde

pelirrojo | pelirroja
red-haired

simpático | simpática
nice

difícil
difficult

Llevo | lleva gafas.
I wear / he / she
wears glasses.

**Llevo | lleva un aparato
en los dientes.**
I have / he /
she has a brace.

Una dieta sana / Healthy eating

**Comer
poco.**
Eat a little.

Comer con moderación.
Eat in moderation.

Comer mucho.
Eat a lot.

la zanahoria
carrot

la manzana
apple

el pollo
chicken

el tomate
tomato

el plátano
banana

la lechuga
lettuce

la naranja
orange

las patatas
potatoes

el arroz
rice

el agua
water

el pan
bread

los espaguetis
spaghetti

el ajo
garlic

el queso
cheese

el helado
ice cream

el zumo de manzana
apple juice

los cereales
cereal

el yogur
yoghurt

los huevos
eggs

Me gustan los caramelos.
I like sweets.

No me gusta el café.
I don't like coffee.

la hamburguesa
burger

las patatas fritas
chips

el chocolate
chocolate

la mermelada
jam

el pastel
cake

la bebida
drink

el azúcar
sugar

las patatas fritas
crisps

El empleo / Jobs

Un día seré ...
One day, I will be ...

Mi padre es piloto.
My dad is a pilot.

Quisiera ser contable.
I would like to be an accountant.

**el maestro / la maestra,
el profesor / la profesora**
teacher

el / la astronauta
astronaut

el fotógrafo / la fotógrafa
photographer

**el bombero /
la bombera**
firefighter

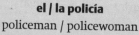

el médico / la médica
doctor

el / la electricista
electrician

**el conductor / la conductora
de autobús**
bus driver

el / la policía
policeman / policewoman

¿Dónde estás? / Where are you?

y and	**o** or	**pero** but	**aunque** though
primero first	**luego** next	**finalmente** finally	**así que** so, therefore

¡Prohibido jugar a la pelota!
No ball games allowed!

¡Socorro!
Help!

en
on

por encima de
over

detrás de
behind

delante de
in front of

en
in

enfrente de
opposite

debajo de
below / under

¡Cuidado con el perro!
Beware of the dog!

Peligro
Danger

Agua no potable.
Do not drink the water.

¡Prohibida la entrada!
Keep out!

Es aburrido.
It's boring.

¡Es estupendo!
It's great!

Estoy triste.
I'm sad.

Gracias.
Thank you.

Tengo hambre.
I'm hungry.

¿Quieres ...? Do you want ...?	**Perdón.** Sorry.	**guay** cool	**No entiendo.** I don't understand.
Sí, por favor. Yes, please.	**Estoy cansado / cansada** I'm tired.	**fácil** easy	**No me importa.** I don't mind.
No, gracias. No, thank you.	**Lo siento.** I'm sorry.	**difícil** difficult	**¡Vale!** OK!
Quizás. Maybe.	**Gracias.** Thank you.	**gracioso / graciosa** funny	**No me apetece.** I don't feel like it.

Una carta / A letter

una carta
a letter

Madrid, 2 de marzo
Madrid, 2nd March

Querida Tía María:
Dear Aunty Mary

Muchas gracias por el regalo estupendo.
Thank you very much for the lovely present.

Con mucho cariño
Lots of love

Carmen

un sobre
an envelope

un sello
a stamp

Un SMS / A text

un móvil
a mobile

un SMS
a text message

¡Hola!
Hi!

bbtt. stas bn?
vams al cin o 1kf mñn?

Buenas tardes.
¿Estás bien?
¿Vamos al cine o a un
café mañana?

Hi. Are you OK?
Do you want to go to the
cinema or a cafe tomorrow?

Un correo electrónico / An email

un ordenador
a computer

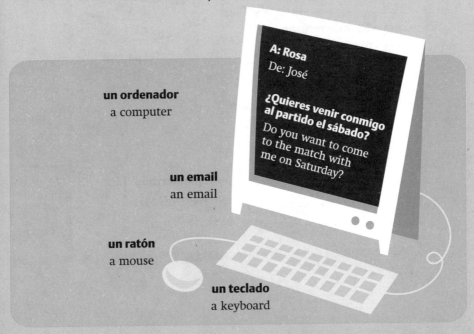

A: Rosa
De: José

¿Quieres venir conmigo
al partido el sábado?
Do you want to come
to the match with
me on Saturday?

un email
an email

un ratón
a mouse

un teclado
a keyboard

El lugar donde vivo / Where I live

Vivo ...
I live ...

en una casa / un piso.
in a house / flat.

Vivo en Londres. Está en el sur de Inglaterra.
I live in London. It is in the south of England.

Hay ...
There is a ...

la oficina de correos
post office

el mercado
market

la oficina de turismo
tourist office

el parque
park

SUPER

el supermercado
supermarket

a pie / en autobús / en tren
on foot / by bus / by train

en el campo / en la ciudad
in the country / in the town

la piscina
pool

la mezquita
mosque

el colegio / la escuela
school

la estación de trenes
railway station

¡Perdón, señor!
Excuse me, sir!

¿Dónde está el / la ... por favor?
Where is the ... please?

el cine
cinema

a iglesia
church

Siga todo recto.
Go straight ahead.

Tome la primera / segunda a la derecha / izquierda.
Take the first / second right / left.

El deporte / Sports

¿Haces deporte?
Do you play sport?

Yo juego al rugby.
I play rugby.

¿Queréis jugar al fútbol?
Do you want to play football?

Mi deporte favorito es …
My favourite sport is …

el tenis
tennis

el fútbol
football

la equitación
horse-riding

la natación
swimming

el bádminton
badminton

el rugby
rugby

la gimnasia
gymnastics

el judo
judo

el baile
dancing

208

Los pasatiempos / Hobbies

el clarinete
clarinet

la flauta
flute

Toco el piano y la batería.
I play the piano and the drums.

Toco la guitarra.
I play the guitar.

el teclado
keyboard

Mi pasatiempo favorito es …
My favourite hobby is…

la lectura
reading

la música
music

la televisión
television

el dibujo
drawing

los juegos de mesa
board games

la informática
computing

los videojuegos
computer games

209

Los cuentos / Story time

el sombrero
hat

la bruja mala
the wicked witch

el gato
cat

la escoba
broomstick

La Bella Durmiente
Sleeping Beauty

Pinocho
Pinocchio

Cenicienta
Cinderella

la casa de pan de jengibre
gingerbread house

Rumpelstiltskin
Rumpelstiltskin

Érase una vez ...
Once upon a time ...

un final feliz
happy ending

fueron felices y comieron perdices
they lived happily ever after

el cuento de hadas
fairy tale

la magia
magic

el mago bueno
the good wizard

Caperucita Roja
Little Red Riding Hood

la varita
wand

El Gato con Botas
Puss in Boots

210

Verb tables

In Spanish there are three main verb types, those ending in **-ar** (like **hablar**), **-er** (like **comer**), and **-ir** (like **vivir**).

You can use the ones on this page as models for other regular verbs as many follow the same patterns. Some verbs don't, so these verb tables also give you some common irregular verbs.

There are also verbs called reflexive verbs. Reflexive verbs are used with a pronoun (like **me**, **te**, **se**) for example, **levantarse** (to stand up): **me levanto** is 'I stand up', **te levantas** is 'you stand up', etc.

You can think of reflexive verbs as those that mean you do something to yourself rather than to someone else.

(-ar) hablar to talk, to speak

present tense

hablo	I talk
hablas	you talk
habla	he/she talks
hablamos	we talk
habláis	you talk
hablan	they talk

past tense

hablé	I talked
hablaste	you talked
habló	he/she talked
hablamos	we talked
hablasteis	you talked
hablaron	they talked

future tense

hablaré	I will talk
hablarás	you will talk
hablará	he/she will talk
hablaremos	we will talk
hablaréis	you will talk
hablarán	they will talk

(-er) comer to eat

present tense

como	I eat
comes	you eat
come	he/she eats
comemos	we eat
coméis	you eat
comen	they eat

past tense

comí	I ate
comiste	you ate
comió	he/she ate
comimos	we ate
comisteis	you ate
comieron	they ate

future tense

comeré	I will eat
comerás	you will eat
comerá	he/she will eat
comeremos	we will eat
comeréis	you will eat
comerán	they will eat

(-ir) vivir to live

present tense

vivo	I live
vives	you live
vive	he/she lives
vivimos	we live
vivís	you live
viven	they live

past tense

viví	I lived
viviste	you lived
vivió	he/she lived
vivimos	we lived
vivisteis	you lived
vivieron	they lived

future tense

viviré	I will live
vivirás	you will live
vivirá	he/she will live
viviremos	we will live
viviréis	you will live
vivirán	they will live

dar to give

present tense

doy	I give
das	you give
da	he/she gives
damos	we give
dais	you give
dan	they give

past tense

di	I gave
diste	you gave
dio	he/she gave
dimos	we gave
disteis	you gave
dieron	they gave

future tense

daré	I will give
darás	you will give
dará	he/she will give
daremos	we will give
daréis	you will give
darán	they will give

decir to say, to tell

present tense

digo	I say
dices	you say
dice	he/she says
decimos	we say
decís	you say
dicen	they say

past tense

dije	I said
dijiste	you said
dijo	he/she said
dijimos	we said
dijisteis	you said
dijeron	they said

future

diré	I will say
dirás	you will say
dirá	he/she will say
diremos	we will say
diréis	you will say
dirán	they will say

estar to be

present tense

estoy	I am
estás	you are
está	he/she is
estamos	we are
estáis	you are
están	they are

past tense

estuve	I was
estuviste	you were
estuvo	he/she was
estuvimos	we were
estuvisteis	you were
estuvieron	they were

future tense

estaré	I will be
estarás	you will be
estará	he/she will be
estaremos	we will be
estaréis	you will be
estarán	they will be

haber to have

present tense

he	I have
has	you have
ha	he/she has
hemos	we have
habéis	you have
han	they have

past tense

hube	I had
hubiste	you had
hubo	he/she had
hubimos	we had
hubisteis	you had
hubieron	they had

future tense

habré	I will have
habrás	you will have
habrá	he/she will have
habremos	we will have
habréis	you will have
habrán	they will have

hacer to do, to make

present tense

hago	I do
haces	you do
hace	he/she does
hacemos	we do
hacéis	you do
hacen	they do

past tense

hice	I did
hiciste	you did
hizo	he/she did
hicimos	we did
hicisteis	you did
hicieron	they did

future tense

haré	I will do
harás	you will do
hará	he/she will do
haremos	we will do
haréis	you will do
harán	they will do

ir to go

present tense

voy	I go
vas	you go
va	he/she goes
vamos	we go
vais	you go
van	they go

past tense

fui	I went
fuiste	you went
fue	he/she went
fuimos	we went
fuisteis	you went
fueron	they went

future tense

iré	I will go
irás	you will go
irá	he/she will go
iremos	we will go
iréis	you will go
irán	they will go

jugar to play

present tense

juego	I play
juegas	you play
juega	he/she plays
jugamos	we play
jugáis	you play
juegan	they play

past tense

jugué	I played
jugaste	you played
jugó	he/she played
jugamos	we played
jugasteis	you played
jugaron	they played

future tense

jugaré	I will play
jugarás	you will play
jugará	he/she will play
jugaremos	we will play
jugaréis	you will play
jugarán	they will play

oír to hear

present tense

oigo	I hear
oyes	you hear
oye	he/she hears
oímos	we hear
oís	you hear
oyen	they hear

past tense

oí	I heard
oíste	you heard
oyó	he/she heard
oímos	we heard
oísteis	you heard
oyeron	they heard

future tense

oiré	I will hear
oirás	you will hear
oirá	he/she will hear
oiremos	we will hear
oiréis	you will hear
oirán	they will hear

poder to be able

present tense

puedo	I can
puedes	you can
puede	he/she can
podemos	we can
podéis	you can
pueden	they can

past tense

pude	I could
pudiste	you could
pudo	he/she could
pudimos	we could
pudisteis	you could
pudieron	they could

future tense

podré	I will be able
podrás	you will be able
podrá	he/she will be able
podremos	we will be able
podréis	you will be able
podrán	they will be able

poner to put

present tense

pongo	I put
pones	you put
pone	he/she puts
ponemos	we put
ponéis	you put
ponen	they put

past tense

puse	I put
pusiste	you put
puso	he/she put
pusimos	we put
pusisteis	you put
pusieron	they put

future tense

pondré	I will put
pondrás	you will put
pondrá	he/she will put
pondremos	we will put
pondréis	you will put
pondrán	they will put

querer to want, to love

present tense

quiero	I want
quieres	you want
quiere	he/she wants
queremos	we want
queréis	you want
quieren	they want

past tense

quise	I wanted
quisiste	you wanted
quiso	he/she wanted
quisimos	we wanted
quisisteis	you wanted
quisieron	they wanted

future tense

querré	I will want
querrás	you will want
querrá	he/she will want
querremos	we will want
querréis	you will want
querrán	they will want

saber to know

present tense

sé	I know
sabes	you know
sabe	he/she knows
sabemos	we know
sabéis	you know
saben	they know

past tense

supe	I knew
supiste	you knew
supo	he/she knew
supimos	we knew
supisteis	you knew
supieron	they knew

future tense

sabré	I will know
sabrás	you will know
sabrá	he/she will know
sabremos	we will know
sabréis	you will know
sabrán	they will know

salir to go out

present tense

salgo	I go out
sales	you go out
sale	he/she goes out
salimos	we go out
salís	you go out
salen	they go out

future tense

saldré	I will go out
saldrás	you will go out
saldrá	he/she will go out
saldremos	we will go out
saldréis	you will go out
saldrán	they will go out

past tense

salí	I went out
saliste	you went out
salió	he/she went out
salimos	we went out
salisteis	you went out
salieron	they went out

sentir to feel

present tense

siento	I feel
sientes	you feel
siente	he/she feels
sentimos	we feel
sentís	you feel
sienten	they feel

past tense

sentí	I felt
sentiste	you felt
sintió	he/she felt
sentimos	we felt
sentisteis	you felt
sintieron	they felt

future tense

sentiré	I will feel
sentirás	you will feel
sentirá	he/she will feel
sentiremos	we will feel
sentiréis	you will feel
sentirán	they will feel

ser to be

present tense

soy	I am
eres	you are
es	he/she is
somos	we are
sois	you are
son	they are

past tense

fui	I was
fuiste	you were
fue	he/she was
fuimos	we were
fuisteis	you were
fueron	they were

future tense

seré	I will be
serás	you will be
será	he/she will be
seremos	we will be
seréis	you will be
serán	they will be

tener to have

present tense

tengo	I have
tienes	you have
tiene	he/she has
tenemos	we have
tenéis	you have
tienen	they have

past tense

tuve	I had
tuviste	you had
tuvo	he/she had
tuvimos	we had
tuvisteis	you had
tuvieron	they had

future tense

tendré	I will have
tendrás	you will have
tendrá	he/she will have
tendremos	we will have
tendréis	you will have
tendrán	they will have

venir to come

present tense

vengo	I come
vienes	you come
viene	he/she comes
venimos	we come
venís	you come
vienen	they come

past tense

vine	I came
viniste	you came
vino	he/she came
vinimos	we came
vinisteis	you came
vinieron	they came

future tense

vendré	I will come
vendrás	you will come
vendrá	he/she will come
vendremos	we will come
vendréis	you will come
vendrán	they will come

ver to see

present tense

veo	I see
ves	you see
ve	he/she sees
vemos	we see
veis	you see
ven	they see

past tense

vi	I saw
viste	you saw
vio	he/she saw
vimos	we saw
visteis	you saw
vieron	they saw

future tense

veré	I will see
verás	you will see
verá	he/she will see
veremos	we will see
veréis	you will see
verán	they will see

levantarse to stand up

present tense

me levanto	I stand up
te levantas	you stand up
se levanta	he/she stands up
nos levantamos	we stand up
os levantáis	you stand up
se levantan	they stand up

past tense

me levanté	I stood up
te levantaste	you stood up
se levantó	he/she stood up
nos levantamos	we stood up
os levantasteis	you stood up
se levantaron	they stood up

future tense

me levantaré	I will stand up
te levantarás	you will stand up
se levantará	he/she will stand up
nos levantaremos	we will stand up
os levantaréis	you will stand up
se levantarán	they will stand up

Aa

a determiner

> 🔑 **LANGUAGE**
> Use **un** before a masculine noun (like **coche**), and **una** before a feminine noun (like **escuela**).

1 **un** *masc.,* **una** *fem.*
   a car un coche
   a school una escuela
   He's a very clever boy. Es un chico muy inteligente.
2 (*when saying how many times*) **al** *masc.,* **a la** *fem.*
   twice a day dos veces al día
   three times a week tres veces a la semana
3 (*no translation*)
   My dad's a doctor. Mi padre es médico.

> 🔑 **LANGUAGE**
> In Spanish you don't use **un** or **una** when saying what somebody's job is.

able adjective

1 **David isn't able to come.** David no puede venir.
2 **Helen isn't able to swim.** Helen no sabe nadar.

> 🔑 **LANGUAGE**
> Translate 'be able to' using the verb **poder** (can) but when it means 'know how to' use **saber**.

about adverb

1 (*with numbers*) **unos** *masc. plural,* **unas** *fem. plural*
   about fifteen boys unos quince chicos
   It costs about a hundred euros. Cuesta unos cien euros.
2 (*with time*) **alrededor de**
   We go to school at about eight. Vamos a la escuela alrededor de las ocho.

about preposition

1 (*on the subject of*) **sobre**
   a book about animals un libro sobre los animales
   What's the book about? ¿De qué trata el libro?
2 (*with 'talk'*) **de**
   to talk about something hablar de algo
3 (*with an infinitive*) **a punto de**
   We're about to go out. Estamos a punto de salir.

above preposition

1 **encima de**
   My grandparents live above a shop. Mis abuelos viven encima de una tienda.
2 (*with verbs showing movement*) **por encima de**
   The plane is flying above the town. El avión vuela por encima de la ciudad.

above adverb
   arriba
   It's on the shelf above. Está en el estante de arriba.

abroad adverb

1 **en el extranjero**
   They live abroad. Viven en el extranjero.
2 (*with verbs showing movement*) **al extranjero**
   to go abroad ir al extranjero
   We always travel abroad. Viajamos siempre al extranjero.

absent adjective
   ausente *masc. & fem.*
   Max is absent today. Max está ausente hoy.

accent noun
   el **acento** *masc.*

• *Languages and nationalities do not take a capital letter in Spanish.*

Marie has a French accent. Marie tiene acento francés.

to **accept** verb
aceptar

accident noun
1 el **accidente** masc.
to have an accident tener un accidente
a car accident un accidente de coche
2 **by accident** sin querer
She did it by accident. Lo hizo sin querer.

accidentally adverb
sin querer
He accidentally knocked over the glass. Tiró el vaso al suelo sin querer.

to **accuse** verb
acusar
They accused me of breaking the window. Me acusaron de haber roto la ventana.

to **ache** verb
My arm aches. Me duele el brazo.
Do your legs ache? ¿Te duelen las piernas?

> ⚷ **LANGUAGE**
> Use **duele** or **duelen** (from **doler** 'to hurt') followed by the name of the thing that aches.

acrobat noun
el or la **acróbata** masc. & fem.

across preposition & adverb
1 (going from one side to the other)
to go across cruzar
Richard went across the road. Richard cruzó la calle.
2 (on the other side) **al otro lado de**
They live across the street. Viven al otro lado de la calle.

to **act** verb
(in a play or film) **actuar**
He acts very well. Actúa muy bien.

action noun
la **acción** fem.

active adjective
activo masc., **activa** fem.

activity noun
la **actividad** fem.

actor noun
el **actor** masc.

actress noun
la **actriz** fem. (plural las **actrices**)

actually adverb
en realidad
Actually, this isn't difficult. En realidad esto no es difícil.

to **add** verb
1 (something extra) **añadir**
We have to add more salt. Hay que añadir más sal.
2 (using numbers) **sumar**
Add up the three numbers. Suma los tres números.

address noun
la **dirección** fem. (plural las **direcciones**)
What's your address? ¿Cuál es tu dirección?

adjective noun
el **adjetivo** masc.

> ⚷ **LANGUAGE**
> English = adjective
> Spanish = adjetivo

adult noun
el **adulto** masc., la **adulta** fem.

adventure noun
la **aventura** fem.

> ⚷ **LANGUAGE**
> English = adventure
> Spanish = aventura

adverb noun
el **adverbio** masc.

• The months of the year and days of the week do not take a capital letter in Spanish.

advert noun
el **anuncio** masc.
There are lots of adverts for sweets. Hay muchos anuncios de caramelos.

advice noun
el **consejo** masc.
Can you give me some advice? ¿Puedes darme un consejo?

aerial noun
la **antena** fem.

aeroplane noun
el **avión** masc. (plural los **aviones**)
to travel on an aeroplane viajar en avión

to **afford** verb
tener dinero para comprar
We can't afford a computer. No tenemos dinero para comprarnos un ordenador.

afraid adjective
1 (scared)
I'm afraid. Tengo miedo.
to be afraid of tener miedo a
He's afraid of his brother. Le tiene miedo a su hermano.
I'm afraid to go out by myself. Me da miedo salir sola.
Don't be afraid! ¡No tengas miedo!

LANGUAGE
English = **I am** afraid.
Spanish = **Tengo** miedo. (I have fear.)

2 (sorry)
I'm afraid she's ill. Lo siento pero está enferma.

LANGUAGE
Use **lo siento** to mean 'I'm afraid' when you are sorry about something.

Africa noun
África fem.

African adjective
africano masc., **africana** fem.

• See the centre section for verb tables.

African noun
el **africano** masc., la **africana** fem.

after preposition & conjunction
después de
after my birthday después de mi cumpleaños
after doing something después de hacer algo
After eating I want to watch TV. Después de comer quiero ver la tele.

after adverb
después
What are you doing after? ¿Qué vas a hacer después?

afternoon noun
la **tarde** fem.
in the afternoon por la tarde
at four o'clock in the afternoon a las cuatro de la tarde
this afternoon esta tarde
I'll see you on Sunday afternoon. Te veré el domingo por la tarde.
on Sunday afternoons los domingos por la tarde

afters noun
el **postre** masc.
What's for afters? ¿Qué hay de postre?

afterwards adverb
después
soon afterwards poco después

again adverb
1 **otra vez**
Are you crying again? ¿Otra vez estás llorando?
I'm going to read it again. Voy a leerlo otra vez.
2 (using **volver**)

LANGUAGE
In Spanish you can also use the verb **volver** (to come back) followed by **a** to say you're doing something again.

to do something again volver a hacer algo

We'll see the film again tomorrow. Volveremos a ver la película mañana.

against preposition
contra
Madrid are playing against Barcelona. El Madrid juega contra el Barcelona.

age noun
la **edad** fem.
They're the same age. Tienen la misma edad.
at the age of ten a la edad de diez años
Helen is eight years of age. Helen tiene ocho años.

ago adverb
hace
I started a week ago. Empecé hace una semana.
a long time ago hace mucho tiempo
not very long ago no hace mucho tiempo

> 🔑 **LANGUAGE**
> Hace goes before the amount of time but 'ago' goes after.

to **agree** verb
estar de acuerdo
I agree. Estoy de acuerdo.
I don't agree with you. No estoy de acuerdo contigo.

ahead adverb
delante
I'll go ahead. Yo voy delante.
There's a river ahead. Hay un río delante de nosotros.
Walk straight ahead. Siga todo recto.

air noun
1 el **aire** masc.
in the open air al aire libre
2 to travel by air viajar en avión

air-conditioned adjective
climatizado masc.,
climatizada fem.

air conditioning noun masc.
el **aire condicionado** masc.

airmail noun
to send something by airmail mandar algo por avión

airport noun
el **aeropuerto** masc.

alarm noun
1 la **alarma** fem.
a fire alarm una alarma contra incendios
2 an alarm clock un despertador masc.

album noun
el **álbum** masc.
a photo album un álbum de fotos

A levels plural noun
los exámenes del final de la enseñanza secundaria masc. plural

> 🌍 **CULTURE**
> Students usually take A levels in the last two years before leaving school. In Spanish schools the last two years are known as el bachillerato, and students take an exam after this if they want to go on to university.

alien noun
el or la **extraterrestre** masc. & fem.

alike adjective
to look alike parecerse
My two brothers look alike. Mis dos hermanos se parecen.

alive adjective
vivo masc., **viva** fem.
Is it alive? ¿Está vivo?

all adjective
todo masc., **toda** fem.
all the cake todo el pastel
all the boys todos los chicos

• Use **el** and **uno** for masculine words and **la** and **una** for feminine words.

all the girls todas las chicas
all week toda la semana

all pronoun
1 (*everything*) **todo**
That's all. Es todo.
He's eaten it all. Se lo ha comido
todo.
2 (*everyone*) **todos** *masc. plural*,
todas *fem. plural*
We're all going. Vamos a ir todos.
All of them are very pretty. Son
todas muy guapas.

all adverb
1 **todo**
I'm all wet. Estoy todo mojado.
2 **completamente**
all by myself completamente solo

allergic adjective
alérgico *masc.*, **alérgica** *fem.*
I'm allergic to milk. Soy alérgico a
la leche.

alleyway noun
el **callejón** *masc.* (plural los
callejones)

alligator noun
el **aligátor** *masc.*, el **caimán** *masc.*
(plural los **caimanes**)

allowed adjective
1 I'm allowed to watch TV.
Me dejan ver la tele.
She's not allowed out. No la dejan
salir.
2 That's not allowed. Está
prohibido.

🔑 **LANGUAGE**
Use *dejar* (to let) for saying somebody is
allowed to do something. Word for word
'I'm allowed to do' is 'They let me do' in
Spanish.

all right adjective & adverb
1 (*good, well*) **bien**
to be all right estar bien
How are you? – All right. ¿Cómo
estás? – Bien.

2 (*not so bad*); **no mal**
to be all right no estar mal
Do you like your teacher? – He's all
right. ¿Te gusta tu maestro? – No
está mal.
3 (*with verbs starting with 'to'*)
Is it all right to open the window?
¿Se puede abrir la ventana?

🔑 **LANGUAGE**
Use *poder* (can) in this meaning (Can I
open the window?).

all right exclamation
1 **¡bueno!**
All right, I'm coming! ¡Bueno, ya
voy!
All right, let's begin. ¡Bueno!
Vamos a empezar.
2 (*saying yes*) **¡vale!**
Do you want to come with us? – All
right! ¿Quieres venir con nosotros?
– ¡Vale!

almost adverb
casi
It's almost finished. Está casi
terminado.

alone adjective
1 **solo** *masc.*, **sola** *fem.*
Don't go out alone. No salgas sola.
We're all alone. Estamos
completamente solos.
2 Leave me alone! ¡Déjame en paz!
Leave my bike alone! ¡No toques
mi bici!

along preposition & adverb
1 **por**
Let's run along the beach. Vamos a
correr por la playa.
2 (*from one end to the other*) **a lo largo de**
There are trees along the street.
Hay árboles a lo largo de la calle.

aloud adverb
en voz alta
Read these words aloud. Lee estas
palabras en voz alta.

a
b
c
d
e
f
g
h
i
j
k
l
m
n
o
p
q
r
s
t
u
v
w
x
y
z

• *Languages and nationalities do not take a capital letter in Spanish.*

alphabet noun
el **alfabeto** *masc.*

alphabetical adjective
Put them in alphabetical order.
Ponlos en orden alfabético.

already adverb
ya
Vicky has already left. Vicky ya se
ha ido.

also adverb
también
I also have a sister. También tengo
una hermana.

although conjunction
aunque
**Although I'm tired, I will help
you.** Aunque estoy cansado, te voy
a ayudar.

altogether adverb
en total
That's fifteen euros altogether.
Son quince euros en total.

always adverb
siempre
I always win! ¡Siempre gano!

am verb SEE **be**
I'm in the garden. Estoy en el
jardín.
I'm English. Soy inglés.

a.m. abbreviation
de la mañana
at six a.m. a las seis de la mañana

amazing adjective
1 (*really good or unusual*)
extraordinario *masc.*,
extraordinaria *fem.*
She's an amazing pupil. Es una
alumna extraordinaria.
2 (*really surprising*) **increíble**
Amazing! ¡Increíble! ·

ambulance noun
la **ambulancia** *fem.*

America noun
1 los **Estados Unidos** *masc. plural*
My grandparents live in America.
Mis abuelos viven en los Estados
Unidos.
2 (*continent*) **América** *fem.*

> **⚿ LANGUAGE**
> Be careful: América can mean the United
> States but it usually means either the
> continent of America or Latin America.

American adjective
norteamericano *masc.*,
norteamericana *fem.*
an American film una película
norteamericana
He's American. Es
norteamericano.

American noun
el **norteamericano** *masc.*,
la **norteamericana** *fem.*
We have an American in our class.
Tenemos un norteamericano en
nuestra clase .

among preposition
entre
She's the only girl among six boys.
Es la única chica entre seis chicos.

amount noun
la **cantidad** *fem.*
a large amount of money una
gran cantidad de dinero

amusement arcade noun
el **salón de juegos** *masc.*

an determiner
un *masc.*, **una** *fem.*
an egg un huevo
an orange una naranja

> **⚿ LANGUAGE**
> Use un before a masculine noun (like
> huevo), and una before a feminine noun
> (like naranja).

· *The months of the year and days of the week do not take a capital letter in Spanish.*

and conjunction
1 y
the tables and chairs las mesas y las sillas
Arthur and Martin Arthur y Martin
2 e
I speak Spanish and English. Hablo español e inglés.

⚷ **LANGUAGE**
Use e instead of y before words beginning with the 'i' sound (pronounced 'ee').

angel noun
el **ángel** masc.

angry adjective
enfadado masc., **enfadada** fem.
I'm angry with you. Estoy enfadado contigo.
to get angry enfadarse
I get angry with my brother. Me enfado con mi hermano.

animal noun
el **animal** masc.

ankle noun
el **tobillo** masc.

anniversary noun
el **aniversario** masc.
It's their wedding anniversary. Es su aniversario de boda.

to **annoy** verb
molestar
My cousin annoys me. Mi primo me molesta.

annoyed adjective
enfadado masc., **enfadada** fem.
I'm annoyed with you. Estoy enfadado contigo.

annoying adjective
to be annoying molestar
This noise is very annoying. Este ruido me molesta mucho.

anorak noun
el **anorak** masc. (plural los **anoraks**)

• See the centre section for verb tables.

another adjective
otro masc., **otra** fem.
another day otro día
Another juice? ¿Otro zumo?
I want another one. Quiero otro.
another ten kilometres diez kilómetros más

answer noun
la **respuesta** fem.
The answer is right. La respuesta es correcta.
The answer is wrong. La respuesta está mal.

to **answer** verb
1 contestar
He doesn't answer. No contesta.
2 contestar a
I can't answer the question. No puedo contestar a la pregunta.

ant noun
la **hormiga** fem.

anthem noun
the national anthem el himno nacional masc.

antibiotic noun
el **antibiótico** masc.
He's on antibiotics. Está tomando antibióticos.

any adjective
(no translation)
Do you have any bread? ¿Tienes pan?
Tell me if you have any problems. Dime si tienes problemas.
Would you like any water? ¿Quieres agua?
I don't have any time. No tengo tiempo.
She doesn't have any money. No tiene dinero.

⚷ **LANGUAGE**
When 'any' is used in questions, with negatives ('not', 'never', etc.), and after 'if', there is usually no translation.

any pronoun
(no translation)
We need to buy some fish but there isn't any. Necesitamos comprar pescado pero no hay.

🔑 **LANGUAGE**
When 'any' refers to singular nouns like 'fish', it is usually not translated.

any adverb
She doesn't come here any more. Ya no viene aquí.
I'm not hungry any more. No tengo más hambre.

🔑 **LANGUAGE**
To mean 'not any more' use ya no or no ... más

anybody pronoun
1 (in questions and with 'if') **alguién**
Has anybody seen my glasses? ¿Alguién ha visto mis gafas?
2 (with negatives and 'if') **nadie**
I don't know anybody. No conozco a nadie.

anyone pronoun SEE **anybody**

anything pronoun
1 (in questions and with 'if') **algo**
Are you looking for anything? ¿Buscas algo?
Tell me if you want anything. Dime si quieres algo.
2 (with negatives and 'if') **nada**
He doesn't do anything. No hace nada.
I don't have anything to do. No tengo nada que hacer.
There isn't anything to eat. No hay nada de comer.

anywhere adverb
1 (in questions and with 'if') **en alguna parte**
Have you seen my gloves anywhere? ¿Has visto mis guantes en alguna parte?
2 (with negatives and 'if') **en ninguna parte**

I can't find them anywhere. No los encuentro en ninguna parte.
We're not going anywhere. No vamos a ninguna parte.

🔑 **LANGUAGE**
When 'anywhere' means 'to' a place use a with parte instead of en.

apart adverb
apart from menos
They're all here apart from him. Todos están aquí menos él.

to **apologize** verb
pedir perdón
He apologized to me. Me pidió perdón.
I apologize! ¡Lo siento!

apostrophe noun
el **apóstrofo** masc.

apple noun
la **manzana** fem.
apple juice el zumo de manzana
an apple tree un manzano

appointment noun
(with a doctor, hairdresser, etc.)
la **hora** fem.
I have a doctor's appointment. Tengo hora en el médico.
My mum has to make an appointment. Mi madre tiene que pedir hora.

April noun
1 **abril** masc.
in April en abril
They arrive on the tenth of April. Llegan el diez de abril.
2 **April Fools' Day** el día de los Santos Inocentes

🌍 **CULTURE**
El día de los Santos Inocentes (the Feast of the Holy Innocents) is similar to April Fools' Day and is celebrated on 28 December. There's a tradition of sticking a paper doll on somebody's back as a joke.

• Use **el** and **uno** for masculine words and **la** and **una** for feminine words.

apron noun
el **delantal** *masc.*

Arab adjective
árabe *masc. & fem.*
the Arab countries los países
árabes

Arab noun
el or la **árabe** *masc. & fem.*

are verb SEE **be**
We're in the kitchen. Estamos en
la cocina.
Where are you? ¿Dónde estás?
They're English. Son ingleses.

area noun
(*of a country, town, etc.*) la **zona** *fem.*
a play area una zona para juegos
infantiles

Argentina noun
Argentina *fem.*

Argentinian adjective
argentino *masc.*, **argentina** *fem.*

Argentinian noun
el **argentino** *masc.*,
la **argentina** *fem.*

to **argue** verb
discutir
They're always arguing. Siempre
están discutiendo.

argument noun
la **discusión** *fem.*
We had an argument. Tuvimos
una discusión.

arm noun
el **brazo** *masc.*

armchair noun
el **sillón** *masc.* (plural los **sillones**)

army noun
el ejército *masc.*
He's in the army. Está en el
ejército.

around preposition & adverb
1 **alrededor de**
We sit around the fire. Nos
sentamos alrededor del fuego.
I get up around seven. Me levanto
alrededor de las siete.
My mum's around forty. Mi madre
tiene unos cuarenta años.
2 (*with places or countries*) **por**
They travel around Europe. Viajan
por Europa.
around here por aquí
My dad's somewhere around.
Mi padre está por ahí.

to **arrive** verb
llegar
I arrive at nine. Llego a las
nueve.

arrow noun
la **flecha** *fem.*

art noun
1 (*in school*) el **dibujo** *masc.*
an art class una clase de
dibujo
2 el **arte** *masc.*
Spanish art el arte español
an art gallery un museo

🔑 **LANGUAGE**
Museo also means 'museum'.

artist noun
el or la **artista** *masc. & fem.*
He's an artist. Es artista.

as conjunction & preposition
1 **como**
as you know como sabes
My teacher treats me as a
friend. Mi maestro me trata como
amigo.
2 as well también
Is Juan coming as well? ¿Viene
Juan también?
3 (*when comparing*)
as ... as tan ... como
I'm as tall as my mother. Soy tan
alta como mi madre.

• *Languages and nationalities do not take a capital letter in Spanish.*

a
b
c
d
e
f
g
h
i
j
k
l
m
n
o
p
q
r
s
t
u
v
w
x
y
z

4 as much tanto *masc.*, tanta *fem.*
I have as much money as you.
Tengo tanto dinero como tú.

5 as many tantos *masc. plural*, tantas *fem. plural*
Paul has as many apples as me.
Paul tiene tantas manzanas como yo.

LANGUAGE
Tanto ... como means 'as much as' in the singular and 'as many as' in the plural.

ashamed adjective
I'm ashamed. Me da vergüenza.
Aren't you ashamed? ¿No te da vergüenza?
She's ashamed of her sister. Le da vergüenza su hermana.

LANGUAGE
Vergüenza means 'shame' so word for word Me da vergüenza is 'It gives me shame'.

Asia noun
Asia *fem.*

Asian adjective
1 (*from India*) **indio** *masc.*, **india** *fem.*
2 (*from Pakistan*) **paquistaní** *masc. & fem.*
3 (*from Asia*) **asiático** *masc.*, **asiática** *fem.*

Asian noun
1 (*from India*) el **indio** *masc.*, la **india** *fem.*
2 (*from Pakistan*) el or la **paquistaní** *masc. & fem.*
3 (*from Asia*) el **asiático** *masc.*, la **asiática** *fem.*

to **ask** verb
1 preguntar
I'm going to ask. Voy a preguntar.
to ask somebody something preguntar algo a alguien
Ask your teacher. Pregúntale a tu maestra.

2 to ask a question hacer una pregunta
Can I ask you a question? ¿Puedo hacerte una pregunta?
3 to ask for something pedir algo
Sophie asked me for a pen. Sophie me pidió un bolígrafo.
4 (*invite*) **invitar**
Jim has asked me to the party. Jim me ha invitado a la fiesta.

asleep adjective
dormido *masc.*, **dormida** *fem.*, **durmiendo**
She's asleep. Está dormida or durmiendo.

assembly noun
la **reunión de maestros y alumnos** *fem.*

CULTURE
Spanish schools do not have assemblies.

assistant noun
1 (*in a shop*) el **dependiente** *masc.*, la **dependienta** *fem.*
2 (*in the classroom*) el **profesor auxiliar** *masc.*, la **profesora auxiliar** *fem.*
3 (*for languages*) el or la **ayudante** *masc. & fem.*

asthma noun
el **asma** *fem.*
I have asthma. Tengo asma.

LANGUAGE
Be careful: you use el with asma but it is not a masculine noun.

astronaut noun
el or la **astronauta** *masc. & fem.*

at preposition
1 en
at school en la escuela
at home en casa
We're at Jason's. Estamos en casa de Jason.
at the station en la estación

• The months of the year and days of the week do not take a capital letter in Spanish.

2 (*with time, ages*) **a**
I go to bed at eight. Me acuesto a las ocho.
at midnight a medianoche
3 at night por la noche
at last por fin

athlete noun
el or la **atleta** *masc. & fem.*

Atlantic noun
el **Atlántico** *masc.*

atlas noun
el **atlas** *masc.* (plural los **atlas**)

attack noun
el **ataque** *masc.*
an asthma attack un ataque de asma

to **attack** verb
atacar

to **attend** verb
to attend school ir a la escuela

attention noun
la **atención** *fem.*
Pay attention! ¡Prestad atención!
Pay attention to what you're doing! ¡Pon or Presta atención en lo que estás haciendo!

attractive adjective
guapo *masc.*, **guapa** *fem.*
a very attractive girl una niña muy guapa

audience noun
el **público** *masc.*

August noun
agosto *masc.*
We're going on holiday in August. Nos vamos de vacaciones en agosto.
The plane leaves on the tenth of August. El avión sale el diez de agosto.

• *See the centre section for verb tables.*

aunt, **aunty** noun
la **tía** *fem.*
She's my aunt. Es mi tía.
my aunt and uncle mis tíos
We've invited Aunty Ruth. Hemos invitado a la tía Ruth.

au pair noun
el or la **au pair** *masc. & fem.*

Australia noun
Australia *fem.*
My cousins live in Australia. Mis primos viven en Australia.

Australian adjective
australiano *masc.*, **australiana** *fem.*
She's Australian. Es australiana.

Australian noun
el **australiano** *masc.*, la **australiana** *fem.*

Austria noun
Austria *fem.*

Austrian noun
el **austriaco** *masc.*, la **austriaca** *fem.*

author noun
el **escritor** *masc.*, la **escritora** *fem.*
He's a well-known author. Es un escritor muy conocido.
the author of the book el autor or la autora del libro

autumn noun
el **otoño** *masc.*
in the autumn en otoño

average adjective
1 medio *masc.*, **media** *fem.*
I'm average height. Soy de estatura media.
2 (*not good or bad*) **regular** *masc. & fem.*
What's the food like? – Average. ¿Qué tal la comida? – Regular.

average noun
1 la **media** *fem.*
an average of four a day una media de cuatro al día
2 el **promedio** *masc.*
twice a week, on average dos veces a la semana, como promedio
Work out the average. Encuentra el promedio.

to **avoid** verb
evitar

awake adjective
despierto *masc.*, **despierta** *fem.*
Are you awake? ¿Estás despierto?

away adverb
1 (*absent*)
The teacher is away today. La maestra no está hoy.
She's away in Spain. Está en España.

My parents are away until tomorrow. Mis padres están fuera hasta mañana.
2 far away lejos
I live far away from school. Vivo lejos de la escuela.
It's five kilometres away. Está a cinco kilómetros.

> **LANGUAGE**
> When you talk about how far something is from something else, use **a** in front of the number.

awful adjective
1 **horrible** *masc. & fem.*
I don't like this awful weather. No me gusta este tiempo horrible.
How awful! ¡Qué horror!
2 (*film, book, concert, etc.*)
malísimo *masc.*, **malísima** *fem.*
This book is awful. Este libro es malísimo.

Bb

baby noun
1 el **bebé** *masc.*
2 el **niño** *masc.*, la **niña** *fem.*
a baby boy un niño
a baby girl una niña
Don't be a baby! ¡No seas niño!

> **LANGUAGE**
> In Spanish **niño** can also mean 'child'.

to **babysit** verb
hacer de canguro
We babysit for our neighbours. Hacemos de canguro para los vecinos.

babysitter noun
el or la **canguro** *masc. & fem.*

back noun
1 (*of a person*) la **espalda** *fem.*

My back hurts. Me duele la espalda.
I sleep on my back. Duermo boca arriba.

> **LANGUAGE**
> Word for word **boca arriba** means 'with your mouth up'!

2 (*of an animal*) el **lomo** *masc.*
3 (*of a house or car*) la **parte de atrás** *fem.*
They're playing at the back of the house. Están jugando en la parte de atrás de la casa.
I'll sit in the back. Yo me siento atrás.
4 (*of a room, drawer, cupboard*) el **fondo** *masc.*
I always sit at the back of the class. Siempre me siento al fondo de la clase.

• Use **el** and **uno** for masculine words and **la** and **una** for feminine words.

back adjective
1 **de atrás**
the back seat el asiento de atrás
the back door la puerta de atrás
2 (page, row) **último** masc.,
última fem.
the back row la última fila

back adverb
1 (using 'volver' for saying that somebody comes back)
I'll be back in ten minutes. Volveré dentro de diez minutos.
When are you back from Madrid? ¿Cuándo vuelves de Madrid?
to come back volver
2 (to look, move, lean) **hacia atrás**
Take two steps back. Dad dos pasos hacia atrás.
3 back to front al revés
You've put your sweater on back to front. Te has puesto el jersey al revés.

backpack noun
la **mochila** fem.

backwards adverb
1 **hacia atrás**
Don't lean backwards. No te eches hacia atrás.
2 **al revés**
Your T-shirt's on backwards. Llevas la camiseta al revés.

bacon noun
el **bacon** masc.
bacon and eggs los huevos con bacon

bad adjective
1 **malo** masc., **mala** fem.
a bad book un libro malo
a very bad idea una idea muy mala

> 🔑 **LANGUAGE**
> You can also use malo and mala before the noun, but then the masculine singular malo becomes mal.

It's bad weather. Hace mal tiempo.
I have bad news. Tengo malas noticias.
Rick is bad at drawing. A Rick se le da mal el dibujo.
2 (serious) **grave** masc. & fem.
a bad accident un accidente grave
3 **fuerte** masc. & fem.
a bad pain un dolor fuerte
I have a bad cough. Tengo mucha tos.
4 Do you like the film? – It's not bad. ¿Te gusta la película? – No está mal.
How are you? – Not bad! ¿Cómo estás? – ¡Bien!

badge noun
1 (made of plastic or metal) la **chapa** fem.
2 (made of cloth) la **insignia** fem.

badly adverb
1 **mal**
The team is playing very badly. El equipo juega muy mal.
2 badly hurt malherido

badminton noun
el **bádminton** masc.
Miguel plays badminton. Miguel juega al bádminton.

bag noun
1 la **bolsa** fem.
a carrier bag una bolsa de plástico
2 el **bolso**
The lady has lost her bag. La señora ha perdido el bolso.

> 🔑 **LANGUAGE**
> When you mean a woman's handbag, use bolso, not bolsa.

bagpipes plural noun
la **gaita** fem.
Alistair plays the bagpipes. Alistair toca la gaita.

• Languages and nationalities do not take a capital letter in Spanish.

a
b
c
d
e
f
g
h
i
j
k
l
m
n
o
p
q
r
s
t
u
v
w
x
y
z

English Spanish

a
b
c
d
e
f
g
h
i
j
k
l
m
n
o
p
q
r
s
t
u
v
w
x
y
z

to **bake** verb
to bake something hacer algo al horno
to bake a cake hacer un pastel
a baked potato una patata asada

baked beans plural noun
las **judías con salsa de tomate** fem. plural

 CULTURE
Baked beans are not eaten in Spain.

baker noun
el **panadero** masc.,
la **panadera** fem.
He's a baker. Es panadero.
the baker's shop la panadería
I'm going to the baker's. Voy a la panadería.

balance noun
el **equilibrio** masc.
I lost my balance. Perdí el equilibrio.

balcony noun
el **balcón** masc. (plural los **balcones**)

bald adjective
calvo masc., **calva** fem.
He's bald. Es calvo.

ball noun
1 (for tennis, rugby, golf, etc.) la **pelota** fem.
a tennis ball una pelota de tenis
2 (for football) el **balón** masc. (plural los **balones**)

ballet dancing noun
el **ballet** masc.

balloon noun
el **globo** masc.
There are lots of balloons for the party. Hay muchos globos para la fiesta.

⚠ **FALSE FRIEND**
a balloon = **un globo** (not un balón)

ballpoint pen noun
el **bolígrafo** masc.

banana noun
el **plátano** masc.

band noun
1 (playing rock or pop music) el **grupo** masc.
a rock band un grupo de rock
They've formed a band. Han formado un grupo.
2 (playing music with trumpets, saxophones) la **orquesta** fem.

bandage noun
la **venda** fem.

bang noun
1 (noise, knock) el **golpe** masc.
Did you hear a bang on the door? ¿Oíste un golpe en la puerta?
2 (of a bomb etc.) la **explosión** fem.

to **bang** verb
1 (to knock)
Jack banged his knee. Jack se dio un golpe en la rodilla.
2 (to slam)
to bang the door dar un portazo
She always bangs the door. Siempre da portazos.

bank noun
1 (for money) el **banco** masc.
Dad's going to the bank. Papá va a ir al banco.
2 (at the side of a river) la **orilla** fem.
I sat down on the river bank. Me senté a la orilla del río.

bar noun
1 (made of metal) la **barra** fem.
an iron bar una barra de hierro
2 (place selling drinks) el **bar** masc.; (counter for buying drinks) la **barra** fem.
3 **a bar of chocolate** una tableta de chocolate
a bar of soap una pastilla de jabón

barbecue noun
la **barbacoa** fem.

• *The months of the year and days of the week do not take a capital letter in Spanish.*

bare adjective
(*arms, walls, etc.*) **desnudo** *masc.*,
desnuda *fem.*
with bare feet descalzo *masc.*,
descalza *fem.*

to **bark** verb
ladrar
Mi perro ladra mucho. My dog
barks a lot.

baseball noun
el **béisbol** *masc.*
Ahmed is playing baseball.
Ahmed juega al béisbol.
a baseball cap una gorra de
béisbol

basement noun
el **sótano** *masc.*

to **bash** verb
William bashed his knee. William
se dio un golpe en la rodilla.

basin noun
(*for washing*) el **lavabo** *masc.*

basket noun
la **cesta** *fem.*
a shopping basket una cesta de la
compra

basketball noun
el **baloncesto** *masc.*
Do you play basketball? ¿Juegas
al baloncesto?

bat noun
1 (*for cricket or baseball*) el **bate** *masc.*
2 (*for table tennis*) la **pala** *fem.*
3 (*flying animal*) el **murciélago** *masc.*

bath noun
1 (*wash*) el **baño** *masc.*
a hot bath un baño caliente
I want to have a bath. Quiero
bañarme., Quiero darme un baño.
2 (*container you sit in*) la **bañera** *fem.*
**There's too much water in the
bath.** Hay demasiada agua en la
bañera.

• *See the centre section for verb tables.*

bathroom noun
el **cuarto de baño** *masc.*

battery noun
(*for a torch, radio, camera, toy*) la **pila** *fem.*

⚠ **FALSE FRIEND**
a battery = una pila (*not* una batería)

battle noun
la **batalla** *fem.*

to **be** verb

⚿ **LANGUAGE**
Be careful: in Spanish there are two main
verbs for translating 'be': ser and estar.

1 ser
I'm English. Soy inglés.
Are you my friend? ¿Eres mi
amigo?
She's tall. Es alta.
It's not a problem. No es
problema.
It's six o'clock. Son las seis.
It's the fifth of June. Es el cinco de
junio.
When is it? ¿Cuándo es?
We're Spanish. Somos españoles.
You're my friends. Sois mis
amigos.
Are you Mrs Sanders? ¿Es usted la
señora Sanders?
They're friendly. Son simpáticos.
Two and two are four. Dos y dos
son cuatro.

⚿ **LANGUAGE**
Use ser when you're talking about
something permanent or saying what
something is, and with time and dates.

2 estar
I'm in the garden. Estoy en el
jardín.
I'm playing the clarinet. Estoy
tocando el clarinete.
How are you, Pete? ¿Cómo estás,
Pete?
Are you sad? ¿Estás triste?
He's in London. Está en Londres.

English Spanish

a
b
c
d
e
f
g
h
i
j
k
l
m
n
o
p
q
r
s
t
u
v
w
x
y
z

We're very tired. Estamos muy cansados.
Are you ready? ¿Estáis listos?
What are they doing? ¿Qué están haciendo?
My father has been ill. Mi padre ha estado enfermo.

> 🔑 **LANGUAGE**
> Use estar when you're talking about where something is, or about something that normally lasts only a short time, and when translating English verbs made up of 'be' and a verb ending in '-ing' (e.g. 'I'm doing' is estoy haciendo).

3 tener
I'm hot. Tengo calor.
Are you sleepy? ¿Tienes sueño?
We're hungry. Tenemos hambre.
I'm eleven. Tengo once años.
She's nine. Tiene nueve años.

> 🔑 **LANGUAGE**
> English = I am hot/cold/hungry/thirsty/scared/6 years old.
> Spanish = Tengo calor/frío/hambre/sed/miedo/6 años.

4 (when talking about the weather) **hacer**
It's hot. Hace calor.
It's very sunny. Hace mucho sol.

> 🔑 **LANGUAGE**
> With the weather 'it is' = hacer

> 🔑 **LANGUAGE**
> To translate questions such as 'isn't it?' or 'aren't you?', you can use either ¿no? or ¿verdad?, e.g. 'She's English, isn't she?' is Es inglesa, ¿no? or Es inglesa, ¿verdad?

beach noun
la **playa** fem.

bean noun
la judía fem.
baked beans las judías con salsa de tomate
green beans las judías verdes

bear noun
el **oso** masc.

beard noun
la **barba** fem.
My dad has a beard. Mi padre tiene barba.

to **beat** verb
1 ganar
to beat somebody ganarle a alguien
I beat my sister at chess. Le gané a mi hermana al ajedrez.
Their team has beaten us. Su equipo nos ha ganado.
2 to beat somebody up golpear a alguien
They beat me up. Me golpearon.

beautiful adjective
1 (very attractive) **precioso** masc., **preciosa** fem.
What a beautiful dress! ¡Qué vestido más precioso!
2 (pretty) **bonito** masc., **bonita** fem.
What a beautiful skirt! ¡Qué falda tan bonita!
3 (baby, girl, woman) **muy guapo** masc., **muy guapa** fem.
a beautiful girl una chica muy guapa

> 🔑 **LANGUAGE**
> You can also say hermoso in Spanish, e.g. una mujer hermosa (a beautiful woman).

4 (very good) **muy bueno** masc., **muy buena** fem.
The weather's beautiful. Hace muy buen tiempo.

because conjunction
1 porque
I can't go out because I'm ill. No puedo salir porque estoy enfermo.
2 because of (when blaming somebody) por culpa de
I was late because of my brother. Llegué tarde por culpa de mi hermano.
because of you por tu culpa

• Use **el** and **uno** for masculine words and **la** and **una** for feminine words.

to **become** verb
1 hacerse
We became friends. Nos hicimos amigos.
She became famous. Se hizo famosa.
2 ponerse
to become very angry ponerse furioso
She became ill. Se puso enferma.
3 llegar a ser
He later became king. Más tarde llegó a ser rey.

bed noun
1 la **cama** *fem.*
I'm in bed. Estoy en la cama.
2 to go to bed acostarse
Claire goes to bed at nine. Claire se acuesta a las nueve.
I'm going to bed. Me voy a la cama.

bedroom noun
el **dormitorio** *masc.*
She's in her bedroom. Está en su dormitorio.

bedtime noun
It's bedtime. Ya es hora de irse a la cama.
Bedtime! ¡A la cama!

bee noun
la **abeja** *fem.*

beef noun
la **carne de vaca** *fem.*

been verb SEE **be**
I've never been to Spain. No he estado nunca en España.
It's been an exciting game. Ha sido un partido emocionante.

beer noun
la **cerveza** *fem.*

beetle noun
el **escarabajo** *masc.*

beetroot noun
la **remolacha** *fem.*

before preposition & conjunction
antes de
before Sunday antes del domingo
before doing something antes de hacer algo
We want to watch TV before doing our homework. Queremos ver la tele antes de hacer los deberes.

before adverb
1 antes
I saw her two weeks before. La vi dos semanas antes.
2 (*already*) **ya**
Have you read this book before? ¿Ya has leído este libro?

to **begin** verb
empezar
My classes begin at nine. Mi clases empiezan a las nueve.
It's beginning to rain. Está empezando a llover.

beginner noun
el or la **principiante** *masc. & fem.*
I'm a beginner. Soy principiante.

beginning noun
el **principio** *masc.*
At the beginning it's very easy. Al principio es muy fácil.

to **behave** verb
portarse
Simon behaves badly in class. Simon se porta mal en clase.

behaviour noun
el **comportamiento** *masc.*

behind preposition & adverb
1 detrás de
behind the door detrás de la puerta
2 detrás
The tallest children behind! ¡Los niños más altos detrás!

being verb SEE **be**
She likes being an only child. Le gusta ser hija única.

• *Languages and nationalities do not take a capital letter in Spanish.*

being noun
  a human being un ser humano

Belgian adjective
  belga masc. & fem.
  He's Belgian. Es belga.

Belgian noun
  el or la **belga** masc. & fem.

Belgium noun
  Bélgica fem.

to **believe** verb
  creer
  I believe you. Te creo.
  Do you believe it? ¿Lo crees?
  They don't believe in ghosts.
  No creen en fantasmas.

bell noun
  1 (on a door or bicycle) el **timbre** masc.
  to ring the bell tocar el timbre
  2 (electric bell in school) el **timbre** masc.
  The bell's gone. Ha sonado el
  timbre.
  3 (of a church) la **campana** fem.
  The church bells are ringing.
  Suenan las campanas.

to **belong** verb
  1 (to somebody) **ser de**
  This bike belongs to David. Esta
  bici es de David.
  Who does this pen belong to?
  ¿De quién es este bolígrafo?
  It belongs to me. Es mío.
  2 (to be part of a group) **ser socio** or **socia
  de**
  Does she belong to any club?
  ¿Es socia de algún club?

below preposition
  debajo de
  the flat below ours el piso debajo
  del nuestro

below adverb
  abajo
  down below in the street abajo en
  la calle

It's on the shelf below. Está en el
estante de abajo.

belt noun
  1 el **cinturón** masc. (plural los
  cinturones)
  2 (seatbelt in a car) el **cinturón de
  seguridad** masc.

bench noun
  el **banco** masc.

bend noun
  (in the road) la **curva** fem.
  a dangerous bend una curva
  peligrosa

to **bend** verb
  1 **doblar**
  You have to bend your knees.
  Tienes que doblar las rodillas.
  Do not bend. No doblar.
  2 **to bend your head** inclinar la
  cabeza
  to bend over inclinarse
  to bend down agacharse

beneath preposition
  debajo de

beside preposition
  al lado de
  beside the table al lado de la mesa
  Sit down beside me. Siéntate a mi
  lado.

besides preposition & adverb
  1 **además de**
  **Besides maths I have to study
  science.** Además de matemáticas
  tengo que estudiar ciencias.
  2 **además**
  Besides, you're too young.
  Además, eres demasiado joven.

best adjective
  mejor masc. & fem.
  She's my best friend. Es mi mejor
  amiga.
  Which are the best ones? ¿Cuáles
  son los mejores?
  It's best to wait. Lo mejor es
  esperar.

• The months of the year and days of the week do not take a capital letter in Spanish.

best noun
el or la **mejor** *masc. & fem.*
This book is the best. Este libro es el mejor.
She's the best in the class. Es la mejor de la clase.

best adverb
mejor
Liam is the one who plays best. Liam es el que juega mejor.
I like this dress best. Éste es el vestido que más me gusta.

🗝 **LANGUAGE**
Say **más** (more) instead of **mejor** when using **gustar** to translate 'like'.

better adjective
mejor *masc. & fem.*
Your idea is better than mine. Tu idea es mejor que la mía.
Yes, that's better. Sí, eso es mejor.
I'm better now. Ya estoy mejor.
Are you feeling better? ¿Te encuentras mejor?

better adverb
mejor
I play better than you. Juego mejor que tú.
to get better mejorar
Your Spanish has got better. Tu español ha mejorado.
Get better soon! ¡Que te mejores!

between preposition & adverb
1 **entre**
between seven and ten o'clock entre las siete y las diez
2 **in between** en medio
Put it down in between. Ponlo en medio.

Bible noun
la **Biblia** *fem.*

bicycle noun
la **bicicleta** *fem.*
I go to school by bicycle. Voy a la escuela en bicicleta.

• *See the centre section for verb tables.*

Can you ride a bicycle? ¿Sabes montar en bicicleta?

big adjective
1 **grande** *masc. & fem.*
a big garden un jardín grande
Our house is big. Nuestra casa es grande.

🗝 **LANGUAGE**
You can use **grande** before the noun, but before a singular noun it becomes **gran**.

a big surprise una gran sorpresa
her big blue eyes sus grandes ojos azules
2 (*older*) **mayor** *masc. & fem.*
She's my big sister. Es mi hermana mayor.

bike noun
la **bici** *fem.*
by bike en bici

🗝 **LANGUAGE**
Bici is short for **bicicleta**.

bikini noun
el **bikini** *masc.*

bilingual adjective
bilingüe *masc. & fem.*

bill noun
1 (*in a restaurant*) la **cuenta** *fem.*
The bill, please! ¡La cuenta, por favor!
2 (*for gas, electricity, etc.*) el **recibo** *masc.*
the phone bill el recibo del teléfono

bin noun
1 (*for rubbish*) el **cubo de basura** *masc.*
Throw this apple in the bin. Tira esta manzana a la basura.
2 (*wastepaper basket*) la **papelera** *fem.*

binoculars plural noun
los **gemelos** *masc. plural*

biology noun
la **biología** *fem.*

bird noun
el **pájaro** masc.

Biro® noun
el **boli** masc.

🔑 **LANGUAGE**
Boli is short for **boligrafo**.

birth noun
el **nacimiento** masc.
What's your date of birth? ¿Cuál es su fecha de nacimiento?

birthday noun
el **cumpleaños** masc.
My birthday is the fifth of October. Mi cumpleaños es el cinco de octubre.
It's my tenth birthday tomorrow. Mañana cumplo diez años.
a birthday card una tarjeta de cumpleaños
a birthday cake una tarta de cumpleaños
a birthday party una fiesta de cumpleaños
Happy birthday! ¡Feliz cumpleaños!

🔑 **LANGUAGE**
Cumpleaños comes from **cumplir años** ('to complete years').

biscuit noun
la **galleta** fem.

bit noun
1 (a piece) el **trozo** masc.
Would you like that bit of bread? ¿Quieres ese trozo de pan?
Mum cut the apple into little bits. Mamá cortó la manzana en trocitos.
2 (not very much of something)
a bit un poco
I'm a bit tired. Estoy un poco cansado.

to **bite** verb
1 **morder**
My dog doesn't bite. Mi perro no muerde.
2 (talking about an insect) **picar**
I've been bitten by a mosquito. Me ha picado un mosquito.

bitter adjective
amargo masc., **amarga** fem.
It has a bitter taste. Tiene un sabor amargo.

black adjective
negro masc., **negra** fem.
a black car un coche negro
She's black. Es negra.
a black coffee un café solo

black noun
el **negro** masc.
Carol likes black. A Carol le gusta el negro.

blackberry noun
la **mora** fem.

blackboard noun
la **pizarra** fem.
on the blackboard en la pizarra

to **blame** verb
I'm not to blame. Yo no tengo la culpa.
I blame my sister. Mi hermana tiene la culpa.
Don't blame me! ¡No me eches la culpa a mí!
You're to blame for the accident. El accidente es culpa tuya.

blanket noun
la **manta** fem.

blazer noun
(of school uniform) la **chaqueta** fem.

to **bleed** verb
My nose is bleeding. Me sale sangre de la nariz.
I'm bleeding. Me sale sangre.

• Use **el** and **uno** for masculine words and **la** and **una** for feminine words.

to **bless** verb
Bless you! ¡Jesús!

 CULTURE
In Spain people say the name of Jesus when somebody sneezes.

blind adjective
ciego *masc.*, **ciega** *fem.*
He's blind. Es ciego.

blind noun
(*on a window*) la **persiana** *fem.*
Pull down the blinds. Baja las persianas.

block noun
a block of flats un bloque de pisos

blond, or **blonde** adjective
rubio *masc.*, **rubia** *fem.*
Jack has blond hair. Jack tiene el pelo rubio.
Sarah is blonde. Sarah es rubia.

blood noun
la **sangre** *fem.*

blouse noun
la **blusa** *fem.*

to **blow** verb
1 **soplar**
Blow hard. Sopla fuerte.
Blow out the candles. Sopla las velas.
2 **to blow a whistle** tocar un silbato
The referee blew his whistle. El árbitro tocó el silbato.
3 **to blow up a balloon** inflar un globo
4 **to blow your nose** sonarse la nariz
Blow your nose. Suénate la nariz.

blue adjective
azul *masc. & fem.*
a blue shirt una camisa azul

blue noun
el **azul** *masc.*
I prefer blue. Prefiero el azul.

to **blush** verb
ponerse colorado *masc.*, **ponerse colorada** *fem.*
You're blushing! ¡Te estás poniendo colorado!

LANGUAGE
Word for word this means 'to go red'.

board noun
1 la **pizarra** *fem.*
Write on the board. Escribe en la pizarra.
2 (*piece of wood*) la **tabla** *fem.*
an ironing board una tabla de planchar
3 **a board game** un juego de mesa

boarding school noun
el **internado** *masc.*

boat noun
1 el **barco** *masc.*
to go by boat ir en barco
2 (*small boat*) la **barca** *fem.*

body noun
el **cuerpo** *masc.*
a dead body un cadáver

to **boil** verb
hervir
The water is boiling. El agua está hirviendo.
to boil the water hervir el agua
a boiled egg un huevo pasado por agua

boiling adjective
boiling water agua hirviendo
This tea is boiling hot. Este té está hirviendo.
It's a boiling hot day today. Hoy hace muchísimo calor.

bone noun
el **hueso** *masc.*
The dog is looking for a bone. El perro está buscando un hueso.

• *Languages and nationalities do not take a capital letter in Spanish.*

a
b
c
d
e
f
g
h
i
j
k
l
m
n
o
p
q
r
s
t
u
v
w
x
y
z

bonfire noun
la **hoguera** *fem.*
My parents lit a bonfire in the garden. Mis padres encendieron una hoguera en el jardín.

CULTURE
Bonfire Night is not celebrated in Spain but there are many festivals where bonfires and fireworks are lit, such as the Fallas in Valencia every year in March.

book noun
1 el **libro** *masc.*
2 (*exercise book*) el **cuaderno** *masc.*
Close your books. Cerrad los cuadernos.
3 **an address book** una libreta de direcciones

to book verb
reservar
I'd like to book a ticket. Quiero reservar un billete.

bookcase noun
la **estantería** *fem.*

bookshelf noun
el **estante** *masc.*

bookshop noun
la **librería** *fem.*

LANGUAGE
Librería and 'library' are both related to libro (book) but a librería is where you buy books, not where you borrow them. Library is la biblioteca.

boot noun
1 **la bota** *fem.*
football boots las botas de fútbol
2 (*of a car*) el **maletero** *masc.*
Put it in the boot. Ponlo en el maletero.

border noun
la **frontera** *fem.*

bored adjective
aburrido *masc.*, **aburrida** *fem.*
I'm bored. Estoy aburrido.
to get bored aburrirse
I'm getting bored. Me aburro.

boring adjective
aburrido *masc.*, **aburrida** *fem.*
It's boring. Es aburrido.

born adjective
to be born nacer
I was born in London. Nací en Londres.

to borrow verb
pedir prestado
I borrowed a pen. Pedí prestado un boli.
Can I borrow the bike? ¿Me prestas la bici?, ¿Me dejas la bici?

LANGUAGE
Spanish doesn't have a word for 'to borrow'. Prestar means means 'to lend' and dejar means 'to leave' so if you want to borrow something you say ¿Me prestas ... ? (Can you lend me ... ?) or ¿Me dejas ... ? (Can you leave me ... ?).

bossy adjective
mandón *masc.*, **mandona** *fem.*
He's very bossy. Es muy mandón.

LANGUAGE
The plural of the masculine mandón is mandones.

both pronoun & adjective
los **dos** *masc. plural*, las **dos** *fem. plural*
Hassan and James are both tired. Hassan y James están cansados los dos.
both my sisters mis dos hermanas
both hands las dos manos

• *The months of the year and days of the week do not take a capital letter in Spanish.*

to **bother** verb
1 (*to disturb, pester*) **molestar**
  I'm sorry to bother you. Siento molestarle.
2 Don't bother, I'm leaving! ¡No te molestes, me voy!
  I can't be bothered to go. No tengo ganas de ir.

bottle noun
  la **botella** *fem.*

bottom noun
1 (*of a glass, bag, river, street, etc.*) el **fondo** *masc.*
  at the bottom of the garden al fondo del jardín
2 (*of a wall, mountain, etc.*) el **pie** *masc.*
  at the bottom of the stairs al pie de las escaleras
3 (*of a list, page*) el **final** *masc.*
  at the bottom of the page al final de la página
4 (*a part of the body*) el **trasero** *masc.*, el **culo** *masc.*

bottom adjective
  de abajo
  the bottom shelf el estante de abajo
  the bottom part la parte de abajo
  He got the bottom mark. Sacó la nota más baja.
  You're bottom of the class. Eres el último de la clase.

to **bounce** verb
  botar
  This ball doesn't bounce. Esta pelota no bota.

bow noun
1 (*in a ribbon or shoelaces*) el **lazo** *masc.*
  to tie a bow hacer un lazo
2 el **arco** *masc.*
  bow and arrow arco y flecha

• *See the centre section for verb tables.*

bowl noun
  el **tazón** *masc.* (plural los **tazones**)
  a bowl of cereal un tazón de cereales

bowling noun
  los **bolos** *masc. plural*
  We go bowling every Friday. Jugamos a los bolos todos los viernes.
  a bowling alley una bolera

box noun
1 la **caja** *fem.*
  a box of chocolates una caja de bombones
  a cardboard box una caja de cartón
2 (*on forms, worksheets, etc.*) la **casilla** *fem.*
  Tick the box. Marca la casilla.

boxer shorts plural noun
  los **calzoncillos** *masc. plural*

boxing noun
  el **boxeo** *masc.*

Boxing Day noun
  el **día después de Navidad** *masc.*

CULTURE
Boxing Day is translated simply as 'the day after Christmas', and is not a holiday in Spain.

boy noun
1 (*young child*) el **niño** *masc.*
  a little boy of five un niño de cinco años
2 (*older child or teenager*) el **chico** *masc.*
  a boy of seventeen un chico de diecisiete años

boyfriend noun
  el **novio** *masc.*

bra noun
  el **sujetador** *masc.*

brace noun
(for teeth) el **aparato** masc.
I wear a brace. Llevo un aparato.

bracelet noun
la **pulsera** fem.

brain noun
el **cerebro** masc.

brainy adjective
inteligente masc. & fem.

brake noun
el **freno** masc.
to put on the brakes frenar

branch noun
la **rama** fem.

brand-new adjective
nuevo masc., **nueva** fem.
I have a brand-new bike. Tengo
una bicicleta nueva.

brave adjective
valiente masc. & fem.

bread noun
el **pan** masc.
I'm eating some bread. Estoy
comiendo pan.
a piece of bread un trozo de pan

break noun
(playtime in school) el **recreo** masc.
We go out for break at eleven.
Salimos al recreo a las once.

to **break** verb
1 to break something romper algo
Shaun has broken a glass. Shaun
ha roto un vaso.
I've broken my arm. Me he roto el
brazo.
2 **romperse**
The plate broke. Se rompió el
plato.
3 to break down estropearse
The car has broken down. Se ha
estropeado el coche.
4 We break up tomorrow.
Terminamos las clases mañana.

breakfast noun
el **desayuno** masc.
to have breakfast desayunar
I have breakfast at seven.
Desayuno a las siete.

breath noun
el **aliento** masc.
He arrived out of breath. Llegó sin
aliento.

to **breathe** verb
respirar

breeze noun
la **brisa** fem.

brick noun
el **ladrillo** masc.
a brick wall una pared de
ladrillo

bride noun
la **novia** fem.
the bride and groom los novios
masc. plural

bridegroom noun
el **novio** masc.

bridesmaid noun
la **dama de honor** fem.

bridge noun
el **puente** masc.

bright adjective
1 (colour) **vivo** masc., **viva** fem.
bright colours colores vivos
2 (light, sun) **brillante** masc. & fem.
a bright light una luz brillante
a very bright room una habitación
con mucha luz
3 (clever) **inteligente** masc. & fem.
He's very bright. Es muy
inteligente.
a bright idea una brillante
idea

• Use **el** and **uno** for masculine words and **la** and **una** for feminine words.

240

brilliant adjective
1 (*really good*) **estupendo** *masc.*, **estupenda** *fem.*
The weather was brilliant. Hizo un tiempo estupendo.
a brilliant idea una idea genial
2 (*very clever*) **brillante** *masc. & fem.*
She's a brilliant student. Es una alumna brillante.

to **bring** verb
1 (*to bring with you*) **traer**
Have you brought your umbrella? ¿Has traído el paraguas?
Bring your best friend. Trae a tu mejor amigo.
2 (*to bring to a place*) **llevar**
Bring this book to your teacher. Lleva este libro al maestro.
3 to bring something back devolver algo
I'll bring back your bike tomorrow. Te devolveré la bici mañana.
to bring somebody back to ... llevar a alguien a ...
Granddad brought me back home by car. Mi abuelo me llevó a casa en coche.

Britain noun
Gran Bretaña *fem.*
We live in Britain. Vivimos en Gran Bretaña.

British adjective
británico *masc.*, **británica** *fem.*
Emma is British. Emma es británica.
the British Isles las Islas Británicas

British noun
the British los británicos *masc. plural*

broccoli noun
el **brécol** *masc.*, el **brócoli** *masc.*

broken adjective
roto *masc.*, **rota** *fem.*
It's broken. Está roto.
She has a broken leg. Tiene la pierna rota.

bronze noun
el **bronce** *masc.*
a bronze medal una medalla de bronce

broom noun
la **escoba** *fem.*

brother noun
el **hermano** *masc.*
Bring your brother. Trae a tu hermano.
Do you have any brothers or sisters? ¿Tienes hermanos?

brown adjective
1 **marrón** *masc. & fem.*
a brown blouse una blusa marrón
brown shoes zapatos marrones

⚷ LANGUAGE
The singular form marrón is the same in the masculine and feminine, and the plural is marrones. 'Maroon' is related to marrón but it means a dark red colour.

2 (*hair*) **castaño** *masc.*, **castaña** *fem.*
Liz has brown hair. Liz tiene el pelo castaño.
3 (*from the sun*) **moreno** *masc.*, **morena** *fem.*
You're getting brown. Te pones moreno.

brown noun
el **marrón** *masc.*
I prefer brown to blue. Prefiero el marrón al azul.

brown bread noun
el **pan integral** *masc.*

•*Languages and nationalities do not take a capital letter in Spanish.*

Brownie noun
la **alita** *fem.*
She's in the Brownies. Pertenece a las alitas.

bruise noun
el **moretón** *masc.* (plural los **moretones**)
I have a bruise on my knee. Tengo un moretón en la rodilla.

brush noun
1 (*for hair, cleaning, etc.*) el **cepillo** *masc.*
2 (*for painting walls etc.*) la **brocha** *fem.*

to **brush** verb
1 (*hair, clothes, etc.*) **cepillar**
I'm brushing my hair. Me estoy cepillando el pelo.
2 **to brush your teeth** lavarse los dientes

Brussels sprouts plural noun
las **coles de Bruselas** *fem. plural*

bubble noun
1 (*in water*) la **burbuja** *fem.*
2 (*in the air*) la **pompa** *fem.*
soap bubbles pompas de jabón

bucket noun
el **cubo** *masc.*
a bucket and spade un cubo y una pala

Buddhist adjective
budista *masc. & fem.*

bug noun
1 (*insect*) el **insecto** *masc.*
2 (*germ*) el **microbio** *masc.*;
(*virus*) el **virus** *masc.* (plural los **virus**)

buggy noun
(*for a baby*)
la **sillita** *fem.*, el **cochecito** *masc.*

to **build** verb
construir

builder noun
1 (*working man*) el **albañil** *masc.*
2 (*somebody who people work for*)
el **constructor** *masc.*,
la **constructora** *fem.*

building noun
el **edificio** *masc.*

bulb noun
la **bombilla** *fem.*
Mum changed the light bulb. Mamá cambió la bombilla.

bull noun
el **toro** *masc.*

bully noun
el **matón** *masc.*, la **matona** *fem.*

🔑 **LANGUAGE**
The plural of **matón** is **matones**.

bump noun
1 (*on your head*) el **chichón** *masc.*
2 (*in the road*) el **bache** *masc.*
3 (*noise*) el **golpe** *masc.*

to **bump** verb
1 (*to knock*) **I bumped my head.** Me di un golpe en la cabeza.
2 (*to hit*) **to bump into something** tropezar contra algo
I bumped into the table. Tropecé contra la mesa.
3 (*to meet*) **to bump into somebody** encontrarse con alguien
We bumped into her in the supermarket. Nos encontramos con ella en el supermercado.

bumpy adjective
(*road, street*) **lleno de baches** *masc.*,
llena de baches *fem.*

bun noun
1 (*sweet*) el **bollo** *masc.*
2 (*for a hamburger*) el **panecillo** *masc.*

bunch noun
1 **a bunch of flowers** un ramo de flores
2 **a bunch of friends** un grupo de amigos

• *The months of the year and days of the week do not take a capital letter in Spanish.*

bunk beds plural noun
la **litera** *fem.*

> 🗝 **LANGUAGE**
> You can also use litera to mean one bunk bed.

burger noun
la **hamburguesa** *fem.*

burglar noun
el **ladrón** *masc.*, la **ladrona** *fem.*
a burglar alarm una alarma antirrobo

> 🗝 **LANGUAGE**
> The plural of ladrón is ladrones.

to **burn** verb
1 to burn something quemar algo
He burned the rubbish. Quemó la basura.
I've burnt my finger. Me he quemado el dedo.
2 (*talking about something that burns*)
quemarse
The house burned down. Se quemó la casa.

burnt adjective
quemado *masc.*, **quemada** *fem.*
The toast is burnt. La tostada está quemada.

to **burst** verb
reventarse
The balloon burst. El globo se reventó.

bus noun
el **autobús** *masc.* (plural los **autobuses**)
We go to school by bus. Vamos a la escuela en autobús.
a bus stop una parada de autobús
the bus station la estación de autobuses
a school bus un autobús escolar

• See the centre section for verb tables.

bush noun
el **arbusto** *masc.*

business noun
los **negocios** *masc. plural*
a business trip un viaje de negocios

busy adjective
1 **ocupado** *masc.*, **ocupada** *fem.*
I'm busy. Estoy ocupado.
2 (*shops, streets, etc.*)
The shops are busy. Hay mucha gente en las tiendas.

but conjunction
1 **pero**
I want to go but my parents won't let me. Quiero ir pero mis padres no me dejan.
2 **sino**
It's not blue but green. No es azul sino verde.

butcher noun
el **carnicero** *masc.*, la **carnicera** *fem.*
He's a butcher. Es carnicero.
the butcher's shop la carnicería
Dad went to the butcher's. Papá fue a la carnicería.

butter noun
la **mantequilla** *fem.*

butterfly noun
la **mariposa** *fem.*

button noun
el **botón** *masc.* (plural los **botones**)

to **buy** verb
comprar
We're going to buy a computer. Vamos a comprar un ordenador.
He bought me some sweets. Me compró caramelos.

by preposition
1 **por**
a book written by Cervantes un libro escrito por Cervantes
one by one uno por uno
by chance por casualidad

a
b
c
d
e
f
g
h
i
j
k
l
m
n
o
p
q
r
s
t
u
v
w
x
y
z

2 **de**
a painting by Goya un cuadro de Goya
a book by Roald Dahl un libro de Roald Dahl
3 (with car, bike, plane, etc.) **en**
by train en tren
by boat en barco
4 (near to) **al lado de**

The restaurant is by the station. El restaurante está al lado de la estación.
5 (not later than) **antes de**
I'll come back by nine. Volveré antes de las nueve.

bye exclamation
¡adiós!

Cc

cab noun
el **taxi** masc.
to go by cab ir en taxi

cabbage noun
la **col** fem.
Do you like cabbage? ¿Te gusta la col?

cable noun
el **cable** masc.
cable television la televisión por cable

cafe noun
la **cafetería** fem.

CULTURE
British cafes do not sell drinks with alcohol in them.

cafeteria noun
la **cafetería** fem.

cage noun
la **jaula** fem.

cake noun
el **pastel** masc.
Amy's eating some cake. Amy está comiendo pastel.
a cake shop una pastelería

to **calculate** verb
calcular

calculator noun
la **calculadora** fem.

calendar noun
el **calendario** masc.

calf noun
(baby cow) el **ternero** masc.

call noun
(phone call) la **llamada** fem.
I have to make a phone call. Voy tiene que hacer una llamada.

to **call** verb
1 **llamar**
I'm going to call the doctor. Voy a llamar al médico.
to call the register pasar lista
2 to be called llamarse
What's your cat called? ¿Cómo se llama tu gato?
3 (to visit somebody) **pasar**
I'll call round at your house. Pasaré por tu casa.

to **call back** verb
volver a llamar
Dad's busy – he'll call back later. Papá está ocupado – volverá a llamar más tarde.

to **call off** verb
suspender
They called off the party. Suspendieron la fiesta.

• Use **el** and **uno** for masculine words and **la** and **una** for feminine words.

calm adjective
tranquilo *masc.*, **tranquila** *fem.*
Keep calm! ¡Tranquilo!

to **calm** verb
to calm down calmarse
Calm down, Bob! ¡Cálmate, Bob!

camcorder noun
la **videocámara** *fem.*

came verb SEE **come**
I came with her. Vine con ella.
He came by bike. Vino en bici.

camel noun
el **camello** *masc.*

camera noun
la **cámara** *fem.*
a digital camera una cámara digital

camp noun
el **campamento** *masc.*
a summer camp un campamento de verano

to **camp** verb
acampar
We camped by the river.
Acampamos cerca del río.

camping noun
el **camping** *masc.*
I like camping. Me gusta ir de camping.
to go camping ir de camping
We went camping in Spain Fuimos de camping a España.

campsite noun
el **camping** *masc.* (plural los **campings**)

can noun
la **lata** *fem.*
a can of sardines una lata de sardinas

can verb
1 **poder**
I can help you. Puedo ayudarte.

Can you turn the volume down? – Yes, I can. ¿Puedes bajar el volumen? – Sí, puedo.
Can she come tomorrow? ¿Puede venir mañana?

🗝 **LANGUAGE**
Translate 'can' using **poder** but when it means 'know how to do something' use **saber**.

2 **saber**
Can you swim? ¿Sabes nadar?
I can't read yet. Aún no sé leer.

3 (*sometimes not translated*)
Can you hear? ¿Oyes?
I can see you. Te veo.
I can't remember. No me acuerdo.

Canada noun
Canadá *masc.*
We're going to Canada. Vamos a Canadá.

Canadian adjective
canadiense *masc. & fem.*
She's Canadian. Es canadiense.

Canadian noun
el or la **canadiense** *masc. & fem.*

canal noun
el **canal** *masc.*

canary noun
el **canario** *masc.*

cancel verb
cancelar
The flight has been cancelled.
El vuelo ha sido cancelado.

cancer noun
el **cáncer** *masc.*
He has cancer. Tiene cáncer.

candle noun
la **vela** *fem.*
Blow out the candles. Sopla las velas.

candyfloss noun
el **algodón de azúcar** *masc.*

• *Languages and nationalities do not take a capital letter in Spanish.*

a
b
c
d
e
f
g
h
i
j
k
l
m
n
o
p
q
r
s
t
u
v
w
x
y
z

cannot verb SEE **can**
I cannot do it. No lo puedo hacer.
He cannot read. No sabe leer.

canoe noun
la **canoa** fem.

can't verb SEE **can**
I can't come. No puedo venir.
She can't swim. No sabe nadar.

canteen noun
(in a school, factory, etc.) el **comedor** masc.

cap noun
la **gorra** fem.
Put your cap on. Ponte la gorra.

capital noun
1 (capital city) la **capital** fem.
Madrid is the capital of Spain.
Madrid es la capital de España.
2 (capital letter) **la mayúscula** fem.
in capitals en mayúsculas

capital adjective
a capital letter una mayúscula
It's written with a capital D. Se escribe con D mayúscula.

captain noun
el **capitán** masc., la **capitana** fem.
the captain of our team el capitán de nuestro equipo

LANGUAGE
The plural of **capitán** is **capitanes**.

car noun
el **coche** masc.,
(Latin America) el **carro** masc.
We will go by car. Iremos en coche.
a car park un aparcamiento

caravan noun
la **caravana** fem.

card noun
1 la **tarjeta** fem.
a birthday card una tarjeta de cumpleaños

a greetings card la tarjeta de felicitación
2 la **carta** fem.
to play cards jugar a las cartas

LANGUAGE
Be careful: **carta** only means card when talking about a playing card.

cardboard noun
el **cartón** masc.
a cardboard box una caja de cartón

cardigan noun
la **chaqueta** fem.

care noun
el **cuidado** masc.
with care con cuidado
Take care crossing the road.
Cuidado al cruzar la calle.
to take care of cuidar
Rachel takes care of the children.
Rachel cuida a los niños.

to **care** verb
I don't care. No me importa.

careful adjective
to be careful tener cuidado
Be careful crossing the road. Ten cuidado al cruzar la calle.
Careful! ¡Cuidado!

carefully adverb
con cuidado
Close the door carefully. Cierra la puerta con cuidado.
We listened carefully.
Escuchamos con atención.

caretaker noun
1 (in a building) el **portero** masc., la **portera** fem.
2 (in a school) el or la **conserje** masc. & fem.

Caribbean adjective
caribeño masc., **caribeña** fem.

Caribbean noun
the Caribbean el Caribe

• The months of the year and days of the week do not take a capital letter in Spanish.

carnival noun

el **carnaval** *masc.*

 CULTURE

Spanish people celebrate the festival known as carnaval in the middle of February just before Christian Lent. They put on fancy dress, play music, and dance. Two famous carnavales are those of Tenerife and Cadiz.

carol noun

a Christmas carol un villancico

carpenter noun

el **carpintero** *masc.*,
la **carpintera** *fem.*
My dad's a carpenter. Mi padre es carpintero.

carpet noun

1 (*wall-to-wall*) la **moqueta** *fem.*
2 (*rug*) la **alfombra** *fem.*

carriage noun

(*on a train*) el **vagón** *masc.* (plural los **vagones**)

carrier bag noun

la **bolsa de plástico** *fem.*

carrot noun

la **zanahoria** *fem.*

to **carry** verb

llevar
Ruth is carrying a bag. Ruth lleva una bolsa.

to **carry on** verb

seguir
Carry on! ¡Sigue!
to carry on doing something
seguir haciendo algo
Do you want to carry on reading?
¿Quieres seguir leyendo?

carton noun

(*of milk or juice*) el **cartón** *masc.* (plural los **cartones**)

• *See the centre section for verb tables.*

cartoon noun

1 (*film*)
a cartoon una película de dibujos animados
Do you like cartoons? ¿Te gustan los dibujos animados?
2 (*funny drawing*) el **chiste** *masc.*

case noun

1 (*luggage*) la **maleta** *fem.*
Have you packed your case? ¿Has hecho la maleta?
2 (*soft cover for glasses, guitar, etc.*) la **funda** *fem.*
Where is my glasses case? ¿Dónde está la funda de mis gafas?
3 (*cover for pencils, make-up, etc.*) el **estuche** *masc.*
4 just in case por si acaso
Take your umbrella just in case.
Llévate el paraguas por si acaso.

cash noun

el **dinero** *masc.*
Do you have any cash? ¿Tienes dinero?
a cash machine un cajero automático

cashier noun

el **cajero** *masc.*, **la cajera** *fem.*

cassette noun

el **casete** *masc.*

castle noun

el **castillo** *masc.*

cat noun

el **gato** *masc.*, **la gata** *fem.*
I have three cats. Tengo tres gatos.

catch verb

1 (*a ball, bus, thief, fish, etc.*) **coger**
We'll catch the bus. Cogeremos el autobús.
I caught a cold. Cogí un resfriado.
Catch! ¡Coge!
2 to catch up with somebody
alcanzar a alguien

a
b
c
d
e
f
g
h
i
j
k
l
m
n
o
p
q
r
s
t
u
v
w
x
y
z

a
b
c
d
e
f
g
h
i
j
k
l
m
n
o
p
q
r
s
t
u
v
w
x
y
z

catching adjective
contagioso masc., **contagiosa** fem.
It's not catching. No es contagioso.

caterpillar noun
la **oruga** fem.

cathedral noun
la **catedral** fem.

Catholic adjective
católico masc., **católica** fem.

cauliflower noun
la **coliflor** fem.

cause noun
la **causa** fem.

cave noun
la **cueva** fem.

CD noun
el **CD** masc. (plural los **CDs**)
a CD player un reproductor CD

ceiling noun
el **techo** masc.

celebrate verb
celebrar
How are you going to celebrate your birthday? ¿Cómo vas a celebrar tu cumpleaños?
Let's celebrate! ¡Vamos a celebrarlo!

celery noun
el **apio** masc.

cello noun
el **violonchelo** masc.
Ambika plays the cello. Ambika toca el violonchelo.

cemetery noun
el **cementerio** masc.

cent noun
1 (part of a euro) el **céntimo** masc.
It costs fifty cents. Cuesta cincuenta céntimos.
2 (part of a dollar etc.) **el centavo** masc.

centigrade adjective
centígrado masc., **centígrada** fem.
fifteen degrees centigrade quince grados centígrados

centimetre noun
el **centímetro** masc.

central adjective
1 **central** masc. & fem.
central heating la calefacción central
2 (near the town centre) **céntrico** masc., **céntrica** fem.

centre noun
el **centro** masc.
in the centre of the room en el centro de la habitación
a shopping centre un centro comercial
I live in the town centre. Vivo en el centro de la ciudad.

century noun
el **siglo** masc.
in the twenty-first century en el siglo veintiuno

cereal noun
los **cereales** masc. plural
We always have cereal for breakfast. Siempre desayunamos cereales.

🔑 **LANGUAGE**
English = cereal is singular
Spanish = los cereales is plural

certain adjective
seguro masc., **segura** fem.
Are you certain? ¿Estás seguro?

certainly adverb
(of course) **por supuesto**
Certainly not! ¡Por supuesto que no!

certificate noun
el **certificado** masc.

chain noun
la **cadena** fem.
a gold chain una cadena de oro

• Use **el** and **uno** for masculine words and **la** and **una** for feminine words.

chair noun
1 la **silla** *fem.*
I sat down on the chair. Me senté en la silla.
2 (*armchair*) el **sillón** *masc.* (plural los **sillones**)

chalk noun
la **tiza** *fem.*
a piece of chalk una tiza

champion noun
el **campeón** *masc.*,
la **campeona** *fem.*
He's a cycling champion.
Es campeón de ciclismo.

⚷ **LANGUAGE**
The plural of campeón is campeones.

chance noun
1 (*something that might happen*) la **posibilidad** *fem.*
We have no chance of winning.
No tenemos ninguna posibilidad de ganar.
2 (*opportunity*) la **oportunidad** *fem.*
Now you have a chance to ask questions. Ahora tenéis la oportunidad de hacer preguntas.
3 (*risk*) el **riesgo** *masc.*
You're taking a big chance. Corres un gran riesgo.
4 by chance por casualidad
I bumped into Jamal by chance.
Me encontré a Jamal por casualidad.

change verb
1 **cambiar**
Can I change this book? ¿Puedo cambiar este libro?
He hasn't changed much. No ha cambiado mucho.
2 **cambiar de**

⚷ **LANGUAGE**
You use cambiar de when you mean to change one thing for another.

Do you want to change places?
¿Quieres cambiar de sitio?

I'm going to change my socks.
Me voy a cambiar de calcetines.
I've changed my mind. He cambiado de idea.
3 (*to put on different clothes*) **cambiarse**
Go and change. Ve a cambiarte.

change noun
el **cambio** *masc.*
I don't have any change for the bus. No tengo cambio para el autobús.
There have been lots of changes.
Ha habido muchos cambios.

changing room noun
1 (*for sports*) el **vestuario** *masc.*
2 (*for trying on clothes*) el **probador** *masc.*

channel noun
(*on TV*) el **canal** *masc.*
What channel is the film on?
¿En qué canal dan la película?
Can I change channels? ¿Puedo cambiar de canal?

Channel noun
el **Canal de la Mancha** *masc.*
the Channel Tunnel el túnel del Canal de la Mancha, el Eurotúnel
the Channel Islands las Islas del Canal de la Mancha

chapter noun
el **capítulo** *masc.*

character noun
1 (*in a book, play, or film*) el **personaje** *masc.*
the character of Harry Potter
el personaje de Harry Potter
the main character in the novel
el protagonista de la novela
2 (*somebody's personality*) el **carácter** *masc.*

charge noun
1 (*money you pay*)
There's no charge. Es gratuito.
There's an extra charge. Hay un suplemento.

• Languages and nationalities do not take a capital letter in Spanish.

2 the person in charge el or la responsable
Who's in charge? ¿Quién es el responsable?
In this house mum's in charge! ¡En esta casa manda mamá!

🔑 **LANGUAGE**
When 'be in charge' means 'be the boss' then use the verb **mandar**, e.g. 'Who's in charge here?' is ¿Quién manda aquí?

---

to **charge** verb
cobrar
They charged us ten euros for breakfast. Nos cobraron diez euros por el desayuno.

chart noun
(*diagram*) el **gráfico** *masc.*

to **chase** verb
perseguir
They chased the thief. Persiguieron al ladrón.

chat noun
la **charla** *fem.*
to have a chat with somebody charlar con alguien

to **chat** verb
charlar
Stop chatting! ¡Deja de charlar!

chatroom noun
el **chat** *masc.*
The chatroom is empty. El chat está vacío.

cheap adjective
barato *masc.*, **barata** *fem.*
a cheap T-shirt una camiseta barata

cheat noun
el **tramposo** *masc.*, la **tramposa** *fem.*
You're a cheat! ¡Eres un tramposo!

to **cheat** verb
hacer trampa
He always cheats. Siempre hace trampa.
That's cheating. Eso es trampa.

to **check** verb
1 (*to make sure*) **comprobar**
Check the date of the concert. Comprueba la fecha del concierto.
2 (*passports or tickets*) **controlar**
3 **to check in** (*at an airport*) **facturar**

check noun
1 el **control** *masc.*
passport check el control de pasaportes
2 (*pattern*) los **cuadros** *masc. plural*
a check skirt una falda de cuadros

checkout noun
(*at a supermarket*) la **caja** *fem.*
There's a queue at the checkout. Hay cola en la caja.

cheek noun
la **mejilla** *fem.*
She kissed me on the cheek. Me dio un beso en la mejilla.

cheeky adjective
descarado *masc.*, **descarada** *fem.*

cheer verb
aplaudir

cheerful adjective
alegre *masc. & fem.*

cheers exclamation
1 (*thanking somebody*) ¡gracias!
2 (*saying goodbye*) ¡hasta luego!

cheese noun
el **queso** *masc.*
He's eating some cheese. Está comiendo queso.
a cheese sandwich un sandwich de queso

chef noun
el **chef** *masc.* (plural los **chefs**)
My father's a chef. Mi padre es chef.

chemist noun
el **farmacéutico** *masc.*, la **farmacéutica** *fem.*
She's a chemist. Es farmacéutica.
the chemist's la farmacia

• *The months of the year and days of the week do not take a capital letter in Spanish.*

He went to the chemist's Fue a la farmacia.

cheque noun
el **cheque** *masc.*

cherry noun
la **cereza** *fem.*

chess noun
el **ajedrez** *masc.*
We play chess. Jugamos al ajedrez.

chest noun
1 el **pecho** *masc.*
My chest hurts. Me duele el pecho.
2 a chest of drawers una cómoda

chestnut noun
la **castaña** *fem.*

chew verb
masticar

chewing gum noun
el **chicle** *masc.*

chick noun
el **pollito** *masc.*

chicken noun
1 (*food*) el **pollo** *masc.*
They're eating chicken. Están comiendo pollo.
a chicken leg un muslo de pollo
2 (*animal*) la **gallina** *fem.*
John's going to feed the chickens. John va a darles de comer a las gallinas.

chickenpox noun
la **varicela** *fem.*
I have chickenpox. Tengo la varicela.

child noun
1 (*boy*) el **niño** *masc.*; (*girl*) la **niña** *fem.*
a child of five un niño de cinco años
2 (*son*) el **hijo** *masc.*; (*daughter*) la **hija** *fem.*
I'm the oldest child. Soy la hija mayor.

childminder noun
la **niñera** *fem.*

children plural noun
1 (*boys and girls*) los **niños** *masc. plural*
There are lots of children. Hay muchos niños.
2 (*sons and daughters*) los **hijos** *masc. plural*
They have four children. Tienen cuatro hijos.

Chile noun
Chile *masc.*

chilly adjective
frío *masc.*, **fría** *fem.*
The weather's chilly. Hace frío.
I'm chilly. Tengo frío.

> **LANGUAGE**
> English = to be chilly   I'm chilly.
> Spanish = tener frío   Tengo frío.

chimney noun
la **chimenea** *fem.*

chin noun
la **barbilla** *fem.*

> **LANGUAGE**
> Note the relation between la barbilla (chin) and la barba (beard).

China noun
China *fem.*

Chinese adjective
chino *masc.*, **china** *fem.*
a Chinese town una ciudad china
a Chinese man un chino
a Chinese woman una china

Chinese noun
1 (*language*) el **chino** *masc.*
Do you speak Chinese? ¿Hablas chino?
2 the Chinese los chinos *masc. plural*

chip noun
la **patata frita** *fem.*
Do you like fish and chips? ¿Te gusta el pescado con patatas fritas?

• *See the centre section for verb tables.*

English Spanish

a
b
c
d
e
f
g
h
i
j
k
l
m
n
o
p
q
r
s
t
u
v
w
x
y
z

choc-ice noun
el **bombón helado** *masc.*

chocolate noun
1 el **chocolate** *masc.*
I love chocolate. Me encanta el chocolate.
a chocolate cake un pastel de chocolate
2 el **bombón** *masc.* (plural los **bombones**)
Would you like a chocolate? ¿Quieres un bombón?

🔑 **LANGUAGE**
Be careful! When you mean one chocolate sweet use **bombón**, not **chocolate**.

---

choice noun
la **elección** *fem.* (plural las **elecciones**)
a good choice una buena elección

choir noun
el **coro** *masc.*
We sing in the choir. Cantamos en el coro.

choose verb
elegir
Choose a card. Elige una carta.

chop noun
la **chuleta** *fem.*
a pork chop una chuleta de cerdo

chopsticks plural noun
los **palillos** *masc. plural*

Christian adjective
cristiano *masc.*, **cristiana** *fem.*

Christmas noun
la **Navidad** *fem.*
at Christmas en Navidad
Where are you spending Christmas? ¿Dónde vas a pasar la Navidad?
Happy Christmas! ¡Feliz Navidad!
a Christmas card una tarjeta de Navidad
Christmas Day el día de Navidad

Christmas dinner la comida de Navidad

 CULTURE
In Spain the main Christmas meal is on Christmas Eve, and it is eaten before Midnight Mass.

Christmas Eve la Nochebuena
a Christmas present un regalo de Navidad

 CULTURE
Spanish children usually receive their Christmas presents on 6th January, known as **el día de Reyes** (the day of the Three Wise Men). Children put out their shoes for the Wise Men to leave the presents in!

---

a Christmas tree un árbol de Navidad

church noun
la **iglesia** *fem.*
to go to church ir a la iglesia

cinema noun
el **cine** *masc.*
We're going to the cinema. Vamos al cine.

circle noun
el **círculo** *masc.*
The children sat down in a circle. Los niños se sentaron en círculo.

circus noun
el **circo** *masc.*
Do you like the circus? ¿Os gusta el circo?

city noun
la **ciudad** *fem.*
the city centre el centro de la ciudad

clap verb
1 (*when you like something*) **aplaudir**
Everyone clapped. Todos aplaudieron.
2 (*with the music*) **dar palmas**
You sing and I clap. Tú cantas y yo doy palmas.

• *Use **el** and **uno** for masculine words and **la** and **una** for feminine words.*

clarinet noun
el **clarinete** *masc.*
Yasmina plays the clarinet.
Yasmina toca el clarinete.

class noun
la **clase** *fem.*
He's in my class. Está en mi clase.
Today we have a Spanish class.
Hoy tenemos clase de español.

classroom noun
el **aula** *fem.*, la **clase** *fem.*
a classroom assistant un or una
auxiliar de aula

> 🔑 **LANGUAGE**
> Be careful: you use **el** with **aula** but it is
> not a masculine noun.

clean adjective
limpio *masc.*, **limpia** *fem.*
The room is clean. La habitación
está limpia.

to **clean** verb
limpiar
Dad's cleaning the house. Papá
está limpiando la casa.
I'm going to clean my teeth. Voy a
lavarme los dientes.

cleaner noun
(*man*) el **hombre de la limpieza**
masc.; (*woman*) la **mujer de la
limpieza** *fem.*

cleaning noun
la **limpieza** *fem.*
I don't like doing the cleaning.
No me gusta hacer la limpieza.

clear adjective
claro *masc.*, **clara** *fem.*
Your explanation is very clear. Tu
explicación es muy clara.

to **clear** verb
1 **to clear the table** quitar la mesa
2 **to clear up** recoger
Clear up your toys! ¡Recoge los
juguetes!

clearly adverb
claramente

clementine noun
la **clementina** *fem.*

clever adjective
inteligente *masc. & fem.*

to **click** verb
hacer clic
Click on the icon. Haz clic en el
icono.

cliff noun
el **acantilado** *masc.*

climate noun
el **clima** *masc.*

> 🔑 **LANGUAGE**
> Be careful: **clima** ends in an **-a** but it is not
> a feminine noun.

to **climb** verb
subir
to climb the stairs subir las
escaleras
to climb a tree subir a un árbol

cloakroom
1 (*for coats*) el **guardarropa** *masc.*
2 (*toilet*) los **servicios** *masc. plural*

> 🔑 **LANGUAGE**
> Be careful: **guardarropa** ends in an **-a** but
> it is not a feminine noun.

clock noun
el **reloj** *masc.*
The kitchen clock is broken.
El reloj de la cocina está roto.
an alarm clock un despertador

close adverb
(*nearby*) **cerca**
We live close by. Vivimos muy
cerca.
close to cerca de
The school is close to the library.
El colegio está cerca de la
biblioteca.

• *Languages and nationalities do not take a capital letter in Spanish.*

a
b
c
d
e
f
g
h
i
j
k
l
m
n
o
p
q
r
s
t
u
v
w
x
y
z

to **close** verb
cerrar
Close the door. Cierra la puerta.
The supermarket closes at ten.
El supermercado cierra a las diez.

closed adjective
cerrado *masc.*, **cerrada** *fem.*
The shops are closed. Las tiendas
están cerradas.

cloth noun
1 (*for cleaning*) el **trapo** *masc.*
2 (*material*) la **tela** *fem.*
Is it made of cloth? ¿Es de tela?

clothes plural noun
la **ropa** *fem.*
Your clothes are dirty. Tu ropa
está sucia.

LANGUAGE
English = **clothes** is plural
Spanish = **la ropa** is singular

cloud noun
la **nube** *fem.*

cloudy adjective
nublado *masc.*, **nublada** *fem.*
It's cloudy today. Hoy está
nublado.

clown noun
el **payaso** *masc.*, la **payasa** *fem.*

club noun
1 el **club** *masc.* (plural los **clubs**)
a football club un club de fútbol
2 (*for dancing*) la **discoteca** *fem.*
My sister went to a club.
Mi hermana fue a una discoteca.

LANGUAGE
The Spanish word **club** is pronounced
'cloob'.

clumsy adjective
torpe *masc. & fem.*
You're so clumsy today! ¡Qué
torpe estás hoy!

coach noun
el **autocar** *masc.*
by coach en autocar
the coach station la estación de
autobuses

coal noun
el **carbón** *masc.*

coast noun
la **costa** *fem.*
**We spend our holidays on the
coast.** Pasamos las vacaciones en
la costa.

coat noun
el **abrigo** *masc.*

cocoa noun
el **cacao** *masc.*

cobweb noun
la **telaraña** *fem.*
full of cobwebs lleno de telarañas

coconut noun
el **coco** *masc.*

cod noun
el **bacalao** *masc.*

code noun
la **clave** *fem.*
a secret code una clave secreta
The message is in code. El mensaje
está en clave.

coffee noun
el **café** *masc.*
a cup of coffee una taza de café
Shall we have a coffee? ¿Tomamos
un café?
a black coffee un café solo
a white coffee un café con leche

coin noun
la **moneda** *fem.*
a one euro coin una moneda de un
euro

coincidence noun
la **casualidad** *fem.*
What a coincidence! ¡Qué
casualidad!

• *The months of the year and days of the week do not take a capital letter in Spanish.*

Coke® noun
la **Coca-Cola®** *fem.*
a can of Coke una lata de Coca-Cola®

cold adjective
frío *masc.*, **fría** *fem.*
The water's cold. El agua está fría.
The weather's cold. Hace frío.
It's cold today. Hoy hace frío.
I'm cold. Tengo frío.
He's very cold. Tiene mucho frío.

> **LANGUAGE**
> English = **to be** cold   **I'm cold.**
> Spanish = **tener** frío   **Tengo frío.**

cold noun
1 (*the cold weather*) el **frío** *masc.*
I don't like the cold. No me gusta el frío.
2 (*illness*) el **resfriado** *masc.*
to catch a cold coger un resfriado
to have a cold estar resfriado *masc.*, estar resfriada *fem.*
Jenny has a cold. Jenny está resfriada.

collar noun
1 el **cuello** *masc.*
my shirt collar el cuello de mi camisa
2 (*on a dog*) el **collar** *masc.*

to **collect** verb
1 (*to pick up*) **recoger**
Can I collect the exercise books? ¿Puedo recoger los cuadernos?
2 (*as a hobby*) **coleccionar**
Do you collect stamps? ¿Coleccionas sellos?

collection noun
la **colección** *fem.* (plural las **colecciones**)
a CD collection una colección de CDs

college noun
la **institución de educación superior** *fem.*

• *See the centre section for verb tables.*

colour noun
el **color** *masc.*
What colour is her hair? ¿De qué color es su pelo?

to **colour** verb
colorear
to colour in a picture colorear un dibujo
a colouring book un cuaderno para colorear

column noun
la **columna** *fem.*

comb noun
el **peine** *masc.*
Do you have a comb? ¿Tienes un peine?

to **comb** verb
to comb your hair peinarse
I haven't combed my hair. No me he peinado.

to **come** verb
venir
Come and see me tomorrow. Ven a verme mañana.
I want to come with you. Quiero venir contigo.
Come with me. Ven conmigo.
The bus is coming. Ya viene el autobús.
I come from Madrid. Soy de Madrid.
Wait for me, I'm coming! ¡Espérame, ya voy!
Come on! ¡Venga!
Has the post come yet? ¿Ya ha llegado el correo?

to **come back** verb
volver
Come back later. Vuelve más tarde.

to **come down** verb
bajar
I'm coming down! ¡Ya bajo!
He came down the stairs. Bajó las escaleras.

a
b
c
d
e
f
g
h
i
j
k
l
m
n
o
p
q
r
s
t
u
v
w
x
y
z

to **come in** verb
entrar
She came into the dining room.
Entró en el comedor.
Come in! ¡Pase!, ¡Adelante!

to **come out** verb
salir
When are you coming out of your
room? ¿Cuándo vas a salir de tu
cuarto?

to **come up** verb
subir
I'm coming up now. Ahora subo.
They came up the stairs. Subieron
las escaleras.

comfortable adjective
(*chair, shoes, etc.*) **cómodo** *masc.*,
cómoda *fem.*
These shoes are very comfortable.
Estos zapatos son muy cómodos.

comic noun
el **cómic** *masc.*
Malcolm loves reading comics.
A Malcolm le encanta leer cómics.

comma noun
la **coma** *fem.*

comments plural noun
(*by teacher on homework etc.*)
los **comentarios** *masc. plural*

common adjective
1 **corriente** *masc. & fem.*
John is a very common name. John
es un nombre muy corriente.
2 in common en común
We have nothing in common.
No tenemos nada en común.

company noun
la **compañía** *fem.*
My mum works in an insurance
company. Mi madre trabaja en
una compañía de seguros.

to **compare** verb
comparar

compass noun
la **brújula** *fem.*

compasses plural noun
a pair of compasses un compás
(plural los **compases**)

competition noun
1 el **concurso** *masc.*
a fancy dress competition
un concurso de disfraces
2 (*for sports*) la **competición** *fem.*
a swimming competition una
competición de natación

competitor noun
el or la **participiante** *masc. & fem.*
the competitors in the race los
participiantes en la carrera

to **complain** verb
quejarse
You're always complaining about
something! ¡Siempre te estás
quejando de algo!

complete adjective
1 (*sentence, list, etc.*) **completo** *masc.*,
completa *fem.*
2 (*change, disaster, etc.*) **total** *masc. & fem.*
complete silence un silencio total

to **complete** verb
1 **terminar**
Have you completed your work?
¿Has terminado tu trabajo?
2 (*to add something missing*) **completar**
Complete this sentence with the
right word. Completa esta frase
con la palabra adecuada.

completely adverb
completamente

complicated adjective
complicado *masc.*,
complicada *fem.*

comprehension noun
(*an exercise in school*) el **ejercicio de
comprensión** *masc.*

comprehensive noun
(*school*) el **instituto de enseñanza
secundaria** *masc.*
My sister goes to a comprehensive.
Mi hermana va al instituto.

• *Use* **el** *and* **uno** *for masculine words and* **la** *and* **una** *for feminine words.*

computer noun
el **ordenador** *masc.*,
(*Latin America*) el **computador** *masc.*,
la **computadora** *fem.*
My parents have bought me a new computer. Mis padres me han comprado un ordenador nuevo.
a computer game un videojuego
a computer program un programa informático
a computer room una sala de ordenadores

to **concentrate** verb
concentrarse
Be quiet, I can't concentrate!
¡Cállate, que no me puedo concentrar!

concert noun
el **concierto** *masc.*
My brother went to a rock concert. Mi hermano fue a un concierto de rock.

condition noun
in good condition en buen estado

conductor noun
(*of an orchestra*) el **director** *masc.*,
la **directora** *fem.*

cone noun
an ice-cream cone un cucurucho

confused adjective
confundido *masc.*,
confundida *fem.*
I'm still confused. Todavía estoy confundido.
to get confused confundirse
I got confused. Me confundí.

congratulations plural noun
la **enhorabuena** *fem.*
Congratulations! ¡Enhorabuena!

conjunction noun
la **conjunción** *fem.* (plural las **conjunciones**)

to **connect** verb

to connect to the Internet
conectarse a Internet
I connect every day. Me conecto a Internet todos los días.
We're connected to the Internet. Estamos conectados a Internet.

conservatory noun
(*room made of glass*) la **galería** *fem.*

console noun
a games console una videoconsola

consonant noun
la **consonante** *fem.*

to **contact** verb
ponerse en contacto con

container noun
el **recipiente** *masc.*

contest noun
el **concurso** *masc.*

continent noun
1 el **continente** *masc.*
How many continents are there?
¿Cuántos continentes hay?
2 (*Europe*)
on the Continent en Europa

to **continue** verb
continuar, **seguir**
I continued reading. Continué leyendo., Seguí leyendo.
Continue with what you're doing. Sigue con lo que estás haciendo.

to **control** verb
controlar
Control yourself! ¡Contrólate!

convenient adjective
1 (*time, place*) **conveniente** *masc. & fem.*
2 **cómodo** *masc.*, **cómoda** *fem.*
It's convenient living near the school. Es cómodo vivir cerca de la escuela.

conversation noun
la **conversación** *fem.* (plural las **conversaciones**)

a b c d e f g h i j k l m n o p q r s t u v w x y z

• Languages and nationalities do not take a capital letter in Spanish.

to **cook** verb
1 cocinar
Do you like cooking? ¿Te gusta cocinar?
What are you cooking? ¿Qué estás cocinando?
2 to cook a meal hacer una comida
Granddad is cooking dinner. El abuelo está haciendo la cena.
3 hacerse
The potatoes are cooking. Las patatas se están haciendo.

cook noun
el **cocinero** masc., la **cocinera** fem.
Mum's a good cook. Mamá es muy buena cocinera.

cookbook noun
el **libro de cocina** masc.

cooked adjective
(cake, chicken, etc.) **hecho** masc., **hecha** fem.
The meat is well cooked. La carne está bien hecha.

cooker noun
la **cocina** fem.
a gas cooker una cocina de gas

cookie noun
la **galleta** fem.

cooking noun
la **cocina** fem.
Spanish cooking la cocina española
to do the cooking cocinar

cool adjective
1 fresco masc., **fresca** fem.
a cool drink una bebida fresca
The weather is cool. Hace fresco.
2 (good or great) **guay** masc. & fem.
He's a really cool guy! ¡Qué chico más guay!
You look cool in that jacket. Esa chaqueta te queda guay.

to **cool down** verb
enfriar
Let the soup cool down. Deja enfriar la sopa.

copy noun
la **copia** fem.
I need two copies. Necesito dos copias.

to **copy** verb
copiar
Can I copy your notes? ¿Puedo copiar tus apuntes?

corn noun
(wheat) el **trigo** masc.

corner noun
1 (of a street, table, page, etc.) la **esquina** fem.
the corner of the table la esquina de la mesa
There's a post office on the corner. Hay una oficina de correos en la esquina.
2 (of a room, drawer, cupboard, etc.) el **rincón** masc.
There's a cupboard in the corner. Hay un armario en el rincón.

LANGUAGE
Be careful: there are two words for corner. Use esquina when you mean the corner from the *outside*, and rincón when you mean the corner from the *inside*.

cornflakes plural noun
los **copos de maíz** masc. plural, los **cereales** masc. plural

Cornwall noun
Cornualles masc.

correct adjective
(amount, number, sentence, etc.) **correcto** masc., **correcta** fem.
Your answer is correct. Tu respuesta es correcta.
Correct! ¡Correcto!

• The months of the year and days of the week do not take a capital letter in Spanish.

to **correct** verb
corregir
You have to correct the mistakes.
Tienes que corregir las faltas.

correction noun
la **corrección** *fem.* (plural las
correcciones)

correctly adverb
correctamente, **bien**

corridor noun
el **pasillo** *masc.*
It's at the end of the corridor. Está
al final del pasillo.

to **cost** verb
costar
How much does it cost? ¿Cuánto
cuesta?
It cost me ten euros. Me costó diez
euros.

costume noun
1 el **traje** *masc.*
a swimming costume un traje de
baño
2 (*fancy dress*) el **disfraz** *masc.* (plural
los **disfraces**)

cot noun
la **cuna** *fem.*

cottage noun
la **casita** *fem.*

⚷ **LANGUAGE**
Casita is the Spanish for 'little house'.

cotton noun
el **algodón** *masc.*
a cotton shirt una camisa de
algodón
cotton wool el algodón

couch noun
el **sofá** *masc.*

cough noun
la **tos** *fem.*
a cough medicine un jarabe para
la tos
I have a cough. Tengo tos.

Alice has a bad cough. Alice tiene
mucha tos.

to **cough** verb
toser
Smoke makes me cough. El humo
me hace toser.

could verb
poder
Could I ask you a question? ¿Puedo
hacerte una pregunta?
Could you open the window?
¿Puedes abrir la ventana?

to **count** verb
contar
Count up to twenty. Cuenta hasta
veinte.
The teacher counted his pupils.
El maestro contó a sus alumnos.

counter noun
1 (*in a shop*) el **mostrador** *masc.*
2 (*in a bank or post office*) la **ventanilla**
fem.
3 (*in a game*) la **ficha** *fem.*

country noun
1 (*Britain, Spain, etc.*) el **país** *masc.*
a foreign country un país
extranjero
Have you visited many countries?
¿Has visitado muchos países?
2 (*not the town*) **el campo** *masc.*
Maite lives in the country. Maite
vive en el campo.

countryside noun
el **campo** *masc.*
in the countryside en el campo

couple noun
1 a couple of un par de
a couple of hours un par de horas
2 (*two people*) **la pareja** *fem.*
a young couple una pareja joven
a married couple una pareja de
casados

• *See the centre section for verb tables.*

courgette noun
el **calabacín** *masc.* (plural los **calabacines**)

course noun
1 (*lessons*) el **curso** *masc.*
a Spanish course un curso de español
My sister's going on a course. Mi hermana va a hacer un curso.
2 (*part of a meal*) el **plato** *masc.*
the main course el plato principal
3 of course claro
Can you help me? – Of course I can! ¿Puedes ayudarme? – ¡Claro que sí!
of course not claro que no

court noun
(*for sports*) la **pista** *fem.*
a tennis court una pista de tenis

cousin noun
el **primo** *masc.*, la **prima** *fem.*

cover noun
(*of a book or magazine*) la **tapa** *fem.*
the covers (*on a bed*) las mantas

to **cover** verb
cubrir
I covered myself with a sheet. Me cubrí con una sábana.
You're covered in mud! ¡Estás cubierta de barro!

cow noun
la **vaca** *fem.*

cowboy noun
el **vaquero** *masc.*

crab noun
el **cangrejo** *masc.*

cracker noun
(*biscuit*) la **galleta salada** *fem.*

> **CULTURE**
> Christmas crackers do not exist in Spain so there is no word for them in Spanish.

crash noun
el **accidente** *masc.*, el **choque** *masc.*
a car crash un accidente de coche
a crash helmet un casco

to **crash** verb
to crash into something chocar con algo
The lorry crashed into a lamp-post. El camión chocó con una farola.

to **crawl** verb
1 (*talking about babies*) **gatear**
2 (*talking about insects*) **andar**

crayon noun
el **lápiz de color** *masc.*, la **crayola**® *fem.*

crazy adjective
loco *masc.*, **loca** *fem.*
You're crazy! ¡Estás loco!
My brother's crazy about football. A mi hermano le encanta el fútbol.

cream noun
1 (*from milk*) la **nata** *fem.*
strawberries and cream fresas con nata
2 (*for your skin*) la **crema** *fem.*

to **create** verb
crear

crèche noun
la **guardería** *fem.*

crew noun
(*on a plane or ship*) la **tripulación** *fem.* (plural las **tripulaciones**)

cricket noun
el **críquet** *masc.*
Do you like playing cricket? ¿Te gusta jugar al críquet?
a cricket bat un bate de críquet

> **CULTURE**
> Spanish people do not play cricket.

• Use **el** and **uno** for masculine words and **la** and **una** for feminine words.

crime noun
1 el **delito** masc.
2 (serious crime, such as murder) el **crimen** masc. (plural los **crímenes**)

criminal noun
1 el or la **delincuente** masc. & fem.
2 (murderer) el or la **criminal** masc. & fem.

crisps plural noun
las **patatas fritas** fem. plural
a bag of crisps una bolsa de patatas fritas

LANGUAGE
Word for word patatas fritas means 'fried potatoes'. The Spanish can also mean 'chips'.

to **criticize** verb
criticar

crocodile noun
el **cocodrilo** masc.

LANGUAGE
English = crocodile
Spanish = cocodrilo

crooked adjective
torcido masc., **torcida** fem.
The picture is crooked. El cuadro está torcido.

to **cross** verb
1 **cruzar**
Let's cross the road. Vamos a cruzar la calle.
Cross your arms. Cruzad los brazos.
2 to cross something out tachar algo

cross noun
la **cruz** fem. (plural las **cruces**)
Put a cross in the box. Pon una cruz en la casilla.

cross adjective
(angry) **enfadado** masc., **enfadada** fem.
Are you cross with me? ¿Estás enfadado conmigo?
to get cross enfadarse

I got cross with my sister. Me enfadé con mi hermana.

crossing
1 (safe place to cross the road) el **paso de peatones** masc.
2 (by boat) **la travesía** fem.

crossroads noun
el **cruce** masc.
at the crossroads en el cruce

crossword noun
el **crucigrama** masc.
I like doing crosswords. Me gusta hacer crucigramas.

LANGUAGE
Be careful: crucigrama ends in an -a but it is not a feminine noun.

crowd noun
a crowd mucha gente fem.
There are crowds of people in the shops. Hay mucha gente en las tiendas.

LANGUAGE
Word for word mucha gente means 'lots of people'. In Spanish you normally say this for a crowd.

crowded adjective
It's crowded. Hay mucha gente.

crown noun
la **corona** fem.

cruel adjective
cruel masc. & fem.
a cruel man un hombre cruel

crumbs plural noun
las **migas** fem. plural

to **crush** verb
aplastar

crust noun
la **corteza** fem.

• Languages and nationalities do not take a capital letter in Spanish.

crutch noun
la **muleta** *fem.*
She's on crutches. Anda con muletas.

to **cry** verb
llorar
Don't cry! ¡No llores!

cub noun
(*young lion, bear, or wolf*) el **cachorro** *masc.*

Cub noun
(*Scout*) el **lobato** *masc.*
He's in the Cubs. Pertenece a los lobatos.

Cuba noun
Cuba *fem.*

cube noun
el **cubo** *masc.*
an ice cube un cubito de hielo

cucumber noun
el **pepino** *masc.*

cup
1 la **taza** *fem.*
a cup of tea una taza de té
2 (*prize*) la **copa** *fem.*
the World Cup la Copa del Mundo

cupboard noun
el **armario** *masc.*

curious adjective
curioso *masc.*, **curiosa** *fem.*

curly adjective
rizado *masc.*, **rizada** *fem.*
I have curly hair. Tengo el pelo rizado.

curriculum noun
the curriculum el plan de estudios

curry noun
el **curry** *masc.* (plural los **currys**)
chicken curry el pollo al curry

cursor noun
el **cursor** *masc.*

curtain noun
la **cortina** *fem.*

curve noun
la **curva** *fem.*

curved adjective
curvo *masc.*, **curva** *fem.*
a curved line una línea curva

cushion noun
el **cojín** *masc.* (plural los **cojines**)

custard noun
las **natillas** *fem. plural*

custom noun
la **costumbre** *fem.*

customer noun
el **cliente** *masc.*, **la clienta** *fem.*

to **cut** verb
1 **cortar**
Cut the cake. Corta el pastel.
I've cut my finger. Me he cortado el dedo.
I've cut my hair. Me he cortado el pelo
2 **to cut something out** recortar algo
Cut this picture out of the paper. Recorta esta foto del periódico.

cut noun
(*on your finger etc.*) el **corte** *masc.*

cutlery noun
los **cubiertos** *masc. plural*

to **cycle** verb
ir en bicicleta
My brother cycles to school. Mi hermano va al colegio en bicicleta.
to go cycling ir en bicicleta
a cycle path un carril bici

cycling noun
(*sport*) el **ciclismo** *masc.*

cyclist noun
el or la **ciclista** *masc. & fem.*

• *The months of the year and days of the week do not take a capital letter in Spanish.*

Dd

dad noun
el **papá** *masc.*, el **padre** *masc.*
Good night, dad. Buenas noches, papá.
My dad works in an office.
Mi padre trabaja en una oficina.
my mum and dad mis papás

daddy noun
el **papá** *masc.*
Bye, daddy! ¡Adiós, papá!

daily adjective
diario *masc.*, **diaria** *fem.*

damage noun
los **daños** *masc. plural*

> 🔑 **LANGUAGE**
> English = damage is singular
> Spanish = los daños is plural

damp adjective
húmedo *masc.*, **húmeda** *fem.*

dance noun
el **baile** *masc.*
She goes to dance classes. Va a clase de baile.

to **dance** verb
bailar
I love dancing. Me encanta bailar.

dancer noun
el **bailarín** *masc.*, la **bailarina** *fem.*

> 🔑 **LANGUAGE**
> The Spanish words are related to the English word 'ballerina'.

danger noun
el **peligro** *masc.*
We're in danger. Estamos en peligro.

dangerous adjective
peligroso *masc.*, **peligrosa** *fem.*

• *See the centre section for verb tables.*

to **dare** verb
atreverse
I don't dare to go out. No me atrevo a salir.

dark adjective
1 (*room, colours, hair, etc.*) **oscuro** *masc.*, **oscura** *fem.*
It's dark here. Está oscuro aquí.
I have dark eyes. Tengo los ojos oscuros.
dark blue dresses vestidos azul oscuro

> 🔑 **LANGUAGE**
> With colours use oscuro and the colour word in the masculine singular form only.

2 (*describing night-time*)
It's dark. Es de noche.
It's getting dark. Se está haciendo de noche.

dark noun
la **oscuridad** *fem.*
I'm afraid of the dark. Me da miedo la oscuridad.

darling exclamation
¡cariño!
Yes, darling! ¡Sí, cariño!

database noun
el **banco de datos** *masc.*

date noun
la **fecha** *fem.*
What's your date of birth? ¿Cuál es tu fecha de nacimiento?
What's the date today? ¿A qué fecha estamos hoy?

daughter noun
la **hija** *fem.*

day noun
1 el **día** *masc.*
two days later dos días más tarde
every day todos los días

What day is it today? ¿Qué día es hoy?
It rained all day. Llovió todo el día.
2 **the day before yesterday** anteayer
the day after tomorrow pasado mañana

> **LANGUAGE**
> Be careful: **día** ends in an **-a** but it is not a feminine noun.

daytime noun
el **día** masc.

dead adjective
muerto masc., **muerta** fem.
He's dead. Está muerto.

> **LANGUAGE**
> Be careful: translate 'be dead' by **estar muerto**, not **ser muerto**, even though you normally use **estar** for something that lasts a short time.

deaf adjective
sordo masc., **sorda** fem.
He's deaf. Es sordo.

dear adjective
1 (person) **querido** masc., **querida** fem.
Dear Tina ... Querida Tina ...
2 (expensive) **caro** masc., **cara** fem.
This blouse is too dear. Esta blusa es demasiado cara.

dear exclamation
Oh dear! ¡Oh, no!

death noun
la **muerte** fem.

December noun
diciembre masc.
I was born in December. Nací en diciembre.
We're going to Valencia on the fifth of December. Vamos a Valencia el cinco de diciembre.

to **decide** verb
decidir
I've decided to learn Spanish. He decidido aprender español.
I can't decide. No puedo decidir.

decision noun
la **decisión** fem. (plural las **decisiones**)
I've made a decision. He tomado una decisión.

> **LANGUAGE**
> Use **tomar** (to take) with **decisión**, not **hacer** (to make).

deckchair noun
la **hamaca** fem.

to **decorate** verb
1 (with pictures, balloons, etc.) **decorar**
We've decorated the classroom. Hemos decorado la clase.
2 **to decorate the Christmas tree** adornar el árbol de Navidad
3 (to paint) **pintar**
We're decorating the dining room. Estamos pintando el comedor.

decorations plural noun
los **adornos** masc. plural
I'm putting up the Christmas decorations. Estoy poniendo los adornos de Navidad.

deep adjective
profundo masc., **profunda** fem.
a deep river un río profundo

deer noun
el **ciervo** masc.

to **defend** verb
defender

definite
(certain) **seguro** masc., **segura** fem.
I can come but it's not definite. Puedo venir pero no es seguro.
a definite date una fecha segura

definitely adverb
yes, definitely sí, claro
Are you coming? – Yes, definitely. ¿Vienes tú? – Sí, claro.
definitely not claro que no

• Use **el** and **uno** for masculine words and **la** and **una** for feminine words.

degree noun
1 (*of temperature*) el **grado** *masc.*
It's twenty-five degrees. Estamos a veinticinco grados.
2 (*university certificate*) el **título universitario** *masc.*

delay noun
el **retraso** *masc.*

to **delay** verb
retrasar
Our flight has been delayed. Nuestro vuelo se ha retrasado.

delete verb
(*a file, word, etc.*) **borrar**
Delete that file. Borra ese fichero.

delicious adjective
delicioso *masc.*, **deliciosa** *fem.*
This cake is delicious. Este pastel está delicioso.

> 🔑 **LANGUAGE**
> In Spanish you can also say **rico/rica**, e.g. **Este pastel está muy rico.**

deliver verb
(*milk, newspapers, pizzas, etc.*) **traer**
Have they delivered the pizzas? ¿Han traído las pizzas?
to deliver a parcel entregar un paquete

denim adjective
vaquero *masc.*, **vaquera** *fem.*
a denim skirt una falda vaquera

dentist noun
el or la **dentista** *masc. & fem.*
I'm going to the dentist. Voy al dentista.

department noun
1 (*in a store*) la **sección** *fem.* (plural las **secciones**)
the toy department la sección de juguetes

> 🔑 **LANGUAGE**
> **Sección** is similar to 'section' in English.

2 (*in a university*) el **departamento** *masc.*
3 **a department store** unos grandes almacenes

departure noun
la **salida** *fem.*

to **depend** verb
depender
That depends on you. Depende de ti.
It all depends. Depende.

deputy head noun
el **subdirector** *masc.*, la **subdirectora** *fem.*

to **describe** verb
describir
Describe your family. Describe a tu familia.

description noun
la **descripción** *fem.* (plural las **descripciones**)

desert noun
el **desierto** *masc.*

to **deserve** verb
merecer
You deserve the prize. Te mereces el premio.

design noun
el **diseño** *masc.*
a flower design un diseño de flores

to **design** verb
diseñar
My mother designs dresses. Mi madre diseña vestidos.

desk noun
1 (*for a pupil*) la **mesa** *fem.*
2 (*in an office, and for a teacher*) el **escritorio** *masc.*

dessert noun
el **postre** *masc.*
What's for dessert? ¿Qué hay de postre?

• *Languages and nationalities do not take a capital letter in Spanish.*

destination noun
el **destino** masc.

to **destroy** verb
destruir

detail noun
el **detalle** masc.
in detail con todo detalle

detective noun
el or la **detective** masc. & fem.
a private detective un detective
privado masc., una detective
privada fem.
a detective story una novela
policíaca

detention noun
to be in detention estar castigado
masc., estar castigada fem.
The teacher gave her a detention.
La maestra la dejó castigada
después de clase.

> **LANGUAGE**
> **Castigar** means 'to punish'; there is no
> word for **detention** in Spanish.

devil noun
el **diablo** masc.

diagram noun
el **diagrama** masc.
to draw a diagram hacer un
diagrama

> **LANGUAGE**
> Be careful: **diagrama** ends in an -**a** but it
> is not a feminine noun.

to **dial** verb
marcar
to dial a number marcar un
número

diamond noun
el **diamante** masc.
a diamond ring un anillo de
diamantes

diary noun
1 (for writing appointments in) la **agenda**
fem.

2 (for writing private things in) el **diario**
masc.
I keep a diary. Escribo un diario.

> **LANGUAGE**
> The Spanish **diario** also means 'daily'
> because you write in it every day.

dice noun
el **dado** masc.
Throw the dice. Tira el dado.

> **LANGUAGE**
> The plural of dice is also 'dice' so 'Throw
> the dice' can also be **Tira los dados**.

dictionary noun
el **diccionario** masc.
**I'm looking up a word in the
dictionary.** Estoy buscando una
palabra en el diccionario.

did verb SEE do
I didn't do it. No lo hice.
He did nothing. No hizo nada.

to **die** verb
morir
My cat died last week. Mi gato
murió la semana pasada.

diet noun
(food) la **dieta** fem.
I have a healthy diet. Llevo una
dieta sana.

difference noun
la **diferencia** fem.
**What's the difference between the
two?** ¿Qué diferencia hay entre los
dos?

different adjective
distinto masc., **distinta** fem.
I'm very different from my sister.
Soy muy distinta a mi hermana.

> **LANGUAGE**
> You can also say **diferente** in Spanish.

difficult adjective
difícil masc. & fem.
It's very difficult. Es muy difícil.

• The months of the year and days of the week do not take a capital letter in Spanish.

to **dig** verb
 cavar
 to dig a hole cavar un agujero

digital adjective
 (*camera, television, watch*) **digital** *masc. & fem.*

dining room noun
 el **comedor** *masc.*

dinner noun
 1 (*in the evening*) la **cena** *fem.*
  What's for dinner? ¿Qué hay de cena?
  to have dinner cenar
  It's dinner time. Es la hora de cenar.
 2 (*at midday*) la **comida** *fem.*
  to have dinner comer
  It's dinner time. Es la hora de comer.
  Do you like school dinners? ¿Te gusta comer en el colegio?

dinosaur noun
 el **dinosaurio** *masc.*

direct adjective
 directo *masc.*, **directa** *fem.*

direction noun
 la **dirección** *fem.* (plural las **direcciones**)
 We're going in the opposite direction. Vamos en dirección contraria.
 Are we going in the right direction? ¿Vamos bien?
 I asked for directions to the station. Pregunté el camino a la estación.

directory noun
 (*phone book*) la **guía telefónica** *fem.*

dirty adjective
 sucio *masc.*, **sucia** *fem.*
 The table is dirty. La mesa está sucia.
 My hands are dirty. Tengo las manos sucias.

• *See the centre section for verb tables.*

disabled adjective
 minusválido *masc.*,
 minusválida *fem.*

to **disagree** verb
 I disagree. No estoy de acuerdo.

to **disappear** verb
 desaparecer
 My pen has disappeared. Mi bolígrafo ha desaparecido.

to **disappoint** verb
 decepcionar
 I'm disappointed. Estoy decepcionada.

disaster noun
 el **desastre** *masc.*

disco noun
 1 (*party where you dance*) el **baile** *masc.*
 2 (*place where you dance*) la **discoteca** *fem.*

to **discover** verb
 descubrir

discovery noun
 el **descubrimiento** *masc.*

to **discuss** verb
 to discuss something hablar de algo

disease noun
 la **enfermedad** *fem.*

disguise noun
 el **disfraz** *masc.* (plural los **disfraces**)

to **disguise** verb
 disfrazar
 I disguised myself as a pirate. Me disfracé de pirata.

disguised adjective
 disfrazado *masc.*, **disfrazada** *fem.*
 I'm disguised as a pirate. Estoy disfrazada de pirata.

disgusting adjective
 asqueroso *masc.*, **asquerosa** *fem.*
 This food's disgusting. Esta comida está asquerosa.

a
b
c
d
e
f
g
h
i
j
k
l
m
n
o
p
q
r
s
t
u
v
w
x
y
z

dish noun
el **plato** masc.
I'm doing the dishes. Estoy lavando los platos.

dishwasher noun
el **lavaplatos** masc. (plural los **lavaplatos**)

disk noun
el **disco** masc.
I copied the files onto a disk. He copiado los archivos en un disco.

to **dislike** verb
I dislike this music. No me gusta esta música.

> **LANGUAGE**
> Gustar means 'to please' so the order of the words in the Spanish sentence is different, e.g. 'I dislike this music' is, word for word, 'This music does not please me'.

to **disobey** verb
desobedecer

to **display** verb
exponer
We're going to display the pictures in the classroom. Vamos a exponer los dibujos en la clase.

distance noun
la **distancia** fem.
What's the distance between London and Madrid? ¿Qué distancia hay entre Londres y Madrid?
in the distance a lo lejos

district noun
1 (in a town) el **barrio** masc.
2 (in a country) la **región** fem. (plural las **regiones**)

to **disturb** verb
molestar
Sorry to disturb you. Siento molestarle.

to **dive** verb
1 (into the water) **tirarse de cabeza**
I dived into the swimming pool. Me tiré de cabeza a la piscina.

2 (under the water) **bucear**
I want to go diving. Quiero ir a bucear.

diver noun
el or la **submarinista** masc. & fem.

to **divide** verb
dividir
Eight divided by two is four. Ocho dividido por dos son cuatro.

divorced adjective
divorciado masc., **divorciada** fem.
My parents are divorced. Mis padres están divorciados.

dizzy adjective
mareado masc., **mareada** fem.
I feel dizzy Estoy mareado

DJ noun
el or la **disc-jockey** masc. & fem.

to **do** verb
1 **hacer**
I do my homework. Hago mis deberes.
What are you doing? ¿Qué estás haciendo?
What have you done with my pen? ¿Qué has hecho con mi boli?
Who did that? ¿Quién hizo eso?

2 (in questions 'do' and 'does' are not translated)
Do you want some bread? ¿Quieres pan?
Where do you live? ¿Dónde vives?
How much does it cost? ¿Cuánto cuesta?

3 (in negative sentences use 'no' before the verb)
I don't know. No sé.
He doesn't like tomatoes. No le gustan los tomates.

> **LANGUAGE**
> To translate questions such as 'doesn't she?' or 'don't you?', you can use ¿no? in Spanish, e.g. 'You play football, don't you?' is Juegas al fútbol, ¿no?

• Use **el** and **uno** for masculine words and **la** and **una** for feminine words.

to **do up** verb
1 (*a coat, jacket, etc.*) **abrochar**
Do up your shirt. Abróchate la camisa.
2 (*shoes*) **atar**
Do up your shoes. Átate los zapatos.
3 (*a room, house, etc.*) **arreglar**

doctor noun
el **médico** *masc.*, la **médica** *fem.*
He's a doctor. Es médico.
I'm going to the doctor. Voy al médico.

dodgems plural noun
los **autos** or los **coches de choque** *masc. plural*

does verb SEE **do**
Dad does the shopping. Papá hace la compra.
She doesn't know. No sabe.

dog noun
el **perro** *masc.*, la **perra** *fem.*
I like dogs. Me gustan los perros.

doll noun
la **muñeca** *fem.*
a doll's house una casa de muñecas

dollar noun
el **dólar** *masc.*

dolphin noun
el **delfín** *masc.* (plural los **delfines**)

dominoes plural noun
el **dominó** *masc.*
to play dominoes jugar al dominó

done verb SEE **do**
I've done my homework. He hecho mis deberes.
Have you done it? ¿Lo has hecho?

donkey noun
el **burro** *masc.*

door noun
la **puerta** *fem.*
Close the door. Cierra la puerta.

doorbell noun
el **timbre** *masc.*
Ring the doorbell. Toca el timbre.

dormitory noun
el **dormitorio** *masc.*

LANGUAGE
Both 'dormitory' and dormitorio are related to the Spanish word dormir (to sleep) because you sleep there.

dot noun
el **punto** *masc.*

double adjective
doble *masc. & fem.*
a double room una habitación doble
a double bed una cama de matrimonio

double-decker noun
el **autobús de dos pisos** *masc.*

LANGUAGE
The plural of autobús is autobuses.

doubt noun
la **duda** *fem.*

to **doubt** verb
dudar
I doubt it. Lo dudo.

dough noun
la **masa** *fem.*

doughnut noun
la **rosquilla** *fem.*, el **donut** *masc.*

down adverb & preposition
abajo
It's down there. Está allí abajo.
I looked down. Miré hacia abajo.
Helen lives just down the road. Helen vive muy cerca.

LANGUAGE
'Down' is often translated as part of a verb such as 'to go down' (bajar) or 'to sit down' (sentarse).

• Languages and nationalities do not take a capital letter in Spanish.

down adjective
(*not working*)
The computers are down. Los ordenadores no funcionan.

to **download** verb
descargar
I downloaded the program. Descargué el programa.

downstairs adverb
abajo
I'm downstairs in the kitchen. Estoy abajo en la cocina.
Come downstairs! ¡Baja!

> **LANGUAGE**
> Use **bajar** to translate 'to come downstairs' or 'to go downstairs'.

dozen noun
la **docena** *fem.*
two dozen dos docenas
a dozen eggs una docena de huevos

> **LANGUAGE**
> When 'dozen' is followed by a noun use **de** before the noun in Spanish.

dragon noun
el **dragón** *masc.* (plural los **dragones**)

draught noun
la **corriente** *fem.*
There's a draught here. Aquí hay corriente.

draughts plural noun
las **damas** *fem. plural*
We're playing draughts. Estamos jugando a la damas.

to **draw** verb
1 **dibujar**
I'm drawing a dog. Dibujo un perro.
to draw a picture hacer un dibujo
2 **to draw the curtains** correr las cortinas
3 (*in a match*) **empatar**

The two teams drew. Los dos equipos empataron.

draw noun
el **empate** *masc.*
The match ended in a draw. El partido acabó en empate.

drawer noun
el **cajón** *masc.* (plural los **cajones**)

> **LANGUAGE**
> **Cajón** comes from **caja** (box) and **-ón** (meaning big) – it's a big box.

drawing noun
el **dibujo** *masc.*
I love your drawing. Me encanta tu dibujo.

drawing pin noun
la **chincheta** *fem.*

dreadful adjective
(*weather, accident, etc.*) **horrible** *masc. & fem.*

dream noun
el **sueño** *masc.*
I've had a strange dream. He tenido un sueño extraño.

to **dream** verb
soñar
I dreamt about you! ¡Soñé contigo!

dress noun
el **vestido** *masc.*
I like your dress. Me gusta tu vestido .

to **dress** verb
1 **to get dressed** vestirse
I'll get dressed. Me voy a vestir.
2 **to dress up** disfrazarse
I want to dress up as a pirate. Quiero disfrazarme de pirata.

dressed adjective
1 **vestido** *masc.*, **vestida** *fem.*
Are you dressed? ¿Estás vestido?
2 **to get dressed** vestirse
She's getting dressed. Se está vistiendo.

• *The months of the year and days of the week do not take a capital letter in Spanish.*

dressing gown noun
la **bata** fem.

drink noun
la **bebida** fem.
a hot drink una bebida caliente
Do you want a drink? ¿Quieres beber algo?

to **drink** verb
beber
I drank a glass of water. Bebí un vaso de agua.

drive noun
1 la **vuelta en coche** fem.
Do you want to go for a drive? ¿Quieres ir a dar una vuelta en coche?
2 (place in front of the house) la **entrada** fem.
They've parked the car in the drive. Han aparcado el coche en la entrada.

to **drive** verb
1 **conducir**
to drive a car conducir un coche
Can you drive? ¿Sabes conducir?
2 (to go somewhere by car) **ir en coche**
We drove to Spain. Fuimos a España en coche.
3 (to take somebody by car) **llevar en coche**
My dad drives me to school. Mi padre me lleva a la escuela en coche.

driver noun
el **conductor** masc., la **conductora** fem.
a taxi driver un or una taxista

driving licence noun
el **permiso de conducir** masc.

drop noun
la **gota** fem.
a drop of water una gota de agua

• See the centre section for verb tables.

to **drop** verb
1 **I dropped the plate.** Tiré el plato.
Don't drop it! ¡No lo tires!

> ⚷ **LANGUAGE**
> You can also use the verb **caerse** (to fall down) in Spanish, so 'I dropped the plate' can be **El plato se me cayó**. Word for word this means 'The plate fell down from me'.

2 (to let somebody out of a car) **dejar**
Can you drop me at the school? ¿Me puedes dejar delante del colegio?

to **drown** verb
ahogarse
He fell into the river and drowned. Se cayó al río y se ahogó.

drum noun
el **tambor** masc.
the drums la batería fem.
My brother plays the drums. Mi hermano toca la batería.

drunk adjective
borracho masc., **borracha** fem.
He's drunk. Está borracho.

dry adjective
seco masc., **seca** fem.
The towels are dry. Las toallas están secas.

to **dry** verb
secar
I'm drying the dishes. Estoy secando los platos.
She's drying her hair. Se está secando el pelo.

duck noun
el **pato** masc.

dull adjective
1 (boring) **aburrido** masc., **aburrida** fem.
2 (weather) **gris** masc. & fem.
It's very dull today. Es un día muy gris.

dumb adjective
(*stupid*) **tonto** *masc.*, **tonta** *fem.*

dummy noun
el **chupete** *masc.*

during preposition
durante
during the class durante la clase

dust noun
el **polvo** *masc.*

dustbin noun
el **cubo de basura** *masc.*

dusty adjective
lleno de polvo *masc.*, **llena de polvo** *fem.*

Dutch adjective
holandés *masc.*, **holandesa** *fem.*
She's Dutch. Es holandesa.

Dutch noun
1 (*language*) el **holandés** *masc.*
2 **the Dutch** los holandeses *masc.*
plural

duvet noun
el **edredón** *masc.* (plural los **edredones**)

DVD noun
el **DVD** *masc.* (plural los **DVDs**)
a DVD player un reproductor DVD

dwarf noun
el **enano** *masc.*, la **enana** *fem.*

dyslexic adjective
disléxico *masc.*, **disléxica** *fem.*
I'm dyslexic. Soy disléxico.

Ee

each adjective
cada *masc. & fem.*
each time cada vez

each pronoun
cada uno *masc.*, **cada una** *fem.*
The pupils have a computer each.
Los alumnos tienen un ordenador cada uno.

each other pronoun
We hate each other! ¡Nos odiamos!
Do you know each other?
¿Os conocéis?
They write to each other.
Se escriben.

eagle noun
el **águila** *fem.*

ear noun
la **oreja** *fem.*, el **oído** *masc.*
The elephant has big ears.
El elefante tiene orejas grandes.
My ear hurts. Me duele el oído.

earache noun
el **dolor de oídos** *masc.*
I have an earache. Tengo dolor de oídos.

• *Use* **el** *and* **uno** *for masculine words and* **la** *and* **una** *for feminine words.*

earlier adverb
más temprano
Wake up earlier tomorrow.
Despiértate más temprano
mañana.

early adjective
I'm having an early night. Me voy
a la cama temprano.

early adverb
temprano, **pronto**
I get up early. Me levanto temprano.
It's too early. Es demasiado
temprano.
to arrive early llegar pronto
You're early. Has llegado pronto.

to **earn** verb
ganar
My mum earns a lot of money.
Mi madre gana mucho dinero.

earring noun
el **pendiente** masc.

earth noun
la **tierra** fem.

earthquake noun
el **terremoto** masc.

easily adverb
fácilmente

east noun & adjective
el **este** masc.
in the east en el este
the east coast la costa este

Easter noun
la **Semana Santa** fem.
I'm going to Madrid at Easter.
Voy a Madrid en Semana Santa.
Easter Day .el Domingo de Pascua
an Easter egg un huevo de Pascua

CULTURE
Word for word Semana Santa is Holy
Week: it means the whole Easter period.
Pascua is Easter Sunday or Monday.
Spanish people take part in religious
processions, such as the famous one in
Seville.

easy adjective
fácil masc. & fem.
It's easy to speak Spanish. Es fácil
hablar español.

to **eat** verb
comer
I'm eating an apple. Estoy
comiendo una manzana.
I want something to eat. Quiero
comer algo.

edge noun
el **borde** masc.
the edge of the table el borde de la
mesa

Edinburgh noun
Edimburgo masc.

education noun
la **educación** fem.
primary education la enseñanza
primaria

educational adjective
(game, toy, etc.) **educativo** masc.,
educativa fem.

effort noun
el **esfuerzo** masc.
Make an effort. Haz un esfuerzo.

e.g. abbreviation
p. ej.

LANGUAGE
e.g. stands for Latin exempli gratia, and
p. ej. is short for Spanish por ejemplo (for
example).

egg noun
el **huevo** masc.
a boiled egg un huevo pasado por
agua
a hard-boiled egg un huevo duro
a fried egg un huevo frito
scrambled eggs los huevos
revueltos

eggcup noun
la **huevera** fem.

a
b
c
d
e
f
g
h
i
j
k
l
m
n
o
p
q
r
s
t
u
v
w
x
y
z

• Languages and nationalities do not take a capital letter in Spanish.

eight number
ocho
I go to bed at eight. Me acuesto a las ocho.
Luke is eight. Luke tiene ocho años.

eighteen number
dieciocho
My brother is eighteen. Mi hermano tiene dieciocho años.

eighth adjective
octavo masc., **octava** fem.
on the eighth floor en el octavo piso
the eighth of June el ocho de junio

eighty number
ochenta

either adverb
tampoco
You can't swim and I can't either. Tú no sabes nadar y yo tampoco.
I don't have any friends either. Yo tampoco tengo amigos.

either pronoun
1 **cualquiera**
Take either of them. Toma cualquiera de los dos.
2 (with negatives) **ninguno** masc., **ninguna** fem.
I don't want either of them. No quiero ninguno.

either conjunction
either ... or o ... o
You can have either meat or fish. Puedes comer o carne o pescado.
I don't like either tea or coffee. No me gusta el té ni el café.

elastic band noun
la **goma** fem.

elbow noun
el **codo** masc.

eldest adjective
mayor masc. & fem.
my eldest sister mi hermana mayor

electric adjective
eléctrico masc., **eléctrica** fem.

electrician noun
el or la **electricista** masc. & fem.
My dad's an electrician. Mi padre es electricista.

electricity noun
la **electricidad** fem.

elephant noun
el **elefante** masc.

eleven number
once
I woke up at eleven. Me desperté a las once.
My friend is eleven. Mi amiga tiene once años.

eleventh adjective
the eleventh floor el piso once
the eleventh of December el once de diciembre

else adverb
1 (using **más**)
nobody else nadie más
nothing else nada más

· The months of the year and days of the week do not take a capital letter in Spanish.

What else? ¿Qué más?
Anything else? ¿Algo más?
2 (using **otra**)
somebody else otra persona
something else otra cosa
somewhere else en otra parte
3 (using **demás**)
everybody else todos los demás
everything else todo lo demás

LANGUAGE
Remember the three main ways to say 'else' in Spanish: **más** means 'more', **otra** means 'other', and **lo demás** means 'the rest'.

email noun
el **email** masc., el **correo electrónico** masc.
I've sent an email. He enviado un email.
an email address una dirección de email

to **email** verb
to email somebody enviar un email a alguien

emergency noun
la **emergencia** fem.
in an emergency en caso de emergencia
an emergency exit una salida de emergencia

empty adjective
vacío masc., **vacía** fem.
The bottle is empty. La botella está vacía.

to **empty** verb
vaciar

encyclopedia noun
la **enciclopedia** fem.

end noun
1 (the last part) el **final** masc.
at the end of the book al final del libro
at the end of July a finales de julio

2 (of a place) el **final** masc., el **fondo** masc.
at the end of the street al final de la calle
at the end of the corridor al fondo del pasillo
at the other end of town al otro extremo de la ciudad

to **end** verb
terminar
The film ends at two. La película termina a las dos.

ending noun
(of a book, film, or play) el **final** masc.
a happy ending un final feliz

enemy noun
el **enemigo** masc., **la enemiga** fem.

energy noun
la **energía** fem.

engaged adjective
1 (going to be married) **prometido** masc., **prometida** fem.
They're engaged. Están prometidos.
2 (talking about a phone) **comunicando**
It's engaged. Está comunicando.
3 (talking about a toilet) **ocupado** masc., **ocupada** fem.

engine noun
1 (in a car) el **motor** masc.
2 (of a train) la **locomotora** fem.

LANGUAGE
Locomotora is related to 'locomotive'.

engineer noun
1 (who designs things) el **ingeniero** masc., la **ingeniera** fem.
2 (who fixes things) el **técnico** masc., la **técnica** fem.

England noun
Inglaterra fem.
We live in England. Vivimos en Inglaterra.
They want to go to England. Quieren ir a Inglaterra.

• See the centre section for verb tables.

a b c d e f g h i j k l m n o p q r s t u v w x y z

275

English adjective
inglés *masc.*, **inglesa** *fem.*
an English town una ciudad inglesa
I'm English. Soy inglés.
She's English. Es inglesa.
my English lesson mi clase de inglés
English people los ingleses

LANGUAGE
The masculine plural of inglés is ingleses.

English noun
1 (*language*) el **inglés** *masc.*
Do you speak English? ¿Habla usted inglés?
2 **the English** los ingleses *masc. plural*

Englishman, **Englishwoman** noun
el **inglés** *masc.* (plural los **ingleses**); la **inglesa** *fem.*

to **enjoy** verb
1 **I enjoy reading.** Me gusta leer.

LANGUAGE
Gustar means 'to please' so the order of the words in the Spanish sentence is different, e.g. 'I enjoy reading' is, word for word, 'It pleases me to read'.

2 **to enjoy yourself** divertirse
I enjoyed myself. Me divertí mucho.

enjoyable adjective
1 **agradable** *masc. & fem.*
enjoyable holidays unas vacaciones agradables
2 **divertido** *masc.*, **divertida** *fem.*
The film is very enjoyable. La película es muy divertida.

enormous adjective
enorme *masc. & fem.*

enough adverb & pronoun
bastante
I've eaten enough. He comido bastante.
Is there enough? ¿Hay bastante?
That's enough! ¡Basta!

enough adjective
bastante *masc. & fem.*, **suficiente** *masc. & fem.*
I have enough money. Tengo bastante dinero.
I don't have enough money. No tengo suficiente dinero.

to **enter** verb
(*a competition, an exam*) **presentarse a**
I'm entering the competition. Me presento al concurso.

entrance noun
la **entrada** *fem.*
Where's the entrance? ¿Dónde está la entrada?
an entrance exam un examen de ingreso

entry noun
'No entry' (*on a door*) 'Prohibida la entrada'

envelope noun
el **sobre** *masc.*

environment noun
el **medio ambiente** *masc.*

episode noun
el **episodio** *masc.*

equal adjective
igual *masc. & fem.*
two equal groups dos grupos iguales

to **equal** verb
ser igual a
Four plus two equals six. Cuatro más dos es igual a seis.

equipment noun
el **equipo** *masc.*

error noun
el **error** *masc.*

escalator noun
la **escalera mecánica** *fem.*

to **escape** verb
escaparse
The rabbit has escaped. Se ha escapado el conejo.

• *Use* **el** *and* **uno** *for masculine words and* **la** *and* **una** *for feminine words.*

especially adverb
especialmente, **sobre todo**
I like Madrid, especially the people. Me gusta Madrid, especialmente la gente.

essay noun
la **redacción** *fem.*

essential adjective
esencial *masc. & fem.*
It's essential to know Spanish. Es esencial saber español.

estate noun
(*housing estate*) la **urbanización** *fem.*
(plural las **urbanizaciones**)
I live on an estate. Vivo en una urbanización.

EU noun
la **UE** *fem.*

euro noun
el **euro** *masc.*
It costs five euros. Cuesta cinco euros.

Europe noun
Europa *fem.*

European adjective
europeo *masc.*, **europea** *fem.*
the European Union la Unión Europea

European noun
el **europeo** *masc.*, la **europea** *fem.*

Eve noun
Christmas Eve la Nochebuena
New Year's Eve la Nochevieja

even adverb
1 **incluso**
Everyone's coming, even my sister. Todos vienen, incluso mi hermana.
2 (*when comparing things*) **aún**, **todavía**
even more difficult aún más difícil, todavía mas difícil

even adjective
an even number un número par

evening noun
1 (*before it gets dark*) la **tarde** *fem.*
In the evening I watch TV. Por la tarde veo la tele.
at six in the evening a la seis de la tarde
this evening esta tarde
tomorrow evening mañana por la tarde
Good evening! ¡Buenas tardes!
2 (*when it's dark*) la **noche** *fem.*
at nine in the evening a las nueve de la noche
Good evening! ¡Buenas noches!
an evening class una clase nocturna

ever adverb
1 **alguna vez**
Have you ever been to Madrid? ¿Has estado alguna vez en Madrid?
2 **nunca**
The cat's fatter than ever. El gato está más gordo que nunca.
I hardly ever eat fish. Casi nunca como pescado.

3 (*always*) **siempre**
for ever para siempre
4 ever since, ever since then desde entonces

• Languages and nationalities do not take a capital letter in Spanish.

English Spanish

a
b
c
d
e
f
g
h
i
j
k
l
m
n
o
p
q
r
s
t
u
v
w
x
y
z

every adjective
1 **todos** *masc. plural*, **todas** *fem. plural*
   every day todos los días
   every week todas las semanas
   every Saturday todos los
   sábados

LANGUAGE
Todos is always followed by **los** and
todas by **las**.

2 **cada** *masc. & fem.*
   **Every pupil has an exercise
   book.** Cada alumno tiene un
   cuaderno.
   every time cada vez

everybody pronoun
   todo el mundo, **todos** *masc. plural*
   Everybody has seen this film.
   Todo el mundo ha visto esta
   película.
   Everybody has come. Todos han
   venido.
   everybody else todos los demás

everyone pronoun
   todo el mundo, **todos** *masc. plural*

everything pronoun
   todo
   That's everything. Eso es todo.
   Everything's ready. Todo está
   listo.
   everything else todo lo demás

everywhere adverb
1 **por todas partes**
   I looked everywhere. Busqué por
   todas partes.
2 (with 'go') **a todas partes**
   I go everywhere by bike. Voy en
   bici a todas partes.

evil adjective
   malo *masc.*, **mala** *fem.*

exact adjective
   exacto *masc.*, **exacta** *fem.*

exactly adverb
   exactamente
   at exactly the same time
   exactamente a la misma hora
   It's exactly ten o'clock. Son las
   diez en punto.

to **exaggerate** verb
   exagerar

exam noun
   el **examen** *masc.* (plural los
   exámenes)
   a Spanish exam un examen de
   español

example noun
   el **ejemplo** *masc.*
   for example por ejemplo

excellent adjective
   excelente *masc. & fem.*

except preposition
   excepto, **menos**
   all the boys except me todos los
   chicos excepto yo, todos los chicos
   menos yo

to **exchange** verb
   cambiar
   **Can I exchange this book for
   another one?** ¿Puedo cambiar este
   libro por otro?

excited adjective
   entusiasmado *masc.*,
   entusiasmada *fem.*

exciting adjective
   (*book, film, etc.*) **emocionante** *masc. &
   fem.*
   an exciting match un partido
   emocionante

exclamation mark noun
   el **signo de admiración** *masc.*

excuse noun
   la **excusa** *fem.*

to **excuse** verb
   Excuse me! ¡Perdón!

• *The months of the year and days of the week do not take a capital letter in Spanish.*

exercise noun
el **ejercicio** *masc.*
a Spanish exercise un ejercicio de español
Do you do exercise? ¿Haces ejercicio?
an exercise book un cuaderno

exhausted adjective
agotado *masc.*, **agotada** *fem.*
I'm exhausted. Estoy agotado.

exhibition noun
la **exposición** *fem.* (plural las **exposiciones**)

to **exist** verb
existir

exit noun
la **salida** *fem.*

to **expect** verb
1 (*to wait for*) **esperar**
I'm expecting my dad. Estoy esperando a mi padre.
She's expecting a baby. Está esperando un niño.
2 (*to suppose*) **suponer**
I expect so. Supongo que sí.

expensive adjective
caro *masc.*, **cara** *fem.*
It's too expensive. Es demasiado caro.

experience noun
la **experiencia** *fem.*

experiment noun
el **experimento** *masc.*
to do an experiment hacer un experimento

expert noun
el **experto** *masc.*, la **experta** *fem.*

to **explain** verb
explicar
I'll explain. Te explico.

explanation noun
la **explicación** *fem.* (plural las **explicaciones**)

• *See the centre section for verb tables.*

to **explode** verb
estallar

to **explore** verb
explorar

explosion noun
la **explosión** *fem.* (plural las **explosiones**)

expression noun
(*sentence, look*) la **expresión** *fem.* (plural las **expresiones**)

extra adjective & adverb
1 (*more*) **más**
We need extra exercise books. Necesitamos más cuadernos.
to pay extra pagar más
2 (*left over*) **de más**
There are three extra sweets. Hay tres caramelos de más.
3 (*in a restaurant*)
Breakfast is extra. El desayuno no está incluido.

extraterrestrial noun
el or la **extraterrestre** *masc. & fem.*

extremely adverb

> 🔑 **LANGUAGE**
> Add **-ísimo** (masculine) or **-ísima** (feminine) to the adjective in Spanish.

extremely difficult dificilísimo
extremely tired cansadísimo

eye noun
el **ojo** *masc.*
I have blue eyes. Tengo los ojos azules.

eyebrow noun
la **ceja** *fem.*

eyelid noun
el **párpado** *masc.*

eyesight noun
la **vista** *fem.*

Ff

fabulous adjective
fabuloso *masc.*, **fabulosa** *fem.*

face noun
la **cara** *fem.*

facing preposition
(*opposite*) **enfrente de**
I sat down facing the teacher.
Me senté enfrente de la maestra.

fact noun
el **hecho** *masc.*

factory noun
la **fábrica** *fem.*
My dad works in a factory.
Mi padre trabaja en una fábrica.

to **fail** verb
suspender
My sister has failed her exam. Mi
hermana ha suspendido el examen.

to **faint** verb
desmayarse
Amy fainted. Amy se desmayó.

fair adjective
1 (*right*) **justo** *masc.*, **justa** *fem.*
It's not fair! ¡No es justo!
2 (*hair*) **rubio** *masc.*, **rubia** *fem.*
I have fair hair. Tengo el pelo
rubio.

fair noun
la **feria** *fem.*
Can I go to the fair ¿Puedo ir a la
feria?

fair-haired adjective
I'm fair-haired. Tengo el pelo
rubio.

fairly adverb
bastante
It's fairly expensive. Es bastante
caro.

fairy noun
el **hada** *fem.*
a fairy tale un cuento de hadas

> **LANGUAGE**
> Be careful: you use **el** with **hada** but it is
> not a masculine noun.

to **fall** verb
1 **caerse**
Be careful, you'll fall! ¡Cuidado, te
vas a caer!
I fell down the stairs. Me caí por la
escalera.
She fell off the chair. Se cayó de la
silla.
2 (*talking about snow, rain, bombs, etc.*) **caer**
The snow is falling. Cae la nieve.

> **LANGUAGE**
> When 'fall' means 'fall down
> accidentally' use **caerse**; otherwise use
> **caer**.

false adjective
falso *masc.*, **falsa** *fem.*
True or false? ¿Verdadero o falso?

family noun
la **familia** *fem.*
the Turner family la familia
Turner
a big family una familia numerosa

famous adjective
famoso *masc.*, **famosa** *fem.*

fan noun
1 (*of a person*) el or la **fan** *masc. & fem.*
(plural los or las **fans**)
I'm a great Harry Potter fan.
Soy un gran fan de Harry Potter.
2 (*of a team*) el or la **hincha** *masc. & fem.*
He's a Manchester United fan.
Es hincha del Manchester United.
3 (*machine for keeping cool*) **el
ventilador** *masc.*

• *Use* **el** *and* **uno** *for masculine words and* **la** *and* **una** *for feminine words.*

to **fancy** verb
apetecer
I fancy an ice cream. Me apetece un helado.

🔑 **LANGUAGE**
The order of the words in the Spanish sentence is different, so 'I fancy an ice cream' is, word for word, 'An ice cream takes my fancy'.

fancy dress noun
el **disfraz** masc. (plural los **disfraces**)
a fancy dress party una fiesta de disfraces
She's in fancy dress. Está disfrazada.

fantastic adjective
estupendo masc., **estupenda** fem.

🔑 **LANGUAGE**
You can also say fantástico/fantástica.

far adjective & adverb
1 **lejos**
Is it far? ¿Está lejos?
It's not very far away. No está muy lejos.
How far is it to York? ¿A qué distancia está York?
2 as far as hasta
I went as far as the bridge. Fui hasta el puente.
so far hasta ahora

farm noun
la **granja** fem.
I live on a farm. Vivo en una granja.

farmer noun
(man) el **agricultor** masc., el **granjero** masc.;
(woman) la **agricultora** fem., la **granjera** fem.

fashion noun
la **moda** fem.
a fashion show un desfile de modas

fashionable adjective
de moda
Black shoes are fashionable. Los zapatos negros están de moda.

fast adverb
1 **rápido**
I read very fast. Leo muy rápido.
Can you go faster? ¿Puedes ir más rápido?
2 She's fast asleep. Está profundamente dormida.

fast adjective
rápido masc., **rápida** fem.
a fast car un coche rápido

to **fast-forward** verb
avanzar
to fast-forward the tape avanzar la cinta

fat adjective
gordo masc., **gorda** fem.
He's very fat. Está muy gordo.

father noun
el **padre** masc.
My father works in a factory. Mi padre trabaja en una fábrica.
my father and mother mis padres
Father Christmas Papá Noel
Father's Day el día del Padre

fault noun
la **culpa** fem.
It's not my fault. No es mi culpa.

favourite adjective
favorito masc., **favorita** fem.
Spanish is my favourite subject. El español es mi asignatura favorita.

fear noun
el **miedo** masc.

feather noun
la **pluma** fem.

• Languages and nationalities do not take a capital letter in Spanish.

February noun
febrero *masc.*
Come to my house in February.
Ven a mi casa en febrero.
It's my birthday on the sixth of February. Es mi cumpleaños el seis de febrero.

fed up adjective
I'm fed up! ¡Estoy harto!
We're fed up with him! ¡Estamos hartos de él!

to **feed** verb
dar de comer a
I've fed the dog. Le he dado de comer al perro.

to **feel** verb
1 (*happy, tired, etc.*) **sentirse**
I don't feel well. No me siento bien.
I feel cold. Tengo frío.

> 🔑 **LANGUAGE**
> English = **to feel** cold   **I feel cold.**
> Spanish = **tener** frío   **Tengo frío.**

2 (*talking about feeling something in your body*) **sentir**
I didn't feel a thing. No sentí nada.
3 (*talking about touching something*) **tocar**
Feel my hands - they're cold.
Tócame las manos - las tengo frías.
4 **to feel like doing something** tener ganas de hacer algo
I feel like going out. Tengo ganas de salir.

> 🔑 **LANGUAGE**
> To say you feel like something, use **apetece** in the singular and **apetecen** in the plural.

I feel like an ice cream. Me apetece un helado.

feet plural noun
los **pies** *masc. plural*
I have cold feet. Tengo los pies fríos.

felt-tip pen noun
el **rotulador** *masc.*

female noun
la **hembra** *fem.*

female adjective
hembra *masc. & fem.*
a female elephant un elefante hembra

feminine adjective
femenino *masc.*, **femenina** *fem.*

> 🔑 **LANGUAGE**
> English = fem**i**nine
> Spanish = fem**e**nino

fence noun
la **valla** *fem.*

ferry noun
el **ferry** *masc.* (plural los **ferries**)

to **fetch** verb
traer
Fetch my glasses. Tráeme las gafas.

few adjective & pronoun
a few algunos *masc. plural*, algunas *fem. plural*
a few books algunos libros
a few of the books algunos de los libros
quite a few bastantes
quite a few mistakes bastantes faltas

fewer adjective & pronoun
menos
fewer dogs menos perros
fewer than ten menos de diez

field noun
(*for wheat, playing football, etc.*) el **campo** *masc.*

fierce adjective
feroz *masc. & fem.* (plural **feroces**)

• *The months of the year and days of the week do not take a capital letter in Spanish.*

fifteen number
quince
My sister is fifteen. Mi hermana tiene quince años.

> 🔑 **LANGUAGE**
> In English you can say just 'fifteen'. In Spanish you must add años.

fifth adjective
quinto masc., **quinta** fem.
on the fifth floor en el quinto piso
the fifth of June el cinco de junio

> 🔑 **LANGUAGE**
> With dates you use cinco (five).

fifty number
cincuenta
My dad is fifty. Mi padre tiene cincuenta años.

> 🔑 **LANGUAGE**
> In English you can say just 'fifty'. In Spanish you must add años.

fight noun
la **pelea** fem.

to **fight** verb
pelearse
Jake and Ben are fighting in the playground. Jake y Ben se están peleando en el patio.

figure noun
(number) la **cifra** fem.
Write the amount in figures. Escribe la suma en cifras.

file
1 (cover for papers) la **carpeta** fem.
I keep my drawings in a file. Guardo mis dibujos en una carpeta.
2 (on a computer) el **archivo** masc.
I've created a file. He creado un archivo.
3 in single file en fila india

• See the centre section for verb tables.

to **fill** verb
llenar
Fill the bucket with water. Llena el cubo de agua.
to fill in a form rellenar un formulario

film noun
1 (in the cinema or on TV) la **película** fem.
Do you like films? ¿Te gustan las películas?
a film star una estrella de cine
2 (in a camera) el **carrete** masc.

final adjective
(last) **último** masc., **última** fem.
the final week la última semana

final noun
la **final** fem.
Our team has won the final. Nuestro equipo ha ganado la final.

to **find** verb
1 **encontrar**
Have you found my pen? ¿Has encontrado mi boli?
I can't find my glasses. No encuentro mis gafas.

> 🔑 **LANGUAGE**
> The word 'can't' is not translated into Spanish. Word for word this Spanish sentence means 'I don't find my glasses'.

2 (to look for) **buscar**
Find page 10. Busca la página diez.
3 (when you want to discover what happened)
to find out descubrir
I've found out who did it. He descubierto quién lo hizo.

fine adjective & adverb
(good, well) **bien**
How are you? – Fine. ¿Qué tal estás? – Bien.
Can I come tomorrow? – That's fine. ¿Puedo venir mañana? – Está bien.
It's working fine. Funciona bien.
The weather's fine. Hace buen tiempo.

a
b
c
d
e
f
g
h
i
j
k
l
m
n
o
p
q
r
s
t
u
v
w
x
y
z

a
b
c
d
e
f
g
h
i
j
k
l
m
n
o
p
q
r
s
t
u
v
w
x
y
z

finger noun
el **dedo** *masc.*
I wear a ring on my finger.
Llevo un anillo en el dedo.

fingerprint noun
la **huella dactilar** *fem.*

to **finish** verb
terminar
I've finished my homework.
He terminado mis deberes.
School finishes at three. El colegio
termina a las tres.
Have you finished eating? ¿Has
terminado de comer?

finish noun
(*in a race*) la **llegada** *fem.*

fire noun
1 el **fuego** *masc.*
Dad lit the fire. Papá encendió el
fuego.
It's on fire. Está ardiendo.
2 (*fire that destroys things*) el **incendio**
masc.
The firemen have put out the fire.
Los bomberos han apagado el
incendio.
a fire alarm una alarma contra
incendios
a fire engine un camión de
bomberos
a fire station un parque de
bomberos

firefighter noun
el **bombero** *masc.*, la **bombera** *fem.*

fireplace noun
la **chimenea** *fem.*

fireworks plural noun
(*display*) los **fuegos artificiales** *masc.*
plural

firm noun
la **empresa** *fem.*

first adjective & pronoun
primero *masc.*, **primera** *fem.*
for the first time por primera vez

I'm the first. Soy el primero.
Bradley came first. (*in the race*)
Bradley quedó primero.

LANGUAGE
Before a masculine singular noun
primero becomes primer.

the first year el primer año
first aid los primeros auxilios
my first name mi nombre

LANGUAGE
With dates you use uno (one).

on the first of March el uno de
marzo

first adverb
1 (*before doing anything else*) **primero**
First I'm going to eat. Primero voy
a comer.
first of all en primer lugar
2 at first al principio

fish noun
1 (*eaten as food*) el **pescado** *masc.*
I like fish. Me gusta el pescado.
fish and chips el pescado frito con
patatas fritas
2 (*alive in the sea or river*) el **pez** *masc.*
(plural los **peces**)
There are lots of fish in the river.
Hay muchos peces en el río.
3 fish fingers los palitos de pescado
a fish shop una pescadería
a fish tank una pecera

to **fish** verb
pescar
Do you like fishing? ¿Te gusta
pescar?
to go fishing ir a pescar

fisherman noun
el **pescador** *masc.*

fishing rod noun
la **caña de pescar** *fem.*

fishmonger noun
el **pescadero** *masc.*,
la **pescadera** *fem.*

• Use **el** and **uno** for masculine words and **la** and **una** for feminine words.

fist noun
   el puño *masc.*

fit adjective
   en forma
   to be fit estar en forma

to **fit** verb
 1 estar bien
   These shoes don't fit me. Estos
   zapatos no me están bien.
 2 to fit into something caber en algo
   My books don't fit into this box.
   Mis libros no caben en esta caja.

five number
   cinco
   We're going to the cinema at five.
   Vamos al cine a las cinco.
   It's five to eight. Son las ocho
   menos cinco.
   It's five past seven. Son las siete y
   cinco.
   I'm five. Tengo cinco años.

> **LANGUAGE**
> In English you can say 'five o'clock' or just
> 'five', 'five years old' or just 'five'. In
> Spanish you must add **las** (for time) and
> **años** (for age).

to **fix** verb
   (*to repair*) **arreglar**
   Dad has fixed my bike. Papá me ha
   arreglado la bici.

fizzy adjective
   con gas
   fizzy water agua con gas

flag noun
   la **bandera** *fem.*

flame noun
   la **llama** *fem.*

flan noun
   la **tarta** *fem.*

flash noun
   a flash of lightning un relámpago

flat adjective
 1 plano *masc.*, **plana** *fem.*
   a flat screen una pantalla plana
   flat shoes zapatos planos
 2 (*when describing land or ground*)
   llano *masc.*, **llana** *fem.*
   a flat country un país llano
 3 to have a flat tyre tener un
   pinchazo

flat noun
   el **piso** *masc.*
   They have a flat in London. Tienen
   un piso en Londres.

flavour noun
   el **sabor** *masc.*
   It has a chocolate flavour. Tiene
   sabor a chocolate.

flight noun
   el **vuelo** *masc.*
   the next flight to Madrid el
   próximo vuelo para Madrid

flip-flop noun
   la **chancleta** *fem.*

to **float** verb
   flotar

flood noun
   la **inundación** *fem.* (plural las
   inundaciones)

floor noun
 1 el **suelo** *masc.*
   on the floor en el suelo
 2 (*a level in a building*) el **piso** *masc.*
   on the second floor en el segundo
   piso
   on the ground floor en la planta
   baja

florist noun
   el or la **florista** *masc. & fem.*

flour noun
   la **harina** *fem.*

to **flow** verb
   (*talking about water or rivers*) **correr**

a b c d e **f** g h i j k l m n o p q r s t u v w x y z

•*Languages and nationalities do not take a capital letter in Spanish.*

flower noun
la **flor** *fem.*
a bunch of flowers un ramo de flores

flowerpot noun
la **maceta** *fem.*

flu noun
la **gripe** *fem.*
I have the flu. Tengo gripe.

fluently adverb
con fluidez
I speak Spanish fluently. Hablo español con fluidez.

flute noun
la **flauta** *fem.*
Jacob plays the flute. Jacob toca la flauta.

to **fly** verb
1 (*talking about birds, planes, balloons, etc.*)
volar
The birds are flying. Los pájaros están volando.
2 (*to go somewhere by plane*) **ir en avión**
We flew to Malaga. Fuimos a Málaga en avión.

fly noun
la **mosca** *fem.*
I hate flies. Odio las moscas.

flying saucer noun
el **platillo volante** *masc.*

fog noun
la **niebla** *fem.*

foggy adjective
It's foggy. Hay niebla.

> ⚷ **LANGUAGE**
> Word for word the Spanish means 'there is fog'.

to **fold** verb
1 **doblar**
to fold something in half doblar algo por la mitad
2 **to fold your arms** cruzar los brazos

folder noun
(*for papers, and on a computer*)
la **carpeta** *fem.*

to **follow** verb
seguir
Follow me. Sígueme.
I'll follow. Yo te sigo.

following adjective
siguiente *masc. & fem.*
the following week la semana siguiente

food noun
la **comida** *fem.*
to buy food comprar comida
English food la comida inglesa
I want some food. Quiero comer algo.

> ⚷ **LANGUAGE**
> Word for word **Quiero comer algo** means 'I want to eat something'.

fool noun
el or la **idiota** *masc. & fem.*

foot noun
el **pie** *masc.*
My foot hurts. Me duele el pie.
on foot a pie
I'm five foot tall. Mido un metro cincuenta.

> 🌎 **CULTURE**
> Spanish measurements are in metres and centimetres; a foot is about 30 centimetres.

football noun
1 (*game*) el **fútbol** *masc.*
I love playing football. Me encanta jugar al fútbol.
football boots las botas de fútbol
2 (*ball*) el **balón de fútbol** *masc.*
(plural los **balones de fútbol**)

footballer noun
el or la **futbolista** *masc. & fem.*
He's a footballer. Es futbolista.

• *The months of the year and days of the week do not take a capital letter in Spanish.*

footprint noun
   la **huella** *fem.*

for preposition
 1 para
   It's for you. Es para ti.
   I need it for tomorrow. Lo necesito
   para mañana.
   What's this for? ¿Para qué es?
 2 (*when giving reasons, or talking about buying
   or selling*) **por**
   They punished me for that. Me han
   castigado por eso.
   I bought it for six euros. Lo compré
   por seis euros.
 3 (*for showing something still going on*)
   I've been living here for a year.
   Hace un año que vivo aquí.

> 🔑 **LANGUAGE**
> You can use the verb **hacer** (to make) to
> say you are still doing something, like
> living somewhere or waiting, so word for
> word **Hace un año que vivo aquí** means
> 'It makes a year that I live here'.

 4 (*for showing something that happened in the
   past*) **durante**
   I lived in Toledo for six months.
   Viví en Toledo durante seis meses.

to **forbid** verb
   prohibir
   **My parents have forbidden me to
   go out.** Mis padres me han
   prohibido salir.
   Smoking is forbidden. Está
   prohibido fumar.

forecast noun
   (*weather forecast*) el **pronóstico** *masc.*

forehead noun
   la **frente** *fem.*

foreign adjective
   extranjero *masc.*, **extranjera** *fem.*
   foreign languages las lenguas
   extranjeras

• *See the centre section for verb tables.*

foreigner noun
   el **extranjero** *masc.*,
   la **extranjera** *fem.*
   I'm a foreigner. Soy extranjero.

forest noun
   el **bosque** *masc.*
   a tropical forest una selva
   tropical

to **forget** verb
 1 olvidarse de
   You always forget my birthday.
   Siempre te olvidas de mi
   cumpleaños.
   I forget everything. Me olvido de
   todo.
 2 olvidarse
   I've forgotten your name. Se me
   ha olvidado tu nombre.
   I forgot! ¡Se me olvidó!

to **forgive** verb
   perdonar
   I forgive you. Te perdono.

fork noun
   el **tenedor** *masc.*

form noun
 1 (*paper*) el **formulario** *masc.*
   to fill in a form rellenar un
   formulario
 2 (*in school*) **la clase** *fem.*

to **form** verb
   formar
   Form a circle! ¡Formad un círculo!

fortnight noun
   quince días *masc. plural*
   in a fortnight dentro de quince
   días

> 🔑 **LANGUAGE**
> Word for word **quince días** is fifteen days
> although a **fortnight** is fourteen.

forty number
cuarenta
My mum is forty. Mi madre tiene cuarenta años.

> 🔑 **LANGUAGE**
> In English you can say just 'forty'. In Spanish you must add **años**.

forward adverb
adelante
I took one step forward. Di un paso adelante.
to move forward avanzar

fountain noun
la **fuente** *fem.*

four number
cuatro
The party starts at four. La fiesta empieza a las cuatro.
Catherine is four. Catherine tiene cuatro años.

> 🔑 **LANGUAGE**
> In English you can say 'four o'clock' or just 'four', 'four years old' or just 'four'. In Spanish you must add **las** (for time) and **años** (for age).

fourteen number
catorce
My brother is fourteen. Mi hermano tiene catorce años.

fourth adjective
cuarto *masc.*, **cuarta** *fem.*
on the fourth floor en el cuarto piso
the fourth of December el cuatro de diciembre

> 🔑 **LANGUAGE**
> With dates you use **cuatro** (four).

fox noun
el **zorro** *masc.*

France noun
Francia *fem.*
Alain lives in France. Alain vive en Francia.
I'm going to France. Me voy a Francia.

freckles plural noun
las **pecas** *fem. plural*
I have freckles. Tengo pecas.

free adjective
1 **libre** *masc. & fem.*
Are you free tomorrow? ¿Estás libre mañana?
This seat is free. Este asiento está libre.
2 (*when you don't pay*) **gratis** *masc. & fem.*
It's free. Es gratis.
a free ticket una entrada gratis

freedom noun
la **libertad** *fem.*

to **freeze** verb
1 (*in the cold weather*) **helarse**
The water has frozen. El agua se ha helado.
2 (*in a freezer*) **congelar**
frozen fish pescado congelado

freezer noun
el **congelador** *masc.*

freezing adjective
I'm freezing! ¡Estoy helado!
It's freezing today. Hoy hace muchísimo frío.

French adjective
francés *masc.*, **francesa** *fem.*
French food la comida francesa
Fabrice is French. Fabrice es francés.
French people los franceses
French fries las patatas fritas

> 🔑 **LANGUAGE**
> The masculine plural of **francés** is **franceses**.

• Use **el** and **uno** for masculine words and **la** and **una** for feminine words.

French noun
1 (*language*) el **francés** *masc.*
Do you speak French? ¿Habla usted francés?
2 **the French** los franceses *masc. plural*

Frenchman, **Frenchwoman** noun
el **francés** *masc.* (plural los **franceses**); la **francesa** *fem.*

fresh adjective
fresco *masc.*, **fresca** *fem.*
fresh eggs huevos frescos

Friday noun
el **viernes** *masc.*
Today is Friday. Hoy es viernes.
on Friday el viernes
I'll see you on Friday. Te veo el viernes.
on Fridays los viernes
It's closed on Fridays. Está cerrado los viernes.

> **LANGUAGE**
> Remember the difference in Spanish between el viernes (one Friday only) and los viernes (every Friday).

fridge noun
el **frigorífico** *masc.*

fried adjective
frito *masc.*, **frita** *fem.*
a fried egg un huevo frito

friend noun
el **amigo** *masc.*, la **amiga** *fem.*
She's my best friend. Es mi mejor amiga.
I'm a friend of his. Soy uno de sus amigos.
I'm friends with him. Somos amigos.

friendly adjective
simpático *masc.*, **simpática** *fem.*
Anne is very friendly. Anne es muy simpática.
I'm friendly with her. Somos amigas.

fries plural noun
las **patatas fritas** *fem. plural*

fright noun
el **susto** *masc.*
You gave me a fright. Me has dado un susto.
What a fright! ¡Qué susto!

to **frighten** verb
asustar
You frightened me Me has asustado

frightened adjective
I'm frightened. Tengo miedo.
She's frightened of the dark. Tiene miedo a la oscuridad.
I'm frightened to go by plane. Tengo miedo de ir en avión.

> **LANGUAGE**
> English = I am frightened.
> Spanish = Tengo miedo = I have fear

fringe noun
el **flequillo** *masc.*
I have a fringe. Llevo flequillo.

frisbee® noun
el **frisbee®** *masc.*

frog noun
la **rana** *fem.*

from
1 **de**
a present from your brother un regalo de tu hermano
It's not far from the airport. No está lejos del aeropuerto.

> **LANGUAGE**
> de + el = del

2 (*starting from a particular time etc.*) **desde**
from today desde hoy
from now on desde ahora
books from five euros libros desde cinco euros

• *Languages and nationalities do not take a capital letter in Spanish.*

a
b
c
d
e
f
g
h
i
j
k
l
m
n
o
p
q
r
s
t
u
v
w
x
y
z

front noun
1 (*the front part of something*) la **parte de delante** *fem.*
There's a light at the front. Hay una luz en la parte de delante.
Sit in the front of the car. Siéntate delante.
2 (*of a classroom, theatre, etc.*) la **primera fila** *fem.*
I always sit at the front. Siempre me siento en primera fila.
3 in front of delante de
in front of my house delante de mi casa

front adjective
1 (*seat, wheel, leg, etc.*) **delantero** *masc.*, **delantera** *fem.*
the front seat el asiento delantero
the front door la puerta de la calle
2 (*page, row*) **primero** *masc.*, **primera** *fem.*
the front row la primera fila

frost noun
la **helada** *fem.*
There's a frost. Ha caído una helada.

frosty adjective
It's frosty. Ha helado.

frozen adjective
1 **helado** *masc.*, **helada** *fem.*
I'm frozen. Estoy helado.
2 (*vegetables, fish, etc.*) **congelado** *masc.*, **congelada** *fem.*

fruit noun
la **fruta** *fem.*
I like fruit. Me gusta la fruta.
a fruit juice un zumo de fruta
a fruit salad una macedonia de frutas

frying pan noun
la **sartén** *fem.* (plural las **sartenes**)

full adjective
1 **lleno** *masc.*, **llena** *fem.*
The glass is full of water. El vaso está lleno de agua.
I'm full. Estoy lleno.
2 a full stop un punto

fun noun
to have fun divertirse
I had a lot of fun. Me divertí mucho.
Have fun! ¡Qué te diviertas!
It's fun! ¡Es divertido!

funeral noun
el **entierro** *masc.*

funfair noun
la **feria** *fem.*

funny adjective
1 (*making you laugh*) **gracioso** *masc.*, **graciosa** *fem.*
2 (*strange*) **raro** *masc.*, **rara** *fem.*

fur noun
(*of an animal*) el **pelo** *masc.*
the cat's fur el pelo del gato

furious adjective
furioso *masc.*, **furiosa** *fem.*
My dad is furious with me. Mi padre está furioso conmigo., Mi padre está muy enfadado conmigo.

🔑 **LANGUAGE**
Word for word **muy enfadado** means 'very angry'.

furniture noun
los **muebles** *masc. plural*
a piece of furniture un mueble

further adverb
1 (*talking about places*) **más lejos**
Madrid is a bit further. Madrid está un poco más lejos.
2 (*more*) **más**
further down más abajo

future noun
el **futuro** *masc.*
in the future en el futuro

• *The months of the year and days of the week do not take a capital letter in Spanish.*

Gg

game noun
1 el **juego** *masc.*
  a board game un juego de mesa
  the Olympic Games los Juegos Olímpicos
  Do you want to play a game? ¿Quieres jugar?
2 (*of chess, hide-and-seek, etc.*) la **partida** *fem.*
  Let's play a game of chess. Vamos a jugar una partida de ajedrez.
3 (*of football, tennis*) el **partido** *masc.*
  a football game un partido de fútbol
4 (*sport when it's a school subject*) **games** el deporte *masc.*
  We have games on Monday. Tenemos deporte los lunes.

gang noun
  la **pandilla** *fem.*
  There's a gang in my neighbourhood. Hay una pandilla en mi barrio.

gap noun
  (*in a fence, wall, etc.*) el **hueco** *masc.*

garage noun
  el **garaje** *masc.*

> ⚷ **LANGUAGE**
> English = gara**g**e
> Spanish = gara**j**e

garden noun
  el **jardín** *masc.* (plural los **jardines**)

gardener noun
  el **jardinero** *masc.*, la **jardinera** *fem.*
  My dad's a gardener. Mi padre es jardinero.

gardening noun
  la **jardinería** *fem.*

garlic noun
  el **ajo** *masc.*

gas noun
  el **gas** *masc.*
  a gas cooker una cocina de gas

gate noun
  la **puerta** *fem.*

to **gather** verb
1 (*to get together*) **reunirse**
  The children gather in the playground. Los niños se reúnen en el patio.
2 (*to come closer*) **acercarse**
  Gather round! ¡Acercaos!

GCSE noun
  el **certificado de estudios** *masc.*

> 🌍 **CULTURE**
> In Spain, children do not do special exams at sixteen as they do in the UK.

geese noun
  los **gansos** *masc. plural*

gender noun
  el **género** *masc.*
  What gender is 'ventana'? ¿De qué género es 'ventana'?

general adjective
  general *masc. & fem.*

generally adverb
  generalmente

generous adjective
  generoso *masc.*, **generosa** *fem.*

genius noun
  el **genio** *masc.*
  You're a genius! ¡Eres un genio!

gentle adjective
1 **dulce** *masc. & fem.*
  Rebecca is very gentle. Rebecca es muy dulce.
2 **to be gentle with something** tener cuidado con algo
  Be gentle with that cup. Ten cuidado con esa taza.

a b c d e f **g** h i j k l m n o p q r s t u v w x y z

• *The months of the year and days of the week do not take a capital letter in Spanish.*

gently adverb
(*carefully*) **con cuidado**
Put it down gently on the table.
Ponlo con cuidado en la mesa.

gents noun
(*toilets*) los **servicios de caballeros**
masc. plural

geography noun
la **geografía** *fem.*

gerbil noun
el **jerbo** *masc.*

German adjective
1 **alemán** *masc.*, **alemana** *fem.*
She's German Es alemana
2 **German measles** la rubeola *fem.*

German noun
1 (*language*) el **alemán** *masc.*
Can you speak German? ¿Hablas alemán?
2 (*person*) el **alemán** *masc.*, la **alemana** *fem.*

> 🔑 **LANGUAGE**
> The plural of alemán is alemanes.

Germany noun
Alemania *fem.*

germs plural noun
los **microbios** *masc. plural*

to **get** verb

> 🔑 **LANGUAGE**
> Be careful in choosing the correct translation of 'get'. Look at the English signpost words until you find the meaning you want.

1 (*to receive*) **recibir**
I got your letter. Recibí tu carta.
He got a knock on his head. Ha recibido un golpe en la cabeza.
2 (*a prize, mark, idea*) **sacar**
I got good marks. Saqué buenas notas.
3 (*a job, some information, money*) **conseguir**

My dad got a job. Mi padre ha conseguido un trabajo.
4 (*as a present*)
I got a computer for my birthday. Me regalaron un ordenador para mi cumpleaños.
5 (*when translating 'have got' or 'has got'*) **tener**
I've got fair hair. Tengo el pelo rubio.
Have you got a bike? ¿Tienes una bici?
They've got a big house. Tienen una casa grande.
6 (*to buy*) **comprar**
Dad got me a CD. Papá me ha comprado un CD.
7 (*a bus, train, cold, thief, etc.*) **coger**
I don't like getting the bus. No me gusta coger el autobús.
Did they get the thief? ¿Han cogido al ladrón?
8 (*to fetch*) **buscar**
Go and get my glasses. Vete a buscar mis gafas.
9 (*to arrive somewhere*) **llegar**
We get to Glasgow at four. Llegamos a Glasgow a las cuatro.
How do you get to the station? ¿Cómo se llega a la estación?
10 (*when translating 'have got' or 'has got to do something'*) **tener que**
I've got to go to the doctor. Tengo que ir al médico.
You've got to open the window. Tienes que abrir la ventana.
11 (*to become*)
to get angry enfadarse
to get tired cansarse
I'm getting hungry. Me está entrando hambre.

> 🔑 **LANGUAGE**
> When 'get' is followed by an adjective, the translation depends on the adjective, e.g. 'dark', 'late', 'old'.

• *See the centre section for verb tables.*

to **get away** verb
escaparse
The thief has got away. Se ha escapado el ladrón.

to **get back** verb
volver
Mum gets back at seven. Mamá vuelve a las siete.

to **get down** verb
bajar
Get down from there! ¡Baja de allí!

to **get in** verb
subir
Get in the car. Sube al coche.
Get in, Jack. Sube, Jack.

to **get off** verb
bajarse
I got off the bus at Richmond. Me bajé del autobús en Richmond.
Get off the bike. Bájate de la bici.

to **get on** verb
1 **subir**, **subirse**
We've got on the bus. Hemos subido al autobús., Nos hemos subido al autobús.
I got on my bike. Subí a mi bici.
2 **to get on with somebody** llevarse bien con alguien
I get on with my mum. Me llevo bien con mi madre.
3 **How are you getting on?** ¿Qué tal te va?
I'm getting on well. Voy bien.

to **get out** verb
1 **salir**
Get out! ¡Sal!
to get out of a car bajarse de un coche
2 **to get something out** sacar algo
Get out your exercise books. Sacad los cuadernos.

to **get up** verb
levantarse
I get up at six. Me levanto a las seis.

ghost noun
el **fantasma** masc.

LANGUAGE
Be careful: fantasma ends in an -a but it is not a feminine noun.

giant noun
el **gigante** masc., la **giganta** fem.

gift noun
el **regalo** masc.
a gift shop una tienda de regalos

gigantic adjective
gigantesco masc., **gigantesca** fem.

ginger adjective
to have ginger hair ser pelirrojo or pelirroja
I've got ginger hair. Soy pelirrojo.

LANGUAGE
Be careful: don't use the word pelo (hair) with pelirrojo.

giraffe noun
la **jirafa** fem.

LANGUAGE
English = giraffe
Spanish = jirafa

girl noun
1 (young child) la **niña** fem.
a little girl of five una niña de cinco años
It's a baby girl. Es una niña.
2 (older child or teenager) la **chica** fem.
a girl of sixteen una chica de dieciséis años

girlfriend noun
la **novia** fem.
My brother has a girlfriend. Mi hermano tiene novia.

to **give** verb
dar
Give me a pen. Dame un boli.
He gave me the book. Me dio el libro.

• Use **el** and **uno** for masculine words and **la** and **una** for feminine words.

a b c d e f g h i j k l m n o p q r s t u v w x y z

to **give back** verb
devolver
I'll give it back to you tomorrow. Te lo devuelvo mañana.

to **give in** verb
entregar
I've given in my homework. He entregado mis deberes.

to **give out** verb
repartir
The teacher gave out the books. La maestra repartió los cuadernos.

to **give up** verb
rendirse
I give up! ¡Me rindo!

glad adjective
to be glad **alegrarse**
I'm glad to see you. Me alegro de verte.
Yes, I'm glad. Sí, me alegro.

glass noun
1 (for drinking) el **vaso** masc.
a glass of milk un vaso de leche
2 el **cristal** masc.
It's made of glass. Es de cristal.
a glass door una puerta de cristal
Careful, there's broken glass. Cuidado, hay cristales rotos.

glasses plural noun
las **gafas** fem. plural,
(Latin America) los **anteojas** masc. plural
I wear glasses. Llevo gafas.

globe noun
el **globo** masc.

glove noun
el **guante** masc.

glue noun
el **pegamento** masc.

go noun
It's your go. Te toca a ti.
Whose go is it? ¿A quién le toca?

LANGUAGE
Use **tocar** (to be somebody's turn). It also means 'to touch'.

to **go** verb
1 **ir**
I want to go to the cinema. Quiero ir al cine.
I'm going to school. Voy a la escuela.
Where are you going? ¿Adónde vas?
She's gone to the doctor. Ha ido al médico.
Let's go! ¡Vamos!
2 (to leave) **irse**
I'm going. Ya me voy.
I went at six. Me fui a las seis.
3 (talking about trains, planes, etc.) **salir**
What time does the train go? ¿A qué hora sale el tren?
4 (used with another verb when talking about the future) **ir**
What are you going to do? ¿Qué vas a hacer?
I'm going to play in the garden. Voy a jugar en el jardín.

to **go away** verb
irse
Go away, Philip! ¡Vete, Philip!

to **go back** verb
volver
I'm going back home. Vuelvo a casa.

to **go down** verb
bajar
I'm going down to the basement. Bajo al sótano.
She went down the stairs. Bajó las escaleras.
The sun is going down. Se pone el sol.

to **go in** verb
entrar
Go in. Entra.
I went into the room. Entré en la habitación.

to **go off** verb
1 (to explode) **estallar**
A bomb has gone off. Una bomba ha estallado.

• Languages and nationalities do not take a capital letter in Spanish.

2 (*to sound*) **sonar**
  Has the alarm clock gone off?
  ¿Ha sonado el despertador?

to **go on** verb
 1 (*to continue*) **seguir**
  to go on doing something seguir
  haciendo algo
  Go on reading. Sigue leyendo.
 2 (*to happen*)
  What's going on? ¿Qué pasa?

to **go out** verb
  salir
  I don't go out much. No salgo
  mucho.
  Go out! ¡Sal!
  Ben's going out with my sister.
  Ben sale con mi hermana.

to **go up** verb
  subir
  I'm going up to my room. Subo a
  mi habitación.
  She went up the stairs. Subió las
  escaleras.

goal noun
 1 el **gol** *masc.*
  They scored two goals. Marcaron
  dos goles.
 2 (*the goalposts*) la **portería** *fem.*

goalkeeper noun
  el **portero** *masc.*, la **portera** *fem.*

goat noun
  la **cabra** *fem.*

God noun
  Dios *masc.*

goddaughter noun
  la **ahijada** *fem.*

godfather noun
  el **padrino** *masc.*

godmother noun
  la **madrina** *fem.*

godson noun
  el **ahijado** *masc.*

goggles plural noun
  (*for swimming*) las **gafas (de
  natación)** *fem. plural*

gold noun
  el **oro** *masc.*
  a gold ring un anillo de oro

goldfish noun
  el **pez de colores** *masc.* (plural los
  peces de colores)

> **LANGUAGE**
> Word for word the Spanish means 'fish of
> colours'.

golf noun
  el **golf** *masc.*
  My uncle plays golf. Mi tío juega
  al golf.
  a golf course un campo de golf

gone verb SEE **go**
  They've gone to the cinema. Han
  ido al cine.
  Amanda has gone. Amanda se ha
  ido.

good adjective
 1 bueno *masc.*, **buena** *fem.*
  Be good! ¡Sé bueno!
  Apples are good for you. Las
  manzanas son buenas para la
  salud.

> **LANGUAGE**
> The masculine singular bueno becomes
> buen when it is used before a noun.

  a good example un buen ejemplo
  Good! ¡Muy bien!
 2 I'm good at Spanish. Se me da bien
  el español.
  Cheryl is no good at numbers.
  Cheryl no es buena para los
  números.
 3 (*when wishing somebody something*)
  Good morning! ¡Buenos días!
  Good afternoon! ¡Buenas tardes!
  Good night! ¡Buenas noches!
  Have a good trip! ¡Buen viaje!

a
b
c
d
e
f
g
h
i
j
k
l
m
n
o
p
q
r
s
t
u
v
w
x
y
z

• *The months of the year and days of the week do not take a capital letter in Spanish.*

English Spanish

a
b
c
d
e
f
g
h
i
j
k
l
m
n
o
p
q
r
s
t
u
v
w
x
y
z

goodbye exclamation
¡adiós!

Good Friday noun
el **Viernes Santo** *masc.*

good-looking adjective
guapo *masc.*, **guapa** *fem.*
He's very good-looking. Es muy guapo.

goodnight exclamation
¡buenas noches!

goose noun
el **ganso** *masc.*

gorilla noun
el **gorila** *masc.*

> **LANGUAGE**
> Be careful: **gorila** ends in an -a but it is not a feminine noun.

got verb SEE **get, have**
I got your postcard. Recibí tu postal.
I've got black hair. Tengo el pelo negro.
We've got to go to the dentist. Tenemos que ir al dentista.

grade noun
(*in school subjects*) la **nota** *fem.*
My brother always gets good grades. Mi hermano siempre saca buenas notas.

graffiti noun
los **graffiti** *masc. plural*

gram noun
el **gramo** *masc.*

grammar noun
la **gramática** *fem.*

grandchildren plural noun
los **nietos** *masc. plural*

granddad, grandpa noun
el **abuelito** *masc.*

granddaughter noun
la **nieta** *fem.*

grandfather noun
el **abuelo** *masc.*

grandma noun
la **abuelita** *fem.*

grandmother noun
la **abuela** *fem.*

grandparents plural noun
los **abuelos** *masc. plural*

grandson noun
el **nieto** *masc.*

granny noun
la **abuelita** *fem.*

grape noun
la **uva** *fem.*

grapefruit noun
el **pomelo** *masc.*

grass noun
la **hierba** *fem.*
I'm sitting on the grass. Estoy sentada en la hierba.

gravy noun
la **salsa de carne** *fem.*
Do you want some gravy? ¿Quieres salsa?

greasy adjective
(*hair, skin, food*) **graso** *masc.*, **grasa** *fem.*

great adjective
estupendo *masc.*, **estupenda** *fem.*
That's great! ¡Estupendo!

Great Britain noun
Gran Bretaña *fem.*
We live in Gret Britain. Vivimos en Gran Bretaña.

Greece noun
Grecia *fem.*

greedy adjective
glotón *masc.*, **glotona** *fem.*
You're very greedy! ¡Eres muy glotón!

> **LANGUAGE**
> The masculine plural of **glotón** is **glotones**.

• *See the centre section for verb tables.*

Greek adjective
griego *masc.*, **griega** *fem.*

Greek noun
1 (*language*) el **griego** *masc.*
He speaks Greek. Hablar griego.
2 (*person*) el **griego** *masc.*,
la **griega** *fem.*

green adjective
verde *masc. & fem.*
I have green eyes. Tengo los ojos
verdes.

green noun
1 el **verde** *masc.*
I love green. Me encanta el verde.
2 greens las verduras *fem. plural*
Eat your greens! ¡Cómete las
verduras!

greengrocer's noun
la **verdulería** *fem.*

grey adjective
gris *masc. & fem.*
a grey shirt una camisa gris

grey noun
el **gris** *masc.*
Grey is my favourite colour. El gris
es mi color favorito.

grocer's noun
the grocer's la tienda de
comestibles *fem.*

groom noun
el **novio** *masc.*
the bride and groom los novios

ground noun
1 el **suelo** *masc.*
I'm sitting on the ground. Estoy
sentado en el suelo.
2 (*for football etc.*) el **campo** *masc.*
a sports ground un campo de
deportes
3 the ground floor la planta baja
I live on the ground floor. Vivo en
la planta baja.

group noun
el **grupo** *masc.*

grow
(*to get bigger*) **crecer**
You've grown a lot! ¡Has crecido
mucho!
My plants are growing well.
Mis plantas crecen muy bien.
I want to be a teacher when I grow
up. Quiero ser profesor cuando sea
mayor.

grown-up noun
el **adulto** *masc.*, la **adulta** *fem.*

grumpy adjective
gruñón *masc.*, **gruñona** *fem.*

> **LANGUAGE**
> The masculine plural of gruñón is
> gruñones.

to **guess** verb
adivinar
Guess what I saw. Adivina lo que
he visto.

guest noun
el **invitado** *masc.*, la **invitada** *fem.*
You're my guest. Eres mi
invitado.

> **LANGUAGE**
> The Spanish means 'person who has been
> invited'.

guide noun
1 (*book*) la **guía** *fem.*
2 (*person*) el or la **guía** *masc. & fem.*

Guide noun
(*Scout*) la **guía** *fem.*
She's in the Guides. Pertenece a las
guías.

guidebook noun
la **guía** *fem.*

guinea pig noun
el or la **cobaya** *masc. & fem.*

• *Use el and uno for masculine words and la and una for feminine words.*

a
b
c
d
e
f
g
h
i
j
k
l
m
n
o
p
q
r
s
t
u
v
w
x
y
z

a
b
c
d
e
f
g
h
i
j
k
l
m
n
o
p
q
r
s
t
u
v
w
x
y
z

guitar noun
la **guitarra** *fem.*
Daniel plays the guitar. Daniel toca la guitarra.

gum noun
(*chewing gum*) el **chicle** *masc.*

gun noun
la **pistola** *fem.*

guy noun
el **tío** *masc.*
He's a nice guy. Es un tío simpático.

gym noun
1 (*PE*) la **gimnasia** *fem.*
We have gym on Tuesdays. Los martes tenemos clase de gimnasia.
2 (*room in a school, health club*)
el **gimnasio** *masc.*
My dad goes to the gym. Mi padre va al gimnasio.

gymnastics noun
la **gimnasia** *fem.*
to do gymnastics hacer gimnasia

Hh

habit noun
la **costumbre** *fem.*
a bad habit una mala costumbre

had verb SEE **have**
I've had an accident. He tenido un accidente.
He had a problem. Tuvo un problema.

hail noun
el **granizo** *masc.*

to **hail** verb
granizar
It's hailing. Está granizando.

hair
el **pelo** *masc.*
I've got black hair. Tengo el pelo negro.
cat hairs pelos de gato

haircut noun
el **corte de pelo** *masc.*
I'm going to have a haircut. Voy a cortarme el pelo.

hairdresser noun
el **peluquero** *masc.*,
la **peluquera** *fem.*
She's a hairdresser. Es peluquera.

I'm going to the hairdresser's. Voy a la peluquería.

hairdryer noun
el **secador de pelo** *masc.*

hairstyle noun
el **peinado** *masc.*

hairy adjective
peludo *masc.*, **peluda** *fem.*

half noun
1 la **mitad** *fem.*
half my apple la mitad de mi manzana
to cut something in half cortar algo por la mitad
2 (*use* **medio** *after numbers*)
six and a half seis y medio
3 (*use* **media** *with times*)
an hour and a half una hora y media
It's half past nine. Son las nueve y media.

half adjective
medio *masc.*, **media** *fem.*
half an hour media hora
half a kilo medio kilo

• *Languages and nationalities do not take a capital letter in Spanish.*

half adverb
medio
She's half asleep. Está medio dormida.

 LANGUAGE
Be careful: the adverb medio does not change when it is in front of a feminine or plural adjective.

half-brother noun
el **hermanastro** masc.

half-sister noun
la **hermanastra** fem.

half-term noun
las **vacaciones de mitad de trimestre** fem. plural

CULTURE
There are no half-term holidays in Spanish schools but summer holidays are longer.

half-time noun
el **descanso** masc.
at half-time en el descanso

halfway adverb
a mitad de camino
It's halfway between Manchester and Leeds. Está a mitad de camino entre Manchester y Leeds.

hall noun
1 (big room) la **sala** fem.
a concert hall una sala de conciertos
2 (in a school) el **salón de actos** masc.
3 (in a house) la **entrada** fem.

Hallowe'en noun
la **víspera del día de Todos los Santos** fem.

CULTURE
The Spanish means 'the Eve of All Saints' Day'. In Spain people do not usually celebrate Hallowe'en, but el día de Todos los Santos is a public holiday.

ham noun
el **jamón** masc. (plural los **jamones**)
a ham sandwich un sándwich de jamón

hamburger noun
la **hamburguesa** fem.

hammer noun
el **martillo** masc.

hamster noun
el **hámster** masc. (plural los **hámsters**)

hand noun
1 la **mano** fem.
Put your hand up. Levantad la mano.
Can you give me a hand? ¿Me puedes echar una mano?
2 (on a clock or watch) la **manecilla** fem.
the hands of the clock las manecillas del reloj

to **hand** verb
1 **pasar**
Hand me the pencil. Pásame el lápiz.
2 to hand in entregar
I've handed in my homework. He entregado mis deberes.
3 to hand out repartir
Edward handed out the exercise books. Edward repartió los cuadernos.

handbag noun
el **bolso** masc.

handkerchief noun
el **pañuelo** masc.

handle noun
1 (on a door) el **picaporte** masc.
2 (on a knife, broom, frying pan) el **mango** masc.
3 (on a cup, bag) el **asa** fem.

LANGUAGE
Be careful: you use el with asa but it is not a masculine noun

• The months of the year and days of the week do not take a capital letter in Spanish.

a
b
c
d
e
f
g
h
i
j
k
l
m
n
o
p
q
r
s
t
u
v
w
x
y
z

a
b
c
d
e
f
g
h
i
j
k
l
m
n
o
p
q
r
s
t
u
v
w
x
y
z

handlebars plural noun
el **manillar** masc.

> **LANGUAGE**
> English = handlebars is plural
> Spanish = el manillar is singular

handsome adjective
guapo masc., **guapa** fem.
Dylan is very handsome. Dylan es
muy guapo.

handwriting noun
la **letra** fem.
You have very good handwriting.
Tienes muy buena letra.

> **LANGUAGE**
> In Spanish letra is also 'letter of the
> alphabet': 'handwriting' is how we write
> letras.

handy adjective
1 (useful) **práctico** masc.,
práctica fem.
My mobile phone is very handy.
Mi móvil es muy práctico.
2 (easy to get at) **a mano**
I always keep a pen handy.
Siempre tengo un bolígrafo a mano.

to **hang** verb
1 **colgar**
I hung the picture on the wall.
Colgué el cuadro en la pared.
The picture is hanging on the wall.
El cuadro está colgado en la pared.
2 Hang on! ¡Espera!

hangman noun
el **ahorcado** masc.
We're playing hangman. Estamos
jugando al ahorcado.

happen verb
pasar
What's happened? ¿Qué ha
pasado?
What happened to dad? ¿Qué le
pasó a papá?

happiness noun
la **felicidad** fem.

happy adjective
feliz masc. & fem. (plural **felices**)
Hassan is very happy. Hassan es
muy feliz.
Happy birthday! ¡Feliz
cumpleaños!
Happy Christmas! ¡Feliz Navidad!
Happy New Year! ¡Feliz Año Nuevo!

harbour noun
el **puerto** masc.

hard adjective
1 (not soft) **duro** masc., **dura** fem.
This bread is very hard. Este pan
está muy duro.
a hard-boiled egg un huevo duro
2 (not easy) **difícil** masc. & fem.
This exercise is hard. Este ejercicio
es difícil.

hard adverb
mucho
I work hard. Trabajo mucho.

hardly adverb
casi
I hardly ever eat meat. Casi nunca
como carne.
hardly anybody casi nadie

> **LANGUAGE**
> Casi is the Spanish word for 'almost'.

hard-working adjective
trabajador masc.,
trabajadora fem.

has verb SEE **have**
She has blue eyes. Tiene los ojos
azules.
He has seen the film. Ha visto la
película.

hat noun
1 el **sombrero** masc.
2 (soft hat, e.g. worn by children)
el **gorro** masc.
a woolly hat un gorro de lana

to **hate** verb
odiar
I hate swimming. Odio la natación.

• See the centre section for verb tables.

300

to **have** verb

1 tener

I have two brothers. Tengo dos hermanos.

I don't have any time. No tengo tiempo.

Do you have a bike? ¿Tienes una bici?

He has a blue shirt. Tiene una camisa azul.

They have a problem. Tienen un problema.

> 🔑 **LANGUAGE**
> 'Have' and 'have got' mean the same, and have the same translation in Spanish.

She's got fair hair. Tiene el pelo rubio.

We've got lots of friends. Tenemos muchos amigos.

2 (to eat or drink) **tomar**

I'm going to have an omelette. Voy a tomar una tortilla.

3 (used for making past tenses) **haber**

I've finished. He terminado.

He has read the book. Ha leído el libro.

4 (when translating 'have to do something' or 'have got to do something') **tener que**

I have to go to the doctor. Tengo que ir al médico.

You've got to help me. Tienes que ayudarme.

5 (when translating questions such as 'hasn't he?' or 'haven't you?') **He's arrived, hasn't he?** Ha llegado, ¿no?

You've finished, haven't you? Has terminado, ¿no?

> 🔑 **LANGUAGE**
> When talking about activities (like having a shower) there are many ways of translating 'have' + noun into Spanish. These expressions are usually given in the dictionary under the noun.

to have a shower ducharse

to have lunch comer

hay noun

el **heno** masc.

hay fever la fiebre del heno

he pronoun

1 (not usually translated)

He's tall. Es alto.

He lives in London. Vive en Londres.

2 él

He's tall but his sister is short. Él es alto pero su hermana es baja.

> 🔑 **LANGUAGE**
> Use él when you want to give special importance to the word he.

head

1 la cabeza fem.

He banged his head. Se dio un golpe en la cabeza.

2 (headteacher) el **director** masc., la **directora** fem.

3 (when throwing a coin) **heads!** ¡cara!

Heads or tails? ¿Cara o cruz?

headache noun

I have a headache. Me duele la cabeza.

> 🔑 **LANGUAGE**
> Word for word the Spanish means 'my head hurts'.

headmistress, headmaster noun

el **director** masc.; la **directora** fem.

headphones noun

los **auriculares** masc. plural

headteacher noun

el **director** masc., la **directora** fem.

health noun

la **salud** fem.

healthy adjective

sano masc., **sana** fem.

I'm healthy. Estoy sano.

to **hear** verb

oír

I hear a noise Oigo un ruido

Can you hear me? ¿Me oyes?

a b c d e f g **h** i j k l m n o p q r s t u v w x y z

• Use **el** and **uno** for masculine words and **la** and **una** for feminine words.

heart noun
1 el **corazón** *masc.* (plural los **corazones**)
It's good for your heart Es bueno para el corazón
2 **to learn something by heart** aprender algo de memoria

heat noun
el **calor** *masc.*

heater noun
la **estufa** *fem.*
an electric heater una estufa eléctrica

heating noun
la **calefacción** *fem.*

heavy adjective
pesado *masc.*, pesada *fem.*
It's very heavy. Es muy pesado.

hedge noun
el **seto** *masc.*

heel noun
el **talón** *masc.* (plural los **talones**)

height noun
1 (*of a person*) la **estatura** *fem.*
2 (*of a wall, building, etc.*) la **altura** *fem.*

helicopter noun
el **helicóptero** *masc.*

hello exclamation
1 ¡hola!
Hello, mum! ¡Hola, mamá!
2 (*when answering the phone*)
¡diga!, ¡dígame!

helmet noun
el **casco** *masc.*

help noun
la **ayuda** *fem.*
I need help. Necesito ayuda.

to **help** verb
1 **ayudar**
Help me make the bed. Ayúdame a hacer la cama.
Help! ¡Socorro!

2 **to help yourself to something** (*food or drinks*) servirse algo
Help yourself! ¡Sírvete!

hen noun
la **gallina** *fem.*

her adjective
1 (*before a singular noun*) **su**
her father su padre
2 (*before a plural noun*) **sus**
her books sus libros
3 (*with parts of the body, clothes, etc.*)
She's washing her hands. Se está lavando las manos.
She put her coat on. Se puso el abrigo.

LANGUAGE
Use se with el, la, los, or las instead of su and sus in these examples.

her pronoun
1 (*after a verb*) **la**
I know her. La conozco.
Have you seen her? ¿La has visto?

LANGUAGE
With commands and infinitives la is joined with the verb to make one word.

Help her. Ayúdala.
I want to see her. Quiero verla.
2 (*to her*) **le**
I have sent a letter to her. Le he mandado una carta.
Give her the pen. Dale el bolígrafo.

LANGUAGE
When le is used with lo or la you use se instead of le.

I've given it to her. Se lo he dado.
Give it to her. Dáselo.
3 (*after a preposition etc.*) **ella**
with her con ella
You're taller than her. Eres más alto que ella.
It's her. Es ella.

• *Languages and nationalities do not take a capital letter in Spanish.*

here adverb

1 **aquí**
   I live here. Vivo aquí.
   Come here! ¡Ven aquí!
   Here he is. Aquí está.

2 (*when you're giving something*)
   Here's the book. Aquí tienes el libro.
   Here are the pens. Aquí tienes los bolis.

> 🔑 **LANGUAGE**
> In Spanish aquí tienes (word for word 'here you have') can be used for 'here is' and 'here are'.

hero noun
   el **héroe** *masc.*

heroine noun
   la **heroína** *fem.*

hers pronoun

1 (*with a singular noun*) el **suyo** *masc.*, la **suya** *fem.*
   My house is bigger than hers.
   Mi casa es más grande que la suya.

2 (*with a plural noun*) los **suyos** *masc. plural*, las **suyas** *fem. plural*
   my friends and hers mis amigos y los suyos

3 (*following 'is'*) **suyo** *masc.*, **suya** *fem.*
   This book is hers. Este libro es suyo.
   This apple is hers. Esta manzana es suya.

4 (*following 'are'*) **suyos** *masc. plural*, **suyas** *fem. plural*
   These books are hers. Estos libros son suyos.

herself pronoun

1 **ella misma**
   She has done it herself. Lo ha hecho ella misma.

2 (*with a reflexive verb*) **se**
   María is washing herself. María se está lavando.

3 by herself sola
   She's sitting by herself. Está sentada sola.

hi exclamation
   ¡hola!

hiccups plural noun
   to have hiccups tener hipo

to **hide**

1 **esconderse**
   I hid behind a tree. Me escondí detrás de un árbol.

2 to hide something esconder algo
   Hide the book. Esconde el libro.

hide-and-seek noun
   el **escondite** *masc.*
   to play hide-and-seek jugar al escondite

hiding place noun
   el **escondite** *masc.*

high adjective
   alto *masc.*, **alta** *fem.*
   This building is very high. Este edificio es muy alto.

high school noun
   el **instituto** *masc.*

hill noun

1 (*in the countryside*) la **colina** *fem.*

2 (*in the town*) la **cuesta** *fem.*

him pronoun

1 (*after a verb*) **lo**
   I know him. Lo conozco.
   Have you seen him? ¿Lo has visto?

> 🔑 **LANGUAGE**
> With commands and infinitives lo is joined with the verb to make one word.

   Call him. Llámalo.
   Can you help him? ¿Puedes ayudarlo?

2 (*to him*) **le**
   I have sent a present to him. Le he mandado un regalo.
   Give him the CD. Dale el CD.

> 🔑 **LANGUAGE**
> When le is used with lo or la you use se instead of le.

   I've given it to him. Se lo he dado.
   Give it to him. Dáselo.

• *The months of the year and days of the week do not take a capital letter in Spanish.*

3 (*after a preposition etc.*) **él**
with him con él
I'm younger than him. Soy más
joven que él.
It's him. Es él.

himself pronoun
1 **él mismo**
He has done it himself. Lo ha hecho
él mismo.
2 (*with a reflexive verb*) **se**
He's washing himself. Se está
lavando.
3 by himself solo
He doesn't go out by himself.
No sale solo.

Hindu adjective
hindú *masc. & fem.* (plural **hindúes**)

hip noun
la **cadera** *fem.*

hip hip hurrah exclamation
¡viva!

hippopotamus noun
el **hipopótamo** *masc.*

to **hire** verb
(*a bike, car, etc.*) **alquilar**

his adjective
1 (*before a singular noun*) **su**
his dog su perro
2 (*before a plural noun*) **sus**
his parents sus padres
3 (*with parts of the body, clothes, etc.*)
He's washing his hands. Se está
lavando las manos.
He took his coat off. Se quitó el
abrigo.

LANGUAGE
Use se with el, la, los, or las instead of su
and sus in these examples.

his pronoun
1 (*with a singular noun*) el **suyo** *masc.*,
la **suya** *fem.*
My house is smaller than his. Mi
casa es más pequeña que la suya.

• See the centre section for verb tables.

2 (*with a plural noun*) los **suyos** *masc.
plural*, las **suyas** *fem. plural*
my toys and his mis juguetes y los
suyos
3 (*following 'is'*) **suyo** *masc.*, **suya** *fem.*
This pen is his. Este bolígrafo es
suyo.
This magazine is his. Esta revista es
suya.
4 (*following 'are'*) **suyos** *masc. plural*,
suyas *fem. plural*
These pens are his. Estos bolígrafos
son suyos.

history noun
la **historia** *fem.*

hit noun
(*song*) el **éxito** *masc.*
It's his latest hit. Es su último
éxito.

to **hit** verb
1 **golpear**
They've hit me! ¡Me han golpeado!
2 **darse un golpe en**
I hit my head. Me di un golpe en la
cabeza.
3 (*to bump into*) **chocar con**
My bike hit a tree. Mi bici chocó
con un árbol.

hobby noun
el **pasatiempo** *masc.*, el **hobby**
masc. (plural los **hobbies**)

hockey noun
el **hockey** *masc.*
I play hockey. Juego al hockey.

to **hold** verb
1 **tener**
What are you holding in your
hand? ¿Qué tienes en la mano?

LANGUAGE
Use tener when you describe what you've
got in your hand, otherwise sostener.

2 **sostener**
Can you hold this box, please?
¿Me sostienes esta caja, por
favor?

3 to hold on (*to wait*) esperar
Hold on a moment! ¡Espera un momento!
4 to hold up (*to lift up*) levantar
Hold up your hands! ¡Levantad la mano!

hold-up noun
(*traffic jam*) el **atasco** *masc.*

hole noun
el **agujero** *masc.*

holiday noun
1 las **vacaciones** *fem. plural*
I'm on holiday. Estoy de vacaciones.
When are you going on holiday? ¿Cuándo te vas de vacaciones?
the Christmas holidays las vacaciones de Navidad
the school holidays las vacaciones escolares
2 (*public holiday*) **la fiesta** *fem.*
Tomorrow is a holiday. Mañana es fiesta.

Holland noun
Holanda *fem.*

holly noun
el **acebo** *masc.*

holy adjective
santo *masc.*, **santa** *fem.*

home noun
1 la **casa** *fem.*
at home en casa
My dad is at home. Mi papá está en casa.
2 (*on web page*) el **inicio** *masc.*
the home page la página de inicio

home adverb
a casa
I'm going home. Me voy a casa.
Mum gets home at six. Mamá llega a casa a las seis.

homeless adjective
a homeless person una persona sin hogar

homework noun
los **deberes** *masc. plural*
my Spanish homework mis deberes de español

🔑 **LANGUAGE**
English = **homework** is singular
Spanish = **los deberes** is plural

honest adjective
(*telling the truth*) **sincero** *masc.*, **sincera** *fem.*

honey noun
la **miel** *fem.*

hood noun
(*on a coat*) la **capucha** *fem.*

hook noun
(*for a picture or clothes*) el **gancho** *masc.*

hooray exclamation
¡hurra!

Hoover® noun
la **aspiradora** *fem.*

to hoover verb
pasar la aspiradora
I've hoovered my room. He pasado la aspiradora por mi habitación.

to hop verb
(*on one leg*) **saltar a la pata coja**

to hope verb
esperar
I hope to see you tomorrow. Espero verte mañana.
I hope so. Espero que sí.
I hope not. Espero que no.

hopeless adjective
muy malo *masc.*, **muy mala** *fem.*
I'm hopeless at maths. Soy muy malo para las matemáticas.

horn noun
1 (*on a bull etc.*) el **cuerno** *masc.*
2 (*on a car*) la **bocina** *fem.*

horrible adjective
horrible *masc. & fem.*

• Use **el** and **uno** for masculine words and **la** and **una** for feminine words.

a
b
c
d
e
f
g
h
i
j
k
l
m
n
o
p
q
r
s
t
u
v
w
x
y
z

horror film noun
la **película de terror** *fem.*

horse noun
el **caballo** *masc.*

hospital noun
el **hospital** *masc.*
My grandfather's in hospital.
Mi abuelo está en el hospital.

hot adjective
caliente *masc. & fem.*
The water's hot. El agua está caliente.
The weather's hot. Hace calor.
It's hot today. Hoy hace calor.
I'm hot. Tengo calor.
He's very hot. Tiene mucho calor.

LANGUAGE
English = to be hot   I'm hot.
Spanish = tener calor   Tengo calor.

hot dog noun
el **perrito caliente** *masc.*

hotel noun
el **hotel** *masc.*

hour noun
la **hora** *fem.*
half an hour media hora
a quarter of an hour un cuarto de hora
two and a half hours dos horas y media

house noun
la **casa** *fem.*
at my house en mi casa
I'm at Parminder's house. Estoy en casa de Parminder.
I'm going to Tom's house. Voy a casa de Tom.

housework noun
la **limpieza** *fem.*
to do the housework hacer la limpieza

how adverb
1 **cómo**
How are you? ¿Cómo estás?
2 how much? ¿cuánto?
How much is it? ¿Cuánto es?
How much money do you have? ¿Cuánto dinero tienes?
3 how many? ¿cuántos?
How many books do you want? ¿Cuántos libros quieres?
4 how often? ¿cada cuánto?
How often do you see your uncle? ¿Cada cuánto ves a tu tío?
5 How old are you? ¿Cuántos años tienes?

huge adjective
enorme *masc. & fem.*

human adjective
humano *masc.*, **humana** *fem.*
a human being un ser humano

humour noun
to have a sense of humour tener sentido del humor

hundred number
1 **cien**
a hundred children cien niños
about a hundred children unos cien niños
2 **ciento**
a hundred and five ciento cinco
hundreds of children cientos de niños
two hundred doscientos or doscientas
two hundred and ten euros doscientos diez euros
five hundred quinientos or quinientas

LANGUAGE
Use cien in front of nouns and ciento for numbers 101 to 199. For numbers 200 to 999 join dos, tres, etc. to cientos to make one word (e.g. doscientos); sometimes the first number has a different form (e.g. quinientos, not cincocientos).

• Languages and nationalities do not take a capital letter in Spanish.

hungry adjective
I'm hungry. Tengo hambre.
He's very hungry. Tiene mucha hambre.

🔑 **LANGUAGE**
English = **to be** hungry I'm hungry.
Spanish = **tener** hambre Tengo hambre.

hurricane noun
el **huracán** *masc.* (plural los **huracanes**)

hurry noun
to be in a hurry tener prisa
I'm in a hurry. Tengo prisa.

to **hurry** verb
darse prisa
Hurry up, granddad! ¡Date prisa, abuelo!

to **hurt** verb
1 My arm hurts. Me duele el brazo.
It hurts a lot. Me duele mucho.
My feet hurt. Me duelen los pies.
2 to hurt somebody hacer daño a alguien
You're hurting me! ¡Me estás haciendo daño!
Have you hurt yourself? ¿Te has hecho daño?

hurt adjective
(*in an accident*) **herido** *masc.*, **herida** *fem.*
He's hurt. Está herido.

husband noun
el **marido** *masc.*

hyphen noun
el **guión** *masc.* (plural los **guiones**)

Ii

I pronoun
1 (*not usually translated in Spanish*)
I'm English. Soy inglés.
I have a dog. Tengo un perro.
2 **yo**
I'm reading a book and my brother's playing. Yo estoy leyendo un libro y mi hermano está jugando.
my father and I mi padre y yo

🔑 **LANGUAGE**
Use **yo** when you want to give special importance to the word 'I'.

ice noun
el **hielo** *masc.*

ice-cold adjective
(*water, hands, etc.*) **helado** *masc.*, **helada** *fem.*

ice cream noun
el **helado** *masc.*
a strawberry ice cream un helado de fresa

ice cube noun
el **cubito de hielo** *masc.*

ice lolly noun
el **polo** *masc.*

ice rink noun
la **pista de hielo** *fem.*

ice-skating noun
el **patinaje sobre hielo** *masc.*
I go ice-skating. Voy a patinar.

icon noun
el **icono** *masc.*
Click on the icon. Haz clic en el icono.

• *The months of the year and days of the week do not take a capital letter in Spanish.*

a
b
c
d
e
f
g
h
i
j
k
l
m
n
o
p
q
r
s
t
u
v
w
x
y
z

ICT noun
las **TIC** *fem. plural*,
la **informática** *fem.*

> **LANGUAGE**
> TIC is short for Tecnologías de la
> información y de la comunicación.

icy adjective
1 (*wind, hands, etc.*) **helado** *masc.*,
helada *fem.*
2 The roads are icy. Hay hielo en la
carretera.

idea noun
la **idea** *fem.*
I have an idea. Tengo una idea.

identical adjective
idéntico *masc.*, **idéntica** *fem.*

idiot noun
el or la **idiota** *masc. & fem.*

if conjunction
si
if you can si puedes
Tell me if you want to come. Dime
si quieres venir.
if not si no

> **LANGUAGE**
> si = if
> sí = yes

ill adjective
enfermo *masc.*, **enferma** *fem.*
I'm ill. Estoy enfermo.

illness noun
la **enfermedad** *fem.*

imaginary adjective
imaginario *masc.*,
imaginaria *fem.*
an imaginary friend un amigo
imaginario

imagination noun
la **imaginación** *fem.*

to **imagine** verb
imaginar
Imagine you have lots of money.
Imagina que tienes mucho dinero.

to **imitate** verb
imitar

immediately adverb
inmediatamente

> **LANGUAGE**
> English = immediately
> Spanish = inmediatamente

important adjective
importante *masc. & fem.*

impossible adjective
imposible *masc. & fem.*

to **improve** verb
mejorar
Your Spanish has improved.
Tu español ha mejorado.
I want to improve my Spanish.
Quiero mejorar mi español.

> **LANGUAGE**
> Mejorar comes from mejor (better).

in preposition & adverb
1 **en**
I'm in the garden. Estoy en el
jardín.
in Spain en España
in Spanish en español
in April en abril
in here aquí dentro
2 (*with 'most' + adjective, or words like 'best',
'biggest'*) **de**
the most intelligent girl in the
class la chica más inteligente de la
clase
the best school in Madrid el mejor
colegio de Madrid
3 (*talking about time in the future*) **dentro
de**
I'm coming back in two days.
Vuelvo dentro de dos días.
4 (*talking about being at home*) **to be in**
estar
Is Nicole in? ¿Está Nicole?
She's not in. No está.

• *See the centre section for verb tables.*

inch noun
I'm two inches taller than you.
Soy cinco centímetros más alto que
tú.

CULTURE
Spanish measurements are in metres
and centimetres; an inch is about 2.5
centimetres.

included adjective
incluido *masc.*, **incluida** *fem.*
The service is included El servicio
está incluido

incorrect adjective
incorrecto *masc.*, **incorrecta** *fem.*

to **increase** verb
aumentar

incredible adjective
increíble *masc. & fem.*

indeed adverb
realmente
I'm very tired indeed. Estoy
realmente cansado.
Thanks very much indeed!
¡Muchísimas gracias!

independent adjective
independiente *masc. & fem.*

India noun
la **India** *fem.*

Indian adjective
indio *masc.*, **india** *fem.*
an Indian town una ciudad india

Indian noun
el **indio** *masc.*, la **india** *fem.*

indoor adjective
(*swimming pool, tennis court, etc.*)
cubierto *masc.*, **cubierta** *fem.*
an indoor pool una piscina
cubierta

indoors adverb
dentro
They're eating indoors. Están
comiendo dentro.
to go indoors entrar

infant school noun
la **guardería** *fem.*

CULTURE
In Spain the guardería is a nursery school
for children before they start primary
school at the age of 6. In Britain the infant
school is for children from 4 to 7 years.

infection noun
la **infección** *fem.* (plural las
infecciones)
a throat infection una infección de
garganta

infinitive noun
el **infinitivo** *masc.*

information noun
la **información** *fem.*

ingredient noun
el **ingrediente** *masc.*

initials plural noun
las **iniciales** *fem. plural*
My initials are BTN. Mis iniciales
son BTN.

injection noun
la **inyección** *fem.* (plural las
inyecciones)
The doctor gave me an injection.
El médico me puso una inyección.

injured adjective
1 (*in an accident etc.*) **herido** *masc.*,
herida *fem.*
There are many injured people.
Hay muchos heridos.
2 (*in sports*) **lesionado** *masc.*,
lesionada *fem.*
The player is injured. El jugador
está lesionado.

injury noun
1 (*in an accident etc.*) la **herida** *fem.*
2 (*in sports*) la **lesión** *fem.*

ink noun
la **tinta** *fem.*
an ink mark una mancha de tinta

• *Use* **el** *and* **uno** *for masculine words and* **la** *and* **una** *for feminine words.*

insect noun
el **insecto** *masc.*

inside preposition
dentro de
inside the box dentro de la caja

inside adverb
dentro
What's inside? ¿Qué hay dentro?
Your socks are inside out. Tus
calcetines están al revés.

to **install** verb
instalar
Have you installed the program?
¿Has instalado el programa?

instead adverb
1 (*not translated*)
Ali's not well so I went instead. Ali
está enfermo así que fui yo.
2 instead of en vez de
I went to the cinema instead of
going to school. Fui al cine en vez
de ir al colegio.

instructions plural noun
las instrucciones *fem. plural*

instructor noun
el **monitor** *masc.*, la **monitora** *fem.*
a ski instructor un monitor de
esquí

instrument noun
el **instrumento** *masc.*
I play an instrument. Toco un
instrumento.

intelligent adjective
inteligente *masc. & fem.*

to **intend** verb
to intend to do something pensar
hacer algo

interest noun
(*hobby*) la **afición** *fem.*
My interests are football and
swimming. Mis aficiones son el
fútbol y la natación.

to **interest** verb
interesar
I'm not interested. No me interesa.
I'm interested in music. Me
interesa la música.

🔑 **LANGUAGE**
To say 'you're interested in something' in
Spanish, you say 'something interests
you'.

interesting adjective
interesante *masc. & fem.*

international adjective
internacional *masc. & fem.*

Internet noun
Internet *masc. & fem.*
on the Internet en Internet
an Internet cafe un cibercafé

🔑 **LANGUAGE**
El or **la** are not used with 'Internet'.

to **interrupt** verb
interrumpir
Don't interrupt me! ¡No me
interrumpas!

interval noun
(*in the cinema or theatre*) el **intermedio**
masc.

into
1 **en**
I went into the classroom. Entré
en la clase.
2 **a**
Get into the car. Sube al coche.
to translate something into
Spanish traducir algo al español

to **introduce** verb
presentar
Are you going to introduce me to
your friend? ¿Me presentas a tu
amiga?

to **invent** verb
inventar

invention noun
el **invento** *masc.*

• *Languages and nationalities do not take a capital letter in Spanish.*

invisible adjective
invisible *masc. & fem.*

invitation noun
la **invitación** *fem.* (plural las invitaciones)

to **invite** verb
invitar

Ireland noun
Irlanda *fem.*
I live in Ireland. Vivo en Irlanda.

Irish adjective
irlandés *masc.*, **irlandesa** *fem.*
an Irish town una ciudad irlandesa
He's Irish. Es irlandés.
Irish people los irlandeses

LANGUAGE
The masculine plural of irlandés is irlandeses.

Irish noun
1 (*language*) el **irlandés** *masc.*
She speaks Irish. Habla irlandés.
2 **the Irish** los irlandeses *masc. plural*

Irishman noun
el **irlandés** *masc.* (plural los irlandeses)

Irishwoman noun
la **irlandesa** *fem.*

iron noun
1 (*metal*) el **hierro** *masc.*
an iron bar una barra de hierro
2 (*for clothes*) la **plancha** *fem.*

to **iron** verb
planchar
I like ironing. Me gusta planchar.

ironing noun
to do the ironing planchar
an ironing board una tabla de planchar

is verb SEE **be**
He's in the kitchen. Está en la cocina.
She's tall. Es alta.

Islamic adjective
islámico *masc.*, **islámica** *fem.*

island noun
la **isla** *fem.*

isle noun
la **isla** *fem.*
the Isle of Man la Isla de Man
the Isle of Wight la Isla de Wight

it pronoun

LANGUAGE
Remember: if 'it' stands for a noun you need to know if it's masculine or feminine.

1 (*not usually translated in Spanish*)
Do you like my shirt? It's red. ¿Te gusta mi camisa? Es roja.
Where's the umbrella? – It's in the car. ¿Dónde está el paraguas? – Está en el coche.
Who is it? – It's me. ¿Quién es? – Soy yo.
It's raining. Está lloviendo.
It's cold. Hace frío.
There's a book behind it. Hay un libro detrás.
2 (*after a verb, standing for a masculine noun*) **lo**
I have a pen. Do you want it? Tengo un bolígrafo. ¿Lo quieres?
It's my book. Bring it to me. Es mi libro. Tráemelo.

LANGUAGE
With commands lo and la must be joined with the verb to make one word.

3 (*after a verb, standing for a feminine noun*) **la**
Here's the letter. I have read it. Aquí está la carta. La he leído.
The film is interesting. I want to see it. La película es interesante. Quiero verla.

LANGUAGE
With infinitives lo and la can be joined with the verb to make one word.

• The months of the year and days of the week do not take a capital letter in Spanish.

a b c d e f g h i j k l m n o p q r s t u v w x y z

4 (*to it*) **le**
The dog is hungry. I gave it a bone.
El perro tiene hambre. Le di un
hueso.
Give it a bone. Dale un hueso.
5 (*talking about the time*)
It's one o'clock. Es la una.
It's four o'clock. Son las cuatro.

🔑 **LANGUAGE**
With the time translate 'it is' by **es** for 'one
o'clock' and by **son** for all other times.

IT noun
la **informática** *fem.*

Italian adjective
italiano *masc.*, **italiana** *fem.*
She's Italian. Es italiana.

Italian noun
1 (*language*) el **italiano** *masc.*
He speaks Italian. Habla italiano.
2 (*person*) el **italiano** *masc.*,
la **italiana** *fem.*

Italy noun
Italia *fem.*

to **itch** verb
picar
My arm itches. Me pica el brazo.

itchy adjective
This T-shirt is itchy. Esta camiseta
me pica.

its adjective
1 (*before a singular noun*) **su**
a dog with its bone un perro con su
hueso
2 (*before a plural noun*) **sus**
the town and its inhabitants
la ciudad y sus habitantes

itself pronoun
1 (*with a reflexive verb*) **se**
The cat's washing itself. El gato se
está lavando.
2 **by itself** solo *masc.*, sola *fem.*

Jj

jacket noun
1 la **chaqueta** *fem.*
2 **a jacket potato** una patata asada
(con la piel)

🔑 **LANGUAGE**
Word for word this means 'potato baked
with the skin'.

jail noun
la **cárcel** *fem.*
in jail en la cárcel

jam noun
1 la **mermelada** *fem.*
strawberry jam la mermelada de
fresa

🔑 **LANGUAGE**
In Spanish **mermelada** is the same word
for 'jam' and 'marmalade'.

2 **a traffic jam** un atasco

jammed adjective
(*drawer, window, etc.*) **atascado** *masc.*,
atascada *fem.*

January noun
enero *masc.*
I'm going to Spain in January.
Voy a España en enero.
**The plane leaves on Monday, the
ninth of January.** El avión sale el
lunes nueve de enero.

Japan noun
Japón *masc.*

Japanese adjective
japonés *masc.*, **japonesa** *fem.*
Japanese food la comida japonesa

🔑 **LANGUAGE**
The masculine plural of **japonés** is
japoneses.

• *See the centre section for verb tables.*

Japanese noun
1 (*language*) el **japonés** *masc.*
My sister speaks Japanese.
Mi hermana habla japonés.
2 **the Japanese** los japoneses *masc. plural*

jar noun
el **bote** *masc.*
a jar of jam un bote de mermelada

jealous adjective
celoso *masc.*, **celosa** *fem.*
My sister is jealous of me.
Mi hermana está celosa de mí.

jeans plural noun
los **vaqueros** *masc. plural*
I'm wearing jeans. Llevo vaqueros.
a pair of jeans unos vaqueros

> ⚷ **LANGUAGE**
> The Spanish word comes from **vaquero**, meaning 'cowboy'.

jelly noun
la **gelatina** *fem.*
There's jelly for dessert. De postre hay gelatina.

jersey noun
1 el **jersey** *masc.* (plural los **jerseys** or **jerséis**)
2 (*for football*) la **camiseta** *fem.*
a football jersey una camiseta de fútbol

jewel noun
la **joya** *fem.*

jewellery noun
las **joyas** *fem. plural*
a jewellery shop una joyería

Jewish adjective
judío *masc.*, **judía** *fem.*

jigsaw puzzle noun
el **rompecabezas** *masc.* (plural los **rompecabezas**)
I'm doing a jigsaw puzzle.
Estoy haciendo un rompecabezas.

job noun
el **trabajo** *masc.*
My sister has found a job.
Mi hermana ha encontrado un trabajo.
Cleaning the house is a difficult job. Limpiar la casa es un trabajo difícil.

jogging noun
el **footing** *masc.*
to go jogging hacer footing

join verb
1 (*a club etc.*) **hacerse socio** or **socia de**
2 **to join in** participar

joke noun
1 (*something silly or funny*)
la **broma** *fem.*
It's a joke! ¡Es una broma!
2 (*a funny story*) **el chiste** *masc.*
I like telling jokes. Me gusta contar chistes.

to **joke** verb
bromear
I'm joking! ¡Estoy bromeando!

journey noun
el **viaje** *masc.*
the bus journey el viaje en autobús
Have a good journey! ¡Buen viaje!

joy noun
la **alegría** *fem.*

a
b
c
d
e
f
g
h
i
j
k
l
m
n
o
p
q
r
s
t
u
v
w
x
y
z

• *Use* **el** *and* **uno** *for masculine words and* **la** *and* **una** *for feminine words.*

joystick noun
(*for computer games*) el **mando** *masc.*

judge noun
el or la **juez** *masc. & fem.*

judo noun
el **judo** *masc.*
Do you do judo? ¿Haces judo?

> 🔑 **LANGUAGE**
> The Spanish **judo** is pronounced with a 'j'
> sound as in English.

jug noun
(*for water, wine, etc.*) la **jarra** *fem.*

to **juggle** verb
hacer malabarismos

juice noun
el **zumo** *masc.*
Do you want an orange juice?
¿Quieres zumo de naranja?

July noun
julio *masc.*
They're going to come in July. Van
a venir en julio.
It's the tenth of July. Es el diez de
julio.

to **jump** verb
saltar
Jump! ¡Salta!
to jump over a fence saltar una valla

jumper noun
el **jersey** *masc.* (plural los **jerseys** or
jerséis)

June noun
junio *masc.*

My birthday is in June.
Mi cumpleaños es en junio.
I was born on the fifth of June.
Nací el cinco de junio,

jungle noun
la **selva** *fem.*

junior school noun
la **escuela primaria** *fem.*

> 🌍 **CULTURE**
> Spanish children go to the escuela
> primaria from age 6 to 11.

just adverb
1 **justo**
just after my birthday justo
después de mi cumpleaños
just in time justo a tiempo
2 (*only*) **sólo**
I just have ten euros. Sólo tengo
diez euros.
3 **to have just done something**
acabar de hacer algo
I've just eaten. Acabo de
comer.

> 🔑 **LANGUAGE**
> English = to have just eaten
>   I've just eaten.
> Spanish = acabar de comer
>   Acabo de comer.

4 (*no translation*)
I'm just coming!
¡Ya voy!
Wait just a moment. Espera un
momento.

Kk

kangaroo noun
el **canguro** *masc.*

karate noun
el **kárate** *masc.*

My brother does karate.
Mi hermano hace kárate.

keen adjective
entusiasmado *masc.*,
entusiasmada *fem.*

• *Languages and nationalities do not take a capital letter in Spanish.*

English Spanish

a
b
c
d
e
f
g
h
i
j
k
l
m
n
o
p
q
r
s
t
u
v
w
x
y
z

to **keep** verb
1 (*a secret, something for somebody, etc.*)
guardar
Can you keep my seat?
¿Me guardas el sitio?
I keep my toys in a box. Guardo los
juguetes en una caja.
2 (*talking about something you don't have to
give back*) **quedarse con**
You can keep this CD. Puedes
quedarte con este CD.
3 (*to carry on*) **seguir**
to keep doing something seguir
haciendo algo
I kept working. Seguí trabajando.
4 (*to stay*)
Keep still! ¡Estate quieto!
Keep quiet! (*to one person*) ¡Cállate!;
(*to more than one person*) ¡Callaos!
to keep fit mantenerse en
forma

kennel noun
la **caseta** *fem.*

kettle noun
la **tetera** *fem.*

CULTURE
Electric kettles are not common in
Spain. Water is normally boiled in a
pan. The Spanish tetera also means
'teapot'.

key noun
1 la **llave** *fem.*
2 (*on a computer or piano*) la **tecla** *fem.*

keyboard noun
el **teclado** *masc.*

kick noun
la **patada** *fem.*

to **kick** verb
dar una patada a
He kicked me. Me ha dado una
patada.

kid noun
1 (*child*) el **niño** *masc.*, la **niña** *fem.*
There are twenty kids in the class.
Hay veinte niños en la clase.
2 (*son or daughter*) el **hijo** *masc.*,
la **hija** *fem.*
They have three kids. Tienen tres
hijos.

to **kill** verb
matar

kilo nóun
el **kilo** *masc.*
four euros a kilo cuatro euros el
kilo

kilometre noun
el **kilómetro** *masc.*
at fifty kilometres an hour
a cincuenta kilómetros por hora

kind noun
el **tipo** *masc.*
What kind of bike do you have?
¿Qué tipo de bici tienes?
all kinds of people todo tipo de
personas

kind adjective
amable *masc. & fem.*
Ahmed is very kind to me. Ahmed
es muy amable conmigo.

king noun
el **rey** *masc.*

kingdom noun
el **reino** *masc.*
the United Kingdom el Reino
Unido

kiss noun
el **beso** *masc.*
Give me a kiss. Dame un beso.

to **kiss** verb
1 **besar**
She kissed me. Me besó.
2 (*to kiss each other*) **besarse**
They're kissing. Se están besando.

a
b
c
d
e
f
g
h
i
j
k
l
m
n
o
p
q
r
s
t
u
v
w
x
y
z

• *The months of the year and days of the week do not take a capital letter in Spanish.*

a
b
c
d
e
f
g
h
i
j
k
l
m
n
o
p
q
r
s
t
u
v
w
x
y
z

kit noun
(*clothes etc.*) el **equipo** *masc.*
my PE kit mi equipo de gimnasia
my football kit mi ropa de fútbol

kitchen noun
la **cocina** *fem.*

kite noun
la **cometa** *fem.*
to fly a kite hacer volar una cometa

> ⚷ **LANGUAGE**
> Do you think a kite looks like a comet? The Spanish words for both are the same but the genders are different – 'comet' is masculine: **el cometa.**

kitten noun
el **gatito** *masc.*, la **gatita** *fem.*

knee noun
la **rodilla** *fem.*

to **kneel** verb
ponerse de rodillas
Kneel down! ¡Ponte de rodillas!
I'm kneeling. Estoy de rodillas.

knickers plural noun
las **bragas** *fem. plural*

knife noun
el **cuchillo** *masc.*

to **knit** verb
hacer punto
I like knitting. Me gusta hacer punto.

knob noun
1 (*on a door etc.*) el **pomo** *masc.*
2 (*on a radio etc.*) el **botón** *masc.* (plural los **botones**)

knock noun
el **golpe** *masc.*
a knock on the door un golpe en la puerta
I got a knock on my head. Me di un golpe en la cabeza.

to **knock** verb
1 (*to hit*) **dar se un golpe en**
I knocked my head. Me di un golpe en la cabeza.
2 (*on a door*) **llamar**
Somebody's knocking on the door. Alguien está llamando a la puerta.
3 **to knock somebody down** (*in a road accident*) atropellar a alguien
to knock something over (*a bottle, glass, ink, etc.*) tirar algo

knot noun
el **nudo** *masc.*
to tie a knot in something hacer un nudo en algo

to **know** verb
1 **saber**
Do you know where she is? ¿Sabes dónde está?
I know. Ya lo sé.
I don't know. No lo sé.
to know how to do something saber hacer algo
Do you know how to swim? ¿Sabes nadar?
2 **conocer**
I know your brother. Conozco a tu hermano.
Andrew knows Barcelona well. Andrew conoce bien Barcelona.

> ⚷ **LANGUAGE**
> As a general guide use **saber** when it is followed by words like 'that', 'if', 'where', or 'how to'. Use **conocer** when you are talking about a person or place, or things like a book, film, or name.

knowledge noun
(*of a subject*) los **conocimientos** *masc. plural*

Koran noun
el **Corán** *masc.*

• *See the centre section for verb tables.*

Ll

label noun
la **etiqueta** *fem.*

lace noun
(*for a shoe*) el **cordón** *masc.* (plural los **cordones**)
to do up your laces atarse los cordones

ladder noun
la **escalera (de mano)** *fem.*
to climb a ladder subirse a una escalera

> 🔑 **LANGUAGE**
> Word for word escalera de mano means 'hand stairs'.

ladies noun
(*toilets*) los **servicios de señoras** *masc. plural*

lady noun
la **señora** *fem.*
a young lady una señorita

ladybird noun
la **mariquita** *fem.*

lake noun
el **lago** *masc.*

lamb noun
el **cordero** *masc.*
a lamb chop una chuleta de cordero

lamp noun
la **lámpara** *fem.*

lamp-post noun
la **farola** *fem.*

land noun
la **tierra** *fem.*

to **land** verb
aterrizar
The plane has landed. El avión ha aterrizado.

lane noun
1 (*in the countryside*) el **camino** *masc.*
2 (*part of a road*) el **carril** *masc.*

language noun
el **idioma** *masc.*
a foreign language un idioma extranjero

> 🔑 **LANGUAGE**
> Be careful: idioma ends in an -a but it is not a feminine noun.

lap noun
las **rodillas** *fem. plural*
Sit on my lap. Siéntate en mis rodillas.

laptop noun
el **ordenador portátil** *masc.*

large adjective
grande *masc. & fem.*
a large house una casa grande

> 🔑 **LANGUAGE**
> You can also use grande before the noun, but before a singular noun it becomes gran.
>
> **a large number of ...** un gran número de ...

> ⚠️ **FALSE FRIEND**
> large = grande (*not* largo)

last adjective & pronoun
1 **último** *masc.*, **última** *fem.*
the last time la última vez
I came last. (*in the race*) Llegué el último.
Are you the last? ¿Eres la última?
2 **pasado** *masc.*, **pasada** *fem.*
last week la semana pasada
last Monday el lunes pasado
last night anoche

• *Use* **el** *and* **uno** *for masculine words and* **la** *and* **una** *for feminine words.*

last adverb
1 (*last of all*) **por último**
I did my homework last. Por último hice los deberes.
2 (*talking about the last time*) **por última vez**
When did you see Jon last? ¿Cuándo viste a Jon por última vez?
3 at last! ¡por fin!

to **last** verb
durar
The holidays last three weeks. Las vacaciones duran tres semanas.

late adjective & adverb
tarde
You're late. Llegas tarde.
I'm late. Voy a llegar tarde.
I'm going to be late for school. Voy a llegar tarde al colegio.
We arrived late. Llegamos tarde.
It's late. Es tarde.
It's getting late. Se está haciendo tarde.

lately adverb
últimamente

later adverb
más tarde
He's coming later. Va a llegar más tarde.
See you later! ¡Hasta luego!

latest adjective
último *masc.*, **última** *fem.*
the latest Disney film la última película de Disney

to **laugh** verb
1 **reírse**
I laughed a lot. Me reí mucho.
Don't laugh. No te rías.
2 **reír**
She makes me laugh. Me hace reír.

lawyer noun
el **abogado** *masc.*, la **abogada** *fem.*
My mum's a lawyer. Mi madre es abogada.

to **lay** verb
to lay the table poner la mesa

lazy adjective
perezoso *masc.*, **perezosa** *fem.*
I'm very lazy. Soy muy perezoso.

lead noun
to be in the lead (*in a race or game*) ir en cabeza

to **lead** verb
to be leading (*in a match etc.*) ir ganando
Our team is leading by two goals. Nuestro equipo va ganando por dos goles.

leader noun
1 (*of a group or gang*) el **jefe** *masc.*, la **jefa** *fem.*
2 (*in a race etc.*) el or la **líder** *masc. & fem.*

leaf noun
la **hoja** *fem.*

to **lean** verb
1 **apoyar**
Lean your bike against the wall. Apoya la bici en la pared.
I'm leaning against the wall. Estoy apoyado en la pared.
2 to lean out of the window asomarse por la ventana
to lean over inclinarse

to **learn** verb
aprender
I'm learning Spanish. Estoy aprendiendo español.
Samuel is learning to swim. Samuel está aprendiendo a nadar.

least adverb, adjective & pronoun
1 **menos**
It's the colour I like least. Es el color que menos me gusta.
the least interesting book el libro menos interesante
It's Jill who has the least ice cream. Jill es la que menos helado tiene.
I have the least. Yo soy el que menos tengo.

•*Languages and nationalities do not take a capital letter in Spanish.*

2 at least por lo menos
I have at least ten books. Tengo por lo menos diez libros.

leather noun
el **cuero** masc.
a leather jacket una chaqueta de cuero

to **leave** verb
1 (to go away) **irse**
I'm leaving tomorrow. Me voy mañana.
We left Scotland on Saturday. Nos fuimos de Escocia el sábado.
2 (to go out) **salir**
The train leaves at five. El tren sale a las cinco.
I leave the house at eight. Salgo de casa a las ocho.
3 **dejar**
Leave the book on the table. Deja el libro en la mesa.
Leave me alone! ¡Déjame en paz!
4 (to forget) **dejarse**
I left my pen at your house. Me dejé el bolígrafo en tu casa.

left adjective
1 **izquierdo** masc., **izquierda** fem.
my left hand mi mano izquierda
2 (left over) **to be left** quedar
I have two chocolates left. Me quedan dos bombones.
There's nothing left. No queda nada.

left noun & adverb
on the left a la izquierda
Our school is on the left. Nuestro colegio está a la izquierda.
We drive on the left. Se conduce por la izquierda.
Turn left. Gira a la izquierda.

left-handed adjective
zurdo masc., **zurda** fem.
Daniel is left-handed. Daniel es zurdo.

left-luggage office noun
la **consigna** fem.

leg noun
1 (of a person) la **pierna** fem.
2 (of an animal) la **pata** fem.
3 (in cooking) **a chicken leg** un muslo de pollo

leisure centre noun
el **polideportivo** masc.

lemon noun
el **limón** masc. (plural los **limones**)
a lemon tea un té con limón

lemonade noun
la **gaseosa** fem.

to **lend** verb
dejar
I lent a book to my friend. Le dejé un libro a mi amiga.
Can you lend me your pen? ¿Puedes dejarme el boli?

length noun
la **longitud** fem.

leopard noun
el **leopardo** masc.

less adverb, adjective & pronoun
1 **menos**
I eat less than you. Como menos que tú.
My book is less interesting than yours. Mi libro es menos interesante que el tuyo.
Less milk, please. Menos leche, por favor.
2 **less than** (with numbers) menos de
less than three hours menos de tres horas

lesson noun
1 la **clase** fem.
We have a Spanish lesson at ten. Tenemos clase de español a las diez.
2 (in a book) la **lección** fem. (plural las **lecciones**)
Lesson two is hard. La lección dos es difícil.

a b c d e f g h i j k l m n o p q r s t u v w x y z

• The months of the year and days of the week do not take a capital letter in Spanish.

 1 **dejar**
  Let me speak. Déjame hablar.
  They don't let me watch TV. No me dejan ver la tele.
  Can you let me in? ¿Me dejas entrar?
  Let go of me! ¡Suéltame!
 2 (*making suggestions*)
  Let's ... Vamos a ...
  Let's play. Vamos a jugar.
  Let's go! ¡Vámonos!

letter noun
 1 la **carta** *fem.*
  I'm writing a letter. Estoy escribiendo una carta.
 2 (*of the alphabet*) la **letra** *fem.*
  the letter D la letra D

letter box noun
 el **buzón** *masc.* (plural los **buzones**)

lettuce noun
 la **lechuga** *fem.*

level noun
 el **nivel** *masc.*

liar noun
 el **mentiroso** *masc.*,
 la **mentirosa** *fem.*

library noun
 la **biblioteca** *fem.*

⚠ **FALSE FRIEND**
a **library** = una **biblioteca** (*not* una librería)

licence noun
 el **permiso** *masc.*
 a driving licence un permiso de conducir

to **lick** verb
 lamer

lid noun
 la **tapa** *fem.*

lie noun
 la **mentira** *fem.*
 Don't tell lies! ¡No digas mentiras!

to **lie** verb
 1 (*to tell lies*) **mentir**
  Ana never lies. Ana nunca miente.
 2 (*to be flat*) **echarse**
  Lie down on the sofa. Échate en el sofá.

life noun
 la **vida** *fem.*
 all my life toda mi vida

lifebelt noun
 el **salvavidas** *masc.* (plural los **salvavidas**)

lift noun
 el **ascensor** *masc.*
 Let's get the lift. Vamos a coger el ascensor.

to **lift** verb
 levantar
 I can't lift this case. No puedo levantar esta maleta.

light noun
 la **luz** *fem.*
 Turn on the light. Enciende la luz.
 Turn off the light Apaga la luz

light adjective
 1 (*not heavy*) **ligero** *masc.*, **ligera** *fem.*
  a light backpack una mochila ligera
 2 (*describing colours*) **claro** *masc.*, **clara** *fem.*
  a light brown skirt una falda marrón claro

🔑 **LANGUAGE**
When **claro** follows the name of a colour (e.g. **verde**, **rojo**), use **claro** and the colour word in the masculine singular form only.

 3 (*talking about daylight*)
  It's light. Es de día.
  It gets light at five. Se hace de día a las cinco.

to **light** verb
 (*the oven, a match, a candle, etc.*)
 encender
 to light a fire encender un fuego

• *See the centre section for verb tables.*

light bulb noun
la **bombilla** *fem.*

lighthouse noun
el **faro** *masc.*

lightning noun
los **relámpagos** *masc. plural*
a flash of lightning un relámpago

to **like** verb
1 I like jam. Me gusta la mermelada.
I like it. Me gusta.
I don't like cats. No me gustan los gatos.
David likes Emma. A David le gusta Emma.
Do you like reading? ¿Te gusta leer?

LANGUAGE
In Spanish gustar means 'to please' so the order of the words in the Spanish sentence is different, e.g. 'I like jam' is, word for word, 'Jam pleases me'.

2 (*to want*) **querer**
I would like ... Quiero ...
I'd like a glass of water, please. Quiero un vaso de agua, por favor.
Would you like ...? ¿Quiere usted ...?, ¿Quieres ...?
What would you like, sir? ¿Qué quiere usted, señor?
What would you like to drink, dad? ¿Qué quieres beber, papá?
if you like si quieres

like preposition
1 **como**
a bike like this una bici como ésta
2 What's it like? ¿Cómo es?
What's your house like? ¿Cómo es tu casa?
What's the weather like? ¿Qué tiempo hace?

LANGUAGE
When como is used in questions you put an accent on it: cómo.

likely adjective
probable *masc. & fem.*

• *See the centre section for verb tables.*

line noun
1 la **línea** *fem.*
a straight line una línea recta
2 (*of people or things*) la **fila** *fem.*
to get into line ponerse en fila

to **line up** verb
(*in the playground etc.*) **ponerse en fila**

link noun
el **enlace** *masc.*
Click on the link. Haz clic en el enlace.

lion noun
el **león** *masc.* (plural los **leones**)

lip noun
el **labio** *masc.*

lipstick noun
el **pintalabios** *masc.* (plural los **pintalabios**)
My sister wears lipstick. Mi hermana se pinta los labios.

LANGUAGE
Word for word pintalabios means 'paints lips'.

liquid noun
el **líquido** *masc.*

list noun
la **lista** *fem.*

to **listen** verb
escuchar
Listen! ¡Escucha!
I like to listen to the radio. Me gusta escuchar la radio.
Listen to me. Escúchame.

LANGUAGE
English = to listen to something/somebody
Spanish = escuchar algo/a alguien

literature noun
la **literatura** *fem.*

litre noun
el **litro** *masc.*

litter noun
(*papers, rubbish*) la **basura** *fem.*
a litter bin una papelera

little adjective, pronoun & adverb
1 (*not big*) **pequeño** *masc.*,
pequeña *fem.*
a little house una casa pequeña
my little sister mi hermana
pequeña
2 (*not much*) **poco** *masc.*, **poca** *fem.*
very little money muy poco dinero
I eat very little. Como muy poco.
3 a little un poco
Do you speak Spanish? – Just a
little. ¿Hablas español? – Un poco.
Would you like a little more?
¿Quieres un poco más?

to **live** verb
vivir
I live in Birmingham. Vivo en
Birmingham.
Where do you live? ¿Dónde vives?
'... and they lived happily ever
after'. (*in stories*) '... y fueron felices y
comieron perdices'.

LANGUAGE
Word for word the Spanish means 'they
were happy and ate partridges'.

lively adjective
(*party, street, person, etc.*)
animado *masc.*, **animada** *fem.*

living room noun
el **salón** *masc.* (plural los **salones**)

lizard noun
1 (*big*) el **lagarto** *masc.*
2 (*small*) la **lagartija** *fem.*

load noun
loads of un montón de
I have loads of things to do. Tengo
un montón de cosas que hacer.

loaf noun
el **pan** *masc.*
a loaf of bread un pan

lock noun
la **cerradura** *fem.*

to **lock** verb
cerrar con llave
The door is locked. La puerta está
cerrada con llave.

locker noun
el **armario** *masc.*

to **log off** verb
1 (*from a computer program*) **salir**
2 (*from the Internet*) **desconectar**

to **log on** verb
1 (*to a computer program*) **entrar**
2 (*to the Internet*) **conectarse a
Internet**

lollipop noun
el **chupachups®** *masc.*,
la **piruleta** *fem.*

lolly noun
(*ice lolly*) el **polo** *masc.*

London noun
Londres *masc.*
I was born in London. Nací en
Londres.

lonely adjective
solo *masc.*, **sola** *fem.*
I feel lonely. Me siento solo.

long adjective & adverb
1 **largo** *masc.*, **larga** *fem.*
I have long hair. Tengo el pelo
largo.
2 a long time mucho tiempo
I've been waiting a long time.
Llevo mucho tiempo esperando.
I didn't stay long. No me quedé
mucho tiempo.
I won't be long. No tardo mucho.
3 a long way lejos
Is it a long way? ¿Está lejos?
4 how long? ¿cuánto tiempo?
How long have you been waiting?
¿Cuánto tiempo llevas esperando?
The journey is three hours long.
El viaje dura tres horas.

LANGUAGE
Word for word this means 'The journey
lasts three hours'.

• Use **el** and **uno** for masculine words and **la** and **una** for feminine words.

loo noun
el **baño** *masc.*

look noun
to have a look mirar
Have a look at this picture. Mira este dibujo.

to **look** verb
1 mirar
Look! ¡Mira!
I'm looking at the photos. Estoy mirando las fotos.
Look at me! ¡Mírame!

🔑 **LANGUAGE**
English = **to look at** something/somebody
Spanish = **mirar** algo/a alguien

2 (*followed by an adjective*) **parecer**
It looks easy. Parece fácil.
3 to look like parecerse a
You look like your dad. Te pareces a tu padre.

to **look after** cuidar
My sister looks after the children. Mi hermana cuida a los niños.

to **look for** buscar
I'm looking for my book. Estoy buscando mi libro.

to **look out** tener cuidado
Look out! ¡Cuidado!

to **look up** buscar
Look it up in the dictionary. Búscalo en el diccionario.

loose adjective
1 (*clothes*) **ancho** *masc.*, **ancha** *fem.*
These jeans are loose on me. Estos vaqueros me están anchos.
2 I have a loose tooth. Se me mueve un diente.

🔑 **LANGUAGE**
Word for word the Spanish means 'A tooth is moving'!

lorry noun
el **camión** *masc.* (plural los **camiones**)
a lorry driver un camionero *masc.*, una camionera *fem.*
My dad's a lorry driver. Mi padre es camionero.

to **lose** verb
perder
I've lost my pen. He perdido el boli.

lost adjective
perdido *masc.*, **perdida** *fem.*
I'm lost. Estoy perdido.
to get lost perderse
I got lost. Me perdí.
lost property los objetos perdidos

lot noun
1 a lot mucho
I read a lot. Leo mucho.
a lot of mucho *masc.*, mucha *fem.*
a lot of people mucha gente
I have a lot of CDs. Tengo muchos CDs.
2 quite a lot bastante
I eat quite a lot. Como bastante.
quite a lot of bastante *masc. & fem.*
I have quite a lot of books. Tengo bastantes libros.

lottery noun
la **lotería** *fem.*
to play the lottery jugar a la lotería
I've won the lottery. Me ha tocado la lotería.

loud adjective & adverb
fuerte *masc. & fem.*
a loud noise un ruido fuerte
The radio's too loud. La radio está muy fuerte.
Speak louder. Habla más fuerte.
in a loud voice en voz alta

• *Languages and nationalities do not take a capital letter in Spanish.*

lounge noun
el **salón** *masc.* (plural los **salones**)

love noun
el **amor** *masc.*
a love story una historia de amor
to be in love with somebody estar enamorado de alguien
They're in love. Están enamorados.
Love, Carol. (*in a letter*) Con mucho cariño, Carol., Un abrazo, Carol.

to **love** verb
1 (*talking about being in love with somebody*) **querer**
He loves her. La quiere.
2 (*talking about liking something very much*) **I love Madrid.** Me encanta Madrid.
I love apples. Me encantan las manzanas.
Sally loves chocolate. A Sally le encanta el chocolate.
I love to read. Me encanta leer.

> **LANGUAGE**
> Encantar means 'to please very much' so the order of the words in the Spanish sentence is different, e.g. 'I love Madrid' is, word for word, 'Madrid pleases me very much'.

lovely adjective
1 (*beautiful*) **precioso** *masc.*, **preciosa** *fem.*
a lovely dress un vestido precioso
2 (*very good*) **buenísimo** *masc.*, **buenísima** *fem.*
The weather's lovely. Hace un tiempo buenísimo.
I had a lovely time. Lo pasé muy bien.

3 (*adorable*) **encantador** *masc.*, **encantadora** *fem.*
They are lovely girls. Son unas niñas encantadoras.

low adjective
bajo *masc.*, **baja** *fem.*
a low ceiling un techo bajo

luck noun
la **suerte** *fem.*
Good luck! ¡Buena suerte!
Bad luck! ¡Qué mala suerte!
It brings me luck. Me trae suerte.

lucky adjective
1 (*talking about people*)
to be lucky tener suerte
I'm always lucky. Siempre tengo suerte.
2 (*talking about things or numbers*)
The number seven is lucky. El número siete trae suerte.
my lucky number mi número de la suerte

luggage noun
el **equipaje** *masc.*
I have lots of luggage. Tengo mucho equipaje.

lunch noun
la **comida** *fem.*
My dad prepares lunch. Mi padre prepara la comida.
What's for lunch? ¿Qué hay para comer?
to have lunch comer
a lunch box una fiambrera

lunchtime noun
la **hora de comer** *fem.*

luxury noun
el **lujo** *masc.*
a luxury car un coche de lujo

• *The months of the year and days of the week do not take a capital letter in Spanish.*

Mm

macaroni noun
los **macarrones** *masc. plural*

machine noun
la **máquina** *fem.*

mad adjective
1 (*crazy*) **loco** *masc.*, **loca** *fem.*
You're mad! ¡Estás loco!
2 (*angry*) **enfadado** *masc.*,
enfadada *fem.*
I'm mad at you. Estoy enfadada
contigo.
3 I'm mad about bikes. Me chiflan
las bicis.
He's mad about football. Le chifla
el fútbol.

madam noun
señora *fem.*
Yes, madam. Sí, señora.

made verb SEE **make**
I made a lot of noise. Hice mucho
ruido.
She has made a cake. Ha hecho un
pastel.

magazine noun
la **revista** *fem.*

magic adjective
mágico *masc.*, **mágica** *fem.*
a magic wand una varita mágica
a magic trick un truco de magia

magic noun
la **magia** *fem.*

magician noun
el **mago** *masc.*, la **maga** *fem.*

magnet noun
el **imán** *masc.* (plural los **imanes**)

magnifying glass noun
la **lupa** *fem.*

mail noun
el **correo** *masc.*
Is there any mail? ¿Hay correo?

to **mail** verb
mandar por correo
Mail the parcel to me. Mándame el
paquete por correo.

mailbox noun
(*for getting email*) el **buzón** *masc.*
(plural los **buzones**)

main adjective
principal *masc. & fem.*
the main road la carretera
principal
That's the main thing. Eso es lo
principal.

make noun
la **marca** *fem.*
What make is your computer?
¿De qué marca es tu ordenador?

to **make** verb
1 **hacer**
I always make the bed. Siempre
hago la cama.
You make me happy. Tú me haces
feliz.
He makes me laugh. Me hace reír.
I've made some sandwiches. He
hecho bocadillos.
2 (*to build*) **fabricar**
to make cars fabricar coches
'Made in Spain.' 'Fabricado en
España.'

a
b
c
d
e
f
g
h
i
j
k
l
m
n
o
p
q
r
s
t
u
v
w
x
y
z

• *See the centre section for verb tables.*

3 (*to get ready*) **preparar**
My mum's making lunch. Mi madre está preparando la comida.
4 (*to earn*) **ganar**
My uncle makes a lot of money. Mi tío gana mucho dinero.
5 (*with some adjectives: nervous, sad, furious, etc.*) **poner**
It makes me sad. Eso me pone triste.
6 (*with hungry, thirsty, sleepy*) **dar**
It makes me hungry. Me da hambre.
It makes me sleepy. Me da sueño.
7 **ser**
Two and three make five. Dos y tres son cinco.
8 **to make up** inventarse
You've made up the story! ¡Te has inventado la historia!

make-up noun
el **maquillaje** *masc.*
She doesn't wear make-up. No lleva maquillaje.

male noun
el **macho** *masc.*

male adjective
macho *masc. & fem.*
a male hamster un hámster macho

mall noun
shopping mall el centro comercial *masc.*

man noun
el **hombre** *masc.*
a man and a woman un hombre y una mujer
a young man un joven
an old man un anciano, un viejo

⚷ **LANGUAGE**
Anciano is a polite word for 'old man'.

manage verb
to manage to do something poder hacer algo
I've managed to open the window. He podido abrir la ventana.

manager noun
1 (*of a company*) el **director** *masc.*, la **directora** *fem.*
2 (*of a shop or restaurant*) el **encargado** *masc.*, la **encargada** *fem.*

manners plural noun
los **modales** *masc. plural*
to have good manners tener buenos modales
bad manners malos modales

many adjective & pronoun
1 **muchos** *masc. plural*, **muchas** *fem. plural*
I don't have many books. No tengo muchos libros.
many people mucha gente
Do you have many? ¿Tienes muchos?
2 **how many?** ¿cuántos? *masc. plural*, ¿cuántas? *fem. plural*
How many times have you seen the film? ¿Cuántas veces has visto la película?
3 **so many** tantos *masc. plural*, tantas *fem. plural*
I've read so many books! ¡He leído tantos libros!
4 **too many** demasiados *masc. plural*, demasiadas *fem. plural*
There are too many apples. Hay demasiadas manzanas.
too many people demasiada gente
That's too many. Son demasiados.

map noun
1 (*of a country*) el **mapa** *masc.*
a map of Spain un mapa de España
2 (*of a town*) el **plano** *masc.*
a map of Madrid un plano de Madrid

⚷ **LANGUAGE**
Be careful: **mapa** ends in an -a but it is not a feminine noun.

• *Use **el** and **uno** for masculine words and **la** and **una** for feminine words.*

marathon noun
el or la **maratón** *masc. & fem.* (plural los **maratones**)
to run in a marathon correr una maratón

marble noun
la **canica** *fem.*
to play marbles jugar a las canicas

March noun
marzo *masc.*
My grandparents are coming in March. Los abuelos llegan en marzo.
We leave on Sunday, the fourth of March. Salimos el domingo cuatro de marzo.

margarine noun
la **margarina** *fem.*

margin noun
el **margen** *masc.*
Don't write in the margin. No escribas en el margen.

mark noun
1 (*in school subjects*) la **nota** *fem.*
I always get good marks. Siempre saco buenas notas.
2 (*stain*) la **mancha** *fem.*
an ink mark una mancha de tinta
3 (*from fingers, on the body, etc.*) la **marca** *fem.*

to **mark** verb
1 (*homework etc.*) **corregir**
Have they marked the exercises? ¿Han corregido los ejercicios?
2 (*to show*) **señalar**
Mark with a cross. Señala con una cruz.

market noun
el **mercado** *masc.*

marmalade noun
la **mermelada (de naranja)** *fem.*

marriage noun
el **matrimonio** *masc.*

married adjective
casado *masc.*, **casada** *fem.*
Are they married? ¿Están casados?
to get married casarse
They're getting married tomorrow. Se casan mañana.

to **marry** verb
casarse con
She has married an Englishman. Se ha casado con un inglés.

Martian noun
el **marciano** *masc.*, la **marciana** *fem.*

masculine adjective
masculino *masc.*, **masculina** *fem.*

mashed potatoes plural noun
el **puré de patatas** *masc.*

mask noun
la **máscara** *fem.*

mass noun
1 (*church service*) la **misa** *fem.*
to go to mass ir a misa
2 masses of un montón de
Angela has masses of friends. Angela tiene un montón de amigas.

massive adjective
enorme *masc. & fem.*

mat noun
1 la **alfombrilla** *fem.*
2 (*doormat*) el **felpudo** *masc.*

match noun
1 la **cerilla** *fem.*
a box of matches una caja de cerillas
2 (*a team game*) el **partido** *masc.*
a football match un partido de fútbol

• *Languages and nationalities do not take a capital letter in Spanish.*

to **match** verb
 1 (talking about clothes etc.) **pegar con**
 This blouse doesn't match the skirt. Esta blusa no pega con la falda.
 These colours don't match. Estos colores no pegan.
 2 (to find similar things)
 Match the words and the pictures. Encuentra la palabra que corresponda a cada dibujo.

mate noun
 el **amigo** masc., la **amiga** fem.

material noun
 (cloth) la **tela** fem.

mathematics noun
 las **matemáticas** fem. plural

maths noun
 las **matemáticas** fem. plural

matter noun
 What's the matter? ¿Qué pasa?
 What's the matter with you? ¿Qué te pasa?
 There's something the matter with this bike. A esta bici le pasa algo.

to **matter** verb
 It doesn't matter. No importa.

mattress noun
 el **colchón** masc. (plural los **colchones**)

maximum noun
 el **máximo** masc.

maximum adjective
 máximo masc., **máxima** fem.

may verb
 (asking for permission) **poder**
 May I open the window? ¿Puedo abrir la ventana?

May noun
 mayo masc.
 We're going on holiday in May. Nos vamos de vacaciones en mayo.

Come to my house on the tenth of May. Ven a mi casa el diez de mayo.
 May Day el uno de mayo

CULTURE
El uno de mayo is a public holiday.

maybe adverb
 quizás, a lo mejor
 Maybe he's left. Quizás se ha ido., A lo mejor se ha ido.
 Maybe not. Quizás no.

mayonnaise noun
 la **mayonesa** fem.

mayor noun
 el **alcalde** masc., la **alcaldesa** fem.

maze noun
 el **laberinto** masc.

me pronoun
 1 (after a verb) **me**
 She knows me. Me conoce.
 Are they looking for me? ¿Me están buscando?

LANGUAGE
With commands and infinitives me is joined with the verb to make one word.

 Call me. Llámame.
 Can you see me? ¿Puedes verme?
 2 (to me) **me**
 Hassan has sent a letter to me. Hassan me ha mandado una carta.
 Give me the pen. Dame el bolígrafo.
 Give it to me. Dámelo.
 3 (after a preposition) **mí**
 without me sin mí
 behind me detrás de mí
 with me conmigo

LANGUAGE
Remember the special word conmigo to translate 'with me'; never say con mí.

 4 (after 'than' and the verb 'to be') **yo**
 She's taller than me. Es más alta que yo.
 It's me. Soy yo.

• The months of the year and days of the week do not take a capital letter in Spanish.

meal noun
la **comida** *fem.*
I have three meals a day. Hago tres comidas al día.
I've had a good meal. He comido bien.

to **mean** verb
1 **querer decir**
What does 'lápiz' mean? ¿Qué quiere decir 'lápiz'?
What do you mean? ¿Qué quieres decir?

> 🔑 **LANGUAGE**
> Word for word querer decir means 'want to say'.

2 **to mean to do something** querer hacer algo
I didn't mean to break it. No quería romperlo.

> 🔑 **LANGUAGE**
> Word for word querer hacer means 'want to do'.

mean adjective
1 (*with money*) **tacaño** *masc.*, **tacaña** *fem.*
He's very mean. Es muy tacaño.
2 (*nasty*) **malo** *masc.*, **mala** *fem.*
Norman is mean to his sister. Norman es malo con su hermana.

meaning noun
el **significado** *masc.*

measles noun
el **sarampión** *masc.*

to **measure** verb
medir

meat noun
la **carne** *fem.*
Do you eat meat? ¿Comes carne?

mechanic noun
el **mecánico** *masc.*,
la **mecánica** *fem.*
My dad's a mechanic. Mi padre es mecánico.

medal noun
la **medalla** *fem.*
a gold medal una medalla de oro

medical room noun
la **enfermería** *fem.*

medicine noun
el **medicamento** *masc.*,
la **medicina** *fem.*
Take the medicine. Toma la medicina., Toma el medicamento.

Mediterranean noun
the Mediterranean el Mediterráneo

medium adjective
mediano *masc.*, **mediana** *fem.*
of medium height de estatura mediana

to **meet** verb
1 (*by chance*) **encontrarse con**
I met her in the street. Me encontré con ella en la calle.
We met in the supermarket. Nos encontramos en el supermercado.
2 (*to plan to meet*) **quedar con**
I'm meeting my friends in the library. He quedado con mis amigos en la biblioteca.
Where shall we meet? ¿Dónde quedamos?
3 (*to go and get*) **recoger**
My dad's meeting me at the airport. Mi padre va a recogerme al aeropuerto.
4 (*to meet for the first time*) **conocer**
I met Juan two years ago. Conocí a Juan hace dos años.

meeting noun
la **reunión** *fem.* (plural las **reuniones**)

melon noun
el **melón** *masc.* (plural los **melones**)

to **melt** verb
derretirse
My ice cream is melting. Mi helado se derrite.

a
b
c
d
e
f
g
h
i
j
k
l
m
n
o
p
q
r
s
t
u
v
w
x
y
z

• *See the centre section for verb tables.*

a
b
c
d
e
f
g
h
i
j
k
l
m
n
o
p
q
r
s
t
u
v
w
x
y
z

member noun
1 el **miembro** *masc.*
2 (*of a club*) el **socio** *masc.*, la **socia** *fem.*

to **memorize** verb
aprender de memoria

memory noun
1 la **memoria** *fem.*
I have a good memory. Tengo buena memoria.
2 (*something you remember*) el **recuerdo** *masc.*
I have good memories of my school. Tengo buenos recuerdos de mi colegio.

men plural noun
los **hombres** *masc. plural*

to **mend** verb
arreglar

menu noun
el **menú** *masc.* (plural los **menús**)

mermaid noun
la **sirena** *fem.*

merry adjective
Merry Christmas! ¡Feliz Navidad!

merry-go-round noun
el **tiovivo** *masc.*

mess noun
el **desorden** *masc.*
Tidy up this mess! ¡Arregla este desorden!
The house is in a mess. La casa está desordenada.

to **mess up** verb
(*papers, books, house, etc.*) **desordenar**
You've messed up the room! ¡Has desordenado la habitación!

message noun
el **mensaje** *masc.*
a text message un mensaje de texto

messy adjective
(*room, house, etc.*)
desordenado *masc.*, **desordenada** *fem.*

metal noun
el **metal** *masc.*
a metal box una caja de metal

metre noun
el **metro** *masc.*

mice plural noun
los **ratones** *masc. plural*

microphone noun
el **micrófono** *masc.*

microscope noun
el **microscopio** *masc.*

microwave noun
el **microondas** *masc.* (plural los **microondas**)

midday noun
el **mediodía** *masc.*
at midday a mediodía

middle noun
1 el **medio** *masc.*
in the middle of the room en medio de la habitación
the middle drawer el cajón de en medio
a middle name un segundo nombre
2 (*talking about when something happens*) la **mitad** *fem.*
in the middle of the night en mitad de la noche

midnight noun
la **medianoche** *fem.*
at midnight a medianoche

might verb
She might have gone out. Quizás ha salido.
Can you come? – I might. ¿Puedes venir? – Quizás.

mild adjective
The weather's mild. No hace frío.

• Use **el** and **uno** for masculine words and **la** and **una** for feminine words.

330

mile noun
I live three miles away. Vivo a cinco kilómetros de aquí.
We've walked for miles. Hemos andado muchos kilómetros.

CULTURE
In Spain they use kilometres for distances: one mile is just over one and a half kilometres.

milk noun
la **leche** *fem.*
a glass of milk un vaso de leche
a milk shake un batido

milkman noun
el **lechero** *masc.*

million noun
el **millón** *masc.*
two million dos millones
a million people un millón de personas

LANGUAGE
English = a million + noun
Spanish = un millón de + noun

millionaire noun
el **millonario** *masc.*,
la **millonaria** *fem.*
He's a millionaire. Es millonario.

mind noun
I've changed my mind. He cambiado de opinión.
to make up your mind decidirse
Make up your mind! ¡Decídete!

to **mind** verb
1 (*to look after*) **cuidar**
Can you mind the baby? ¿Puedes cuidar al niño?
2 **do you mind ...?** ¿le importa ...?
Do you mind if I close the window? ¿Le importa si cierro la ventana?
I don't mind. No me importa.
Never mind! ¡No importa!
3 (*to watch out*)
Mind your head! ¡Cuidado con la cabeza!

mine pronoun
1 (*with a singular noun*) el **mío** *masc.*, la **mía** *fem.*
Your mum is younger than mine. Tu madre es más joven que la mía.
2 (*with a plural noun*) los **míos** *masc. plural*, las **mías** *fem. plural*
her toys and mine sus juguetes y los míos
3 (*following 'is'*) **mío** *masc.*, **mía** *fem.*
This CD is mine. Este CD es mío.
This bike is mine. Esta bici es mía.
4 (*following 'are'*) **míos** *masc. plural*, **mías** *fem. plural*
These books are mine. Estos libros son míos.

mine noun
la **mina** *fem.*
My dad works in a mine. Mi padre trabaja en una mina.

mineral water noun
el **agua mineral** *fem.*

LANGUAGE
Be careful: you use el with agua but it is not a masculine noun.

minibus noun
el **microbús** *masc.* (plural los **microbuses**)

minimum noun
el **mínimo** *masc.*

minimum adjective
mínimo *masc.*, **mínima** *fem.*

miniskirt noun
la **minifalda** *fem.*

mint noun
1 (*sweet*) el **caramelo de menta** *masc.*
2 (*plant*) la **menta** *fem.*

minus preposition
menos
Five minus two is three. Cinco menos dos son tres.
It's minus three today. Hoy hace tres grados bajo cero.

• *Languages and nationalities do not take a capital letter in Spanish.*

English Spanish

a b c d e f g h i j k l **m** n o p q r s t u v w x y z

minute noun
el **minuto** *masc.*
Wait a minute. Espera un minuto.
I'll be back in a minute. Enseguida vuelvo.

miracle noun
el **milagro** *masc.*

mirror noun
el **espejo** *masc.*

to **misbehave** verb
portarse mal
Holly misbehaves in class. Holly se porta muy mal en clase.

mischief noun
to get up to mischief hacer travesuras

miserable adjective
1 (*sad*) **triste** *masc. & fem.*
Why are you miserable? ¿Por qué estás triste?
2 **The weather's miserable.** Hace un tiempo fatal.

to **miss** verb
1 (*the bus, train, etc.*) **perder**
I don't want to miss the bus. No quiero perder el autobús.
2 (*the party, film, etc.*) **perderse**
I've missed the film. Me he perdido la película.

> **LANGUAGE**
> Use **perder** when you mean you don't catch the bus etc., and **perderse** when you're too late to go somewhere.

3 (*to feel sad*)
I miss you. Te echo de menos.
I miss her. La echo de menos.
I miss my parents. Echo de menos a mis padres.

miss noun
(*talking about your teacher etc.*)
la **señorita** *fem.*
Miss is very nice. La señorita es muy simpática.
Please, miss! ¡Por favor, señorita!
Yes, miss. Sí, señorita.

Miss noun
la **señorita** *fem.*
Good afternoon, Miss Price.
Buenas tardes, señorita Price.

> **LANGUAGE**
> **Señorita** is usually written on an envelope as **Srta.**, e.g. **Srta. Price.**

missing adjective
1 **to be missing** faltar
There's a page missing. Falta una página.
the missing page la página que falta
2 **to go missing** desaparecer

mist noun
la **neblina** *fem.*

mistake noun
1 el **error** *masc.*
I've made a mistake. He cometido un error.
by mistake por error
2 (*in your writing, spelling, or typing*)
la **falta** *fem.*
to make a spelling mistake cometer una falta de ortografía

mistletoe noun
el **muérdago** *masc.*

> **CULTURE**
> In Spain it isn't a tradition to kiss under the mistletoe at Christmas.

misty adjective
It's misty. Hay neblina.

> **LANGUAGE**
> Word for word the Spanish means 'there is mist'.

to **mix** verb
1 **mezclar**
Mix these colours together.
Mezcla estos colores.
You've mixed up all the photos!
¡Has mezclado todas las fotos!
2 (*to confuse*) **confundir**
I get her and her sister mixed up.
La confundo con su hermana.

• *The months of the year and days of the week do not take a capital letter in Spanish.*

mixture noun
la **mezcla** *fem.*

to **moan** verb
(*to complain*) **quejarse**

mobile noun
el **móvil** *masc.*
You can call me on the mobile.
Puedes llamarme al móvil.
a mobile phone un móvil

model noun
1 (*a copy of a bigger thing*) la **maqueta** *fem.*
a model plane una maqueta de avión
2 (*a type of thing*) el **modelo** *masc.*
It's the latest model. Es el último modelo.
3 (*a person*) el or la **modelo** *masc. & fem.*
She's a model. Es modelo.

modern adjective
moderno *masc.*, **moderna** *fem.*

moment noun
el **momento** *masc.*
Just a moment! ¡Un momento!
at the moment en este momento
I'll be back in a moment.
Enseguida vuelvo.

Monday noun
el **lunes** *masc.*
Today is Monday. Hoy es lunes.
on Monday el lunes
We're going to the cinema on Monday. Vamos al cine el lunes.
on Mondays los lunes
We have games on Mondays.
Tenemos deporte los lunes.

> **LANGUAGE**
> Remember the difference in Spanish between el lunes (one Monday only) and los lunes (every Monday).

money noun
el **dinero** *masc.*
It costs a lot of money. Cuesta mucho dinero.
a money box una hucha

• *See the centre section for verb tables.*

monitor noun
(*computer screen*) el **monitor** *masc.*

monkey noun
el **mono** *masc.*, **la mona** *fem.*

monster noun
el **monstruo** *masc.*

month noun
el **mes** *masc.*
I'm leaving in a month. Me voy dentro de un mes.
this month este mes
last month el mes pasado
next month el mes que viene

mood noun
el **humor** *masc.*
Are you in a good or bad mood?
¿Estás de buen o de mal humor?

moon noun
la **luna** *fem.*

more adverb, adjective & pronoun
1 **más**
more interesting más interesante
I read more than you. Leo más que tú.
More water, please. Más agua, por favor.
a bit more un poco más
I don't want any more. No quiero más.
ten more days diez días más
2 **more than** (*with numbers*) más de
more than ten books más de diez libros
3 (*talking about something you did but don't do now*)
I don't come here any more. Ya no vengo aquí.
I'm not playing with you any more. No juego más contigo.

> **LANGUAGE**
> To mean 'not any more' use ya no or no ... más.

a
b
c
d
e
f
g
h
i
j
k
l
m
n
o
p
q
r
s
t
u
v
w
x
y
z

morning noun
la **mañana** *fem.*
In the morning I go to school. Por la mañana voy al colegio.
at eight o'clock in the morning a las ocho de la mañana
this morning esta mañana
tomorrow morning mañana por la mañana
Good morning! ¡Buenos días!

mosque noun
la **mezquita** *fem.*

mosquito noun
el **mosquito** *masc.*
a mosquito bite una picadura de mosquito

most adverb, adjective & pronoun
1 más
I like Spanish most. Lo que más me gusta es el español.
the most boring book el libro más aburrido
the most expensive ones los más caros
It's Andrew who has the most cake. Andrew es el que más pastel tiene.
I have the most. Yo soy la que más tengo.
2 (*over half*) **la mayoría de**
most children la mayoría de los niños
most people la mayoría de la gente
most of my friends la mayoría de mis amigos
3 (*almost all*) **casi todo** *masc.*, **casi toda** *fem.*
I've eaten most of the ice cream. He comido casi todo el helado.
I've eaten most of it. He comido casi todo.
most of the time la mayor parte del tiempo

moth noun
la **mariposa de la luz** *fem.*

mother noun
la **madre** *fem.*
My mother is a dentist. Mi madre es dentista.
my mother and father mis padres
Mother's Day el día de la Madre

> **CULTURE**
> In Spain Mother's Day is the first Sunday in May; it's in March in Britain.

motorbike noun
la **moto** *fem.*

motorcycle noun
la **motocicleta** *fem.*

motorcyclist noun
el or la **motorista** *masc. & fem.*

motorist noun
el or la **automovilista** *masc. & fem.*

> ⚠ **FALSE FRIEND**
> motorist = automovilista (*not* motorista)

motorway noun
la **autopista** *fem.*

mountain noun
la **montaña** *fem.*
a mountain bike una bicicleta de montaña

mouse noun
el **ratón** *masc.* (plural los **ratones**)
a mouse mat una alfombrilla de ratón

> **LANGUAGE**
> As in English, a ratón is an animal and a part of your computer.

moustache noun
el **bigote** *masc.*
He has a moustache. Tiene bigote.

mouth noun
la **boca** *fem.*

move noun
1 (*in a game*)
It's your move. Te toca a ti.
2 Get a move on! ¡Date prisa!

• *Use **el** and **uno** for masculine words and **la** and **una** for feminine words.*

to **move** verb
1 **mover**
  Can you move your hand? ¿Puedes mover la mano?
2 (*to move your body*) **moverse**
  Don't move. No te muevas.
  I can't move. No puedo moverme.
3 (*to put out of the way*) **quitar**
  Move your things off the table. Quita tus cosas de la mesa.
  Move your bag. Quita tu bolso de aquí.
4 (*to move house*) **mudarse**
  We're moving tomorrow. Nos mudamos mañana.

to **move forward** verb
  avanzar

to **move over** verb
  correrse
  Move over a bit. Córrete un poco.

movement noun
  el **movimiento** *masc.*

movie noun
  la **película** *fem.*
  Do you like movies? ¿Te gustan las películas?
  to go to the movies ir al cine
  a movie star una estrella de cine

Mr noun
  el **señor** *masc.*
  Good morning, Mr Short. Buenos días, señor Short.

🔑 **LANGUAGE**
Señor is usually written on an envelope as Sr., e.g. Sr. Short.

Mrs noun
  la **señora** *fem.*
  Goodbye, Mrs Patel. Adiós, señora Patel.

🔑 **LANGUAGE**
Señora is usually written on an envelope as Sra., e.g. Sra. Patel.

Ms noun
  la **señora** *fem.*
  Good morning, Ms Solomon. Buenos días, señora Solomon.

🌐 **CULTURE**
You use 'Ms' when you don't want to say whether a woman is married or not. There is no special word in Spanish for this, but señora can always be used.

much adverb, adjective & pronoun
1 **mucho**
  I don't read much. No leo mucho.
  much bigger mucho más grande
  very much mucho
2 **mucho** *masc.*, **mucha** *fem.*
  I don't have much chocolate. No tengo mucho chocolate.
  There's not much snow. No hay mucha nieve.
  Thank you very much! ¡Muchas gracias!
3 how much? ¿cuánto? *masc.*, ¿cuánta? *fem.*
  How much is it? ¿Cuánto es?
  How much milk? ¿Cuánta leche?
4 so much tanto *masc.*, tanta *fem.*
  Not so much milk! ¡No tanta leche!
5 too much demasiado *masc.*, demasiada *fem.*
  too much work demasiado trabajo
  I eat too much. Como demasiado.

mud noun
  el **barro** *masc.*

muddy adjective
  (*hands, shoes, etc.*) **lleno de barro** *masc.*, **llena de barro** *fem.*

mug noun
  (*of tea or coffee*) la **taza** *fem.*

to **multiply** verb
  multiplicar
  Four multiplied by two is eight. Cuatro multiplicado por dos son ocho.

• *Languages and nationalities do not take a capital letter in Spanish.*

English Spanish

a b c d e f g h i j k l **m** n o p q r s t u v w x y z

mum noun
la **mamá** *fem.*, la **madre** *fem.*
Yes, mum. Sí, mamá.
My mum works in an office.
Mi madre trabaja en una oficina.,
Mi mamá trabaja en una oficina.
my mum and dad mis papás

mummy noun
la **mamá** *fem.*
Hello, mummy! ¡Hola, mamá!

mumps noun
las **paperas** *fem. plural*

murder noun
el **asesinato** *masc.*

to **murder** verb
asesinar

🔑 **LANGUAGE**
The English word assassinate is like asesinar and means 'to murder somebody important or famous'.

murderer noun
el **asesino** *masc.*, la **asesina** *fem.*

muscle noun
el **músculo** *masc.*

museum noun
el **museo** *masc.*

mushroom noun
el **champiñón** *masc.* (plural los **champiñones**)

music noun
la **música** *fem.*
I'm listening to music. Estoy escuchando música.

musical adjective
a musical instrument un instrumento musical

musician noun
el **músico** *masc.*, la **música** *fem.*

Muslim adjective
musulmán *masc.*, **musulmana** *fem.*

mussels plural noun
los **mejillones** *masc. plural*

must verb
1 **tener que**
I must leave. Tengo que irme.
You must do it. Tienes que hacerlo.
2 **deber**
He must not tell lies. No debe mentir.
I must leave right away. Debo irme enseguida.

🔑 **LANGUAGE**
Use deber when the sentence is negative, or as a stronger way of saying 'must'.

3 (*for saying something is probably true*)
deber de, deber
You must be tired. Debes de estar cansado., Debes estar cansado.

mustard noun
la **mostaza** *fem.*

my adjective
1 (*before a singular noun*) **mi**
my brother mi hermano
2 (*before a plural noun*) **mis**
my toys mis juguetes
3 (*with parts of the body, clothes, etc.*)
I'm washing my hands. Me estoy lavando las manos.
I put my coat on. Me puse el abrigo.

🔑 **LANGUAGE**
Use me with el, la, los, or las instead of mi and mis in these examples.

myself pronoun
1 **yo mismo** *masc.*, **yo misma** *fem.*
I wrote it myself. Lo escribí yo mismo.
2 (*with a reflexive verb*) **me**
I'm washing myself. Me estoy lavando.
3 **by myself** solo *masc.*, sola *fem.*
I'm at home by myself. Estoy solo en casa.

mysterious adjective
misterioso *masc.*, **misteriosa** *fem.*

mystery noun
el **misterio** *masc.*

• *The months of the year and days of the week do not take a capital letter in Spanish.*

Nn

nail noun
1 la **uña** *fem.*
   I bite my nails. Me muerdo las uñas.
   nail varnish el esmalte de uñas
2 el **lavo** *masc.*
   with a hammer and nails con un martillo y unos clavos

naked adjective
desnudo *masc.*, **desnuda** *fem.*

name noun
el **nombre** *masc.*
I don't remember your name. No me acuerdo de tu nombre.
What's your name? ¿Cómo te llamas?
My name's Karim. Me llamo Karim.
What's his name? ¿Cómo se llama?

nanny noun
(*who looks after children*) la **niñera** *fem.*

nap noun
la **siesta** *fem.*
to have a nap echarse una siesta

napkin noun
la **servilleta** *fem.*

nappy noun
el **pañal** *masc.*

narrow adjective
estrecho *masc.*, **estrecha** *fem.*

nasty adjective
1 (*bad, cruel*) **malo** *masc.*, **mala** *fem.*
   It's nasty weather. Hace un tiempo muy malo.
   He's nasty to his sister. Es malo con su hermana.
2 (*horrible*) **horrible** *masc. & fem.*
   a nasty accident un accidente horrible

• *See the centre section for verb tables.*

national adjective
nacional *masc. & fem.*
the national anthem el himno nacional

nationality noun
la **nacionalidad** *fem.*
What nationality are you? ¿De qué nacionalidad eres?

natural adjective
natural *masc. & fem.*

nature noun
la **naturaleza** *fem.*

naughty adjective
malo *masc.*, **mala** *fem.*
Naughty boy! ¡Malo!

navy blue adjective
azul marino *masc. & fem.*
navy blue socks calcetines azul marino

> 🔑 **LANGUAGE**
> Azul marino is the same in the masculine, feminine, and plural.

near adjective
cercano *masc.*, **cercana** *fem.*
the nearest supermarket el supermercado más cercano

near adverb & preposition
1 **cerca**
   I live very near. Vivo muy cerca.
2 (*with nouns and pronouns*) **cerca de**
   near the school cerca del colegio
   near me cerca de mí

nearby adverb
cerca
The station is nearby. La estación está cerca.

a
b
c
d
e
f
g
h
i
j
k
l
m
n
o
p
q
r
s
t
u
v
w
x
y
z

nearly adverb
casi
It's nearly five o'clock. Son casi las cinco.

neat adjective
1 (room, person) **ordenado** masc., **ordenada** fem.
2 (clothes, hair) **arreglado** masc., **arreglada** fem.

necessary adjective
necesario masc., **necesaria** fem.

neck noun
el **cuello** masc.

necklace noun
el **collar** masc.

nectarine noun
la **nectarina** fem.

to **need** verb
1 **necesitar**
I need some money. Necesito dinero.
2 (talking about something you must do) **tener que**
I need to go home. Tengo que irme a casa.

needle noun
la **aguja** fem.

negative noun
(in grammar) el **negativo** masc.

neighbour noun
el **vecino** masc., la **vecina** fem.

neighbourhood noun
el **barrio** masc.

neither pronoun & conjunction
1 **ninguno** masc., **ninguna** fem.
Do you want the red dress or the green one? – Neither. ¿Quieres el vestido rojo o el verde? – Ninguno.
2 neither ... nor **ni ... ni**
Neither one nor the other. Ni el uno ni el otro.
3 (in replies) **tampoco**

I don't want to go. – Neither do I.
No quiero ir. – Yo tampoco.
I don't like cheese. – Neither do I.
No me gusta el queso. – A mí tampoco.

nephew noun
el **sobrino** masc.

nerve noun
1 el **nervio** masc.
She gets on my nerves. Me pone los nervios de punta.
2 (being rude) la **cara** fem.
You've got a nerve! ¡Qué cara tienes!

🔑 **LANGUAGE**
Word for word this means 'What a face you have!'

nervous adjective
nervioso masc., **nerviosa** fem.
Are you nervous? ¿Estás nervioso?

nest noun
el **nido** masc.

net noun
1 (for fishing, tennis, etc.) la **red** fem.
2 the Net la **Red**
to surf the Net navegar por la Red

netball noun

🌐 **CULTURE**
Girls do not play netball in Spain; instead girls – and boys – play basketball (**el baloncesto**).

Netherlands noun
the Netherlands los Países Bajos

never adverb
nunca
I never go out alone. No salgo nunca sola.
Never again! ¡Nunca más!
Never mind! ¡No importa!

🔑 **LANGUAGE**
no + verb + nunca, for example: No salgo nunca

• Use **el** and **uno** for masculine words and **la** and **una** for feminine words.

new adjective
1 **nuevo** *masc.*, **nueva** *fem.*
my new friends mis nuevos amigos
I have a new bike. Tengo una bici nueva.
2 **the New Year** el Año Nuevo
Happy New Year! ¡Feliz Año Nuevo!
New Year's Day el día de Año Nuevo
New Year's Eve la Nochevieja

> **CULTURE**
> On New Year's Eve Spanish people eat twelve grapes (one for each month of the year) just as the clock strikes twelve.

news noun
1 la **noticia** *fem.*
That's good news. Es una buena noticia.
I have bad news. Tengo malas noticias.

> 🔑 **LANGUAGE**
> **las noticias** = more than one piece of news

2 (*on TV or the radio*) **las noticias** *fem. plural*
I watch the news. Veo las noticias.

newsagent's noun
la **tienda de periódicos** *fem.*

newspaper noun
el **periódico** *masc.*

news-stand noun
el **kiosco de periódicos** *masc.*

New Zealand noun
Nueva Zelanda *fem.*

next adjective
1 (*in time*) **próximo** *masc.*, **próxima** *fem.*
next time la próxima vez
the next stop la próxima parada
2 (*week, month, year, Monday, etc.*) **que viene**, **próximo** *masc.*, **próxima** *fem.*

next week la semana que viene, la próxima semana

> 🔑 **LANGUAGE**
> Word for word **la semana que viene** means 'the week that comes'.

3 (*following on*) **siguiente** *masc. & fem.*
on the next page en la página siguiente
the next day el día siguiente
Next, please! ¡El siguiente!
Who's next? ¿Quién es el siguiente?

next adverb
1 (*after this*) **luego**
What did you do next? ¿Qué hiciste luego?
2 (*now*) **ahora**
What shall we do next? ¿Qué hacemos ahora?
3 **next to** al lado de
Sit next to your brother. Siéntate al lado de tu hermano.
next to me a mi lado
next door al lado
He lives next door. Vive al lado.

nice adjective
1 (*good*) **bueno** *masc.*, **buena** *fem.*
The soup's very nice. La sopa está muy buena.
It's nice weather. Hace buen tiempo.
He's very nice to me. Es muy bueno conmigo.
2 (*pretty*) **bonito** *masc.*, **bonita** *fem.*
a very nice dress un vestido muy bonito
3 (*friendly*) **simpático** *masc.*, **simpática** *fem.*
My teacher is very nice. La maestra es muy simpática.

nickname noun
el **apodo** *masc.*

• *Languages and nationalities do not take a capital letter in Spanish.*

niece noun
la **sobrina** *fem.*

night noun
la **noche** *fem.*
all night toda la noche
at night por la noche
at nine o'clock at night a las nueve de la noche
last night anoche
Good night! ¡Buenas noches!

nightdress, **nightie** noun
el **camisón** *masc.* (plural los **camisones**)

nightmare noun
la **pesadilla** *fem.*
to have a nightmare tener una pesadilla

night-time noun
la **noche** *fem.*

nil noun
el **cero** *masc.*
We've won two nil. Hemos ganado dos a cero.

nine number
nueve
We ate at nine. Comimos a las nueve.
Ben is nine. Ben tiene nueve años.

> **LANGUAGE**
> In English you can say 'nine o'clock' or just 'nine', 'nine years old' or just 'nine'. In Spanish you must add **las** (for time) and **años** (for age).

nineteen number
diecinueve
My cousin is nineteen. Mi primo tiene diecinueve años.

ninety number
noventa

ninth adjective
noveno *masc.*, **novena** *fem.*
on the ninth floor en el noveno piso
the ninth of January el nueve de enero

> **LANGUAGE**
> With dates you use **nueve** (nine).

no adverb
no
Do you live in London? – No. ¿Vives en Londres? – No.
No thanks. No, gracias.

no adjective
1 (*not any*) **no**
I have no time. No tengo tiempo.
There's no more milk. No hay más leche.
No problem! ¡Sin problema!
2 (*on signs*)
'No smoking.' 'Prohibido fumar.'

nobody pronoun
nadie
Who wants to play? – Nobody! ¿Quién quiere jugar? – ¡Nadie!
There's nobody in the garden. No hay nadie en el jardín.
Nobody knows me. Nadie me conoce.

> **LANGUAGE**
> **no** + *verb* + **nadie**, for example: **No** veo a **nadie**

noise noun
el **ruido** *masc.*
to make a noise hacer ruido

noisy adjective
It's noisy here. Hay mucho ruido aquí.
My computer is very noisy. Mi ordenador hace mucho ruido.

none pronoun
1 **ninguno** *masc.*, **ninguna** *fem.*
How many CDs do you have? – None. ¿Cuántos CDs tienes? – Ninguno.

• *The months of the year and days of the week do not take a capital letter in Spanish.*

There are none left. No queda
ninguno.
none of the children ninguno de
los niños
2 **nada**
How much bread is left? – None.
¿Cuánto pan queda? - Nada.

> **LANGUAGE**
> Use ninguno when talking about plural
> nouns, and nada with singular nouns such
> as 'bread', 'money', or 'chocolate'.

nonsense noun
las **tonterías** *fem. plural*,
la **tontería** *fem.*
You're talking a lot of nonsense!
¡Dices muchas tonterías!
What nonsense! ¡Qué tontería!

noodles plural noun
los fideos *masc. plural*

noon noun
el **mediodía** *masc.*
at noon a mediodía
It's noon. Es mediodía.

no-one, **no one** pronoun
nadie
Who wants to help me? – No-one!
¿Quién quiere ayudarme? - ¡Nadie!
There's no-one in the shop. No hay
nadie en la tienda.
No-one knows me. Nadie me
conoce.

> **LANGUAGE**
> no + *verb* + nadie, for example: No veo a
> nadie.

nor conjunction
1 neither ... nor ni ... ni
Neither Yasmina nor her sister are
at home. Ni Yasmina ni su
hermana están en casa.
2 **tampoco**
I don't want to do it. - Nor do I.
No quiero hacerlo. - Yo tampoco.
I don't like fish. - Nor do I. No me
gusta el pescado. - A mí tampoco.

• *See the centre section for verb tables.*

normal adjective
1 **normal** *masc. & fem.*
That's not normal. No es normal.
2 (*time or place*) **de siempre**
at the normal time a la hora de
siempre

north noun & adjective
1 el **norte** *masc.*
in the north en el norte
the north coast la costa norte
2 North America Norteamérica *fem.*
the North Pole el Polo Norte
the North Sea el Mar del Norte

Northern Ireland noun
Irlanda del Norte *fem.*
I live in Northern Ireland. Vivo en
Irlanda del Norte.

nose noun
la **nariz** *fem.* (plural las **narices**)

nosy adjective
curioso *masc.*, **curiosa** *fem.*

not adverb
no
I'm not tired. No estoy cansado.
He hasn't come. No ha venido.
It's not big. No es grande.
Do you want some ice cream or
not? ¿Quieres helado o no?
not yet todavía no
not much no mucho

> **LANGUAGE**
> When you use a verb remember to put no
> in front of the verb in Spanish.

note noun
1 (*message*) la **nota** *fem.*
Dad has left you a note. Papá te ha
dejado una nota.
2 notes los apuntes *masc. plural*
The students are taking notes.
Los alumnos toman apuntes.
3 (*paper money*) **el billete** *masc.*
a five-pound note un billete de
cinco libras

a
b
c
d
e
f
g
h
i
j
k
l
m
n
o
p
q
r
s
t
u
v
w
x
y
z

notebook noun
el **cuaderno** *masc.*

notepad noun
el **bloc** *masc.* (plural los **blocs**)

nothing pronoun
nada
What do you want? – Nothing.
¿Qué quieres? – Nada.
There's nothing in the box. No hay nada en la caja.
It's nothing. No es nada.
Nothing has changed. Nada ha cambiado.
nothing much no mucho

LANGUAGE
no + verb + nada, for example: No hay nada.

to **notice** verb
notar
Do you notice the difference?
¿Notas la diferencia?

notice noun
(*on a wall, door, etc.*) el **letrero** *masc.*
notice board el tablón de anuncios (plural los **tablones de anuncios**)

noun noun
el **nombre** *masc.*

novel noun
la **novela** *fem.*

November noun
noviembre *masc.*
in November en noviembre
My grandparents are arriving in November Mis abuelos llegan en noviembre.
I'm going to Valencia on the ninth of November. Voy a Valencia el nueve de noviembre.

now adverb
ahora
Where are you now? ¿Dónde estás ahora?
from now on de ahora en adelante
now and again de vez en cuando
She left just now. Acaba de irse.

nowhere adverb
a or **en ninguna parte**
Where are you going? – Nowhere.
¿Adónde vas? – A ninguna parte.
The book is nowhere in the house.
El libro no está en ninguna parte de la casa.

number noun
(*of a house, page, etc.*) el **número** *masc.*
my phone number mi número de teléfono
I live at number twenty-five. Vivo en el número veinticinco.
a large number of un gran número de

nun noun
la **monja** *fem.*

nurse noun
el **enfermero** *masc.*,
la **enfermera** *fem.*
My mother's a nurse. Mi madre es enfermera.

nursery noun
la **guardería** *fem.*
a nursery rhyme una canción infantil
nursery school la guardería

nut noun
el **fruto seco** *masc.*

LANGUAGE
Word for word the Spanish means 'dried fruit'.

• Use **el** and **uno** for masculine words and **la** and **una** for feminine words.

Oo

oats plural noun
la **avena** *fem.*

to **obey** verb
1 obedecer
My dog obeys me. Mi perro me obedece.
2 to obey the rules respetar las reglas

object noun
el **objeto** *masc.*

obvious adjective
evidente *masc. & fem.*

obviously adverb
claro
Do you want to come? – Obviously!
¿Quieres venir? – ¡Claro!

occasion noun
la **ocasión** *fem.*
a very special occasion una ocasión muy especial

occasionally adverb
de vez en cuando

occupation noun
(job) el **empleo** *masc.*

ocean noun
el **océano** *masc.*

o'clock adverb
at eight o'clock a las ocho
It's one o'clock. Es la una.
It's four o'clock. Son las cuatro.

October noun
octubre *masc.*
I'm going camping in October.
Me voy de camping en octubre.

It's my birthday on Tuesday, the tenth of October. Es mi cumpleaños el martes diez de octubre.

octopus noun
el **pulpo** *masc.*

odd adjective
1 *(strange)* **raro** *masc.*, **rara** *fem.*
2 an odd number un número impar

of preposition

1 de
a glass of water un vaso de agua
a boy of six un niño de seis años
a page of the book una página del libro
the door of the house la puerta de la casa
2 *(no translation when 'of' is followed by 'it' or 'them')*
Give me some of it. Dame un poco.
I've eaten a lot of it. He comido mucho.
There are ten of them. Hay diez.

of course adverb
claro
Do you have lots of friends? – Of course I do! ¿Tienes muchos amigos? – ¡Claro que sí!
of course not claro que no

off adjective
1 *(light, TV, radio, etc.)* **apagado** *masc.*, **apagada** *fem.*
The TV is off. La tele está apagada.
2 *(tap, gas)* **cerrado** *masc.*, **cerrada** *fem.*
The tap is off. El grifo está cerrado .
3 *(cancelled)*
The match is off. El partido se ha suspendido.

• *Languages and nationalities do not take a capital letter in Spanish.*

a
b
c
d
e
f
g
h
i
j
k
l
m
n
o
p
q
r
s
t
u
v
w
x
y
z

a
b
c
d
e
f
g
h
i
j
k
l
m
n
o
p
q
r
s
t
u
v
w
x
y
z

off adverb & preposition
1 (*going somewhere*) **to be off** irse
   I'm off now. Ahora me voy.
2 (*away from school or work*) **a day off**
   un día libre
   I'm off school. No he ido al colegio.
   We have a week off. Tenemos una
   semana de vacaciones.
3 (*from*) **de**
   I fell off the chair. Me caí de la
   silla.
   I got off the bus. Me bajé del
   autobús.

> ⚷ **LANGUAGE**
> 'Off' is often translated as part of a verb
> such as 'to switch off' (**apagar**) or 'to take
> off' (**quitar**).

to **offer** verb
   ofrecer
   to offer somebody something
   ofrecer algo a alguien

office noun
   la **oficina** *fem.*
   My mum works in an office. Mi
   madre trabaja en una oficina.

often adverb
   a menudo
   I often go to the cinema. Voy al
   cine a menudo.
   **How often do you see your
   grandfather?** ¿Cada cuánto ves a
   tu abuelo?

ogre noun
   el **ogro** *masc.*

oil noun
   el **aceite** *masc.*

okay adjective & adverb
1 (*good, well*) **bien**
   to be okay estar bien
   How are you? – Okay. ¿Cómo
   estás? – Bien.
   I sing okay. Canto bien.
2 (*not so bad*); **no mal**
   to be okay no estar mal

Do you like the film? – It's okay.
¿Te gusta la película? – No está mal.
3 (*with verbs starting with 'to'*)
   Is it okay to close the window? ¿Se
   puede cerrar la ventana?

> ⚷ **LANGUAGE**
> Use **poder** (can) in this meaning (Can I
> close the window?).

okay exclamation
1 **¡bueno!**
   Okay, I'm coming! ¡Bueno, ya voy!
2 (*saying yes*) **¡vale!**
   **Do you want to come with us? –
   Okay!** ¿Quieres venir con
   nosotros? – ¡Vale!

old adjective
1 **viejo** *masc.*, **vieja** *fem.*
   an old bicycle una bicicleta vieja
   an old man un hombre viejo
2 (*when being polite about people*) **mayor**
   masc. & fem.
   My grandfather is very old.
   El abuelo es muy mayor.
   an old lady una anciana
   old people los ancianos
3 (*talking about ages*) **How old are you?**
   ¿Cuántos años tienes?
   Hakim is six years old. Hakim
   tiene seis años.
4 (*from your past*) **antiguo** *masc.*,
   antigua *fem.*
   my old school mi antiguo colegio

older adjective
   (*talking about people*) **mayor** *masc. &
   fem.*
   I'm older than you. Soy mayor que
   tú.
   She's two years older than me.
   Es dos años mayor que yo.

oldest noun
   el or la **mayor** *masc. & fem.*
   I'm the oldest in the class. Soy el
   mayor de la clase.

• *The months of the year and days of the week do not take a capital letter in Spanish.*

old-fashioned adjective
(*clothes, person, etc.*) **anticuado** *masc.*, **anticuada** *fem.*

olive noun
la **aceituna** *fem.*

Olympic adjective
the **Olympic Games** los Juegos Olímpicos *masc. plural*

omelette noun
la **tortilla** *fem.*

on preposition
1 **en**
Write it on the board. Escríbelo en la pizarra.
on the beach en la playa
on TV en la tele
2 **a**

> 🔑 **LANGUAGE**
> a + el = al

I got on the bus. Subí al autobús.
on foot a pie
on a horse a caballo
3 (*talking about books, films, etc.*) **sobre**
a film on dinosaurs una película sobre los dinosaurios
4 on Sunday el domingo
on Sundays los domingos
on the ninth of December el nueve de diciembre
on Christmas Day el día de Navidad

> 🔑 **LANGUAGE**
> With days and dates you don't translate 'on' in Spanish but the determiner **el** (plural **los**) is used instead.

on adjective & adverb
1 (*light, TV, computer, etc.*) **encendido** *masc.*, **encendida** *fem.*
The TV is on. La tele está encendida.
2 (*tap, gas*) **abierto** *masc.*, **abierta** *fem.*
The tap is on. El grifo está abierto.
3 (*wearing something*) I've got my glasses on. Llevo mis gafas.
I don't have a watch on. No llevo reloj.

• *See the centre section for verb tables.*

He has nothing on! ¡Está desnudo!

> 🔑 **LANGUAGE**
> 'On' is often translated as part of a verb such as 'to switch on' (**encender**) or 'to put on' (**poner**).

once adverb
1 **una vez**
once a day una vez al día
once again otra vez
2 at once **enseguida**
Come at once. Ven enseguida.
3 (*a long time ago*) **antes**
'Once upon a time there was …' (*in stories*) 'Érase una vez …'

one number & pronoun
uno *masc.*, **una** *fem.*

> 🔑 **LANGUAGE**
> **Uno** becomes **un** in front of a masculine noun.

One and one are two. Uno y uno son dos.
one euro un euro
It's one o'clock. Es la una.
The baby is one. El niño tiene un año.
one of my friends uno de mis amigos
Do you want one? ¿Quieres uno?
Take the blue one. Coge el azul.

onion noun
la **cebolla** *fem.*

online adjective
en línea, **conectado** or **conectada a Internet** *masc. & fem.*

online adverb
en línea
to buy online comprar en línea

only adjective
único *masc.*, **única** *fem.*
the only book el único libro
It's the only one I have. Es el único que tengo.
He's an only child. Es hijo único.
She's an only child. Es hija única.

only adverb
sólo
I only have one pen. Sólo tengo un boli.

onto preposition
1 **a**
It's fallen onto the floor. Se ha caído al suelo.
2 **en**
Put it onto the table. Ponlo en la mesa.

open adjective
abierto *masc.*, **abierta** *fem.*
The museum is open. El museo está abierto.

to **open** verb
abrir
Open the window. Abre la ventana.
The shops open at nine. Las tiendas abren a las nueve.

operation noun
I'm going to have an operation. Van a operarme.

opinion noun
la **opinión** *fem.* (plural las **opiniones**)
in my opinion en mi opinión

opportunity noun
la **oportunidad** *fem.*

opposite adjective
1 (*page, wall, etc.*) **de enfrente**
the opposite house la casa de enfrente
on the opposite side of the road al otro lado de la calle
2 (*different*) **opuesto** *masc.*, **opuesta** *fem.*
in the opposite direction en la dirección opuesta
3 the opposite of lo contrario de
'Big' is the opposite of 'small'. 'Big' es lo contrario de 'small'.

opposite adverb & preposition
1 **enfrente**
We live opposite. Vivimos enfrente.
2 (*with nouns and pronouns*) **enfrente de**
opposite the school enfrente del colegio
She's sitting opposite me. Está sentada enfrente de mí.

optician noun
el or la **oculista** *masc. & fem.*
to go to the optician's ir a la óptica

or conjunction
1 **o**
yes or no sí o no

> **LANGUAGE**
> O becomes u in front of a word starting with o or ho.

ten or eleven diez u once
2 (*in sentences with 'not', 'never', etc.*) **ni ... ni**
I don't have any brothers or sisters. No tengo ni hermanos ni hermanas.

orange noun
1 (*fruit*) la **naranja** *fem.*
an orange juice un zumo de naranja
2 (*colour*) el **naranja** *masc.*
I don't like orange. No me gusta el naranja.

orange adjective
naranja *masc. & fem.*
orange shirts camisas naranja

> **LANGUAGE**
> Naranja is the same in the masculine, feminine, and plural.

orchestra noun
la **orquesta** *fem.*

order noun
1 el **orden** *masc.*

• Use **el** and **uno** for masculine words and **la** and **una** for feminine words.

Put the names in alphabetical order. Pon los nombres en orden alfabético.
They're in the right order. Están ordenados.
They're in the wrong order. Están desordenados.
2 (*talking about a machine, lift, etc.*)
It's out of order. No funciona.

to **order** verb
(*in a restaurant*) **pedir**
We ordered fish. Pedimos pescado.

ordinary adjective
normal *masc. & fem.*

organize verb
organizar

original adjective
(*idea, version, etc.*) **original** *masc. & fem.*

orphan noun
el **huérfano** *masc.*, la **huérfana** *fem.*

other adjective & pronoun
otro *masc.*, **otra** *fem.*
the other day el otro día
other countries otros países
the other one el otro *masc.*, la otra *fem.*
the others los otros *masc. plural*, las otras *fem. plural*

otherwise conjunction
si no
Hurry, otherwise you'll be late.
Date prisa, si no vas a llegar tarde.

ouch exclamation
¡ay!

ought verb
deber
You ought to work harder.
Deberías trabajar más.

our adjective
1 (*before a singular noun*) **nuestro** *masc.*, **nuestra** *fem.*
our school nuestro colegio
2 (*before a plural noun*) **nuestros** *masc. plural*, **nuestras** *fem. plural*

our friends nuestros amigos
3 (*with parts of the body, clothes, etc.*)
We're washing our hands. Nos estamos lavando las manos.
We put our coats on. Nos pusimos el abrigo.

> 🔑 **LANGUAGE**
> Use **nos** with **el**, **la**, **los**, or **las** in these examples instead of **nuestro** and **nuestros**.

ours pronoun
1 (*with a singular noun*) el **nuestro** *masc.*, la **nuestra** *fem.*
Their house is bigger than ours. Su casa es más grande que la nuestra.
2 (*with a plural noun*) los **nuestros** *masc. plural*, las **nuestras** *fem. plural*
your parents and ours tus padres y los nuestros
3 (*following 'is'*) **nuestro** *masc.*, **nuestra** *fem.*
This bike is ours. Esta bici es nuestra.
4 (*following 'are'*) **nuestros** *masc. plural*, **nuestras** *fem. plural*
These books are ours. Estos libros son nuestros.

ourselves pronoun
1 **nosotros mismos** *masc. plural*, **nosotras mismas** *fem. plural*
We've made it ourselves. Lo hemos hecho nosotros mismos.
2 (*with a reflexive verb*) **nos**
We're washing ourselves. Nos estamos lavando.
3 **by ourselves** solos *masc. plural*, solas *fem. plural*
We're at home by ourselves. Estamos solas en casa.

out adverb
1 (*outside*) **fuera**
I'm out here. Estoy aquí fuera.
It's cold out. Fuera hace frío.
I go out. Salgo.
I'm looking out of the window. Estoy mirando por la ventana.

• *Languages and nationalities do not take a capital letter in Spanish.*

a
b
c
d
e
f
g
h
i
j
k
l
m
n
o
p
q
r
s
t
u
v
w
x
y
z

2 (*from*)
It's made out of wood. Es de madera.
Take the letter out of my pocket. Saca la carta de mi bolsillo.
I've got fifteen out of twenty. He sacado quince sobre veinte.

🔑 **LANGUAGE**
'Out' is often translated as part of a verb such as 'to go out' (**salir**) or 'to take out' (**sacar**).

out adjective
1 (*talking about not being at home*) **to be out** no estar
Karim is out. Karim no está.
2 (*light, fire*) **apagado** *masc.*, **apagada** *fem.*
The lights are out. Las luces están apagadas.
3 (*in games*) **You're out!** ¡Fuera!

outdoor adjective
(*swimming pool etc.*) **al aire libre**
outdoor games juegos al aire libre

outdoors adverb
fuera

outer space noun
el **espacio** *masc.*

outing noun
la **excursión** *fem.* (plural las **excursiones**)
to go on an outing ir de excursión

outside adverb & preposition
1 fuera
Wait outside. Espera fuera.
2 (*in front of*) **delante de**
Wait for me outside the school. Espérame delante del colegio.

outside noun
el **exterior** *masc.*
The outside is dirty. El exterior está sucio.

oval adjective
ovalado *masc.*, **ovalada** *fem.*

oven noun
el **horno** *masc.*

over preposition & adverb
1 sobre
a bridge over the river un puente sobre el río
The helicopter flew over the town. El helicóptero voló sobre la ciudad.
2 por encima de
The ball has gone over the wall. La pelota ha pasado por encima del muro.
I looked over the wall. Miré por encima del muro.

🔑 **LANGUAGE**
Use **por encima de** with verbs of movement like 'go' or 'jump'.

3 (*more than*) **más de**
I'm over ten. Tengo más de diez años.
4 (*during*) **durante**
over the summer durante el verano
5 (*everywhere*)
all over por todas partes
all over the house por toda la casa
6 over here aquí
over there allí
7 (*talking about somebody's house*)
Come over tomorrow. Ven a mi casa mañana.

🔑 **LANGUAGE**
'Over' is often translated as part of a verb such as 'to be left over' (**quedar**) or 'to come over' (**venir**).

over adjective
(*finished*)
to be over terminar
The film's over. Ha terminado la película.
The holidays are over. Han terminado las vacaciones.

to **overtake** verb
(*in a car*) **adelantar**

• *The months of the year and days of the week do not take a capital letter in Spanish.*

to **owe** verb
deber
I owe you two euros. Te debo dos euros.

owl noun
el **búho** *masc.*

own adjective
propio *masc.*, **propia** *fem.*
Do you have your own computer? ¿Tienes tu propio ordenador?

own pronoun
1 I've got a room of my own. Tengo mi propia habitación.

2 on your own solo *masc.*, sola *fem.*
They've left me on my own. Me han dejado solo.

to **own** verb
tener
He owns three bikes. Tiene tres bicis.

owner noun
el **dueño** *masc.*, la **dueña** *fem.*

oxygen noun
el **oxígeno** *masc.*

Pp

Pacific noun
el **Pacífico** *masc.*

to **pack** verb
1 (*one case only*) **hacer la maleta**
I'm going to pack. Voy a hacer la maleta.
2 (*more than one case*) **hacer las maletas**

pack noun
a pack of cards una baraja *fem.*

package noun
el **paquete** *masc.*

packed lunch noun
la **comida** *fem.*
Do you take a packed lunch? ¿Te llevas la comida al colegio?

 CULTURE
In Spain children do not have packed lunches in school; comida is the Spanish word for 'lunch'.

packet noun
el **paquete** *masc.*
a packet of biscuits un paquete de galletas

a packet of crisps una bolsa de patatas fritas

page noun
la **página** *fem.*
on page five en la página cinco

pain noun
el **dolor** *masc.*
I'm in a lot of pain. Tengo mucho dolor.
I have a pain in my arm. Me duele el brazo.

painful adjective
My leg is painful. Me duele la pierna.
Is it very painful? ¿Te duele mucho?
My shoes are painful. Me hacen daño los zapatos.

paint noun
1 la **pintura** *fem.*
a tin of paint un bote de pintura
2 paints las pinturas *fem. plural*; (*watercolours*) las acuarelas *fem. plural*
a box of paints una caja de acuarelas

• See the centre section for verb tables.

English Spanish

a
b
c
d
e
f
g
h
i
j
k
l
m
n
o
p
q
r
s
t
u
v
w
x
y
z

to **paint** verb
pintar
I love to paint. Me encanta pintar.
I want to paint it blue. Quiero
pintarlo en azul.

paintbrush noun
1 (*for pictures*) el **pincel** *masc.*
2 (*for painting walls etc.*) la **brocha** *fem.*

painter noun
el **pintor** *masc.*, la **pintora** *fem.*
My dad's a painter. Mi padre es
pintor.

painting noun
1 (*picture*) el **cuadro** *masc.*
a painting by Dalí un cuadro de
Dalí
2 (*hobby*)
I like painting. Me gusta pintar.

pair noun
1 (*of shoes, gloves, etc.*) el **par** *masc.*
a pair of socks un par de calcetines
2 (*two people*) la **pareja** *fem.*
to work in pairs trabajar en
parejas
3 a pair of jeans unos vaqueros
a pair of trousers unos pantalones

Pakistan noun
Paquistán *masc.*

Pakistani adjective
paquistaní *masc. & fem.*

Pakistani noun
el or la **paquistaní** *masc. & fem.*

palace noun
el **palacio** *masc.*

pale adjective
pálido *masc.*, **pálida** *fem.*
You look very pale. Estás muy
pálida.

palm tree noun
la **palmera** *fem.*

pan noun
1 (*saucepan*) la **cacerola** *fem.*
2 (*frying pan*) la **sartén** *fem.* (plural las
sartenes)

pancake noun
el **crepe** *masc.*
Pancake Day el martes de
Carnaval

> **CULTURE**
> **El martes de Carnaval** is Shrove
> Tuesday, when children in Britain eat
> pancakes. In Spain children dress up for
> **Carnaval**, dance, and play music but
> they don't eat pancakes!

panda noun
el **panda** *masc.*, el **oso panda** *masc.*

> **LANGUAGE**
> Be careful: **panda** ends in an **-a** but it is
> not a feminine noun.

to **panic** verb
Don't panic! ¡Calma!

pantomime noun
la **comedia para niños** *fem.*

pants plural noun
los **calzoncillos** *masc. plural*

paper noun
1 el **papel** *masc.*
a sheet of paper una hoja de papel
a piece of paper un papel
a paper bag una bolsa de papel
paper chains las cadenetas
2 (*newspaper*) el **periódico** *masc.*
a paper boy un repartidor de
periódicos
I do a paper round. Reparto
periódicos.
a paper shop una tienda de
periódicos

paperback noun
el **libro de bolsillo** *masc.*

paperclip noun
el **clip** *masc.* (plural los **clips**)

parachute noun
el **paracaídas** *masc.* (plural los
paracaídas)

parade noun
el **desfile** *masc.*

• Use **el** and **uno** for masculine words and **la** and **una** for feminine words.

paragraph noun
el **párrafo** masc.

parcel noun
el **paquete** masc.

pardon noun
Pardon? ¿Perdón?

🔑 **LANGUAGE**
Use **perdón** when you want somebody to say something again.

parents plural noun
los **padres** masc. plural
my parents mis padres

⚠️ **FALSE FRIEND**
parents = los padres (not los parientes)

🔑 **LANGUAGE**
In the singular **padre** means 'father'.

park noun
1 el **parque** masc.
Let's go to the park. Vamos al parque.
2 **a car park** un aparcamiento masc.

to **park** verb
aparcar
to park the car aparcar el coche
You can park here. Puedes aparcar aquí.

parking noun
'No parking' 'Prohibido aparcar'
a parking space un aparcamiento

parrot noun
el **loro** masc.

part noun
1 la **parte** fem.
the last part of the book la última parte del libro
2 (in a play or film) el **papel** masc.
I play the part of the witch. Hago el papel de la bruja.
3 **to take part in something** participar en algo

parting noun
(in hair) la **raya** fem.

partly adverb
en parte

partner noun
(in a game, school play, etc.) la **pareja** fem.

party noun
la **fiesta** fem.
I'm having a party. Voy a dar una fiesta.
a birthday party una fiesta de cumpleaños
a Christmas party una fiesta de Navidad

to **pass** verb
1 (to go past) **pasar por**
I passed your house. Pasé por tu casa.
2 (to give) **pasar**
Pass me the chocolates, please. ¿Me pasas los bombones, por favor?
3 **to pass an exam** aprobar un examen

passenger noun
el **pasajero** masc., la **pasajera** fem.

passport noun
el **pasaporte** masc.

password noun
la **contraseña** fem.

past preposition & adverb
1 (in front of) **por delante de**
The bus goes past the school. El autobús pasa por delante del colegio.
I went past on my bike. Pasé en bici.
2 (after) **después de**
My house is just past the library. Mi casa está justo después de la biblioteca.
3 (talking about the time)
It's ten past nine. Son las nueve y diez.

• Languages and nationalities do not take a capital letter in Spanish.

a
b
c
d
e
f
g
h
i
j
k
l
m
n
o
p
q
r
s
t
u
v
w
x
y
z

It's a quarter past one. Es la una y cuarto.
It's half past six. Son las seis y media.

past adjective
1 **último** masc., **última** fem.
the past two weeks las últimas dos semanas
2 the past tense el pasado masc.

past noun
the past el pasado masc.
in the past en el pasado

pasta noun
la **pasta** fem.
I like pasta. Me gusta la pasta.

pastry noun
el **pastel** masc.
Would you like a pastry? ¿Quieres un pastel?

path noun
el **camino** masc.

patient adjective
paciente masc. & fem.
My sister's very patient. Mi hermana es muy paciente.

patient noun
(of a doctor) el or la **paciente** masc. & fem.

pattern noun
el **dibujo** masc.

pavement noun
la **acera** fem.

paw noun
la **pata** fem.

pay noun
el **sueldo** masc.

to **pay** verb
1 **pagar**
Pay at the checkout. Paga en caja.
to pay for something pagar algo
I've paid for the ticket. He pagado el billete.
2 to pay attention poner atención

Pay attention to what you're doing! ¡Pon atención en lo que estás haciendo!

PC noun
el **ordenador** masc., el **PC** masc. (plural los **PCs**)

PE noun
la **gimnasia** fem.
to do PE hacer gimnasia
We have PE on Thursdays. Los jueves tenemos clase de gimnasia.

pea noun
el **guisante** masc.

peace noun
la **paz** fem.
Let me have some peace! ¡Déjame en paz!
I want some peace and quiet. Quiero estar tranquilo.

peaceful adjective
tranquilo masc., **tranquila** fem.
a very peaceful spot un sitio muy tranquilo

peach noun
el **melocotón** masc. (plural los **melocotones**)

peanut noun
el **cacahuete** masc.
peanut butter la mantequilla de cacahuete

pear noun
la **pera** fem.

pearl noun
la **perla** fem.
a pearl necklace un collar de perlas

pedal noun
el **pedal** masc.

pedestrian noun
el **peatón** masc. (plural los **peatones**)

to **peel** verb
(apple, banana, etc.) **pelar**

• The months of the year and days of the week do not take a capital letter in Spanish.

peel noun
la **piel** fem.

peg noun
(hook for coats) la **percha** fem.

pen noun
1 (ballpoint) el **bolígrafo** masc.,
el **boli** masc.
2 (fountain pen) la **pluma** fem.

pence plural noun
los **peniques** masc. plural
fifty pence cincuenta peniques

pencil noun
el **lápiz** masc. (plural los **lápices**)
in pencil a lápiz
a coloured pencil un lápiz de colores
a pencil case un estuche
a pencil sharpener un sacapuntas
(plural **sacapuntas**)

penfriend noun
el **amigo por correspondencia** or
por correo masc., la **amiga por
correspondencia** or **por correo**
fem.

penguin noun
el **pingüino** masc.

penknife noun
la **navaja** fem.

penny noun
el **penique** masc.

people plural noun
1 la **gente** fem.
a lot of people mucha gente
most people la mayoría de la
gente

LANGUAGE
Gente is a singular noun in Spanish.

2 (talking about numbers of people) **las
personas** fem. plural
how many people? ¿cuántas
personas?
five people cinco personas

• See the centre section for verb tables.

pepper noun
1 la **pimienta** fem.
Would you like salt or pepper?
¿Quieres sal o pimienta?
2 (vegetable) el **pimiento** masc.
a green pepper un pimiento verde

per cent adverb
por ciento
ten per cent diez por ciento

perfect adjective
perfecto masc., **perfecta** fem.
Vincent speaks perfect Spanish.
Vincent habla un español perfecto.

perfectly adverb
perfectamente

performance noun
1 (of a film) la **sesión** fem. (plural las
sesiones)
2 (of a play) la **representación** fem.
(plural las **representaciones**)

perfume noun
el **perfume** masc.

perhaps adverb
quizás, a lo mejor
Perhaps she's missed the bus.
Quizás ha perdido el autobús.,
A lo mejor ha perdido el autobús.

period noun
1 el **periodo** masc.
a period of six months un periodo
de seis meses
the holiday period la época de
vacaciones
2 (school lesson) la **clase** fem.
We have a Spanish period now.
Ahora tenemos clase de español.

permission noun
el **permiso** masc.
I don't have permission to go out.
No tengo permiso para salir.

person noun
la **persona** fem.
a friendly person una persona
simpática

English Spanish

a
b
c
d
e
f
g
h
i
j
k
l
m
n
o
p
q
r
s
t
u
v
w
x
y
z

personality noun
la **personalidad** fem.

pest noun
el **pesado** masc., la **pesada** fem.
She's a real pest. Es muy pesada.

pet noun
1 el **animal** masc.
Do you have any pets at home?
¿Tienes animales en casa?
2 la **mascota** fem.
I have a hamster as a pet. Tengo
un hámster como mascota.
3 the teacher's pet el favorito masc.
de la maestra, la favorita fem. de la
maestra

petrol noun
la **gasolina** fem.
to get petrol echar gasolina
a petrol station una gasolinera

pharmacy noun
la **farmacia** fem.

phone noun
1 el **teléfono** masc.
The phone's ringing. Suena el
teléfono.
I'm on the phone. Estoy hablando
por teléfono.
2 the phone book la guía telefónica
a phone box una cabina telefónica
a phone call una llamada
telefónica
to make a phone call hacer una
llamada
a phone number un número de
teléfono

to **phone** verb
llamar (por teléfono)
Phone me. Llámame por teléfono.
I'll phone you later. Te llamo más
tarde.

photo noun
la **foto** fem.
to take photos hacer fotos
I've taken a photo of my bike.
He hecho una foto de mi bici.

I've taken a photo of my teacher.
Le he hecho una foto a mi maestra.

LANGUAGE
You can also use sacar instead of hacer,
e.g. He sacado una foto.

photocopier noun
la **fotocopiadora** fem.

photocopy noun
la **fotocopia** fem.

to **photocopy** verb
fotocopiar

photograph noun
la **fotografía** fem.
to take a photograph hacer una
fotografía
I've taken a photograph of my
teacher. Le he hecho una
fotografía a mi maestra.

LANGUAGE
You can also use sacar instead of hacer,
e.g. Le he sacado una fotografía.

photographer noun
el **fotógrafo** masc.,
la **fotógrafa** fem.

phrase noun
la **frase** fem.
a useful Spanish phrase una frase
útil en español
a phrase book un libro de frases

physical adjective
físico masc., **física** fem.

pianist noun
el or la **pianista** masc. & fem.

piano noun
el **piano** masc.
I play the piano. Toco el piano.

pick noun
Take your pick! ¡Elige!, ¡Escoge!

• Use **el** and **uno** for masculine words and **la** and **una** for feminine words.

to **pick** verb
1 (*to choose*) **elegir**, **escoger**
I've picked the green one. He
elegido el verde., He escogido el
verde.
2 (*apples, flowers, etc.*) **recoger**

to **pick up** verb
1 **recoger**
Pick up your toys! ¡Recoge tus
juguetes!
I'm going to pick up Daniel from
school. Voy a recoger a Daniel al
colegio.
2 **coger**
I picked up my books and left.
Cogí mis libros y salí.
3 (*something heavy*) **levantar**
I can't pick it up! ¡No lo puedo
levantar!

picnic noun
el **picnic** *masc.* (plural los **picnics**)
to have a picnic hacer un picnic
to go for a picnic ir de picnic

picture noun
1 (*drawing*) el **dibujo** *masc.*
I've drawn a picture of my dog.
He hecho un dibujo de mi perro.
2 (*by a painter*) el **cuadro** *masc.*
a picture by Dali un cuadro de
Dalí
3 (*photo*) la **foto** *fem.*
to take pictures hacer fotos
4 (*on TV screen*) la **imagen** *fem.*
5 (*in a book*) la **ilustración** *fem.* (plural
las **ilustraciones**)

pie noun
el **pastel** *masc.*
an apple pie un pastel de manzana

piece noun
1 (*bit of something*) el **trozo** *masc.*
a piece of bread un trozo de pan
2 (*in a jigsaw puzzle*) la **pieza** *fem.*
a puzzle of one hundred pieces
un rompecabezas de cien piezas

pierced adjective
She has her ears pierced. Tiene
agujeros en las orejas.

⚷ **LANGUAGE**
Word for word the Spanish means 'She
has holes in her ears'.

pig noun
el **cerdo** *masc.*

pigeon noun
la **paloma** *fem.*

piggy bank noun
la **hucha** *fem.*

pigtails plural noun
las coletas *fem. plural*
She has pigtails. Lleva coletas.

pile noun
el **montón** *masc.* (plural los
montones)
a pile of books un montón de libros

pill noun
la **pastilla** *fem.*
to take pills tomar pastillas

pillow noun
la **almohada** *fem.*

pilot noun
el or la **piloto** *masc. & fem.*

pimple noun
el **grano** *masc.*

pin noun
(*for sewing*) el **alfiler** *masc.*

to **pinch** verb
(*to steal*) **quitar**
Who pinched my book? ¿Quién me
ha quitado el libro?

pineapple noun
la **piña** *fem.*

ping-pong noun
el **ping-pong** *masc.*
to play ping-pong jugar al
ping-pong

a
b
c
d
e
f
g
h
i
j
k
l
m
n
o
p
q
r
s
t
u
v
w
x
y
z

• *Languages and nationalities do not take a capital letter in Spanish.*

English Spanish

a
b
c
d
e
f
g
h
i
j
k
l
m
n
o
P
q
r
s
t
u
v
w
x
y
z

pink adjective
rosa *masc. & fem.*
pink dresses vestidos rosa

> **LANGUAGE**
> Rosa is the same in the masculine, feminine, and plural.

pink noun
el **rosa** *masc.*
I like pink. Me gusta el rosa.

> **LANGUAGE**
> Don't confuse el rosa with la rosa (rose): it's the same word in Spanish for the colour and the flower.

pint noun
la **pinta** *fem.*

> **CULTURE**
> In Spain litres and centilitres are used instead of pints. A pint is just over half a litre.

pirate noun
el or la **pirata** *masc. & fem.*

pitch noun
el **campo** *masc.*
a football pitch un campo de fútbol

pity noun
What a pity! ¡Qué lástima!

pizza noun
la **pizza** *fem.*

place noun
1 el **sitio** *masc.*
Can you keep my place? ¿Me guardas el sitio?
I've changed places. Me he cambiado de sitio.
2 el **lugar** *masc.*
I finished in second place. Terminé en segundo lugar.
It's a beautiful place. Es un lugar precioso.

plain adjective
1 **sencillo** *masc.*, **sencilla** *fem.*
She's wearing a very plain dress. Lleva un vestido muy sencillo.
2 (*with no special flavour*) **natural** *masc. & fem.*
a plain yoghurt un yogur natural

plaits plural noun
las **trenzas** *fem. plural*
She has plaits. Lleva trenzas.

plan noun
1 el **plan** *masc.*
Do you have any plans for tomorrow? ¿Tienes planes para mañana?
2 (*map of a building*) el **plano** *masc.*
the plan of a house el plano de la casa

to **plan** verb
1 (*a journey, party, etc.*) **planear**
My parents are planning a trip to Spain. Mis padres están planeando un viaje a España.
2 **to plan to do something** pensar hacer algo
Are you planning to go? ¿Piensas ir?

plane noun
el **avión** *masc.* (plural los **aviones**)
to go by plane ir en avión
a plane crash un accidente de avión

planet noun
el **planeta** *masc.*

> **LANGUAGE**
> Be careful: planeta ends in an -a but it is not a feminine noun.

plant noun
la **planta** *fem.*

to **plant** verb
plantar

plaster noun
1 (*for a cut, burn, etc.*) la **tirita** *fem.*
2 la **escayola** *fem.*
in plaster escayolado *masc.*, escayolada *fem.*

· *The months of the year and days of the week do not take a capital letter in Spanish.*

I've got my arm in plaster. Tengo el brazo escayolado.

plastic noun
el **plástico** *masc.*
It's made of plastic. Es de plástico.
a plastic bag una bolsa de plástico

Plasticine® noun
la **plastilina®** *fem.*

plate noun
el **plato** *masc.*

platform noun
(*at a train station*) el **andén** *masc.*
(plural los **andenes**)

play noun
(*for acting in*) la **obra** *fem.*
to put on a play hacer una obra

to **play** verb
1 **jugar**
I play with my friends on Saturdays. Juego con mis amigas los sábados.
2 (*games and sports*) **jugar a**
We play football. Jugamos al fútbol.
3 (*an instrument*) **tocar**
Daniel plays the guitar. Daniel toca la guitarra.
to play a tune tocar una melodía

🔑 **LANGUAGE**
Tocar also means 'to touch'.

4 (*a CD, DVD, or tape*) **poner**
Can you play me your new CD?
¿Me puedes poner tu nuevo CD?

player noun
1 el **jugador** *masc.*, la **jugadora** *fem.*
a football player un jugador de fútbol
2 el **reproductor** *masc.*
an MP3 player un reproductor MP3, un MP3 *masc.*

• *See the centre section for verb tables.*

playground noun
1 (*in school*) el **patio de recreo** *masc.*
The children are playing in the playground. Los niños están jugando en el patio.
2 (*in the park*) los **columpios** *masc. plural*
I want to go to the playground.
Quiero ir a los columpios.

🔑 **LANGUAGE**
Columpios means 'swings' and is often used to mean the whole playground.

playgroup noun
la **guardería** *fem.*

playing field noun
el **campo de deportes** *masc.*

playtime noun
el **recreo** *masc.*

pleasant adjective
agradable *masc. & fem.*

please exclamation
por favor
Two ice creams, please. Dos helados, por favor.

pleased adjective
contento *masc.*, **contenta** *fem.*
I'm very pleased with the presents. Estoy muy contento con los regalos.

plenty pronoun
1 (*a lot*)
plenty of mucho *masc.*, mucha *fem.*
You have plenty of books. Tienes muchos libros.
You've given me plenty. Me has dado mucho or muchos.
2 (*enough*)
plenty of bastante *masc. & fem.*
There are plenty of chocolates for everybody. Hay bastantes bombones para todos.
That's plenty. Eso es suficiente.

to **plug in** verb
enchufar
Is the TV plugged in? ¿Está enchufada la tele?

a
b
c
d
e
f
g
h
i
j
k
l
m
n
o
p
q
r
s
t
u
v
w
x
y
z

a
b
c
d
e
f
g
h
i
j
k
l
m
n
o
p
q
r
s
t
u
v
w
x
y
z

plum noun
la **ciruela** fem.

plumber noun
el **fontanero** masc.,
la **fontanera** fem.
My dad's a plumber. Mi padre es fontanero.

plural noun
el **plural** masc.
The sentence is in the plural. La frase está en plural.

plus preposition
más
Three plus five is eight. Tres más cinco son ocho.

p.m. abbreviation
1 (from midday until evening) **de la tarde**
at 2 p.m. a las dos de la tarde
2 (from evening until midnight) **de la noche**
at 9 p.m. a las nueve de la noche

pocket noun
el **bolsillo** masc.
Keep your pen in your pocket. Guarda el bolígrafo en el bolsillo.
pocket money la paga

poem noun
el **poema** masc.

LANGUAGE
Be careful: poema ends in an -a but it is not a feminine noun.

poet noun
el or la **poeta** masc. & fem.

point noun
1 (in a game) el **punto** masc.
I've scored three points. He sacado tres puntos.
2 (of a pencil, knife, etc.) la **punta** fem.
3 (decimal point) la **coma** fem.
four point five cuatro coma cinco

LANGUAGE
In Spanish you use a comma in decimal numbers, e.g. 4.5 is 4,5.

4 (the reason for something) el **sentido** masc.
There's no point. No tiene sentido.

to **point** verb
(with your finger) **señalar**
Point to the picture. Señala el cuadro.

to **point out** verb
señalar
Can you point out your school? ¿Me puedes señalar tu escuela?

poison noun
el **veneno** masc.

poisonous adjective
(snake, plant, etc.) **venenoso** masc., **venenosa** fem.
a poisonous mushroom una seta venenosa

Poland noun
Polonia fem.

polar bear noun
el **oso polar** masc.

Pole noun
1 the North Pole el Polo Norte
the South Pole el Polo Sur
2 (Polish person) el **polaco** masc., la **polaca** fem.

police noun
la **policía** fem.
to call the police llamar a la policía
The police have come. La policía ya ha llegado.
a police car un coche de policía
a police station una comisaría

LANGUAGE
Use the verb in the singular with policía.

policeman noun
el **policía** masc.
My dad's a policeman. Mi padre es policía.

• Use **el** and **uno** for masculine words and **la** and **una** for feminine words.

policewoman noun
  la **policía** fem.
  My mum's a policewoman.
  Mi madre es policía.

Polish adjective
  polaco masc., **polaca** fem.
  She's Polish. Es polaca.

Polish noun
  (the language) el **polaco** masc.

polite adjective
  educado masc., **educada** fem.
  She's very polite. Es muy educada.

polluted adjective
  contaminado masc.,
  contaminada fem.

pollution noun
  la **contaminación** fem.

pond noun
  (in a garden or park) el **estanque** masc.

pony noun
  el **poni** masc.

ponytail noun
  la **cola de caballo** fem.,
  la **coleta** fem.
  She has a ponytail. Lleva una cola
  de caballo., Lleva coleta.

> **LANGUAGE**
> Word for word cola de caballo means
> 'horse's tail'.

pool noun
  la **piscina** fem.
  an indoor swimming pool una
  piscina cubierta

poor adjective
1 **pobre** masc. & fem.
  They're poor. Son pobres.
  a poor family una familia pobre
  Your poor mum! ¡Tu pobre madre!

> **LANGUAGE**
> Use pobre after the noun when it means
> the opposite of 'rich', and before the noun
> when you feel sad about somebody.

2 (bad) **malo** masc., **mala** fem.
  I always get poor marks. Siempre
  saco malas notas.
  The weather's poor. Hace mal
  tiempo.

> **LANGUAGE**
> Before a masculine singular nouns malo
> becomes mal.

pop noun
  (music) el **pop** masc.
  My sister likes pop. A mi hermana
  le gusta el pop.

pop adjective
  (song, singer, music, etc.) **pop** masc. & fem.
  pop music la música pop
  a pop group un grupo de
  pop
  a pop star una estrella del
  pop

> **LANGUAGE**
> The Spanish adjective pop is the same in
> the masculine, feminine, and plural.

popcorn noun
  las **palomitas** fem. plural

> **LANGUAGE**
> English = popcorn is singular
> Spanish = las palomitas is plural

Pope noun
  el **Papa** masc.

> **LANGUAGE**
> Be careful: Papa ends in an -a but it is not
> a feminine noun.

popular adjective
  popular masc. & fem.

porch noun
  el **porche** masc.

pork noun
  el **cerdo** masc.
  a pork chop una chuleta de
  cerdo

• Languages and nationalities do not take a capital letter in Spanish.

a
b
c
d
e
f
g
h
i
j
k
l
m
n
o
p
q
r
s
t
u
v
w
x
y
z

porridge noun
los **copos de avena** *masc. plural*

> **LANGUAGE**
> English = porridge is singular
> Spanish = los copos de avena is plural

port noun
el **puerto** *masc.*

portable adjective
(*television etc.*) **portátil** *masc. & fem.*

portion noun
(*of food*) la **ración** *fem.* (plural las **raciones**)
a portion of potatoes una ración de patatas

portrait noun
el **retrato** *masc.*

Portugal noun
Portugal *masc.*

Portuguese adjective
portugués *masc.*, **portuguesa** *fem.*
Portuguese food la comida portuguesa

> **LANGUAGE**
> The masculine plural of portugués is portugueses.

Portuguese noun
1 (*language*) el **portugués** *masc.*
Do you speak Portuguese? ¿Hablas portugués?
2 **the Portuguese** los portugueses *masc. plural*

posh adjective
(*hotel, restaurant, etc.*) **elegante** *masc. & fem.*

position noun
la **posición** *fem.* (plural las **posiciones**)

positive adjective
(*certain*) **seguro** *masc.*, **segura** *fem.*
Are you positive? ¿Estás seguro?

possible adjective
posible *masc. & fem.*
It's possible. Es posible.
as soon as possible lo más pronto posible

possibly adverb
(*maybe*) **quizás**

post noun
1 (*letters*) el **correo** *masc.*
The post has come. Ha llegado el correo.
2 **to send something by post** mandar algo por correo

to **post** verb
1 (*to put into the postbox etc.*) **echar al correo**
Can you post this for me? ¿Me puedes echar esto al correo?
2 (*to send by post*) **mandar por correo**
Can you post the parcel to me? ¿Me puedes mandar el paquete por correo?

postbox noun
el **buzón** *masc.* (plural los **buzones**)

> **CULTURE**
> In Spain postboxes are usually yellow.

postcard noun
la **postal** *fem.*

postcode noun
el **código postal** *masc.*

poster noun
el **póster** *masc.* (plural los **pósters**); el **cartel** *masc.*

postman noun
el **cartero** *masc.*
Has the postman been? ¿Ha venido el cartero?

> **LANGUAGE**
> Cartero is related to carta (letter).

• *The months of the year and days of the week do not take a capital letter in Spanish.*

post office noun
Correos *masc.*, la **oficina de correos** *fem.*
to go to the post office ir a Correos, ir a la oficina de correos

🔑 **LANGUAGE**
Be careful: **Correos** is spelt with a capital **C** and ends with an **s**. Never use **el** with it.

postwoman noun
la **cartera** *fem.*
My mum's a postwoman.
Mi madre es cartera.

🔑 **LANGUAGE**
Cartera is related to **carta** (letter).

pot noun
1 (*teapot*) la **tetera** *fem.*
to make a pot of tea hacer té en una tetera
2 (*for flowers*) la **maceta** *fem.*
3 (*for cooking*) la **cacerola** *fem.*
the pots and pans los cacharros *masc. plural*

potato noun
la **patata** *fem.*,
(*Latin America*) la **papa** *fem.*
baked potatoes patatas asadas
boiled potatoes patatas hervidas

pound noun
1 (*money*) la **libra** *fem.*
ten pounds diez libras
2 (*weight*)
a pound of apples medio kilo de manzanas

🌍 **CULTURE**
Spanish weights are in kilos and grams; a pound is just under half a kilo.

to **pour** verb
1 **echar**
Pour the milk into the glass.
Echa la leche en el vaso.
2 (*to serve*) **servir**
Pour the soup. Sirve la sopa.

• *See the centre section for verb tables.*

3 **It's pouring with rain.** Está lloviendo a cántaros., Llueve mucho.

power cut noun
el **apagón** *masc.* (plural los **apagones**)

powerful adjective
poderoso *masc.*, **poderosa** *fem.*

practically adverb
(*almost*) **casi**

practice noun
1 (*sports training*) el **entrenamiento** *masc.*
I have football practice today.
Hoy tengo entrenamiento de fútbol.
2 (*on an instrument*) los **ejercicios** *masc. plural*
to do piano practice hacer los ejercicios de piano

to **practise** verb
1 (*a language or instrument*) **practicar**
I have to practise my Spanish.
Tengo que practicar mi español.
2 (*to do a sport*) **entrenar**
Our team practises every day.
Nuestro equipo entrena cada día.

prawn noun
la **gamba** *fem.*

to **pray** verb
rezar

prayer noun
la **oración** *fem.* (plural las **oraciones**)

to **prefer** verb
preferir
I prefer apples to oranges. Prefiero las manzanas a la naranjas.
I prefer to read. Prefiero leer.

pregnant adjective
embarazada *fem.*
She's five months pregnant. Está embarazada de cinco meses.

prehistoric adjective
prehistórico masc., **prehistórica** fem.

to **prepare** verb
preparar
Dad's preparing lunch. Papá está preparando la comida.

preposition noun
la **preposición** fem. (plural las **preposiciones**)

present adjective
1 **presente** masc. & fem.
Is Zafir present? ¿Está presente Zafir?
2 the present tense el presente masc.

present noun
1 (gift) el **regalo** masc.
What a lovely present! ¡Qué regalo tan bonito!
a birthday present un regalo de cumpleaños
2 (the time now) el **presente** masc.
the present and the past el presente y el pasado

president noun
el **presidente** masc., la **presidenta** fem.

to **press** verb
1 (a button, doorbell, etc.) **pulsar**
Press the button. Pulsa el botón.
2 **empujar**
Press here to open the door. Empuja aquí para abrir la puerta.

to **pretend** verb
1 **fingir**
He's pretending to be asleep. Finge dormir.
2 (to imagine) **imaginar**
Pretend you are a lion. Imagina que eres un león.

pretty adjective
1 (thing, town, animal, etc.) **bonito** masc., **bonita** fem.
a pretty skirt una falda bonita
2 (girl, woman) **guapo** masc., **guapa** fem.
a very pretty girl una niña muy guapa

pretty adverb
(fairly) **bastante**
a pretty good book un libro bastante bueno

to **prevent** verb
(an accident, a problem, etc.) **evitar**

price noun
el **precio** masc.
a price list una lista de precios

priest noun
el **sacerdote** masc.

primary school noun
la **escuela primaria** fem.

CULTURE
Spanish children go to the escuela primaria from the ages of 6 to 12. In Britain children go to primary school at around the age of 4 until they are 11.

Prime Minister noun
el **primer ministro** masc., la **primera ministra** fem.

prince noun
el **príncipe** masc.

princess noun
la **princesa** fem.

to **print** verb
1 (on a computer etc.) **imprimir**
Can you print out this page? ¿Me puedes imprimir esta página?
2 (to write in big letters) **escribir en mayúsculas**
Print your name. Escribe tu nombre en mayúsculas.

• Use **el** and **uno** for masculine words and **la** and **una** for feminine words.

printer noun
la **impresora** *fem.*
The printer isn't working.
La impresora no funciona.

prison noun
la **cárcel** *fem.*
He's in prison. Está en la cárcel.

prisoner noun
(*in prison*) el **preso** *masc.*,
la **presa** *fem.*

private adjective
1 **privado** *masc.*, **privada** *fem.*
a private school una escuela
privada
2 (*lesson, teacher*) **particular** *masc. & fem.*
private lessons clases particulares

prize noun
el **premio** *masc.*
to win a prize ganar un premio
the prize-giving la entrega de
premios

prizewinner noun
el **ganador** *masc.*, la **ganadora** *fem.*

probably adverb
probablemente

problem noun
el **problema** *masc.*
No problem! ¡No hay problema!

LANGUAGE
Be careful: problema ends in an -a but it
is not a feminine noun.

to **produce** verb
(*to make, create*) **producir**

profession noun
la **profesión** *fem.* (plural las
profesiones)

program noun
(*on a computer*) el **programa** *masc.*
a computer program un programa
informático

LANGUAGE
Be careful: programa ends in an -a but it
is not a feminine noun.

programme noun
(*on TV or radio, for concert etc.*)
el **programa** *masc.*
a TV programme un programa de
televisión

LANGUAGE
Be careful: programa ends in an -a but it
is not a feminine noun.

progress noun
to make progress mejorar
I'm making progress in Spanish.
Mi español está mejorando.

promise noun
la **promesa** *fem.*
You made a promise! ¡Me has
hecho una promesa!
I've kept my promise. He
cumplido mi promesa.
That's a promise. Te lo prometo.

to **promise** verb
prometer
You promised to come tomorrow.
Has prometido venir mañana.
I promise. Te lo prometo.

pronoun noun
el **pronombre** *masc.*

to **pronounce** verb
pronunciar
How do you pronounce it in
Spanish? ¿Cómo se pronuncia en
español?

pronunciation noun
la **pronunciación** *fem.*

properly adverb
(*well*) **bien**
I read properly. Leo bien.

to **protect** verb
proteger

Protestant adjective
protestante *masc. & fem.*

• Languages and nationalities do not take a capital letter in Spanish.

proud adjective
orgulloso masc., **orgullosa** fem.
We're proud of you. Estamos orgullosos de ti.

proverb noun
el **proverbio** masc.

prune noun
la **ciruela pasa** fem.

⚷ **LANGUAGE**
Word for word the Spanish means 'dried plum'.

pub noun
el **bar** masc., el **pub** masc.

public noun
el **público** masc.
It's open to the public. Está abierto al público.

public adjective
1 **público** masc., **pública** fem.
a public library una biblioteca pública
public transport el transporte público
2 **a public holiday** un día de fiesta
Tomorrow is a public holiday. Mañana es fiesta.
3 **a public school** un colegio privado

⚠ **FALSE FRIEND**
a public school = un colegio privado (not una escuela pública)

pudding noun
1 el **pudín** masc. (plural los **pudines**)
2 (dessert) el **postre** masc.

puddle noun
el **charco** masc.

to **pull** verb
tirar
Don't pull so hard. No tires tan fuerte.
to pull something tirar de algo
I pulled her hair. Le tiré del pelo.

to **pull down** verb
bajar
Pull down the blinds. Baja las persianas.

to **pull off** verb
(a lid, cover, etc.) **quitar**
I pulled off my socks. Me quité los calcetines.

to **pull out** verb
(a plug, tooth, etc.) **sacar**
What did you pull out of your pocket? ¿Qué has sacado del bolsillo?

pullover noun
el **jersey** masc. (plural los **jerseys** or **jerséis**)

pump noun
la **bomba** fem.
a bicycle pump una bomba de bicicleta

to **pump** verb
to pump up a tyre inflar una rueda

pumpkin noun
la **calabaza** fem.

punch noun
el **puñetazo** masc.

to **punch** verb
to punch somebody dar un puñetazo a alguien
She punched me. Me ha dado un puñetazo.

punctual adjective
puntual masc. & fem.
I'm very punctual. Soy muy puntual.

⚷ **LANGUAGE**
English = **punc**tual
Spanish = **pun**tual

• The months of the year and days of the week do not take a capital letter in Spanish.

punctuation noun
la puntuación *fem.*

> ⚷ **LANGUAGE**
> English = **punc**tuation
> Spanish = **pun**tuación

to **punish** verb
castigar
I've been punished. Me han castigado.

punishment noun
el **castigo** *masc.*

pupil noun
el **alumno** *masc.*, la **alumna** *fem.*
all the pupils in my class todos los alumnos de mi clase

puppet noun
el **títere** *masc.*, la **marioneta** *fem.*

puppy noun
el **cachorro** *masc.*, la **cachorra** *fem.*

pure adjective
puro *masc.*, **pura** *fem.*

purple adjective
morado *masc.*, **morada** *fem.*
a purple skirt una falda morada

purple noun
el **morado** *masc.*
I love purple. Me encanta el morado.

purpose noun
on purpose a propósito
I didn't do it on purpose. No lo he hecho a propósito.

purse noun
el **monedero** *masc.*
I have ten euros in my purse. Tengo diez euros en el monedero.

to **push** verb
1 **empujar**
Don't push me! ¡No me empujes!
Push the door. Empuja la puerta.
2 (*a button, doorbell, etc.*) **pulsar**
Push the button. Pulsa el botón.

• *See the centre section for verb tables.*

pushchair noun
la **sillita** *fem.*

to **put** verb
poner
Put your book on the table. Pon tu libro en la mesa.
Where have you put it? ¿Dónde lo has puesto?

to **put away** verb
guardar
Put your toys away. Guarda los juguetes.

to **put back** verb
volver a poner
Put the CD back in the box. Vuelve a poner el CD en la caja.

to **put down** verb
1 **poner**
Put it down on the floor. Ponlo en el suelo.
2 (*your hand, the blind, etc.*) **bajar**
Put the window down. Baja la ventanilla.

to **put off** verb
1 **apagar**
I've put the light off. He apagado la luz.
2 **aplazar**
They've put off the game. Han aplazado el partido.

to **put on** verb
1 (*clothes, music, a CD, etc.*) **poner**
Put the TV on. Pon la tele.
I'm putting my socks on. Me pongo los calcetines.
2 to put the light on encender la luz
3 to put on a play hacer una obra

to **put out** verb
(*a light etc.*) **apagar**
They've put out the fire. Han apagado el incendio.

to put up verb

(*a picture, decorations, etc.*) **poner**
I've put up photos in my room.
He puesto fotos en mi habitación.
to put your hand up levantar la mano
to put up the price subir el precio

puzzle noun

el **rompecabezas** *masc.* (plural los **rompecabezas**)

puzzled adjective

confuso *masc.*, **confusa** *fem.*

Qq

quality noun
la **calidad** *fem.*

quantity noun
la **cantidad** *fem.*

to quarrel verb
discutir
They're always quarrelling.
Siempre están discutiendo.

quarter noun
1 la **cuarta parte** *fem.*
a quarter of the pupils una cuarta parte de los alumnos
2 (*talking about time, weights, etc.*)
el **cuarto** *masc.*
a quarter of an hour un cuarto de hora
It's a quarter past seven. Son las siete y cuarto.
at a quarter to seven a las siete menos cuarto
an hour and a quarter una hora y cuarto

queen noun
la **reina** *fem.*

question noun
la **pregunta** *fem.*

pyjamas plural noun
el **pijama** *masc.*
I'm in pyjamas. Estoy en pijama.
a pair of pyjamas un pijama

> 🔑 **LANGUAGE**
> English = **pyjamas** is plural
> Spanish = **el pijama** is singular

> 🔑 **LANGUAGE**
> Be careful: **pijama** ends in an **-a** but it is not a feminine noun.

pyramid noun
la **pirámide** *fem.*

to ask a question hacer una pregunta
Can I ask you a question? ¿Puedo hacerte una pregunta?
a question mark un signo de interrogación

queue noun
la **cola** *fem.*
We're standing in the queue.
Estamos haciendo cola.

> 🔑 **LANGUAGE**
> The Spanish word **cola** also means 'tail': queues can be long or short like tails.

to queue verb
hacer cola
You have to queue up. Tienes que hacer cola.

quick adjective
rápido *masc.*, **rápida** *fem.*
It's quicker by bike. Es más rápido en bici.
Quick! ¡Rápido!
Be quick! ¡Date prisa!

quickly adverb
rápido, **rápidamente**

• *Use* **el** *and* **uno** *for masculine words and* **la** *and* **una** *for feminine words.*

quiet adjective
1 (*peaceful*) **tranquilo** *masc.*,
tranquila *fem.*
a quiet street una calle tranquila
2 (*not noisy*) **silencioso** *masc.*,
silenciosa *fem.*
a quiet car un coche silencioso
Quiet, please! ¡Silencio, por favor!
Be quiet!, Keep quiet! (*to one
person*) ¡Cállate!; (*to more than one
person*) ¡Callaos!

quietly adverb
1 (*without noise*) **sin hacer ruido**, **en
silencio**
2 (*to talk, say, etc.*) **en voz baja**

quite adverb
1 (*fairly*) **bastante**
quite often bastante a menudo
quite a good film una película
bastante buena
2 (*completely*) **totalmente**
quite different totalmente distinto
3 **quite a lot** bastante
I read quite a lot. Leo bastante.
quite a lot of bastante *masc. & fem.*
I have quite a lot of friends. Tengo
bastantes amigas.

quiz noun
(*on TV etc.*) el **concurso** *masc.*
a quiz show un programa concurso

Rr

rabbi noun
el **rabino** *masc.*, la **rabina** *fem.*

rabbit noun
el **conejo** *masc.*

race noun
1 la **carrera** *fem.*
Let's have a race to the house.
Te echo una carrera hasta la casa.
2 (*people*) la **raza** *fem.*
the human race la raza humana

racing car noun
el **coche de carreras** *masc.*

racket noun
la **raqueta** *fem.*
a tennis racket una raqueta de
tenis

radiator noun
el **radiador** *masc.*

🔑 **LANGUAGE**
English = radiator
Spanish = radiador

radio noun
la **radio** *fem.*

Put on the radio. Pon la radio.
on the radio en la radio
I heard it on the radio. Lo oí por la
radio.
a radio station una emisora de
radio

rail noun
to go by rail ir en tren

railway carriage noun
el **vagón** *masc.* (plural los **vagones**)

railway line noun
1 (*between two places*) la **línea de
ferrocarril** *fem.*
2 (*the metal bars*) la **vía** *fem.*
**You're not allowed to play on the
line.** Está prohibido jugar en la vía.

railway station noun
la **estación de trenes** *fem.* (plural
las **estaciones de trenes**)

rain noun
la **lluvia** *fem.*
Don't go out in the rain. No salgas,
que está lloviendo.
a rain forest una selva tropical

a
b
c
d
e
f
g
h
i
j
k
l
m
n
o
p
q
r
s
t
u
v
w
x
y
z

• *Languages and nationalities do not take a capital letter in Spanish.*

a
b
c
d
e
f
g
h
i
j
k
l
m
n
o
p
q
r
s
t
u
v
w
x
y
z

to **rain** verb
llover
It's raining. Está lloviendo.

rainbow noun
el **arco iris** *masc.*

raincoat noun
el **impermeable** *masc.*

rainy adjective
lluvioso *masc.*, **lluviosa** *fem.*
a rainy day un día lluvioso
It's always rainy in Norwich.
Siempre llueve en Norwich.

to **raise**
levantar
Raise your hand. Levanta la mano.

raisin noun
la **pasa** *fem.*

ramp noun
(*for a wheelchair*) la **rampa** *fem.*

rap noun
el **rap** *masc.*

rare adjective
poco común *masc. & fem.*
These animals are rare. Estos
animales son poco comunes.

rarely adverb
casi nunca
I rarely see my uncle. Casi nunca
veo a mi tío.

rash noun
el **sarpullido** *masc.*
I've got a rash. Me ha salido un
sarpullido.

raspberry noun
la **frambuesa** *fem.*
raspberry jam la mermelada de
frambuesa

rat noun
la **rata** *fem.*

rather adverb
1 (*talking about preferring something*)
I would rather wait. Prefiero
esperar.
**I don't want the red dress. I'd
rather have the green one.** No
quiero el vestido rojo. Prefiero el
verde.

🔑 **LANGUAGE**
Use the verb **preferir** for this meaning.

2 (*instead*)
rather than en vez de
**Choose the jeans rather than the
skirt.** Elige los vaqueros en vez de
la falda.
3 (*fairly*) **bastante**
a rather good book un libro
bastante bueno
rather a lot of bastante *masc. & fem.*
rather a lot of presents bastantes
regalos

raw adjective
crudo *masc.*, **cruda** *fem.*
a raw carrot una zanahoria cruda

razor noun
la **máquina de afeitar** *fem.*

to **reach** verb
1 (*to get to*) **llegar a**
We reached Madrid at two.
Llegamos a Madrid a las dos.
2 (*by stretching your arm*)
alcanzar, **llegar a**
I can't reach the shelf. No alcanzo
al estante., No llego al estante.

to **read** verb
leer
I read a lot. Leo mucho.
What are you reading? ¿Qué estás
leyendo?

reading noun
la **lectura** *fem.*
a reading book un libro de lectura
I like reading. Me gusta leer.

• *The months of the year and days of the week do not take a capital letter in Spanish.*

ready adjective
1 **listo** *masc.*,
lista *fem.*, **preparado** *masc.*,
preparada *fem.*
I'm ready. Estoy listo or
preparado.
We're ready to leave. Estamos
listas or preparadas para salir.
2 (*food*) **preparado** *masc.*,
preparada *fem.*
Lunch is ready. La comida está
preparada.
3 **to get ready** prepararse
Get ready! ¡Prepárate!
to get something ready preparar
algo

real adjective
verdadero *masc.*, **verdadera** *fem.*
my real name mi verdadero
nombre

really adverb
(*with adjectives and adverbs*) **muy**
My bike is really old. Mi bici es
muy vieja.
really well muy bien
Are you tired? - Not really. ¿Estás
cansado? - No mucho.

reason noun
la **razón** *fem.* (plural las **razones**)
For what reason? ¿Por qué razón?

reasonable adjective
1 (*person, price, idea, etc.*) **razonable**
masc. & fem.
Zafir's very reasonable. Zafir es
muy razonable.
2 (*meal, work, etc.*) **bastante**
bueno *masc.*, **bastante buena** *fem.*
reasonable weather un tiempo
bastante bueno

⚠ **LANGUAGE**
Use razonable when you mean
'sensible', and bastante bueno when you
mean 'fairly good'.

• *See the centre section for verb tables.*

to **receive** verb
recibir
I've received your letter. He
recibido tu carta.

recent adjective
reciente *masc. & fem.*

recently adverb
recientemente

reception noun
(*desk in a hotel*) la **recepción** *fem.*
I'm waiting at reception. Estoy
esperando en recepción.

receptionist noun
el or la **recepcionista** *masc. & fem.*

recipe noun
la **receta** *fem.*

to **recognize** verb
reconocer
I don't recognize you. No te
reconozco.

to **recommend** verb
recomendar

record noun
1 (*for music*) el **disco** *masc.*
My granddad has lots of records.
Mi abuelo tiene muchos discos.
2 (*in sport*) el **récord** *masc.* (plural los
récords)
to beat the world record batir el
récord mundial

to **record** verb
(*pictures, sounds, etc.*) **grabar**
Shall we record the film?
¿Grabamos la película?
It's recording. Está grabando.

recorder noun
la **flauta dulce** *fem.*
to play the recorder tocar la flauta
dulce

⚠ **LANGUAGE**
Word for word flauta dulce means
'sweet flute'.

---

a
b
c
d
e
f
g
h
i
j
k
l
m
n
o
p
q
r
s
t
u
v
w
x
y
z

rectangle noun
el **rectángulo** *masc.*

red adjective
1 **rojo** *masc.*, **roja** *fem.*
red socks calcetines rojos
2 (*in the face*) **colorado** *masc.*,
colorada *fem.*
You're going red! (*blushing*) ¡Te estás
poniendo colorado!
3 a red wine un vino tinto
4 to have red hair ser pelirrojo *masc.*;
ser pelirroja *fem.*

red noun
el **rojo** *masc.*
I prefer red. Prefiero el rojo.

redhead noun
el **pelirrojo** *masc.*, la **pelirroja** *fem.*

to **redo** verb
volver a hacer
You have to redo it. Tienes que
volver a hacerlo.

to **reduce** verb
(*price, number, etc.*) **reducir**

referee noun
el **árbitro** *masc.*, la **árbitra** *fem.*

reflexive adjective
(*in grammar*)
a reflexive verb un verbo reflexivo

> ⚷ **LANGUAGE**
> In Spanish a reflexive verb is a verb that is
> used with a pronoun, e.g. levantarse (to
> get up): me levanto is 'I get up', te
> levantas is 'you get up', etc.

refrigerator noun
el **frigorífico** *masc.*

to **refuse** verb
to refuse to do something no
querer hacer algo
He refuses to eat. No quiere comer.

region noun
la **región** *fem.* (plural las **regiones**)

register noun
la **lista** *fem.*
to take the register pasar lista

registration noun
(*in school*)
Registration is at eight o'clock.
Pasan lista a las ocho.

> ⚷ **LANGUAGE**
> There is no word in Spanish for
> registration. Use pasar lista (to take the
> register) instead.

regular adjective
1 **regular** *masc. & fem.*
at regular intervals a intervalos
regulares
2 (*customer, time*) **habitual** *masc. & fem.*
3 (*size, model*) **normal** *masc. & fem.*
One regular fries, please. Una
porción normal de patatas fritas,
por favor.

rehearsal noun
el **ensayo** *masc.*

reindeer noun
el **reno** *masc.*

related adjective
1 (*ideas, problems, etc.*)
relacionado *masc.*,
relacionada *fem.*
2 (*people*)
to be related ser parientes
David and Daniel are related.
David y Daniel son parientes.
3 (*words*) **de la misma familia**
'Rainbow' and 'rainy' are related.
'Rainbow' y 'rainy' son de la misma
familia.

relation noun
el or la **pariente** *masc. & fem.*
my relations mis parientes

relative noun
el or la **pariente** *masc. & fem.*
my relatives mis parientes

• *Use* **el** *and* **uno** *for masculine words and* **la** *and* **una** *for feminine words.*

to **relax** verb
relajarse, **descansar**
I watch TV to relax. Veo la tele para relajarme., Veo la tele para descansar.
Relax! (*don't worry*) ¡Tranquilo!
Music is relaxing. La música me relaja.

relaxed adjective
relajado *masc.*, **relajada** *fem.*
I feel relaxed. Estoy relajado.

religion noun
la **religión** *fem.* (plural las **religiones**)

religious adjective
religioso *masc.*, **religiosa** *fem.*

to **remain** verb
1 (*to stay*) **quedarse**
Remain in the classroom. Quédate en la clase.
2 (*to be left*) **quedar**
It's all that remains. Esto es todo lo que queda.

to **remember** verb
1 **acordarse**
I don't remember. No me acuerdo.
Do you remember? ¿Te acuerdas?
2 **to remember something** acordarse de algo
I remember your name. Me acuerdo de tu nombre.

to **remind** verb
recordar
You remind me of my brother. Me recuerdas a mi hermano.
This reminds me of the summer. Esto me recuerda el verano.

remote control noun
el **mando (a distancia)** *masc.*

to **remove** verb
quitar
Remove your toys from the table! ¡Quita tus juguetes de la mesa!

to **rent** verb
(*a flat, car, etc.*) **alquilar**

to **repair** verb
arreglar, **reparar**
They've repaired the TV. Han arreglado la tele., Han reparado la tele.

to **repeat** verb
repetir
Can you repeat the question? ¿Puede repetir la pregunta?

to **replace** verb
1 (*to change*) **cambiar**
Have you replaced the batteries? ¿Has cambiado las pilas?
2 (*to put back*) **volver a poner**

reply noun
la **respuesta** *fem.*
I haven't got a reply. No he tenido respuesta.

to **reply** verb
responder
She's replied to my letter. Ha respondido a mi carta.

report noun
a school report un boletín de notas
I've got a good report. He sacado buenas notas.

reptile noun
el **reptil** *masc.*

to **rescue** verb
salvar
The firemen rescued her from the fire. Los bomberos la salvaron del incendio.

to **reserve** verb
reservar
This seat is reserved. Este asiento está reservado.

resort noun
(*for holidays*) el **centro turístico** *masc.*
a ski resort una estación de esquí

respect noun
el **respeto** *masc.*

• Languages and nationalities do not take a capital letter in Spanish.

to **respect** verb
respetar

responsibility noun
la **responsabilidad** fem.

responsible adjective
responsable masc. & fem.
She's a very responsible girl.
Es una niña muy responsable.
Who's responsible? ¿Quién es el responsable?

🔑 **LANGUAGE**
English = respon**s**ible
Spanish = respon**s**able

rest noun
1 (talking about something left over)
the rest el resto masc.
the rest of the week el resto de la semana
2 (talking about other people)
the rest los otros masc. plural, las otras fem. plural
The rest have left. Los otros se han ido.
the rest of the boys los otros niños
3 (time to relax) el **descanso** masc.
I need some rest. Necesito descanso.
to have a rest descansar

to **rest** verb
descansar
I rested for an hour. Descansé una hora.

restaurant noun
el **restaurante** masc.

result noun
el **resultado** masc.
the exam results los resultados de los exámenes

to **retire** verb
jubilarse
My granddad retires in May.
Mi abuelo se jubila en mayo.
My grandma is retired. Mi abuela está jubilada.

return noun
1 la **vuelta** fem.
the return to school la vuelta al colegio
the return journey el viaje de vuelta
2 (ticket) el **billete de ida y vuelta** masc.
A return to York, please. Un billete de ida y vuelta a York, por favor.
a return ticket un billete de ida y vuelta
3 **Many happy returns!** ¡Feliz cumpleaños!

to **return** verb
1 (to come or go back) **volver**
When do you return to Barcelona?
¿Cuándo vuelves a Barcelona?
She hasn't returned. No ha vuelto.
2 (to give back) **devolver**
Return the book to the library.
Devuelve el libro a la biblioteca.

to **reverse** verb
(in a car) **dar marcha atrás**

reverse adjective
in reverse order en orden inverso

to **revise** verb
repasar
My sister's revising for her exams.
Mi hermana está repasando para los exámenes.

revision noun
el **repaso** masc.
a revision exercise un ejercicio de repaso
to do revision repasar

reward noun
la **recompensa** fem.
a fifty-euro reward una recompensa de cincuenta euros

to **rewind** verb
rebobinar
Rewind the video. Rebobina el vídeo.

• The months of the year and days of the week do not take a capital letter in Spanish.

rhinoceros noun
el **rinoceronte** *masc.*

rhyme noun
la **rima** *fem.*

to **rhyme** verb
rimar
'House' rhymes with 'mouse'.
'House' rima con 'mouse'.

rhythm noun
el **ritmo** *masc.*

rib noun
la **costilla** *fem.*

ribbon noun
la **cinta** *fem.*

rice noun
el **arroz** *masc.*
Would you like some rice?
¿Quieres arroz?
rice pudding el arroz con leche

rich adjective
rico *masc.*, **rica** *fem.*
They're very rich. Son muy ricos.

rid adjective
1 to get rid of (*to throw away*) tirar
I've got rid of my old magazines.
He tirado las revistas viejas.
2 to get rid of (*to take away*) quitar
to get rid of a stain quitar una
mancha

riddle noun
la **adivinanza** *fem.*

ride noun
1 (*in a car, on a horse, etc.*) la **vuelta** *fem.*
to go for a ride dar una vuelta
I went for a ride on my bike. Fui a
dar una vuelta en bici.
2 (*at a funfair*)
We went on lots of rides. Nos
subimos a muchos aparatos.

to **ride** verb
1 to ride a bike montar en bici
Can you ride a bike? ¿Sabes
montar en bici?
to ride a horse montar a caballo

2 (*to travel somewhere on a bicycle, horse, etc.*)
ir
I ride my bike to school. Voy a la
escuela en bici.

ridiculous adjective
ridículo *masc.*, **ridícula** *fem.*

riding noun
la **equitación** *fem.*
to go riding hacer equitación

right adjective
1 (*correct*) **correcto** *masc.*,
correcta *fem.*
the right answer la respuesta
correcta
2 (*not translated*)
This is the right house. Ésta es la
casa.
Do you have the right time?
¿Tienes hora?
3 (*true*)
That's right. Es verdad.
4 (*at the beginning of a sentence*) **¡bueno!**
Right! I'm leaving. ¡Bueno! Me voy.
5 (*talking about people*) to be right tener
razón
You're right, Emma. Tienes razón,
Emma.
6 (*the opposite of left*) **derecho** *masc.*,
derecha *fem.*
my right hand mi mano derecha

right adverb
1 (*correctly*) **bien**
Am I doing it right? ¿Lo estoy
haciendo bien?
2 (*in time or place*) **justo**
right before my birthday justo
antes de mi cumpleaños
right away ahora mismo
3 (*the opposite of left*) **a la derecha**
Turn right. Gira a la derecha.

right noun
on the right a la derecha
The school is on the right.
La escuela está a la derecha.
We drive on the right. Se conduce
por la derecha.

• *See the centre section for verb tables.*

a
b
c
d
e
f
g
h
i
j
k
l
m
n
o
p
q
r
s
t
u
v
w
x
y
z

English Spanish

a
b
c
d
e
f
g
h
i
j
k
l
m
n
o
p
q
r
s
t
u
v
w
x
y
z

right-handed adjective
to be right-handed escribir con la mano derecha

ring noun
1 (*for your finger*) el **anillo** *masc.*
a gold ring un anillo de oro
2 (*phone call*)
to give somebody a ring llamar a alguien

to **ring** verb
1 (*to call on the phone*) **llamar**
Ring me tomorrow. Llámame mañana.
2 (*talking about a phone, bell, etc.*) **sonar**
The phone's ringing. El teléfono está sonando.
The bell rang. Ha sonado el timbre.
to ring the bell tocar el timbre
Somebody's ringing the doorbell. Llaman a la puerta.

rink noun
an ice rink una pista de hielo

ripe adjective
maduro *masc.*, **madura** *fem.*

to **rise** verb
salir
The sun is rising. Está saliendo el sol.

river noun
el **río** *masc.*
the River Severn el río Severn

road noun
1 (*between towns etc.*) la **carretera** *fem.*
the road to Bilbao la carretera de Bilbao
a road accident un accidente de tráfico
a road map un mapa de carreteras
a road sign una señal de tráfico
2 (*a street in a town or village*) la **calle** *fem.*
They live across the road. Viven al otro lado de la calle.

roadworks plural noun
las **obras** *fem. plural*

to **roar** verb
rugir
The lion is roaring. El león ruge.

to **rob** verb
1 (*a person*) **robar**
We've been robbed. Nos han robado.
2 (*a bank, shop, etc.*) **asaltar**, **robar**

robber noun
el **ladrón** *masc.*, la **ladrona** *fem.*

> 🔑 **LANGUAGE**
> The plural of **ladrón** is **ladrones**.

robbery noun
el **robo** *masc.*

robot noun
el **robot** *masc.* (plural los **robots**)

rock noun
1 (*big stone*) la **roca** *fem.*
2 (*music*) el **rock** *masc.*
a rock group un grupo de rock
rock music la música rock
a rock star una estrella del rock

rocket noun
el **cohete** *masc.*

rocking horse noun
el **caballito de balancín** *masc.*

rod noun
a fishing rod una caña de pescar

role-play noun
el **juego de roles** *masc.*

roll noun
1 (*of paper etc.*) el **rollo** *masc.*
2 (*bread roll*) el **panecillo** *masc.*

to **roll** verb
rodar
Roll the ball. Rueda la pelota.
The ball has rolled under the bed. La pelota ha rodado por debajo de la cama.

Rollerblades® plural noun
los **patines en línea** *masc. plural*

• Use **el** and **uno** for masculine words and **la** and **una** for feminine words.

roller coaster noun
la **montaña rusa** *fem.*

🔑 **LANGUAGE**
Word for word the Spanish means
'Russian mountain': there are plenty of
ups and downs.

roller skates plural noun
los **patines de ruedas** *masc. plural*

roller-skating noun
el **patinaje sobre ruedas** *masc.*
to go roller-skating ir a patinar

Roman adjective
romano *masc.*, **romana** *fem.*
a Roman road una calzada
romana

Roman noun
the Romans los romanos *masc.*
plural

roof noun
el **tejado** *masc.*

room noun
1 (*in a house*) la **habitación** *fem.* (plural
las **habitaciones**)
I'm in my room. Estoy en mi
habitación.
2 (*in school*) la **sala** *fem.*
the computer room la sala de
ordenadores
3 (*space*) el **sitio** *masc.*
There's no room. No hay sitio.
to make room hacer sitio

root noun
la **raíz** *fem.* (plural las **raíces**)

rope noun
la **cuerda** *fem.*

rose noun
la **rosa** *fem.*

rotten adjective
1 (*apple, pear, etc.*) **podrido** *masc.*,
podrida *fem.*
2 (*film, food, weather, etc.*)
malísimo *masc.*, **malísima** *fem.*

rough adjective
1 (*person, behaviour, game*)
violento *masc.*, **violenta** *fem.*
2 (*hands, towel*) **áspero** *masc.*,
áspera *fem.*
3 (*life, voice*) **duro** *masc.*, **dura** *fem.*
4 (*area of town*) **peligroso** *masc.*,
peligrosa *fem.*

roughly adverb
más o menos
It weighs roughly ten kilos. Pesa
diez kilos más o menos.

round adjective
redondo *masc.*, **redonda** *fem.*
He has a round face. Tiene la cara
redonda.

round preposition & adverb
1 **alrededor de**
a trip round the world un viaje
alrededor del mundo
They live round the corner. Viven
muy cerca.
round here por aquí
round about ten o'clock alrededor
de la diez
2 (*talking about somebody's house*)
Come round tomorrow. Ven a mi
casa mañana.

roundabout noun
1 (*merry-go-round*) el **tiovivo** *masc.*
2 (*for traffic*) la **rotonda** *fem.*

row noun
1 (*of people in the cinema etc.*) la **fila** *fem.*
in the front row en la primera fila
in the back row en la última fila
2 (*of chairs, houses, trees, etc.*) la **hilera**
fem.

to **row** verb
(*in a boat*) **remar**

rowing boat noun
el **bote de remos** *masc.*

a
b
c
d
e
f
g
h
i
j
k
l
m
n
o
p
q
r
s
t
u
v
w
x
y
z

• *Languages and nationalities do not take a capital letter in Spanish.*

English Spanish

a
b
c
d
e
f
g
h
i
j
k
l
m
n
o
p
q
r
s
t
u
v
w
x
y
z

royal adjective
real *masc. & fem.*
the royal family la familia real

rubber noun
la **goma** *fem.*
Do you have a rubber? ¿Tienes una goma?
It's made of rubber. Es de goma.
a rubber band una goma elástica

rubbish noun
1 (*food, papers, etc. thrown out*) la **basura** *fem.*
to put out the rubbish sacar la basura
a rubbish bin un cubo de basura
2 (*nonsense*) las **tonterías** *fem. plural*, la **tontería** *fem.*
to talk rubbish decir tonterías
What rubbish! ¡Qué tontería!

rubbish adjective
(*very bad*) **to be rubbish** ser una porquería
The book is rubbish. El libro es una porquería.

to **rub out** verb
borrar
Rub this word out with your rubber. Borra esta palabra con tu goma.

rude adjective
maleducado *masc.*,
maleducada *fem.*
to be rude to somebody ser maleducado con alguien
That's rude. Eso es de mala educación.
a rude word una palabrota

rug noun
(*carpet*) la **alfombra** *fem.*

rugby noun
el **rugby** *masc.*
to play rugby jugar al rugby

to **ruin** verb
(*a dress, toy, etc.*) **estropear**
You're going to ruin that shirt. Vas a estropear esa camisa.

ruins plural noun
(*of a castle etc.*) las **ruinas** *fem. plural*

rule noun
1 (*in grammar etc.*) la **regla** *fem.*
the rules of the game las reglas del juego
2 (*in a school, office, etc.*)
the rules el reglamento
the school rules el reglamento del colegio
It's against the rules. Está prohibido.

ruler noun
la **regla** *fem.*

run noun
to go for a run ir a correr

to **run** verb
1 **correr**
Jamal runs very fast. Jamal corre muy rápido.
I ran down the hill. Bajé la cuesta corriendo.

🔑 **LANGUAGE**
Word for word the Spanish means 'I went down the hill running'.

---

2 (*activities, classes, etc.*) **organizar**

to **run away** verb
escaparse
The children have run away. Los niños se han escapado.

to **run into** verb
chocar con
The car ran into a tree. El coche chocó con un árbol.

to **run over** verb
atropellar
Be careful, you'll get run over! ¡Cuidado, te van a atropellar!

• *The months of the year and days of the week do not take a capital letter in Spanish.*

runner ➜ salad

runner noun
  el **corredor** *masc.*,
  la **corredora** *fem.*

running noun
  el **footing** *masc.*
  to go running hacer footing

runny adjective
  to have a runny nose tener mocos

runway noun
  (*for planes*) la **pista** *fem.*

to **rush** verb
  correr
  Don't rush! ¡No corras!
  You're always rushing. Siempre estás corriendo.

rush noun
  1 **to be in a rush** tener prisa
  2 **in the rush hour** a la hora punta

Russia noun
  Rusia *fem.*

Russian adjective
  ruso *masc.*, **rusa** *fem.*
  She's Russian. Es rusa.

Russian noun
  1 (*language*) el **ruso** *masc.*
  2 (*person*) el **ruso** *masc.*, la **rusa** *fem.*

rusty adjective
  (*bike, wire, etc.*) **oxidado** *masc.*, **oxidada** *fem.*

Ss

sack noun
  el **saco** *masc.*

sad adjective
  triste *masc. & fem.*
  I'm sad. Estoy triste.

saddle noun
  1 (*on a horse*) la **silla de montar** *fem.*
  2 (*on a bicycle*) el **sillín** *masc.* (plural los **sillines**)

sadness noun
  la **tristeza** *fem.*

safe adjective
  1 (*not dangerous, not in danger*)
  seguro *masc.*, **segura** *fem.*
  His car isn't very safe. Su coche no es muy seguro.
  You're safe here. Estás segura aquí.
  It's not safe to go out. Es peligroso salir.
  2 (*not hurt*) **sano y salvo** *masc.*, **sana y salva** *fem.*
  Mum came back safe. Mamá volvió sana y salva.

safe noun
  (*for money*) la **caja fuerte** *fem.*

safely adverb
  1 (*without danger*)
  They've arrived safely. Han llegado sin problemas.
  to drive safely conducir con cuidado
  2 (*in a safe place*) **en un sitio seguro**

safety noun
  la **seguridad** *fem.*

sailing noun
  la **vela** *fem.*
  to go sailing hacer vela
  a sailing boat un barco de vela

sailor noun
  el **marinero** *masc.*

saint noun
  el **santo** *masc.*, la **santa** *fem.*

salad noun
  la **ensalada** *fem.*
  a chicken salad una ensalada de pollo

• *See the centre section for verb tables.*

English Spanish

a
b
c
d
e
f
g
h
i
j
k
l
m
n
o
p
q
r
s
t
u
v
w
x
y
z

sale noun
1 'For sale'. 'Se vende'.
   'Bicycle for sale'. 'Se vende
   bicicleta'.
2 **the sales** las rebajas *fem. plural*
   to buy something in the sales
   comprar algo en las rebajas

salt noun
   la **sal** *fem.*
   Put on some salt. Echa un poco de
   sal.

salty adjective
   salado *masc.*, **salada** *fem.*
   The food is salty. La comida está
   salada.

same adjective & pronoun
1 **mismo** *masc.*, **misma** *fem.*
   I've got the same dress as you.
   Tengo el mismo vestido que tú.
   I've got the same one. Tengo el
   mismo.
   at the same time al mismo tiempo
   It's not the same. No es lo mismo.
2 *(describing things that look the same)*
   igual *masc. & fem.*
   They look the same. Parecen
   iguales.
   You're the same as your dad.
   Eres igual a tu padre.

sand noun
   la **arena** *fem.*
   a sand castle un castillo de arena

sandal noun
   la **sandalia** *fem.*
   a pair of sandals un par de
   sandalias

sandwich noun
   el **sándwich** *masc.* (plural los
   sándwiches)
   a cheese sandwich un sándwich de
   queso

Santa Claus noun
   Papá Noel *masc.*

satellite noun
   el **satélite** *masc.*
   satellite television la televisión
   vía satélite
   a satellite dish una antena
   parabólica *fem.*

Saturday noun
   el **sábado** *masc.*
   Today is Saturday. Hoy es sábado.
   on Saturday el sábado
   They come back on Saturday.
   Vuelven el sábado.
   on Saturdays los sábados
   It's closed on Saturdays. Está
   cerrado los sábados.

> **LANGUAGE**
> Remember the difference in Spanish
> between el sábado (one Saturday only)
> and los sábados (every Saturday).

sauce noun
   la **salsa** *fem.*

saucepan noun
   la **cacerola** *fem.*

saucer noun
   el **platillo** *masc.*
   a flying saucer un platillo volante

sausage noun
   la **salchicha** *fem.*

to **save** verb
1 *(from danger)* **salvar**
   They saved the dog from the fire.
   Han salvado al perro del incendio.
2 *(to keep)* **guardar**
   Save me a place. Guárdame un
   sitio.
3 *(money, time)* **ahorrar**
   I've saved twenty pounds.
   He ahorrado veinte libras.
   ... to save time ... para ahorrar
   tiempo
4 *(a computer file etc.)* **grabar**
   I've saved the file onto a disk.
   He grabado el archivo en un disco.
   I've saved my work. He guardado
   mi trabajo.

• *Use* **el** *and* **uno** *for masculine words and* **la** *and* **una** *for feminine words.*

to **save up** verb
ahorrar
I'm saving up for a computer.
Estoy ahorrando para un
ordenador.

to **say** verb
1 **decir**
He says it's raining. Dice que está
lloviendo.
I didn't say anything. No he dicho
nada.
How do you say 'boy' in Spanish?
¿Cómo se dice 'boy' en español?
2 (*to repeat*) **repetir**
Say these words after me. Repetid
estas palabras después de mí.

saying noun
el **refrán** *masc.* (plural los **refranes**)

scales noun
la **báscula** *fem.*
I weighed myself on the scales.
Me he pesado en la báscula.

scanner noun
el **escáner** *masc.*

scar noun
la **cicatriz** *fem.* (plural las **cicatrices**)

scared adjective
I'm scared. Tengo miedo.
I'm scared of the dark. Tengo
miedo a la oscuridad.
She's scared of her teacher.
Le tiene miedo a su maestra.
He's scared to go out by himself.
Le da miedo salir solo.

> **LANGUAGE**
> English = I am scared.
> Spanish = Tengo miedo = I have fear

scarf noun
1 (*long and warm*) la **bufanda** *fem.*
a woolly scarf una bufanda de
lana
2 (*thin headscarf*) el **pañuelo** *masc.*
a silk scarf un pañuelo de seda

scary adjective
(*story, monster, etc.*) **que da miedo**
Spiders are very scary. Las arañas
me dan mucho miedo.
a scary film una película de miedo

scenery noun
(*in the countryside*) el **paisaje** *masc.*

school noun
la **escuela** *fem.*
at school en la escuela
to go to school ir a la escuela
a school bus un autobús escolar
the school holidays las vacaciones
escolares
the school year el año escolar
a school uniform un uniforme
escolar

> **LANGUAGE**
> You can also say el colegio, e.g. 'at
> school' is en el colegio.

schoolbag noun
1 (*carried on your back*) la **mochila** *fem.*
2 (*carried in your hand*) la **cartera** *fem.*

schoolbook noun
el **libro de texto** *masc.*

schoolboy noun
el **colegial** *masc.*

schoolchildren noun
los **colegiales** *masc. plural*

schoolgirl noun
la **colegiala** *fem.*

science noun
la **ciencia** *fem.*
I like science. Me gustan las
ciencias.

> **LANGUAGE**
> When science is a school subject, use the
> plural in Spanish.

scientist noun
el **científico** *masc.*, la **científica** *fem.*
She's a scientist. Es científica.

a
b
c
d
e
f
g
h
i
j
k
l
m
n
o
p
q
r
s
t
u
v
w
x
y
z

• *Languages and nationalities do not take a capital letter in Spanish.*

English Spanish

a
b
c
d
e
f
g
h
i
j
k
l
m
n
o
p
q
r
s
t
u
v
w
x
y
z

scissors plural noun
las **tijeras** *fem. plural*
a pair of scissors unas tijeras

scooter noun
1 (*for children*) el **patinete** *masc.*
2 (*motorcycle*) el **scooter** *masc.* (plural los **scooters**)

score noun
(*in sports*) el **resultado** *masc.*
The score was four two. El resultado fue cuatro a dos.
What's the score? ¿Cómo van?

to **score** verb
1 (*in football etc.*) **marcar**
Mohammed has scored a goal. Mohammed ha marcado un gol.
2 (*in a competition etc.*) **sacar**
I've scored ten points. He sacado diez puntos.

Scot noun
el **escocés** *masc.*, la **escocesa** *fem.*

🔑 **LANGUAGE**
The plural of escocés is escoceses.

Scotland noun
Escocia *fem.*
We live in Scotland. Vivimos en Escocia.

Scotsman noun
el **escocés** *masc.* (plural los **escoceses**)

Scotswoman noun
la **escocesa** *fem.*

Scottish adjective
escocés *masc.*, **escocesa** *fem.*
a Scottish footballer un futbolista escocés
She's Scottish. Es escocesa.
Scottish people los escoceses

🔑 **LANGUAGE**
The masculine plural of escocés is escoceses.

Scout noun
el **scout** *masc.*
I'm a Scout. Soy scout.

scrapbook noun
el **álbum de recortes** *masc.*

to **scratch** verb
1 (*an arm, leg, etc. that itches*) **rascarse**
I'm scratching my back. Me rasco la espalda.
2 (*to hurt*) **arañar**
The cat scratched me. El gato me arañó.

to **scream** verb
gritar, **chillar**

screen noun
la **pantalla** *fem.*
on the screen en la pantalla

sea noun
el **mar** *masc.*
at the bottom of the sea en el fondo del mar
to travel by sea viajar en barco

seafood noun
el **marisco** *masc.*

seagull noun
la **gaviota** *fem.*

seal noun
(*animal*) la **foca** *fem.*

to **search** verb
buscar
I'm searching for my glasses. Estoy buscando mis gafas.
I've searched everywhere. He buscado por todas partes.

seashore noun
la **orilla del mar** *fem.*

seashell noun
la **concha** *fem.*

seasick adjective
mareado *masc.*, **mareada** *fem.*
I'm seasick. Estoy mareado.
I get seasick. Me mareo.

• *The months of the year and days of the week do not take a capital letter in Spanish.*

seaside noun
  la **playa** *fem.*
  to go to the seaside ir a la playa

season noun
  1 (*of the year*) la **estación** *fem.* (plural
  las **estaciones**)
  2 (*for sports etc.*) la **temporada** *fem.*
  the football season la temporada
  de fútbol

seat noun
  el **asiento** *masc.*
  the front seat el asiento delantero
  This seat is taken. Este asiento está
  ocupado.
  Save me a seat. Guárdame un
  asiento.

seatbelt noun
  el **cinturón de seguridad** *masc.*
  (plural los **cinturones de seguridad**)

second adjective
  segundo *masc.*, **segunda** *fem.*
  for the second time por segunda vez
  I came second. (*in the race*) Quedé
  segunda.
  I'm the second one. Soy el
  segundo.
  on the second of August el dos de
  agosto

LANGUAGE
With dates you use **dos** (two).

second noun
  el **segundo** *masc.*
  two minutes and ten seconds dos
  minutos y diez segundos

secondary school noun
  el **instituto de enseñanza**
  secundaria *masc.*

secret noun
  el **secreto** *masc.*
  Shall I tell you a secret?
  ¿Te cuento un secreto?

secret adjective
  secreto *masc.*, **secreta** *fem.*
  a secret door una puerta secreta

• *See the centre section for verb tables.*

secretary noun
  el **secretario** *masc.*,
  la **secretaria** *fem.*
  My mum's a secretary. Mi madre
  es secretaria.

section noun
  1 (*in a big store etc.*) la **sección** *fem.*
  the toy section la sección de
  juguetes
  2 (*part of something*) la **parte** *fem.*
  the first section of the book
  la primera parte del libro

to **see** verb
  1 **ver**
  I can see the sea. Veo el mar.
  Have you seen the film? ¿Has visto
  la película?
  I saw her yesterday. La vi ayer.
  2 **See you!** ¡Hasta luego!
  See you soon! ¡Hasta pronto!
  See you on Monday! ¡Hasta el
  lunes!

LANGUAGE
Use **hasta** in Spanish to translate 'See
you ...!'. It means 'until'.

seed noun
  la **semilla** *fem.*

to **seem** verb
  parecer
  It seems a good idea to me.
  Me parece una buena idea.

seesaw noun
  el **balancín** *masc.* (plural los
  balancines)

to **select** verb
  seleccionar

selfish adjective
  egoísta *masc. & fem.*
  He's selfish. Es egoísta.

to **sell** verb
  vender
  They sell bicycles. Venden
  bicicletas.

I've sold my computer to my cousin. He vendido mi ordenador a mi primo.
The tickets are sold out. No hay billetes.

Sellotape® noun
el **celo** *masc.*
Stick down the photo with Sellotape. Pega la foto con celo.

semicircle noun
el **semicírculo** *masc.*
in a semicircle en semicírculo

semifinal noun
la **semifinal** *fem.*

to **send** verb
mandar
Send me a photo. Mándame una foto.
to send something back devolver algo

sense noun
el **sentido** *masc.*
It doesn't make sense. No tiene sentido.
My mum has a sense of humour. Mi madre tiene sentido del humor.

sensible adjective
sensato *masc.*, **sensata** *fem.*
Anne is very sensible. Anne es muy sensata.

⚠ **FALSE FRIEND**
sensible = sensato (*not* sensible)

sensitive adjective
sensible *masc. & fem.*
Chen is very sensitive. Chen es muy sensible.

sentence noun
la **frase** *fem.*, **la oración** *fem.*
(plural las **oraciones**)

separate adjective
1 (*different*) **distinto** *masc.*, **distinta** *fem.*
Put them in separate piles. Ponlos en montones distintos.

2 (*another*) **otro** *masc.*, **otra** *fem.*
It's in a separate building. Está en otro edificio.

to **separate** verb
separar
The teacher separated the two boys. La maestra ha separado a los dos niños.

separated adjective
separado *masc.*, **separada** *fem.*
Her parents are separated. Sus padres están separados.

September noun
septiembre *masc.*
I'm going in September. Voy en septiembre.
It's my birthday on Saturday, the tenth of September. Mi cumpleaños es el sábado diez de septiembre.

series noun
la **serie** *fem.*
a TV series une serie de televisión

serious adjective
1 **serio** *masc.*, **seria** *fem.*
a serious man un hombre serio
I'm serious. Estoy hablando en serio.
2 (*accident, problem, etc.*) **grave** *masc. & fem.*
a serious illness una enfermedad grave
a serious mistake un error grave

seriously adverb
gravemente
to be seriously ill estar gravemente enfermo

to **serve** verb
servir
Can I serve the food? ¿Puedo servir la comida?

serviette noun
la **servilleta** *fem.*

• *Use* **el** *and* **uno** *for masculine words and* **la** *and* **una** *for feminine words.*

set noun
a chess set un ajedrez
a train set un tren de juguete
a TV set una televisión (plural
las **televisiones**)

to **set** verb
1 poner
to set the table poner la mesa
Have you set the alarm? ¿Has
puesto el despertador?
to set fire to something prender
fuego a algo
2 ponerse
The sun is setting. Se está poniendo
el sol.

to **set off** **salir**
We set off for Madrid. Salimos
para Madrid.

to **set out** verb
salir

settee noun
el **sofá** *masc.*

to **settle down** verb
Settle down, boys! ¡Niños!
¡Tranquilos!

seven number
siete
We're going to the library at
seven. Vamos a la biblioteca a las
siete.
I'm seven. Tengo siete años.

> **LANGUAGE**
> In English you can say 'seven o'clock' or
> just 'seven', 'seven years old' or just
> 'seven'. In Spanish you must add **las** (for
> time) and **años** (for age).

seventeen number
diecisiete
My sister is seventeen. Mi
hermana tiene diecisiete años.

seventh adjective
séptimo *masc.*, **séptima** *fem.*
on the seventh floor en el séptimo
piso
the seventh of November el siete
de noviembre

> **LANGUAGE**
> With dates you use **siete** (seven).

seventy number
setenta
My grandmother is seventy.
Mi abuela tiene setenta años.

> **LANGUAGE**
> In English you can say just 'seventy'. In
> Spanish you must add **años**.

several adjective & pronoun
varios *masc. plural*, **varias** *fem. plural*
several times varias veces
several of the books varios libros

to **sew** verb
coser
I like to sew. Me gusta coser.

shade noun
la **sombra** *fem.*
to sit in the shade sentarse a la
sombra

shadow noun
la **sombra** *fem.*

shady adjective
It's shady here. Aquí hay sombra.

to **shake** verb
1 (*a person, tree, towel, etc.*) **sacudir**
He shook the carpet. Sacudió la
alfombra.
2 to shake hands with somebody
dar la mano a alguien
I shake hands with him. Le doy la
mano.
They shake hands. Se dan la mano.
3 (*talking about a building, your hand, etc. that shakes*) **temblar**
You're shaking! ¡Estás temblando!

• *Languages and nationalities do not take a capital letter in Spanish.*

shall verb
> **Shall I close the door?** ¿Cierro la puerta?
> **Shall we go for a walk?** ¿Vamos a dar un paseo?

🔑 **LANGUAGE**
When you ask a question using 'Shall I?', just use the verb in the present tense in Spanish, e.g. 'Shall I close ...?' is ¿Cierro ...? When you ask a question using 'Shall we?', you can often use vamos (= 'let's go').

shallow adjective
> **poco profundo** masc., **poco profunda** fem.

shame noun
> **What a shame!** ¡Qué pena!

shampoo noun
> el **champú** masc.

shape noun
> la **forma** fem.
> **What shape is it?** ¿Qué forma tiene?
> **in the shape of a star** en forma de estrella

to **share** verb
> **compartir**
> **I share the sweets with my friends.** Comparto los caramelos con mis amigas.

shark noun
> el **tiburón** masc. (plural los **tiburones**)

sharp adjective
> **These scissors are very sharp.** Estas tijeras cortan muy bien.
> **This knife isn't sharp.** Este cuchillo no corta.
> **This pencil is sharp.** Este lápiz tiene mucha punta.

🔑 **LANGUAGE**
In Spanish you often use cortar (to cut) to translate sharp.

to **sharpen** verb
> **to sharpen a pencil** sacarle punta a un lápiz

sharpener noun
> el **sacapuntas** masc. (plural los **sacapuntas**)

she pronoun
> 1 (not usually translated in Spanish) **She's tired.** Está cansada.
> **She has lots of books.** Tiene muchos libros.
> 2 **ella**
> **She's tall but her brother is small.** Ella es alta pero su hermano es pequeño.

🔑 **LANGUAGE**
Use ella when you want to give special importance to the word 'she'.

shed noun
> (in the garden) la **caseta** fem.

sheep noun
> la **oveja** fem.

sheet noun
> 1 (on a bed) la **sábana** fem.
> 2 **a sheet of paper** una hoja de papel

shelf noun
> el **estante** masc.

shell noun
> 1 (of an egg or nut) la **cáscara** fem.
> 2 (on the beach, of a snail, etc.) la **concha** fem.

shield noun
> el **escudo** masc.

to **shine** verb
> **brillar**
> **The sun is shining.** Brilla el sol.

shiny adjective
> (metal, hair, etc.) **brillante** masc. & fem.

ship noun
> el **barco** masc.
> **by ship** en barco

• The months of the year and days of the week do not take a capital letter in Spanish.

shirt noun
1 la **camisa** *fem.*
  a clean shirt una camisa limpia
2 (*for football, rugby*) la **camiseta** *fem.*
  a football shirt una camiseta de fútbol

to **shiver** verb
  temblar, **temblar de frío**

shoe noun
  el **zapato** *masc.*
  a pair of shoes un par de zapatos
  a shoe shop una zapatería

shoelace noun
  el **cordón de zapato** *masc.*
  Can you do up your shoelaces?
  ¿Sabes atarte los cordones?

shop noun
  la **tienda** *fem.*
  a clothes shop una tienda de ropa
  a shop assistant un
  dependiente *masc.*, una
  dependienta *fem.*
  a shop window un escaparate

shopkeeper noun
  el or la **comerciante** *masc. & fem.*
  My dad's a shopkeeper. Mi padre
  es comerciante.

shopping noun
  la **compra** *fem.*
  to do the shopping hacer la
  compra, hacer las compras
  to go shopping ir de compras
  a shopping bag una bolsa de la
  compra
  a shopping centre un centro
  comercial
  a shopping list una lista de la
  compra

short adjective
1 (*dress, visit, grass, etc.*) **corto** *masc.*,
  corta *fem.*
  to have short hair tener el pelo corto
  a short time ago hace poco tiempo
  Mike is short for Michael. Mike es
  el diminutivo de Michael.

• *See the centre section for verb tables.*

2 (*person*) **bajo** *masc.*, **baja** *fem.*
  I'm quite short. Soy bastante bajo.

short cut noun
  el **atajo** *masc.*

shorts plural noun
  los **shorts** *masc. plural*
  I'm wearing blue shorts. Llevo
  unos shorts azules.
  a pair of shorts unos shorts

short-sighted adjective
  miope *masc. & fem.*
  I'm short-sighted. Soy miope.

should verb
  deber
  You should go. Deberías ir.

shoulder noun
  el **hombro** *masc.*

to **shout** verb
  gritar
  Stop shouting! ¡Deja de gritar!
  Don't shout! ¡No grites!

to **show** verb
  enseñar
  Show me the dress. Enséñame el
  vestido.
  Show me how to do it Enséñame
  cómo se hace

show noun
1 (*with actors, musicians, etc.*)
  el **espectáculo** *masc.*
  a children's show un espectáculo
  para niños
2 (*on TV*) el **programa** *masc.*
  a quiz show un programa concurso

🔑 **LANGUAGE**
Be careful: **programa** ends in an **-a** but it
is not a feminine noun.

shower noun
1 la **ducha** *fem.*
  I want to have a shower. Quiero
  ducharme.
  I'm in the shower. Me estoy
  duchando.

a b c d e f g h i j k l m n o p q r s t u v w x y z

2 (*rain*) el **chaparrón** *masc.* (plural los **chaparrones**)
It's only a shower. Sólo es un chaparrón.

Shrove Tuesday noun
el **martes de Carnaval** *masc.*

 CULTURE
This is the last day before Christian Lent and in Spain children celebrate by dressing up, dancing, and playing music.

to **shut** verb
cerrar
Shut your eyes. Cierra los ojos.
The museum shuts at six. El museo cierra a las seis.

shut adjective
cerrado *masc.*, **cerrada** *fem.*
The door's shut. La puerta está cerrada.

to **shut up** verb
callarse
Shut up! ¡Cállate!

shuttle noun
the space shuttle el transbordador espacial

shy adjective
tímido *masc.*, **tímida** *fem.*

sick adjective
1 (*ill*) **enfermo** *masc.*, **enferma** *fem.*
I'm sick. Estoy enferma.
2 to feel sick tener ganas de devolver
I'm going to be sick. Voy a devolver.

side noun
1 el **lado** *masc.*
on this side of the road a este lado de la calle
on the other side al otro lado
2 (*edge*) el **borde** *masc.*
by the side of the road al borde de la carretera
3 (*team*) el **equipo** *masc.*
He's on our side. Está en nuestro equipo.

sightseeing noun
el **turismo** *masc.*
to go sightseeing hacer turismo

sign noun
1 (*on a door, wall, etc.*) el **letrero** *masc.*
2 (*on a road*) la **señal** *fem.*
a road sign una señal de tráfico
The policeman made a sign. El guardia hizo una señal.

to **sign** verb
firmar
Your parents sign here. Tus padres firman aquí.

signal noun
la **señal** *fem.*

signature noun
la **firma** *fem.*

sign language noun
el **lenguaje de signos** *masc.*
to talk in sign language hablar por señas

Sikh adjective
sij *masc. & fem.*

silence noun
el **silencio** *masc.*

silent adjective
silencioso *masc.*, **silenciosa** *fem.*

silk noun
la **seda** *fem.*
a silk blouse una blusa de seda

silly adjective
tonto *masc.*, **tonta** *fem.*
You're so silly! ¡Tú eres tonto!

silver noun
la **plata** *fem.*
a silver bracelet una pulsera de plata

similar adjective
parecido *masc.*, **parecida** *fem.*
Your bike is similar to mine. Tu bici es parecida a la mía.

• *Use **el** and **uno** for masculine words and **la** and **una** for feminine words.*

simple adjective
1 (*dress, problem, etc.*) **sencillo** *masc.*, **sencilla** *fem.*
2 (*easy*) **fácil**

since preposition & adverb
desde
I haven't seen her since Sunday. No la he visto desde el domingo.
since then, ever since desde entonces
I've been waiting since three o'clock. Estoy esperando desde las tres.

> 🔑 **LANGUAGE**
> For showing something still going on, use the present tense in Spanish, not the past.

to **sing** verb
cantar
I like to sing. Me gusta cantar.
singing lessons clases de canto

singer noun
el or la **cantante** *masc. & fem.*

single adjective
1 **solo** *masc.*, **sola** *fem.*
He hasn't got a single friend. No tiene ni un solo amigo.
2 (*bed, portion, etc.*) **individual** *masc. & fem.*
a single room una habitación individual
3 in single file en fila india
a single ticket un billete de ida

single noun
(*ticket*) el **billete de ida** *masc.*
a single to Cambridge un billete de ida para Cambridge

singular noun
el **singular** *masc.*
'Mouse' is in the singular. 'Mouse' está en singular.

sink noun
1 (*in the kitchen*) el **fregadero** *masc.*
2 (*in the bathroom*) el **lavabo** *masc.*

to **sink** verb
hundirse
The boat sank. El barco se hundió.

sir noun
(*talking about your teacher etc.*) **señor** *masc.*
Please, sir! ¡Por favor, señor!
Yes, sir. Sí, señor.

sister noun
la **hermana** *fem.*
my big sister mi hermana mayor

to **sit** verb
1 **sentarse**
Sit next to your sister. Siéntate al lado de tu hermana.
2 to be sitting estar sentado *masc.*, estar sentada *fem.*
She's sitting on the sofa. Está sentada en el sofá.

to **sit down** verb
sentarse
I sat down on the floor. Me senté en el suelo.
Sit down, Dylan. Siéntate, Dylan.
Sit down, children. Niños, sentaos.

site noun
1 (*website*) el **sitio web** *masc.*
I like this site. Me gusta este sitio.
2 a camping site un camping (plural los **campings**)

sitting room noun
el **salón** *masc.* (plural los **salones**)

situation noun
la **situación** *fem.* (plural las **situaciones**)

six number
seis
I went out at six. Salí a las seis.
I'm six. Tengo seis años.

> 🔑 **LANGUAGE**
> In English you can say 'six o'clock' or just 'six', 'six years old' or just 'six'. In Spanish you must add **las** (for time) and **años** (for age).

• *Languages and nationalities do not take a capital letter in Spanish.*

a
b
c
d
e
f
g
h
i
j
k
l
m
n
o
p
q
r
s
t
u
v
w
x
y
z

a
b
c
d
e
f
g
h
i
j
k
l
m
n
o
p
q
r
s
t
u
v
w
x
y
z

sixteen number
dieciséis
My cousin is sixteen. Mi prima tiene dieciséis años.

sixth adjective
sexto *masc.*, **sexta** *fem.*
on the sixth floor en el sexto piso
the sixth of March el seis de marzo

> 🔑 **LANGUAGE**
> With dates you use seis (six).

sixty number
sesenta
My uncle is sixty. Mi tío tiene sesenta años.

> 🔑 **LANGUAGE**
> In English you can say just 'sixty'. In Spanish you must add años.

size noun
1 el **tamaño** *masc.*
What size is it? ¿De qué tamaño es?
2 (*of clothes*) la **talla** *fem.*
What size do you take? ¿Qué talla usas?
3 (*of shoes*) el **número** *masc.*
What size do you take? ¿Qué número usas?

to **skate** verb
(*on ice*) **patinar**

skateboard noun
el **monopatín** *masc.* (plural los **monopatines**)

skateboarding noun
to go skateboarding montar en monopatín

skating noun
(*on ice*) el **patinaje sobre hielo** *masc.*
to go skating ir a patinar
a skating rink una pista de hielo

skeleton noun
el **esqueleto** *masc.*

ski noun
el **esquí** *masc.*
a pair of skis un par de esquís

ski boots las botas de esquí
a ski slope una pista de esquí

to **ski** verb
esquiar

skiing noun
el **esquí** *masc.*
I like skiing. Me gusta el esquí.
to go skiing ir a esquiar

skin noun
la **piel** *fem.*

to **skip** verb
(*with a rope*) **saltar a la cuerda**, **jugar a la comba**
a skipping rope una cuerda, una comba

skirt noun
la **falda** *fem.*

sky noun
el **cielo** *masc.*

skyscraper noun
el **rascacielos** *masc.* (plural los **rascacielos**)

to **slam** verb
to slam the door dar un portazo

> 🔑 **LANGUAGE**
> Word for word the Spanish means 'to give a bang with the door' (puerta is 'door').

sledge noun
el **trineo** *masc.*

to **sleep** verb
dormir
He's sleeping. Está durmiendo.
a sleeping bag un saco de dormir

> 🔑 **LANGUAGE**
> The verb dormir is related to the English word 'dormitory' (a room where lots of people sleep).

sleep noun
el **sueño** *masc.*
eight hours' sleep ocho horas de sueño
to go to sleep dormirse
Go to sleep! ¡Duérmete!

• The months of the year and days of the week do not take a capital letter in Spanish.

sleepover noun
I went for a sleepover at Jessica's.
Me quedé a dormir en casa de
Jessica.

sleepy adjective
to be sleepy tener sueño

sleeve noun
la **manga** *fem.*
a shirt with short sleeves una
camisa de manga corta

slice noun
1 la **rebanada** *fem.*
a slice of bread una rebanada de
pan
2 (*of cake, cheese*) el **trozo** *masc.*

to slide verb
deslizarse
They're sliding down the slide.
Se deslizan por el tobogán.

slide noun
(*in a playground*) el **tobogán** *masc.*
(plural los **toboganes**)

slight adjective
1 (*pain, accent, taste*) **ligero** *masc.*,
ligera *fem.*
2 (*problem, change, chance*)
pequeño *masc.*, **pequeña** *fem.*

slightly adverb
un poco
slightly bigger un poco más
grande

slim adjective
delgado *masc.*, **delgada** *fem.*

to slip verb
resbalarse
I slipped on the floor. Me resbalé
en el suelo.

• *See the centre section for verb tables.*

slipper noun
la **zapatilla** *fem.*
a pair of slippers un par de
zapatillas

slippery adjective
to be slippery resbalar
This floor's slippery. Este suelo
resbala.

slope noun
la **cuesta** *fem.*

slow adjective
lento *masc.*, **lenta** *fem.*

slowly adverb
despacio
Speak more slowly. Habla más
despacio.

smack noun
1 (*on the backside*) el **azote** *masc.*
2 (*on the face*) la **bofetada** *fem.*

small adjective
pequeño *masc.*, **pequeña** *fem.*
You're smaller than me. Eres más
pequeña que yo.

smart adjective
1 (*clothes, shop, etc.*) **elegante** *masc. &
fem.*
You're very smart today. Estás
muy elegante hoy.
2 (*clever*) **listo** *masc.*, **lista** *fem.*
She's a very smart girl. Es una
chica muy lista.

to smash verb
romper

smell noun
el **olor** *masc.*
a nasty smell un mal olor

a b c d e f g h i j k l m n o p q r s t u v w x y z

to **smell** verb
  1 oler
    I can't smell anything. No huelo nada.
    I can smell fish. Huele a pescado.
    It smells lovely! ¡Qué bien huele!
    It smells bad here. Aquí huele mal.
  2 to smell of something oler a algo
    It smells of fish. Huele a pescado.

> 🔑 **LANGUAGE**
> The Spanish for 'I can smell fish' is, word for word, 'It smells of fish'.

smelly adjective
  Your socks are smelly. Tus calcetines huelen mal.

to **smile** verb
  sonreír
    He smiled at me. Me sonrió.

smile noun
  la **sonrisa** fem.

smoke noun
  el **humo** masc.

to **smoke** verb
  fumar
    My parents don't smoke. Mis padres no fuman.
    'No smoking.' 'Prohibido fumar.'

smooth adjective
  liso masc., **lisa** fem., **suave** masc. & fem.

snack noun
  to have a snack comer algo
  a snack bar una cafetería fem.

> 🌍 **CULTURE**
> Spanish people sometimes have a snack in mid-morning (el almuerzo) or late afternoon (la merienda).

snail noun
  el **caracol** masc.

snake noun
  la **serpiente** fem.

to **sneeze** verb
  estornudar

> 🌍 **CULTURE**
> In Spain people say ¡Jesús! (Jesus) when somebody sneezes.

to **snore** verb
  roncar

snow noun
  la **nieve** fem.

to **snow** verb
  nevar
    It's snowing. Está nevando.

snowball noun
  la **bola de nieve** fem.

snowflakes plural noun
  los **copos de nieve** masc. plural

snowman noun
  el **muñeco de nieve** masc.

so conjunction
  (giving a reason) **así que**
    I'm ill, so I can't come. Estoy enfermo, así que no puedo venir.

so adverb
  1 (so very much) **tan**
    I'm so tired! ¡Estoy tan cansado!
  2 (also) **también**
    Miguel is Spanish and so am I. Miguel es español y yo también.
    I like football and so does she. A mí me gusta el fútbol y a ella también.

> 🔑 **LANGUAGE**
> Word for word yo también means 'me too' and ella también means 'she too'. To translate words like 'so am I', 'so does she', use también with the correct pronoun.

  3 (after 'think', 'hope', etc.)
    I think so. Creo que sí.
  4 so much (with nouns) tanto masc., tanta fem.
    He has so much money. Tiene tanto dinero.

• Use **el** and **uno** for masculine words and **la** and **una** for feminine words.

5 so much (*with verbs*) **tanto**
I like it so much. Me gusta tanto.

6 so many tantos *masc. plural*,
tantas *fem. plural*
I have so many friends. Tengo
tantas amigas.

soaking wet adjective
empapado *masc.*, **empapada** *fem.*

soap noun
1 el **jabón** *masc.*
    a bar of soap una pastilla de jabón
2 (*TV programme*) la **telenovela** *fem.*

soccer noun
    el **fútbol** *masc.*
    to play soccer jugar al fútbol

sock noun
    el **calcetín** *masc.* (plural los
    calcetines)

sofa noun
    el **sofá** *masc.*

soft adjective
1 (*cushion, butter, bed, etc.*) **blando** *masc.*,
    blanda *fem.*
    a soft mattress un colchón blando
2 (*cloth, music, voice, etc.*) **suave** *masc. &*
    fem.
    soft skin la piel suave
3 **a soft drink** un refresco *masc.*

software noun
    el **software** *masc.*

solar adjective
    solar *masc. & fem.*
    the solar system el sistema solar

sold verb SEE **sell**
    I've sold my bike. He vendido mi
    bici.

soldier noun
    el or la **soldado** *masc. & fem.*
    He's a soldier. Es soldado.

solicitor noun
    el **abogado** *masc.*, la **abogada** *fem.*
    My mum's a solicitor. Mi madre es
    abogada.

to **solve** verb
    resolver

some adjective & pronoun
1 (*usually not translated*)
    I'm eating some fish. Estoy
    comiendo pescado.
    I've bought some sweets. He
    comprado caramelos.
    **Do you want some water? – No, I
    have some.** ¿Quieres agua? – No,
    ya tengo.
    I've eaten some of it. He comido un
    poco.
2 (*compared to others*) **algunos** *masc.*
    plural, **algunas** *fem. plural*
    Some books are very expensive.
    Algunos libros son muy caros.
    I like some of my teachers. Me
    gustan algunos de mis maestros.
    Some of them have come. Han
    venido algunos.

somebody pronoun
    alguien
    There's somebody at the door.
    Hay alguien en la puerta.
    somebody else otra persona

someone pronoun SEE **somebody**

something pronoun
    algo
    I've eaten something. He comido
    algo.
    something else otra cosa

sometimes adverb
    a veces

somewhere adverb
    en or **a alguna parte**
    to be somewhere estar en alguna
    parte
    to go somewhere ir a alguna parte
    somewhere else en otra parte
    I want to go somewhere else.
    Quiero ir a otra parte.

🔑 **LANGUAGE**
When 'somewhere' means 'in' a place use
en with **parte** and when it means 'to' use
a instead.

• *Languages and nationalities do not take a capital letter in Spanish.*

son noun
el **hijo** masc.

song noun
la **canción** fem. (plural las **canciones**)
to sing a song cantar una canción

soon adverb
pronto
See you soon! ¡Hasta pronto!
as soon as possible lo más pronto posible
soon after poco después

sore adjective
I have a sore throat. Me duele la garganta.
It's sore. Me duele.

🔑 **LANGUAGE**
Word for word me duele means 'It hurts me'.

sorry adjective
1 I'm sorry. Lo siento.
I'm very sorry, I can't come. Lo siento mucho, no puedo venir.
2 (meaning 'excuse me!' when being polite or not hearing)
Sorry! Did I hurt you? ¡Perdón! ¿Te he hecho daño?
Sorry, what did you say? ¿Perdón, cómo has dicho?

sort noun
1 el **tipo** masc.
What sort of book is it? ¿Qué tipo de libro es?
2 a sort of una especie de
It's a sort of hat. Es una especie de sombrero.

to **sort out** verb
(to fix or to tidy) **arreglar**
to sort out a problem arreglar un problema
Sort out your room! ¡Arregla tu habitación!
Sort out your toys! ¡Guarda los juguetes!

sound noun
1 (noise) el **ruido** masc.
the sound of traffic el ruido del tráfico
2 (from the TV, music, etc.) el **sonido** masc.
the sound of a guitar el sonido de una guitarra
3 (volume) el **volumen** masc.
Turn down the sound. Baja el volumen.

to **sound** verb
1 (to seem) **parecer**
That sounds a good idea to me. Me parece una buena idea.
It sounds good. Me parece bien.
2 (to make a sound) **sonar**
His name sounds French. Su nombre suena francés.

soup noun
la **sopa** fem.
vegetable soup la sopa de verduras

sour adjective
agrio masc., **agria** fem.

south noun & adjective
1 el **sur** masc.
in the south en el sur
the south coast la costa sur
2 South Africa Sudáfrica fem.
the South Pole el Polo Sur

South America noun
Sudamérica fem.

South American adjective
sudamericano masc., **sudamericana** fem.

South American noun
el **sudamericano** masc., la **sudamericana** fem.

souvenir noun
el **recuerdo** masc.
a souvenir shop una tienda de recuerdos

• The months of the year and days of the week do not take a capital letter in Spanish.

space noun
el **espacio** *masc.*
Leave a space. Deja un espacio.
There's enough space. Hay
suficiente espacio.
a journey into space un viaje en el
espacio

spaceship noun
la **nave espacial** *fem.*

spade noun
la **pala** *fem.*
a bucket and spade un cubo y una
pala

spaghetti noun
los **espaguetis** *masc. plural*
I like spaghetti. Me gustan los
espaguetis.

🔑 **LANGUAGE**
English = spaghetti is singular
Spanish = los espaguetis is plural

Spain noun
España *fem.*
They live in Spain. Viven en
España.
I'm going to Spain. Voy a España.

Spaniard noun
el **español** *masc.,* la **española** *fem.*

Spanish adjective
español *masc.,* **española** *fem.*
Spanish cooking la comida
española
He's Spanish. Es español.
my Spanish lesson mi clase de
español
Spanish people los españoles

Spanish noun
1 (*language*) el **español** *masc.*
I speak Spanish. Hablo español.
2 the Spanish los españoles *masc.*
plural

spare adjective
1 a spare room un cuarto de
invitados
spare time el tiempo libre

2 (*extra*) **de más**
Do you have a spare ticket?
¿Tienes una entrada de más?

to **speak** verb
hablar
I speak Spanish. Hablo español.
'English spoken.' 'Se habla inglés.'
to speak to somebody hablar con
alguien
to speak about something hablar
de algo

speaker noun
(*for sound and music*) el **altavoz** *masc.*
(plural los **altavoces**)

special adjective
especial *masc. & fem.*

specially adverb
especialmente

speech noun
el **discurso** *masc.*
to make a speech dar un discurso
the parts of speech las partes de la
oración

speed noun
la **velocidad** *fem.*
What speed are you doing? ¿A qué
velocidad vas?

to **speed up** verb
ir más rápido

to **spell** verb
1 (*to write*) **escribir**
You've spelled my name wrong.
Has escrito mal mi nombre.
How do you spell 'enough'?
¿Cómo se escribe 'enough'?
2 (*to say out loud*) **deletrear**
Can you spell it? ¿Me lo deletreas?

spell noun
a magic spell un hechizo

spelling noun
la **ortografía** *fem.*
a spelling mistake una falta de
ortografía

• See the centre section for verb tables.

a
b
c
d
e
f
g
h
i
j
k
l
m
n
o
p
q
r
s
t
u
v
w
x
y
z

to **spend** verb
1 (*money*) **gastar**
   How much have you spent?
   ¿Cuánto has gastado?
2 (*time*) **pasar**
   I spent two weeks in Valencia.
   Pasé dos semanas en Valencia.

spicy adjective
(*curry, sauce, etc.*) **picante** *masc. & fem.*

spider noun
la **araña** *fem.*

to **spill** verb
tirar
I've spilled water on the floor. He tirado agua en el suelo.

spinach noun
las **espinacas** *fem.plural*

🔑 **LANGUAGE**
English = spinach is singular
French = las espinacas is plural

to **spit** verb
escupir

spite noun
in spite of a pesar de

to **split** verb
dividir
They've split us into two groups. Nos han dividido en dos grupos.

to **spoil** verb
1 (*plans, holidays, shirt, etc.*) **estropear**
2 (*a child*) **mimar**
   spoilt children niños mimados

spoilsport noun
el or la **aguafiestas** *masc. & fem.*
(plural los or las **aguafiestas**)

sponge noun
la **esponja** *fem.*

spooky adjective
(*place, house, etc.*) **que da miedo**
It's spooky here! ¡Da miedo estar aquí!

spoon noun
la **cuchara** *fem.*

sport noun
1 el **deporte** *masc.*
   I play a lot of sport. Hago mucho deporte.
2 a sports bag una bolsa de deporte
   a sports car un coche deportivo
   a sports centre un polideportivo
   a sports club un club deportivo
   sports day el día de competiciones deportivas
   a sports ground un campo de deportes

sportsman, sportswoman noun
el **deportista** *masc.*;
la **deportista** *fem.*

sporty adjective
deportista *masc. & fem.*

spot noun
1 (*pimple*) el **grano** *masc.*
   I'm full of spots. Estoy lleno de granos.
2 (*dot*) **el lunar** *masc.*
   a green blouse with black spots una blusa verde con lunares negros
3 (*place*) **el sitio** *masc.*
   a quiet spot un sitio tranquilo

to **spot** verb
1 (*to find*) **encontrar**
2 (*to see*) **ver**

to **sprain** verb
I've sprained my ankle. Tengo un esguince en el tobillo.

to **spread** verb
(*butter, glue, a towel, etc.*) **extender**

spring noun
la **primavera** *fem.*
in the spring en primavera

sprouts plural noun
las **coles de Bruselas** *fem. plural*

spy noun
1 el or la **espía** *masc. & fem.*
2 I spy el veo veo *masc.*
   to play I spy jugar al veo veo

• *Use* **el** *and* **uno** *for masculine words and* **la** *and* **una** *for feminine words.*

square adjective
cuadrado *masc.*, **cuadrada** *fem.*
a square room una habitación
cuadrada

square noun
1 (*shape*) el **cuadrado** *masc.*
2 (*in a town or village*) la **plaza** *fem.*
the village square la plaza del
pueblo
3 (*in crosswords etc.*) la **casilla** *fem.*

squash noun
1 (*sport*) el **squash** *masc.*
to play squash jugar al squash
2 (*drink*)
an orange squash una naranjada
fem.

squirrel noun
la **ardilla** *fem.*

stable noun
la **cuadra** *fem.*

stack noun
el **montón** *masc.* (plural los
montones)
a stack of books un montón de
libros

stadium noun
el **estadio** *masc.*

staff room noun
la **sala de profesores** *fem.*

stain noun
la **mancha** *fem.*

staircase noun
la **escalera** *fem.*

stairs plural noun
las **escaleras** *fem. plural*,
la **escalera** *fem.*
I went down the stairs. Bajé las
escaleras., Bajé la escalera.

stamp noun
el **sello** *masc.*
a stamp album un álbum de sellos
a stamp collection una colección
de sellos

to **stamp** verb
to stamp your foot dar una patada
en el suelo

to **stand** verb
1 **estar de pie**, **estar**
**I'm sitting but my sister's
standing.** Estoy sentada pero mi
hermana está de pie.
I'm standing outside the school.
Estoy delante del colegio.
2 (*to get up*) **levantarse**
Stand up! ¡Levántate!
3 (*to go and stand somewhere*) **ponerse**
Stand by the board, Amy. Ponte
delante de la pizarra, Amy.
Go and stand in line. Poneos en fila.
4 (*to hate something*) **soportar**
I can't stand that music. No
soporto esta música.

to **stand for** verb
significar
What does 'PE' stand for? ¿Qué
significa 'PE'?

staple noun
la **grapa** *fem.*

stapler noun
la **grapadora** *fem.*

star noun
(*in the sky, shape, person*) la **estrella** *fem.*
a film star una estrella de cine

start noun
1 el **principio** *masc.*
at the start of the film al principio
de la película
at the start of the year a principios
del año
2 (*of a race*) **la salida** *fem.*

to **start** verb
1 **empezar**
Shall we start? ¿Empezamos?
The holidays start tomorrow.
Las vacaciones empiezan
mañana.
I've started to learn Spanish.
He empezado a aprender español.

• *Languages and nationalities do not take a capital letter in Spanish.*

a
b
c
d
e
f
g
h
i
j
k
l
m
n
o
p
q
r
s
t
u
v
w
x
y
z

English Spanish

a
b
c
d
e
f
g
h
i
j
k
l
m
n
o
p
q
r
s
t
u
v
w
x
y
z

2 (*talking about a car*) **arrancar**
The car won't start. El coche no
arranca.
3 (*a group, club, etc.*) **formar**

to **starve** verb
I'm starving! ¡Me muero de
hambre!

🔑 **LANGUAGE**
Word for word the Spanish means 'I'm
dying of hunger'.

States plural noun
the States Estados Unidos *masc.*
They live in the States. Viven en
Estados Unidos.

station noun
1 (*for trains etc.*) la **estación** *fem.* (plural
las **estaciones**)
at the station en la estación
a tube station una estación de
metro
a bus station una estación de
autobuses
2 a radio station una emisora *fem.*
a police station una comisaría *fem.*

stationery noun
(*paper*) el **papel** *masc.*

statue noun
la **estatua** *fem.*

stay noun
la **estancia** *fem.*
my stay in Madrid mi estancia en
Madrid

to **stay** verb
1 **quedarse**
Stay five more minutes. Quédate
cinco minutos más.
I stayed with my brother.
Me quedé en casa de mi
hermano.
Stay still. (*don't move*) No te
muevas.
2 (*in a hotel etc.*) **alojarse**
We stayed in a hotel. Nos
alojamos en un hotel.

3 (*to spend time*) **pasar**
We're going to stay a week in
Toledo. Vamos a pasar una
semana en Toledo.

to **stay in** verb
(*in the house*) **quedarse en casa**

to **stay up** verb
(*not to go to bed*) **no acostarse**
I want to stay up late. Quiero
acostarme tarde.

steak noun
el **bistec** *masc.*
steak and chips el bistec con
patatas fritas

to **steal** verb
robar
He stole a bike. Robó una bici.

steam noun
el **vapor** *masc.*

steep adjective
(*slope, stairs, etc.*) **empinado** *masc.*,
empinada *fem.*
This hill is steep. Esta cuesta es
empinada.

steering wheel noun
el **volante** *masc.*

step noun
1 (*with your foot*) el **paso** *masc.*
Take two steps forward. Da dos
pasos hacia adelante.
2 (*of stairs*) el **escalón** *masc.* (plural los
escalones)
Mind the step! ¡Cuidado con el
escalón!

stepbrother noun
el **hermanastro** *masc.*

stepdaughter noun
la **hijastra** *fem.*

stepfather noun
el **padrastro** *masc.*

stepmother noun
la **madrastra** *fem.*

• *The months of the year and days of the week do not take a capital letter in Spanish.*

396

stepsister noun
la **hermanastra** *fem.*

stepson noun
el **hijastro** *masc.*

stereo noun
el **equipo de música** *masc.*

stew noun
el **estofado** *masc.*

stick noun
1 (*for hitting etc.*) el **palo** *masc.*
2 (*walking stick*) el **bastón** *masc.* (plural los **bastones**)

to **stick** verb
(*with glue etc.*) **pegar**
Stick the stamps on the envelope. Pega los sellos en el sobre.

to **stick out** verb
to stick out your tongue sacar la lengua

sticker noun
la **pegatina** *fem.*

sticky adjective
1 (*dirty*) **pegajoso** *masc.*, **pegajosa** *fem.*
My hands are sticky. Tengo las manos pegajosas.
2 (*paper, label, etc.*) **adhesivo** *masc.*, **adhesiva** *fem.*
sticky tape la cinta adhesiva

stiff adjective
(*leg, arm, etc.*) **agarrotado** *masc.*, **agarrotada** *fem.*
I'm stiff. (*after doing sport*) Tengo agujetas.

still adverb
todavía
She's still eating. Todavía está comiendo.
That's better still. Es todavía mejor.

still adjective
quieto *masc.*, **quieta** *fem.*
Keep still!, Sit still! ¡Estate quieto!

• *See the centre section for verb tables.*

to **sting** verb
picar
I've been stung by a wasp. Me ha picado una avispa.

sting noun
la **picadura** *fem.*
a wasp sting una picadura de avispa

to **stink** verb
apestar
It stinks of fish. Apesta a pescado.

stink noun
el **mal olor** *masc.*
What a stink! ¡Qué mal olor!

stitch noun
el **punto** *masc.*
I had three stitches. Me dieron tres puntos.

stomach noun
el **estómago** *masc.*

stomach ache noun
I have a stomach ache. Me duele el estómago.

> 🔑 **LANGUAGE**
> Word for word the Spanish means 'my stomach hurts'.

stone noun
1 la **piedra** *fem.*
He's throwing stones at me. Me está tirando piedras.
2 (*when weighing people*)
I weigh four stone. Peso unos veinticinco kilos.

> 🌏 **CULTURE**
> In Spain they use kilos for weighing. A stone is about 6.3 kilos.

stool noun
el **taburete** *masc.*

stop noun
la **parada** *fem.*
a bus stop una parada de autobús

stop verb
1 **parar**
I stopped in front of the school.
Paré delante del colegio.
The bus stops here. El autobús
para aquí.
It's stopped raining. Ha parado de
llover.
2 (to stop working) **pararse**
The clock has stopped. Se ha
parado el reloj.
3 to stop something parar algo
Stop the car. Para el coche.
Stop it! ¡Basta!, ¡Para!
4 to stop doing something dejar de
hacer algo
Stop annoying your sister. Deja de
molestar a tu hermana.

store noun
(big shop) la **tienda** fem.
a department store unos grandes
almacenes

🔑 **LANGUAGE**
English = a department store is singular
Spanish = unos grandes almacenes is
plural

storey noun
el **piso** masc., la **planta** fem.
a five-storey building un edificio
de cinco pisos, un edificio de cinco
plantas

storm noun
la **tormenta** fem.

stormy adjective
It's stormy. Hay tormenta.

story noun
1 la **historia** fem.
a true story una historia verdadera

🔑 **LANGUAGE**
In Spanish historia also means 'history'.

2 (for children) el **cuento** masc.
Tell me a story. Cuéntame un
cuento.

straight adjective
1 (road, nose, etc.) **recto** masc., **recta**
fem.
a straight line una línea recta
2 (talking about pictures, hats, etc.)
derecho masc., **derecha** fem.
The picture isn't straight.
El cuadro no está derecho.
3 to have straight hair tener el pelo
liso

straight adverb
1 (without stopping) **directamente**
I went straight to school. Fui
directamente al colegio.
2 (immediately) **enseguida**
I'm coming straight back. Vuelvo
en seguida.
straight away en seguida
3 Go straight ahead. Sigue todo
recto.

strange adjective
raro masc., **rara** fem.

🔑 **LANGUAGE**
You can also say extraño/extraña in
Spanish.

stranger noun
el **desconocido** masc.,
la **desconocida** fem.
Don't talk to strangers. No hables
con desconocidos.

strap noun
1 (on a watch, handbag, etc.) la **correa** fem.
2 (on a dress, swimsuit, etc.) el **tirante**
masc.

straw noun
1 la **paja** fem.
a straw hat un sombrero de paja
2 (for drinking) la **pajita** fem.
to drink with a straw beber con
una pajita

strawberry noun
la **fresa** fem.
strawberry jam la mermelada de
fresa

• Use **el** and **uno** for masculine words and **la** and **una** for feminine words.

stream noun
el **arroyo** *masc.*

street noun
la **calle** *fem.*
in the street en la calle

strength noun
la **fuerza** *fem.*

to **stretch** verb
1 (*after waking up etc.*) **estirarse**
I stretched. Me estiré.
2 (*arm, hand*) **extender**
She stretched out her hand.
Extendió la mano.

strict adjective
estricto *masc.*, **estricta** *fem.*

string noun
(*for tying things, and for a guitar etc.*)
la **cuerda** *fem.*

stripe noun
la **raya** *fem.*
a skirt with green stripes una
falda con rayas verdes

striped adjective
de rayas
a striped shirt una camisa de rayas

to **stroke** verb
(*a cat, dog, etc.*) **acariciar**

strong adjective
fuerte *masc. & fem.*
My brother is very strong. Mi
hermano es muy fuerte.

stubborn adjective
terco *masc.*, **terca** *fem.*

stuck adjective
(*drawer, window, etc.*) **atascado** *masc.*,
atascada *fem.*

student noun
el or la **estudiante** *masc. & fem.*
My sister's a student. Mi hermana
es estudiante.

to **study** verb
estudiar
My cousin is studying Spanish.
Mi primo estudia español.

stuff noun
1 (*things*) las **cosas** *fem. plural*
I've left my stuff on the floor.
He dejado mis cosas en el suelo.
2 (*thing*) la **cosa** *fem.*
What's this green stuff called?
¿Cómo se llama esta cosa verde?

stupid adjective
tonto *masc.*, **tonta** *fem.*
to do something stupid hacer una
tontería

> **LANGUAGE**
> You can also say estúpido/estúpida but
> it is much stronger than 'stupid' in English.

subject noun
1 (*in school*) la **asignatura** *fem.*
My favourite subject is Spanish. Mi
asignatura favorita es el español.
2 (*of a book etc.*) el **tema** *masc.*

> **LANGUAGE**
> Be careful: tema ends in an -a but it is not
> a feminine noun.

submarine noun
el **submarino** *masc.*

subtitles plural noun
los **subtítulos** *masc. plural*

to **subtract** verb
restar
Subtract five from ten. Resta cinco
de diez.

suburbs plural noun
las **afueras** *fem. plural*
I live in the suburbs. Vivo en las
afueras.

subway noun
el **paso subterráneo** *masc.*

success noun
el **éxito** *masc.*
a great success un gran éxito

• *Languages and nationalities do not take a capital letter in Spanish.*

a
b
c
d
e
f
g
h
i
j
k
l
m
n
o
p
q
r
s
t
u
v
w
x
y
z

successful adjective
to be successful tener éxito
The book is very successful. El libro tiene mucho éxito.

such adverb & adjective
1 **tan**
She's such a pretty girl! ¡Es una niña tan guapa!
They're such pretty girls! ¡Son niñas tan guapas!
2 **such a lot** (*with nouns*) tanto *masc.*, tanta *fem.*
such a lot of money tanto dinero
3 **such a lot** (*with verbs*) tanto
I have to study such a lot. Tengo que estudiar tanto.
4 **such as** como
sports such as football deportes como el fútbol

sudden noun
all of a sudden de repente

suddenly adverb
de repente

to **suffer** verb
sufrir

sugar noun
el **azúcar** *masc.*
I don't take sugar. No tomo azúcar.

suggestion noun
la **sugerencia** *fem.*

suit noun
1 (*for a man*) el **traje** *masc.*
2 (*for a woman*) el **traje de chaqueta** *masc.*

to **suit** verb
(*when talking about clothes etc.*)
to suit somebody quedar bien a alguien
Green suits you. El verde te queda bien.

suitcase noun
la **maleta** *fem.*

sum noun
la **suma** *fem.*
to do sums hacer sumas
I'm good at sums. Soy bueno en aritmética.

summer noun
el **verano** *masc.*
in the summer en verano
the summer holidays las vacaciones de verano

sun noun
el **sol** *masc.*
in the sun al sol
The sun's out. Hace sol.

to **sunbathe** verb
tomar el sol

sunburnt adjective
quemado por el sol *masc.*,
quemada por el sol *fem.*
I don't want to get sunburnt. No quiero quemarme con el sol.

Sunday noun
el **domingo** *masc.*
Today is Sunday. Hoy es domingo.
on Sunday el domingo
I come back on Sunday. Vuelvo el domingo.
on Sundays los domingos
I play football on Sundays. Juego al fútbol los domingos.

> **LANGUAGE**
> Remember the difference in Spanish between el domingo (one Sunday only) and los domingos (every Sunday).

sunflower noun
el **girasol** *masc.*

sunglasses plural noun
las **gafas de sol** *fem. plural*

sunny adjective
(*room, beach, etc.*) **soleado** *masc.*,
soleada *fem.*
a sunny day un día de sol
It's sunny. Hace sol.

• *The months of the year and days of the week do not take a capital letter in Spanish.*

sunshade noun
la **sombrilla** *fem.*

sunshine noun
el **sol** *masc.*
in the sunshine al sol

suntan noun
el **bronceado** *masc.*
to get a suntan ponerse
moreno *masc.*, ponerse morena *fem.*

super adjective
genial *masc. & fem.*
That's a super idea! ¡Es una idea
genial!

supermarket noun
el **supermercado** *masc.*

superstar noun
la **gran estrella** *fem.*

superstore noun
el **hipermercado** *masc.*

supper noun
la **cena** *fem.*
to have supper cenar

to **support** verb
(*a team*) **ser hincha de**
Alex supports Liverpool. Alex es
hincha del Liverpool.

to **suppose** verb
1 **suponer**
I suppose you're right. Supongo
que tienes razón.
I suppose so. Supongo que sí.
2 (*using 'deber'*)
You're supposed to be at school.
Deberías estar en la escuela.
I'm not supposed to do that. No
debería hacer eso.
3 (*using 'decir'*)
It's supposed to be a good film.
Dicen que es una buena película.

sure adjective
seguro *masc.*, **segura** *fem.*
Are you sure? ¿Estás seguro?
I'm not sure. No estoy seguro.
Sure! ¡Claro!

to **surf** verb
to surf the Internet navegar en
Internet

surface noun
la **superficie** *fem.*

surname noun
el **apellido** *masc.*

surprise noun
la **sorpresa** *fem.*
What a surprise! ¡Qué sorpresa!

to **surprise** verb
sorprender

surprised adjective
sorprendido *masc.*,
sorprendida *fem.*
I'm surprised. Estoy sorprendido.

to **surround** verb
rodear
surrounded by trees rodeado de
árboles
surrounded by a wall rodeado por
un muro

to **swallow** verb
tragar

swan noun
el **cisne** *masc.*

to **swap** verb
cambiar
**I want to swap my book for your
CD.** Quiero cambiar mi libro por tu
CD.
I've swapped places. Me he
cambiado de sitio.

to **swear** verb
decir palabrotas

to **sweat** verb
sudar

sweater noun
el **jersey** *masc.* (plural los **jerseys** or
jerséis)

sweatshirt noun
la **sudadera** *fem.*

a
b
c
d
e
f
g
h
i
j
k
l
m
n
o
p
q
r
s
t
u
v
w
x
y
z

• *The months of the year and days of the week do not take a capital letter in Spanish.*

sweet noun
1 el **caramelo** *masc.*
I like sweets. Me gustan los caramelos.
a sweet shop una tienda de golosinas
2 (*part of a meal*) el **postre** *masc.*

sweet adjective
1 (*like sugar*) **dulce** *masc. & fem.*
This cake's very sweet. Este pastel es muy dulce.
2 (*nice, kind*) **encantador** *masc.*, **encantadora** *fem.*
She's a very sweet girl. Es una niña encantadora.

sweetcorn noun
el **maíz** *masc.*

swim noun
to go for a swim ir a nadar

swim verb
nadar
I can swim. Yo sé nadar.

swimmer noun
el **nadador** *masc.*, la **nadadora** *fem.*
He's a good swimmer. Es buen nadador.

swimming noun
1 la **natación** *fem.*
I love swimming. Me encanta la natación.
to go swimming ir a nadar
2 a swimming costume un traje de baño, un bañador
a swimming pool una piscina
swimming trunks un bañador, un traje de baño

swimsuit noun
el **traje de baño** *masc.*

swing noun
el **columpio** *masc.*

Swiss adjective
suizo *masc.*, **suiza** *fem.*

Swiss noun
the Swiss los suizos *masc. plural*

• *See the centre section for verb tables.*

switch noun
1 (*for turning or pressing*) el **botón** *masc.* (plural los **botones**)
Press the switch. Pulsa el botón.
2 (*up-down type*) el **interruptor** *masc.*

to **switch** verb
1 (*to change*) **cambiar**
to switch channels cambiar de canal
I've switched to the other channel. He cambiado al otro canal.
2 (*a TV, computer, etc.*) to switch off apagar
Switch the light off. Apaga la luz.
3 (*a TV, computer, etc.*) to switch on encender
I've switched the light on. He encendido la luz.

Switzerland noun
Suiza *fem.*

swollen adjective
(*leg, arm, etc.*) **hinchado** *masc.*, **hinchada** *fem.*

sword noun
la **espada** *fem.*

syllable noun
la **sílaba** *fem.*

symbol noun
el **símbolo** *masc.*

synagogue noun
la **sinagoga** *fem.*

system noun
el **sistema** *masc.*

> 🔑 **LANGUAGE**
> Be careful: **sistema** ends in an **-a** but it is not a feminine noun.

Tt

table noun
1 la **mesa** *fem.*
  on the table en la mesa
  table tennis el tenis de mesa
  to play table tennis jugar al tenis de mesa
2 **the times tables** las tablas de multiplicar
  the five-times table la tabla del cinco

tablecloth noun
  el **mantel** *masc.*

tablespoon noun
  la **cuchara de servir** *fem.*

tablet noun
  la **pastilla** *fem.*
  to take a tablet tomar una pastilla

tadpole noun
  el **renacuajo** *masc.*

tail noun
1 *(of an animal)* la **cola** *fem.*
2 *(when throwing a coin)* **tails!** ¡cruz!
  Heads or tails? ¿Cara o cruz?

to **take** verb
1 *(with your hand, go by car, etc.)* **coger**, **tomar**
  Take a chocolate. Coge un bombón., Toma un bombón.
  I took the bus. Cogí el autobús., Tomé el autobús.
2 *(a medicine, photo, course, etc.)* **tomar**
  Do you take sugar? ¿Tomas azúcar?
  I've taken the antibiotics. He tomado los antibióticos.
3 *(to take to another place)* **llevar**
  Take this book to Yasmina. Lleva este libro a Yasmina.
  My dad takes me to school. Mi padre me lleva al colegio.
  Who's taken my bike? ¿Quién se ha llevado mi bici?

4 **to take an exam** hacer un examen
  What size do you take? ¿Qué talla usas?

to **take away** verb
1 **quitar**
  Take your toys away. Quita tus juguetes de aquí.
2 **llevar**
  Eat here or take away? ¿Para comer aquí o para llevar?

to **take back** verb
  devolver
  I took the book back to the library. Devolví el libro a la biblioteca.

to **take down** verb
1 **bajar**
  Can you take down that book for me? ¿Me puedes bajar ese libro?
2 *(from a wall)* **quitar**
  Take down the picture. Quita el cuadro.

to **take off** verb
1 **quitar**
  I've taken my coat off. Me he quitado el abrigo.
2 **despegar**
  The plane has taken off. El avión ha despegado.

to **take out** verb
  sacar
  I took the toys out of the box. Saqué los juguetes de la caja.

to **take up** verb
  (from downstairs etc.) **subir**
  Can you take up the suitcase? ¿Puedes subir la maleta?

takeaway noun
  (meal) la **comida para llevar** *fem.*

take-off noun
  (of a plane) el **despegue** *masc.*

a b c d e f g h i j k l m n o p q r s t u v w x y z

• Use **el** and **uno** for masculine words and **la** and **una** for feminine words.

tale noun
el **cuento** *masc.*
a fairy tale un cuento de hadas

talk noun
la **charla** *fem.*
to give a talk dar una charla

to **talk** verb
hablar
to talk to somebody hablar con
alguien
to talk about something hablar de
algo

talkative adjective
hablador *masc.*, **habladora** *fem.*

tall adjective
alto *masc.*, **alta** *fem.*
I'm tall. Soy alta.
How tall are you? ¿Cuánto
mides?
I'm five feet tall. Mido un metro
cincuenta.

tan noun
el **bronceado** *masc.*
to get a tan ponerse moreno *masc.*,
ponerse morena *fem.*

tangerine noun
la **mandarina** *fem.*

tank noun
1 (*used in war*) **el tanque** *masc.*
2 **a fish tank** una pecera

tanned adjective
moreno *masc.*, **morena** *fem.*
I'm tanned. Estoy moreno.

tap noun
el **grifo** *masc.*
The tap is off. El grifo está cerrado.

tape noun
la **cinta** *fem.*
**Do you have a tape to record the
film?** ¿Tienes una cinta para
grabar la película?
sticky tape la cinta adhesiva
I've got it on tape. Lo tengo
grabado.

a tape measure un metro
a tape recorder un magnetófono

to **tape** verb
grabar
Can you tape the film? ¿Puedes
grabar la película?
It's taping. Está grabando.

tart noun
la **tarta** *fem.*
an apple tart une tarta de
manzana

taste noun
el **sabor** *masc.*
It has a lovely taste. Tiene muy
buen sabor.
Can I have a taste? ¿Puedo
probarlo?

to **taste** verb
1 (*to eat or drink*) **probar**
Taste this. Prueba esto.
2 (*to have a flavour*) **tener sabor**
It tastes bitter. Tiene un sabor
amargo.
It tastes of strawberry. Tiene
sabor a fresa.
It tastes nice. Está delicioso.

tasty adjective
delicioso *masc.*, **deliciosa** *fem.*

tattoo noun
el **tatuaje** *masc.*
He's got a tattoo on his arm. Tiene
un tatuaje en el brazo.

taxi noun
el **taxi** *masc.*
by taxi en taxi
a taxi driver un or una taxista

tea noun
1 el **té** *masc.*
to have a cup of tea tomar una
taza de té
a tea with milk un té con
leche
a lemon tea un té con limón
2 (*afternoon snack*) la **merienda** *fem.*
to have tea merendar

• *Languages and nationalities do not take a capital letter in Spanish.*

3 (*evening meal*) la **cena** *fem.*
to have tea cenar

 CULTURE
In Spain people usually have lemon rather than milk in their tea.

teabag noun
la **bolsita de té** *fem.*

to **teach** verb
enseñar
Mr Delgado teaches Spanish. El señor Delgado enseña español.
They've taught me to swim. Me han enseñado a nadar.

teacher noun
1 (*in a primary or nursery school*)
el **maestro** *masc.*, la **maestra** *fem.*
My dad's a teacher. Mi padre es maestro.
2 (*in a secondary school*)
el **profesor** *masc.*, la **profesora** *fem.*
My mum's a teacher. Mi madre es profesora.
a Spanish teacher un profesor de español

teacup noun
la **taza de té** *fem.*

team noun
el **equipo** *masc.*
a football team un equipo de fútbol

teapot noun
la **tetera** *fem.*

tear noun
(*when you cry*) la **lágrima** *fem.*

to **tear** verb
romper
I've torn my shirt! ¡Me he roto la camisa!
She tore up the letter. Rompió la carta.

teaspoon noun
la **cucharita** *fem.*

teatime noun
1 (*afternoon snack*) la **hora de merendar** *fem.*
2 (*evening meal*) la **hora de cenar** *fem.*

teddy bear noun
el **osito de peluche** *masc.*

LANGUAGE
Word for word the Spanish means 'little bear made out of plush' (plush is a soft material).

teenager noun
el or la **adolescente** *masc. & fem.*

teens plural noun
to be in your teens ser adolescente

tee-shirt noun
la **camiseta** *fem.*

teeth plural noun
los **dientes** *masc. plural*
I'm brushing my teeth. Me estoy lavando los dientes.

telephone noun
el **teléfono** *masc.*
I'm on the telephone to mum. Estoy hablando por teléfono con mamá.
a telephone call una llamada telefónica
the telephone directory la guía telefónica
a telephone number un número de teléfono

telescope noun
el **telescopio** *masc.*
to look through the telescope mirar por el telescopio

television noun
la **televisión** *fem.* (plural las **televisiones**)
to watch television ver la televisión
on television en televisión
a television set una televisión

a
b
c
d
e
f
g
h
i
j
k
l
m
n
o
p
q
r
s
t
u
v
w
x
y
z

• *The months of the year and days of the week do not take a capital letter in Spanish.*

to **tell** verb
1 **decir**
I'm telling the truth. Digo la verdad.
He's telling lies. Dice mentiras.
What did he tell you? ¿Qué te ha dicho?
Can you tell the time? ¿Sabes decir la hora?
2 (to talk about) **hablar**
Tell me about your family. Háblame de tu familia.
3 (a story, secret, joke) **contar**
Tell me a story. Cuéntame un cuento.
4 to tell off regañar

telly noun
la **tele** fem.
to watch telly ver la tele

temper noun
to lose your temper enfadarse mucho
He lost his temper. Se enfadó mucho.

temperature noun
1 la **temperatura** fem.
the temperature of the water la temperatura del agua
2 to have a temperature tener fiebre

temple noun
el **templo** masc.
a Sikh temple un templo sij

ten number
diez
It starts at ten. Empieza a las diez.
It's ten to nine. Son las nueve menos diez.
It's ten past six. Son las seis y diez.
I'm ten. Tengo diez años.

LANGUAGE
In English you can say 'ten o'clock' or just 'ten', 'ten years old' or just 'ten'. In Spanish you must add **las** (for time) and **años** (for age).

• See the centre section for verb tables.

tennis noun
el **tenis** masc.
I play tennis. Juego al tenis.
a tennis ball una pelota de tenis
a tennis court una pista de tenis
a tennis racket una raqueta de tenis

tense noun
the present tense el presente masc.
the past tense el pasado masc.
the future tense el futuro masc.

tent noun
la **tienda** fem.
to put up a tent montar una tienda

tenth adjective
décimo masc., **décima** fem.
on the tenth floor en el décimo piso
the tenth of May el diez de mayo

LANGUAGE
With dates you use **diez** (ten).

term noun
el **trimestre** masc.
the last day of term el último día del trimestre

terrible adjective
terrible masc. & fem.

LANGUAGE
You can also say **espantoso/espantosa**.

terrific adjective
estupendo masc., **estupenda** fem.

terrified adjective
aterrorizado masc., **aterrorizada** fem.
to be terrified of tener mucho miedo a
She's terrified of her teacher. Le tiene mucho miedo a su maestra.

test noun
(in school) la **prueba** fem., el **examen** masc. (plural los **exámens**)

text noun
(*text message*) el **SMS** *masc.*,
el **mensaje (de texto)** *masc.*
to send a text enviar un
SMS, enviar un mensaje

to **text** verb
to text somebody enviar un SMS a
alguien, enviar un mensaje a
alguien

textbook noun
el **libro de texto** *masc.*

Thames noun
the Thames el Támesis *masc.*

than conjunction
1 **que**
I'm taller than you. Soy más alto
que tú.
2 (*with numbers*) **de**
more than twenty más de v
einte

to **thank** verb
to thank somebody dar las gracias
a alguien
Thank you! ¡Gracias!
Thank you very much! ¡Muchas
gracias!
Thank you for the present. Gracias
por el regalo.

thanks exclamation
¡gracias!
Thanks for the ice cream. Gracias
por el helado.
No thanks. No, gracias.

that conjunction
que
I think that it's a good film. Creo
que es una buena película.

that adjective
1 **ese** *masc.*, **esa** *fem.*
that cat ese gato
that house esa casa
that one ése *masc.*, ésa *fem.*
Take that one. Toma ése.

2 (*talking about something further away*)
aquel *masc.*, **aquella** *fem.*
that book over there aquel libro
that lady aquella señorita
that one aquél *masc.*, aquélla *fem.*

that pronoun
1 **ése** *masc.*, **ésa** *fem.*
That's not my book. Ése no es mi
libro.
That's my bike. Ésa es mi bici.
2 **eso**
What's that? ¿Qué es eso?
That's true. Eso es cierto.
Don't do that. No hagas eso.
3 (*talking about something further away*)
aquél *masc.*, **aquélla** *fem.*
That's my brother over there.
Aquél es mi hermano.
That's my house. Aquélla es mi
casa.
4 **aquello**
What's that over there? ¿Qué es
aquello?
5 **que**
the boy that I met el niño que
conocí
the toys that are in the box los
juguetes que están en la caja

the determiner
1 (*before a masculine noun*) **el** (plural **los**)

> 🔑 **LANGUAGE**
> de + el = de
> la + el = al

the car el coche
the cars los coches
a page of the book una página del
libro
to go to the cinema ir al cine
at the end of the film al final de la
película
2 (*before a feminine noun*) **la** (plural **las**)
the window la ventana
the windows las ventanas

theatre noun
el **teatro** *masc.*

• *Use **el** and **uno** for masculine words and **la** and **una** for feminine words.*

English Spanish

a
b
c
d
e
f
g
h
i
j
k
l
m
n
o
p
q
r
s
t
u
v
w
x
y
z

their adjective
1 (before a singular noun) **su**
  their school su colegio
2 (before a plural noun) **sus**
  their friends sus amigos
3 (with parts of the body, clothes, etc.)
  They're washing their hands. Se están lavando las manos.
  They put their shoes on. Se pusieron los zapatos.

🔑 **LANGUAGE**
Use se with el, la, los, or las in these examples instead of su and sus.

theirs pronoun
1 (with a singular noun) el **suyo** masc., la **suya** fem.
  our dog and theirs nuestro perro y el suyo
  Our house is bigger than theirs. Nuestra casa es más grande que la suya.
2 (with a plural noun) los **suyos** masc. plural, las **suyas** fem. plural
  Our parents are Spanish and theirs too. Nuestros padres son españoles y los suyos también.
  our photos and theirs nuestras fotos y las suyas
3 (following 'is') **suyo** masc., **suya** fem.
  This house is theirs. Esta casa es suya.
4 (following 'are') **suyos** masc. plural, **suyas** fem. plural
  These pens are theirs. Estos bolígrafos son suyos.

them pronoun
1 (after a verb) **los** masc., **las** fem.
  Do you know my brothers? – Yes, I know them. ¿Conoces a mis hermanos? – Sí, los conozco.
  My glasses, have you seen them? ¿Mis gafas, las has visto?

🔑 **LANGUAGE**
With commands and infinitives los and las are joined with the verb to make one word.

  Call them. Llámalos.
  I want to help them. Quiero ayudarlas.
2 (to them) **les**
  I've sent a letter to them. Les he mandado una carta.
  Give them the book. Dales el libro.

🔑 **LANGUAGE**
When les is used with lo or la you use se instead of les.

  I've given it to them. Se lo he dado.
  Give it to them. Dáselo.
3 (after a preposition etc.) **ellos** masc., **ellas** fem.
  with them con ellos
  Hazel and Claire? I'm taller than them. ¿Hazel y Claire? Yo soy más alta que ellas.
  It's them. Son ellos.

theme park noun
  el **parque temático** masc.

themselves pronoun
1 **ellos mismos** masc., **ellas mismas** fem.
  They've done it themselves. Lo han hecho ellos mismos.
2 (with a reflexive verb) **se**
  They're washing themselves. Se están lavando.
3 **by themselves** solos masc., solas fem.
  They don't go out by themselves. No salen solos.

then adverb
1 (next) **luego**
  I went to school and then to the cinema. Fui al colegio y luego al cine.
2 (at that time) **entonces**
  I was in Madrid then. Entonces estaba en Madrid.
3 (so) **entonces**
  What shall we do then? Entonces, ¿qué hacemos?

• Languages and nationalities do not take a capital letter in Spanish.

there adverb
1 (fairly close to you) **ahí**
Sit there. Siéntate ahí.
over there ahí
up there ahí arriba
2 (further away) **allí**
Sit there. Siéntate allí.
over there allí
up there allí arriba
3 there is hay
There's a book on the table.
Hay un libro en la mesa.
There isn't any sugar. No hay
azúcar.
4 there are hay
There are thirty children in my
class. Hay treinta niños en mi
clase.

> **LANGUAGE**
> Hay is used for 'there is' and 'there
> are'.

5 (when shouting, or pointing to something)
¡ahí!
There he is! ¡Ahí está!

thermometer noun
el **termómetro** masc.

these adjective
estos masc., **estas** fem.
these CDs estos CDs
these pages estas páginas
these ones éstos masc., éstas fem.
I want these ones. Quiero
éstos.

these pronoun
éstos masc., **éstas** fem.
Which dresses do you want? –
These. ¿Qué vestidos quieres? –
Éstos
These are my photos. Éstas son mis
fotos.

they pronoun
1 (not usually translated in Spanish)
Have you seen my glasses? –
They're here. ¿Has visto mis gafas?
– Están aquí.

2 **ellos** masc., **ellas** fem.
They're going to the cinema but
I'm going swimming. Ellos van al
cine pero yo voy a la piscina.

> **LANGUAGE**
> Use ellos and ellas when you want to
> give special importance to the word
> 'they'.

thick adjective
1 (wall, slice, etc.) **grueso** masc.,
gruesa fem.
2 (soup, fog, smoke) **espeso** masc.,
espesa fem.

thief noun
el **ladrón** masc., la **ladrona** fem.

> **LANGUAGE**
> The plural of ladrón is ladrones.

thin adjective
1 **delgado** masc., **delgada** fem.
I'm thin. Soy delgado.
2 (slice, paper, line) **fino** masc., **fina** fem.
a thin slice una rebanada fina

thing noun
la **cosa** fem.
I have lots of things to do. Tengo
muchas cosas que hacer.
Put your things on the table. Pon
tus cosas en la mesa.

to **think** verb
1 **pensar**
What are you thinking? ¿Qué
piensas?
I'm thinking about the holidays.
Pienso en las vacaciones.
2 (to believe) **creer**
I think you're tired. Creo que estás
cansada.
I think so. Creo que sí.
I don't think so. Creo que no.

• The months of the year and days of the week do not take a capital letter in Spanish.

third adjective

tercero *masc.*, **tercera** *fem.*
for the third time por tercera vez
I came third. (*in the race*) Quedé tercero.
on the third floor en el tercer piso
on the third of November el tres de noviembre

> 🔑 **LANGUAGE**
> Use tercer instead of tercero before a masculine singular noun.

> 🔑 **LANGUAGE**
> With dates you use tres (three).

third noun

la **tercera parte** *fem.*
a third of the class una tercera parte de la clase

thirsty adjective

I'm thirsty. Tengo sed.
She's very thirsty. Tiene mucha sed.

> 🔑 **LANGUAGE**
> English = to be thirsty I'm thirsty.
> Spanish = tener sed Tengo sed.

thirteen number

trece
My cousin is thirteen. Mi prima tiene trece años.

> 🔑 **LANGUAGE**
> In English you can say just 'thirteen'. In Spanish you must add años.

thirty number

treinta
My dad is thirty. Mi padre tiene treinta años.

> 🔑 **LANGUAGE**
> In English you can say just 'thirty'. In Spanish you must add años.

• *See the centre section for verb tables.*

this adjective

este *masc.*, **esta** *fem.*
this dog este perro
this chair esta silla
this one éste *masc.*, ésta *fem.*
I want this one. Quiero éste.

this pronoun

1 **éste** *masc.*, **ésta** *fem.*
This is not my pen. Éste no es mi boli.
This is my bike. Ésta es mi bici.
2 **esto**
What's this? ¿Qué es esto?
Don't do this. No hagas esto.

those adjective

1 **esos** *masc.*, **esas** *fem.*
those children esos niños
those tables esas mesas
those ones ésos *masc.*, ésas *fem.*
Take those ones. Toma ésos.
2 (*talking about something further away*)
aquellos *masc.*, **aquellas** *fem.*
those men over there aquellos hombres
those houses aquellas casas
those ones aquéllos *masc.*, aquéllas *fem.*

those pronoun

1 **ésos** *masc.*, **ésas** *fem.*
Which dresses do you want? – Those. ¿Qué vestidos quieres? – Ésos.
Those are my photos. Ésas son mis fotos.
2 (*talking about something further away*)
aquéllos *masc.*, **aquéllas** *fem.*
Which jeans? – Those. ¿Qué vaqueros? – Aquéllos
Those are the girls. Aquéllas son las niñas.

though conjunction

aunque
though I'm tired aunque estoy cansado

though adverb

pero
It's cold, though. Pero hace frío.

thousand number
mil
a thousand euros mil euros
two thousand euros dos mil euros
thousands of people miles de personas

three number
tres
I'll come back at three. Vuelvo a las tres.
I'm three. Tengo tres años.

> **LANGUAGE**
> In English you can say 'three o'clock' or just 'three', 'three years old' or just 'three'. In Spanish you must add **las** (for time) and **años** (for age).

throat noun
la **garganta** *fem.*
I have a sore throat Me duele la garganta

> **LANGUAGE**
> Word for word the Spanish means 'my throat hurts'.

throne noun
el **trono** *masc.*

through preposition
por
to look through the window mirar por la ventana
to go through the park ir por el parque

through adverb
to get through pasar
Let me through! ¡Déjame pasar!
Go through! ¡Pasa!

to **throw** verb
tirar
Throw the ball to me. Tírame la pelota.
She's throwing stones at me. Me está tirando piedras.

to **throw away** verb
tirar (a la basura)
Throw this newspaper away. Tira este periódico.

to **throw out** verb
tirar (a la basura)

to **throw up** verb
devolver
I feel like throwing up. Tengo ganas de devolver.

thumb noun
el **pulgar** *masc.*

thunder noun
los **truenos** *masc. plural*
There's thunder and lightning. Hay truenos y relámpagos.

thunderstorm noun
la **tormenta** *fem.*

Thursday noun
el **jueves** *masc.*
Today is Thursday. Hoy es jueves.
on Thursday el jueves
Come to my house on Thursday. Ven a mi casa el jueves.
on Thursdays los jueves
It's open on Thursdays. Está abierto los jueves.

> **LANGUAGE**
> Remember the difference in Spanish between **el jueves** (one Thursday only) and **los jueves** (every Thursday).

tick noun
la **cruz** *fem.*

to **tick** verb
(*an answer, name, etc.*) **marcar con una cruz**

ticket noun
1 (*for train, plane, bus, etc.*) el **billete** *masc.*
   a bus ticket un billete de autobús
2 (*for cinema, museum, etc.*) la **entrada** *fem.*
3 a ticket office una taquilla *fem.*

• Use **el** and **uno** for masculine words and **la** and **una** for feminine words.

a
b
c
d
e
f
g
h
i
j
k
l
m
n
o
p
q
r
s
t
u
v
w
x
y
z

to **tickle** verb
to tickle somebody hacer cosquillas a alguien

ticklish adjective
I'm ticklish. Tengo cosquillas.

tide noun
la **marea** fem.
The tide's in. La marea está alta.
The tide's out. La marea está baja.

tidy adjective
(room or house) **ordenado** masc., **ordenada** fem.
a tidy bedroom una habitación ordenada

to **tidy** verb
(a room, toys, etc.) **recoger**
to tidy up recoger las cosas

tie noun
1 la **corbata** fem.
to wear a tie llevar corbata
2 (in a match) el **empate** masc.
It was a tie. Terminó en empate.

to **tie** verb
(a parcel, an animal, etc.) **atar**
Tie your laces. Átate los cordones.
to tie a knot hacer un nudo

tiger noun
el **tigre** masc.

tight adjective
ajustado masc., **ajustada** fem.
tight jeans unos vaqueros ajustados

tights plural noun
las **medias** fem. plural
a pair of tights unas medias

till noun
la **caja** fem.
There's a queue at the till. Hay cola en la caja.

till preposition
hasta
Wait till Tuesday. Espera hasta el martes.

time noun
1 (an amount of time) el **tiempo** masc.
I don't have time. No tengo tiempo.
at the same time al mismo tiempo
a long time mucho tiempo
a very long time ago hace mucho tiempo
to have a nice time divertirse
I had a nice time. Me divertí mucho.
2 (on the clock) la **hora** fem.
What time is it? ¿Qué hora es?
Do you have the right time? ¿Tienes hora?
What time do you go to school? ¿A qué hora vas a la escuela?
It's time to eat. Es hora de comer.
to arrive on time llegar puntual
3 (a point in time) el **momento** masc.
at this time en este momento
4 (an occasion) la **vez** fem.
for the first time por primera vez
how many times? ¿cuántas veces?
three times tres veces
this time esta vez
Two times five is ten. Dos por cinco son diez.

timetable noun
el **horario** masc.

tin noun
la **lata** fem.
a tin of tomatoes una lata de tomates
a tin of paint un bote de pintura

tinfoil noun
el **papel de aluminio** masc.

tiny adjective
muy pequeño masc., **muy pequeña** fem.

tip noun
(end) la **punta** fem.
the tip of my nose la punta de la nariz

tiptoe noun
on tiptoe de puntillas

• Languages and nationalities do not take a capital letter in Spanish.

tired adjective
cansado *masc.*, **cansada** *fem.*
I'm tired. Estoy cansada.

tissue noun
el **pañuelo de papel** *masc.*
Do you have a tissue? ¿Tienes un pañuelo?

title noun
el **título** *masc.*

to preposition
1 **a**
to the station a la estación
to Spain a España
I'm going to the doctor. Voy al médico.
It's started to rain. Ha empezado a llover.
2 (*to a person, when giving, sending, etc.*) **a**
I've given the pencil to Dave. Le he dado el lápiz a Dave.
Give the book to me. Dame el libro.

🔑 **LANGUAGE**
a + el = al

3 (*with 'road'*) **de**
the road to Burgos la carretera de Burgos
4 (*often not translated with infinitives*)
I want to eat. Quiero comer.
It's difficult to do it. Es difícil hacerlo.
5 (*showing a reason*) **para**
Give me some money to buy sweets. Dame dinero para comprar caramelos.
6 (*with 'have' and infinitive*) **que**
I have nothing to do. No tengo nada que hacer.
I have a lot to do. Tengo mucho que hacer.
I have to study. Tengo que estudiar.
7 (*following adjectives like 'kind', 'nasty', 'cruel'*) **con**
She's very nice to me. Es muy buena conmigo.

8 (*talking about the time*)
It's ten to eight. Son las ocho menos diez.

toad noun
el **sapo** *masc.*

toast noun
el **pan tostado** *masc.*
a slice of toast una tostada *fem.*

today adverb
hoy
Today is my birthday. Hoy es mi cumpleaños.
What's the date today? ¿A qué fecha estamos hoy?

toe noun
el **dedo del pie** *masc.*
my big toe el dedo gordo del pie

🔑 **LANGUAGE**
Word for word dedo del pie means 'finger of the foot'!

together adverb
juntos *masc. plural*, **juntas** *fem. plural*
We always play together. Siempre jugamos juntos.

toilet noun
1 el **baño** *masc.*
to go to the toilet ir al baño
toilet paper el papel higiénico
2 (*in a hotel, restaurant, etc.*) el **servicio** *masc.*
Where are the toilets? ¿Dónde están los servicios?

tomato noun
el **tomate** *masc.*
tomato sauce la salsa de tomate

tomorrow adverb
mañana
See you tomorrow! ¡Hasta mañana!
tomorrow morning mañana por la mañana
tomorrow night mañana por la noche
the day after tomorrow pasado mañana

• *The months of the year and days of the week do not take a capital letter in Spanish.*

a
b
c
d
e
f
g
h
i
j
k
l
m
n
o
p
q
r
s
t
u
v
w
x
y
z

tongue noun
 la **lengua** *fem.*

tonight adverb
 esta noche

tonsillitis noun
 las **anginas** *fem. plural*
 I've got tonsillitis. Tengo anginas.

too adverb
 1 (*as well*) **también**
 I'm going too. Yo también voy.
 You too? – Yes, me too. ¿Tú también? – Sí, yo también.
 2 (*more than something*) **demasiado**
 It's too big. Es demasiado grande.
 3 **too much** (*with nouns*)
 demasiado *masc.*, demasiada *fem.*
 too much milk demasiada leche
 4 **too much** (*with verbs*) demasiado
 I eat too much. Como demasiado.
 5 **too many** demasiados *masc. plural*, demasiadas *fem. plural*
 too many cars demasiados coches
 There are too many. Hay demasiados.

tools plural noun
 las **herramientas** *fem. plural*

tooth noun
 el **diente** *masc.*
 the tooth fairy el ratoncito Pérez

LANGUAGE
Diente is related to the English word 'dentist' (somebody who looks after teeth).

🌎 **CULTURE**
Spanish children just like British ones leave their tooth under the pillow at bedtime and in the morning find some money or a present there instead. The difference is it's not the tooth fairy but a little mouse (ratoncito) whose name is Pérez that comes and takes the tooth away.

• *See the centre section for verb tables.*

toothache noun
 I have a toothache. Tengo dolor de muelas.

toothbrush noun
 el **cepillo de dientes** *masc.*

toothpaste noun
 la **pasta de dientes** *fem.*

top noun
 1 (*of a hill, tree, ladder, etc.*) lo **alto** *masc.*
 to get to the top of the hill llegar a lo alto de la colina
 the top of the mountain la cima de la montaña
 2 (*of a box, page, swimsuit, etc.*) la **parte de arriba** *fem.*
 on the top of the cupboard en la parte de arriba del armario
 3 (*blouse*) la **blusa** *fem.*
 4 (*jacket*) **la chaqueta** *fem.*
 5 **on top of** encima de
 It's on top of the bed. Está encima de la cama.

top adjective
 de arriba
 the top shelf el estante de arriba
 the top floor el último piso
 I've got the top mark. He sacado la nota más alta.
 You're top of the class. Eres la mejor de la clase.

torch noun
 la **linterna** *fem.*

tortoise noun
 la **tortuga** *fem.*

total noun
 el **total** *masc.*

touch verb
 tocar
 Don't touch the glass. No toques el cristal.

tough adjective
 1 (*not soft*) **duro** *masc.*, **dura** *fem.*
 This meat's tough. Esta carne está dura.
 2 (*not easy*) **difícil** *masc. & fem.*

tour noun
1 (of a town, museum, etc.) la **visita** fem.
2 (of a country) el **viaje** masc.

tourist noun
el or la **turista** masc. & fem.
a tourist office una oficina de turismo

towards preposition
hacia
He ran towards me. Corrió hacia mí.

towel noun
la **toalla** fem.

tower noun
la **torre** fem.
a tower block un bloque de pisos

town noun
la **ciudad** fem.
to go into town ir a la ciudad
the town centre el centro de la ciudad

toy noun
el **juguete** masc.
a toy shop una juguetería fem.

to **trace** verb
(with tracing paper) **calcar**
to trace a picture calcar un dibujo
tracing paper el papel de calco

track noun
1 (for races) la **pista** fem.
2 (railway line) la **vía** fem.

tracksuit noun
el **chándal** masc.

tractor noun
el **tractor** masc.

traffic noun
el **tráfico** masc.
There's a lot of traffic. Hay mucho tráfico.
a traffic jam un atasco
the traffic lights el semáforo
The traffic lights are green.
El semáforo está verde.

train noun
el **tren** masc.
by train en tren
the train to ... el tren para ...
a train set un tren de juguete

to **train** verb
(for football, running, etc.) **entrenar**
He trains every day. Entrena todos los días.

trainers plural noun
las **zapatillas de deporte** fem. plural

🔑 **LANGUAGE**
In Spanish zapato means 'shoe', so word for word this means 'little sports shoes'.

training noun
(for football etc.) el **entrenamiento** masc.

tram noun
el **tranvía** masc.

🔑 **LANGUAGE**
Be careful: tranvía ends in an -a but it is not a feminine noun.

trampoline noun
el **trampolín** masc. (plural los **trampolines**)

to **translate** verb
traducir
Translate this sentence into Spanish. Traduce esta frase al español.

translation noun
la **traducción** fem. (plural las **traducciones**)

transport noun
public transport el transporte público masc.

trap noun
la **trampa** fem.

a b c d e f g h i j k l m n o p q r s t u v w x y z

• Use **el** and **uno** for masculine words and **la** and **una** for feminine words.

to **travel** verb
viajar
I like to travel. Me gusta viajar.

travel agent's noun
la **agencia de viajes** fem.

tray noun
la **bandeja**

to **tread** verb
to tread on something pisar algo
to tread on somebody's foot pisar
a alguien

treasure noun
el **tesoro** masc.

LANGUAGE
English = treasure
Spanish = tesoro

treat noun
a treat algo especial
It's a birthday treat. Es algo
especial para mi cumpleaños.

tree noun
el **árbol** masc.

triangle noun
el **triángulo** masc.

trick noun
1 (using magic etc.) el **truco** masc.
a magic trick un truco de magia
2 (a joke) la **broma** fem.
to play a trick on somebody gastar
una broma a alguien

tricky adjective
(difficult) **difícil** masc. & fem.

trip noun
1 (by plane, boat, etc.) el **viaje** masc.
to go on a trip hacer un viaje
Have a good trip! ¡Buen viaje!
2 (short trip by bus etc.) la **excursión** fem.
(plural las **excursiones**)
We're going on a trip to the
seaside. Vamos de excursión a la
playa.

to **trip** verb
tropezar

trolley noun
(for shopping) el **carro** masc.

trouble noun
los **problemas** masc. plural
I'm in trouble. Tengo problemas.
I have trouble walking. Tengo
problemas para andar.

trousers plural noun
los **pantalones** masc. plural
I'm wearing trousers. Llevo
pantalones.
a pair of trousers unos pantalones

truck noun
el **camión** masc. (plural los
camiones)
a truck driver un camionero masc.,
una camionera fem.

true adjective
verdadero masc., **verdadera** fem.
a true story una historia verdadera
That's true. Es verdad.

trumpet noun
la **trompeta** fem.
to play the trumpet tocar la
trompeta

trunk noun
1 el **tronco** masc.
a tree trunk un tronco
2 la **trompa** fem.
the elephant's trunk la trompa del
elefante

trunks plural noun
el **bañador** masc.
a pair of trunks un bañador

LANGUAGE
English = trunks is plural
Spanish = el bañador is singular

truth noun
la **verdad** fem.
It's the truth. Es la verdad.

• Languages and nationalities do not take a capital letter in Spanish.

to **try** verb
1 **intentar**
to try to do something intentar hacer algo
Try again. Inténtalo otra vez.
2 (food, machine, etc.) **probar**
Try this soup. Prueba esta sopa.

to **try on** verb
probarse
Try these jeans on. Pruébate estos vaqueros.

T-shirt noun
la **camiseta** fem.

tube noun
1 el **tubo** masc.
2 (underground) el **metro** masc.
to go by tube ir en metro

Tuesday noun
el **martes** masc.
Today is Tuesday. Hoy es martes.
on Tuesday el martes
Can I go to the cinema on Tuesday?
¿Puedo ir al cine el martes?
on Tuesdays los martes
I play tennis on Tuesdays. Juego al tenis los martes.

LANGUAGE
Remember the difference in Spanish between el martes (one Tuesday only) and los martes (every Tuesday).

tumble-dryer noun
la **secadora** fem.

tummy noun
el **estómago** masc.,
la **barriga** fem., el **vientre** masc.

tummy ache noun
I have a tummy ache. Me duele el estómago.

tuna noun
el **atún** masc.
a tuna sandwich un sándwich de atún

tune noun
la **melodía** masc.

tunnel noun
el **túnel** masc.
to go through a tunnel pasar por un túnel

turkey noun
el **pavo** masc.

turn noun
el **turno** masc.
It's my turn. Es mi turno.
It's Jamal's turn. Es el turno de Jamal.
Whose turn is it? ¿A quién le toca?

to **turn** verb
1 **girar**
Turn right. Gira a la derecha.
She turned the steering wheel. Giró el volante.
2 (a page, corner) **dar la vuelta a**
Turn the page. Da la vuelta a la página.
3 (to become) **ponerse**
He turned red. Se puso rojo.
The prince turned into a frog! ¡El príncipe se convirtió en rana!

to **turn back** verb
volver
We have to turn back. Tenemos que volver.

to **turn down** verb
(a TV, the heating, etc.) **bajar**
Turn down the sound. Baja el volumen.

to **turn off** verb
1 (a TV, computer, etc.) **apagar**
Turn the light off. Apaga la luz.
2 to turn off the tap cerrar el grifo

to **turn on** verb
1 (a light, computer, etc.) **encender**
Turn the TV on. Enciende la tele.
2 to turn on the tap abrir el grifo

a b c d e f g h i j k l m n o p q r s t u v w x y z

• The months of the year and days of the week do not take a capital letter in Spanish.

to **turn out** verb
to turn out the light apagar la luz

to **turn over** verb
(a page, mattress, etc.) **dar la vuelta a**

to **turn round** verb
darse la vuelta
I turned round. Me di la vuelta.

to **turn up** verb
(a radio, the heating, etc.) **subir**
Turn up the sound. Sube el volumen.

turning noun
la **calle** fem.

turtle noun
la **tortuga (de mar)** fem.

TV noun
la **tele** fem.
on TV en la tele
a TV set una tele

twelfth adjective
the twelfth floor el piso doce
the twelfth of February el doce de febrero

> **LANGUAGE**
> In Spanish you usually use doce (twelve).

twelve number
doce
I eat at twelve. Como a las doce.
I'm twelve. Tengo doce años.

> **LANGUAGE**
> In English you can say 'twelve o'clock' or just 'twelve', 'twelve years old' or just 'twelve'. In Spanish you must add las (for time) and años (for age).

twentieth adjective
the twentieth floor el piso veinte
the twentieth of July el veinte de julio

> **LANGUAGE**
> In Spanish you usually use veinte (twenty).

twenty number
veinte
It's twenty to seven. Son las siete menos veinte.
It's twenty past eight. Son las ocho y veinte.
My sister is twenty. Mi hermana tiene veinte años.

> **LANGUAGE**
> In English you can say just 'twenty'. In Spanish you must add años.

twice adverb
dos veces
twice a week dos veces a la semana

twin noun
el **mellizo** masc., la **melliza** fem.
They're twins. Son mellizos.
identical twins los gemelos masc. plural, las gemelas fem. plural
my twin sister mi hermana melliza

to **twist** verb
torcer
I've twisted my ankle. Me he torcido el tobillo.

two number
dos
The film begins at two. La película empieza a las dos.
Harry's two. Harry tiene dos años.

> **LANGUAGE**
> In English you can say 'two o'clock' or just 'two', 'two years old' or just 'two'. In Spanish you must add las (for time) and años (for age).

type noun
el **tipo** masc.
What type of bike do you have? ¿Qué tipo de bici tienes?

to **type** verb
(a letter etc. on a computer) **escribir**
to type in (a password etc.) teclear

tyre noun
el **neumático** masc.

• See the centre section for verb tables.

Uu

UFO noun
el **OVNI** *masc.*

ugly adjective
feo *masc.*, **fea** *fem.*
The dog is very ugly. El perro es muy feo.

UK noun
el **Reino Unido** *masc.*
I live in the UK. Vivo en el Reino Unido.

Ulster noun
el **Ulster** *masc.*
I live in Ulster. Vivo en el Ulster.

umbrella noun
el **paraguas** *masc.* (plural los **paraguas**)

umpire noun
(*in cricket, tennis, etc.*) el **árbitro** *masc.*, la **árbitra** *fem.*

unable adjective
to be unable to do something no poder hacer algo
Sally's unable to come. Sally no puede venir.

unbelievable adjective
increíble *masc. & fem.*

uncle noun
el **tío** *masc.*
He's my uncle. Es mi tío.
my uncle and aunt mis tíos

uncomfortable adjective
(*chair, shoes, etc.*) **incómodo** *masc.*, **incómoda** *fem.*
I'm uncomfortable in this armchair. Estoy incómodo en este sillón.

under preposition
1 **debajo de**
under the table debajo de la mesa
2 **por debajo de**
I went under a ladder. Pasé por debajo de una escalera.

underground noun
el **metro** *masc.*
to go by underground ir en metro

underground adjective
subterráneo *masc.*, **subterránea** *fem.*
an underground car park un aparcamiento subterráneo

underline verb
subrayar

underneath preposition
1 **debajo de**
underneath the bed debajo de la cama
2 **por debajo de**
The train goes underneath the bridge. El tren pasa por debajo del puente.

underneath adverb
debajo
Look underneath. Mira debajo.

*Use **el** and **uno** for masculine words and **la** and **una** for feminine words.*

a
b
c
d
e
f
g
h
i
j
k
l
m
n
o
p
q
r
s
t
u
v
w
x
y
z

understand verb
entender
I don't understand. No entiendo.
Do you understand Spanish?
¿Entiendes el español?

underwater adverb
(to swim etc.) **debajo del agua**

underwear noun
la **ropa interior** fem.

🔑 **LANGUAGE**
Word for word the Spanish means 'inside clothes'.

to **undo** verb
1 (shoelaces, parcel, etc.) **desatar**
Your laces are undone. Tienes los cordones desatados.
2 (a coat, jacket, etc.) **desabrochar**
Undo your shirt. Desabróchate la camisa.
3 (to cancel on a computer) **cancelar**

to **undress** verb
desnudarse
to get undressed desnudarse

unemployed adjective
parado masc., **parada** fem.
My dad's unemployed. Mi padre está parado.

unexpected adjective
inesperado masc.,
inesperada fem.

unfair adjective
injusto masc., **injusta** fem.
That's unfair. Es injusto.

to **unfold** verb
(a map, newspaper) **desplegar**

unfriendly adjective
antipático masc., **antipática** fem.
He's very unfriendly. Es muy antipático.

unhappy adjective
(sad) **triste** masc. & fem.
I'm unhappy. Estoy triste.

unhealthy adjective
(food, person, etc.) **no muy sano** masc.,
no muy sana fem.
This diet is unhealthy. Esta dieta no es muy sana.

uniform noun
el **uniforme** masc.
I'm wearing my school uniform.
Llevo el uniforme del colegio.

🌎 **CULTURE**
In Spain schoolchildren don't usually wear uniforms.

Union Jack noun
la **bandera del Reino Unido** fem.

United Kingdom noun
el **Reino Unido** masc.
We live in the United Kingdom.
Vivimos en el Reino Unido.

United States plural noun
Estados Unidos masc.
I'm going to the United States.
Voy a Estados Unidos.

🔑 **LANGUAGE**
Estados Unidos is usually singular, and los (the) is not usually given.

universe noun
el **universo** masc.

university noun
la **universidad** fem.
My brother goes to university.
Mi hermano va a la universidad.

unless conjunction
si no
I'm going to the cinema unless it rains. Voy al cine si no llueve.

• Languages and nationalities do not take a capital letter in Spanish.

unlikely adjective
poco probable *masc. & fem.*

to **unlock** verb
(*a door, car, etc.*) **abrir**

unlucky adjective
1 (*talking about people*)
to be unlucky tener mala suerte
He's unlucky. Tiene mala suerte.
2 (*talking about things or numbers*)
The number thirteen is unlucky.
El número trece trae mala suerte.

to **unpack** verb
1 (*one case only*) **deshacer la maleta**
I've unpacked my case.
He deshecho mi maleta.
2 (*more than one case*) **deshacer las maletas**

unpleasant adjective
desagradable *masc. & fem.*

to **unplug** verb
desenchufar
Can you unplug the computer?
¿Puedes desenchufar el ordenador?

unsafe adjective
(*dangerous*) **peligroso** *masc.*,
peligrosa *fem.*
an unsafe place un sitio peligroso

untidy adjective
(*room or house*) **desordenado** *masc.*,
desordenada *fem.*
My bedroom's untidy. Mi
habitación está desordenada.

to **untie** verb
(*parcel, knot, etc.*) **desatar**
Untie your laces. Desátate los
cordones.

until preposition
hasta
Wait until tomorrow. Espera
hasta mañana.

untrue adjective
falso *masc.*, **falsa** *fem.*

unusual adjective
1 (*word, name, etc.*) **poco corriente**
masc. & fem.
2 (*strange*) **raro** *masc.*, **rara** *fem.*

LANGUAGE
You can also say **extraño/extraña**.

to **unwrap** verb
(*presents etc.*) **abrir**

up adverb & preposition
1 **arriba**
I looked up. Miré hacia arriba.
up here aquí arriba
Hands up, children! ¡Niños,
levantad la mano!
It's up the hill. Está en lo alto de la
colina.
2 **up to** hasta
to count up to twenty contar hasta
veinte
up to now hasta ahora
That's up to you. Depende de ti.
What are you up to? ¿Qué estás
haciendo?

LANGUAGE
'Up' is often translated as part of a verb
such as 'to go up' (**subir**) or 'to get up'
(**levantarse**).

up adjective
(*out of bed*) **levantado** *masc.*,
levantada *fem.*
Are you up? ¿Estás levantada?

upset adjective
1 (*sad*) **triste** *masc. & fem.*
2 (*angry*) **enfadado** *masc.*,
enfadada *fem.*
3 **I have an upset stomach.** Tengo
mal el estómago.

to **upset** verb
1 **to upset somebody** enfadar a
alguien
2 (*water, tea, etc.*) **tirar**
I've upset the milk. He tirado la
leche.

a b c d e f g h i j k l m n o p q r s t u v w x y z

• *The months of the year and days of the week do not take a capital letter in Spanish.*

English Spanish

a
b
c
d
e
f
g
h
i
j
k
l
m
n
o
p
q
r
s
t
u
v
w
x
y
z

upside down adjective
al revés
The picture is upside down. El cuadro está al revés.

upstairs adverb
arriba
I'm upstairs. Estoy arriba.
Go upstairs! ¡Sube!

🔑 **LANGUAGE**
Use subir to translate 'to come upstairs' or 'to go upstairs'.

up-to-date adjective
(computer, camcorder, etc.)
moderno masc., **moderna** fem.

urgent adjective
urgente masc. & fem.

us pronoun
1 (after a verb) **nos**
They know us. Nos conocen.
Has he seen us? ¿Nos ha visto?

🔑 **LANGUAGE**
With commands and infinitives nos is joined with the verb to make one word.

Call us. Llámanos.
Can you help us? ¿Puedes ayudarnos?
2 (to us) **nos**
She has sent a present to us. Nos ha mandado un regalo.
Give us the book. Danos el libro.
Give it to us. Dánoslo.
3 (after a preposition etc.) **nosotros** masc., **nosotras** fem.
with us con nosotros
They're taller than us. Son más altos que nosotros.
It's us. Somos nosotros.

US plural noun
Estados Unidos masc.
I'm going to the US. Voy a Estados Unidos.

🔑 **LANGUAGE**
Estados Unidos is usually singular, and los (the) is not usually given.

USA noun
Estados Unidos masc.

to **use** verb
usar
Use a hammer. Usa un martillo.
Can I use the toilet? ¿Puedo ir al baño?

use noun
It's no use ... Es inútil ...
It's no use shouting. Es inútil gritar.

used adjective
1 (bicycle, clothes, etc.) **usado** masc., **usada** fem.
a used car un coche usado
2 to be used to something estar acostumbrado or acostumbrada a algo
I'm used to taking the bus. Estoy acostumbrado a coger el autobús.

useful adjective
útil masc. & fem.
It's very useful. Es muy útil.

useless adjective
1 (ideas, effort, etc.) **inútil** masc. & fem.
useless things cosas inútiles
2 (knife, book, etc.) **que no sirve para nada**
Those scissors are useless. Esas tijeras no sirven para nada.
3 (really bad) **muy malo** masc., **muy mala** fem.
He's a useless player. Es un jugador muy malo.

usual adjective
1 **normal** masc. & fem.
the usual price el precio normal
2 (time, place, etc.) **de siempre**
at the usual time a la hora de siempre
as usual como siempre

usually adverb
normalmente

• See the centre section for verb tables.

Vv

to **vacuum** verb
  pasar la aspiradora
  I've vacuumed the carpet. He
  pasado la aspiradora por la
  alfombra.
  a vacuum cleaner una aspiradora

valley noun
  el **valle** masc.

valuable adjective
  valioso masc., **valiosa** fem.
  This picture is very valuable. Este
  cuadro es muy valioso.

van noun
  la **furgoneta** fem.

vanilla noun
  la **vainilla** fem.
  a vanilla ice cream un helado de
  vainilla

> **⚷ LANGUAGE**
> English = vanilla
> Spanish = vainilla

to **vanish** verb
  desaparecer

various adjective
  varios masc. plural, **varias** fem. plural
  I've seen him in various films. Lo
  he visto en varias películas.

varnish noun
  el **barniz** masc.
  nail varnish el esmalte de uñas

vase noun
  el **jarrón** masc. (plural los **jarrones**)

vegetable noun
  la **verdura** fem.
  vegetable soup sopa de verduras

vegetarian adjective
  vegetariano masc., **vegetariana**
  fem.

vegetarian noun
  el **vegetariano** masc.,
  la **vegetariana** fem.
  I'm a vegetarian. Soy vegetariana.

vending machine noun
  la máquina expendedora fem.

verb noun
  el **verbo** masc.

very adverb
  1 muy
  very tired muy cansado
  very well muy bien
  very much mucho
  I like it very much. Me gusta mucho.
  2 mucho masc., **mucha** fem.
  I'm very hungry. Tengo mucha
  hambre.
  It's very hot. Hace mucho calor.

> **⚷ LANGUAGE**
> English = to be **very** hungry
> Spanish = tener **mucha** hambre
> English = to be **very** hot
> Spanish = hacer **mucho** calor

vest noun
  la **camiseta** fem.

vet noun
  el **veterinario** masc.,
  la **veterinaria** fem.

vicar noun
  el **párroco** masc.

video noun
  1 el **vídeo** masc.
  to watch a video ver un vídeo
  on video en vídeo
  a video game un videojuego
  a video recorder un vídeo
  2 (music video) el **clip** masc.

> **⚷ LANGUAGE**
> **Vídeo** means the film you watch, the
> cassette you buy, and the machine you
> watch the film on, just as in English.

• Use **el** and **uno** for masculine words and **la** and **una** for feminine words.

a
b
c
d
e
f
g
h
i
j
k
l
m
n
o
p
q
r
s
t
u
v
w
x
y
z

view noun
la **vista** *fem.*

village noun
el **pueblo** *masc.*

vinegar noun
el **vinagre** *masc.*

violin noun
el **violín** *masc.* (plural los **violines**)
to play the violin tocar el violín

virus noun
el **virus** *masc.* (plural los **virus**)
a computer virus un virus
informático

visit noun
la **visita** *fem.*
a visit to the museum una visita al
museo

to **visit** verb
visitar
I'm going to visit my cousins.
Voy a visitar a mis primos.

visitor noun
la **visita** *fem.*
We have visitors. Tenemos visitas.

vocabulary noun
el **vocabulario** *masc.*

voice noun
la **voz** *fem.* (plural las **voces**)
to speak in a loud voice hablar en
voz alta
Can you keep your voice down?
¿Puedes bajar la voz?

volcano noun
el **volcán** *masc.* (plural los **volcanes**)

volleyball noun
el **voleibol** *masc.*
to play volleyball jugar al
voleibol

volume noun
el **volumen** *masc.*
Turn down the volume. Baja el
volumen.

volunteer noun
el **voluntario** *masc.*,
la **voluntaria** *fem.*

to **vote** verb
votar

voucher noun
a gift voucher un vale de regalo

vowel noun
la **vocal** *fem.*

Ww

to **wag** verb
mover
It's wagging its tail. Mueve la cola.

waist noun
la **cintura** *fem.*

waistcoat noun
el **chaleco** *masc.*

to **wait** verb
esperar
Wait a minute! ¡Espera un
momento!

I'm waiting for you. Te estoy
esperando.
Wait for me. Espérame.
a waiting room una sala de espera

> **LANGUAGE**
> English = **to wait for** somebody
> Spanish = **esperar** a alguien

waiter noun
el **camarero** *masc.*

waitress noun
la **camarera** *fem.*

• Languages and nationalities do not take a capital letter in Spanish.

to **wake up** verb
1 despertarse
I wake up at seven. Me despierto a las siete.
Wake up! ¡Despiértate!
2 despertar
Wake me up at nine. Despiértame a las nueve.

Wales noun
Gales *masc.*
I live in Wales. Vivo en Gales.

walk noun
el **paseo** *masc.*
to go for a walk ir de paseo, ir a dar un paseo
to take the dog out for a walk sacar a pasear al perro

to **walk** verb
1 andar
You walk too fast. Andas demasiado rápido.
2 (*to go on foot, not by bike, bus, etc.*) **ir a pie**
I walk to school. Voy al colegio a pie.
3 to walk with somebody acompañar a alguien
to walk in entrar
to walk out salir
to walk across the road cruzar la calle

walking noun
Walking is good for you. Andar es muy sano.
I like walking. Me gusta andar.
a walking stick un bastón (plural **bastones**)

wall noun
1 (*of a house or room*) la **pared** *fem.*
There's a picture on the wall. Hay un cuadro en la pared.
2 (*in a garden, field, etc.*) el **muro** *masc.*
Jump off the wall. Salta del muro.

wallet noun
la **cartera** *fem.*

wallpaper noun
el **papel pintado** *masc.*

walnut noun
la **nuez** *fem.* (plural las **nueces**)

wand noun
la **varita** *fem.*
a magic wand una varita mágica

to **want** verb
querer
I want an ice cream. Quiero un helado.
Do you want some water? ¿Quieres agua?
I want to watch TV. Quiero ver la tele.
What do you want to do, children? Niños, ¿qué queréis hacer?

war noun
la **guerra** *fem.*

wardrobe noun
el **armario** *masc.*

warm adjective
caliente *masc. & fem.*
My room is warm. Mi habitación está caliente.
These gloves are very warm. Estos guantes son muy calientes.
It's warm today. Hoy hace calor.
I'm warm. Tengo calor.

🔑 **LANGUAGE**
English = to be warm I'm warm.
Spanish = tener calor Tengo calor.

to **warn** verb
advertir
I'm warning you! ¡Te lo advierto!

a
b
c
d
e
f
g
h
i
j
k
l
m
n
o
p
q
r
s
t
u
v
w
x
y
z

• The months of the year and days of the week do not take a capital letter in Spanish.

was verb SEE **be**
I was tired. Estaba cansado.
Yesterday was my birthday. Ayer fue mi cumpleaños.

wash noun
to have a wash lavarse

to **wash** verb
1 (clothes, a floor, car, etc.) **lavar**
Have you washed the blouse? ¿Has lavado la blusa?
2 (your hands etc.) **lavarse**
I get up and wash. Me levanto y me lavo.
I've washed my hands. Me he lavado las manos.
He's washing his face. Se está lavando la cara.

to **wash up** verb
fregar los platos, lavar los platos

washbasin noun
el **lavabo** masc.

washing noun
(clothes) la **ropa** fem.
the dirty washing la ropa sucia
to do the washing lavar la ropa
a washing machine una lavadora
washing powder el detergente

washing-up noun
los **platos sucios** masc. plural
to do the washing-up fregar los platos

wasp noun
la **avispa** fem.

waste noun
It's a waste of time. Es una pérdida de tiempo.

to **waste** verb
perder
You're wasting your time. Estás perdiendo el tiempo.

watch noun
el **reloj** masc.
I don't have a watch. No tengo reloj.

to **watch** verb
1 (to look at) **mirar**
Watch me. Mírame.
2 (a film, programme, etc.) **ver**
I'm watching TV. Estoy viendo la tele.
3 (to look after) **cuidar**
Can you watch the children? ¿Puedes cuidar a los niños?

to **watch out** verb
tener cuidado
Watch out for flies! ¡Cuidado con las moscas!

water noun
el **agua** fem.
Do you want some water? ¿Quieres agua?

LANGUAGE
Be careful: you use el with agua but it is not a masculine noun.

to **water** verb
regar
I'm watering the plants. Estoy regando las plantas.

watermelon noun
la **sandía** fem.

wave noun
(in the sea) la **ola** fem.

to **wave** verb
(to say hello) **saludar con la mano**
She waved goodbye to me. Me hizo adiós con la mano.

wavy adjective
to have wavy hair tener el pelo ondulado

• See the centre section for verb tables.

way noun

1 (*to a place*) el **camino** *masc.*
I know the way. Yo sé el camino.
to ask the way to ... preguntar el camino a ...
Do you know the way to the library? ¿Sabes cómo se llega a la biblioteca?
It's a long way. Está muy lejos.
You're in my way! ¡No me dejas pasar!
the way in la entrada
the way out la salida

2 (*direction*)
We're going the opposite way. Vamos en dirección contraria.
Which way is it? ¿Por dónde es?
this way por aquí
that way por ahí

3 (*a way of doing something*) la **manera** *fem.*
which way? ¿de qué manera?
Do it this way. Hazlo de esta manera.
You're doing it the wrong way. Lo estás haciendo mal.
You've done it the right way. Lo has hecho bien.

we pronoun

1 (*not usually translated in Spanish*)
We're English. Somos ingleses.
We want an ice cream. Queremos un helado.

2 **nosotros** *masc.*, **nosotras** *fem.*
They watch TV but we read books. Ellos ven la tele, pero nosotros leemos libros.

> 🔑 **LANGUAGE**
> Use nosotros/nosotras when you want to give special importance to the word 'we'.

weak adjective
débil *masc. & fem.*
I feel weak. Me siento débil.

to **wear** verb

1 **llevar**
I'm wearing a blue dress. Llevo un vestido azul.

2 **ponerse**
What are you going to wear? ¿Qué te vas a poner?

> 🔑 **LANGUAGE**
> Use ponerse (to put on) rather than llevar when you talk about the clothes you are going to put on.

weather noun
el **tiempo** *masc.*
What's the weather like? ¿Qué tiempo hace?
The weather's nice. Hace buen tiempo.
The weather's cold. Hace frío.
the weather forecast el tiempo, el pronóstico del tiempo

web noun

1 (*spider's web*) la **telaraña** *fem.*

2 (*the Internet*) la **web** *fem.*
a web page una página web

website noun
el **sitio web** *masc.*
to visit a website visitar un sitio web

wedding noun
la **boda** *fem.*
a wedding anniversary un aniversario de boda
a wedding dress un vestido de novia

Wednesday noun
el **miércoles** *masc.*
Today is Wednesday. Hoy es miércoles.
on Wednesday el miércoles

a b c d e f g h i j k l m n o p q r s t u v **w** x y z

• Use **el** and **uno** for masculine words and **la** and **una** for feminine words.

a
b
c
d
e
f
g
h
i
j
k
l
m
n
o
p
q
r
s
t
u
v
w
x
y
z

I'm going swimming on Wednesday. Voy a la piscina el miércoles.
on Wednesdays los miércoles
We play football on Wednesdays. Jugamos al fútbol los miércoles.

> **LANGUAGE**
> Remember the difference in Spanish between el miércoles (one Wednesday only) and los miércoles (every Wednesday).

weed noun
la **mala hierba** fem.

> **LANGUAGE**
> Word for word the Spanish means 'bad grass'.

week noun
la **semana** fem.
We're leaving in a week. Nos vamos dentro de una semana.
this week esta semana
last week la semana pasada
next week la semana que viene
during the week entre semana

weekday noun
on weekdays entre semana

weekend noun
el **fin de semana** masc.
last weekend el fin de semana pasado
next weekend el fin de semana que viene

to **weigh** verb
pesar
I weigh thirty kilos. Peso treinta kilos.

weight noun
el **peso** masc.
to put on weight engordar
to lose weight adelgazar

welcome adjective
bienvenido masc., **bienvenida** fem.
Welcome! ¡Bienvenido!
Welcome to Madrid! ¡Bienvenidos a Madrid!
Thank you! – You're welcome! ¡Gracias! – ¡De nada!

> **LANGUAGE**
> Remember to use ¡Bienvenida! if you're talking to a girl or woman, and ¡Bienvenidos! if you're talking to two people or more.

well adverb & adjective
1 **bien**
You draw well. Dibujas bien.
Well done! ¡Muy bien!, ¡Bien hecho!
2 (in good health)
I'm well. Estoy bien.
I don't feel well. No me encuentro bien.
Get well soon! ¡Que te mejores!
3 as well también
I'm going as well. Yo voy también.

well exclamation
¡bueno!
Well, I'm going! ¡Bueno, me voy!

well noun
el **pozo** masc.
to get water from the well sacar agua del pozo

well-behaved adjective
He's well-behaved. Se porta bien.

wellingtons plural noun
las **botas de goma** fem. plural

well-known adjective
conocido masc., **conocida** fem.

Welsh adjective
galés masc., **galesa** fem.
a Welsh actor un actor galés
She's Welsh. Es galesa.
Welsh people los galeses

> **LANGUAGE**
> The masculine plural of galés is galeses.

• Languages and nationalities do not take a capital letter in Spanish.

Welsh noun
1 (language) el **galés** masc.
Rhys speaks Welsh. Rhys habla galés.
2 the Welsh los galeses masc. plural

Welshman noun
el **galés** masc. (plural los **galeses**)

Welshwoman noun
la **galesa** fem.

went verb SEE **go**
I went to school. Fui al colegio.
She went to Spain. Fue a España.

were verb SEE **be**
We were at home. Estábamos en casa.
You were ill. Estabas enfermo.
They were kind to me. Fueron amables conmigo.

west noun & adjective
el **oeste** masc.
in the west en el oeste
the west coast la costa oeste

western noun
la **película del oeste** fem.

West Indies plural noun
las **Antillas** fem. plural

wet adjective
1 **mojado** masc., **mojada** fem.
The towel is wet. La toalla está mojada.
to get wet mojarse
2 (rainy) **lluvioso** masc., **lluviosa** fem.
a wet day un día lluvioso
I don't go out when it's wet. No salgo cuando llueve.

whale noun
la **ballena** fem.

what pronoun & adjective
1 (in questions) **qué**
What are you doing? ¿Qué estás haciendo?
What is it? ¿Qué es?
What time is it? ¿Qué hora es?
What chocolates do you want? ¿Qué bombones quieres?
What? ¿Qué?
What for? ¿Para qué?
What are you talking about? ¿De qué hablas?
2 **cuál** (plural **cuáles**)
what is ...? ¿cuál es ...?
what are ...? ¿cuáles son ...?
What's your address? ¿Cuál es tu dirección?
What's the problem? ¿Cuál es el problema?
What's the Spanish for 'house'? ¿Cómo se dice 'house' en español?
3 (when there isn't a question) **lo que**
I don't know what you want. No sé lo que quieres.
Tell me what happened. Dime lo que ha pasado.
4 (in exclamations) **qué**
What a pity! ¡Qué lástima!
What a pretty girl! ¡Qué niña tan guapa!

wheat noun
el **trigo** masc.

wheel noun
la **rueda** fem.
the front wheel la rueda delantera
the steering wheel el volante

wheelchair noun
la **silla de ruedas** fem.

a
b
c
d
e
f
g
h
i
j
k
l
m
n
o
p
q
r
s
t
u
v
w
x
y
z

• The months of the year and days of the week do not take a capital letter in Spanish.

a
b
c
d
e
f
g
h
i
j
k
l
m
n
o
p
q
r
s
t
u
v
w
x
y
z

when adverb & conjunction
1 (*in questions*) **cuándo**
When are you leaving? ¿Cuándo te vas?
2 (*when there isn't a question*) **cuando**
I don't go out when it rains No salgo cuando llueve

LANGUAGE
Remember to put the accent on cuándo in questions.

where adverb
1 (*in questions*) **dónde**
Where are you? ¿Dónde estás?
Where are you going? ¿Adónde vas?, ¿Dónde vas?
I don't know where it is. No sé dónde está.
2 (*when there isn't a question*) **donde**
This is the street where I live. Ésta es la calle donde vivo.

LANGUAGE
Remember to put the accent on dónde in questions.

whether adverb
si
I don't know whether it's possible. No sé si es posible.

which adjective
1 **qué**
Which book are you reading? ¿Qué libro lees?
Which house is it? ¿Qué casa es?
2 **cuál** (plural **cuáles**)
I have two CDs. Which of them do you want? Tengo dos CDs. ¿Cuál quieres?
which one? ¿cuál?
Which one do you want? ¿Cuál quieres?
which ones? ¿cuáles?
Which ones do you like best? ¿Cuáles te gustan más?

• *See the centre section for verb tables.*

which pronoun
que
the book which is on the table el libro que está en la mesa
the bike which I want la bici que quiero

while conjunction
mientras
Wait here while I wash my hands. Espérame aquí mientras me lavo las manos.

while noun
a short while un momento
a long while mucho tiempo
I lived in Spain for a while. Viví una temporada en España.

whiskers plural noun
(*of a cat*) los **bigotes** *masc. plural*

to **whisper** verb
susurrar

whistle noun
el **silbato** *masc.*
to blow a whistle tocar un silbato

to **whistle** verb
silbar

white adjective
blanco *masc.*, **blanca** *fem.*
a white dress un vestido blanco
a white coffee un café con leche

white noun
el **blanco** *masc.*
I like white. Me gusta el blanco.

whiteboard noun
la **pizarra blanca** *fem.*
on the whiteboard en la pizarra

who pronoun
1 **quién** (plural **quiénes**)
Who wants an ice cream? ¿Quién quiere un helado?
Who's that? ¿Quién es?
I don't know who they are. No sé quiénes son.
2 **que**

my uncle who lives in Sheffield mi tío que vive en Sheffield

whole adjective
todo *masc.*, **toda** *fem.*
the whole village todo el pueblo
my whole family toda mi familia

> 🔑 **LANGUAGE**
> Todo is the usual Spanish word for 'all' so, word for word, todo el pueblo is 'all the village'.

whose pronoun
de quién (plural de quiénes)
Whose bike is this? ¿De quién es esta bici?
Whose is it? ¿De quién es?
Whose are they? ¿De quiénes son?

why adverb
por qué
Why are you sad? ¿Por qué estás triste?
Why not? ¿Por qué no?

wicked adjective
1 (*evil*) malo *masc.*, mala *fem.*
He's very wicked. Es muy malo.
2 (*very good*) genial *masc. & fem.*
Wicked! ¡Genial!

wide adjective
1 ancho *masc.*, ancha *fem.*
This road is very wide. Esta calle es muy ancha.
2 wide awake completamente despierto *masc.*, completamente despierta *fem.*

wife noun
la mujer *fem.*
my brother's wife la mujer de mi hermano

wild adjective
salvaje *masc. & fem.*
wild animals animales salvajes

• *See the centre section for verb tables.*

will verb
1 (*for talking about the very near future*) ir
I'll be late. Voy a llegar tarde.
What will you do? ¿Qué vas a hacer?
2 (*translated by the future tense in Spanish*)
I'll see you tomorrow. Te veré mañana.
It won't rain. No lloverá.
3 (*when asking*) querer
Will you have a Coke? ¿Quieres una Coca-Cola?
Will you behave yourself? ¿Quieres portarte bien?
4 (*when you mean 'does not or do not want to'*)
no querer
She won't help me. No quiere ayudarme.

to win verb
ganar
Have you won? ¿Has ganado?

wind noun
el viento *masc.*

windmill noun
el molino de viento *masc.*

window noun
1 la ventana *fem.*
Open the window. Abre la ventana.
2 (*the glass of a window*) el cristal *masc.*
to break a window romper un cristal
3 (*of a car*) la ventanilla *fem.*
4 (*shop window*) el escaparate *masc.*

windy adjective
It's windy. Hace viento.

wine noun
el vino *masc.*
red wine el vino tinto

wing noun
el ala *fem.*

> 🔑 **LANGUAGE**
> Be careful: you use el with ala but it is not a masculine noun.

English Spanish

a
b
c
d
e
f
g
h
i
j
k
l
m
n
o
p
q
r
s
t
u
v
w
x
y
z

winner noun
el **ganador** *masc.*, la **ganadora** *fem.*

winter noun
el **invierno** *masc.*
in the winter en invierno

to **wipe** verb
(*a table, your hands, etc.*) **limpiar**

wire noun
1 (*of TV, phone, etc.*) el **cable** *masc.*
an electric wire un cable eléctrico
2 (*of a cage, fence, etc.*) el **alambre** *masc.*

wise adjective
sabio *masc.*, **sabia** *fem.*

wish noun
el **deseo** *masc.*
to make a wish pedir un
deseo
Best wishes on your birthday!
¡Felicidades!
With best wishes, Jenny. (*in a letter*)
Saludos de Jenny.

to **wish** verb
desear
I wish you a happy birthday.
Te deseo un feliz cumpleaños.

witch noun
la **bruja** *fem.*

with preposition
1 **con**
with a knife con un cuchillo
Come with me. Ven conmigo.
He went with you. Fue contigo.
2 (*at somebody's house*) **en casa de**
I stayed with my sister. Me quedé
en casa de mi hermana.

without preposition
sin
without me sin mi
without an umbrella sin paraguas
without looking sin mirar

wizard noun
el **mago** *masc.*

wolf noun
el **lobo** *masc.*
the big bad wolf el lobo feroz

LANGUAGE
Little Red Riding Hood is the same in Spain
but the 'big bad wolf' is the 'fierce wolf'.

woman noun
la **mujer** *fem.*
men and women los hombres y las
mujeres
a young woman una joven
an old woman una anciana, una
vieja

LANGUAGE
Anciana is a polite word for 'old woman'.

wonderful adjective
maravilloso *masc.*,
maravillosa *fem.*

wood noun
1 la **madera** *fem.*
It's made of wood. Es de madera.
2 (*little forest*)
the woods el bosque *masc.*
I walked through the woods. Fui
de paseo por el bosque.

wooden adjective
de madera
a wooden chair una silla de madera

wool noun
la **lana** *fem.*

woolly adjective
de lana
a woolly jumper un jersey de lana

word noun
la **palabra** *fem.*
What does this word mean?
¿Qué quiere decir esta palabra?
What's the Spanish word for 'tree'?
¿Cómo se dice 'tree' en español?
the words of a song la letra de una
canción

work noun
el **trabajo** *masc.*

• Use **el** and **uno** for masculine words and **la** and **una** for feminine words.

lots of work mucho trabajo
Mum's at work. Mamá está en el trabajo.
to go to work by car ir al trabajo en coche

to **work** verb
1 **trabajar**
   I work hard. Trabajo mucho.
2 (*talking about machines*) **funcionar**
   The TV isn't working. La tele no funciona.

to **work out** verb
1 (*to calculate*) **calcular**
   Have you worked it out? ¿Lo has calculado?
2 (*in the gym*) **hacer ejercicio**

worker noun
1 (*in a factory etc.*) el **trabajador** *masc.*, la **trabajadora** *fem.*
2 (*in an office*) el **empleado** *masc.*, la **empleada** *fem.*
3 (*on a building site*) el **obrero** *masc.*, la **obrera** *fem.*

worksheet noun
   la **hoja de ejercicios** *fem.*

workshop noun
   (*for learning, doing repairs, etc.*) el **taller** *masc.*

world noun
   el **mundo** *masc.*
   the best in the world el mejor del mundo
   to travel all over the world viajar por todo el mundo

worm noun
   el **gusano** *masc.*

worried adjective
   preocupado *masc.*,
   preocupada *fem.*
   to be worried about estar preocupado por
   Mum's worried about her. Mamá está preocupada por ella.

to **worry** verb
   preocuparse

Don't worry! ¡No te preocupes!

worse adjective
   peor *masc. & fem.*
   Your Spanish is worse than mine. Tu español es peor que el mío.
   I'm feeling worse. Me encuentro peor.

worse adverb
   peor
   They sing worse than us. Cantan peor que nosotros.

worst adjective
   peor *masc. & fem.*
   He's the worst pupil in the class. Es el peor alumno de la clase.
   the worst one el or la peor

worst noun
   el or la **peor** *masc. & fem.*
   This book is the worst. Este libro es el peor.

worth adjective
   to be worth valer
   It's worth a lot of money. Vale mucho dinero.
   It's worth doing it. Vale la pena hacerlo.
   It's not worth it. No vale la pena.

would verb
1 (*when asking for something*)
   I would like ... Quiero ..., Quisiera ...
   I'd like to say something. Quiero decir algo., Quisiera decir algo.
2 (*in questions*)
   Would you like ...? ¿Quieres ...?, ¿Quiere ...?
   Would you like some Coke®? ¿Quieres Coca-Cola®?
   Would you like something to eat? ¿Quieres comer algo?
   Would you like anything else, sir? ¿Quiere usted algo más, señor?
3 (*when telling somebody politely*)
   Would you help me, dad? ¿Puedes ayudarme, papá?

a
b
c
d
e
f
g
h
i
j
k
l
m
n
o
p
q
r
s
t
u
v
w
x
y
z

• *Languages and nationalities do not take a capital letter in Spanish.*

Would you wait here, please?
¿Puede usted esperar aquí, por favor?

🔑 **LANGUAGE**
Use the verb querer for meanings 1 and 2, and poder for meaning 3.

to **wrap** verb
envolver
to wrap up a present envolver un regalo
wrapping paper el papel de regalo

wrist noun
la **muñeca** fem.

to **write** verb
escribir
She's written me an email.
Me ha escrito un email.
We write to each other.
Nos escribimos.

to **write back** verb
contestar
He didn't write back. No me contestó.

to **write down** verb
apuntar
I've written down the date.
He apuntado la fecha.

writer noun
el **escritor** masc., la **escritora** fem.

writing noun
la **letra** fem.

I can't read your writing.
No entiendo tu letra.
a writing pad un bloc (plural los **blocs**)

wrong adjective
1 (not correct) **equivocado** masc., **equivocada** fem.
the wrong answer la respuesta equivocada
2 (not true) **falso** masc., **falsa** fem.
That's wrong! ¡Eso es falso!
3 (no translation)
This is the wrong house. Ésta no es la casa.
The book's in the wrong place. El libro no está en su sitio.
4 (talking about people) **to be wrong** estar equivocado masc., estar equivocada fem.
You're wrong, Carol. Estás equivocada, Carol.
5 **What's wrong?** ¿Qué pasa?
What's wrong with you? ¿Qué te pasa?
There's something wrong with the computer. El ordenador no funciona bien.

wrong adverb
(not correctly) **mal**
I've done it wrong. Lo he hecho mal.

Xx

Xmas noun
la **Navidad** fem.

X-ray noun
la **radiografía** fem.
I've had an X-ray. Me han hecho una radiografía.

to **X-ray** verb
(an arm, leg, etc.) **hacer una radiografía de**

They've X-rayed my leg. Me han hecho una radiografía de la pierna.

xylophone noun
el **xilófono** masc.
to play the xylophone tocar el xilófono

• The months of the year and days of the week do not take a capital letter in Spanish.

Yy

yard noun
It's a hundred yards away. Está a unos cien metros de aquí.

 CULTURE
Spanish measurements are in metres and centimetres; a yard is about 90 centimetres.

to **yawn** verb
bostezar

year noun
el **año** masc.
this year este año
last year el año pasado
next year el año que viene
the New Year el Año Nuevo
Happy New Year! ¡Feliz Año Nuevo!
I'm in year five. Estoy en quinto de primaria.
I'm eight. Tengo ocho años.

LANGUAGE
English = **to be** eight years old
    I'm eight years old.
Spanish = **tener** ocho años
    Tengo ocho años.

yellow adjective
amarillo masc., **amarilla** fem.
a yellow blouse una blusa amarilla

yellow noun
el **amarillo** masc.
Yellow suits you. El amarillo te queda bien.

yes adverb
sí

yesterday adverb
ayer
yesterday morning ayer por la mañana
yesterday night ayer por la noche
the day before yesterday anteayer

• See the centre section for verb tables.

yet adverb
1 **not yet** todavía no
I haven't seen her yet. Todavía no la he visto.
2 (in questions) **ya**
Are you ready yet? ¿Ya estás listo?

yoghurt noun
el **yogur** masc.
a plain yoghurt un yogur natural

yolk noun
la **yema** fem.

you pronoun

LANGUAGE
There are different ways of saying 'you' in Spanish: there's a familiar way (for talking to friends, people in your family, and people your own age) and a polite way (for grown-ups and strangers). There are also singular and plural words in Spanish – if you're talking to one person or more than one.

1 (not usually translated when it's the subject of the sentence)
You're my friend. Eres mi amigo.
Do you want some cake, children? ¿Niños, queréis un poco de tarta?
Would you like anything else, sir? ¿Quiere algo más, señor?
2 (familiar form) **tú**, (after preposition) **ti** (plural **vosotros** masc., **vosotras** fem.)
I'm ten. How old are you? Yo tengo diez años. ¿Cuántos años tienes tú?
I'm taller than you. Soy más alta que tú.
We're going to the cinema, and you? Nosotras vamos al cine, ¿y vosotras?

a
b
c
d
e
f
g
h
i
j
k
l
m
n
o
p
q
r
s
t
u
v
w
x
y
z

Can we play with you? ¿Podemos jugar con vosotros?

A present for you, mum. Un regalo para ti, mamá.

Can I go with you, dad? ¿Puedo ir contigo, papá?

> **LANGUAGE**
> Use **tú** and **vosotros/vosotras** when you want to give special importance to the word 'you'; use **ti** and **vosotros/vosotras** after a preposition ('with', 'for, etc.); use **tú** and **vosotros/vosotras** after the word 'than'. Remember the special word **contigo** to translate 'with you'.

3 (*polite form*) **usted** (plural **ustedes**)

What would you like? ¿Qué quiere usted?

What would you like? (*plural*) ¿Qué quieren ustedes?

for you para usted

for you (*plural*) para ustedes

4 (*familiar form: after a verb*) **te** (plural **os**)

I know you. Te conozco.

I want to help you. Quiero ayudarte.

I know you. (*plural*) Os conozco.

I want to help you. (*plural*) Quiero ayudaros.

> **LANGUAGE**
> With infinitives **te** and **os** are joined with the verb to make one word.

5 (*familiar form: to you*) **te** (plural **os**)

I've written to you. Te he escrito.

I've written to you. (*plural*) Os he escrito.

6 (*polite form: after a verb*) **lo** *masc.* (plural **los**); **la** *fem.* (plural **las**)

I saw you, Mr Brown. Lo vi, señor Brown.

I saw you, Mrs Patel. La vi, señora Patel.

I saw you both. Los vi.

I want to help you both. Quiero ayudarlos.

> **LANGUAGE**
> With infinitives, **lo/los** and **la/las** are joined with the verb to make one word.

> **LANGUAGE**
> You can also use **le** and **les** in Spanish instead of **lo** and **los**, e.g. 'I saw you' can be Lo vi or Le vi.

7 (*polite form: to you*) **le** (plural **les**)

They've sent a letter to you. Le han mandado una carta.

They've sent a letter to you. (*plural*) Les han mandado una carta.

They want to send a letter to you. Quieren mandarle una carta.

They've sent it to you. Se la han mandado.

> **LANGUAGE**
> When **le** or **les** are used with **lo/los** or **la/las** you use **se** instead.

young adjective
joven *masc. & fem.*
My sister's very young. Mi hermana es muy joven.
a young man un joven
a young woman una joven
young people los jóvenes

younger adjective
más joven *masc. & fem.*
I'm younger than you. Soy más joven que tú.
You're a year younger than me. Tienes un año menos que yo.

youngest adjective
menor *masc. & fem.*
I'm the youngest daughter. Soy la hija menor.

youngest noun
el or la **menor** *masc. & fem.*
I'm the youngest in the family. Soy el menor de la familia.

• Use **el** and **uno** for masculine words and **la** and **una** for feminine words.

your adjective
1 (*familiar form: talking to one person*) **tu** (plural **tus**)
your book tu libro
your sisters tus hermanas
2 (*familiar form: talking to more than one person*) **vuestro** *masc.*, **vuestra** *fem.*
your house vuestra casa
your toys vuestros juguetes
3 (*polite form*) **su** (plural **sus**)
Mr Clarke, here is your coat. Señor Clarke, aquí está su abrigo.
Where are your suitcases, miss? ¿Dónde están sus maletas, señorita?
4 (*with parts of the body, clothes, etc.*)
Have you washed your hands, David? ¿Te has lavado las manos, David?
Wash your hands, children. Niños, lavaos las manos.
Would you like to take your coat off, sir? ¿Quiere quitarse el abrigo, señor?

🔑 **LANGUAGE**
Use te, os, and se with el, la, los, or las in these examples.

yours pronoun
1 (*familiar form: talking to one person*) el **tuyo** *masc.*, la **tuya** *fem.*
my book and yours mi libro y el tuyo
My bike is older than yours. Mi bici es más vieja que la tuya.
That's yours. Eso es tuyo.
2 (*familiar form: talking to more than one person*) el **vuestro** *masc.*, la **vuestra** *fem.*
our CD and yours nuestro CD y el vuestro
our friends and yours nuestras amigas y las vuestras
These pens are yours. Estos bolis son vuestros.
3 (*polite form*) el **suyo** *masc.*, la **suya** *fem.*

my house and yours mi casa y la suya
These are yours, miss. Éstos son suyos, señorita.

yourself pronoun
1 (*familiar form*) **tú mismo** *masc.*, **tú misma** *fem.*
Do it yourself. Hazlo tú mismo.
2 (*familiar form: with a reflexive verb*) **te**
Go and wash yourself. Lávate.
3 (*polite form*) **usted mismo** *masc.*, **usted misma** *fem.*
Have you done it yourself, sir? ¿Lo ha hecho usted mismo, señor?
4 (*polite form: with a reflexive verb*) **se**
Have your hurt yourself, miss? ¿Se ha hecho daño, señorita?
5 by yourself solo *masc.*, sola *fem.*
Do you go out by yourself? ¿Sales sola?

yourselves pronoun
1 (*familiar form*) **vosotros mismos** *masc. plural*, **vosotras mismas** *fem. plural*
Have you written it yourselves? ¿Lo habéis escrito vosotros mismos?
2 (*familiar form: with a reflexive verb*) **os**
Go and wash yourselves. Lavaos.
3 (*polite form*) **ustedes mismos** *masc. plural*, **ustedes mismas** *fem. plural*
Have you seen it yourselves, ladies? ¿Lo han visto ustedes mismas, señoras?
4 (*polite form: with a reflexive verb*) **se**
Have you enjoyed yourselves? ¿Se han divertido?
5 by yourselves solos *masc. plural*, solas *fem. plural*
Do you go out by yourselves? ¿Salís solos?

youth hostel noun
el **albergue juvenil** *masc.*

yo-yo noun
el **yoyó** *masc.*

• Languages and nationalities do not take a capital letter in Spanish.

a b c d e f g h i j k l m n o p q r s t u v w x y z

Zz

zebra noun
la **cebra** *fem.*

zero noun
el **cero** *masc.*

zip noun
la **cremallera** *fem.*
to undo the zip abrir la cremallera

zoo noun
el **zoo** *masc.*, el **zoológico** *masc.*
I'm going to the zoo. Voy al zoo.

a
b
c
d
e
f
g
h
i
j
k
l
m
n
o
p
q
r
s
t
u
v
w
x
y
z

• *The months of the year and days of the week do not take a capital letter in Spanish.*